BEYOND CRACKING *the* CODING INTERVIEW

PASS TOUGH CODING INTERVIEWS, GET NOTICED, AND NEGOTIATE SUCCESFULLY

INTERVIEW CHECKLIST

OPENING CHAT

Understand the Problem
- Read the statement (twice)
- Work through examples out loud
- Ask clarifying questions
  - Edge cases
  - Input/output format
  - Scale constraints

1 →

Design the Algorithm
- Minimally sketch naive solution
- Identify upper & lower bounds
- Look for triggers
- Employ boosters

2

Problem-solving boosters

Boosters	**B**ruce force optimization
Help	**H**unt for properties
Developers	**D**ecrease the difficulty
Crack	**C**ycle through the Catalog
Algorithms	**A**rticulate your blocker

Get Buy-In
- The Magic Question™

4 ←

Explain the Solution
- Examples
- Indented English
- Name & Justify

3

Code the Solution
- Main logic
- Helper functions
- *Stop if you get lost*

5 →

Verify the Solution
- Top-to-bottom pass
- Tricky expressions
- Run through with tiny input
- Check edge cases
- Verify analysis

6

CLOSING CHAT & QUESTIONS FOR INTERVIEWER

Common Mistakes
Testing the concept, not code
Not thinking as you go

STUDY PLAN

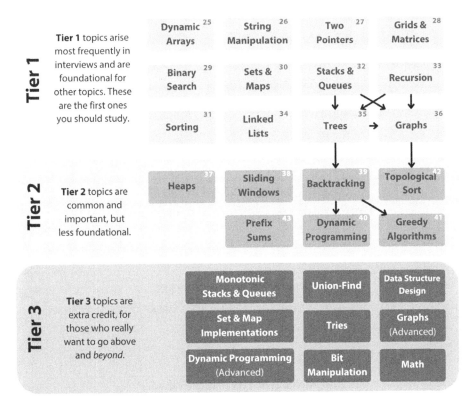

Tier 1 topics arise most frequently in interviews and are foundational for other topics. These are the first ones you should study.	Dynamic Arrays [25]	String Manipulation [26]	Two Pointers [27]	Grids & Matrices [28]
	Binary Search [29]	Sets & Maps [30]	Stacks & Queues [32]	Recursion [33]
	Sorting [31]	Linked Lists [34]	Trees [35] →	Graphs [36]

Tier 1

Tier 2

Tier 2 topics are common and important, but less foundational.

Heaps [37]	Sliding Windows [38]	Backtracking [39]	Topological Sort [42]
	Prefix Sums [43]	Dynamic Programming [40]	Greedy Algorithms [41]

Tier 3

Tier 3 topics are extra credit, for those who really want to go above and *beyond*.

Monotonic Stacks & Queues	Union-Find	Data Structure Design
Set & Map Implementations	Tries	Graphs (Advanced)
Dynamic Programming (Advanced)	Bit Manipulation	Math

BOOSTERS

If boundary & trigger thinking don't point you to the right approach, start with the brute force

Bruce Force Optimization
- Preprocessing Pattern
- Data Structure Pattern
- Skip Unnecessary Work

1

If you need a new approach...

Hunt for Properties
- DIY
- Case Analysis
- Reverse Engineer the Output Pattern
- Sketch a Diagram
- Reframe the Problem

2

If you can't find any approach...

Decrease the Difficulty
- Tackle an Easier Version
- Break Down the Problem

3

Solution might be in your blindspot

Cycle Through the Catalog
- *Think: Could ___ be useful?*

4

If you are still stuck...

Articulate Your Blocker
- Don't Say "Hint"
- Show Your Work

5

CRACKING THE CODING INTERVIEW
189 PROGRAMMING QUESTIONS AND SOLUTIONS

CRACKING THE PM CAREER
THE SKILLS, FRAMEWORKS, AND PRACTICES TO BECOME A GREAT PRODUCT MANAGER

CRACKING THE PM INTERVIEW
HOW TO LAND A PRODUCT MANAGER JOB IN TECHNOLOGY

CRACKING THE TECH CAREER
INSIDER ADVICE ON LANDING A JOB AT GOOGLE,
MICROSOFT, APPLE, OR ANY TOP TECH COMPANY

BEYOND CRACKING

the

CODING INTERVIEW

GAYLE L. MCDOWELL
MIKE MROCZKA
ALINE LERNER
NIL MAMANO

CareerCup, LLC
Palo Alto, CA

BEYOND CRACKING THE CODING INTERVIEW

Published by CareerCup, LLC, Palo Alto, CA. Compiled Jan 22, 2025.

For more information, or to enquire about bulk or university copies, contact support@careercup.com.

Please report bugs or issues at beyondctci.com.

978-1955706001 (ISBN 13)

To my favorite coders, Davis and Tobin—
Gayle

To my dog, my wife, and our readers (and not necessarily in that order)—
Mike

To my two wonderful kids (or if I have more, then whichever two are the most wonderful)—
Aline

Als meus pares—
Nil

WHAT'S INSIDE

You can access all of our online materials and bonus chapters here:

Talk with the authors, get help if you're stuck, and geek out with us on Discord.

bctci.co

bctci.co/discord

__INIT__()

PART I

Watch for these speech-bubble icons, which mean there is online content.

✦ **AI Interviewer:** Each problem can be tried online with the AI Interviewer.

▶ **Interview Replay:** Recordings of actual mock interviews.

🗋 **Snippet:** Material to copy/paste online, including email templates and code recipes.

☑ **Resource:** Bonus chapters, worksheets, and other material.

__INIT__()

README

This is a big book, and yes, it needs an instruction manual. We ask (beg?) you to read this. We'll keep it short and to the point. We also know lots of books have online materials, and they're often junk. We promise this isn't the case with ours.

Before we do that, we'd like to address the relationship between this book and interviewing.io. You'll see a lot of references to it. This book is not *from* interviewing.io, but we do partner with them for access to lots of data, interview replays, and an AI Interviewer. Because of this relationship, we know that sometimes mentioning interviewing.io might sound promotional. We've tried to avoid that as much as we could. We hope—trust—that you'll forgive this in exchange for access to lots of data, resources, and tools (and the discount code).

The book is roughly split into two segments: the first segment (Parts I–V) is the soft squishy stuff (backed up by a lot of qualitative and quantitative data). The second segment (Parts VI and onwards) is the technical content, which has its own README (pg 168). Please read it before diving into those parts.

ONLINE MATERIALS AND DISCUSSION

You can access all of our online materials and bonus chapters here:

Talk with the authors, get help if you're stuck, and geek out with us on Discord.

bctci.co

bctci.co/discord

ICONS

Whenever you see an icon wrapped in a speech bubble, it means that there's online content that goes with it, like so:

- **Problems, Solutions, and AI Interviewer:** Each problem in the book has a Python solution (without any fancy Python-specific tricks). We also provide Java, JavaScript, and C++ solutions online. We encourage you to try each problem with AI Interviewer and to only look at the solution if you get stuck.

- **Interview Replay:** These are recordings of actual mock interviews from interviewing.io's collection, conducted by engineers from FAANG and other top companies. We use them to showcase real-life examples of successes and mistakes.

- **Snippet:** These are snippets that you can copy and paste. Sometimes they're code. Sometimes they're text that you can steal verbatim (e.g., emails to recruiters).

- **Resource or document:** These are bonus chapters, downloadable problem sets, or worksheets (e.g., an equity calculator, a calculator to help you figure out the order in which to approach companies).

BUGS, QUESTIONS, AND CONTACT

Website:	beyondctci.com
Bugs:	bctci.co/bugs
Errata:	bctci.co/errata
Email:	beyond@gayle.com

Get $50 off anonymous mock interviews on interviewing.io

While this book gives you the tools and strategies to tackle tough technical questions, it is essential to put these tools into practice. With the purchase of this book, you get $50 off on interviewing.io mock interviews. There, you can practice anonymously with FAANG interviewers.

Even if you don't use interviewing.io, find a way to practice with another person; grinding problems by yourself quickly reaches the point of diminishing returns.

bctci.co/discount-X3A4

HELLO WORLD. HELLO READER.

The only thing worse than technical interviews is
not having technical interviews.

Oscar Wilde(ish)

Always stay gracious, best revenge is your paper.

Beyoncé Knowles-Carter

Cracking the Coding Interview (*CtCI*) has been the industry leader in teaching engineers how to get into top tech companies for over a decade. It's referenced in almost every major interview prep source, including books, podcasts, blogs, and online courses, as the source of truth on how to get into the major tech companies in our industry. And—although this was never the intention—it's even been used as a classroom textbook and a question bank for companies to draw on.

So, why write *another* interview prep book? And why now?

While CtCI remains an excellent foundation for interview preparation, the landscape of technical interviews has evolved dramatically since its publication. Online interview resources have changed how candidates practice, and the questions asked in interviews have grown both in difficulty and variety. And, as more candidates are preparing for interviews than ever before, the bar for passing has risen accordingly.

But it's not just the questions that have changed. The process of landing a job at top tech companies has grown even more competitive. The technical interview format has sparked increasing debate, and AI is reshaping how people apply for jobs, how companies screen candidates, and even how interviews are conducted.

Amidst these shifts, we felt it was time to take a step back and rethink what a modern interview prep book should look like—one that complements existing resources and patches the gaps between what candidates are doing and what they need to be doing. We realized that a new edition wouldn't cut it. It would have to be a brand new book, and this book would have to:

- **Focus on understanding, not memorization.** We aim to teach you the computer science fundamentals *and* the interview skills needed to excel, regardless of your educational background. By building a deep understanding of these concepts, you'll be prepared to tackle problems you've never seen before—something memorization alone can't achieve.

- **Cover important non-technical topics.** CtCI only briefly touched on what some call the "squishy" stuff—resumes, negotiation, and managing your job search. This book devotes ~150 pages to these topics because they are now critical to success. We'll guide you through technical recruiting with practical advice, down to exactly what to say in the situations you're likely to encounter.
- **Ground our advice in data.** This book draws on a decade of insights from real-world interviews, including a corpus of over 100,000 interviews conducted on interviewing.io by senior engineers from FAANG+ companies. You'll get a data-driven perspective on what technical interviews look like at top companies today.

Now, to address the angry elephant in the room: technical interviews are flawed, right? Absolutely. We don't just acknowledge that; we're going to dive into a candid discussion of everything wrong with technical interviews, and what you can do about it.

Despite what some have suggested, CtCI didn't invent this format—nor is BCtCI going to end it. As far as we can tell, technical interviewing isn't going anywhere. But we hope to make the process a little less daunting and a lot more transparent—by leveling the playing field and giving you access to what was previously insider knowledge. We hope that you're able to put away your hatred of the format, read this book with an open mind, put in the work, and get your revenge... by nailing your interviews, fearlessly negotiating, and landing the high-paying, challenging, awesome job that you deserve.

Before we get on with the real stuff, we have one request for you. Do not *read* this book—at least not in the traditional sense of left-to-right, top-to-bottom, page-to-page. Rather, we implore you to *do* this book. Use it. Interact with it. This is so important that we have a literal README on how to use it.

We hope you enjoy ~~reading~~ doing this book, inasmuch as one can enjoy a book about interviews and job searches. We really enjoyed ~~writing~~ building it.

CRASH & LEARN: OUR FAILED INTERVIEWS

Everyone loves a success story, but failure is often the best teacher. We will share here our most humbling interview experiences—times we bombed, blanked, or were simply unprepared. These stories aren't just about the mistakes we made; they're about the lessons we learned and how those failures shaped us.

Our hope is that by sharing these moments, you'll see that even "experts" have stumbled, arguably in career-altering ways. More importantly, you'll learn that just as these interview failures don't reflect on *our* skills as engineers, nor do yours.

GAYLE

Entering my fourth year of a five-year undergrad/master's program, I was fortunate to have three Microsoft internships behind me. Determined to try something new for my final internship, I sent countless cold emails and resumes into the void of online applications. Somehow, Google picked mine. I was thrilled.

From the bits I'd heard about technical interviewing, questions could be anything from implementing an ArrayList to the heavy-ball brainteaser[1]. Imagine my surprise when, instead, I got a math question: "What is 2^20?" My answer was the always-brilliant "Um, I don't know? Can I use a calculator?"

All I could think about was what a stupid question this was and how I definitely didn't know the answer. And why should I? Who cares? *Just look it up if you need to know it.* (Sound familiar?)

What I didn't realize then was that—probably—my interviewer wasn't expecting me to just *know* this. Most likely, she wanted me to start from what I did know, perhaps that 2^{10} is about 1000. From there, if I knew my exponent rules, I could solve it: $2^{20} = 2^{10} * 2^{10}$ is about 1000 * 1000… so approximately 1 million.

In *her* mind, it was a problem-solving question—albeit one that relied on a lot of math[2]. But in *my* mind, I didn't know the answer, and I was supposed to, and <*PANIC*>. All I needed to do was focus on what I *could* solve rather than what I *knew*.

Still a stupid question though[3].

---

1 Given a balance (i.e., a scale that only tells you which side is heavier) and eight balls—all the same weight other than one which is slightly heavier—find the heavy ball in as few measurements as possible.

2 In general, asking math-heavy questions is a no-no for interviews. However, I'll let her off the hook here, a little. I was a computer science major with a math minor. If I didn't know exponent rules, something had gone very wrong.

3 Why is this a bad question? Put aside the "it's not relevant" part. The relevant factor is: is it predictive? Approached the right way, this *could be* a problem solving question. However, it didn't feel like that to me—and perception matters. Additionally, even if I had approached it as a problem-solving question, there is very little "meat" to the question; what distinguishes between good and bad other than understanding how to break up the exponents?

MIKE

In my first year of college as a CS student, I was the only student to get an opportunity to interview at Google for their internship position[4]—and I was ecstatic about it. The problem? I hadn't taken my data structures and algorithms class yet. My GPA took a colossal hit that semester as I spent way too much time cutting class to watch YouTube lectures on sorting algorithms and NP-hard problems in an attempt to prepare for my interview.

The interview day came, and I had two back-to-back meetings with different Googlers. I described the optimal solution for my first interview, which I nervously coded in C++ with a hashmap—but then the second interviewer stumped me with a binary tree question[5]. After much fumbling, the interviewer walked me through a viable way to solve the problem, which I coded, but I knew I had bombed my chance at a Google internship.

A few years later, I passed Google's full-time interviews twice—declining the first offer for a remote role at Salesforce and accepting the second for a permanent position at Google.

ALINE

After graduating from MIT, I spent three years cooking professionally. While my culinary detour could fill a book, I wasn't good enough at it to make it a career. Out of money, I returned to coding. Coming off three years of flipping pans, chopping food, and drinking nightly, I found myself back in a well-lit office, standing at a whiteboard, asked to reverse a linked list.

Not only had I forgotten what these interviews were like (I was expecting to talk about my past projects), but I completely blanked on what a linked list was, much less how to reverse one. And this particular interview was with Sasha Aickin, Redfin's CTO, back when they were like five people. It's one of the things I still kick myself for, every now and again.

To his credit, Sasha patiently explained how linked lists work, and, through a series of hints, got me to change pointer directions. I clumsily erased and redrew arrowheads, but I don't think I wrote much code. It was too little, too late.

I never forgot how shitty failing that interview felt. I also never forgot how gracious Sasha was, in the face of my failure, and how he patiently walked me through the problem by asking leading questions. Both of those experiences helped me come up with the idea for interviewing.io: a place where people could fail privately, without the stigma, and learn from those failures, by pairing with kind, empathetic people who care.

NIL

Nil insists that he's never failed an interview. We would like to clarify that it's because he's only done one—and passed. True to his name, Nil has exactly zero failure stories to share. Classic edge case.

---

4 For the curious, I sent over 100+ cold email messages to former alumni until someone was willing to refer me. Even back then, I was using the techniques we show you in this book.

5 I was asked to compute the maximum sum of any path in the tree, which did not necessarily start at the root but could include it. For a variant of that problem, see Problem 35.1: Aligned Chain (pg 437).

UGLY TRUTHS & HIDDEN REALITIES
PART II

Watch for these speech-bubble icons, which mean there is online content.

✦ **AI Interviewer:** Each problem can be tried online with the AI Interviewer.

▶ **Interview Replay:** Recordings of actual mock interviews.

📄 **Snippet:** Material to copy/paste online, including email templates and code recipes.

↗ **Resource:** Bonus chapters, worksheets, and other material.

UGLY TRUTHS & HIDDEN REALITIES

WHY JOB SEARCHES SUCK

Job searches suck—*especially* for engineers, who are, by and large, rational, well-intentioned people who expect the world to function according to some set of predictable rules. Why do job searches suck so much?

- **Job searches are not deterministic, and neither are interview outcomes.** In job searches, effort doesn't always correlate with results. For technical interviews specifically, there's little predictability in how the same person will perform from interview to interview (pg 26).

- **No feedback loop.** When you apply online and don't get a response, you can't tell if you weren't a fit or if no one even saw your application. Your insecurities can convince you that not only did a human look, but they quickly sized you up, saw right through you, and lasered in on every single flaw to conclude (correctly, in your mind) that you're unfit for the job. When you interview, whether you pass or get rejected, you often don't know why, which makes it difficult to know how to prepare the next time.

- **The content of your resume is often eclipsed by the brands in it. If you don't have brand-name companies or schools, it's much harder to get noticed.** Recruiters are notoriously bad at making value judgments based on resumes[1]. Despite these shortcomings, resumes are still the gold standard, and that means candidates from non-traditional backgrounds enter the game with a significant disadvantage.

- **To get in the door, you very likely have to know someone.** Surprisingly, this is even true for candidates who look good on paper; recruiters often ignore online applications because the signal-to-noise ratio is so poor. But it's especially true if you don't look good on paper.

- **Technical interviews are notoriously flawed and not representative of the actual engineering work you do every day.** This one is especially rough, and it bears out in our data. Senior engineers often do *worse* than juniors in their first few interviews because junior engineers have more recently completed an algorithms class or have done extensive interview prep. Senior engineers have been in the trenches, often focusing on building applications; there are very few engineering roles where you're doing the types of academic problems that you get in interviews day in and day out.

These are just a few of the challenges, but the strategies in this book will help you navigate them and achieve success—however you define it.

Given all these flaws, you might ask: How did we get here, where our technical interviews feel so divorced from the work and so unpredictable in their outcomes? For that, let's take a brief look at the history of technical interviewing.

---

1   See https://www.reddit.com/r/recruitinghell/comments/qhg5jo/this_resume_got_me_an_interview/

## CHAPTER 1

A BRIEF HISTORY OF TECHNICAL INTERVIEWS

A definitive work on the history of technical interviewing was surprisingly hard to find, but we were able to piece together a narrative by scouring books like *How Would You Move Mount Fuji*, *Programming Interviews Exposed*, and the bounty of the internets. The story goes something like this.

Technical interviewing has its roots as far back as the 1950s, at Shockley Semiconductor Laboratories in Mountain View, California. William Shockley's[1] interviewing methodology came out of the need to keep up with the innovative, rapidly moving, Cold War-fueled tech sector, something that traditional hiring approaches taken from established, skills-based assembly line industries simply couldn't handle.

And so, Shockley relied on questions that could gauge analytical ability, intellect, and potential quickly. One canonical question[2] in this category has to do with coins:

> You have eight identical-looking coins, except one is lighter than the rest. Figure out which one it is with just two weighings on a pan balance.

The techniques that Shockley developed were adopted by Microsoft during the 1990s, as the success of the desktop computer, and later, the first dot-com boom spurred an explosion in tech hiring. Like Shockley, Microsoft also needed to quickly and scalably assess high volumes of candidates for potential. As software engineering became increasingly complex, it was no longer possible to have a few centralized expert programmers manage the design and then delegate away the minutiae. Even rank-and-file developers needed to be able to produce under a variety of rapidly evolving conditions, where just mastery of specific skills wasn't enough.

The puzzle format, in particular, was easy to standardize because individual hiring managers didn't have to come up with their own interview questions, and a company could quickly build up its own interchangeable question repository. Over time, most companies did away with puzzle questions[3] for engineers, and moved to algorithmic questions: these questions seemed more relevant but still assessed problem-solving skills.

At many top companies, such as Google, this need for interchangeable parts ultimately carried over to the interview process as well—rather than having individual teams run their own processes and pipelines,

---

1   We are acutely aware that this is the same William Shockley who became the poster boy for eugenics. He was a pretty awful person.

2   A first attempt—if you're an engineer—is to do something akin to binary search: split the coins into two sets of four coins each. Then, take the lighter set, and divide it into two sets of two coins each. Then, split in half again. But that will be *three* weighings, not two. To reduce a weighing, consider that the balance will also tell us if the sets are equal. We can divide the coins into *three* sets.

3   https://www.nytimes.com/2013/06/20/business/in-head-hunting-big-data-may-not-be-such-a-big-deal.html

companies standardized it. This way, in addition to questions, you could effectively plug and play the interviewers themselves—any interviewer within your org could be quickly trained up and assigned to speak with any candidate, independent of the prospective team.

At the same time, companies didn't always create incentives for engineers to work hard at being good interviewers, and as you'll see later in this book, we believe that much of the flak that algorithmic interviews get is due to the interviewers conducting them (and, often, lack of training or proper incentives).

So where does this leave us? Technical interviews are, at best, a *proxy* for the day-to-day tasks that a software engineer actually does, and not all interviewers are good. But, regardless, do technical interviews work? Well, that's complicated and depends a lot on your definition of "work." For whom, the candidate or the company? For what type of company? Compared to what?

We would argue that interviewing as a whole is flawed, and it's really a matter of picking your poison. However, even the most ardent defenders[4] of these sorts of technical interviews agree that false negatives—great engineers who get rejected—are common. FAANGs and other companies who adopt these processes tolerate a high false negative rate, under the rationale that it's better to reject a good candidate than to hire a bad one. The process is optimized to reduce false positives.

For you, the candidate, that kind of sucks. But it is what it is, and that's what this book is here for: to help you avoid being one of those false negatives.

---

4 Let's call out the elephant in the room. Some might assume that, as authors of a coding interview book, we must adamantly believe in the value of coding interviews. Not so. Not only has our intimate look at coding interviews exposed many flaws, but the entire existence of coding interview prep means that coding interviews are, at least, a little bit broken.

## CHAPTER 2

WHAT'S BROKEN ABOUT CODING INTERVIEWS

This chapter dives into the systemic flaws of technical interviews, from the prevalence of bad questions and bad interviewers to the randomness of interview outcomes and the growing interview-industrial complex. But it's not all doom and gloom. Once you understand the challenges and accept that the system is flawed, you'll be able to operate within it and win (and do so with confidence and integrity).

IT'S NOT THE WORK YOU DO EVERY DAY

One of the most persistent critiques of technical interviews is that they feel disconnected from the work you do every day. If interviews were like the work you did every day, we'd expect that senior engineers would outperform juniors in interviews. As it turns out, that's not the case: frustratingly, the more experienced you are, the worse you perform.

We actually have data for this. If you look at performance in their first mock interview on interviewing.io, junior engineers significantly outperform senior ones. In the upcoming graph, you can see the average score that candidates got in their first mock interview on interviewing.io, broken out by seniority. Not only do junior engineers significantly outperform experienced engineers,[1] but experienced engineers perform the worst out of all the groups.

---

1 At this point, you're probably thinking that the bar is different for more junior engineers. At some companies, it is. At some, it is not. Our interviewers know the experience level of their candidates and adjust their bar accordingly when giving feedback. With that in mind, new grads likely do the best in interviews because they're fresh off a data structures and algorithms course.

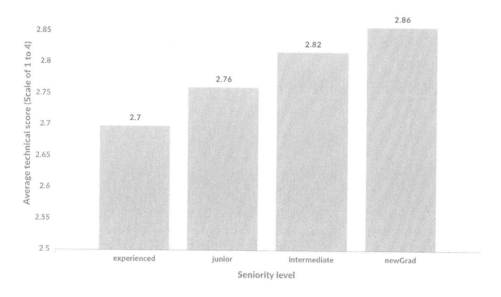

Performance in first interview, by seniority level

This effect gets less pronounced as people practice more; once everyone has done a bunch of mock interviews, they all roughly converge, as you can see in the next graph. But, out of the gate, recency with the material gives you a significant advantage.

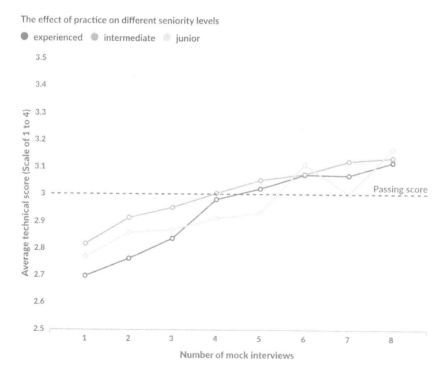

The effect of practice on different seniority levels

You might also notice in this graph that it takes about five mock interviews, on average, to start passing these interviews (pg 40).

BAD QUESTIONS (AND MEMORIZATION OVER UNDERSTANDING)

There is so much vitriol targeted toward technical interview questions that rehashing it in detail probably isn't worth the paper this book is printed on. If you've ever read any thread on Hacker News about interviewing, you know the main points:[2]

- **Questions are too academic and obscure.** You've probably never had to invert a binary tree at work.
- **Bad questions.** Many questions require a serendipitous "Ah-ha!" moment to solve, which even the best engineers may not be able to guarantee. Some questions aren't well-formulated or require too much domain-specific knowledge.
- **Too much memorization.** With how interviewing works today, it's rational to memorize a bunch of common questions, which turns the exercise into a test of memorization rather than understanding or ability.

We do not disagree with any of these points, and yes, these flaws are real. We've already talked about how we got here and why technical interviews are the way they are. It's easier for huge companies to scale if they can reduce interviewer training time and not have to come up with original questions/use LeetCode questions verbatim. Sadly, smaller companies often "cargo cult" large company practices, not realizing that they hire good candidates despite their processes and not because of them.

It's also true that memorizing helps a lot. On interviewing.io, after every interview, both interviewers and interviewees fill out a feedback form. One of the things we ask interviewees is whether they've seen this question before. We don't share whether they have or not with interviewers, so there's no reason to lie.

Here is a graph of the pass rate for algorithmic interviews as a function of whether candidates have seen the question before.

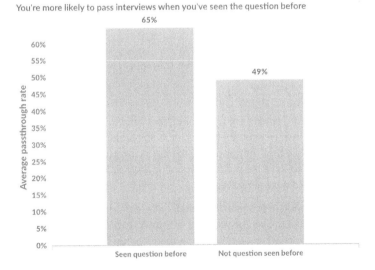

You're more likely to pass interviews when you've seen the question before

---

2 We've also surveyed our users, as part of some research we did to figure out what makes someone a good interviewer: https://interviewing.io/blog/best-technical-interviews-common

As you can see, familiarity with a question before gives you a serious edge in interviews: you are 33% more likely to pass. We expect that this disparity would be even higher if we had rephrased our feedback form to say something like, "Have you *practiced* this question before?"

The fact that memorizing questions gives you an edge is ironic, given that the whole purpose of modern technical interviewing is to evaluate one's ability to think like an engineer, rather than come to the table with a bunch of specific skills. It's also one of the things that makes it harder to stomach practicing for interviews. It's a tough pill to swallow to know that, ultimately, you're competing with memorizers.

In this book, we'll arm you with the kind of foundational understanding that will make memorization less important (but will be just as effective at improving your performance).

BAD INTERVIEWERS WHO DON'T WANT TO BE THERE

> Good interviewers can get good signal from a bad question. Bad interviewers cannot even get good signal from a good question. For a good interviewer, the question is just a tool to guide the discussion into interesting areas. For bad interviewers, the question is an absolute to which they must hear the exact answer they have in mind.
>
> Jos Visser, Member of Technical Staff at OpenAI, and formerly of Google, Facebook, and Amazon

Yes, bad questions are bad. However, bad interviewers are, in our minds, the biggest problem with technical interviews. A terrible question, in the hands of a skilled, engaged interviewer, can yield meaningful signal. A great question asked by an unskilled, disconnected interviewer will always be bad.

We talked about how large companies adopted modern technical interviewing in part because of the "interchangeable parts" approach to provisioning interviewers. However, human beings are not gears or sprockets—each comes with their own unique hangups and proclivities. It's naive to think that you can swap one interviewer for another and achieve the same result.

> In our experience hiring professional mock interviewers, we saw very quickly that whether someone likes to conduct interviews is bimodal: either they love it or they hate it, with not much in between.

The people who like interviewing tend to enjoy teaching. They tend to have higher-than-average empathy, they remember a time when they were on the other side of the table, and they want to make that experience less painful for their candidates. They also tend to approach interviews with a certain curiosity. They are curious about novel ways to solve the problem, about new rabbit holes their candidates will inevitably go down, and about the candidates themselves.

The people who hate interviewing treat it as a disruption—a necessary evil between shipping features. They do the bare minimum, and it shows. Over the years, we've listened to a lot of interviews. You can immediately identify when an interviewer is checked out. You'll hear them typing. You'll hear them go silent for a while. They'll often need to ask the candidate to repeat themselves. You certainly won't hear them collaborating with their candidate or gently guiding them away from a perilous rabbit hole. Most of us have been on the receiving end of an interviewer's callous indifference and know what it feels like.

Bad interviewers are common across companies, even top-tier ones,[3] and there is an added complication: companies don't usually track who their best interviewers are,[4] nor do they reward them. Sadly, it's often the opposite—bad interviewers get rewarded because they focus on writing code instead of conducting interviews. In other words, curmudgeons who alienate their recruiting team (and get scheduled less often as a result) get rewarded. Engineers who end up being less present in their interviews because their mind is elsewhere, still churning through the code they were writing when they got interrupted, get rewarded. In the rare instances where we've seen companies really care about interviewer quality, it's because an eng leader there has taken it upon themselves, as a labor of love.

Why does it matter if an interviewer is bad, outside of it being a poor experience for candidates? In this graph, you can see the average interview pass rates on interviewing.io, broken out by interviewer quality.[5]

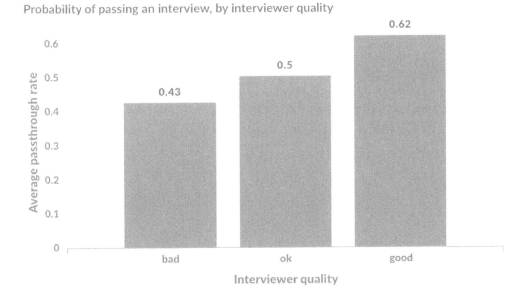

Probability of passing an interview, by interviewer quality

Interviewer quality matters because the purpose of a technical interview is not to see if you can get the perfect answer. You're not just solving a coding problem online by yourself. As such:

- Bad interviewers miss out on critical two-way interactions with the candidate. You're meant to discuss approaches with your interviewer and ask questions, all in the service of determining if you're the kind of person who can pick up new skills in a rapidly changing landscape and work well with other smart people. When your interviewer is not holding up their end, it's much harder for you to hold up yours, and it turns into a contest of who's memorized the most questions.

---

3 Some people assume that top-tier companies invest more into interviewer training than others. In our experience, that isn't true. We won't throw specific companies under the bus in this book, but if you read interviewing.io's guide to FAANG interview processes (https://interviewing.io/guides/hiring-process), you'll see how much or how little some of them invest in interviewer training.

4 https://interviewing.io/blog/best-technical-interviews-common

5 We determine quality as a function of how highly rated interviewers are by their candidates with respect to question quality, hint quality, and how excited the candidate would be to work with that person. It's a "candidate experience" score, in other words. Candidates submit these ratings before they know how they did. This graph is also not about interviewer leniency—for what it's worth, the best-calibrated interviewers tend to be the best-rated, and those who are too lenient tend to be among the worst.

- Bad interviewers are incentivized to be unnecessarily harsh. Better to say no to a good candidate than risk hiring a bad one, right?

- Bad interviewers will judge too much on superficial grounds, which is especially unfair to candidates who come from a non-traditional background or lack some little bit of institutional knowledge.

For all their perceived objectivity (and certainly they're more objective than ones where you talk about your experience), coding interviews are a complex interaction between two humans. When one of the parties isn't truly present, the candidate pipeline suffers, and you end up with fewer candidates to choose from and, ultimately, worse hires.

NON-DETERMINISTIC OUTCOMES

Anyone who's done multiple technical interviews has probably felt in their gut that outcomes are somewhat arbitrary. So much depends on serendipity and, well, clicking! *Did you click with your interviewer? Did something click in your head at the right time when trying to solve the problem?*

If you've felt like this, you're not alone, and we have the data to prove it. On interviewing.io, after every interview, you get a technical score from your interviewer, on a scale of 1 to 4. The same candidate can do multiple interviews, each of which is with a different interviewer and/or different company, and this opens the door for some pretty interesting and somewhat controlled comparative analysis.

With that in mind, we looked at how the same person performed from interview to interview.

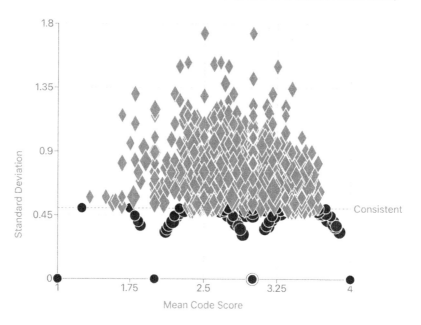

Standard Dev vs. Mean Interview Performance (33,052 Interviews, 7,161 Interviewees)

● Consistent (StdDev ≤ 0.5)   ◆ Inconsistent (StdDev > 0.5)

We analyzed interviewing.io's data to understand how individuals performed across multiple interviews (for this analysis, we included people who did between 3 and 20 interviews). Each circle or diamond represents people with that specific average score and standard deviation across their interviews.

The y-axis is the standard deviation of performance; a higher standard deviation reflects more volatility. Some surprising takeaways from this analysis:

- Only 25% of people are consistent from interview to interview (standard dev of <= 0.5). Everyone else is all over the place.
- 64% of the people who scored at least one 4 have also scored at least one 1 or one 2.

So, what did the most highly volatile performers have in common? The answer appears to be, well, nothing. About half were working at top companies. About 60% had attended top schools. And years of experience didn't have much to do with it either—a plurality of interviewees had between 2 and 6 years of experience, with the rest all over the board (varying between 1 and 20 years).

When we corrected for interviewer strictness, the effect didn't go away either.

Why is this bad? This inconsistency means randomness significantly impacts your career. In a way, interviews serve the same function as standardized tests—giving an organization a way to make a value judgment about someone's ability relatively quickly and without a lot of priors, in a way that's consistent and repeatable. For all their flaws and biases, standardized testing providers have made a lot of effort to make sure that their results are repeatable because their results often determine the social mobility and livelihoods of millions of students every year. Even though they have a similar impact on outcomes for millions of engineers, tech companies have not done the same for their interviews.

BUCKETED SCORING

Imagine that we wanted to evaluate whether students in a given classroom were tall or short. But rather than measuring people's heights, we first bucketed them into "very short," "short," "tall," or "very tall." Inevitably, there will be many cases where two students are nearly the same height, but a few millimeters make the difference between "short" and "tall."

Any bucketed scoring will lose precision and create arbitrariness, but it's even worse when we have few buckets and split the middle zone—which is common. That is, if, rather than providing a bucket for "average height" (where most people might fall), we split these people into "short" and "tall" depending on whether they cross some threshold. Now, we don't just have some arbitrary scores; we have a lot of them.

This is effectively what's happening in many technical interviews. In fact, it can be a triple-whammy.

- **Bucketed Scoring:** Interviewers don't score you as a 2.6; almost always, interviewers are forced into bucketed scores, such as 1, 2, 3, or 4 (or its qualitative equivalent: strong no-hire, no-hire, hire, strong hire).
- **Risk-Averse Scoring:** Interviewers are encouraged to be risk-averse: "better to reject a good one than hire a bad one," they say. That 2.6 interview is more likely to be reported as a 2 than a 3.
- **Splitting the Middle:** In many cases, interviewers are bucketed into just *four* buckets— with no place for "average" or "maybe." The average score is often around a 2.5 to 2.7, so a four-point scale splits the middle candidates. This means that *a lot* of people will get rounded up or down into "hire" or "no-hire."

A candidate who gets {3.2, 3.3, 2.7, 3.4} on a four-point scale may be hired, but the candidate who gets {3/hire, 3/hire, 2/no-hire, 3/hire} (a possible risk-averse rounding equivalent) may not be. We've effectively lost the information that the "no-hire" was actually really close to a "hire."

No matter how you bucket, bucketed scoring effectively forces interviewers to translate very typical scores into something more extreme and loses fidelity in the process. No wonder we have so much variability in interviews!

INTERVIEW PREP BEGETS INTERVIEW PREP

Technical interviewing has given rise to a booming preparation industry. This is somewhat ironic, as it defeats the purpose of this form of interviewing; the goal was to understand the candidate's aptitude, independent of what they currently know.

The reality is that—as we've shown—interview prep *works*. We might not like it, but people do better with preparation. That's why interview prep is a multi-billion dollar industry, including everything from books and courses to asynchronous coding challenges and mock interviews. This also means that you are being compared to candidates who are prepping for interviews (and, in many cases, simply memorizing a ton of questions), which means that the expectations for *you* have gone up too. What do you do about this? You, of course, prepare for interviews too.

It's an unfortunate cycle; interview prep begets interview prep.[6] But for the record, memorizing problems without *also* working on understanding goes against our preparation philosophy, and it's honestly not that effective.

All that said, it's time to change our lens and talk about how to work the system. Technical interviews are here to stay, and if you want a job at a top-tier tech company, you have to jump through this hoop.

---

6   Would it be better if we did the impossible and magically got rid of all interview prep? Probably not. Before today's industry, there were still some books and resources—but it relied more on word of mouth and "inside" sources (friends telling you what to expect). This favored people with connections. The bar might have been lower, but the playing field was more unfair.

## CHAPTER 3

WHAT RECRUITERS WON'T TELL YOU

Show me the incentives, and I'll show you the outcome.

Charlie Munger

It is difficult to get a man to understand something when his salary depends on his not understanding it.

Upton Sinclair

Even though recruiters try to position themselves as your advocate, remember this: recruiters are not your friend, and they don't work for you.

I (Aline) used to be a recruiter. I ran my own third-party agency, and I also worked in-house before starting interviewing.io. That means I've had to struggle with the tangled incentive structure[1] that comes with being a recruiter. There's always tension; recruiters are, by and large, good human beings who genuinely want to help their candidates, but they also have an employer they're beholden to, as well as a comp/bonus structure that rewards certain behaviors, some of which run counter to candidates' best interests.

There's some distinction between in-house recruiters and third-party recruiters (recruiters who work for an agency that does placement, rather than a specific company that's hiring engineers).

THIRD-PARTY RECRUITERS

Working with third-party recruiters (also known as agency recruiters) is, at best, mixed. The most important thing to realize about them is that you are not the customer. The employer is. As such, even when they're paid a commission based on your salary, their incentives are, at best, *sometimes* aligned with yours.

Ultimately, a recruiter's incentive is to *get the deal done*, not to get you the best possible deal. Here's why.

A recruiter, depending on market conditions, gets anywhere from 8% - 25% of a candidate's base salary when they make a placement. However, that cut is going to the recruiting agency as a whole rather than to the individual recruiter; you will almost always end up working with large agencies rather than a single person.

Let's say that you get an offer. You talk to your third-party recruiter and tell them that you would like more money. The recruiter may go to the hiring manager and try to advocate for you, but they're not going to

---

1 https://blog.alinelerner.com/if-youre-an-engineer-who-wants-to-start-a-recruiting-business-read-this-first/

push very hard because the incremental difference in their cut is going to be pretty small[2], and to them the thing that matters is making the hire. After all, they're evaluated on the number of hires they make, first and foremost, independent of compensation. Third-party recruiters are incentivized to get the deal done, not to risk the deal by negotiating hard for you.

This means:

- If they have multiple clients potentially matching the same company, and they know you're less likely to take their offer, they'll fight for the other candidates more than you.
- They may expose information to the company that reveals whether you'll demand a high salary. Remember: they're paid by the company, not you. If the company likes them, that's good for them.
- They may encourage you to take a lower salary. Sure, they get a slightly higher commission if you negotiate a higher salary, but they get *no* commission until the deal is done.
- They may encourage an employer to lowball you, if they think you'll take it.[3]

So, when you work with third-party recruiters:

- Do not tell them *anything* about your job search.
- Do not share your compensation history/expectations.
- Always deal directly with the companies they introduce you to, once you establish a point of contact there.
- Assume that anything you tell your recruiter is going to get back to every company you're working with.

IN-HOUSE RECRUITERS

Some in-house recruiters get a bonus for hires, but this bonus is rarely tied to your compensation. In fact, in some cases, they may get a bigger bonus if they're able to negotiate you down.

At big companies, in particular, in-house recruiters follow a playbook, and are evaluated accordingly. They're trained to make offers within specific bands, and they're trained to mobilize such that they don't lose candidates to other big companies; if you wave a Facebook counteroffer in front of Google, they will act. If you tell them you're interviewing at a startup, they will not, because they know that startups don't pay as much.

Because of this playbook[4]—and because they are working for the employer—their incentives do not align with yours. They're incentivized, first and foremost, to follow the rules their head of department sets for them. This is true for how they evaluate candidates, who they let through, and how they read resumes. And it's definitely true for how they negotiate.

Generally speaking, recruiters want to help, and many are rooting for their candidates. But they're also operating inside a box, and that box isn't set up to put your interests first.

---

2   Understanding that, let's do the math anyway. Let's say your offer has a base salary of $150k. Say that your recruiter goes to bat for you and tries to get you up to $165k. Before, the agency would have gotten paid $15k. Now the agency gets paid $16.5k. That incremental $1.5k isn't worth risking a deal over (even a few thousand dollars would not justify jeopardizing the deal). On top of that, the individual recruiter is only going to maybe get a few hundred dollars total from that increase.

3   Why would a recruiter recommend that an employer not pay you more? It seems counterintuitive, but remember that the employer is their customer, not you. A savvy business person will often take a short-term hit in the service of building an enduring relationship with their customer. Telling an employer that they don't need to pay a candidate more (even though paying the candidate more would get the recruiter marginally more money) builds trust and makes it more likely that that employer will keep coming back to them for future searches. Employers often work with several agencies at once and cycle between agencies, so anything agencies can do to retain employers is a win.

4   For more insight, watch this video on how recruiting leaders think about looking at resumes, debriefing interviews, and extending offers. https://www.youtube.com/watch?v=dHSufqvgUqY

A NOTE ABOUT IN-HOUSE RECRUITER TENURES

Many recruiters at FAANG companies are contractors. The longer a contractor works, the more their role may resemble that of a full-time employee. To avoid legal risks, companies often limit contract durations to around 6 months. While this practice is most common in California due to its strict labor laws, similar limitations are applied in other states, though the typical contract length may vary.

Why do recruiter tenures matter to you?

- Never assume that the recruiter you're talking to now will still be there in a few months, when you're ready to interview.
- Build good rapport with your recruiter. Odds are good that, even if you don't pursue their current company, you might be interested in their future company.
- Don't lie about other offers—it's not super likely your recruiter is checking whether you have the offers you say you do, but chances are, because recruiters have short tenures and work at lots of companies, your recruiter knows someone there. We've seen it happen.

We'll talk a *lot* more about how to work well with recruiters in future chapters, and now you'll understand why we give the advice that we do.

RECRUITERS WILL TRY TO CALL/TEXT. USE EMAIL INSTEAD.

Recruiters are notorious for calling and texting instead of using email. Why?

The generous interpretation is that recruiters generally want to move things along quickly. If they can get you to respond quickly, through a synchronous medium like phone or text, then they can likely move you through the process faster as well.

There is one other, less generous interpretation—phone and text give recruiters the upper hand. Even the worst recruiters, if they have any work experience at all, quickly become seasoned negotiators. Even inexperienced recruiters have an edge because they are following a script and playbook. They've been told what to say in a variety of situations, and they interact with candidates multiple times a day, over years.

You, on the other hand, do one job search every few years.

Email lets you level the playing field. You can craft every word, and figure out what to say and how much to reveal. Over email, you can play it cool, and you can take the time to get advice from friends or experts.

When a recruiter calls you on the phone, they get your impromptu responses. They can see if you're excited about the money, and possibly get you to answer questions that you might not have otherwise answered (e.g., your salary expectations). The phone will keep you off balance.

While texting allows you to think longer about your response, its casual nature lulls you into a false sense of security. Moreover, the fact that texts interrupt you from something else puts you at a disadvantage—when you get interrupted, your instinct is to quickly respond to make the interruption go away. But knee-jerk responses are rarely the right ones, and you end up giving away information you shouldn't have.

We encourage you to stick to email as much as possible. You will have to get on the phone eventually, of course, likely when they are ready to extend an offer, but you never have to text.

## CHAPTER 4

WHAT INTERVIEWERS WON'T TELL YOU

Much of interviewing advice takes an idealistic stance: interviewers are fundamentally well-intentioned rational actors who want to run a fair process, and any flaws in the process itself are circumstantial or occur because of very rare bad actors.

That's not strictly true. As we previously discussed (pg 24), most employers don't reward strong interviewing skills, so interviewers have little motivation to improve.

Here are some additional interviewing tropes, which may or may not be true. We'll discuss them all and address them with data. Can you guess which ones are true?

- It's not about whether you get the right answer. Rather it's about demonstrating your thought process.
- Interviewers decide early on if you've passed the interview.
- If you're a great communicator and build rapport with your interviewer, you can pass the interview, even if your technical skills are wobbly.

IS IT REALLY ABOUT DEMONSTRATING YOUR THOUGHT PROCESS, OR DO YOU NEED TO GET TO AN OPTIMAL SOLUTION?

On interviewing.io, candidates who clearly and correctly explained their approach but failed to reach an acceptable working solution received a "thumbs up" only 32% of the time, compared to the platform's overall average of 51%. This means that failing to produce a working solution reduces your chances of passing the interview by 37%.[1]

How Interview Replays Work and How to Use Them

Interview replays come from mock interviews on interviewing.io. Replays are shared with the permission of both participants. Each replay includes the interviewer's feedback. You can watch just the relevant snippet, but we include the entire interview.

We strongly recommend pausing your reading and watching these replays. Hearing real people interview lets you learn from their mistakes—so that you aren't doomed to repeat them.

Where we know it (and where enough time has elapsed since they did mock interviews), we'll share the candidate's outcome.

---

1 To be clear, if you've gotten to the optimal solution and have *mostly* working code (maybe some small syntax errors or an off by one error), we believe most interviewers would still give a Hire rating. But if it's not working, it has to be very close.

▶ NOT GETTING A WORKING SOLUTION, DESPITE DESCRIBING IT SUCCESSFULLY INTERVIEW REPLAY

View Online:	bctci.co/interviewers-replay-1 @ 45:50 - end
The Question:	Given an array of integers, are there elements a, b, c such that $a + b + c = 0$? Find all unique triplets which give the sum of zero.
What You'll See:	Although the candidate explained the solution well, their code had bugs. The interviewer offered some suggestions on how to improve coding speed and discussed the importance of writing compilable code.
Who:	*Interviewer*: Staff Software Engineer at Lyft *Candidate*: 4 years of experience

So, why do many interviewers insist on saying that it's about your thought process rather than the end result? That's complicated, but there are a few reasons:

1. It *feels good* to say. Interviewers *want* to believe that they're grading on something deeper and more qualitative than getting the right answers to really hard questions.

2. It is true, in a sense; interviewers prioritize your *solving ability*, not the answer itself. If you just spit out the right answer because you already know it, this won't be impressive to a good interviewer and could even lead you to getting eliminated for "cheating."

3. It *used to* be even more true. As standards have increased, there has been a bit less forgiveness for a candidate who made good progress but didn't get to the best solution.

The reality is that interviewers *are* looking for strong problem solvers, and—for a good interviewer—it *is* about the process, not the solution. However, it's often hard to convince them that you're a strong problem solver if you can't reach the optimal solution.

Either way, this trope stresses the importance of practice—the more you practice, the faster you'll get, and the more likely you get to an acceptable solution.

FIRST IMPRESSIONS AREN'T PREDICTIVE. EARLY PERFORMANCE IS.

You might have heard that the interviewers decide in the first few minutes whether you've passed the interview; we've certainly heard that plenty. But even supposing that's true, is it true for technical interviews? Given that technical interviews are focused on problem solving, it would be troubling if interviewers did in fact make such snap judgments *before the problem solving had even happened*.

At interviewing.io, we looked into this claim by analyzing sentiment—interviewers can make a comment during the interview (we call these "annotations") with an associated sentiment (positive, neutral, or negative), which the candidate will see afterwards.

05:01

TC clarified if it is okay to distribute less than 6M burgers and also explained how this might simplify their design.

communication

09:20

TC could have talked about non-functional requirements like availability, consistency, latency.

technical skill

Those who believe that the first impression is make-or-break might be reassured by this: the interviewer's first annotation is aligned with the outcome just 56% of the time—barely better than a coin flip. The first annotation occurs at an average of 13 minutes into the interview, which means the chit-chat is done and we've kicked off the problem solving portion. We can't speak for what happens in non-eng interviews, but at least for eng interviews: no, interviewers do *not* decide in the first few minutes. Whew!

However, your interviewer's impression of you by the 18-minute mark *is* predictive.

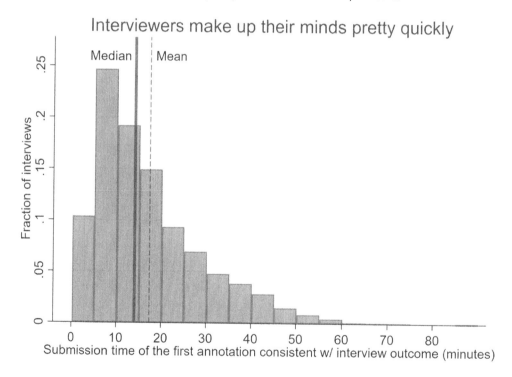

Figure 1. This graph is based on 7,883 interviews with annotations from the interviewing.io corpus. You can see when the first annotation that was predictive of the interview outcome happened. Most happen in the first 18 minutes.

Moreover, the average sentiment gets worse over time for both successful and unsuccessful candidates, with the sharpest decline occurring in the first 15 minutes.

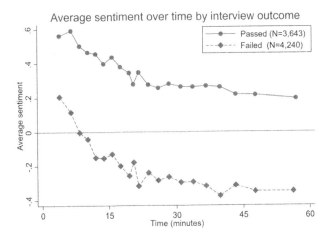

Figure 2. This graph is based on 7,883 interviews with annotations from the interviewing.io corpus.

You could interpret these findings cynically—all candidates do badly, and interviewers get stuck in preconceived (or at least early) notions. But as authors who have—collectively—spoken with thousands of candidates and interviewers, we see this in a more positive light.

Good interviewers[2] adjust their guidance based on your performance: when you do well, they give you less assistance; when you struggle, they give you more. It's like a live version of computer adaptive testing. This means that while you might do well in the first 10 minutes (mostly chit-chat and explaining the problem), *good* interviewers will adjust so that you struggle just enough. Perhaps seeing that struggle is why sentiment generally gets more negative over time; a good interviewer is purposefully putting you into situations that challenge you, thus creating more room for negative sentiment[3]. But that's part of the interview process.

\#   This means, for you, don't panic when things get more challenging. *Embrace the struggle.* Struggling doesn't mean that you're doing poorly; it can just mean that your interviewer is doing their job. They've given a problem of appropriate difficulty and adjusted their guidance to suit your abilities.

We also believe, optimistically, that it's a good thing early-formed opinions are predictive. At the 18 minute mark, we're about 10 minutes into the problem solving portion, by which point our interviewer has seen some of our skills. If the first 10 minutes of problem solving were not predictive of the next 30 minutes, that would be a further indictment of the interview process. After all, it's not like we're magically becoming better or worse problem solvers, so our performance at the beginning *should* typically be predictive of the rest.

It's good that we see consistency. It means that our interviewers, if they're good, are actually looking at our problem solving process, not quantitative metrics like "number of minutes to solution" or "did you get it perfect right away", nor dinging us because we have some tiny bug.

\#   This means, again, there's no reason to panic at little mistakes; these aren't making interviewers flip flop. Not all interviewers are good interviewers (unfortunately), but still—interviewers are generally looking at your performance as a *process*.

---

2   Fortunately, this data set is limited to interviewers who were rated well by their candidates. Our interpretations of the data do not hold for bad interviewers. As we discussed earlier (pg 24), there are many bad interviewers who aren't engaged and check out after the first few minutes.

3   However, this doesn't mean that you are *truly* doing worse. A good interviewer will also be looking at signal (pg 180), which means that they are taking into account the complexity of the problem.

COMMUNICATION SKILLS ARE NICE, BUT TECHNICAL SKILLS ARE NICER

Communication in technical interviews boils down to two aspects: rapport-building at the start (about yourself, your projects, etc) and clear communication throughout the interview.

RAPPORT-BUILDING AT THE START

Look, this isn't the kind of thing you usually say in an interview prep book, but the chit-chat in the first few minutes does not matter… *much*. Data shows positive communication in the first five minutes increases pass rates by 6 percentage points for underperforming candidates, compared to a 25-point boost from strong technical performance. Be enthusiastic and personable, but don't stress this unless small talk is a challenge for you. The technical stuff really does matter more.

COMMUNICATION THROUGHOUT THE INTERVIEW

Although many candidates believe in coding as soon as possible, the data shows the opposite: successful candidates actually code *slightly* later (about two minutes later[4] in a one-hour interview). This difference is small, but extra surprising given that many unsuccessful candidates will be quite delayed in coding because they lack a working approach. So why would coding later be linked to better outcomes? Communication, essentially. Candidates who explain their approach do better in interviews, but communication takes time.

Thinking out loud is essential in technical interviews, but beyond a baseline, communication may not significantly impact outcomes—at least for roles below Staff. On interviewing.io, candidates are rated on technical skills, problem-solving ability, and communication skills (all on a 1 - 4 scale), alongside a pass/fail score. Our analysis found that once a candidate scores 2 / 4 in communication, additional improvements yield diminishing returns. In contrast, boosting technical or problem-solving scores by 1 or 2 points can increase the odds of passing by 1.5X to 2.4X, emphasizing the greater importance of these skills.

As roles become more senior though, communication and behavioral skills play an increasingly critical role in interview outcomes. At the Staff level and beyond, our anecdotal experience—supported by feedback from interviewers—shows that the evaluation criteria shift significantly to emphasize these skills.

All that said, we can't fully tease apart technical ability and communication skills; when a candidate can't communicate their solution, interviewers are also less likely to be impressed by their approach—and they are less able to give you hints to help you along.

Where does this leave you?

- Don't worry about practicing specifically for the first 5 minutes of the interview. You can prepare for it a little, but don't stress about it.
- Get used to thinking out loud.
- Spend the bulk of your time getting better at solving problems.

Fortunately, practicing thinking out loud doesn't come at the cost of practicing solving problems. You can quite literally do them at the same time.

---

4   Candidates with successful interviews first run code 27% of the way through the interview, whereas candidates with unsuccessful interviews first run code 23.9% of the way into the interview. This difference is small, but nonetheless statistically significant. https://interviewing.io/blog/we-analyzed-thousands-of-technical-interviews-on-everything-from-language-to-code-style-here-s-what-we-found#user-content-fnref-3

## CHAPTER 5

MINDSET AND THE NUMBERS GAME

No matter how good an engineer you are, if you get too much in your head during interviews, you'll fail. We've seen countless candidates self-sabotage because they jumped into the interview prep material before they accepted some fundamental truths about the journey. This chapter is about how to approach these interviews, and we encourage you to take it seriously. It's not woo-woo nonsense. It's our way of making sure you can apply your full potential for the rest of the book. With that in mind, here are the things you need to internalize and truly believe before you begin your studies.

TECHNICAL INTERVIEWING IS A NUMBERS GAME

Technical interviews are a numbers game, but many engineers underestimate just how much. It takes doing many interviews, and even more importantly, access to a peer group going through the same thing, to really internalize it. Here, we'll try to short-circuit all of that and convince you that failing an interview doesn't reflect on your engineering skills or potential; it's often the byproduct of a broken system.

Remember the graph (pg 26) where we showed that most people's technical interview performance is all over the place? Here it is again (Figure 1). Only 25% of people performed consistently, and about two thirds of people who got at least one 4 also got at least one 1 or 2.

Due to this inconsistency, even great engineers routinely fail interviews. This is a particularly big issue in technical phone screens, where interviewers must decide if someone gets to onsite based on *just one data point*.

Many candidates go into the process assuming it's repeatable, like a standardized test—a reasonable but flawed assumption. The truth is, unless you've been through the wringer, and unless you have people around you who have *also* been through the wringer, you're unlikely to realize just how unpredictable and variable the process can be.

For me (Aline), this became clear when I was a student at MIT. Attending a top-tier computer science program offered a number of advantages, but one of the most important (and least obvious) was access to a peer group that was going through the same things.

Having this group around me meant that we could all practice with each other, share our successes and failures, and have multiple shots on goal at top companies. Everyone was interviewing everywhere, and we quickly learned that bombing a Microsoft interview did not mean that you weren't meant to be an engineer. It just meant that you needed to work some more problems, do some more mock interviews, and try again at Google.

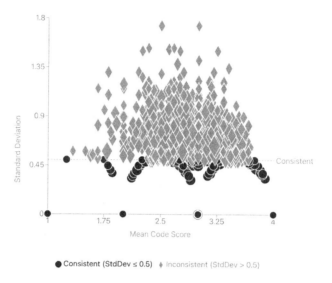

Figure 1. Standard deviation vs. mean interview performance (33,052 interviews; 7,161 interviewees). We analyzed interviewing.io's data to understand how individuals performed across multiple interviews (for this analysis, we included people who did between 3 and 20 interviews). Each circle or diamond represents people who had that specific average score and standard deviation across their interviews.

One of the most critical things to internalize is that if you fail an interview, that's all it is. It is *not* a well-reasoned indictment of your potential as an engineer. Keep practicing and try again.

Unfortunately, dusting yourself off and trying again is harder for some groups than for others.

PERSEVERANCE AFTER FAILURE IS HARDER FOR ENGINEERS FROM NON-TRADITIONAL BACKGROUNDS

Many years ago, we noticed that on interviewing.io, women were performing significantly worse in technical interviews than men. This disparity still exists today. But before you jump to conclusions, the reason is *not* that women are actually technically weaker. Let us explain.

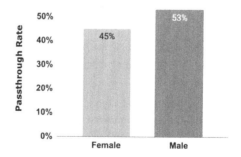

Figure 2. Gender differences in interview passthrough rate.

When we first noticed this disparity, we wondered if it was due to bias against women. So, we ran an experiment[1] using a real-time voice modulator that could change the pitch of the user's voice (making women sound like men, and vice versa).

Contrary to what we expected, masking gender had *no effect* on interview performance.

Perhaps the women were less senior? Doing different work? Nope. Neither of those factors seemed to differ meaningfully between groups.

What *was* different then? Women left interviewing.io roughly seven times as often as men after they do badly in an interview. And the numbers for two bad interviews aren't much better.[2]

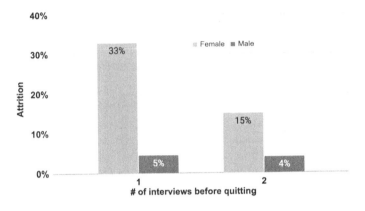

Figure 3. Attrition after poor interview performance.

When you correct for attrition, the difference between men and women goes away entirely.[3]

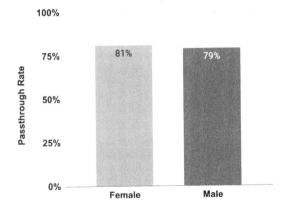

Figure 4. Average passthrough rate by gender when correcting for people who drop out after two failures.

---

1 We split our users into three groups: unmodulated (the control group), modulated *without* pitch change (another control; we needed it because modulated voices sound somewhat processed, and the last thing we wanted was for interviewers to guess the gender of their interviewees because anyone who sounded processed and male must actually be a woman and vice versa), and modulated *with* pitch change. This last one was the treatment group. https://interviewing.io/blog/voice-modulation-gender-technical-interviews

2 The differences between men and women are extremely statistically significant with P < 0.00001.

3 We have not studied this effect in race or in socioeconomic status, but we'd expect that you'd see a disparity in perseverance between groups, with engineers from non-traditional backgrounds being more likely to quit.

We are calling this out because we want it to change your behavior: everyone fails these interviews, regardless of background. If you're a woman, and very likely if you're from a non-traditional background, know that failure isn't a career end. Accept the system's flaws and learn to navigate them.

This means learning as much as you can, practicing as much as you can, then learning some more, and then practicing some more.

End-to-end, the practice journey may take anywhere from two to six months, depending on where you start and your previous exposure to algorithms and data structures. But, no matter who you are, you will need to practice, and you will fail some interviews. This is an axiom of our book.

It might take two failures before things turn around. It might take fifteen. But we implore you to exert yourself and keep going. If you approach technical interviewing from a place of curiosity, we *promise* that you'll get through it and find success at the end… which brings us to our final point.

PRACTICE IS ~~REALLY IMPORTANT~~ CRITICAL

It's all well and good to talk about who is doing well in mock interviews, but at the end of the day, your goal is to do well in *real* interviews. To understand what is driving strong performance in real interviews, we surveyed interviewing.io users about how well they did in real interviews at Google, Meta, and Amazon and compared their performance at these companies against their past total interview count (both mock and real), gender, whether they had a computer science degree, and how they learned to code.

The factor that stood out most was how many technical interviews an engineer had done in the past. Across all users, people who had completed five or more interviews had higher rates of passing a phone interview than those who had done fewer. The number of interviews mattered more than people's starting technical proficiency, and it also mattered more than gender and pedigree (those factors didn't actually matter).[4]

Probability of Passing a Technical Phone Screen	1 - 4 Interviews Beforehand	5+ Interviews Beforehand
Amazon	65%	81%
Meta	40%	71%
Google	51%	80%

Figure 5. The probability of passing phone screens at Amazon, Google, and Meta, as a function of how many technical interviews candidates had done previously, based on data from interviewing. io users. Practice helps, and the "tipping point" is five interviews.

But what, specifically, is it about practice that is so impactful? According to survey results, it's about direct feedback (when candidates were fortunate enough to get it; most often it was in mock interviews, rarely in real ones).

Engineers typically can't gauge how they did in interviews,[5] so they probably can't gauge *why* they passed or failed—although, unfortunately, they often *think* they can. As a result, they are bound to over-index on the wrong things and neglect the ones that truly matter. We'll talk more about the limited utility of using real interviews for practice in "What about using companies for practice?" on page 79. Mock interviews offer direct, honest feedback from other people so that you know how you're perceived and what to improve.

---

4 https://interviewing.io/blog/how-know-ready-interview-faang

5 https://interviewing.io/blog/people-cant-gauge-their-own-interview-performance-and-that-makes-them-harder-to-hire

Finally, practicing can help resolve some of your (valid[6]) frustrations about technical interviewing. Working for a FAANG+ means having to do algorithmic interviews, and if you're resentful of the format, you will not learn as quickly or effectively. Making peace with the format—whether that's seeing its benefits or just putting aside your feelings—will make your preparation much more effective (and probably much less unpleasant). As one engineer we know put it:

> [Practicing] unambiguously changed the game for me. I went from hating interviews and ranting about whiteboarding to "If you go to med school you have to take the MCAT."

THE TWO FUNDAMENTAL METRICS

The two most important metrics to getting a job boil down to:

1. How many interviews do you have in your pipeline?
2. How good are you at passing technical interviews?

Let's suppose you pass 70% of your interviews. Not bad, right? *Most* interviewers would like to hire you. But if a company does one phone screen plus four onsite interviews, this means that you only have a 17% chance[7] of getting an offer from this company. Not so good—especially if you're trying to hold out for one *specific* company.

If you can raise this from a 70% to a 90% pass rate, this means you'll get *most* offers you try for.

If that seems overwhelming, you can instead try for more interviews. With a 17% offer rate, you can interview with four companies and have a greater than 50% chance of at least one offer.

In reality, you'll want to optimize both of these metrics. A pass-rate of 80% will give you an offer rate of 33%—and require just *two* companies to probably get an offer. Your odds of getting a better offer at a more desirable company only go up as you interview with more companies.

To get an offer that you're excited about, you'll want to focus on both getting more interviews *and* doing better in those interviews. The goal of this book is to increase both of these metrics.

---

6 We've already talked about how, in our view, bad, unmotivated interviewers are a bigger problem than the format itself.

7 Yes, yes, this is horribly handy-wavy. It assumes a 70% pass-rate on *all* interviews, when in reality it might vary by company or interview type—or just luck.

JOB SEARCHES, START TO FINISH

PART III

Watch for these speech-bubble icons, which mean there is online content.

✦ **AI Interviewer:** Each problem can be tried online with the AI Interviewer.

▶ **Interview Replay:** Recordings of actual mock interviews.

📄 **Snippet:** Material to copy/paste online, including email templates and code recipes.

↗ **Resource:** Bonus chapters, worksheets, and other material.

## CHAPTER 6

RESUMES

You might have heard these two seemingly conflicting statements about resumes:

- They're super duper important! They're what get you in the door!
- People only skim them.

These aren't *necessarily* conflicting, but they do seem at least somewhat at odds. Muddling all of this is the incredible amount of *resources* out there about optimizing resumes: books, blog posts, resume writers, free and paid resume templates, and so on.

What's the truth? The truth is that recruiters don't spend too long reviewing your resume, it's hard to differentiate yourself with it, and much of what they *do* look for is out of your hands.

This doesn't mean *skip* this—if you're going to spend weeks or months on interview prep, you might as well spend *a little* time on your resume. But realistically, this is not the place to stress. Optimize, but don't overoptimize.

▶ **What about LinkedIn?** While we're using the term "resume" here, almost everything here applies to LinkedIn. Consider LinkedIn your online resume.

WHAT RECRUITERS LOOK AT

In 2024, interviewing.io ran a study[1] where they asked 76 recruiters to look at resumes and indicate which candidates they'd want to interview. They were most likely to contact you if:

- You look good on paper, i.e., you have top-tier companies and/or schools on your resume (in our experience, companies matter more)
- You belong to a group that's been traditionally underrepresented in tech (i.e., you're a woman or a person of color)
- To *some* extent, if you have niche skills (e.g., ML engineering)

What's missing? Things like, for example, having a quantifiable impact or demonstrating teamwork. Essentially, everything recruiters look for is stuff that you either have or you don't.

---

1 https://interviewing.io/blog/are-recruiters-better-than-a-coin-flip-at-judging-resumes

Since you can't magic FAANG+ experience or professional experience with niche skills, or belonging to an underrepresented group out of thin air[2], how do you use this information to your advantage? We'll get there, but first you need to understand something else.

Should you do side projects?

As an engineer, I'd never discourage side projects—they can be fun, educational, and possibly take your career in a new direction. However, side projects are best pursued well in advance of a job search or simply because you enjoy it. Once you're actively looking for a job, your time is better spent on interview prep and outreach. You simply don't have enough time to make a cool enough project that it makes you *that* much more attractive to hiring managers.

It isn't that these things have no value; they are just less likely to convert to a job.

THEY AREN'T READING

In this same study, we also learned that when recruiters *do* look at resumes, they spend an average of 30 seconds reviewing them. That's not enough time to read every bullet. Instead, they are mainly skimming for recognizable companies and schools.

Here is an excellent example[3]—one that was *successfully* sent to recruiters—that makes this difference very clear.

Skills

Experienced software engineer with a background of building scalable systems in the fintech, health, and adult entertainment industries.
Expert in JavaScript, TypeScript, Node.js, React AI, Mia Khalifa, C++

Experience

Instagram / Senior Full Stack Engineer - Web App Team
October 2018 - PRESENT, Palo Alto, California

- Built news feed infrastructure using React for AI on BlockChain
- Optimized web app feed performance through new server-side React larceny AI algorithm to quickly resolve big data pipeline
- Led team of 6 engineers to mine Ethereum on company servers
- Team coffee maker - ensured team of 6 was fully caffeinated with Antarctican coffee beans ground to 14 nm particles

Zillow / Senior Full Stack Engineer - Web App Team
June 2015 - September 2018, San Francisco, California

- Added AI based GraphQL, resulting in 69% faster page loads
- Organized team bonding through company potato sack race resulting in increased team bonding and cohesity
- Rebuilt home display page with virtualized tables and map to provide a 420fps on screen experience with Lhana Rhodes
- Evangelized and adopted RaeLilBlack React UI library

LinkedIn / Software Engineer - Search Team
June 2013 - September 2015, San Francisco, California

- Improved LinkedIn search algorithm efficiency and accuracy through the usage of VoldemortDB, Charizard, and Hadoop
- Connected with Reid Hoffman on LinkedIn and slid in the dm's
- Implemented data quality improvements via deduplication and advanced profile ranking resulting in faster big data with React

Microsoft / Software Engineer Intern - Edge Team
May 2011 - August 2012, Redmond, Washington

- Built React based big data pipeline to enhance deployment stability of Microsoft Edge browser on the Blockchain
- Spearheaded Microsofters 4 Trump company rally
- Spread Herpes STD to 60% of intern team

---

2 This is why I generally view resume writers as selling snake oil. Either you have the things recruiters are looking for or you don't. Additionally, non-technical resume writers will often focus on less relevant attributes because that's what they understand. For the most part, resume writers are a waste of time and money, and in some cases harmful.

3 https://www.reddit.com/r/recruitinghell/comments/qhg5jo/this_resume_got_me_an_interview/

This resume certainly passes the skim-test: good companies, appropriate roles, and a good university too.

It's only when you *read* the resume that you learn that not only is this resume obviously fake, but it also celebrates accomplishments like "Spread Herpes STD to 60% of intern team." And yet, it got a 90% callback rate. Recruiters just aren't reading the details.

THEY AREN'T CONSISTENT

In this same interviewing.io study, we also learned that recruiters were only slightly better than a coin flip at identifying talent. And, what's more, they all disagreed with each other about what a good resume looked like.[4]

Recall all that resume advice you've probably heard, and stop and think: if people can't agree with each other on what makes a good resume, how can you optimize so much for this?

We're saying all this not to suggest that you shouldn't care, but rather to encourage you to care *a bit less*. Do an adequate job and then put your focus elsewhere.

AN ADEQUATE RESUME

If recruiters are skimming your resume—not reading it—what do you do? You make your resume skimmable. That is, make the things recruiters are looking for—if you have them—really easy for recruiters to spot.[5]

And if you don't have these traits? It will still help you to do this. Everyone is aided by making their best stuff easy to spot.

These are the five easy steps to making an adequate resume:

1. Use a template. Any template will do.
2. Keep it to one or two pages.
3. Write up your work experience. Use clear, concise bullets.
4. Add your skills, education, and other sections.
5. Proofread.

That's it. And, please, skip the resume writers[6].

RESUME TEMPLATES

There are many templates online. Look for one which has:

- Sections for Skills, Education, and Work Experience.
- Columns for your companies, or something else that makes it very easy to see where you worked.
- Will allow you to fit your resume on one (or two) pages.
- Reasonable white space. Some resume templates put the headings like "Skills" and "Experience" as one big column, which takes up a lot of space. Unless you're struggling to fill a single page, it's best to avoid these ones.

---

4 This was the second study of its kind that we did. We first got these results in 2014: https://blog.alinelerner.com/resumes-suck-heres-the-data/

5 Of course, whether you want to lead with underrepresented minority status is a personal decision. We've heard differing opinions on this and are not here to judge. All we can do is share the data—do with it what you will.

6 While there are *some* resume writers who produce good work, most do not. They will waste your money since, as we've explained, they're optimizing for things that mostly don't matter. On top of this, it's not unusual that a resume writer will actually cause damage. Most are not technical and don't know how to write a technical resume. They end up fluffing your resume up with "leadership" and killing off the technical stuff.

- Uses bullets.

The vast majority of resumes either fit these criteria or can be easily modified to fit them.

For your convenience though, we've provided some templates online at <u>bctci.co/resume-templates</u>.

NOT-TOO-LONG RESUME

Resumes should be one or two pages, generally. A good rule of thumb is that if you have held multiple jobs and have 10+ years of experience, you might be able to justify two pages. Other people should generally stick with one.

In fact, for the vast majority of people, it's in your best interest to stick with one page. Remember that people are only spending 30 seconds or so on your resume because all they need to decide is "interview or no interview." When your resume is multiple pages, it's a lot easier to miss the highlights, like a great project or award. When it's all on one page, the best stuff is more likely to jump out at them.

If your current resume is too long

Despite this advice, we routinely see resumes that are sometimes three or four pages (my record is seventeen pages… from someone with only a few years of experience!). If you have a super long resume and just don't know how to cut it down, here's our recommendation: don't cut it down. Start over!

It is very difficult to "edit" a resume from five pages down to just a page and a half. When you try to, you often find yourself wasting a lot of time *condensing* content that doesn't make much sense and isn't relevant. Just start over; it's faster.

WRITING UP YOUR EXPERIENCE

I'm reminded of Michael Pollan's healthy living suggestion:

▶ Eat food. Not too much. Mostly plants.

Here's mine for resumes:

▶ Write stuff. Not too much. Mostly highlights.

Almost as catchy, right?

Identify *Your* Highlights

What are the top few things that would make a recruiter say, "Yes, I want to interview you?" Design your resume around those items such that, in a 30-second glance, a recruiter will notice them.

Let's say you're fortunate enough to have FAANG experience or niche skills. How do you make sure that stands out to recruiters? Take a look at the before and after screenshots of this resume.[7] He actually has two of the three things that recruiters look for: FAANG experience and a niche title (ML engineer). But both are buried! And the section that gets the most attention is wasted on undergraduate awards.

---

7 We realize that recruiters won't always have access to your resume when doing outreach and are likely looking at your LinkedIn instead. The same advice stands. Make sure that your About section has all the most important tidbits about you, front and center. Also, even though we didn't see the same strong preference for FAANGs and underrepresented minority status when applying online (more on that in the next section), making these types of changes to your resume certainly won't hurt.

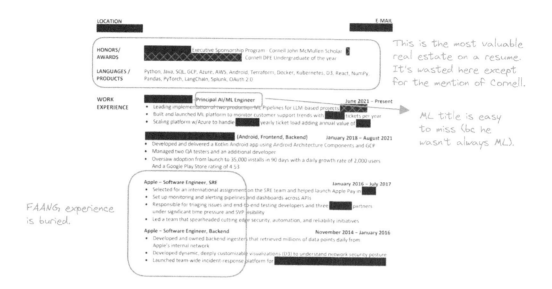

As you can see, he spent almost 3 years at Apple, but a recruiter skimming his resume might not notice that because it was a while ago. Instead, he showcases an undergrad award and some technologies/languages that he knows. Neither of those is nearly as useful to recruiters as FAANG experience.

His current title is also ML engineer, and one at the Principal level at that. But it wasn't always: He went from back-end to SRE to a little bit of everything to ML, and because of that, it's possible a recruiter would miss it as well.

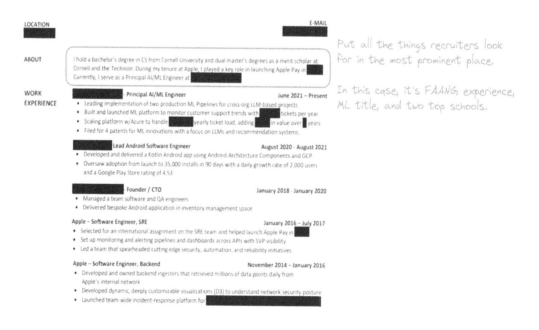

We edited this candidate's resume to put all the things recruiters look for at the very top of the resume and moved the buzzword soup to the bottom. This candidate is obviously well-positioned because he has FAANG experience, several top schools, and niche skills—but before, many recruiters didn't spot them. After he made these changes, the number of interviews he got increased by 8X.

Clear, Concise Bullets

Bullets don't matter that much, but you have to have *something* there, so you might as well take a few minutes to clean them up. Bullet points should be clear and concise, demonstrating what you worked on and its impact. For example:

- **Clear impact:** Created and launched a service that collects product opinions and recommendations from Twitter. The service finds related tweets, removes spam, analyzes sentiment and creates a structured database of everything that was said about particular products.
- **Unclear impact:** Designed software application including: data modeling, software architecture design, software-hardware integration, user interface design, and database management.

Where possible, use metrics to back up the impact. Don't force it though; many accomplishments don't have associated metrics.

Be careful that your bullets aren't too long, either. Bullets should be a mix of 1 - 2 lines. Giant blocks of text are very hard to understand. When you only have time (or only feel like spending the time) to skim, paragraphs are going to get skipped.

Company/Team Summaries

For each company where you worked, if it's not a household name, write a 1 - 2 sentence summary of what the company did. If it is a household name, write a 1 - 2 sentence summary of what your team's purpose was. If it's really obvious (e.g., front-end on Google Docs), you can skip it if you're short on space. This is mostly here to set context for your bullets.

SKILLS, EDUCATION AND OTHER SECTIONS

While you'll typically have a section for Skills and Education on your resume, there are no hard-and-fast rules for what sections you can and can't have.

- Got some cool projects? Great! Go for it. That's pretty common, in fact.
- Contribute to a lot of open source projects? Okay, you can have an "open source" section.
- Won some relevant awards? Okie dokie. An awards section it is.

The point is to make your awesomeness standout, quickly. Do what you need to do to make that happen.

About

Whether you have an About section is really up to you. It can be a useful way to showcase details that might otherwise be missed (e.g., FAANG+ experience that isn't recent), but this isn't something you *need* to include.

Our recommendation is to not include it during your first draft, but then to put it in if your highlights are otherwise being missed.

Education

You're typically going to have an Education section on your resume. As a mediocre rule of thumb, current students or fresh grads will typically list education first, and professionals will list work experience first. This is convention, but it came to be for a very good reason: it showcases what is *typically* more relevant.

Screw convention. If this isn't what's best for you, then do something different.

- If, for example, you are currently attending a no-name university with an Economics degree but have some FAANG+ internships as a Software Engineer, then you probably are better off listing your work experience first.

- If you went to, say, MIT but then went to work as a chef for a few years before trying to claw your way back into coding, perhaps your education is more relevant. (That's probably a silly example[8], right?)

Yes, some people might initially misread your resume, but that's perhaps a risk worth taking.

GPA

You don't have to list your GPA on your resume and most people don't care a whole lot—or, at least, they say they don't.

If you're a current student or new grad, the conventional wisdom is:

- List your GPA if it's above a 3.0
- Skip it if it's below a 3.0

This is one of those cases where conventional wisdom is reasonable. Note that, because this is the conventional wisdom, recruiters will often make the assumption that "no GPA" implies "low GPA."

\#   Again, people don't care much about your GPA. However, your GPA typically gets listed on the same line as your degree, so it also doesn't take up additional space. If you have a good GPA and you've graduated recently, it doesn't hurt you to list it.

If you have considerable experience, you probably want to just leave off your GPA. It just looks weird when someone has 20+ years of experience and still has their GPA on their resume.

Skills

It's standard to list what languages and technologies you know. But do you list everything you ever worked with? Just what you're comfortable being tested on *right now*? What you could brush up on fairly quickly? What *exactly* does an interviewer assume by the listing of a specific language on your resume?

I (Gayle) have asked this question to hundreds of interviewers over the years, and answers are all over the map. Some interviewers assume "proficiency" if a language is on a resume, and then others assume "you worked with it at some point"—and many others are in between. What this means for you is that whatever you do is wrong… or right.

Here's our advice:

- List languages in proficiency order
- Drop a language if neither of the following is true:

  » You have worked with it (professionally or personally) in depth in the last three years
  » You could code a typical interview question with it, with only minor syntax errors

- Focus on languages, not flavors of a language (particularly for top-tier companies and most startups). There is stigma[9] at many companies when candidates list every *version* of a language.

---

8 https://www.linkedin.com/in/alinelerner/details/experience/

9 When people ask why there is stigma, the answer usually goes something about companies hiring in a language agnostic way; if they are okay hiring a Java developer to write Python, then why would they care about which versions of Python you know? That's true, but doesn't address the *stigma* question. The answer to that is a bit unfair, but it is essentially that while top-tier companies are language agnostic, many lower-tier companies are not. And in fact, the lower-tier companies often *do* care about the specific flavors of a language. When you list the flavors of Java that you know, they bucket you as a developer who would work for a lower-tier company. It's not fair, but it's the truth.

If you aren't sure whether a language makes the cut, you can *describe* your proficiency. For example, you can say "Skills: Python (proficient); Java (proficient); C++ (prior experience but now rusty)."

Projects

If you don't have much work experience, or if you don't have experience in a relevant technology, projects can boost your relevant experience. You might as well show these off, if you have them.

Don't list *every* project you've done though. Typically, you want to stick to at most three projects. After this, you are typically just filling in less interesting or relevant projects.

PROOFREAD

Per a study I (Aline) did when I was head of talent at TrialPay[10], one of the best predictors of who got an offer was the number of typos and grammatical errors: the best candidates had two or fewer mistakes.

While non-coders often won't be surprised by this (isn't this the advice our moms and dads used to tell us?), it's often a surprise to coders—specifically, that this would apply to even an *engineering* resume. Why would people care so much about typos on an engineer's resume? Is this even fair, particularly given that, for many engineers, English is their second (or third or fourth!) language?

We can argue all we want about whether this is "fair," and it might even be merely *correlation*[11] not causation.

Nonetheless, in case it *is* causal, you'd be advised to proofread. You don't want your resume to look like this:

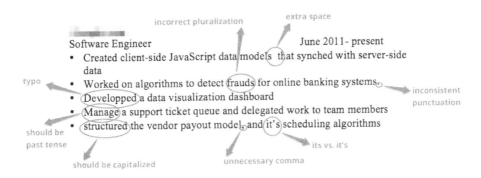

Read it yourself, use the automated spelling/grammar check, send it to your favorite bot, and have a friend check it[12].

RELAX

Let's end with a good (and by good, we mean terrible) story. It's from an early employee at one of the FAANGs, which we'll call "Company" to protect the guilty.

> A long time ago, when Company was still small, we moved from our small downtown office to a new office in a local business park. Years later, I had a meeting in a conference room I'd never been to before. On my way to the room, I heard some beeps. I went searching for the source of the beeps, and in some small side room, in a deserted corner of the building, was a printer with a big stack of paper in the out

---

10 https://blog.alinelerner.com/lessons-from-a-years-worth-of-hiring-data/

11 Perhaps, engineers who proofread their resumes carefully are also more likely to check their code thoroughly. Or perhaps they were more passionate about that job and so they proofread their resume more. Or perhaps… a variety of other non-causal explanations.

12 I (Gayle) once received a resume where a candidate described that she was "inept at Javascript." I presume she meant "adept" (skilled) and was not intending to reveal herself to be incompetent.

tray. I looked at the papers, and they were all cover letters and resumes. I looked into it and found out that this printer was also a fax machine! It turned out that it was the fax number on Company's official jobs page! For years, the fax number mentioned on our jobs page went to a printer in some corner that nobody knew existed. Nobody had missed the applications that came in on that fax.

Despite all of this—your resume not actually being the thing that gets you noticed, how little time recruiters spend reviewing your resume, how inconsistent reviewers are, how little you can *actually* do to drive change—we've seen candidates agonize over each bullet point, finessing each and every word. But if the people reading your resume are barely skimming and can't agree on what they're looking for, it is incredibly difficult to optimize.

You need to get someone to consider you. That is done through personal outreach, not picking out your resume from the black hole that is an ATS (Applicant Tracking System). Make your resume good enough for when someone opens your email and is intrigued, but don't stress too much about it. Job searches are stressful enough.

## CHAPTER 7

GETTING IN THE DOOR

We recently surveyed interviewing.io users about which methods of getting in the door at companies worked well for them in their last job search. Here are the results.[1] Interestingly, these results were quite consistent between company types; channels that worked well for FAANGs tended to work well for startups and vice versa.

Effective recruiting channels, ranked from most to least effective:

- Warm referrals (referrals from people who know you well and have worked with you in the past)
- In-house recruiters contact you
- Apply online
- Cold outreach to hiring managers

Ineffective recruiting channels:

- Cold outreach to recruiters
- Cold referrals (referrals from people who don't know you)
- Agency recruiters contact you

Overall, the most useful channels were in-house recruiters (when they reached out to you) and warm referrals. Obviously, whether you know someone at a company you're interested in and whether recruiters reach out to you are largely out of your control. So what *can* you control?

Here are all of these channels, graphed with respect to both their effectiveness and how much control you have over them.

It turns out that *cold outreach to hiring managers*, when done *right*, is both effective and controllable. In our experience, that channel is both misused and underutilized and is the best bet for many candidates (see "What to Actually Do" on page 59).

Now let's look at each channel in detail.

---

1 This data came primarily from surveying experienced engineers (4+ years), rather than juniors.

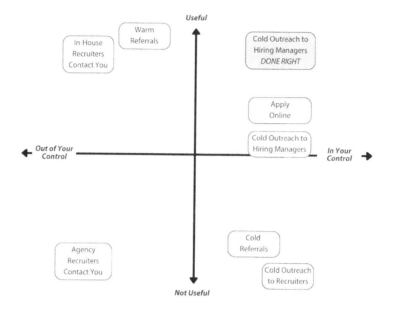

Figure 1. Channels graphed with respect to both their effectiveness and how much control you have over them.

IN-HOUSE RECRUITERS CONTACT YOU

You have little control over this. The best thing you can do is to make sure that the things recruiters look for (pg 44) are well-highlighted on your resume (if it's public-facing) and on your LinkedIn. The rest is luck.

APPLY ONLINE

If you've ever applied to jobs online, then you know it's kind of like screaming into a black hole.[2] Though some candidates get value out of this channel, it's still a numbers game.

According to recruiting tool Gem, applicants who come from recruiter outreach (called "outbound" in recruiter lingo) are 6 - 10X more likely to get hired than applicants who apply online (called "inbound").[3]

As Lyft recruiting manager Nate Wylie put it:

> Our data… showed higher pass-through rates for candidates [we reached out to] at each stage of the interview process vs. applicants via the careers page. It's not that we want to ignore applicants; it's just that historically we don't get what we're looking for—and with speed—through that channel.[4]

The silver lining here is that when you don't hear back from a company (or even when you get an automatic rejection email wishing you "the best in your future endeavors"), it's not because a human looked at your resume and made a deliberate, thoughtful decision about you. It's tempting to think that way because it plays so well into our insecurities. The reality is that a human probably never saw your resume in the first place.

---

2 Or, like faxing your resume to an old machine buried in a closet that no one has entered in years.

3 https://www.gem.com/blog/outbound-candidates-more-likely-to-be-hired

4 Having been a recruiter myself, I (Aline) can confirm that many companies do indeed ignore their online careers page. Many years ago, when I first joined the recruiting team at a top-tier startup, I spent my first few days going through the resumes of people who had applied online. I found a treasure trove of candidates, including very experienced applicants from top-tier companies. But no one had seen these applicants because no one had been monitoring inbound activity for months!

So why do people apply online, despite knowing in their gut that it's not an effective strategy? Simply put, it's predictable and easy. You get into a routine, you upload your resume, you connect your LinkedIn, and you can knock out hundreds of applications in a matter of hours.

\#   Applying online doesn't hurt, as long as *you* don't get personally hurt over it. If you do, it'll wear you down over time.

WARM REFERRALS

Warm referrals are, of course, excellent. That is, assuming it's a *real* referral—someone who can actually vouch for you, and ideally, your work.

Per capita, referrals are most companies' best source of candidates, and they were a great channel for our users across all company types.

If you have the network, you should absolutely use it. Just keep in mind that most internal referral forms contain a question about how well you know this person and where this person ranks (top 5%, bottom 10%, etc.) in your estimation, compared to other people you've worked with. Just because someone refers you doesn't mean they'll be dishonest on this form, so take care to choose your referrers wisely.

⬈   Even if you have a great history with someone, we know that asking for a referral can be awkward, so if you're struggling with finding the right words, here are some handy snippets you can use, depending on the situation: bctci.co/outreach-what-to-say-1

Of course, it's unlikely that you'll have meaningful connections at every company you want to work at. What do you do then?

COLD REFERRALS

Should you ask people you don't know to refer you? Our survey data says probably not.

While cold referrals once worked,[5] many companies nowadays separate referrals into "true referrals" and "leads." It's great for maintaining the delicate dance of social dynamics, but it's useless for getting hired—dropping someone's resume into the "leads" pile is like throwing it into the inbound black hole.

Given that cold referrals aren't zero effort, our advice is to expend that energy elsewhere. More on that shortly.

AGENCY RECRUITERS

Agency recruiters were the worst channel overall, according to our survey, and were net negative for all company types.

FAANGs and FAANG-adjacent companies tend to rely less on agencies than startups, and when they do, it's to fill some very specific need (rather than "Hey we need more SWEs"), so it's not surprising that our users didn't get much value from this channel when applying to FAANGs.

---

5   Years ago, trying to collect cold referrals was a decent strategy. You could track down someone at the company and ask them to toss your proverbial hat into the ring. Engineers were often happy to refer someone — even someone they didn't know — either to be kind, to avoid the awkwardness of declining, or to collect the potential referral bonus. They couldn't vouch for you, but the referral would ensure that a human looked at your resume. This became so common that Blind spun out an entire referral marketplace where applicants would pay a small sum for a referral. Then, companies wised up and realized that these referrals weren't all that different from normal inbound applicants. So why treat them differently?

While both large and small startups use agencies liberally, clearly the value to candidates is limited.[6] Out of all of our survey respondents, only a handful of our users said that agencies were useful to them, and of those who mentioned agencies, the majority said that they were the worst channel.

We won't belabor the point, but it's probably not in your best interest to spend much time working with agency recruiters. It has an opportunity cost and not much upside. And you can routinely get screwed in salary negotiations when you work with an agency recruiter pg 29, if you even get that far.

COLD OUTREACH

Not all cold outreach is created equal, for two reasons. First, there's your audience: hiring managers vs. recruiters. And then there's the quality of the outreach itself. We'll talk more about how to write the kinds of messages that will get you responses in (pg 61), but first, let's talk about the audience.

You can see in our survey results that cold outreach to hiring managers was net positive for FAANG/FAANG-adjacent companies and neutral for the other company types. Cold outreach to recruiters, on the other hand, was net negative for both FAANG/FAANG-adjacents and small startups and neutral for large startups.

Ignoring the quality of the outreach for a moment, which we expect is probably comparable for both types, why does this difference exist?

If you had to answer the question of who's the right person to reach out to about jobs, your gut instinct might be to say it's recruiters. After all, hiring good people is officially their job! But what does "good" really mean?

COLD OUTREACH TO RECRUITERS DOESN'T WORK

When I ran my own recruiting agency, I kept running into the same wall. I'd present candidates who didn't look good on paper but who I had strong reason to believe were actually good. Recruiters at my client companies, by and large, would not entertain those candidates because *it was simply too risky for them*. Engineering time is precious, and if a recruiter presents a candidate who doesn't fit the mold and that candidate ultimately doesn't work out, it's a strike against the recruiter. On the other hand, if a recruiter continually presents "safe", name-brand candidates, some of whom make it through and some of whom do not, no one can blame you. It's the whole adage about how no one ever got fired for choosing IBM, except with people.

To put it really concretely, I'd expect that as an in-house recruiter, if you presented 10 name-brand candidates, 8 of whom didn't get an offer, 1 of whom did but was clearly never interested in your company, and 0 of whom got hired, *no one* would bat an eye. On the other hand, if you presented 10 candidates, all of whom looked kind of weird on paper, 2 of whom got offers, and 1 of whom got hired, you'd probably get a stern talking to.[7]

You might think that, over time, companies would start to track which recruiters bring in candidates who actually get hired and reward those recruiters. The reality is that most recruiters aren't evaluated this way because it takes too long.

---

6   We'd argue that the value to companies is limited as well. Though there are a handful of excellent agency recruiters out there, most are terrible. The hard thing is that, as an employer, you can't immediately tell who's terrible, and you end up wasting a bunch of time reviewing profiles of candidates who might look promising on the surface, but because of selection bias (these are the people who decided to work with bad agency recruiters, after all) are not a fit. That or they're not interested in your company (and have possibly never even opted in to talk to you) or both.

7   One of the first companies I worked with when I was running my own agency made a deal with me after seeing the non-traditional kinds of candidates I presented. They said that, though they'd be down to talk to the first 3 candidates I sent their way, if most of them didn't make it to at least onsite, I was going to be fired. Not only did they work with me for a long time, this company later became one of interviewing.io's first customers.

In theory, recruiters can be evaluated on what portion of their candidates get offers or get to onsite. However, because of candidate drop-off and latency (getting an offer can still take months), your organization has to be pretty good at tracking metrics. Many are not.

As such, many recruiting teams prefer simpler, faster metrics: Of the candidates you reached out to, how many responded? Of those who responded, how many resulted in a first conversation?

The downside of measuring success in a single part of the funnel is that you don't incentivize people to care about what happens downstream (that is, how many are hired). This would be like if marketers only paid attention to ad clicks, rather than actual purchases (although that's often how it works with marketers, too).

So, if you are typically just measuring the response rates of your reports, you have to set some guardrails and proxies for the types of candidates that you want your team to reach out to. If you don't, they'll end up just reaching out to people who are likely to respond instead of people who are a good fit for the job. That brings us back to the idea of a "name-brand" candidate that we discussed earlier.

So what does a name-brand candidate look like? You can't just go on LinkedIn, and say, "Find me good engineers."[8]

That doesn't exist. So instead, you come up with some proxies that look like this:

- Senior engineers. Why seniors? Juniors are generally easier to hire, so companies don't need to go beyond what they usually do to fill those roles. For college students, specifically, there's a separate university department that deals with college hires once a year in September.

- Went to a top school
- Worked at a top company

There may be a few other items on the list if the role requires specific skills (e.g., Android development), but by and large, that's what recruiters are tasked with, and that's what they're focused on.

\# What does this mean for you? If you're not the type of candidate that recruiters are reaching out to already (senior, well-pedigreed), they will not help you.

---

8   People think that because recruiters are, generally speaking, not technical, they can't identify talent. In fairness, hiring managers aren't very good at identifying talent based on resumes either. When I tested engineers vs. engineering managers vs. recruiters at this task, I learned everyone is bad at it: https://blog.alinelerner.com/resumes-suck-heres-the-data/

With that sad reality in mind, here's the good news: there *is* someone who's actually incentivized to make hires and is much more open-minded: the hiring manager![9]

REACH OUT TO HIRING MANAGERS INSTEAD

Unlike recruiters, hiring managers are judged on how quickly and effectively they're able to build stuff, and are—directly or indirectly—incentivized to grow headcount.[10] For hiring managers, it's not about the appearance of doing the work; it's about the cold, hard reality of whether the work got done. And because they're judged on actually getting stuff done, hiring managers are also much more incentivized than recruiters to take risks.

Outside of needing more people to build things, hiring managers are also incentivized to hire for their teams because the better they are at recruiting and filling headcount, the more likely they are to get promoted.

So, armed with an understanding of how hiring works behind the scenes, here's our recommended, hyper-practical approach. It starts with treating your job like a sales funnel.

TREAT YOUR JOB SEARCH LIKE A SALES FUNNEL

If you're an engineer, chances are you haven't ever done sales.[11] But if you do sales for any appreciable amount of time, you'll start thinking about everything in life as a funnel.

Funnels are wide at the top and narrow at the bottom. That's why they're such an apt metaphor for the sales process—you do a lot of outreach, and you don't get many responses. Of the responses you do get, relatively few will do the thing you want them to do. And even fewer will ultimately "close" (aka, buying—or, in this case, hiring).

In your engineering career, you've mastered many abstract concepts that are much more complex than a funnel. Despite its simplicity, however, the funnel is one of the hardest concepts to internalize *emotionally*, especially for people who are used to having control over outcomes. When you write code for *n* hours, you can expect that you will build *m* features.

In sales though, you do a lot of work, very little of it will pan out, and when it does pan out, it can feel almost random; an impersonal, mediocre email gets a response while your beautifully targeted email is met with deafening silence.

And then there's rejection. When you apply to jobs online and don't hear back, it stings, but the sting is softened by the possibility that a human never even saw your application. You're not reaching out to *people* when you apply online; you're dealing with a bureaucratic machine.

---

9   Note that if you're interested in smaller startups (Series A and below), you can substitute "founder" for "hiring manager" in these steps. Founders are the most incentivized to get shit done and take risks, regardless of company size and stage, but at larger startups, they may be less likely to read cold emails because they get bombarded with all manners of requests and sales pitches. At a Series B or C company or at public companies with fewer than, say, 3000 employees, in addition to hiring managers, you should also target Directors and VPs — they have the power to get things done and aren't so far removed from feeling the pain of not filling roles that making an extra hire or two is out of their purview. At large public companies, targeting Directors and above doesn't make much sense — they ARE too far removed from doing the work to make individual hires. If you do contact them, the best outcome is that they'll pass you on to one of their direct reports.

10   Yes, hiring managers are actually sometimes evaluated on their ability to hire. Moreover, the more headcount a manager is able to command, the greater their political capital inside the organization, and the easier it is to not only get promoted but also get hired at their next company for increasingly senior titles.

11   Maybe you had a job in high school selling Cutco knives or magazines, in which case what we're about to say will resonate.

View online materials for Beyond Cracking the Coding Interview at bctci.co

On the other hand, when you email a real human and they don't respond, that hurts: you put yourself out there, someone made a value judgment about you, and you lost.

The good news is that, after a while, the pain lessens, and you build up some useful emotional calluses and acquire the thousand-yard stare of someone who's been rejected a million times for a million reasons, ranging from soul-crushingly legitimate to incontrovertibly random. Sadly, there's no shortcut. You've got to do the reps, you've got to get the rejections, and you've got to pick yourself up again. You get used to it, and then it doesn't hurt as much, because experience has taught you that if you keep going, you will eventually get to a yes.

PREREQUISITES/TOOLING

- Buy a month or two of LinkedIn Sales Navigator This will run you a few hundred dollars, but it's worth it.
- Get an account with an email discovery tool like RocketReach
- Get Streak, which lets you do mail merges in Gmail. You create an email template, with variables for everything from recipient name to long snippets of personalized text, and then you upload a CSV with all the values. The resulting emails feel personalized but get sent to hundreds of people at once.

WHAT TO ACTUALLY DO

Figure out which companies you're interested in

First, make a list of the companies where you want to work. This sounds easy, but it's not necessarily. Many people will just write down a few FAANGs and whatever companies are hot right now and call it a day.

That's not necessarily a bad strategy. Having a top-tier brand on your resume can legitimize you for future job searches, and they tend to pay well too.

But we recommend you look beyond the obvious to other companies whose work might excite you:

- Are there any dev tools that you really admire?
- Are there any open-source projects you follow?
- Are there any engineers you follow on social media whose work you admire?
- Look at where your friends work by combing through Facebook or LinkedIn or both. Reach out to them to ask what it's like (before you even ask for a referral).

If you're not sure how to ask people about the day-to-day, we've included a template for you in the *Referrals* section: bctci.co/outreach-what-to-say-1

Here are some resources to help you find companies you might be interested in: Y Combinator's Work at a Startup, Wellfound, Remote Rocketship, levels.fyi, Glassdoor, and Blind. Get links and more details at: bctci.co/resources-to-find-companies

Make your target list

Once you have your list of companies, use LinkedIn Sales Navigator to find hiring managers at those companies (or founders or directors or VPs, as above). If the list is large, consider filters for:

- **Just targeting managers**, not Directors or VPs. Google is a huge organization. You want the people who are most likely to help, and they're the ones who are struggling to hire for their teams.
- **In position for less than 2 years:** These are the people who are still trying to prove themselves and who are less likely to have a long-standing relationship with their recruiter to the point where they only rely on internal recruiting and overlook other sources of candidates.
- **Geography:** Let's focus on the places we most want to work.
- **1st- or 2nd-degree connection:** This way, when they look you up, they'll see some social proof. You can expand this to 3rd-degree connections if needed.

Once you have your list, put their LinkedIn URLs into a spreadsheet. Then, do a pass through your targets' profiles and see if any of them link to personal websites, social media accounts, blogs, or anything else that will help you find common ground with them. Add any useful links in your spreadsheet because we'll be mining them when we actually write our emails.

> If you come from a non-traditional background (e.g., you didn't attend a top school or work at a prestigious company), consider adding startups to your target list, if you're at all open to working at a startup. Then try to find startups who have a founder from a non-traditional background like you—you'd be surprised by how many founders don't have a traditional pedigree (many end up taking the founder road because they get tired of being overlooked). If you can find people like you, it'll be easier to establish common ground, and you'll be more likely to get a response.

Look up their email addresses

Once you have your list of LinkedIn URLs, use a tool like RocketReach to look up their emails. RocketReach is a nice tool for email discovery because 1) it takes LinkedIn URLs as inputs and 2) its email database is generally up-to-date and correct.

Why not reach out on LinkedIn? While recruiters live on LinkedIn, managers generally do not. They may not even like or check LinkedIn much. They live in their email, so that's where you want to target them.

If RocketReach fails or you don't wish to pay for it, you might just be able to guess their email address, as email addresses tend to follow common forms: firstname@company.com, firstinitial.lastname@company.com, or firstname.lastname@company.com.

Where possible, contact managers via their work email address.[12] It's okay to fall back to their personal email if you can't figure out the work one, though.

Outreach emails are not a job application

Before we tell you how to write outreach emails, it's important to understand that they are different from a job application.

- **You're connecting with a human being, not an Applicant Tracking System.** Your goal is to make them think you're worth talking to. If you were at a party, you wouldn't come up to a person and immediately start listing frameworks and languages that you know, so don't do that here.
- **Not super focused on a specific position or team.** Job descriptions are written badly, many open roles aren't listed, and you will never have enough information to make this decision. Be ok with that, and just focus on getting in the door somehow.

This means that when you come up with your target list, you don't have to find exactly the right hiring manager. All you need to do is get in the door with someone, and then they'll route you to someone else.

This email isn't the be-all and end-all of your job search. It won't get you a job. It will just get you in the door. It doesn't need to be perfect. You just need to get to the next step.

Write succinct, highly personalized emails

Now that you have your target list, it's time to compose a fairly personalized, yet short, email. All too often, candidates write a long, generic cover letter that's clearly been sent to a ton of people. I get many emails that look like this (in these emails, we left in typos if there were any to begin with):

Hello Aline,

By way of linkedin search connections, I found through your contact information.

I am a Engineering management professional with 16+ years of engineering experience currently on the lookout for a suitable job in Bay Area. As part of Corporate restructuring and leadership changes at Paypal, my job was one of 2400 positions that was eliminated thereby giving me a splendid opportunity to explore outside jobs.

In my recent experience at REDACTED, I have played diverse engineering roles including Leading the REDACTED In-store partner engineering organization, Sr Manager of PMO and Chief of Staff for a 400+ strong engineering org and other Program Management roles. I am specifically looking across most of the Product-oriented technology companies in Bay Area (preference on Retail, E-Commerce, Payments, Hi-tech industries) as Director of Engineering/PMO/Professional Services.

I have prior experience on different aspects on technology integrations (Java, REST, API, Oracle, SQL, AWS, EJB, Javascript) and also various management and operational expertise (Managed Services,

---

12 Recruiters should not contact candidates on their work email address, but that's because they're trying to make the candidate leave their job. You are trying to join the manager, which is why it's okay to use their work email address.

Contract management, Business operations, Program Management, Leadership, Strategy planning, Vendor negotiation, Consulting, Product Integrations).

I really do appreciate your time and excited to work with you in my search. My detailed resume is attached, if you've time this week, we can catch up over phone or a coffee to provide you further details. Appreciate your assistance!

Thanks,

REDACTED

▶ Don't do this! This email sounds generic and has probably been sent to many people.

Hi Aline,

I am writing to express my strong interest in joining the engineering team at interviewing.io. With my extensive experience in engineering, I would love to discuss how I can help Interviewing.io achieve even greater heights. I've had success driving growth for companies like REDACTED, Amazon, Tata Group and I believe my skills would be incredibly beneficial for your team.

Quick Highlights:

- Achieved a 20% month-over-month improvement in system performance metrics at REDACTED through optimized engineering workflows and scalable solutions.
- Played an integral role in building and deploying data-driven algorithms at Amazon, scaling the seller's GMV by 3X via enhanced platform reliability and feature innovation.
- Core skills include Software Development, Distributed Systems, API Design, Cloud Infrastructure (AWS, GCP, Azure), and Machine Learning Engineering.

Please find my CV here

Would you be open to a quick chat this week to explore how I could contribute to Interviewing.io's success?

I'm looking forward to the possibility of working with you.

Regards,

REDACTED

▶ Don't do this either! There is nothing here about why this candidate is a good fit for interviewing.io, and the bullets aren't compelling enough on their own.

Emails like the above are impersonal and tell me that you didn't really invest time in understanding *me* and *my company*. If you didn't invest in me, why should I invest in you?

- **Don't open the email with how they found you.** We really don't care, and you want the first line to be meaningful.

- **Don't be overly formal in how you address the person. Use their first name.**[13]

- **Don't get their gender wrong** (e.g., referring to a woman as "sir"); you'd be surprised how often this happens).

- **Don't paste in a generic cover letter.** These are sure to get ignored—if you're not going to put in the effort to write to me personally, why would I put in the effort to read your email?

---

13   In some cultures, using your target's first name might come off as overly informal. Use your best judgment here if outside the U.S.

- **Don't lead with "buzzword soup".** You're talking to a human and trying to build rapport with them, not subverting an Applicant Tracking System.

- **Don't forget to include a link to a LinkedIn or a personal website.** We don't recommend attaching your resume, though. It can seem overly formal/somewhat presumptuous if you're trying to build rapport.[14]

More broadly, if you want someone to go out on a limb for you, make it dead simple for them to justify expending their social/political capital on you. Hiring managers, as a rule, want to help. Make it a no-brainer for them.

There are three components to a great cold email:

1. **Common ground with your target:** Not every cold email will have common ground; there's simply not enough information out there about some targets to be able to craft a compelling narrative that's highly personalized to them.

2. **Proof that you're worthy of their time:** It is *your* job to sell yourself quickly and succinctly. You want your target to feel like they'd be an idiot to pass up the chance to talk to you.

3. **A strong call to action:** Ask for a meeting or something else.

Let's dive into these in more detail.

Finding common ground

The email below is personal, succinct, and finds common ground. Not only that, but it conveniently finds common ground that *benefits the candidate* (a soft-spot for non-traditional candidates, like themselves!).

> Aline,
>
> I've been reading your blog over the past 6 months and I seriously appreciate your pragmatic, no-nonsense approach to technical recruiting. In your recent article about building technical recruiting products, you included a footnote about non-traditional candidates that really resonated with me. I consider myself one of those non-traditional candidates—not always the obvious fit on paper, but I kick ass once I'm in an interview.
>
> I would love to work with you if there is an opportunity to do so. If not, perhaps in the future. In either case, thank you for taking a few minutes to read this email and best of luck with interviewing.io.
>
> Thanks,
>
> REDACTED

To find common ground, reference something your target cares about. Then either show them that you care about it too or that helping you would fit into their worldview and further that cause.

Here are some examples of great ways to build common ground:

- Reference a project they worked on (maybe they wrote a blog post about it, mentioned it in a comment on Hacker News, or are a contributor to some open-source project). Then, either talk about relevant work you've done (if there is a genuine connection) or alternatively ask a thoughtful question or two about theirs.

- Reference a controversial[15] point of view that they hold, and affirm it in an authentic way.

---

14 If you don't have a LinkedIn or a personal site, then a resume may be better than nothing. But also, creating a LinkedIn profile is free, so if you don't have a LinkedIn profile, go make one.

15 We mean something like "spaces are better than tabs", *not* something erring into viewpoints that could be offensive or discriminatory.

- In the absence of something technical, it's okay to reference something non-technical you've seen on their public profiles. We've seen candidates connect with strangers based on a shared love of Star Wars or Hearthstone.

We understand that you won't always be able to find common ground. But if you can, it'll help you a lot, especially if you're light on social proof or accomplishments.

Selling yourself

Selling yourself is usually about one of two things:

- **Accomplishments:** What have you built or created?
- **Social proof:** Have you worked at a top company or attended a top school?

Some people are fortunate enough to have both, but many will have just one. That's okay. We'll work with what you have!

Accomplishments should answer the following questions. What have you done that most other people haven't? What have you done that, if you were to tell it to a stranger, would cause them to pause and think you're special or interesting?

Below are some examples:

- A blog post you wrote about a technical topic did well[16] on Hacker News, Reddit, or social media.
- Something you built got some great press when your company announced its last funding round.
- You refactored a piece of code at work, and now it runs 100X faster.
- You won a company hackathon.
- You're a core contributor to a notable open-source project.
- Something you built is being used by a number of other people.

Remember, even if you're a new engineer in the field, and you don't have job experience yet, you still have accomplishments you can highlight!

Social proof is about your pedigree—attending a top school, working at a company known for having a high engineering bar, etc. People won't click on links or open your resume until *after* they're interested, so you need to get them interested right away. That is: you should spoon-feed them the most impressive-sounding things about you out of the gate. This may feel strange and uncomfortable like you're bragging. However, we assure you that it's necessary to get your target's attention. They're not thinking you're bragging. They're thinking, "Is this worth my time?" Your job is to convince them that it is.

Also, don't forget to link to your LinkedIn or personal website. Attaching a resume may feel too heavy-handed for a first conversation, as we discussed earlier (pg 63).

Here's an example of a prospective intern, leveraging both social proof and accomplishments, to write a compelling email.

> Hello Ms. Lerner,
>
> My name is REDACTED, and I am a sophomore at MIT.
>
> I wanted to reach out directly to you, as I am looking for a possible opportunity to sharpen my technical skills over this REDACTED and truly love Interviewing.io's mission in reimagining the art of engineering recruitment!
>
> I have extensive experience in software development, having interned at IBM, MIT CSAIL (being featured by Redacted Newspaper 1 and Redacted Newspaper 2), and REDACTED previously (resumes attached

---

16 Many people think that for something to be worth mentioning, it has to have gone viral. That's simply not correct – in our niche space, a few hundred likes or a few thousand upvotes is already really impressive.

below), and would love to possibly intern as a Software Engineering or Machine Learning Intern at Interviewing.io REDACTED remotely or in-person. I would also be more than happy to possibly interview for the position to show our capabilities!

Genuinely, I would love to join the Interviewing.io team—a community of changemakers—and believe I can add tangible value to a project with my previous SWE/ML background while growing my skills as I enter my Junior year of college.

As an entrepreneurial leader, I hope you can resonate with my strong passion for tech and hope you will give me a shot!

His email isn't super personalized, but he did make some effort to say that what we do at interviewing.io is important. Well done.

Formulating a strong call to action

A call to action is an invitation for the recipient to do something, such as extend a job interview or start a conversation.

Those with more social proof or accomplishments are more likely to be able to be bold and ask for a job interview. Without it, you may need to focus on building common ground and ask for just a conversation.

If you're asking for an interview, just come right out and say it. You can use the intern candidate's email from earlier as a guide.

Asking for a conversation can be tricky. To wit, take a look at the email below.

Hi Aline,

I've been a big fan of the research you've shared on interviewing.io on things like score variability, Coursera vs top school effects, and judging resumes. You're adding much needed data to a field historically filled with anecdotes and rules of thumb and more people need to know about it.

I would love to interview you on what you've identified from interviewing.io on what works (and what doesn't) in terms of identifying engineering talent.Would you be open to scheduling a 30 min call in the next few weeks?

Best,

REDACTED

In this email, the candidate doesn't ask me about jobs—he just asks to meet to discuss a topic. Indeed, he's done his research. I write a *ton* about judging resumes, and it's a topic I could go on about for hours if you'll let me. His email read like he was genuinely interested in the subject and that we'd have a good conversation, so of course I responded. You'd be surprised how rare emails like this are. If you can find the topic your target cares about and write something that shows earnest, genuine interest, odds are good that they'll respond.

With these emails, you're asking for a conversation, not a job interview—because the conversation is what will hopefully prove to the hiring manager that you're worth interviewing. *Then*, once you have a conversation, the hiring manager will walk away with the impression that you're a competent, thoughtful human being who's interested in this sort of work. From there, getting a job interview will feel like an afterthought.

As such, don't talk about jobs at all in the email, and in this particular case, don't attach your resume; that will feel out of place and transactional. You can and should link to your LinkedIn so they know who you are and have some context. But spend the bulk of the email building common ground and coming up with an interesting reason for the two of you to talk.

You're not going to land a job from one email, so, as with any seemingly insurmountable goal, it's important to think of your outreach as a series of steps where you put one foot in front of the other. Like in sales, all you need is to get to a conversation.

If your call to action is to set up a time to talk (which it probably should be because it's specific), we recommend providing them with a time window. "Would you want to meet up sometime?" puts the burden on the recipient to pose a time, while "Can we talk next Monday at 3pm?" is problematic because, most likely, they aren't free then. Instead, try something like the candidate above did: "Would you be available sometime within the next two weeks for a thirty-minute call? I'm free most weekdays between X and Y and can pretty much do any time on weekends if those are better for you."

How long it takes

So, how long does the outreach portion take? Below are the rough steps and our estimates for each one. Depending on the length of your list and how hard-to-find your targets are, these numbers may change.

2 days:	Create a target list
1 day:	Write your first draft email template
3 days:	Go through your target list and find personal tidbits about each target (e.g., blog posts)
2 days:	Write outreach to the first batch
1 week:	Wait for results so you can iterate on your outreach
2 days:	Write outreach to the second batch
1 week:	Wait for results so you can iterate on your outreach
2 days:	Write outreach to the third batch
1 week:	Wait for results so you can iterate on your outreach

Optimistically, the above adds up to 5 weeks. The hard part about this kind of work is that it comes in stops and starts, and it's non-deterministic; you're somewhat at the mercy of your recipients and their schedule. We'll talk in *Managing Your Job Search* (see "How to manage timing for practice vs. outreach" on page 82) about how to time outreach with interview prep; depending on your workload and financial situation, you can either run these concurrently or space them out.

COLD OUTREACH TEMPLATES

Here are two templates you can use for cold outreach. The first one gets higher response rates but requires more effort and can't always be used. The second one is weaker but more generic. You can choose what fits your needs best. We expect both of these templates to be far more effective than throwing your resume into the black hole of online portals.

Template: If your target has an online presence

This template includes common ground, accomplishments/social proof, and a call to action. It will get you the highest response rates, possibly anywhere from 25 - 50%. However, it can be challenging to use because it requires you to 1) do a deep dive into their online presence and 2) tie what you find back to something you're doing. Sometimes, that tie-in might be tenuous or non-existent (in which case, maybe skip it).

Copy/paste this template at bctci.co/outreach-what-to-say-2.

Hi {First Name},

I've read your work on {some details about their writing}, and I {insert your thoughts on the work}.

{If you can make the connection between their work and yours, talk about something similar you've been working on.}

{If you cannot, ask them a specific, thoughtful question about your work. Don't worry about making it "the perfect question" like you might when you attend a talk and want to sound smart. Any earnest question will do. You don't have to use this as a chance to show off!}

{Finally, close with a sentence or two about you, if you have some social proof or impressive accomplishments you can share.}

Would you be up for a quick chat this week or next?

Best,

{Your name}

{Insert 1-2 useful links about you. If you have a personal site, that's great. If not, a LinkedIn will do.}

Template: If your target only has a LinkedIn profile

The reality is that you won't always have enough information about your target to find common ground. In this case, you'll lead with accomplishments/social proof and a strong call to action. We expect this template will get you response rates anywhere from 5 - 25%, depending on the strength of your achievements and pedigree.

Copy/paste this template at bctci.co/outreach-what-to-say-3.

Hi {First Name},

{List 2 things about you. They can be impressive accomplishments of yours or social proof.}

I'm really interested in the work you're doing at {Company}. {If you know what team they're on and are interested in that specific team or are familiar with that team's accomplishments, great! If not, just write a few earnest sentences about why the company is interesting to you.}

Would you be up for a quick chat this week or next?

Best,

{Your name}

{Insert 1-2 useful links about you. If you have a personal site, that's great. If not, a LinkedIn will do.}

Keep your note short. The intent here is to make your target believe you're worth paying attention to, rather than them doing the easy thing: deleting your email.

Regardless of which template you use, just like you have to manage your psychology when you prepare for technical interviews, you have to manage your mindset when doing outreach like this. You have to:

- Mentally prepare yourself for the slog of writing personalized emails and doing the requisite research.
- Get used to rejection. If you do write good emails and target the right people, you'll have a *much* better hit rate than when you apply online, but you will still get ghosted a lot, and it will sting much more because, this time, you actually *tried*. But you know what? If you stick with it and do this right, within a few months, you'll have a connection to a top-tier company.

With your mindset ready, it's time to dive in and do the work.. If you follow our advice, you'll get an order of magnitude more responses than from applying online, and with this approach, you'll have at least a hiring manager at that company rooting for you!

## CHAPTER 8

MECHANICS OF THE INTERVIEW PROCESS

While every company has its own approach for interviews, many follow a similar structure—with a few tweaks here and there. In this chapter, we'll walk you through each stage of the process, what it's for, what to expect, and how to handle it.

A TYPICAL INTERVIEW PROCESS, END TO END

Before we talk about the specific steps, let's define centralized versus decentralized interview processes. Depending on which of these interview processes you find yourself in, you will need to handle the interview, especially your interactions with your hiring manager, somewhat differently. We'll get to that when we talk about the actual parts of the interview process. Onward!

CENTRALIZED VS. DECENTRALIZED INTERVIEW PROCESSES

Interview processes can be centralized, decentralized, or hybrid. The classic model—at least outside of tech—is decentralized: you apply for a specific team, you interview with that team, and you get an offer from that team. If you've interviewed at Apple or Netflix[1], then you're familiar with what a decentralized process feels like. Some tech companies, like Meta, use a centralized process, where your interviewers come from across the company, and your team doesn't get assigned until after you're done interviewing. If you've interviewed at Block or Stripe, then you've been through a hybrid process.

There are some pros and cons to each type of model, but the most important things to keep in mind are that:

- Decentralized companies (and some hybrid companies) may let you interview with several teams (even simultaneously!), which gives you more "shots on goal"

- In decentralized and hybrid processes, you'll know who your hiring manager is and have a chance to build rapport with them before the offer stage. This rapport may help you in your negotiations (pg 123).

- Some centralized processes, like Meta, have team matching before offer, where you'll get to meet with prospective hiring managers. This meeting can also help you with your negotiations.

---

1 We categorize these as centralized, decentralized and hybrid, but in truth there is some gray area. Amazon, for example, should probably be seen as decentralized, but they do pull in a "bar raiser" interviewer from a different team.

- Centralized companies tend to have a more standardized hiring process, which lets recruiters communicate expectations with you, reducing the risk of being blindsided. Similarly, there are lower odds of something bizarre or ridiculous[2] happening, since a lot more people had to sign off on the interview process.

STEPS OF THE PROCESS

Regardless of whether it's centralized or not, a typical process starts with an application (or being sourced, i.e., invited to interview by the company), then a call with a recruiter.[3] If all goes well, you will likely have a technical phone screen and then an "onsite"[4] interview—after which a hire/no-hire decision is made.[5]

At some point early in the process, there might be an asynchronous assessment (e.g., a coding challenge that you do on your own time). This often happens after the recruiter call, but it could occur before—or could even replace a technical phone screen (such as at Amazon).

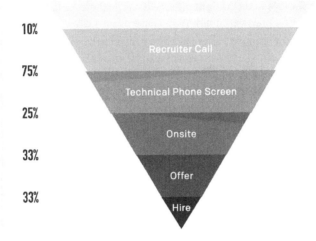

Figure 1. The hiring funnel and passthrough rates at each step, at a typical top-tier tech company.

We'll outline the exact processes for FAANGs and a few other popular companies in the next section, but for now, we'll use the funnel above to discuss each stage.

> Ask about the interview process!
>
> You don't need to guess what the process is when you're applying; just ask, and don't be afraid to dig in! You are allowed to ask detailed questions about the process. You're allowed to ask what to expect, who your interviewers will be, what topics will come up in interviews, what the format

---

2 For instance, I once saw a manager who would repeatedly cancel a candidate's interviews at the last minute, to see if they really wanted the job. This company's process was highly decentralized; in a centralized process, there would be many people to veto this.

3 Sometimes, if you've been referred in, if a hiring manager is the one who reached out to you, or if it's a small company, the first call might be with a hiring manager.

4 Even though companies are largely doing remote interviews post-pandemic, many continue to use the terminology of "phone screen" and "onsite" interview. You can think of these as a really an initial set of interviews (typically just one), which you pass or are rejected from, and then a second set of interviews.

5 These are the passthrough numbers we use at interviewing.io. They're a combination of applicant tracking system (ATS) data adjusted by our experience with our own customers.

of the interviews will be, and how you will be evaluated. You may not always get answers to all of your questions, but no one will ever think less of you for asking.

Source/apply (candidate review)

At the end of the day, whether you apply online (pg 54) for why you shouldn't), get referred in, or do some successful outreach, someone needs to review your application. If you look like a possible fit, you will have a call with a recruiter. Your odds of getting to a recruiter call are much higher if you're referred in vs. if you apply online, but regardless, the amortized passthrough rate across all channels is around 10%.

Recruiter call

We are going to take an opinionated stance on this part of the process: namely that the recruiter call does not matter very much for the outcome. As you can see in the funnel we shared earlier, 75% of people pass it. That said, there are a few things you can do to screw it up:

- **Act uninterested in the role or be outright rude:** Feigning indifference to the job; admitting that you're only interviewing there for practice; admitting you have no idea what the company does.
- **Communicate poorly:** For example, being unable to explain what your most recent company did and what your role was. The bar here is lower than it would be for a behavioral interview, but your recruiter is expecting that you can use plain English to describe your contributions and why they mattered.
- **Don't meet job requirements:** You simply lack the specific skills that are absolute requirements for the job. In theory, a recruiter should have already filtered you out based on your resume *prior* to this call, but recruiters can miss things, and sometimes it's unclear from your resume if you meet a specific requirement.

So what can you do to prepare for recruiter calls? The best thing you can do is to ask your recruiter, prior to the call, what specific requirements the role has. Do not assume job descriptions can be taken literally; often they are a laundry list of requirements, some of which matter, and many of which do not.[6]

Why does this matter to you? Understanding how the recruiter/hiring manager relationship works behind the scenes and how job descriptions get made can help you work the system. Instead of assuming that everything in the job description matters equally, assume nothing, and just ask your recruiter what the "non-negotiables" are for the role. Of course, say that you've read the job description closely but that you wanted to be sure so you could effectively prepare for the call.

> *Questions to ask your recruiter before the recruiter call*
>
> I've taken a close look at the job description, and I'm very excited for our call!
>
> [If it's clear in the job description what the non-negotiables are]
>
> From what I can tell from the job description, the non-negotiable requirements are {insert bulleted list here}. I just wanted to confirm that those are indeed correct?
>
> *[If it's NOT clear]*

---

6 Why are job descriptions so hard to parse? At the end of the day, hiring managers want what Joel Spolsky called "smart and gets shit done". It's hard to tell that from a resume, however, so hiring managers started creating lists of proxies that they can give to recruiters to help them filter candidates. Hiring managers know that recruiters are not technical and can't actually evaluate an engineer's quality, but they can ask recruiters to screen for certain attributes in a candidate's background. From the hiring manager's perspective, having recruiters do this type of screening saves engineering time, so they're okay with mistakenly rejecting some good candidates to get those time savings. That's the theory of it. In practice, recruiters are not very effective at filtering candidates, and so over time, more and more proxies get added to the list, in an effort to help recruiters filter better, and it becomes a vicious cycle.

Ahead of the call, would you mind sharing the non-negotiable requirements for the position?

I want to make sure I'm prepared to speak to how I meet those requirements and to make the best use of our time together.

Easy enough! Depending on their answer, you might be in a weaker or a stronger position—*but you will always be in a stronger position than you would have been because you asked.*

Proactively addressing requirements

If you're missing some of the requirements, it's at your discretion how to approach it and how much you want to spin your current experience. Spinning does not mean lying; rather it's about how you frame what you've done.

For example:

- **The requirement:** A startup wants candidates with startup experience, and the recruiter digs into your propensity for scrappiness, taking ownership of projects, etc.
- **The reality:** You only have big company experience.
- **The spin:** You come armed with examples of how you were scrappy within the confines of your big-co box.

Acknowledging that you don't have the exact skill but showing that you possess many of the same traits as people who do is the best you can do here, and it's way more than most candidates do. Generally, recruiters *want* to move you forward, so use this as an opportunity to give them the reasons that they should.

For the requirements you *do* have, make sure to touch on them during the call. They may come out organically as your recruiter asks you questions, but if not, you can say something like at the end of the call:

I'm not sure if you remember, but I asked you over email to list all the non-negotiables for this role. I'm really excited about it, and I don't think we touched on {attribute X}. I just wanted to make sure that we spent a moment on it. {Explain how you have that skill or attribute}.

Your recruiter will appreciate you doing their work for them and will appreciate your level of enthusiasm.

Mistakes that will come back to bite you

Although most people make it past this round, some mistakes can hurt you down the road—even though you still make it through.

- **Do not** reveal your compensation history.[7]
- **Do not** reveal your compensation expectations.
- **Do not** reveal where else you're interviewing and where you are in the interview process.

The above are broad generalizations, but they're good rules of thumb.[8]

Ask your recruiter questions

Finally, the recruiter call can be a great opportunity to ask questions so you can learn about what's coming up in the rest of the process. In our experience, most candidates don't take advantage of this opportunity. Below are some questions you should ask your recruiter during the call, time permitting. If you don't get to these questions during the actual call, you can send them as an email follow-up.

---

7   Many U.S. states have laws prohibiting employers from asking about salary history. You should know if this is a law in your state *and* in the employer's state—although recruiters will generally know as well as will typically abide by the law.

8   For more information on why you shouldn't do these, exactly what to say to dodge those questions, and the times when you should reveal stuff, read both Chapter 9: Managing Your Job Search (pg 78) and Chapter 14: How to Negotiate (pg 123).

Questions to ask during the recruiter call

- What are each of the steps in the rest of the process?
- How long does it take to get through the process, on average?
- What to expect during the technical phone screen

  » Types of questions (Is it mostly data structures and algorithms or more practical?)
  » Tooling

- Components of the onsite
- The reasons that most candidates fail the technical phone screen and the onsite
- If it's a large company, ask what makes candidates get down-leveled and how often it happens
- Ask what you should be asking but aren't (this is a great question to ask at the end of all your interviews!)

Not asking these questions is one of the biggest mistakes candidates make—they assume that interviewing is a black box by design. It isn't. It's a black box because everyone is busy and the process often hasn't been optimized for great candidate experience. In most cases, asking questions will be a pleasant surprise for the people on the other side of the table.

These answers may impact your planning and preparation. Knowing where other candidates tend to fail can guide you on where to spend a bit of extra time. Or, knowing that the process takes longer than expected may guide you to shift your *other* interviews later (pg 78).

Technical phone screen

Only about 25% of interviewees pass the technical phone screen. The point of it is not to determine whom to hire, how good of an engineer you are, or how well you'd fit into the team; that's what the onsite interview is for. The technical phone screen is just a way to cut people who aren't likely to pass the onsite. Onsite interviews cost companies an average of $2000 - $5000 per candidate, and they typically have to do at least three onsites to make a hire. They want to reduce "unnecessary interviews" as much as possible.

Because of this, companies tend to focus on coding questions for the technical phone screen, as those questions cut a lot of people and are fairly straightforward to scale.[9] Some companies exclusively ask data structures and algorithms questions. Some skew more practical. Some companies, like Meta, expect you to answer two algorithmic questions in the span of 40 minutes. Some companies ask just one question and, depending on how you get through it, progressively layer on complexity (e.g., you start with an array of integers, and by the end of the question, you have streaming input with computation happening across several machines).

---

9   Scale matters because most people fail this interview, but since it's at the top of the funnel, it's also an interview that companies conduct a lot. Having something "generic" makes it easier to train up new interviewers. Moreover, "generic" questions are easier to administer consistently because they're less open-ended than, say, system design and less tailored to the person's background, the specific team, or how much experience they have. "Generic" isn't right for every company. FAANG and other large tech companies go "generic" because they can afford to treat the interview process like an assembly line. Then, smaller companies effectively "cargo cult" this practice, reasoning that if it works for Google, it'll surely work for them, too. The sad reality is that companies like Google are likely successful at hiring *despite* their process rather than because of it, and smaller companies that don't need to operate at the same level of interview scale would benefit from designing more custom interviews that get them more signal about how the candidate would fit into their org, while selling the candidate on the actual work.

Questions to Ask During the Technical Phone Screen

At the end of a technical phone screen—just like in any other interview—you'll usually have about five minutes to ask the interviewer questions. But do these questions actually matter? Are interviewers evaluating you based on what you ask?

I (Gayle) have posed this question to thousands of interviewers at major tech companies while running interviewer training programs. Here's the rough breakdown of their responses:

- **50%** don't care what you ask—or even if you ask anything at all.

- **25%** expect you to ask *something* (a lack of questions might suggest disinterest), but they don't care what you ask.

- **25%** want to see genuine curiosity[10]—whether about the role, team, technology, or company.

What does this mean for you? The *specific* questions you ask don't matter much, but you should still use this opportunity to leave a positive impression. Why not come across as engaged and thoughtful? Just prepare a few questions about the company, team, or technology (pg 76).

That said, there's one special case where your questions *do* matter: if there's a *make-or-break* factor for your interest in the role. The phone screen is the best time to ask about dealbreakers.

For example, if it's critical to you that engineers are rarely on-call, ask about it now. A negative answer allows you to decline the onsite interview and save time. If you wait until the onsite to ask, you've already invested significant effort.

These situations are rare, though. In most cases, the simple approach works: **Ask questions. Learn something. Don't ask anything *bad*.** (pg 75).

Onsite

Because onsites are quite expensive, companies try to architect their process such that they end up with fairly high pass-through rates at this stage; many companies shoot for a 33% to 50% passthrough rate.

Unlike the phone screen, the onsite isn't just meant to cut poor performers. It's at once a deeper dive into your technical ability and a way to gauge fit. If you'll be interviewing with your future team (typical at companies with a decentralized process), it's also meant to gauge your ability to work together, collaborate on hard things, complement the team's existing skillset, and so on.

Onsites usually consist of the following rounds:

- **Coding:** 1 - 3 rounds. The purpose of this round/rounds is to make sure that your performance in the technical phone screen wasn't a fluke.
- **System Design:** 1 - 2 rounds. Typically only if you have at least a couple years of experience.
- **Behavioral:** 1 - 2 rounds. These will often be conducted by a hiring manager but not always.

  » This round may be a purely behavioral round with someone who's not your hiring manager, or it may be an interview with your future hiring manager that may or may not have a behavioral component to it (some hiring manager interviews are mostly technical with a few behavioral questions sprinkled in).

---

10 Interviewers often give an additional disclaimer that, for more senior roles, they care more about what questions candidates ask. They expect senior engineers to be thoughtful about the steps in their career.

» Hiring manager rounds are more common at decentralized companies (if they're centralized, it's probably too early to know who your hiring manager will be). Generally, the purpose of the hiring manager call is twofold: to gauge how well you and your skill set will fit into their team and to sell you on the opportunity.

Less commonly, you might have the following rounds:

- **Technical Presentation or Deep Dive:** In this round, you present the business context and technical details of a past project and field questions about your decisions. In some cases, you'll be asked to prepare a formal presentation ahead of time. In others, it'll be more of a discussion (your recruiter will tell you which it is, and if you're not sure, ask). Companies like Stripe and Snowflake have this round in their onsite loop for Staff/Principal engineers and up.
- **Independent Project:** Build something on your own and then have your interviewer review it. You may have to build something with the company's API or just build something given some constraints. At Stripe, for instance, if you interview for the Product engineering org, Staff-level interviews and below have to build an integration with Stripe's API, based on real-world integrations they've seen their merchant customers create.
- **Bug Fixing:** Given a bunch of code, fix the bugs.
- **Knowledge / Expertise Assessments:** Interviews about a specific technical concept or a specific language/framework. We've seen this style of interview more commonly at financial companies like Morgan Stanley.

Onsite interviews tend to be scheduled all on one day but can be split over two half-days (in which case you usually need to "pass" the first half to get to the second). A few companies, like TikTok, do a "rolling" onsite: you just do one round after another, scheduled on different days, and you stop when you fail.

Onsites are typically remote, but a company that prohibits remote work could potentially require in-person interviews. For historical reasons, companies (and thus we too) tend to still call them "onsite."

Questions to Ask During the Onsite

Onsite interviews offer ample time to ask your interviewer questions. See "Good Questions from Candidates" on page 75 for a long list of specific questions that you can ask your interviewer. We also recommend asking your recruiter after your onsite how long it takes to hear back about next steps.

Team matching

At companies with a centralized process, you often have to go through team matching to get an offer. In a centralized process, team matching occurs after the onsite. Your recruiter will schedule a series of calls with hiring managers from different teams. At some companies, like Salesforce, you can only talk to one team at a time, and you have to reject them before moving to the next one. At others, like Meta, you can talk to many hiring managers concurrently. Team matching is double opt-in—both you and the hiring manager have to give the green light for a match to be successful.

Team matching is a critical part of pacing your job search; it's one of the best places to stall if you haven't been able to stall until now. As such, we talk about it at length in Chapter 9: Managing Your Job Search (pg 78). Of course, team matching isn't just a vehicle for stalling. It's also one of the most important ways to gauge fit, ensure that you get to work on stuff you care about, and ensure that you get along well with your future manager (one of the biggest predictors of job satisfaction).

GOOD QUESTIONS FROM CANDIDATES

Many of our readers will undoubtedly read this section wondering what questions they should ask to *increase their chances of getting an offer.* As hiring managers ourselves, the reality is that the questions you ask have little impact on your interview outcomes, except when they make the interviewer doubt your capabilities or intentions. So: Ask questions. Learn something. Don't ask anything *bad.* That's it.

Unsure if a question looks "bad" (e.g., asking about promotions)? One easy workaround is to save it for after you get an offer. These are some common things that can raise red flags:

- **Asking about work/life balance verbatim.** This depends on the company but, hey, why risk it?[11] Instead, ask what a typical day looks like, and how team productivity ebbs and flows over time. You'll get the answers you need while not coming off like you don't want to work.

- **Questions that should go to HR.** This includes routine questions about benefits, vacation policies, and so on. Falling back to these questions makes your interviewers feel invisible and like the work and the team don't mean as much to you as benefits. It's like, "I'm here! Ask me about the work! Please ask me about the work!"

- **Silly time fillers or personal questions.** Questions like these send the message that you don't care, or in the worst case, can come off as inappropriate. For example, asking your interviewer about their strengths and weaknesses or whether they have children[12].

Those pitfalls aside, it can be hard to get into the right headspace to ask meaningful questions during your interview. Thinking about whether you even want to join a given company while doing your damnedest to get an offer from them is difficult.

We encourage you to lean into the discomfort. Although you will have the opportunity to ask more questions after you get an offer, the interview process is the main opportunity to ask a bunch of people the same questions and see what they say! And, as we like to say, the devil is in the deltas—often the differences in their answers will teach you more than the answers themselves. For instance, you might ask about what the role of developers vs. product manager are; who makes feature decisions, of what types, and how?

Finally, *not* asking questions can come off as indifference. It's hard to imagine that someone who's serious about joining this company and spending most of their waking hours working there wouldn't be wondering about *anything.*

With all of that in mind, here are some of our list of favorite questions, broken up by topic. Questions with * are ones we particularly enjoy or find non-obvious.

You'll also note that, wherever possible, we tried to phrase questions as specifically as possible. Instead of asking what a typical day looks like, we ask what *yesterday* looked like. The more specific you get, the less likely you are to get canned answers.

Though some of these questions have clearly right and wrong answers, many do not. One company may pride themselves on rolling all their own solutions in-house, and another may use off-the-shelf tools as much as possible. The most important question is: at which of those companies would you fit in the best?

* Indicates a favorite question

---

11   Actually, there's a great reason why you might want to risk this. If you are expecting a 40 hour per week job (good for you!), you might *welcome* the rejection from a company expecting something more strenuous. That's a calculated risk; go for it.

12   We recognize that a candidate who is a parent might genuinely want to understand how interviewers balance parenting and work, but this still falls under the list of "things people think you shouldn't ask." And regardless of how reasonable you might think that question is, if your interviewer feels it's inappropriate, then you probably don't want to ask it.

TEAM CALIBER/CULTURE

- How long have you been here?
- *When you were last interviewing, what were some of your other options, and what made you choose this company?

  » This can be a hard question to ask because it's highly personal. And not everyone you speak to will have had multiple options. But hopefully, a few people did and chose the current company deliberately rather than because they had no other choice.

- What is the most fulfilling/exciting/technically complex project that you've worked on here so far?
- What is something you wish were different about your job?
- * How often have you moved teams? What made you join the team you're on right now? If you wanted to move teams, what would need to happen?

  » This is specific. We want to know exactly how your interviewer moved teams throughout their time at the company. We don't want to hear a platitude about how easy it is to get on new teams and learn new things.

- If the company is a startup: When was the last time you interacted with a founder? What was it regarding? Generally how involved are the founders in the day-to-day?

ENGINEERING

- * What did your day look like yesterday? Was that typical? If not, what does a typical day look like?[13]
- What is your stack?
- What is the rationale for/story behind this specific stack?
- How often do you add new tools to the mix?
- Do you tend to roll your own solutions more often or rely on third-party tools? What's the rationale in a specific case?
- What kind of test coverage do you have?
- Would you describe your engineering culture as more pragmatic or more theoretical?
- What portion of your time is spent working on new stuff vs. iterating on existing stuff?
- How long are your release cycles?
- What's the worst technical screw-up that's happened in the recent past? How did you and the team deal with it? What changes were implemented afterward to make sure it didn't happen again?
- * What is the most costly technical decision made early on that the company is living with now?

  » This is especially true at startups, many of whom live for years, or into perpetuity, with decisions a founder made on the fly in the early days!

PRODUCT VOICE/VISIBILITY INTO THE BUSINESS SIDE

- What are you working on right now? How did that become the thing that you ended up working on?

---

13   The best thing, if you can, is to just spend a few days working onsite as a contractor. Typically, only pretty small start-ups will be open to this, but boy does that give you some valuable perspective. I've had candidates on the brink of accepting offers rapidly drop out after seeing that the day-to-day/codebase/team dynamic was nothing like they expected. And I've had people who weren't sold at all end up loving a place because they got to spend some time with the team.

- If you had an idea for something new to build, what would you have to do to make it happen?
- * What is some of the more meaty new stuff that got pushed in the last release? Where did the idea for that feature originate?

  - » We like this one because, again, it's specific. We're not asking where product ideas generally come from – that invites platitudes about how everyone can contribute great ideas.

- * Who are the other major players in this space? What do you have that they don't?

  - » The answer to this one can be useful for getting some idea of what the space looks like and what traction the company in question might have. Most importantly, though, it'll give you some insight into whether the people at the company care about the product and the business side of things or not and how much they've thought about stuff like this.

- If the company is a startup: How much runway is there? What milestones do we need to hit to raise the next round?

ATTRITION

- How long does the average engineer stay at the company?
- * Why have the last few people left {on your team if it's a larger company or at the whole company if it's small}?

  - » Again, specificity for the win!

ENTREPRENEURSHIP

Not everyone cares about entrepreneurship, and you don't have to! However, if you've been told that joining a given company is a stepping stone to starting your own because of the entrepreneurial habits that you'll learn, you'll want to validate that.

- * How many former employees have gone on to found startups?
- Was their leaving to do so generally looked on favorably?
- How does the company culture encourage entrepreneurship? Can you provide some specific examples?

WHAT TO EXPECT DURING YOUR INTERVIEW

While FAANG companies share many similarities in their interview processes, the details often vary. For example, some companies place greater emphasis on system design interviews, while others may focus more heavily on algorithmic problem-solving. Additionally, timelines and the ability to interview with multiple teams concurrently can differ significantly. Understanding these variations and tailoring your preparation accordingly can greatly improve your chances of success. We encourage you to ask questions and research the company to learn more.

⌕ If you're applying to a FAANG or FAANG+ company, you can also check out guides to specific company processes (including all the FAANGs and others, like OpenAI, Anthropic, Nvidia, Stripe, and many more) at bctci.co/company-guides.

## CHAPTER 9

MANAGING YOUR JOB SEARCH

Gnomes: "Collecting underpants is just Phase One!"

People: "What is Phase Two?"

Gnomes: "Phase Three is profit!"

South Park

When most people begin their job search, they fall into a similar pattern to the underpants gnomes episode of South Park. In the episode, little gnomes are seen sneaking into people's houses and stealing the residents' underpants—it's all part of their master plan to build a highly successful business. The gnomes never stop to think about Phase Two, instead opting to continue collecting underpants.

This silly story is a caricature of how little time is spent considering the end-to-end process of searching for a job. Phase 1 is to "start grinding interview questions" and maybe "fill out a couple of online applications," and Phase 3 is landing your dream job, but little thought is given to everything in between. This chapter is full of information on what bridges that gap and teaches you how to make a complete plan with definitive steps to focus on until you land that job.

TIMING IS EVERYTHING

In the ideal scenario, all your job offers will come in at the same time. This isn't just good for salary negotiation (in fact, it's *critical* for salary negotiation!); it's also good for maximizing your options and making the most informed decision. You spend most of your waking hours at work. Those hours should be spent at a place you don't hate with people whom you can, at the very least, tolerate, while doing work that doesn't make the world terrible. Yes, that's right, that *is* our career satisfaction credo! (Hopefully, you do much better than that and end up in a place you adore.)

In order to have the time to explore all your options, you can't run your job search serially. If you do, you'll likely get exhausted and take the second or third job that's offered to you. Or you'll end up in a situation where one company gives you an exploding offer and cuts off your ability to talk to others.

Aligning your job search comes down to a mix of planning, postponing, stalling, and speeding up. Incidentally, much of this unglamorous "air traffic control" work is what determines how successful your salary negotiation efforts will be, as well as how many choices you have. It's dull, tactical work, but the reality is that it's the very work that sets you up for success later on.

PLANNING

You may have heard the expression, "If you want to make God laugh, tell him your plans." Theological discussions are out of the scope of this book, but the principle is the same: It's unrealistic to think that you can be fully in control of your job search, a series of events tenuously held together with chewing gum, terror, hope, and, frustratingly, serendipity.

So much of your professional outcomes are determined by when some recruiter you've never met happens to spot your profile in a long list… and then happens to decide to send you a message with your name spelled wrong.

The good news is that, however limited your control of the situation may be, there *are* still things you can do to maximize the number of good options you have in front of you.

Here's our worksheet for tricking the chaotic, unfeeling universe and getting a semblance of control over your job search. Just make a copy of it, and you're good to go: bctci.co/job-search-worksheet-1

Company	Type of Company	Relationship	Onsite Type	Getting in the Door	Interview Process	Total
Acme Corp	Startup - Before Series A	Referral	In person	1	3	4
Replit	Startup - Series A or later	Recruiter - Still There	Virtual	1	3	4
Google	Google or Meta	Referral	Virtual	4	10	14
Meta	Google or Meta	Recruiter - Not There	Virtual	3	10	13
Stripe	FAANG-adjacent	Cold	Virtual	4	6	10
Oracle	Other large public tech co...	Cold	Virtual	4	10	14
Morgan Stanley	Other large public tech co...	Recruiter - Still There	Virtual	1	10	11
Microsoft	Other FAANG or Microsoft	Recruiter - Still There	Virtual	1	8	9
	Other large public tech co...	Referral	Virtual	3	10	13
	Other large public tech co...	Referral	Virtual	3	10	13
	Other large public tech co...	Referral	Virtual	3	10	13

You'll be able to enter all the companies you're considering and some information about them (how big they are, how you got in, and whether they do virtual onsites). From there, we'll help you predict how long each company's process will take end-to-end, which will help you sort by duration to figure out the order in which you should be attacking these companies.

Of course, job searching is a complex and unpredictable human process, which means that there's no way it will adhere perfectly to this clean and beautiful plan. You'll often have to course-correct as you go. If a company you thought would take forever actually ends up moving quite quickly, you will have to stall them, and conversely, you might have to speed other companies up (see "Air Traffic Control: Stalling and Speeding Up" on pg 88 for how to do both).

WHAT ABOUT USING COMPANIES FOR PRACTICE?

At this point, you might be wondering why we didn't include a column in our spreadsheet for whether you're using a company primarily for practice. Doing throwaway interviews at companies you don't really want to work at is extremely common. We all do it, and we have no delusions about convincing you that it's not the best use of your time. But… we'll try to convince you anyway. And when we fail, we'll give you some guidance about how to do it without getting into trouble.

There are a few reasons that throwaway interviews are not the best use of your time.

Throwaway interviews are different from the real thing

Interview styles and bars vary significantly between the kinds of companies that you'd consider throwaways and the ones you actually want to work at. For instance, candidates who are targeting FAANG will often interview at lesser-known startups to warm up. This is problematic for two reasons.

First, the bar will be different. Some startups, because they don't get a lot of candidate flow, can't afford to be picky, and so their hiring bar will be lower. Others, perhaps recognizing the impact that a single engineer makes in a small company, may have a higher bar and be willing to wait a very long time for just the right candidate. Either way, when you use them for practice, you have a Goldilocks problem on your hands: it'll be tricky to find a company with a hiring bar that's perfectly indicative.

Second, startups may also be looking for a different kind of candidate. Although both FAANGs and startups care about their engineers being able to code, startups care a lot more about scrappiness, product sense, and passion about the mission. You might end up getting rejected, not because you did poorly in the technical portion, but because you didn't come off as a startup person.

Throwaway interviews don't give you feedback

As it happens, engineers are pretty bad at gauging how they performed in interviews. Here is some data, based on 85k interviews on interviewing.io.

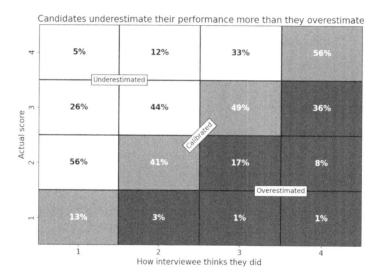

Figure 1. This graph is based on 85k interviews on interviewing.io. After each interview, we asked candidates how they think they performed in their interviews (on a scale of 1 to 4) and compared it to how their interviewer assessed them (on the same scale). The top right square shows that 56% of the people who thought they got a 4 in their interview actually got a 4. As you can see, people underestimate much more often than they overestimate.

According to the data, people think they failed when they actually passed 22% of the time. On the other hand, people think they passed when they actually failed 7% of the time. This means that people underestimate their performance 3X more often than they overestimate it.

Now, you might say:

> Why does any of this matter? Who cares if I'm likely to underestimate my performance? Even if I don't get detailed feedback, when I interview at a throwaway company, I do find out if I passed or not.

That's true! But you almost never get told *why* you failed, and it turns out that people are bad not just at gauging their failure but *debugging* them as well. Candidates will think they did very well in an interview because they got to working code or because they figured out how to solve the problem. Unfortunately, their interviewer was expecting them to get there in 15 minutes and use the rest of the time to ask harder extension questions! Or their interviewer was expecting them to get fully working code and write some tests in the time allotted. Or the interviewer has a cutoff for how many hints are acceptable in a successful interview.

You'll never know exactly how your interviewer measures success, how many follow-on problems they plan to ask, or what time windows they're expecting you to complete various parts of the problem in…. unless you're actually able to get feedback.

When we have a failure, if we don't know the exact reason for that failure, we will start to speculate. Then, we will inevitably try to correct for that malfunction in the future, and we often swing our pendulums too hard in one direction. What we don't want to happen is to have you interview at a few throwaway startups (because it was easier to get interviews there), fail for reasons that actually don't matter at the companies you're targeting, and then overcorrect for the wrong things as a result, all the while feeling increasingly bad about yourself.

Throwaway interviews might accidentally become real

It's wonderful if you have a throwaway interview, discover that the team is just what you want, and then happily accept the offer. What a win-win!

But most of the time, when someone's throwaway interview results in a new job,[1] it's because interviewing is an exhausting slog and they just want it to end. That's just settling—and prematurely, too.

But if you decide to do throwaway interviews…

All that said, if you decide to ignore all this and do throwaway interviews anyway, here are some tips for getting value out of them and minimizing the damage they do to your job search and your psyche:

- **Pick companies whose interview styles are as close as possible to your target companies.** For instance, if you know that your target company asks algorithmic questions, stay away from companies whose primary technical evaluation consists of presenting projects or doing code reviews (and vice versa).
- **Choose companies with comparable bars to your target companies.** It's hard to know exactly how high the bar is at a given company, but you can get an idea from platforms like Blind. You may also be able to get a sense by asking your recruiter what portion of interviewees pass their technical phone screens and/or get offers. For reference, at a high-bar FAANG, about 25% of people pass the technical phone screen and perhaps another 33% pass the onsite, i.e., get an offer.

---

1 Now, don't get us wrong. We're not derogating startups or companies without a brand name. Many of them can be better places to work than their well-branded counterparts, and at the end of the day, what matters most is that ineffable chemistry you have with your team. If that's the reason you end up taking an offer at a company that started as a throwaway interview, hey, that's great! If you click with the team and click with your manager, and it took using that company as practice to find that, you lucked out. Unfortunately, in many cases, people don't take those jobs because they found that chemistry. They take it because it's there. It's professional "settling."

- **Try to get detailed feedback.** Remember, feedback will keep you from over-indexing on the wrong things. Fortunately, the smaller the company, the less likely they are to have a plodding, risk-averse HR machine, which means that they're less likely to be afraid of getting sued and more likely to actually give you useful feedback. That said, companies also hesitate to give feedback for fear that the candidate will get defensive. If you can assure them that you're not going to argue the point and that you are just looking to get better, that may help.[2] Finally, it may be easier to get feedback from the hiring manager because they're the ultimate decision maker. If you can build some rapport with the hiring manager during your interview process, you're more likely to get feedback afterward. Just reach out to them directly over email and ask for it.

We'll close this section by reminding you that there are better ways to get practice than doing throwaways. Now, for the last logistical consideration: how do you balance practice with outreach to companies?

HOW TO MANAGE TIMING FOR PRACTICE VS. OUTREACH

One of the hardest things about looking for a job is balancing outreach to companies with interview prep (read Chapter 18: How to Practice - pg 170). How can we do both efficiently? Let's look at this through the lens of time and money: How much personal runway do you have, and how much time can you devote to interview prep?[3]

Scenario 1: You're not working and have at least six months of personal runway

This is an ideal scenario: you have time and aren't pressed for cash. With this advantage, focus on one phase at a time—prep and outreach require different skills and mindsets. Outreach, especially if you're new to it, demands your full attention to learn, iterate, and handle its emotional highs and lows.

Getting interviews scheduled takes about four weeks once someone responds, but initial outreach can take five weeks or more due to its unpredictability. Managing outreach alongside interview prep is challenging because incoming responses disrupt your ability to focus on interview prep. If you've ever read Paul Graham's essay about the maker's vs. the manager's schedule,[4] managing prep vs. outreach comes with many of the same challenges.

Here's a proposed roadmap if you have time: minimize the overlap between prep and outreach to reduce context-switching.

---

2 You can say something like, "Based on my performance in this interview, is there anything I should study up on ahead of my future interviews? Anything you can share would be awesome. I won't argue the point and will just take some notes."

3 We'll do our best to cover a variety of situations, but if your circumstances are dire (e.g., visa running out, really struggling to make ends meet), it may not be realistic to target the types of companies that require weeks to months of juggling outreach and prep.

4 http://www.paulgraham.com/makersschedule.html

		MONTH 1	MONTH 2	MONTH 3	MONTH 4	MONTH 5	MONTH 6
Outreach to companies		Focus on outreach until you have a repeatable system that gets you responses		Keep doing outreach in the background until you're confident you'll get an offer that you'd take			
Learn/review the material			Learn and/or de-rust. Work problems on your own			Ongoing maintenance	
Interview simulation	**Solo practice**			Continue to work problems on your own, but try to simulate the interview experience as much as possible			
	Mock interviews				Start mock interviews	Do as many as possible	
System design prep				Work on this weekly as time permits			
Behavioral prep					Fill in behavioral matrix	Review periodically	
Schedule interviews & do recruiter calls				Stay on top of emails & communication			
Company-specific prep					Before each interview		
Actually interview					Phone screens & onsites		

A few notes:

- Some candidates don't start outreach until they feel ready to interview. We recommend *starting* with it. Outreach can drag on for months, giving you enough time to study after you find your rhythm. Remember that if you need to, you can always postpone your technical interviews and onsites if you need to (see "Postponing your interviews if you're not ready" on pg 87 for what to say).

- If you don't hear back from companies after a month or two, it's time to take a long hard look at the quality of your messages, make another target list, and start over.

- During Month 2, it's time to start studying, reviewing data structures and algorithms, and working problems on your own.

- Once you're comfortable with common data structures and algorithms (we will give you both a list and a detailed study plan in Chapter 18: How to Practice - pg 170), you should kick your solo practice up a notch by closely simulating a real interview. Time yourself, and practice walking through your thought process out loud.

- There are diminishing returns to grinding problems on your own, and once you find your footing, it's best to add mock interviews with another person to your practice regimen. If you have access to experienced interviewers, great. If not, peers or friends are good, too. Aim for a few mock interviews weekly. Shooting for 10+ mock interviews before your onsites is an excellent goal.

- System design requires a lot of knowledge: early prep and a solid plan to help you **retain** what you learn will give you an edge. Juniors, who are increasingly asked system design questions, tend to focus on it more **after** passing the phone screens, as system design rounds are typically reserved for onsite interviews. However, trying to cram for it in a few days is a terrible idea—early studying will pay off in spades. We have more to say about practicing system design on page 177.

- Behavioral interviews need less time than you'd expect but more than you'd like. Preparing responses in the behavioral matrix (see "Behavioral Category Matrix" on page 148) should take about two weeks— after that, you can revisit it from time to time to stay interview ready.

- Start scheduling your interviews and making recruiter calls around Month 3. In all of our scenarios, we've combined scheduling interviews and doing recruiter calls. Short of getting used to not revealing your compensation expectations or where else you're interviewing (see pg 116 for exactly what to say to recruiters when they ask you about these things), recruiter calls don't require much preparation, and you can knock them out while you're still getting ready.

- Once you get interview invites, prioritize company-specific prep. For instance, Amazon emphasizes leadership principles, Netflix focuses on system design, and Google has tougher coding questions.[5] It isn't uncommon to be told before an onsite that ideal candidates have experience with a particular technology or API.[6]

- Then, depending on how your preparation has gone, you can begin real interviews in Month 4. If you find, after your first few interviews, that you're not fully prepared, you can always postpone the rest (see "Postponing your interviews if you're not ready" on pg 87 for exactly what to say). The important thing is to get in the door, and once you're in, you can control your pacing.

- Try to finish all prep, except company-specific work, before onsites begin. Onsite interviews will drain your mental and emotional energy, making it hard to keep up with practice once you start doing them.

Scenario 2: You're not working and need to find a job in the next few months

If you're not working, you have time to practice, but you may still care about getting your next job by some specific date. If your situation dictates that you have to do prep and outreach simultaneously, then know that it's an uphill battle… and know that, even though it probably doesn't help much, we feel your pain.

In this unenviable situation, here's what we recommend:

		WEEK 1	WEEK 2	WEEK 3	WEEK 4	WEEK 5	WEEK 6	WEEK 7	WEEK 8
Outreach		Get a system in place and complete a first pass of your network		Don't stop until onsite week		Tweak messaging			
Learn/review the material		Superficial pass on common technical topics				Work problems during any remaining free time			
Interview simulation	Solo practice			Continue to work problems on your own, but try to simulate the interview experience as much as possible					
	Mock interviews			As many mock interviews as possible					
System design prep		Work on this daily as time permits							
Behavioral prep					Fill in behavioral matrix				
Schedule interviews & do recruiter calls					Stay on top of emails & communication				
Company-specific prep							Do some of this, time-permitting		
Actually interview								Phone screens	Onsites

This schedule is seriously condensed, compared to the last one (this scale is in weeks, not months). In this schedule, you will be heads-down, working very hard, and juggling many different types of tasks. The most important thing, going into it, is to embrace the suck and accept that the next eight weeks will be very rough.

---

5   If you're not sure what to focus on, check out the company-specific guides at interviewing.io: bctci.co/company-guides

6   Of course, dedicating weeks of studying for just one role is inefficient, and we recommend limiting this as much as possible—scale effort based on how much you want that particular job.

- Spend the first week on immersive outreach—come up with your target list, do all the work to personalize it, and write as many emails as you can in the first few days. We're taking the outreach sequence from above and condensing the hell out of it. We'd strongly advise doing as much experimentation and iteration on your outreach in the first few days of the first week as possible, so you learn what works by the time you get into the second week.

- After Week 1, while you're waiting for responses, start working problems on your own, and continue your outreach in parallel. You won't have time to cover everything, so you'll need to prioritize based on the most common data structures and algorithms (see pg 171 for details).

- In this condensed schedule, we recommend starting to practice with another human as soon as you reasonably can—hopefully by Week 3 at the latest. We're doubling down on mock interviews because a good mock interview is as valuable as spending a week grinding on your own. We still recommend shooting for 10+ mock interviews before your onsites because of how valuable they can be.

- System design and behavioral interview prep mostly stay the same, just on a tighter timeline. Both are as your schedule permits because they get used for leveling more often than they're used to determine success. Better to get down-leveled than fail because you didn't spend enough time preparing for coding interviews.

- Company-specific prep will be challenging to do on such a tight timeline, so it needs to be focused on as soon as you know for sure you'll have onsites.

- Finally, in this condensed schedule, we're having you start scheduling interviews while you're still doing outreach and interview prep—not ideal, but still doable if you're focused.

Scenario 3: You are working

There are a few advantages to running your job search while still being employed. The obvious first one is the safety net—if you know you have your fallback in place, you will be calmer. And, if you have steady income, you can theoretically run your search indefinitely.

Of course, in reality, that's not true. Outreach, prep, and actual interviewing are hard enough by themselves, and having to slot them in while working a full-time job is exhausting, as is the psychological dance of having to take time off to interview without tipping off your manager.

Should you tell your manager that you're interviewing?

Depending on the rapport you have with your manager and the culture of your company, it might be OK to admit that you're looking for work. If you pull this off, you won't have to slink around conference rooms and take a suspicious number of sick days and dentist appointments. We know it sounds crazy to tell your manager, but we've seen it work—chances are, your manager suspects it,[7] and admitting that it's happening can be a big relief for both sides.

However, telling your manager that you're looking is not always the right course of action. Some managers are vindictive, and some cultures are not tolerant of deviation or transparency. You don't want to end up in a situation where you tell your manager you're looking and then get preemptively let go.

Ultimately, it's a judgment call: in engineer-friendly environments with trust, openness, and precedent for others openly looking, sharing may work. In political cultures where engineers feel replaceable, it's better to stay discreet.

---

7   Kind of a funny aside, many years ago, when I (Aline) first started my recruiting business, I found myself visiting a lot of companies and meeting with a lot of founders and in-house recruiting teams. I'd often get swag during these visits, and soon I had an eclectic collection of men's startup T-shirts, which I re-gifted to my then-husband. He started wearing these shirts to work, and he quickly got a raise. We found out later that it was because his manager was convinced he was actively interviewing at all of these companies and wanted to retain him.

If you're working, you will have limited time and limited mental bandwidth to do outreach and practice. However, you will have more runway and can take a month longer than in the scenario where you're running out of cash. That said, we tried not to exceed three months in our proposed schedule because managing a job search, especially a clandestine one, is quite tiring, and we advise you not to take any longer than you have to because you'll eventually run out of steam.[8]

WEEK		1	2	3	4	5	6	7	8	9	10	11	12
Outreach		Focus on outreach until you have a repeatable approach that gets you responses											
Learn/review the material				Learn and/or de-rust. Work problems on your own					Ongoing maintenance				
Interview simula-tion	Solo practice							3 mock interviews per week, with the remaining time dedicated to solo practice that simulates the feel of an interview					
	Mock inter-views												
System design prep						Work on this weekly as time permits							
Behavioral prep						Fill in behavioral matrix & two weeks of focused prep				Review periodically			
Schedule interviews & do recruiter calls						Stay on top of emails & communication							
Company-specific prep										Before each interview			
Actually interview										Phone screens & onsites			On-sites

- In this schedule, we've dedicated three weeks to outreach, with no disruptions (after the first three weeks, you continue outreach as you start working on prep). Hopefully this will give you enough time to get used to writing cold emails and to start iterating on your messaging.

- By Week 3, begin learning and reviewing the material. Here, we have you just practicing on your own for four weeks, which seems lengthy, except that when you're working full-time, it's unrealistic to expect that you'll be putting in the same amount of effort day to day. When you have a hard day at work, you will probably not be able to grind at the same efficiency as you can when that's all you're doing.

- By Week 7, we advise you to dedicate time to solo simulated practice and mock interviews. This still gives you plenty of time to complete 10+ mock interviews before your real interviews begin. Given the logistical challenges of interviewing while working and your limited time during the day, we expect these calls to be spaced out more than in the previous scenario.

- For your own sanity, because you're working, we advise wrapping up scheduling and recruiter calls before starting your technical interviews. This also gives you some time to keep practicing with another human before your interviews begin.

These schedules are starting points, and your mileage will vary. You might need extra practice or multiple outreach attempts. The key is to be deliberate with your time and track what works so you can adjust as needed.

---

8   As an interview coach, I (Mike) have seen that most people underestimate the toll of job searching. It is easy to look at an empty calendar and assume you can make any schedule work, but being realistic with an end date is important. Burnout is the norm, and sustaining a full-time job search while working is incredibly hard. Life gets in the way, so we strongly advise against **planning** for more than three months of job searching.

What about <x>?

Are you considering ML, front-end, or other specialist roles? Depending on the type of role you are looking for, you may need to add an extra row to the schedule for role-specific prep and budget the time for it. For example, sometimes front-end interviews are less DS&A-focused, so you can allocate some of the DS&A time to learning (or de-rusting on) a framework like React.

POSTPONING YOUR INTERVIEWS IF YOU'RE NOT READY

One of the biggest and costliest mistakes candidates make is not postponing interviews when they're unprepared. Here's how it plays out.

> A recruiter from a FAANG company contacts you out of the blue and invites you to interview. The recruiter call goes well, and then they schedule your technical phone screen. You haven't practiced enough, but you are scared to tell the recruiter that you want to postpone the interview by a few months (?!). So, you plow ahead, do the phone screen, fail it, and then you're frozen out for a year.

Even if you *do* get an offer anyway, interviewing when you're unprepared may lead to you getting down-leveled, particularly if you didn't perform well in system design.[9]

Here are a few little-known facts about timing and how interview timing works internally.

1. Recruiters don't *really* care when you interview. Though they'd prefer that you interview sooner rather than later so they can hit their numbers, at the end of the day, they'd rather be responsible for successful candidates than unsuccessful ones.

2. If you're interviewing at large companies, most engineering roles will be evergreen, i.e., they will always be around. Sure, perhaps one team will have filled their spot, but another one will pop up in its place.

If you're applying to a very small company that has just one open headcount, it is possible that postponing will cost you the opportunity because they'll just go with another candidate. However, you can ask how likely that is to happen, upfront.

In our combined decades of experience, we've never heard of a candidate regretting their decision to postpone the interview. On the other hand, we've heard plenty of stories where candidates regretted rushing into it. As such, we strongly recommend telling your recruiter that you need some time to prepare. Because this stuff is hard, here's what you can say, word for word.

⧉   Copy/paste this snippet from bctci.co/job-search-what-to-say-1.

> Hey [name], I'm really excited about interviewing at [company name]. Unfortunately, if I'm honest, I haven't had a chance to practice as much as I'd like. I know how hard and competitive these interviews are, and I want to put my best foot forward. I think I'll realistically need a couple of months to prepare. How about we schedule my interview for [date]?

One important thing to note about this template. We do recommend actually scheduling your interview at the time you postpone, rather than leaving it open. Even though it's very uncommon for companies to implement hiring freezes, it is *quite* common for recruiters to leave their company every few months (see "A

---

9   This is a bit over-simplistic, but generally how you perform in algorithmic interviews determines whether you get an offer, and how you perform in system design (and often in behavioral) interviews determines how you're leveled.

note about in-house recruiter tenures" on page 31), and you don't want to end up in a situation months later where you're ready to reschedule but have lost your contact point.

If you end up getting close to the new date and you still feel unprepared, you can always postpone the interview again. Better that than failing.

The next two sections, *Stalling* and *Speeding Up,* will talk about what to do once you get an offer. Getting good at these skills, as well as salary negotiation, could earn you extra millions of dollars over your lifetime.

AIR TRAFFIC CONTROL: STALLING AND SPEEDING UP

In this section, we'll talk about how to get recruiters to move faster and how to get them to slow down. Imagine this situation. You're interviewing at Google and have your onsite coming up in a few days. You also just finished a phone screen at a small startup and finally heard back from Stripe. Finally, you've just gotten an offer from Amazon. You know by now that ideally you want all of your offers to come in around the same time. What do you do?

From our worksheet, you can see that Google's interview process takes about ten weeks. By the time you pass the onsite, though, an offer is probably just a few weeks away. Stripe's process takes something like 4-6 weeks. By contrast, a small startup can get everything wrapped up in 1-2 weeks. Clearly, you will need to speed up Stripe and slow down both the startup and Amazon.

In the sections below, we'll explain the theory of how to speed up and slow down. In each section, we also have a table that tells you exactly what to say to speed up or slow down.

SPEEDING UP

The best way to get a company to move quickly is to be (mostly) upfront with them. Email your recruiter,[10] and mention that you're wrapping up onsites at a few companies, including Google and Amazon, and that you'll hold them off as long as you can but that you'd really appreciate it if they could expedite your interview.

When you do send that email, it's better to talk about wrapping up onsites rather than mentioning offers. The last thing you want is for Stripe to get spooked and write you off—if they think you're already at the offer stage with Amazon, they may assume that they can't move fast enough to compete and won't want to waste their time. Purposely keeping your situation vague by saying that you're at the onsite stage will galvanize them without scaring them off.

Note that we specifically named both FAANGs. This was a deliberate decision; FAANG-adjacent companies like Stripe don't want to lose candidates to FAANG, and planting that seed is an effective way to mobilize them.

On the other hand, if you're interviewing at an earlier stage startup, you definitely DO NOT want to use your FAANG onsites as leverage. Whether it's justified or not, startups tend to have a bias against candidates who are also interviewing at FAANG. This bias is intellectually inconsistent, as many startups also try to recruit from FAANG, but it goes something like this: FAANG candidates are expecting to make FAANG $$ and are likely just using us for practice.

Sometimes startups will also double-down on this bias by assuming that FAANG engineers and engineers who want to work at FAANG are less scrappy, less willing to work hard, and are more academic than their startup counterparts. However, whether these stereotypes hold water or not, it does you no good to play into them. The last thing you want is for your speeding-up strategy to backfire because your startup recruiter decided to write you off.

---

10 We always suggest using email to communicate with recruiters rather than phone or text—email levels the playing field (they do this all the time; you do not) and keeps them from asking a bunch of followup questions about compensation or where else you're interviewing. For more information about why email is better and how to get recruiters to email you instead of calling, see page 31.

What about using the fact that you're interviewing at a competitor as leverage? If you're interviewing at a direct competitor of a small startup, don't mention it. Startups may be turned off by your lack of serious interest/loyalty (*especially* if you're talking to a founder[11]). On the other hand, if you're interviewing at a direct competitor of a large startup (and NOT talking directly to the founder) or a large company, we'd advise mentioning it—once you hit a certain size, these things stop being personal. If you do use a competitor as leverage, you can soften it by saying, "...That said, I'd prefer to work with you, but if it doesn't work out, I'd like to stay in this space."

Exactly what to say

The table below assumes that you're somewhere between a recruiter screen and offer at a few companies and that the company you're trying to speed up is lagging. No matter where you are in the process with the other companies, we recommend saying that you're wrapping up onsites. Depending on which companies they are, where you are in the process with the lagging company, and how big the lagging company is, you'll say different things.

Copy/paste this snippet from bctci.co/job-search-what-to-say-2.

If you need to speed up an early-stage startup

> At the moment, I'm wrapping up final interviews at a few companies and expect to make a decision in the next 2 weeks. Would it be possible to expedite the process? I'm really excited about {Company name} and want to make sure I don't miss out on the chance to work with you all.

Note: We don't mention specific companies where you're interviewing, regardless of who they are. For early stage startups, it's generally not useful, as we discussed above. You also don't need to be super specific in your request to expedite—early stage startups are nimble and should be able to adjust their schedule and figure it out.

If you need to speed up a late-stage startup or a large company

> At the moment, I'm wrapping up onsites at {If you have FAANG or competitors offers, list them here. Otherwise just say "a few companies"} and expect to make a decision in the next 2 weeks.

> [If you're pre-phone screen] Would it be possible to schedule my technical phone screen as soon as possible or perhaps go straight to onsite? Alternatively, maybe we can schedule the phone screen and tentatively schedule the onsite in parallel and then cancel if the phone screen doesn't go well?

> [If you're post-phone screen] Would it be possible to schedule my final interview rounds as soon as possible?

> I'm really excited about {Company name} and want to make sure I don't miss out on the chance to work with you all.

SLOWING DOWN

Let's say you find yourself in this situation. You've passed the onsite at Meta, and you're proceeding to team matching. However, you're at early stages with a few companies, including Stripe and Square—you've done recruiter calls but haven't yet scheduled your technical phone screens.

You know that it's going to take at least four weeks to get through Stripe and Square's process. Can you reasonably stall Meta for that long? And can you get Stripe and Square to move faster? Fortunately, the answer is yes!

---

11 We'll talk more about how to talk to founders vs. recruiters later on page 133.

That said, there are some cases where the answer will be no. If you were just starting the process with another FAANG or another large, slow-moving company and already had the offer from Meta, it would be unrealistic to stall Meta for another two to three months. Look, you can always try, and sometimes it works, but in that scenario, you'll have to steel yourself for the possible outcome that Meta won't wait forever.

Whether stalling this much will work for you is a function of five things:

- **Market conditions:** In the heady days of a hiring boom, candidates have a lot of leverage, and it's possible to get FAANGs to wait over a month before accepting an offer *just by asking them to wait*. Though your recruiter might halfheartedly grumble about how they're talking to other candidates, you'd both know that all roles are evergreen, that all FAANGs are always hiring, and that they would ultimately wait as long as needed. In a team matching scenario, in ideal market conditions, it wouldn't make sense for a recruiter to pressure you to accept because a certain team only has so many open roles (they'd still try, of course, but these threats didn't have teeth). In a down market, it's harder. Companies may not be hiring all the time. Certain teams may freeze. And there are many more candidates competing for fewer slots, which means teams really do fill up, and recruiter threats aren't always idle.
- **Stage:** The best time to slow down is before the onsite. At large companies with evergreen roles, you can often postpone the onsite indefinitely, as long as they're still hiring.
- **Company size:** Startups are often more flexible with timelines for two reasons: they want to avoid losing candidates to larger, higher-paying companies, and their less rigid processes allow for exceptions.
- **Whether you're interviewing for a specific team:** Slowing down after an onsite is toughest when you're interviewing at a company with a decentralized process, i.e., you've applied to a specific team. Ideally, you'd already have delayed the onsite, but there's still some room to maneuver at the offer stage. Keep in mind, slowing down may risk losing the chance to work with that specific team, so weigh your options carefully. It doesn't hurt to ask to slow down—at worst, the recruiter might refuse, leaving you to decide if joining this team is worth losing other opportunities or negotiation leverage. If you're applying to a centralized company with team matching, your best bet is to slow-play that part of the process.

Team matching (for centralized processes)

Once you get to team matching, the company knows they want you, but they can't yet hold an offer deadline over you.

At Meta and other centralized companies, once you commit to a team, recruiters will get quite aggressive and will push hard to have you accept an offer. Meta, in particular, has been known to give very tight deadlines of just a couple days. Why are recruiters so aggressive at this stage?

- By picking a team, you've effectively committed, which shows that you're likely to accept an offer. Every day that you don't sign, the deal loses momentum, and your odds of signing drop.
- A spot is being held for you on that specific team, which impedes the company's ability to extend offers to others.
- Recruiters are also evaluated on how many candidates they close, so it's in their interest to create a false sense of scarcity, to rush you, and to use high-pressure sales tactics.

Therefore, if you need to slow things down, it's important to take your time *before you commit to a team*. Here's what we recommend:

- **Build rapport with hiring managers:** More on that in the next section.

- **Spread out the conversations:** Even if the company lets you talk to multiple hiring managers concurrently, try to serialize those conversations as much as possible. Space them a few days apart, if you can.[12]
- **Request to speak with individual contributors:** Not just as a stalling tactic, but to understand the job and team dynamics. These are your future colleagues, and they're less likely to hard-sell. Ask thoughtful questions to gain insight (). Just like with hiring manager calls, if you need to slow things down, we recommend scheduling calls with your peers a few days apart.

Build rapport with hiring managers

Hiring managers are your best defense against any recruiter pressure, so building rapport with them is key.

As we said above, recruiters are trying to close the deal. That's their job. Hiring managers, on the other hand, are trying to lay the groundwork for a good working relationship with you. Of course, they still want to close you, but it's not worth it to them to employ high-pressure tactics, and it's not something they're trained in or used to (many of them have been on the other end of it when they were looking for work and don't like it either).[13]

As such, hiring managers will generally be much more transparent about when you actually have to make a decision by, and their answers will likely differ dramatically[14] from information you gleaned from recruiters.

Questions to ask during team matching

We list hiring manager questions in their own section (because they may come up either during the onsite or team matching, depending on the type of process the company has).

For everyone:

- Choose some questions from our list on page 75, and ask the same questions of everyone to see how their responses differ.

Questions to ask your hiring manager(s)

Even though this is part of the bigger *Slowing down* section, these questions are not just meant to stall or build rapport in order to get an extension on your offer deadline. They serve a much more important purpose: getting insight into what it'd actually be like to work on the team and specifically for this person. Rapport with your manager is one of the key predictors of job satisfaction, and although these questions are dual-purpose, the more important purpose is the one that helps you decide if this is the right team for you.

For hiring managers to build rapport and gauge fit:

- Which project on the roadmap are you personally most excited about, and why?
- What can I do to minimize my onboarding time and become effective as fast as possible?

---

12 Don't worry about this making you seem less serious. The biggest risk you run is losing the chance to work on a specific team. If you find the perfect fit, do prioritize that call. However, in almost every case, there will be a next team and many choices. If you're unsure about team supply, you can always ask your recruiter up front how many teams recent candidates have had the chance to talk to, on average. The only time we saw this advice backfire was when companies started to freeze hiring aggressively in mid-2022; if you didn't get matched before the ax came down, you were left out in the cold. This is obviously an unfortunate situation, but it's extremely rare, and in our humble opinion, not worth optimizing for or worrying about. In most cases, you will not be dealing with an impending freeze.

13 Of course, some hiring managers will use high-pressure sales tactics or create false timelines to try to close you. But that's the exception rather than the rule. You can decide if that's something that you want to weigh when judging whether you want to work for them or not.

14 We've advised all of our Meta candidates to ask their prospective hiring managers about when they realistically have to make a decision by, and the differences between what the hiring manager has told them ("Take your time; you have a few weeks at least.") and what their recruiter has told them ("We're talking to a lot of candidates for that team. To ensure your spot, you should make a decision in the next few days.") are stark.

- What have been some failure modes for past hires? What are things I should make sure to avoid doing?
- What's your preferred mode of communication? Email? Messaging?
- If there are several project options when I join, which would help the team most for me to take on?
- There are even more questions you can ask in our list (pg 75).

For hiring managers to gauge when you have to *actually* make a decision by (regardless of what recruiters tell you):

- How many more people are you trying to hire for your team this quarter?

  » This is a specific question that hiring managers don't get that much and, as such, may not have a rehearsed response/will be more likely to answer honestly. Even if you don't get an answer to the next question, it'll give you some idea of how urgently you have to make a decision.

- From everything I've heard about your team and from getting to know you, I think it could be a great fit. That said, this is a decision I'm taking really seriously. I know you're talking to other candidates, but would you mind sharing when you think I'll need to make a decision by? I promise not to draw things out, but I want to make the best decision I can and then give 100% to the team I join.

  » This is really important. As we discussed above, you're much more likely to get honest answers from hiring managers than from recruiters.

- Would you be comfortable sharing your contact info (e.g., email) with me? I promise not to abuse it.[15]

Exactly what to say

We've made a table that tells you what to say to stall.[16] But first, let's see how long you can reasonably stall, as a function of company type and where you are in the process.

	HOW LONG YOU CAN STALL	
	BEFORE THE ONSITE	**AFTER THE ONSITE/AT OFFER**
Startup	Indefinitely, if the company has head-count	At least 6 weeks, likely more, if the company has open headcount
Large company (specific team)	Indefinitely, but you may be routed to a different team	2 weeks
Large company (centralized / has team matching)	Indefinitely, provided they have open headcount	4 weeks

Now here's exactly what to say.

 Copy/paste the snippets below from bctci.co/job-search-what-to-say-3 and bctci.co/job-search-what-to-say-4.

---

15 We recommend asking for your hiring manager's email because they very likely check their email much more often than they check their LinkedIn, and when you need to get in touch with them, it may be time-sensitive. However, it's also a good idea to add them on LinkedIn. People change jobs fairly often, and if you end up having good rapport with this manager, they may be able to refer you to their next company in the future.

16 With respect to market conditions, we're assuming that some hiring is happening, but candidates have less leverage than during a boom. In better conditions, you'll be able to stall for longer with less worry about missing out on teams or roles.

	WHERE IN THE PROCESS YOU NEED TO SLOW DOWN	
	Before the onsite	**After the onsite/at offer**
Startup	I would really appreciate it if we could postpone the onsite by a few weeks. I would like a bit more time to prepare. As you can imagine, I'm taking this opportunity very seriously and want to do everything I can to maximize my chances. If doing so would hurt my chances of getting hired because you have limited headcount right now, please let me know, and I'll think it through carefully.	I'm currently wrapping up interviews with a few other companies. As you can imagine, this is a decision I'm not taking lightly, and I'd like to have as much information as possible. I expect to collect offers by {DATE} and make a decision by {DATE}. I promise not to accept any offers without discussing them with you.
Large company (applying for a specific team)	I would really appreciate it if we could postpone the onsite by a few weeks. I would like a bit more time to prepare. As you can imagine, I'm taking this opportunity very seriously and want to do everything I can to maximize my chances. If doing so would hurt my chances of ending up on {TEAM}, let me know, and I'll think it through carefully. If there's a chance that I can end up on a different team, please let me know (this would not be my preference, as I'm very excited about this team; just trying to think through my options).	I'm currently wrapping up interviews with a few other companies. As you can imagine, this is a decision I'm not taking lightly, and I'd like to have as much information as possible. I expect to collect offers by {DATE} and make a decision by {DATE}. If doing so would hurt my chances of ending up on {TEAM}, let me know, and I'll think it through carefully. If there's a chance that I can end up on a different team, please let me know (this would not be my preference, as I'm very excited about this team; just trying to think through my options). Regardless, I promise not to accept any offers without discussing them with you.
Large company (centralized/has team matching)	I would really appreciate it if we could postpone the onsite by a few weeks. I would like a bit more time to prepare. As you can imagine, I'm taking this opportunity very seriously and want to do everything I can to maximize my chances.	[Here, we recommend slow-playing team matching.]

EXAMPLES

Let's get back to the two examples we referenced earlier.

Example #1: Upcoming Google onsite

You're interviewing at Google and have your onsite coming up in a few days. You also just finished a phone screen at a small startup and finally heard back from Stripe. Lastly, you've just gotten to team matching at Amazon. What do you do?

You'll need to use a combination of tactics! You'll need to speed up everyone except Amazon, and you'll need to slow Amazon down. Let Stripe know that you've just wrapped up your Amazon onsite and will be done with Google's shortly as well. They will likely get you on a recruiter call the next day and possibly skip the phone screen in favor of moving straight to onsite in the next few days. That or they'll schedule the phone screen right away and tentatively schedule the onsite right after. Let Google know that you have started talking numbers with Amazon and ask them if you can move the onsite up by a few days to ensure that you'll be reviewed the very next time the hiring committee meets. Let the small startup know that you're wrapping up onsites with other companies without mentioning that they're FAANGs.

With Amazon, slow play the team matching step: serialize the conversations, make sure to build rapport with the hiring manager for each team, ask to talk to peers on each team, and space out those conversations as much as possible.

Example #2: Team matching at Meta

You're at team matching at Meta and have yet to schedule your technical phone screens at Stripe and Square. What do you do?

Again, you'll need to use a combination of tactics! You'll need to slow Meta down by slow-playing team matching, as above. In parallel, you'll want to reach out to both Stripe and Square, mention that you're wrapping up your Meta onsite, and ask them if they could please either skip the phone screen and go straight to onsite OR schedule the phone screen ASAP and optimistically schedule the onsite a few days after it as well.

OFFERS & NEGOTIATION

PART IV

Watch for these speech-bubble icons, which mean there is online content.

✦ **AI Interviewer:** Each problem can be tried online with the AI Interviewer.

▶ **Interview Replay:** Recordings of actual mock interviews.

🗋 **Snippet:** Material to copy/paste online, including email templates and code recipes.

🗗 **Resource:** Bonus chapters, worksheets, and other material.

OFFERS & NEGOTIATION

## CHAPTER 10

COMPONENTS OF THE OFFER

Once you get the offer, the trickiest part is dealing with negotiation. However, there are a few foundational things to know about offers that will help you value them and think about how you want to approach negotiation.

Offers usually consist of four components: base salary, equity, signing bonus, and performance bonus. When you add together the value of all of these, you get something called total compensation or TC.[1]

In this section, we'll break down each of the offer components. We'll also talk about whether having a written offer matters, what happens if you renege on an offer, and under what circumstances we've seen companies rescind offers (spoiler: it doesn't happen much).

OFFER COMPONENTS

Not every offer will have all of the components below. But we'll teach you how to reason about each one and explain which ones are easiest (or hardest) for companies to give out.

BASE SALARY

Base salary is among the hardest aspects of your offer to negotiate, with increases rarely being more than 10% - 20%. That's not bad, of course, but it's nothing compared to equity where people can sometimes double their initial offer.

Here's why base salary is hard to negotiate:

1. When a company hires you, they're committing to pay you *at least* that salary for your entire tenure—if not more, due to raises.[2]

2. It tends to have the least variance across people with the same title—employers assume that people will talk about their compensation, and it's not a good look to have two people with the same title making hugely different salaries.

---

1 If you've ever read posts on Blind, you've probably seen an undue obsession with TC with people routinely saying something like, "TC or GTFO!" to people who forgot to include their TC in their posts. Now you know what they're referring to.

2 Though some companies have successfully pulled off pay cuts, they're hard to do and almost always result in significant employee attrition. Keeping salaries within some predetermined range is a cash flow move. There is also the expectation that you will get a raise every few years. Studies have shown that raises add up to much less cash than switching jobs every few years—according to Zippia, "the average salary increase when changing jobs is 14.8%, while wage growth is 5.8%". However, raises are still expected and something employers have to budget for.

Unlike the base salary, the other components of an offer usually have more wiggle room.

EQUITY

Very few people understand equity. This includes people who give it out and people who have it. There's no shame in not understanding it. It's hard, understanding it involves understanding securities law and tax law, and the rules change from time to time. In this book, we'll just cover the quick and dirty practical bits and help you understand equity well enough to be able to negotiate it. Fortunately, there's an excellent book out there, *The Holloway Guide to Equity Compensation*,[3] that goes into a ton of detail. Also, for a good explanation of how stock options work, read Alex MacCaw's *An Engineer's Guide to Stock Options*.[4]

Equity needs to be thought about differently depending on whether you're dealing with a public or private company.

- **At a private company:** Your equity is basically Monopoly money until it's not. It may have some kind of value eventually, but in most cases, you can't cash out until there's a liquidity event—most commonly an acquisition or an IPO—and there's no assurance there will ever be one. Valuing equity is incredibly difficult, but we'll give you some rough guidelines for how to reason about your startup equity stake later in this chapter.
- **At a public company:** Your equity has a real, tangible cash value: the stock price.

Equity most commonly comes as either stock options or restricted stock units (RSUs). If you're a very early startup employee, you may get a restricted stock grant.

Vesting schedules: Equity is granted on a vesting schedule, which is a timeline (usually several years) on which your equity gets doled out. Employers are reluctant to hand you all your equity on day one, because they want to create an incentive for you to stay as long as possible.[5]

- **Cliffs:** Most companies do a four-year vesting schedule with a one-year cliff. This means that if you leave before the one-year mark, you don't get any equity. If you stay for a year or longer, you usually get your remaining equity in linear, monthly chunks (so 1/36th of the remaining stock every month… because you already got the first 1/4th when you stayed for the first year).

Fair market value vs. preferred price: These terms only apply to companies that are not publicly traded— once you're publicly traded, your shares have just one price.

- Preferred price is a company's valuation from its latest funding round divided by the number of shares outstanding. This is the price investors pay for preferred stock (as opposed to common stock), which typically includes some special rights for investors, such as the right to be paid back first in the event of a low exit. If you've read press pieces about funding rounds or watched *Silicon Valley*, you'll know that companies' valuations are often inflated and that in a boom market, they can get absurdly high. Although valuations vary quite a bit depending on market conditions and how many investors are interested, the valuation will generally be 10-15X revenue at a SaaS (software-as-a-service) company. These valuations are meant to be (aspirational) proxies for what the company would be worth if it were to IPO or get acquired today.

---

3 https://www.holloway.com/g/equity-compensation

4 https://blog.alexmaccaw.com/an-engineers-guide-to-stock-options/

5 This approach also has the added benefit of selectively retaining the employees who are most optimistic about the company's success.

- Fair market value is the result of an independent third-party's assessment (called a 409A valuation) of what your company's common stock might be worth on the open market. The fair market value, unlike the preferred price, is not meant to be aspirational. In fact, founders want to drive their 409A valuations as low as possible, for tax purposes. So, after the third party comes to you with an estimate of the share price, you push back a few times, citing a litany of financial fails: poor revenue, market downturns, poor cash flow, and so on.

This creates a funny situation where founders are trying to inflate their preferred price (for investors) while trying to squash their fair market value (which sets the strike price for employee options). FMV is often as low as 5X lower than the preferred price.

Restricted stock awards. These are actual shares of the company, and they're relatively rare because they're usually issued just to founders and very early employees.

Stock options. With the exception of some late-stage startups, equity in startups tends to be issued in the form of stock options. Stock options aren't actually stock. They are a promise that you can eventually buy ("exercise") stock at whatever the fair market value (FMV) was when the options were issued (around when you started the job, in most cases).

- **Vesting schedules:** Stock options, just like stock grants, are generally subject to some kind of vesting schedule; you usually can't exercise them until they are vested.
- **What your offer might look like:** 20,000 options with a strike price of $0.50 vesting over four years with a one-year cliff.

Recently, many not-yet-public startups have started presenting the stock options portion of their offer in the same way that public companies present their equity: as a dollar value. For instance, you may see a startup offer include "$400k in stock options." This is potentially misleading for several reasons:

1. Given the simultaneous existence of a preferred price and the FMV, it's not necessarily clear what calculation the company is doing to arrive from that promise to the number of shares in your option grant.
2. This potentially fosters a faux apples-to-apples comparison between their stock options (which are, well, Monopoly money) and publicly traded shares of stock (which have an accepted dollar value). Don't be fooled. We're not saying stock options can't be valuable. We're just advising you not to take the dollar value literally and to do your own math. We'll show you how to do that in a bit.

If there's a liquidity event (acquisition or IPO) and you haven't exercised your vested options, they may either get cashed out (basically like exercising the option and then turning around and immediately selling the share) or they may be converted to acquirer stock options.

Unvested options may get replaced with acquirer options or they may disappear entirely, depending on how employee-favorable the acquisition is. In rare cases, they might get accelerated.

Should you exercise your options, and if so, when? The hard thing about valuing stock options is that you don't know how much your shares will eventually be worth (if anything at all!). The *strike price* (which is the FMV at the time of grant) tells you how much you can purchase a share for. But what will you sell it for? The closest guess we have is the preferred price. When you sell, your "profit" will be the delta between the strike price and the then-sale price (also called "the spread"). The *hope* is that by the time you sell, each share will be worth much more than the current preferred price, but of course, you have no idea.

There are two things you need to think about when deciding if you want to exercise:

- How long your startup's exercise window is
- How long you're willing/able to wait to see if your company will be worth something, and how that plays out with respect to taxation (you can get taxed a lot or a little, depending on how long you wait)

In order to be able to sell, you first have to exercise your options. If you leave the company with vested, but unexercised options, you typically have a window in which you can exercise those options (the "exercise window"), which is anywhere from 90 days to 10 years, though in rare cases, it's been as little as 30 days. The longer the window, the better for you because the longer you can wait before you decide if you want to spend money on your options. (The exercise window is one of the things you'll definitely want to ask about. We'll include a handy list of questions about equity at the end of this section.)

Waiting to exercise stock options may seem appealing, as you can assess your company's success over a typical 9-year startup exit timeline before committing. However, waiting until the last moment can lead to significant tax burdens. At the same time, exercising early requires you to have the cash to buy something *right then and there*.

We'll leave the topic of taxation to the tax professionals, but when you exercise your options is something you do control. So when you consider your offer, look at the exercise window; it matters. And when you exercise matters, too, because it determines how much you get taxed, which will, in turn, inform how hard you want to negotiate for equity vs. cash.

Restricted stock units (RSUs). If you're applying to late-stage startups or public companies, you'll likely get your equity in the form of restricted stock units (RSUs).

Startups move to RSUs from options at some point because as the company gets bigger, more successful, and closer to exiting, the delta between the fair market value and the preferred price gets smaller and smaller, making your possible "profit" on options smaller as well. Also, as the fair market value goes up, so does your strike price, which means that exercising your options could be more expensive than most people can spend (tens or hundreds of thousands of dollars). RSUs are a good way to incentivize employees when options no longer look like a clear win.

- **Vesting schedule:** Once you vest, you get taxed on your RSUs like they're income. At a public company, vesting is usually straightforward: a four-year vest with a one-year cliff. If you're at a late-stage startup, you'll usually see something called "double trigger" vesting, where your RSUs can only vest (still on some schedule) when there's an exit. Either way, the amount of income is the value times the number of RSUs. Your employer will likely withhold some portion of your RSUs to cover tax.
- **Value of RSUs:** If you're at a public company, the value of your RSUs is the actual stock price. If you're at a late-stage startup, the value is the fair market value, just like it is for options and stock grants. However, if you have double trigger vesting (which you likely do), you will not be taxed on your RSUs until an exit.
- **What your offer might look like:** $225K in RSUs, vesting over 4 years with a 1-year cliff.

So how do you actually make money on your RSUs? At some point, you decide to sell them. Then, you get taxed *again* (the first time was income tax when you vested). This time it's going to be short or long-term capital gains, depending on whether you held on to them for at least a year before selling or not.

How to actually value your equity. This is really hard. It's not realistic to promise that we can teach you to accurately value startup equity. If you could do that every time, you wouldn't need to write code or practice for interviews because you'd be raking in the dough in the financial markets. However, we *can* teach you enough to empower you to ask the right questions of your recruiters, to negotiate confidently, and to know when someone is blowing smoke up your butt.

The first thing you need to look at is this graph from Prospect, a startup that helps individuals value their equity.

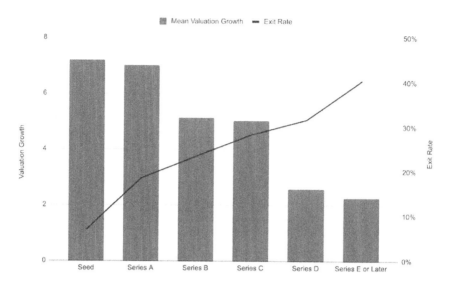

Figure 1. The probability that a startup will exit, as well as its likely valuation multiple. Taken from Prospect's blog post: What stage startup offers the best risk-reward tradeoff?[6]

In this graph, you can see the probability that a startup will exit, as well as how much its valuation is likely to grow between now and exit. For instance, a Series B startup has a 30% exit rate, and when they exit, their valuation is likely to be ~5X higher than it is now.

You can use these numbers to compute the probability-weighted expected value of your equity. Fortunately, we built you an equity calculator so you don't have to do the work. It looks like this, and it can figure out the probability-weighted value of your equity by the time the company exits (either gets acquired or goes public).

⬀   Use our equity calculator to figure out the expected value of your equity. It may be much lower than you think, primarily because most startups fail: bctci.co/offer-components-worksheet-1.

Fill in the yellow boxes!	
Startup stage	Seed ▾
Current valuation	$16,000,000
Equity type	Stock options ▾
How many shares/options/units you're getting	6,000
Number of shares outstanding	1,000,000
How many more rounds of funding they plan to raise before exiting (if you don't know, that's ok, we'll use our best guess, which is the value that's already filled in)	5 OPTIONAL
Strike price for your options (if not getting options, leave this blank)	$0.15
Probability-weighted expected value of your equity at exit (before taxes)	**$14,750**

The calculator works by figuring out the probability that your company will exit (based on what stage it's at right now), how much we expect the valuation to go up by then (based on Prospect's figures above),

---

6   Source: Blog post from Prospect: What stage startup offers the best risk-reward tradeoff?. https://www.joinprospect. com/blog/which-stage-startup

and how much we expect you to get diluted between now and then— generally it's by 20% every time a company raises a round.

Of course, if you have some privileged information about how likely your company is to exit, our calculations go out the window. But, in most cases, you won't have that info, and for that, using industry averages is a good first-pass approach.

As you play around with the numbers, you might be surprised by how low the expected value of your equity is, relative to what your recruiter is telling you. The difference is that your recruiter's estimates are *not* probability-weighted. They are best-case scenario estimates and do not factor in the (fairly reasonable) chance that the company's equity will be worthless.

Of course, you may know (or know of) people who have gotten very rich from joining startups. Generally, the earlier you join, the more likely you are to make a life-changing amount of money. But the less likely it is that you'll make any money overall. The later you join, the more likely you are to make *some* money. But it probably won't be a life-changing amount.

Finally, the calculator also assumes a 1X liquidation preference. If your company has anything more than that, you will probably never see a dime.

One big gotcha: liquidation preference. We can't leave the topic of equity without covering one very important concept: liquidation preference. In the event of a liquidity event, such as an exit, it allows investors with this right to choose to have their investment amount (and sometimes a multiple of that amount) repaid *before* other shareholders get anything. In practice, this means that if a startup has a low (or just "okay") exit, the investors will get repaid first with the exit proceeds—and there may not be much (or anything) left for employee shareholders.

If it's a "participating" liquidation preference, investors get their investment out and also a portion of what's left over, further reducing what's left for founders and employees. While this mainly applies in the event of a relatively low exit, it can be devastating. It's not really possible to value your equity without taking it into account, especially if the liquidation preference involves more than a 1X multiple.

Here's a real-life example. In 2013, Meebo was acquired by Google for an impressive $100 million, after they had raised $70 million. However, due to liquidation preference, employees didn't make any money in this sale. Meebo's co-founder, Elaine Wherry, explains it better than I can in her blog post called, *top 10 myths of silicon valley*.[7] We've reproduced the relevant portion here:

> Founders [and employees] don't pocket the incredible dollar figures in headlines. It's possible for an acquisition in the hundreds of millions to leave nothing for the founders depending upon how much has been raised, how much was allotted to employees, the number of founders, whether the exit included stock or cash, and the liquidation preferences.

> Given how important they are, it's surprising that liquidation preferences aren't discussed more… When a company folds or is acquired, liquidation preferences protect the investors' investment. At a minimum, a liquidation preference simply specifies that the investors receive their money back (1x non-participating). At the other extreme, investors might have a 2x multiple (meaning that investors want double back) and if there's anything left over, they are also entitled to a cut of the remainder based upon their ownership (2x participating).

> With a 2x participating liquidation preference, it's possible for a company that raised a total of $50M for 50% ownership to sell for $100M and for the team to have nothing. Participating also means that the investors always get more than just 50%. When the exit is huge, the liquidation preference matters less. But huge exits are rarer.

---

7   https://elainewherry.com/2014/08/07/top-10-myths-of-silicon-valley/

Liquidation preferences can be brutal[8] for founders and employees. Recruiters usually don't volunteer the liquidation preference and often don't know themselves. But it's something you absolutely need to ask. As we said before, if it's anything above 1X, you should assume the odds of payout for you are slim.

Equity tends to be one of the easier aspects of your offer to negotiate because it's easier for employers to give it away than cash. We'll talk about how much more equity is appropriate to ask for in Chapter 14: How to Negotiate (pg 123).

Questions to ask about equity
Ask this ALWAYS:

- What's the vesting schedule?

If the company isn't public yet, ask these questions (doesn't matter what type of equity you're getting):

- What percent of the company am I getting (based on fully diluted numbers)? *Many recruiters won't share this with you,[9] but you can't value your equity without it.*

  » As we said above, when you get an offer that includes stock options, it's usually presented as some number of options or possibly a dollar value. What that dollar value is based on is unknown. Some companies use the current valuation, but many use an aspirational valuation that they might have when they IPO. Either way, valuation will likely change over time, and you won't be able to reason about future value without knowing what your percentage ownership is. Giving you the number of options or the dollar value is like offering you some amount of money in a foreign currency without telling you the conversion rate. If a recruiter won't tell you the percentage you're getting, you can still get at it by asking:

    - What is the number of fully diluted shares?

      » If you're given this amount, you can just divide your number of shares or options by the total amount of fully diluted shares to calculate your percentage ownership.

---

8 Why would a company ever accept greater than 1X liquidation preference? The reality is that fundraising is really hard, and relatively few companies have the luxury of juggling multiple investor offers. If you find yourself fundraising while you're running out of cash, in a hard market, you may have no choice but to accept bad terms. Though having high liquidation preferences has gone out of fashion on the west coast, we've heard about them coming back in style during the 2022-2023 downturn, especially if dealing with firms who aren't based in the Bay Area.

For an investor's perspective on why investors sometimes offer greater than 1X liquidation preferences, read Leo Polovets' (of Susa Ventures) excellent post on LinkedIn: https://www.linkedin.com/posts/lpolovets_i-wrote-a-post-about-liquidation-preferences-activity-7171583604102275073-o9Qq. The gist is that, sometimes, an investor will give a company a choice: take a down round OR include a multiple on the liquidation preference. Founders may actively choose the multiple because the optics of a down-round can be brutal.

9 Why don't recruiters share what percent of the company you're getting? It seems absurd because, as we mentioned above, you can't value your equity without it. In my experience (and it's something I've had some screaming matches about over the years, when I worked in-house), they're told not to by legal or by the executive team because the less they share, the less liability they open themselves up to if, later, they have to make ownership changes (the most extreme example of this is in the movie *The Social Network* where they dilute the hell out of Eduardo Saverin). That's not to say that every company has ill intent, but it's probably fair to say that every company wants to protect themselves and hedge against the possibility that they'll act with ill intent at some point in the future (the moral equivalent of packing condoms for your business trip). The second reason is that, in concert with it being a liability to share percentages, companies can often get away with NOT sharing them because very few candidates ask about their percentage ownership. We hope that everyone reading this book will make it a habit to ask.

Incidentally, you might be curious about why the percent of the company doesn't go into an offer letter. Fortunately, the reason for that is much less insidious. It's because, over time, your percent ownership will change. As the company raises future rounds of funding, they will create more options, and you'll get diluted. Dilution is factored into our equity calculator above, and it's usually about 20% for every round of funding.

- What is the preferred price per share?
- What was the valuation of the company at the last funding round?

  » If you're given the valuation and the preferred price, you can divide them to figure out the number of fully diluted shares. Once you have that, you can calculate your percentage ownership.

- Are there any liquidation preferences?

  » We discussed this above. If it's anything more than 1X, it's much less likely you'll ever see cash for your equity because investors are guaranteed to get paid out more than they put in. In other words, having a >1X liquidation preference raises the bar on how high the sale price of the company has to be.

If your company is issuing restricted stock awards or options (i.e., not RSUs):

- Is it possible to early exercise and do an 83(b) election?
- If stock awards: What is the fair market value per share?
- If options:

  » What is the strike price?
  » What is the preferred price per share?

    - Multiplying the preferred price times the number of shares outstanding will give you the latest investor valuation.

If your company is issuing RSUs and isn't public:

- When is the IPO likely to be?
- How many more rounds of funding are expected before the IPO?

  » You can plug this information into our equity calculator to get a more accurate value.

PERFORMANCE BONUS

There's not a lot to say about performance bonuses, honestly. In our experience, they are not negotiable and vary significantly from company to company. Moreover, they're only a sure thing at large public companies; startups generally have too much uncertainty in their yearly performance and cash flow to promise a bonus.

At large companies, your performance bonus is likely to be somewhere between 10% and 20% of your base salary. Meta's is 15%, for instance.

SIGNING BONUS

A signing bonus (also called a sign-on bonus) is a one-time bonus you get for deciding to accept an offer, and it usually comes with some strings: if you leave or get fired before your one-year anniversary, you have to pay it back.

Because signing bonuses are a one-time payment (unlike salary, you don't have to pay it every year) and are largely de-risked for employers (if you don't work out, they get it back), they are one of the easier aspects of your offer to negotiate.

RELOCATION BONUS

If the company you're applying to doesn't have a remote option, you may have to move for your job. If that happens, your company may offer you a relocation bonus. Some companies will combine the signing and relocation bonuses into one. Some will give you one separately. Usually it's somewhere between $5k and $10k. At smaller companies, your relocation bonus is almost always negotiable. At larger companies, there's usually a set package.

OFFER MECHANICS: WRITTEN VS. VERBAL, RENEGING, RESCINDING

By now we've covered a lot of material on the components of an offer. Let's switch gears and talk about actual offer mechanics. How do written vs. verbal offers work? What happens if you renege on an offer? And how likely are companies to rescind your offer for negotiating?

WRITTEN VS. VERBAL OFFERS

Many of our negotiation clients believe that an offer isn't real until they get an offer letter. While it's generally a good idea not to assume anything until an offer letter is *signed* (we advise all of our clients to keep their options open until that moment), expecting to get offer letters from all the companies you're talking to is unrealistic. The main reason is that offers usually change at least once and sometimes several times before both sides agree. Drafting a letter each time is both time-consuming and opens up the possibility of signing the wrong document.

As such, just because you don't get a formal offer letter does not mean that the company is trying to screw you over. Rather, they're waiting for you to verbally accept before they put in the effort to send out the paperwork.

Sometimes, recruiters will put your offer numbers into an email. Other times, you'll get the numbers on the phone. While phone calls are not contractually binding, for your own sanity, we recommend assuming that the numbers they propose are real. If you'd like, you can always jot an email to your recruiter with the numbers they gave you and ask them to confirm if those are correct.

Once you get the numbers, you can negotiate, and once you're happy with the outcome, your recruiter will send you a formal offer letter.

RENEGING ON AN OFFER

We are not fans of reneging on offers, primarily because in most cases, it's the last in a series of completely avoidable errors. With proper negotiation techniques, you should not get to the point where you need to renege[10]. See Chapter 14: How to Negotiate (pg 123).

Are there any tangible negative consequences to reneging on an offer? Not really. Of course, if you're inter-viewing at a small startup and dealing directly with the founder, your name may be seared into the depths of their soul forever.

But do large companies maintain an official candidate blacklist? The answer is no, at least from what we've heard. It's true that there will be a note in their Applicant Tracking System about how you reneged, and that note may keep recruiters from reaching out to you or trying proactively to get you back. But there's no system in place, as far as we know, that blocks your application, if you end up applying again. That said, we'll

---

10 There's one notable exception. If you're in the US on a visa and you lose your job, you have something like 60 days to get a new job before you have to leave. Given that just the FAANG interview process, never mind the preamble to it, can take more than 60 days, in our minds, in a catastrophic situation such as this, all bets are off, and you need to do whatever you can to ensure your livelihood and ability to stay. Antiquated and unfair immigration policies are not your fault and something you're largely powerless to change, as a non-citizen, so do what you have to do.

again advise you not to renege because it's a symptom of mishandling your negotiations and also, because if you're mishandling them this way, you're likely mishandling them in other ways, leaving money on the table.

OFFERS GETTING RESCINDED

We'll talk more later about conditions under which your offer might be rescinded for negotiating (see pg 108). For now, let's just say that unless you're a giant jerk or unless the company literally has one open headcount for your role, your job offer will not get rescinded because you negotiated.

So, negotiating aside, under what circumstances do job offers get rescinded? If you were job hunting during an economic downturn, then you probably know the answer—it's when companies unexpectedly freeze hiring.

One of the most stark examples comes from Meta, which rescinded offers from both summer interns and new grads (as well as possibly other full-time hires), between October of 2022 and January of 2023.[11] Flexport rescinded about 50 eng offers in early 2023 as well.[12]

All that said, we don't advise worrying about or planning for these types of events. They are completely out of your control, they're unlikely, and they don't happen because you negotiated. As such, adjusting your negotiation strategy to factor in economic downturns will, nine times out of ten, mean that, rather than being prudent and world-wise, you'll actually be leaving a bunch of money on the table.

---

11   https://www.theverge.com/2023/1/11/23550302/meta-layoffs-hiring-freeze-tech-recession-labor
12   https://www.cnbc.com/2023/09/08/flexport-ceo-ryan-petersen-rescinds-hiring-offers-cuts-office-space.html

## CHAPTER 11

THE WHAT & WHY OF NEGOTIATION

We hear lots of excuses from candidates about why they didn't negotiate. The offer was fair. They don't want their offer to be rescinded. They didn't think they were allowed to. And, often, they just really hate negotiating.

We acknowledge those reasons and would like to counter with this: suck it up, and do it anyway! Your offer will not be rescinded, your future manager won't hate you for it, no one needs to give you "permission" to negotiate, and any discomfort is easily worth it for the increased pay. If you're still unsure about it, just picture yourself being paid $10,000—and likely *much* more—to put up with a few awkward conversations.

Plus, it's good training for the future, and the importance of negotiating will only increase over time.

YOU SHOULD ALWAYS NEGOTIATE. GET USED TO IT EARLY IN YOUR CAREER, WHILE THE STAKES ARE LOW.

If you're early in your career, you might say that negotiation isn't worth the hassle—after all, junior roles have pretty narrow salary bands. There are a few reasons this view is short-sighted and wrong.

First, though it's pretty unlikely in the grand scheme of things if you're applying to a startup, there might come a magical day when your equity is worth something. This is especially true if you're an early employee— with a good exit, an extra 0.1% in equity could translate into hundreds of thousands of dollars.

But, let's get real, your equity is likely worthless. So let me give you a better, more immediate reason to learn to haggle early in your career. Humans are frighteningly adaptable creatures. Scared of public speaking? Give three talks. The first one will be gut-wrenchingly horrific, the stuff of nightmares. Your voice will crack, you'll mumble, and the whole time, you'll want to vomit. The next one will be nerve-wracking. The last one will mostly be okay. And after that, you'll be just fine. The same thing applies to approach anxiety, mathematical proofs, dancing, sex, and, you guessed it, salary negotiation!

So, make all the awkward, teeth-cringing mistakes now, while the stakes are low and it doesn't matter, and when failure will cost you only $5K or $10K a year.[1] Because the further along you get in your career, the bigger the impact will be. Not only will the salary bands be wider for senior roles, but as you get more senior, more of your compensation (we'll refer to it as "comp" from now) comes from equity—effectively negotiating equity can make a six figure difference (or more). Learn these skills early in your career, where the stakes are low and where screwing it up won't bite you. Moreover, there's no real downside to negotiating. We've helped

---

1 Sometimes it's more, because new grad signing bonuses at some FAANGs can get high, but that's the exception, not the rule.

hundreds of candidates negotiate their salaries at interviewing.io, and there are only two scenarios where an offer might get pulled for negotiating. Note that both of these scenarios are serious outliers.

1. You're applying for an intern or new grad role at a very small startup. In this situation, it's very possible that the startup literally just has one headcount, and in that scenario, they may just go with the candidate who accepts their offer first. To avoid this scenario, ask how many open headcount the position has. If it's small and if you're junior, then skipping the negotiation portion makes sense.

2. You're a giant jerk during negotiations or you blatantly waste the company's time. When we say "giant jerk," we mean being straight-up rude to your recruiter. We do not mean advocating for yourself or asking for more money. And when we talk about wasting the company's time, we mean drawing out the negotiation process for months, asking to talk to more than five people on the team, and still not being able to make up your mind.

If you don't find yourself in either of these situations, your offer will not be rescinded.[2]

Since we can stop worrying about your offer getting rescinded, we can talk about the real reason you want to negotiate: to get more money for not that much more effort. Companies rarely give their best possible offer right away, so by not negotiating, you are likely leaving money on the table. Here is a graph that shows the median increase in compensation for interviewing.io's negotiation clients. Even in the worst markets, candidates were getting $40k more in cash—and in better months it cleared $150k.

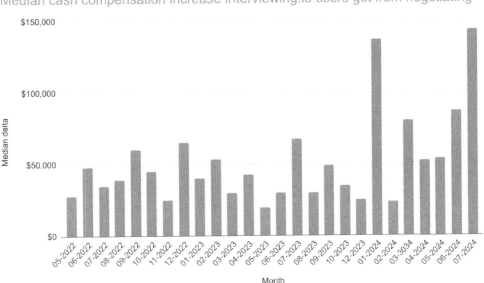

Median cash compensation increase interviewing.io users got from negotiating

How long did it take? On average, 19 calendar days. Notably, there's no correlation between how long a negotiation takes and its outcome.

Even if you're not an expert negotiator, with just a little bit of effort, you should be able to increase your compensation by at least $10k. That's pretty nice pay for a few uncomfortable conversations.

---

2   Harvard Business Review has the data. Candidates seriously overestimate the likelihood of their offers being rescinded: https://hbr.org/2024/05/research-negotiating-is-unlikely-to-jeopardize-your-job-offer

NEGOTIATION IS MOSTLY PREPARATION AND LEVERAGE.

Probably because of bad books and airplane magazine ads (for those of you old enough to remember those), people often think that negotiation is all about saying the right thing, or how firm your handshake is, or any other amount of silly nonsense. The reality is that negotiation is all about preparation and leverage.

Preparation and leverage means:

- Doing the work to make sure that you have multiple offers
- Ensuring all your offers come in at the same time
- Not tipping your hand too early
- Not sharing anything with recruiters until you're ready to negotiate
- Not negotiating before you're ready

Laying this foundation is 80% of the work. It's the unglamorous effort of slowing some companies down, speeding some companies up, and holding off questions from recruiters until you're ready to negotiate—and not before. If you do this right, the actual negotiation part will be easy and almost a foregone conclusion.

## CHAPTER 12

PRE-OFFER NEGOTIATION MISTAKES

Having coached hundreds of engineers through salary negotiation over the years, we've seen the same two mistakes over and over. These mistakes are costly, and they make it harder for us to help. Both mistakes involve how you talk to recruiters at the start of your job search, way before there's an offer:

1. Revealing information too early in the game
2. Negotiating before you're ready

MISTAKE #1: REVEALING INFORMATION BEFORE YOU'RE READY TO NEGOTIATE

You've probably never been arrested, but if you're like me, you've watched a lot of police procedurals on TV. You know the bit where they read the suspect their Miranda rights? They start like this:

> You have the right to remain silent. Anything you say can and will be used against you in a court of law…

Talking to recruiters is exactly the same, and one of the biggest mistakes we see our users make is sharing information too early. And unfortunately, this is a mistake you can't walk back. Specifically, do not share with recruiters any information about:

- Your salary history[1]
- Your comp expectations
- Where else you're interviewing
- How far along in the process you are with other companies

In short, don't share *any* information about money or other interviews.

When you're ready to negotiate, you're doing so deliberately because you already know the state of the world, and you're choosing to reveal the parts that set you up for success. Before that, you're just revealing stuff that can be used against you.

The main question recruiters ask up front is: "What are your compensation expectations?" They claim that it's because they want to make sure that you're not so far off that you're wasting each other's time. This is a nonsense reason—very few companies pay so much below market that it would be a non-starter. Those companies know who they are, and they know to give you a heads up that they pay below market. Moreover,

---

1 Though it's illegal in many U.S. states to ask about salary history directly, there are indirect ways of asking, and many still do.

with the recent advent of companies sharing salary bands, you'll have some idea if they're grossly below market before you interview. The real reason recruiters ask about compensation expectations is so that they can use it against you later in negotiations. (See "Exactly what to say to recruiters at the beginning of the process" on page 116 for how to handle this question.)

Naming a number puts a ceiling on your offer. Do not utter a single number to a recruiter until you're ready to negotiate. Do NOT go on levels.fyi, pick something within the range listed there, and say that's what you're looking for, even if you're currently underpaid and an average offer from them would be life-changing. Do not say a number first—ever.

Revealing other interviews also risks losing leverage. Smaller companies might back off, fearing they can't compete with FAANG. Or, companies may lowball you if they sense limited options. Worse, they could issue an exploding offer to force a premature decision.

Let's see some examples.

EXAMPLE #1: YOU'RE INTERVIEWING AT GOOGLE, META, AND TWO STARTUPS

Let's say that you're currently interviewing at Google, Meta, and two startups (let's call them A and B). You're at the onsite stage with Google, you're doing technical phone screens at both startups, and you're just doing your first recruiter call with Meta. This is actually a very strong position to be in! Of course, your Meta recruiter asks you about your comp expectations and where else you're interviewing.

If you reveal your comp expectations, it will be hard to walk them back.

Let's say that you currently work at a startup and make $150k in cash with some amount of equity. You go to levels.fyi or a similar site and look up Meta's salary bands for the role you're targeting. Let's say those bands for total comp are $250k-$350k. Hell, that's way more cash than you're making now, so you decide to share that range, thinking that if those are their bands already, it does no harm. That's reasonable, except that let's say Google ends up making you an offer, and it's $400k (we've seen this scenario happen to a bunch of our users). Now you have to walk back what you said, in which case your recruiter will invariably ask why. And now you have to reveal, before you're ready, that you have a Google offer, which means you'll probably end up revealing that it's for $400k. Now you've set an artificial ceiling for your Meta counteroffer at around $400k as well, when in reality that ceiling may have been closer to $450k or even $500k.

If you reveal that you're at the onsite stage with Google and talking to some startups, here's what will happen:

- Your recruiter will do the math and start asking you in a few weeks if you got to team matching.
- Now Meta knows that Google is the only possible offer on the table that they should be worried about. They (and other big companies) don't take startup offers nearly as seriously because equity is monopoly money until it's not… and even if you don't reveal the cash portion of your comp, they'll assume it's smaller than what they're offering.
- If you didn't pass the onsite, it's going to be hard to not share that when you're persistently asked about it, unless you lie (which we absolutely do not condone). Now you've lost leverage because Meta knows that you cannot possibly have any other big tech company offers.
- If you *do* perform well in your Google onsite, that's great, but team matching can take a while. So now if Meta is about to make you an offer, they can set an artificially fast expiration date to run out the clock.

Though you started in a strong position with multiple interviews, including at companies that are known to pay well, you've now weakened that position by sharing details.

Here's another thing that could happen in this scenario. Let's say that it's the same set of companies, but this time you're talking to the recruiter from startup A. The recruiter asks you where else you're interviewing. If you mention that you're interviewing at both Google and Meta, they might get spooked. Dropping FAANG names can be a good power move, or it can shoot you in the foot, and which it'll be depends on the situation. Many small startups view FAANG candidates as risky because they know they can't compete on comp and are worried that you're going to walk the moment that you get a FAANG offer. This may or may not be true (not everyone is motivated just by comp!), but it's not to your advantage to reveal it. *You* should be in control of if and when we play the FAANG card. We talk at length about how to play these cards to control the timing of your job search in Chapter 9: Managing Your Job Search (pg 78).

EXAMPLE #2: YOU'RE INTERVIEWING AT A STARTUP AND ARE ALSO UP FOR A PROMOTION

Here's a different example. Let's say that you work at a startup, and you're up for a promotion soon. You figured it'd make sense to see what's out there as well, so you've started interviewing with another startup.

Your recruiter asks you in your first call about where else you're interviewing and what your comp expectations are. You may be tempted to mention that you're up for a promotion because that feels like it'll give you leverage—if you get a promotion, the startup will have to work harder to entice you to leave, after all. Not so fast!

If you mention that you're up for a promotion, your recruiter will start checking in consistently on whether you got it. Promotions always take longer than you think, and the increase in your comp may not be what you expect. At some point, if you haven't gotten it yet, the recruiter will assume it's not coming, and then you actually lose leverage because they know that you're going to be more likely to walk.

If you mention that you're not interviewing anywhere else, that's just a giveaway that you have no leverage. Promotion or not, many of our users assume that they have leverage because "I don't have to leave my job, so my current job is leverage." That's not true, though—in both good and bad hiring climates, an engineer having another job is table stakes. Almost every candidate you're competing with will be currently employed. So even if having a job gives you a little bit of leverage, it gets canceled out when everyone has the same exact thing.

The details may differ in your case, but the fundamental mechanics are the same. When you reveal information before you know what hand you've been dealt, it can only hurt you.

The one exception to revealing information is this: Sometimes, it can be useful to give your recruiter a rough estimate for when you'll be collecting offers, if you expect that time will be pretty far in the future. For example:

> I've just started interviewing. I expect to get through all my interviews and onsites in the next 6 weeks and start collecting offers roughly 2 months from now. Does that timeline work for you?

> You can estimate roughly how long your job search process will take by using the spreadsheet at bctci.co/job-search-worksheet-1 (pg 79).

This technique can be helpful for aligning expectations up front and then keeping recruiters off your back, as they won't need to chronically text you to make sure you haven't taken another offer yet (we'll talk more about texting with recruiters in the next section). But note that even in this example, we're not actually revealing any information about where you're interviewing, how long it's taking, or compensation. You're just setting a timeline based on hypotheticals without giving out any details that can be used against you later. When you share the actual timeline you're working with, you no longer control the timing of your job search, and a huge part of negotiation is controlling timing so you can make all your offers come in at the same time.

MISTAKE #2: NEGOTIATING BEFORE YOU'RE READY

> Don't fire until you see the whites of their eyes!
>
> Unknown officer at the Battle of Bunker Hill

Just as you don't want to reveal information too early, you also don't want to negotiate too early. They're two sides of the same coin.

Think of it like a hand of cards. At the beginning, you have no idea what you're going to draw. The longer you wait to negotiate, assuming you've timed things correctly, the more information you have. Then, when you're ready to negotiate, you can look at your hand and selectively share information that puts you in the strongest position. For instance, if you have a high base salary from one company, a great equity package from a public company, and a signing bonus from a third company, you can strategically share those portions of the offers without sharing the weaker parts. Each negotiation is different, and it's hard to give catch-all advice, but that's generally the situation you should set yourself up to be in.

With that in mind, we are firm believers in negotiating when you're ready and not before. Until you know what else is on the table, it's really hard to:

1. Have the bravado that comes with actually having multiple offers (this is possible to fake, but it's hard) *and*

2. Negotiate effectively—you will never know as well as your recruiter what salary bands are like, what market comp is, and so on.

There are two ways to combat this power imbalance: have as many of your interactions be asynchronous as possible (we'll talk more about that in the next section), and do everything you can to negotiate when you're at the point of maximum information, and not before. Daniel Biales, an engineer with multiple offers, explained the latter really well.[2]

> When I received a low offer, my first inclination was to start the negotiating process. [This would not have been] the best course of action. The problem with this approach is that I wanted to start negotiating before receiving my highest offer. If I negotiated an increase then, I would have had to renegotiate when I received the higher offer. This will cause negotiating fatigue for you and the company. They will be less likely to negotiate a second time because they don't know how many times you will ask them for more. First, focus on strategies to draw out your decision. Then, when you have all your offers, start negotiating. There may be a couple of back-and-forth communications, but they will be over a short time span rather than drawn out.

Ideally, you wait until all your offers come in, and then you negotiate once, at the end. As with any complicated human process, there are some exceptions, but by and large, it's best to ask any given company to raise their offer just once. Going back and forth is not only exhausting, it's also ineffective.

EXAMPLE #1 REVISITED: YOU'RE INTERVIEWING AT GOOGLE, META, AND TWO STARTUPS

Let's review our first example again. Imagine that you're interviewing at Google, Meta, and two startups, A and B, just like before. Startup A makes you an offer: $160k base, 0.1% of the company in options over four years, and no signing bonus. You react to it and say that you were hoping for a signing bonus. The recruiter quickly comes back with a $10k signing bonus and pressures you to make a decision, saying that they have other candidates waiting.

---

2 https://levelup.gitconnected.com/learn-how-to-negotiate-your-salary-with-expert-help-5afedd11a178

By starting to negotiate, you accelerated their timeline, and this is going to make it hard to go back and ask for more signing bonus.

You try to stall, and then a few days later, Google makes you an offer that includes a $25k signing bonus. You're still excited about the startup for reasons other than compensation, but now you have to go back to them and say that you actually got a $25k signing bonus at Google. They are unlikely to move again.

So, don't negotiate until you're ready. It's hard to walk things back. That doesn't mean it's not possible to negotiate in stages and gradually start bringing up all your offers. However, this is a much more difficult maneuver, takes way more experience, is much more stressful for the candidate, and often ends up with the same results as laying a solid foundation and just negotiating once at the end.

So what do you say when you get asked pointed questions by your recruiter about your comp expectations or where you're interviewing? And how do you delay negotiation until you're ready?

ENTER "PASSIVE INFORMATION GATHERING" MODE—INSTEAD OF TALKING, LISTEN

Until you're ready to negotiate, your default mode should be "passive information gathering." This means that you listen rather than talk. We coach all of our negotiation clients to be in this mode when they get on a call with a recruiter.

Note that all of these points hold for the whole process, not just the beginning—you should be polite and gracious both on the first call and the last. But for now, we'll focus on the beginning of the process and provide separate advice for the end (when you're receiving offers) later on.

- **Be polite and gracious to a fault.** Thank your recruiter for their time and for their help so far, whether it's scheduling interviews or answering your questions.
- **Express genuine enthusiasm**. Express excitement about the company or the interview process if there's something idiosyncratically cool about it. And be genuine. Every process and company will have something exciting about it.
- **Use email (not phone when possible and *definitely* not texts) to interact with recruiters.** Leave your phone number off your resume, and if required for a form, use a Google Voice number. During your first conversation, tell the recruiter you prefer email because you have your phone on "do not disturb" during work hours and don't want to miss anything important from them. If they call or text, respond after a few hours via email and remind them that email is best. Why does this matter? Phone calls and texts are disruptive, and they pressure you into quick, often poor responses. Texting, in particular, can lull you into a false sense of security. Negotiations require time to think and seek advice, so "train" recruiters early to use email. By offer time, they'll be less likely to catch you off guard with calls.
- **Don't feel pressure to answer questions directly.** Being in "passive information gathering" mode does not mean you can't ask questions. We give you a list of things to ask your recruiter on page 72. What we mean by passive here is that you don't need to react to what recruiters tell you, and you don't need to answer *their* questions.

WHY YOU SHOULD GET COMFORTABLE WITH NOT ANSWERING RECRUITER QUESTIONS

When I was in high school, I was on the debate team. If you're a nerd like me, maybe you were too. In formal debates, there's a specific, structured way you have to present your arguments. The first side goes, and while they're making their argument, you write down each of their points. When it's your turn to rebut, you reiterate their points and offer a counter-argument for each one.

Many engineers are, not surprisingly, hyper-rational linear thinkers whose instincts are to treat their interactions with recruiters the same way they'd treat a debate tournament. A recruiter poses a series of questions in an email, you break up each question into its own line, and you write a response. That's what makes you a good engineer… and a terrible negotiator.

Here's a real recruiter email one candidate got.

> Hey _____,
>
> It was a pleasure speaking with you today. Can you please let me know where you are with your other opportunities and any onsites you have coming up in particular? Also, I'm working on scheduling your technical phone screen and will get back to you with details.

The candidate's first instinct was to do exactly what we described above: answer each question methodically. The truth is that you don't have to answer anything your recruiter asks you! Of course, you should never be rude or flippant, but you can safely ignore most of the questions that come your way. For instance, to the email above, you can say something like:

> It was a pleasure speaking with you as well. I'm looking forward to next steps. I promise to keep you posted on any updates and will not accept any offers without discussing them with you first.

We completely dodged providing details but were able to address the recruiter's worry that they're going to lose out on you. If you can address that worry, you don't have to say anything else! With that in mind, in the next section, we'll tell you exactly what to say in a variety of situations.

Before we dive into specifics, let's address awkwardness. Stonewalling recruiters or refusing to share information can feel uncomfortable, especially since recruiters are skilled at building rapport (though, as discussed in Chapter 3: What Recruiters Won't Tell You (pg 29), they're not your friends). When someone seems friendly, it's harder to say no.

Here's a simple mindset shift: stop thinking about awkwardness as bad. It's perfectly okay for conversations to feel awkward. As long as you're kind and enthusiastic, you won't put off your recruiter. So embrace the awkwardness; it's much better than revealing information that could hurt your position.

We promise you that over time, these techniques will feel second nature to you. It just takes a bit of practice!

EXACTLY WHAT TO SAY TO RECRUITERS AT THE BEGINNING OF THE PROCESS

In all these snippets, you'll notice that they end with the same sentence: *I promise not to accept other offers until I have a chance to discuss them with you.* This is a great way to address recruiter concerns about losing you to a different company without directly answering their questions or providing them with details that they can use against you later. If you can speak to that worry head-on, there's not much they can say back.

    Copy/paste these snippets from bctci.co/negotiation-mistakes-what-to-say-1.

For questions about comp expectations

> At this point, I don't feel equipped to throw out a number because I'd like to find out more about the opportunity first—right now, I simply don't have the data to be able to say something concrete. If you end up making me an offer, I would be more than happy to iterate on it if needed and figure out something that works. I promise not to accept other offers until I have a chance to discuss them with you.

For when a recruiter provides you a salary range and asks you to comment on it

Thank you for sharing that with me. Right now I don't know enough about the opportunity to value it concretely, and I honestly haven't done my market research. If you end up making me an offer, I would be more than happy to iterate on it if needed and figure out something that works. I promise not to accept other offers until I have a chance to discuss them with you.

In both of these cases, the goal is to avoid locking yourself into a number too early while keeping the conversation open. By emphasizing your willingness to discuss an offer later, you maintain flexibility without shutting down the discussion.

Copy/paste these snippets from bctci.co/negotiation-mistakes-what-to-say-2.

For questions about where else you're interviewing

I'm currently speaking with a few other companies. I'll let you know if I get to the point where I have an exploding offer, and I promise not to accept other offers until I have a chance to discuss them with you.

It's best to keep your answer vague while reassuring them that they won't be blindsided by another offer.

FIELDING QUESTIONS ABOUT YOUR TIMELINE

Recruiters will often ask you how far along you are with other companies, at the same time that they ask you where you're interviewing. Up until now, we've advised being as vague as possible. However, when it comes to the timeline, sometimes it can serve you to be specific. And other times being vague is the right call. Here's how to decide which one is right for you.

1. Ask your recruiter during this call how long the process takes on average (pg 72). This is good information for you to have because it'll inform how you field the timeline question.

2. Use our spreadsheet at bctci.co/job-search-worksheet-1 to estimate how long the process will take at each of the companies you're interviewing with (pg 79 for more information)

Once you know both numbers, rough though they may be, you can apply the following rule:

\# If the company you're talking to is among the slowest, don't reveal your timeline. If they are faster than a few of the companies you're talking to, you should reveal your timeline.

Here's why:

- **Fast-moving companies:** It's a good idea to manage your recruiter's expectations upfront that it may take you a bit longer to get to a decision. By doing this, you're playing defense—later in the process, if they start to apply time pressure, they'll have no leg to stand on.
- **Slower companies:** Revealing your timeline doesn't serve you because there is nothing the recruiter can do to speed up the process… except try to apply high-pressure tactics to make you walk from the other companies.

Now here's exactly what to say in both scenarios.

Copy/paste these snippets from bctci.co/negotiation-mistakes-what-to-say-3.

For questions about timeline, in cases where you want to share it (i.e., when the company you're talking to is faster than some of the others)

> I'm actively interviewing right now, and I expect to wrap up interviews in the next {n} weeks and then make a decision {m} weeks from now. How does that sound?

For questions about timeline, in cases where you don't (i.e., when the company you're talking to is among the slowest)

> I'm at various stages with a number of different companies, but based on what you told me, it sounds like there won't be any timing challenges. I promise to keep you posted if anything comes up.

These snippets should get you through the beginning of the process and keep you from divulging information or entering a negotiation before you're ready. Now, let's switch gears and talk about the other thing you need to do to negotiate successfully: get multiple offers that come in at the same time.

MULTIPLE OFFERS: THE BEST WAY TO GET MORE MONEY

The best way to get more money is to have other offers. We know, we know—interviewing sucks and is a giant gauntlet-slog, but in many cases, having just one other offer (so, I don't know, spending a few extra days of your time spread over a few weeks) can get you at least $10K more, even without being a great negotiator. It's a pretty rational, clear-cut argument for biting the slog-bullet and doing a few more interviews.

> Why do offers matter so much? From an employer's perspective, for every offer you have, your odds of accepting their offer drop significantly.

One anecdote I'll share on the subject goes like this. A few years ago, a close friend of mine who's notoriously bad at negotiation and hates it with a passion was interviewing at one of the FAANGs. I was trying to talk him into getting out there just a little bit, and for the love of god, to talk to at least one more company. I ended up introducing him to a mid-sized startup where he quickly got an onsite interview. Just mentioning that he had an onsite to his FAANG recruiter increased his signing bonus by $5K.

Offers are better than onsites, of course, but in a pinch, even onsites may be enough… because every onsite increases your odds of not accepting the offer from the company you're negotiating with. Offers really are better though. Here's a particularly poignant story about why.

> Many years ago, an engineer friend of mine, whom we'll call Alex, applied to work at a sexy ed-tech non-profit. His brother, whom we'll call Sam, was also an engineer, and he decided to apply as well. Both did well in their interviews and both got offers. Here's where things got interesting.
>
> Both brothers tried to negotiate. Alex simply asked for more money. He had no other offers, and he didn't try to pretend he did. He just looked the CEO in the eye and said he thought he deserved more money. Sam also asked for more money, but he mentioned he had an offer from a top-tier startup that was significantly higher than what the non-profit offered. The company reacted very differently to these requests.
>
> The CEO looked right back at Alex, and without batting an eye, told him that any money he'd be getting would be routed out of the hands of students and teachers. The same CEO responded to Sam by increasing his base salary by $30k, a bold move on his part, given that he must surely have known that the two brothers would talk.

Now, this is a particularly blatant example, but, while I find this CEO's behavior reprehensible (especially setting up the false dichotomy that either you get the money or the kids do—that's not how budgets work), the reality is that, behind the scenes, this is how decision-makers think. Leverage is the most significant bit in these conversations, and it's louder than emotional appeals and even market research.

If you've ever gotten negotiation advice in the past, chances are you've been advised to research what market compensation looks like so that you can rationally and cogently present those figures to your future employer when you negotiate. Let me tell you a secret. I don't really know what market compensation looks like for many of the jobs and titles I help candidates negotiate.

So how many interviews do you need to do to ensure that you get multiple competitive offers? As with many things in this book, it's a function of the hiring climate. In a boom market, the rule of thumb you should use is that you'll get an offer for every four companies where you do a technical phone screen.[3] In a rougher market, you may get an offer for every six companies where you do a technical phone screen. Of course, preparation is the biggest lever you can pull here, and the math can get much more favorable. But at a first pass, use these rules of thumb.

HAVING A JOB ISN'T LEVERAGE

We touched on this already, but we'd like to reiterate it because it's such a common misconception. Many candidates, after hearing how important it is to have multiple offers, will come back with, "But I have a great job. Can't I just use that as leverage and say that if my offer isn't good enough, I just won't leave?"

Sadly, this approach rarely works... simply because, regardless of whether the job market is hot or cold, most engineers who are actively interviewing are still employed. When almost everyone else has something, it's no longer considered leverage.

Moreover, recruiters know that if you were committed to your current employer, you wouldn't be looking around. After all, interviewing is quite unpleasant (that's why this book exists!), and most people only do it if they're seriously considering leaving their job.

That said, there *are* a few exceptions. Sometimes, if you're walking away from a guaranteed bonus (e.g., for quant traders, a significant portion of their compensation comes from an annual bonus), you might be able to squeeze out a (larger) signing bonus. However, in these cases, it's still more likely that your new company will accommodate it by pushing out your start date until you get the guaranteed bonus.

The other exception is a scenario where you're walking away from a guaranteed promotion, an impending stock vest, or a refresher stock grant. In those scenarios, you may be able to leverage a signing bonus or an equity increase. However, the limited negotiating power you'd get from these exceptions will not match the increase in overall compensation you'd get from having multiple offers in hand.

HOW TO MAKE SURE YOUR OFFERS COME IN AT THE SAME TIME

Hopefully, by now, you believe us that having multiple offers matters. Read Chapter 9: Managing Your Job Search (pg 78), if you haven't already, and then come back here—it explains everything from how to order the companies you interview with, based on how long they take. Armed with all of those techniques, you'll be in good shape to air traffic control your job search and make sure that your offers all come in at roughly the same time. Once you've done that hard work, the negotiation piece will feel like an afterthought.

We'll talk about how to actually negotiate in a moment, but first, let's talk about what to do when you get an offer.

---

3   As you know from the Chapter 7: Getting in the Door (pg 53), the math is much harsher for job applications, and there's much more variance there as well, depending on how you actually get in the door. Here, to keep it simple, we'll start the funnel at the interview stage.

## CHAPTER 13

GETTING THE OFFER: EXACTLY WHAT TO SAY

Up until the negotiation stage, you should single-mindedly be air traffic controlling the process to maximize the number of offers you have in hand. Your goal is to create options and leverage, not decide where you want to work yet. Be calculating, and prioritize optionality over excitement about specific companies. Once you have multiple offers, you can decide where to go.

With that in mind, let's go through exactly what to say to create maximum optionality.

Your recruiter will likely want to extend the offer over the phone. Some recruiters will send you numbers over email, but almost all prefer to do it live so they 1) can gauge your reaction and 2) make it more likely that you'll accept on the spot.

The most important thing to remember about getting offers is that, even though your recruiter wants you to respond to it immediately, you should not. Even though your recruiter may act like it's normal to accept an offer right away (most recruiters get evaluated primarily on how many offers they turn into hires, so, of course, they want to do everything to get you to say yes), know that it's not normal or expected.

Why do you want to buy time? First of all, this really is an important decision. Even if it's your only offer, you probably still want to sleep on it. Secondly, if you're planning to negotiate, you need time to formulate a plan, and you definitely don't want to negotiate over the phone, on the spot. Email, as we've said, is the best way to level the playing field, between you, who's done this a few times, and a recruiter, who does this a few times a day.

As always, stay in passive information-gathering mode. Learn about the offer details without reacting. Be gracious, express enthusiasm, and buy yourself time to make an informed decision.

EXACTLY WHAT TO SAY WHEN YOU GET AN OFFER

To wit, here's exactly what to say in a few situations you're likely to encounter on an offer call. Responding like this will buy you time without committing you to anything.

Copy/paste these snippets from bctci.co/getting-the-offer-what-to-say-1.

When a recruiter makes you an offer without a hard deadline

Thank you so much, and thank you for all your help with this process so far! This is really exciting! I'll need some time to process and talk to my {family, partner, spouse}. I will get back to you as soon as I can, and I may have some questions as well.

HOW TO DEAL WITH EXPLODING OFFERS

Exploding offers are a high-pressure tactic aimed at preventing you from exploring elsewhere by imposing tight deadlines. The idea is that if you have less time, you're less likely to speak with other companies.

Imposing *some* kind of deadline makes sense when you're hiring for a position with a specific timeline and/or limited headcount, but even then, exploding offers are hard to justify, especially in a market where companies are perpetually hiring. In that scenario, they're entirely an artificial construct, and trust me, they're arbitrary. Having been a recruiter, I know just how arbitrary they are, having set them myself in the past.[1] Joel Spolsky, creator of Trello and Stack Overflow, said it well:[2]

> Here's what you're thinking. You're thinking, well, that's a good company, not my first choice, but still a good offer, and I'd hate to lose this opportunity. And you don't know for sure if your number one choice would even hire you. So you accept the offer at your second-choice company and never go to any other interviews. And now, you lost out. You're going to spend several years of your life in some cold dark cubicle with a crazy boss who couldn't program a twenty out of an ATM, while some recruiter somewhere gets a $1000 bonus because she was better at negotiating than you were.

Even for internships, deadlines don't need to be as aggressive as they often are, and many college career centers now oppose this practice. Here's how to respond if you are given an exploding offer.

📋   Copy/paste these snippets from bctci.co/getting-the-offer-what-to-say-2.

When you get an exploding offer

> Thank you so much, and thank you for all your help with this process so far! This is really exciting! I would very much appreciate having a bit more time. I'll need a bit of time to process and to talk to my {family, partner, spouse}. Know that I'm very excited about Company X. At the same time, choosing where I work is extremely important to me. Of course, I will not drag things out, and I will continue to keep you in the loop, but I hope you can understand my desire to make as informed of a decision as possible. How about I make a decision by…?

EXACTLY WHAT TO SAY WHEN YOU GET MORE QUESTIONS OR A SALARY RANGE INSTEAD OF AN OFFER

Sometimes, you'll get on what you think is an offer call, only to find that your recruiter isn't ready to share numbers quite yet. Instead, they may use the opportunity to get you on the phone as a way to ask you again about comp expectations or where else you're interviewing. They may also, in lieu of committing to an offer, try to first gauge your reaction to a hypothetical compensation range.

Here's what to say if either of these comes up. At the end of the day, our goal is to get a concrete offer because then, and only then, can we start negotiating.

---

1 I'm embarrassed to admit it. I remember a time when an eng leader and I were in a conference room, trying to figure out exactly what day we should make an offer explode to maximize the chances that a candidate wouldn't have time to finish up another process.

2 https://www.joelonsoftware.com/2008/11/26/exploding-offer-season/

Copy/paste these snippets from bctci.co/getting-the-offer-what-to-say-3.

For questions about comp expectations at the end of the process

It sounds like there's an offer coming, and I'm really excited about it. I'm not sure exactly what number I'm looking for, but if you'd be able to share what an offer package might look like, then I will gladly iterate on it with you if needed and figure out something that works. I promise not to accept other offers until I have a chance to discuss them with you.

For when a recruiter provides you a salary range and asks you to comment on it at the end of the process

Thank you for sharing that with me. I haven't done enough research to say definitively what I'm expecting. If you end up making me a concrete offer, I would be more than happy to iterate on it if needed and figure out something that works. I promise not to accept other offers until I have a chance to discuss them with you.

Copy/paste these snippets from bctci.co/getting-the-offer-what-to-say-4.

For questions about where else you're interviewing at the end of the process

I'm wrapping things up with a few companies and in process with a few more. I promise to keep you in the loop, and I promise not to accept other offers until I have a chance to discuss them with you.

If you follow these tips, you'll end up with concrete offer numbers without having to immediately react.

At some point, your recruiter might ask you, "What will it take to get you to accept?" Many candidates take this to mean, "Name your price!" But, unfortunately, that's not what it means. Some candidates make the mistake of naming an ambitious number, and then when the recruiter balks, they panic, backpedal and accept less than they would have otherwise. Instead of seeing this question as a blank check, treat it like you would if your recruiter asked you about comp expectations.

Now, you can take the time to ask any questions over email. You will likely want to ask questions about equity. See "Equity" on page 99 for a comprehensive explanation of different equity types and a long list of questions to ask, as well as a calculator, to help you value your equity.

You can also take some time to come up with your plan of attack and speed up some of the companies you're talking to that haven't made you an offer yet (see "Speeding up" on page 88).

Now that you've set yourself up for success, we'll talk about how to negotiate. If you don't have multiple offers, don't worry, we'll talk about what to do in that situation, too.

## CHAPTER 14

HOW TO NEGOTIATE

It's impossible to cover every possible scenario in a single chapter (or even in a book), and getting great at negotiation, just like technical interviewing, takes a bunch of practice. That said, we hope that reading through this section will give you a grasp of the theory and that, in many cases, you'll be able to use our suggestions for what to say verbatim.[1]

HOW TO NEGOTIATE IF YOU DON'T HAVE MULTIPLE OFFERS

If we're realists, we can safely assume that some of you will not have been able to line everything up perfectly and may just have one offer in hand. Let's talk about what you can do to negotiate, because all may not be lost (but it is a lot harder to get results). Then we'll spend the rest of this section focused on how to negotiate with multiple offers.

If you're in this unenviable position, there are still some things you can do. How likely they are to succeed depends on how strong the hiring market is right now. In a booming market, you can be successful at negotiating with just one offer. In a less ideal market, it's not likely.

Which tactics you should use depends on whether you're actively interviewing at other companies, even if you don't have offers. That said, we'll repeat this one more time: please avoid this situation. Plan ahead so you end up with multiple offers. It's a non-trivial investment of time and effort, but we'd argue that a few months of work is worth an extra $40k - $150k per year.[2]

IF YOU'RE ACTIVELY INTERVIEWING, PLAY COMPANIES OFF EACH OTHER

We mentioned before that having looming onsites may be enough to negotiate a small increase in your compensation. This technique is especially effective if you're interviewing at a competitor of your target company, or at a company that your target hates losing candidates to.

A classic example is playing one FAANG against another. Let's say that you just got an offer from Amazon and are either about to do an onsite at Google or have recently wrapped one up. If you're sure that you want to work at Amazon, here's what you can do (this is a variant of the Reverse Used Car Salesman technique that we'll discuss in more detail in the next section).

---

1   If you happen to be interviewing at Meta when you read this, take a look at this blog post about how to negotiate with them specifically. They are more aggressive than most companies, but fortunately, they run their negotiations in a predictable way: bctci.co/negotiate-with-meta

2   These are the median increases interviewing.io users have seen when negotiating (large range because the increase is largely a function of how hot the hiring market is).

Reach out to your Amazon recruiter *over email* (always over email—it levels the playing field!), and say something like this:

> Hey [name],
>
> Transparently, right now I'm wrapping up onsites at Google and Meta. However, from what I've seen so far, I'm most excited about Amazon and about the [insert team name here] team. [Insert a few authentic reasons why you're excited about both Amazon and the team.]
>
> As such, after having given it some serious thought, I'd be ready to stop interviewing everywhere else and sign immediately if we can do the following:
>
> - Increase the base salary to X
> - Increase the equity to Y
> - Increase the signing bonus to Z/Add a meaningful signing bonus
>
> Thank you so much, and I look forward to hopefully working together soon!

You'll notice two things about this approach.

1. **You're *wrapping up onsites*, not already wrapped them up.** It's important to create the feeling that you're *not* about to find out the results. Think about it—if you were expecting offers soon, you'd likely stall to gain leverage and you wouldn't be pulling this move. Instead, paint a picture that you're still in the interview process, unsure of the outcomes, and simply eager to complete your job search and get on with your life. If they suspect you know the results, they might assume you're stalling because you didn't perform well.

2. **You asked for three things**. That may seem like a lot when you have no leverage, but it's intentional. We'll talk more about why we're asking for all three in the *Reverse Used Car Salesman* section (pg 126). We'll also talk in that section about why the "I'll sign today if you do this" approach is particularly effective. Note that we're not saying we'll walk if they don't do it. We're just saying we'll sign right now if they do indeed give us everything we want. As for how much to ask for, weigh your willingness to keep interviewing against the chances of more offers and Amazon's willingness to wait. The strategy's effectiveness depends on the market. In a boom, you might secure a larger signing bonus or small equity bump; in a tougher market, you may only get a minor bonus or nothing. Still, it never hurts to ask.

IF THIS IS YOUR ONLY OFFER, AND YOU HAVE NO OTHER INTERVIEWS, YOU'RE IN A TOUGH SPOT. BUT YOU MIGHT STILL HAVE SOME OPTIONS.

The first thing we'll say is that you should not be in this position. It is very difficult, if not impossible to negotiate a meaningful comp increase without leverage. Getting to this point is the culmination of a series of lapses in planning.

Is it the end of the world? Of course not. If you have a job offer from a company you're excited about, that's great. But, in this section, it's our job to help you negotiate. And from a negotiation perspective, it's not good.

So, what can you do? You have four choices, none of which are great:

1. **You could lie about offers.** We're mentioning this only because you're probably already thinking about it and wondering if you can get away with it. We do *not* recommend this approach and cannot, in good conscience, advise you to do it. There are a few reasons why:

a. You will likely be caught in the lie. For your negotiations to be meaningful, you need offers from companies that are known to pay well. If you haven't interviewed there, you will not be familiar with how their offers look or what their process is like. Your recruiter, however, probably is. We already talked about how recruiters change jobs quite often and tend to accrue lots of brands on their resumes. Chances are, they either know someone who's worked at that company, or it's possible they've worked there themselves.

b. Recruiting is a small industry, and people talk. For the same reason—recruiters have worked at a lot of companies with fairly short tenures—and because they're professional networkers, recruiters tend to know other recruiters. It's not likely they're back-channeling your offers, but we've seen it happen. Though getting blacklisted from companies isn't common, lying about your offers is one of the few reasons it can happen.

c. It's unethical. This is the main reason we oppose lying about your offers. Getting into a situation where you have to lie is completely avoidable in this case, and that makes it even harder to justify.

2. **You could lie about interviews.** This is arguably less egregious than blatantly making up specific offers, but all the points from (1) still apply. What you *can* do is abstain from mentioning other companies and instead be vague in your email. Take the template above and replace the details with: *"I'm wrapping up a few onsites and have several phone screens coming up."*

3. **Bring up your existing compensation.** Mention your current compensation only if it's significantly higher than the offer—it's your best chance of leverage in this case. While having a job isn't good leverage on its own (recruiters know you wouldn't be out interviewing if you planned to stay), pointing out higher pay or unvested stock and upcoming bonuses can help. However, if your current pay is lower, selectively mentioning bonuses can backfire and lead to unwanted questions, even if such questions are illegal in some states.

4. **Try to negotiate without bringing up other companies.** If you take this route, you're taking the moral high ground, but you also have the lowest odds of success. Your best bet here is to ask for a signing bonus. Sometimes it works. We recently had a candidate who interviewed at Meta, and he ended up with no other offers. After his offer was extended, he emailed his recruiter and asked, verbatim: *I'm close to making a decision. Is there any possibility we could attach a signing bonus to my offer? If so, I'd be willing to sign immediately.*

The recruiter came back with a $20k signing bonus. Depending on how the hiring market is, getting signing bonuses may be the exception and not the rule, but asking certainly doesn't hurt.

HOW TO NEGOTIATE IF YOU HAVE MULTIPLE OFFERS

Hopefully, you end up in a strong position, with multiple offers in hand. You've successfully defended against your recruiter's attempts to start negotiating before you were ready, you've stalled some companies and sped up others, and you have not divulged any information about where you're interviewing or your compensation expectations.

You've done the hard work! Now, let's put the cherry on the cake.

Once you have multiple offers, there are a few approaches you can take. The first approach (and, incidentally, my favorite approach) is the aforementioned "Reverse Used Car Salesman." This approach is extremely effective in boom markets and, in that climate, will get you almost all the way there with 20% of the effort.

The other approach is what I call the "Ladder." The Ladder is way more work than the Reverse Used Car Salesman, and in a boom market, the extra work has diminishing returns. However, in a down market, it's the best strategy and can routinely get you 50% more than the Reverse Used Car salesman. You'll see why in a moment. Note that for both of these approaches, you're going to need all your offers in hand.

BOOM MARKETS: THE REVERSE USED CAR SALESMAN

To run this play, ask yourself which company would be your first choice if money were off the table. Once you decide, approach your first choice with the following. See why I call it the Reverse Used Car Salesman?

Copy/paste this snippet from bctci.co/how-to-negotiate-what-to-say-1.

> {I have 5 offers, including ones from Company X and Company Y/I have several strong offers} and am wrapping up the process with {Company M and Company Z/a few more}, but I'm really excited about this opportunity and will drop my other stuff and sign immediately if you can do the following:
>
> - Increase the base to X
> - Increase equity to Y
> - Add a $Z signing bonus
>
> Thank you so much, and I look forward to hearing from you. Hopefully, we'll be working together soon!

There's a lot to unpack here, so let's go through it step by step.

First, after clutching our cards tightly to our chests this entire time, we are finally revealing information about where we're interviewing and where we have offers from. How do we decide if we're going to name specific companies? And if so, why now?

How much to reveal about your other offers

The rules here are the same as in the *Managing Your Job Search* chapter (pg 88). Here's a summary:

- If you're interviewing at a FAANG or FAANG-adjacent company and have offers from other companies in this category, name them. These companies hate losing candidates to their counterparts.
- If you're interviewing at a startup, we recommend NOT naming FAANGs or FAANG-adjacents because they're likely to get spooked for fear of not being able to compete on compensation (or might think you're not a serious candidate).
- If you're interviewing at a direct competitor, name them, depending on company size.

Is this approach too aggressive?

The next thing I'd like to draw your attention to is what you're promising: you're saying that you'll sign immediately if they do what you ask. When some of our users see this wording, they panic because it feels aggressive and because they are used to negotiation being about bluffing that you'll walk. But that's not what we're doing; there's a subtlety here. You're *not* saying that you'll walk if they don't meet your demands. You're just saying that if they meet your demands, you'll sign right now. This way, if they don't (and they very likely won't give you everything you ask for), you can still sign without losing face.[3]

What to ask for in your email: more of everything

In the email template, I propose asking for an increase on three parts of your offer:

- Equity
- Salary
- Signing bonus

---

3   There is one notable edge case. In my entire negotiation career, I've only seen a company rescind an offer once when a candidate was aggressive with this technique, and that was when the candidate was negotiating with a founder. We talk about the differences between negotiating with founders and recruiters on page 133.

Why these three things? They are the ones you can affect, as opposed to say, the performance bonus or the size of your relocation package, which are almost always standard and don't change. And why ask for three things (rather than one or two)? You likely won't get all three, but when you ask for a list of stuff, you're giving the person you're negotiating with some options. In my experience, you'll likely get two of them.

So, what amounts should you ask for? Whatever you ask for, chances are that your recruiter will meet you halfway. We refer to this as the "law of midpoints," and it holds for equity, signing bonuses, and base salaries. We've padded our suggested amounts accordingly.

- **Equity:** As you know from the Offers chapter, it's usually easier to negotiate up equity and bonuses than salary (because those are easier for employers to grant). It's not crazy to ask for a 50-100% increase. If your best competing offer has even more equity than that, and the equity types are comparable (e.g., they're both RSUs), you can ask for 1.5X the equity from your best competing offer.[4]

- **Signing bonus:** For the signing bonus, a lot depends on the size of the company and what your other offers look like. For a seed stage company, regardless of other offers, just ask for a "meaningful signing bonus." If you're talking to a startup that's beyond seed stage, you can safely ask for at least 15% of your base salary as a signing bonus. If you're interviewing at a large company, you can safely ask for at least 25% of your base salary (and a lot more than that if you're talking to a FAANG that's known for giving big signing bonuses, like Meta or Amazon. If you're interviewing at a large company AND have a big signing bonus in one of your competing offers, ask for the greater of the following two values: the amount you just came up with and 1.2X the competing signing bonus.

- **Base salary:** How much of a base salary increase to ask for is a bit trickier. It's the hardest for employers to grant, but you also don't want to be too conservative because of the law of midpoints. If you started at a $160k base and you ask for $200k, you will get something in the neighborhood of $180k. If you really want a shot at $200k, it's best to ask for $220k or more.

One thing we encourage you *not* to over-index on is the salary ranges that you see published online, especially if you're talking to large companies (which are the ones that would have published bands, anyway). We've routinely seen companies exceed the top of their bands by $100k or more when a candidate has strong leverage. Think of those bands as polite suggestions. They should not impact how much you ask for; if you find yourself thinking, "I can't ask for a $250k base because the top of the band on levels.fyi is $220k," stop.

You might be surprised that we're not asking you if you value cash or equity more before giving you advice. In our experience, it's good to ask for a lot across all three dimensions, and you'll find that the company will adjust and grant what they're going to grant.

You might worry that asking for specific amounts could backfire. In a boom market with multiple offers, it's safe—and smart—to overshoot others due to the midpoint rule, avoiding a cap on your negotiation potential.

Why is the Reverse Used Car Salesman approach best for boom markets? Provided you list a few offers (like in the email template), recruiters won't ask a lot of questions. If you've listed the right companies, they will assume your offers are very competitive (in a boom market, offers tend to be), and they will scramble to get you the best possible offer.

This approach is basically one big, yet polite, flex. It's very little work on your part, and it's extremely effective when companies are hiring like crazy, have unlimited headcount, and are fighting a full-on war for talent. But, sometimes, you'll be surprised by a no. If the company says no to all or most of these and is a big enough brand to where you don't have much of a leg to stand on? You can still get creative. One of our users told

---

4 Even if they're not comparable, sometimes you can play dumb and compare apples to oranges if it's in your favor. Let's say one company is offering you stock options and claiming that in a few years they'll be worth $2M. Let's say the other company is close to IPO and offering you RSUs. You can still claim that you're getting $2M and wait for your recruiter to call you on it. In many cases they will, but sometimes they will not.

me about a sweet deal he came up with—he said he'd sign today if he got to choose the team he could join and had a specific team in mind...

But what do you do when the market isn't booming? If you use the Reverse Used Car Salesman in a down market, your recruiter will start asking you for offer details from the other companies. And then, assuming you have higher offers, they will match or slightly exceed them. If you don't have higher offers, you will be in the unpleasant position of having to decline to share… which will telegraph a message to your recruiter that you don't have competitive offers, and then they likely won't budge.

In a down market, you'll find recruiters to be fastidious, conservative, and brimming with endless prying questions. It will also take much more work to get results. The good news is that you can still negotiate a significant increase with a technique called the Ladder.

THE LADDER (BEST STRATEGY FOR A DOWN MARKET)

The Ladder has the same prerequisites as the Reversed Used Car Salesman—you get multiple offers, and you air traffic control your job search so they all come in around the same time. You've been in passive information gathering mode, haven't reacted to your offers, and haven't prematurely negotiated. You have all your cards in front of you.

Let's say you have initial offers from Google,[5] Stripe, Bloomberg LP, and a couple of smaller startups. And let's say the offers look like this:

- **Google:** $190k base, $450k equity, no signing bonus
- **Stripe:** $220k base, $200k equity, no signing bonus
- **Bloomberg LP:** $172k base, no equity, $30k signing bonus
- **Startup1:** $165k base, $350k in stock options (as presented by the company, not an actual dollar value),[6] no signing bonus
- **Startup2:** $187k base, $440k in stock options (as presented by the company, not an actual dollar value), $10k signing bonus

With the Reversed Used Car Salesman, we asked you to pick your first choice. With the Ladder, you'll need to make two sets of rankings: one based on your excitement about the company/role itself (if money were no object) and the other based on just the initial offer size.

For the second list, we recommend using first year's total compensation (TC) for public companies and *only* using cash compensation (salary and any bonuses) for startups (unless you have a ton of conviction they're going to exit soon… which is why we decided to make an exception and include the equity in Stripe's offer).

Let's say your ranked lists look something like this:

---

5   Note that we chose Google in this example deliberately. If you're interviewing at a company like Meta, this configura-tion may be difficult to pull off because Meta doesn't like to give out numeric offers until team matching is over… but team matching is also the part of the process where you have the most control over timing—once they make you an offer, they'll do their best to get you to sign within a few days. As such, what you may want to do in a situation like this is to start running the Ladder without Meta's numbers and assume that Meta will probably give you the highest or second-highest offer. Then, once you get to the point in the Ladder where you're ready to start negotiating with Meta, you finalize the team and get the offer. Even though they may initially pressure you to accept within a few days, once you start negotiating, especially if you can bring other offers to the table, the clock effectively resets.

6   Remember that even if you're presented with a dollar value for stock options, in the same way that you might see a dollar value for your equity at a public company, the dollar value is speculative and likely way overestimated. We recommend using our equity calculator (pg 102) for a dose of reality.

View online materials for Beyond Cracking the Coding Interview at bctci.co

Most Exciting	**Best Initial Offer**
1. Stripe	1. Google ($302k)
2. Google	2. Stripe ($270k; if we weren't including equity, it'd be $220k)
3. Startup1	3. Bloomberg LP ($202k)
4. Startup2	4. Startup2 ($197k)
5. Bloomberg LP	5. Startup1 ($165k)

Now that we have both of these lists, we can glom them together. This is more art than science, but it might look something like this. The goal is to try to get comp ordered from highest to lowest while still being cognizant of how excited you are about these companies. This might look something like this:

Merged List (aka the Ladder)

1. Google
2. Stripe
3. Bloomberg LP
4. Startup2
5. Startup1

Now that we have our merged list, here's how the Ladder works. Essentially, we'll negotiate the companies off each other, starting with the bottom.

In this case, you start with Startup1 and negotiate with them first. So, you might reach out with something like:

Copy/paste this snippet from bctci.co/how-to-negotiate-what-to-say-2.

> Thank you so much for your offer and for all your help with this process so far. I'm excited about this opportunity, but I have several other strong offers in hand, from a mix of startups and larger companies. I know you can't match FAANG salaries in cash, and I'm not expecting it (there are plenty of great reasons to choose startups over FAANGs), but it'd be great to see a significant increase in both the cash and the equity component, as well as a meaningful signing bonus.
>
> Can you please let me know what's possible? I'd appreciate it very much.

Your recruiter may come back and ask you about your other offers. You don't have to reveal offer-by-offer detail, but the great news is that, because they're the bottom rung on your Ladder, *all* your offers are by definition better. So you can respond with something like this. The exact numbers don't matter. They're already significantly higher than the offer you received from the startup, making any increase a clear improvement.

Copy/paste this snippet from bctci.co/how-to-negotiate-what-to-say-3.

> As I mentioned, I have offers from a mix of startups and large companies. Most base salaries are around $200k, and I have a few strong signing bonuses as well. Equity is in the $400k-$500k range.

In general, when sharing competing offer details, we always want to paint the most favorable picture that we can. If one offer has a very high signing bonus but a low base, you can cherry-pick the signing bonus to mention. If another offer has a huge equity component but a lackluster base, just mention the equity. You're in charge of how much information to divulge, and you just want to let them see the good stuff.

While you're waiting for updated numbers from Startup1, you can start negotiating with the second-most bottom rung on your Ladder, Startup2. You can send them pretty much the same initial email that you sent to Startup1 and pretty much the same follow-up email if your recruiter presses you for competing offer details.

While you wait for offer details from the first two startups, it's time to start negotiating with Bloomberg.[7] You can write to them with something like this:

📋   Copy/paste this snippet from bctci.co/how-to-negotiate-what-to-say-4.

> Thank you so much for your offer and for all your help with this process so far. I'm excited about this opportunity, but I have several other strong offers in hand, from a mix of startups and larger companies, including Stripe and Google. I know that you likely can't match FAANG salaries in cash, and I'm not expecting it, but it'd be great to see a significant increase in both the base salary and the signing bonus.

You probably noticed that we mentioned specific companies this time. Why? It's to light a fire under Bloomberg LP—they're not going to want to lose candidates to FAANG and Stripe. We do need to tread carefully here, however, because Bloomberg's compensation can't match FAANG. That's why we mentioned that we're also interviewing at startups—to give the impression that it's not all about money. We go on to say that explicitly as well. We also don't ask for equity because it doesn't come with Bloomberg's offers.

As before, you'll likely get a question about competing offer details. You can respond with something similar to what you used with Startup1. By now, you may have heard back from Startup1 and Startup2, and if either of them offered you a signing bonus that's greater than Bloomberg's, you can include that amount explicitly in your email.

Then, while you're waiting on Bloomberg, it's time to start negotiating with the heavy hitters. You can send something like the following to Stripe:

📋   Copy/paste this snippet from bctci.co/how-to-negotiate-what-to-say-5.

> Thank you so much for your offer and for all your help with this process so far. I'm excited about this opportunity, but I have several very strong offers in hand, including one from Google. It would be great to see a significant increase in both the cash and the equity component of the offer, as well as a meaningful signing bonus.
>
> Can you please let me know what's possible? I'd appreciate it very much.

Now, of course your recruiter will ask you for Google offer details. What do you say?

📋   Copy/paste this snippet from bctci.co/how-to-negotiate-what-to-say-6.

> The main component of the offer I'd like to focus on is that Google has offered me more than double the equity of Stripe's current offer. Please let me know what you can do. Thank you again for your help!

The reason we have chosen not to divulge specific numbers here is that Google will likely increase its equity component when you negotiate with them, and you don't want to box yourself in. However, if your Stripe

---

7 You don't need to wait on the startups to start with Bloomberg because you still have two other initial offers that are higher than Bloomberg's initial offer.

recruiter pushes you, it's ok to divulge the $450k—it's so much higher than what Stripe is offering that sharing it could be quite impactful.

Now, before you negotiate with the top rung on the Ladder, Google, we should pause and wait for some counter-offers to start rolling in.

Let's say that your new offer lineup looks like this:

- **Stripe:** $225k base, $380k in equity, $30k signing bonus
- **Bloomberg LP:** $185k base, $50k signing bonus
- **Startup1:** $175k base, $480k in stock options, $10k signing bonus
- **Startup2:** $190k base, $540k in stock options, $20k signing bonus

So the good news is that the company you're most excited about (if money were no object) has just raised your first year's TC from $270k to $350k. That's not bad! But what do we do with Google? Here's what we recommend:

Copy/paste this snippet from bctci.co/how-to-negotiate-what-to-say-7.

> Thank you so much for your offer and for all your help with this process so far. I'm excited about this opportunity, but I have several very strong offers in hand, including one from Stripe with a significantly higher TC. It would be great to see a significant increase in both the cash and the equity component of the offer, as well as a meaningful signing bonus.
>
> Can you please let me know what's possible? I'd appreciate it very much.

Your Google recruiter will *definitely* ask you for offer details. Here's how we'd recommend responding:

Copy/paste this snippet from bctci.co/how-to-negotiate-what-to-say-8.

> Of course, happy to share. Stripe has offered me a $225k base with a $30k signing bonus. The equity component of the offer is comparable. I also have an offer from Bloomberg LP that includes a $50k signing bonus. And I have offers from several startups that include a $20k signing bonus and over $500k in equity.

The above should be enough to get Google to move. We expect they'll come back with something like this:

▸ **Google:** $200k base, $480k equity, $20k signing bonus

Ok, now we're getting somewhere. Google's TC has just gone up from $302k to $340k.

Now, we do the final step! Because we haven't yet shared Google's numbers with Stripe, we can respond to their offer update like so:

Copy/paste this snippet from bctci.co/how-to-negotiate-what-to-say-9/

> Thank you for that increase. I really appreciate it. At the moment, Google has offered me $480k in equity. That said, Stripe is my first choice, and I'm ready to sign immediately if we can increase either the equity component or the cash component.

At this point, Stripe may budge once more or they may not, but they likely will, and your final offer from Stripe is likely to be in the $370k range, or $100k more than when we started.

So, why go through all this trouble? We warned you that the Ladder was MUCH more labor intensive than the Reverse Used Car Salesman. It's also more stressful. We've glossed over the fine details of managing all the recruiter time pressure you'll get as you run this play and all the air traffic control you'll have to do. Our users who have successfully run the Ladder have described it as among the most stressful week or two of their lives because of all the recruiter calls and emails and follow-ups… while managing your own fear that your offers will get rescinded (they won't).

So why put in this much work at all? Our honest answer is that, when possible, the Reverse Used Car Salesman is preferable, but in a down market, you will have to run the Ladder more often than not because recruiters are in a different, more scarce mindset and will often need an extra push—read: details of other offers—to take your negotiations seriously. This approach is the best way to maximize as many offer details at once.

One last note about the Ladder. Though we ran you through a very specific example in order to illustrate how this play works, the details of your own Ladder will vary each time. It's impossible to cover every possible scenario in a single chapter (or even in a book), and getting great at this technique takes, just like technical interviewing, a bunch of practice. That said, we hope that reading through this scenario and exactly what to say will give you enough of an idea to start negotiating.

CLOSING OUT YOUR NEGOTIATIONS (AND ONE LAST OPPORTUNITY TO DRIVE UP YOUR COMP)

Regardless of which play you decide to use, at some point, you'll get to a place where you're ready to accept an offer. If you recall, in many of our email templates, we've included the following line:

I promise not to accept other offers until I have a chance to discuss them with you.

This is a very powerful way of getting recruiters off your back, but it also signs you up for some additional work at the end of your job search, if you're the kind of person who wants to keep your word.

And should you keep our word? Our answer is a resounding YES! There is no downside to doing so except a fairly small time investment. Before you sign that offer letter, send the following email to the other recruiters you've been working with:

 Copy/paste this snippet from bctci.co/how-to-negotiate-what-to-say-10.

> Thank you for all your help throughout this process. I've been thinking long and hard about what to do. It hasn't been an easy decision, but I'm very strongly leaning toward accepting an offer from {Company}. They've made me a very strong offer that looks like this: {Share details}
>
> I promised you that I would discuss with you any offers before accepting them, so I'd like to keep my word.
>
> Please let me know if you'd like to chat. And regardless of outcome, thank you again.

When you send this email, you'll find that all of a sudden, there's a flurry of recruiter activity! A minority will respond to wish you well and thank you for the heads up without budging on their numbers, but most will immediately want to talk and present stronger offers.

How much you want to engage here is up to you. If you're sick and tired of negotiating and are really excited about your top choice, you don't have to do much. But it may be worth listening to what they have to say—at the zero hour, we've seen offers go up by *another* $50k or more.[8] We recommend budgeting 3 - 5 days for this final close-out portion.

THE EITHER-OR FALLACY: WHY CHOOSE BETWEEN SALARY AND EQUITY WHEN YOU CAN ASK FOR BOTH?

You may, at times, toward the end of your negotiation, find yourself in a situation where a recruiter lets you choose between two things. For instance, at startups, you may get two ranges before your offer: one for base salary and one for equity. The idea is that you can decide which one matters more to you and take more cash and less equity or vice versa. Your recruiter may say something like, "We have a range of $130k to $170k for base and 0.1% to 0.3% of the company in options."

Or you might end up in a situation where you ask for an offer increase, and your recruiter says, "We can either get you a $25k signing bonus or $50k more in RSUs."

The either-or is a fallacy. Whenever you're given two choices, even if you don't negotiate for anything else, just ask for both.

In the first scenario, even if you do nothing else, say that you'd like $170k and 0.3%. They may not give you both, but you'll end up in a better place than if you hadn't asked.

In the second scenario, you can say, "Would it be possible to have both the signing bonus and the equity increase?" 99 times out of 100, your recruiter will say yes to both.

Though this advice holds even if you do have multiple offers, the leverage you have from multiple offers will likely overshadow the gains you'd get from asking for both. So it's most impactful when you just have one.

OFFER DEADLINES AND HOW NEGOTIATION RESETS THE CLOCK

Here's a practical secret that may help you, regardless of which technique you use. Often, recruiters will give you a deadline by which you must accept or reject a given offer. What they don't tell you is that every time you start to negotiate, the clock resets. We think of it as each "negotiating instance" resetting the clock—every time you send an email for the Ladder or every time you send your one Reverse Used Car Salesman email, the offer deadline disappears.

You'll also find that, even though a recruiter gives you a pretty aggressive deadline, once the ball is back in their court (i.e., after you've countered), they may take much longer to get back to you. At Meta, as we've mentioned, once you accept a team, your recruiter will usually give you a couple of days to make a decision. If you counter, they kick your request to the compensation committee, which we've seen take *weeks* in some cases. Obviously, those weeks don't count against you. The clock really does reset.

NEGOTIATING WITH FOUNDERS VS. RECRUITERS

So far, in all of our negotiation advice, we've assumed that you'll be negotiating with recruiters, and indeed, most of the time, you will be.

The one notable exception is young startups (seed and possibly Series A). These companies often don't have a recruiting team. Until a startup hires a recruiting team, usually, one of the founders handles important hiring-related tasks, such as negotiation. Even if they do have one or two recruiters on staff, sometimes the founder hasn't handed over the negotiation reins to them yet.

In case you do find yourself negotiating with a founder, we wanted to talk about how to handle it because if you treat them just like recruiters, the results could be disastrous.

---

8   Seeing how much of a difference being on the brink of accepting another offer makes will likely make you cynical about the whole process but will also drive home how important leverage really is.

Here's the most important difference between recruiters and founders. Recruiters are doing a job, and at larger companies, they're often following a script. Though we always advise you to be enthusiastic, gracious, and courteous (and we take great pains in our copy to do so), at the end of the day, there's an undercurrent in our negotiations: if you read between the lines, we're practically shouting, "Look! Here's my leverage! I'm cold and calculating and indifferent! Money talks!"

For founders, everything is *personal*. The company is their baby, and talking to them like they're a recruiter may upset them and make them think you're wasting their time. Moreover, many founders are not experienced at hiring, especially if it's their first company, and may not have had many candidate conversations. The playing field between you and a founder is, in this way, much more level than it would be with a recruiter.

Here's a real story to drive these points home.

> One candidate had just wrapped up the onsite at a seed-stage startup. The final step was to meet (once more) with the founders. During the call, they asked him where else he was interviewing. Using our playbook, he was deliberately vague and said that he's interviewing with a number of companies, at various stages, and is unable to share more information at this time.

> The founders dug in and asked several more times if he was interviewing with big tech companies. He held the line, even though the founders were visibly surprised in the meeting that he wasn't more forthcoming.

> After the meeting, the candidate got an email from their recruiter saying that they wouldn't be moving forward because "we aren't sure what you're looking for."

What happened here? Here's our best guess.

After spending several weeks of interviews telling them how interested he was in their startup, the founders were shocked to find that he wasn't fully bought in and was still considering other companies. Moreover, going into the conversation, the founders were probably worried that this candidate was interviewing at FAANGs and other big companies and that there was no way they'd be able to match big company compensation. We talked about this bias earlier (pg 88). It's a real thing.

As such, they made the calculated decision to stop investing in this candidate because they'd be unlikely to close him.[9] Their time is limited and the opportunity cost of any time spent is very high. Moreover, as we discussed earlier, they're not recruiters—they have less experience navigating these conversations, and for them it's personal.

So how do you deal with founders? Here's what we recommend.[10]

- When founders ask where else you're interviewing, you can use our recommended copy but soften it. Say that you're excited about this company and that you're talking to a mix of startups and big companies.

- If they ask you about your comp expectations and/or if they push on the big company thing, and especially if you've previously worked at one, say *up front* that you understand startups can't pay the same thing as FAANG, and that you're sure that they'll make you a fair offer.

---

9   As a founder, I (Aline) can relate—it makes our blood boil when it feels like someone is wasting your time. But as a founder, this decision *also* strikes me as naive—if a candidate is spending time with you, it's on you to sell them, and you sell until the last minute! However, not all founders feel this way.

10   Incidentally, the advice below assumes that you're okay with the cash hit you'd invariably take when working at a startup and that you're going into it with your eyes open. If you're not actually okay with it, please don't waste founders' time! And if you're using small startups for interview practice, shame on you. Not only is it unethical (in our book, wasting small startups' time is much more *personal* than big companies'), but the types of questions and feedback you'll get will likely be non-indicative of what you'll see at big companies (pg 87).

- If they give you a compensation range at the beginning of the process, take it seriously. Large company ranges are often fungible (we've seen FAANGs go $100k+ above their ranges with proper negotiation). Startup ranges are much less so, when it comes to cash. You may be able to negotiate a lot more equity, but if you don't want equity, think seriously about whether you even want to continue with the process.

BEHAVIORAL INTERVIEWS
PART V

Watch for these speech-bubble icons, which mean there is online content.

✦ **AI Interviewer:** Each problem can be tried online with the AI Interviewer.

▶ **Interview Replay:** Recordings of actual mock interviews.

📋 **Snippet:** Material to copy/paste online, including email templates and code recipes.

↗ **Resource:** Bonus chapters, worksheets, and other material.

BEHAVIORAL INTERVIEWS

## CHAPTER 15

WHEN AND HOW THEY MATTER

As often happens with nuanced topics, the answer to whether behavioral interviews matter is… it's complicated. How much companies care about your behavioral interview performance varies quite a bit.

At one extreme is Google, where some of interviewing.io's Google interviewers[1] joke that the bar is "don't be a serial killer." At the other extreme is Amazon. At Amazon, behavioral questions aren't confined to a single round and come up in pretty much every interview that you do, no matter how technical. Amazon also has a codified set of Leadership Principles[2] that they've trained their interviewers on, and they expect you to answer questions in a way that very clearly speaks to those principles.

Most companies are somewhere in the middle, both with respect to how much they weigh this interview type and how much effort they've put into designing their behavioral interviews and training their interviewers.

Part of the complexity is in what actually counts as a "behavioral interview." Certainly questions like "tell me about a conflict you faced" fall under the "behavioral" umbrella. But what about questions that cover your past (technical) projects? Most top-tier companies consider those types of questions to be "behavioral" as well, and in this book, so do we.

Here is a continuum of how much behavioral interviews matter at some indicative companies, from "not at all" to "a whole lot."

How Much Behavioral Interviews Matter

Figure 1. Importance of behavioral interviews at various companies, based on conversations with their interviewers

---

1 https://interviewing.io/guides/hiring-process/google#google-s-interview-types-in-detail

2 https://interviewing.io/guides/amazon-leadership-principles

Note that this is addressing situations where your behavioral interview is *mediocre* but your technical performance is strong; do you get an offer? A catastrophic fail (e.g., blaming your coworkers for every failure you have) will often merit a rejection, even in companies on the left side of this spectrum. And, conversely, a fantastic behavioral interview with a poor technical interview will typically not result in an offer, even for companies on the right side of this spectrum.

We have a bit of data about this as well. On the interviewing.io platform, about 82% of people pass their behavioral mock interviews, as compared to about 50% of people passing technical mock interviews.[3] Moreover, from talking to some interviewers at Amazon (which is among the pickiest when it comes to behavioral interviews) about 20% of people who passed their technical rounds end up getting rejected because they failed the behavioral portion.

However, before you assume that behavioral interviews don't matter that much and just blow them off entirely, a few words of caution:

- The bar is rising for behavioral interviews, as more people have been preparing specifically for this interview type.
- Behavioral interviews are often used for leveling. Especially in tough hiring climates, where companies are frequently down-leveling engineers because they can, don't give them a reason to![4]
- Technical interviews often start off with a few behavioral questions. Although these do not *significantly* affect your score (barring when you reveal major red flags)[5], they likely still affect your interviewer's impression of you leading into the technical questions.

So, even though behavioral interviews and questions don't matter as much as the technical ones, they can still significantly affect your outcomes... and your career trajectory and compensation!

WHAT GOES WRONG

Before diving into what you should do right, let's first explore some data on the most common mistakes candidates make in behavioral interviews. Take a look at this histogram, which highlights the most frequent errors observed in mock behavioral interviews on interviewing.io.[6]

---

3   50% is probably higher than you expected. In the wild, top-tier companies' passthrough rates for the technical screen are somewhere between 20% and 30%. Why are they higher on interviewing.io? We think it comes down to two factors: selection bias and pre-interview prep. The users who invest in interview prep are a specific, self-selected slice of the population. Moreover, many of our users practice on their own before practicing with a human.

4   The difference between, say an L4 and an L5 role at Google is on the order of $100k per year, and if you come in at a lower level, at the larger companies, it'll likely be at least 2 years before you get a promotion.

5   We quantify how much the chit-chat at the beginning of the interview matters for outcomes in "Rapport-Building at the Start" on page 36.

6   Interviewers in this data set come from FAANG and FAANG+ companies, with about half coming from either Meta or Amazon. The data set contains ~500 interviews.

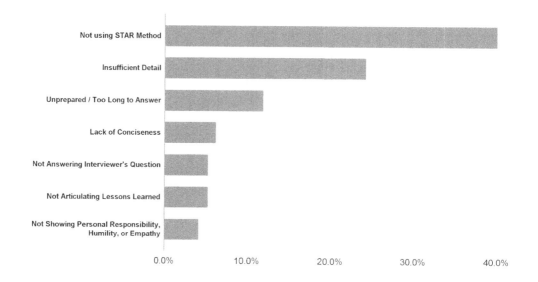

Figure 1. Frequency of mistakes in behavioral interviews.

As you can see, there are a lot of different things that can go wrong; behavioral questions are *not* just a casual conversation. Are these mistakes more in content (what to say) or communication though?

Well, they're both. When a candidate misses the mark on technical depth—giving too much or too little—their communication is weak. However, in many cases, the issue really arose from a mismatch in the *content*. The candidate didn't understand what the importance of their own story was or what message they were trying to send. No wonder they couldn't communicate well.

To show you how to tackle this effectively, we'll start with teaching you *what to say* and then dive into *how to say it*.

## CHAPTER 16

CONTENT: WHAT TO SAY

If I had to pick *one* thing that goes wrong with behavioral questions, it would be this: candidates tackle these like they are (falling) rock climbers… or like they are tackling a technical question. These seem like very different things, but allow me to explain.

Let's take a question like this:

> Tell me about a challenging project you have tackled.

When I'm coaching candidates for behavioral questions, this is often the first question I ask. It should be so incredibly easy. *Everyone* should have an answer here.

And that's exactly what goes wrong. You get a question; you deliver an answer. Like a (falling) rock climber looking for a hold, or an engineer looking to find a starting place on a technical question, they find a starting place and they just *go*.

In rock climbing, this is fine; you didn't want to fall, right? In a technical question, this is also okay; it's a starting point from which you iterate. But in a behavioral question, there's no *iteration*. This isn't a rough draft that you improve on. This is your answer.

So you spit out the answer and—often—one of these things goes wrong:

1. You had more challenging situations but didn't think of them. This is a fault in *preparation* (pg 164).
2. You thought of these other challenges, but didn't select the most relevant one. This is a fault in *selecting* (pg 144) and possibly dealing with *leveling* too (pg 150).
3. You picked a great challenge, but you failed to send a compelling message about what was truly challenging. This is a fault in *signal* (pg 141).
4. You said the right stuff, but your story was disorganized. This is a fault in *communication*; that's the next chapter (pg 154).

We'll tackle each of these in detail, starting with signal.

SIGNAL

Sometimes, the answer isn't the answer, and the question isn't the question. Take the earlier interview question like: "Tell me about a challenging project you have tackled." This *should be* an easy question—and it is, for a candidate who is prepared *and* understands signal.

Unfortunately, what many candidates do is they simply answer the question:

> At a previous job, I worked on overhauling our legacy authentication system to implement single sign-on (SSO) across multiple applications. The project involved integrating with an external identity provider and ensuring compatibility with our existing user database.
>
> I designed a system to support OAuth 2.0 and OpenID Connect protocols, enabling secure token-based authentication while maintaining backwards compatibility with older APIs. I also implemented a custom middleware to handle session management and token validation. Additionally, I collaborated with the front-end team to update the login flow and improve the user experience. The result was a seamless authentication process across all applications with enhanced security features.

This candidate has literally answered the question. Project? Check. Challenging? Check. Described it? Check.

The issue is the answer—while not awful—falls a little flat. A good, attuned interviewer will recognize this and probe for more information, but unfortunately, many interviewers aren't this good. Instead, they just move on, not really understanding what they missed out on.

What's missing in this answer is that the *real* question wasn't just to describe a project that was challenging. It was really something more like "show me that you're smart / creative / persistent by walking me through the specific details of a challenge." The candidate has not done this. Because they didn't really understand the real question, they didn't deliver the real answer.

This is where *signal* comes in.

WHAT IS SIGNAL?

Signal is not literally *what* happened ("built an authentication system"). Signal is about *who you are*. What does this story show about you? Does it show that you are smart? Persistent? Creative? Empathetic? A good mentor? Data-driven? Scrappy? Thorough?

In a perfect world, your stories should demonstrate things about you. Your interviewer should walk away from each story with a feeling of "wow, they are a [something good] sort of person!"

Let's take a look at this answer to a question about a challenging problem at work:

> In one project, our team needed to improve the load time of our customer-facing dashboard, which had been a frequent source of user complaints. I started by collecting detailed performance metrics using tools like Chrome DevTools and New Relic to identify where the bottlenecks were occurring.
>
> The data showed that over 60% of the load time was tied to inefficient API calls that fetched data redundantly. To address this, I analyzed usage patterns in our analytics platform to determine which data was accessed most frequently. Using this information, I implemented server-side caching for the most common queries and reduced the number of API calls by aggregating multiple requests into a single optimized endpoint.
>
> After deployment, I tracked metrics over several weeks and saw a 40% reduction in average load time, which correlated with a significant drop in user complaints and a 15% increase in customer satisfaction ratings, according to our feedback surveys. This data-driven approach allowed us to focus on the most impactful changes and validate the improvements quantitatively.

This person sounds pretty data-driven to me.

Now here's a very similar story, but highlighting a different attribute:

> Our team needed to improve the load time of our customer-facing dashboard, which had become a significant issue for users. Using tools like Chrome DevTools and New Relic, I identified that redundant API calls were causing over 60% of the delays. However, when I proposed a caching strategy to address the issue, my manager initially pushed for a quicker fix, suggesting we focus on front-end optimizations instead.

While I understood the desire for a rapid solution, I believed a deeper back-end overhaul would have a more lasting impact. I presented a detailed analysis of the performance data to my manager, demonstrating that front-end changes alone would only marginally improve load times. Even when she was convinced, there was still pushback from more senior management who were concerned about the timeline for delivery. I spent the weekend working on a clear implementation plan and risk mitigation strategies to ensure we could execute the back-end changes effectively. After several discussions and pushback, we agreed to proceed with the proposed caching solution.

Implementing the changes came with its own set of challenges, including debugging inconsistencies in data updates during testing. I worked closely with the team to refine the system and ensure its reliability. After deployment, the metrics spoke for themselves: a 40% reduction in load time, fewer user complaints, and a 15% improvement in customer satisfaction. This experience not only solved an immediate problem but also led to a shift in our engineering practices, including improved monitoring pipelines, automated performance regression tests, and stricter standards for API design.

From this story, we learn that the candidate is persistent and collaborative.

MATCHING QUESTIONS TO SIGNALS

Some behavioral questions aren't so much questions as they are open-ended discussions about a project. Others are more specific: *Tell me about a time when you …*

In this latter type, the interviewer typically has a specific signal—or set of signals—they're trying to measure. Your job then is to deliver that signal to them.

Assess Yourself

See if you can identify which signal(s) the interviewer is trying to measure in these questions. Note that there can be many signals in any one question, and multiple ways to describe an attribute.

1. Describe a situation where you had to collaborate with a difficult team member. How did you handle it, and what was the outcome?[1]
2. Tell me about a time when you disagreed with a decision made by your manager or team. How did you handle the situation?[2]
3. Tell me about a time when you were working on a project that was behind schedule.[3]
4. Tell me about a time when you made a mistake.[4]
5. Tell me about a time when you had to balance the needs of multiple stakeholders.[5]
6. Tell me about a time when you influenced an individual or team.[6]
7. Tell me about a time when you identified a performance issue in code.[7]

The answers are in the footnotes (no peeking!).

For more junior engineers, much of the relevant signal is around technical skills. But as people get more senior, they'll see more questions diving into particular aspects of communication, influence, and leadership.

---

1 Empathy, conflict management, and ability to tailor communication or approach.

2 Knowing how to speak up; influencing others; ability to understand other people's reasoning; knowing when to *stop* arguing.

3 Prioritization; communication about challenges; time management

4 Ability to admit that you made that you made a mistake (really, that's the #1 thing); the self-reflection to learn from mistakes

5 Empathy; communication; prioritization

6 Empathy; ability to adjust communication and approach

7 Technical skills related to identifying performance issues and fixing them

SIGNAL IN OPEN-ENDED QUESTIONS

Some behavioral questions are less questions and more like *prompts*. The interviewer has simply asked you to tell them about a project. Does signal still matter? Absolutely!

The difference is that it's up to you to choose what signal you want to demonstrate. As we saw earlier, the same project could be used to demonstrate influence, being data-driven, or persistence, or almost anything else.

What you should demonstrate depends a bit on you, the company, and the role. You might, for example, match your stories to the company's values, if it's a very culture-driven company. But when in doubt, these are always good signals to hit:

1. Being smart / creative
2. Being persistent
3. Being technically knowledgeable
4. Can lead / Has accomplished things at the level of this role

What company *doesn't* want an engineer who is smart, works hard, knows a lot, and can lead / work at the appropriate level?

PICKING THE RIGHT PROJECTS

Your interviewer isn't necessarily looking for you to have been on the most impactful projects; often, that is entirely out of your control. Rather, they want your project to demonstrate *your skills*, either at a technical or interpersonal level. This might mean assessing your technical competence, or it might mean assessing how you work with or lead others. Your interviewer might be asking open-ended questions about a past project, or they might be assessing a particular skill, like your ability to handle conflict.

In either case, it is important to show that you understand the purpose of the project, can reason about your individual contribution, and can discuss what went well and what didn't.

WHAT MAKES A GOOD PROJECT?

With that in mind, here are the criteria for what projects make good behavioral interview fodder:

1. **Recency and familiarity.** You should have worked on this project recently enough and at enough depth to be able to answer detailed questions about it. Your interviewer may ask you about tooling or about specific metrics. They may also change up constraints on the fly to see how you'd change your approach. If you don't remember details, you will fumble.

2. **Large contribution.** This should be a project where your part was meaningful. You want to give the interviewer enough for them to sink their teeth into and be able to discuss with you at length.

3. **Part of a team.** Ideally, you'll be able to talk about being part of a team—at least for most of your stories.[8] Part of the intent of behavioral interviews is to suss out whether you're able to work well with others. At more senior levels, this would morph into working with several other teams or leading several teams.

4. **Difficult, open-ended task.** Your interviewer wants to know if you can thrive in ambiguous circumstances. The more uncertainty there was going into the project, the better, provided you're able to tell a story about how you tamed the chaos.

---

8   If your interviewer wants to hear about an individual project, they will specifically ask for it. This is sometimes the case, especially when applying to a very small startup where your ability to work independently is a key factor. If you're unsure whether to focus on an individual project or a team effort, don't hesitate to ask your interviewer.

5. **Successes *and* failures.** Some companies, like Amazon, will explicitly ask about both success and failure stories; others don't care much whether your story ends happily. Optimize for the stories that demonstrate positive attributes about you (pg 141). If you do tell a failure story (and you absolutely should when asked about failures), be sure to talk about what you learned, and if possible, how you made it right or how you avoided similar mistakes.

6. **Signal-sending stories.** Interviewers are often looking for stories that demonstrate particular attributes, such as being adaptable, prioritizing the customer, or being data-driven. They are often related to the company's values. Especially if the company is known for doing values-based interviewing (e.g., Amazon and their Leadership Principles), we recommend looking up the company's values and identifying stories that demonstrate those attributes.

7. **Appropriate scope for the level you're targeting** Use this interview as an opportunity to show your interviewer that you're already doing the job and thinking at the level of the role that you're applying for. We'll talk more about this in the upcoming section about leveling specifically.

8. **High visibility, if possible.** If you've worked on something high-profile, all other things being equal, choose that project. Your interviewer is human and not impervious to being impressed by projects that touch products they admire. However, don't choose high visibility projects at the expense of the other things on this list. If you had a negligible role in something impressive-sounding, for example, it's better to pick a more obscure project where you contributed meaningfully.

Though this list is long, it's not going to cover every scenario. If you're ever not sure what your interviewer is looking for, just ask! You can say something like, "I have a project in mind that demonstrates X and another project that demonstrates Y. Which one would you rather hear about?" If you're *ever* not sure about what your interviewer is looking for, in *any* type of interview, just ask.

INTERVIEW REPLAYS

Here, we have some interview replays where candidates chose good projects to talk about… and one replay where the project choice could have been better.

How Interview Replays Work and How to Use Them

Interview replays come from mock interviews on interviewing.io (in this section, they're all behavioral mock interviews). Replays are shared with the permission of both participants. Each replay includes the interviewer's feedback. You can watch just the relevant snippet, but we include the entire interview.

We strongly recommend pausing in your reading and watching these replays. Hearing real people interview lets you learn from their mistakes—so that you aren't doomed to repeat them.

Where possible, we'll share what role the candidate was targeting and whether they got the job.

▶ MENTORSHIP SESSION ON HOW TO DISCUSS PAST PROJECTS   INTERVIEW REPLAY

View Online:	bctci.co/behavioral-content-replay-1 @ 11:00 - 22:56
The Question:	Tell me about a recent project.
What You'll See:	The candidate worked on infrastructure for the Gmail Spam team. This conversation decouples the quality of the project itself from how well the candidate talked about it. The candidate chose a recent, difficult, highly visible, and impactful project where they personally did a lot of the work, and their interviewer mentored them through how to better tell the story.
Role:	Senior Software Engineer at a FAANG or FAANG+ company
Who:	*Interviewer*: Senior Software Engineer at Dropbox *Candidate*: 4 years of experience
Outcome:	The candidate got three offers from FAANG+ companies, two for mid-level roles and one for senior.

▶ TURNING A DIFFICULT SITUATION INTO A GOOD STORY   INTERVIEW REPLAY

View Online:	bctci.co/behavioral-content-replay-2 @ 8:20 - 13:36
The Question:	Tell me about the last time when you thought of a new program from scratch.
What You'll See:	Even though this project is high-profile (rack migration and retirement at AWS' EC2), it would have still been a good choice even if it was at a company no one had ever heard of. It was recent, part of a team, showed ownership and a large contribution, and, because of the circumstances (was given minimal direction and didn't have people to ask because a bunch of engineers on their team had left) was a difficult and open-ended task.
Role:	E4 at Meta
Who:	*Interviewer*: Technical Program Manager at Meta *Candidate*: 3 years of experience
Outcome:	The candidate got the job at Meta!

View Online:	bctci.co/behavioral-content-replay-3 @ 39:45 - 43:15
The Question:	What is the time that you had a large failure, something you were so sure but didn't work out? And how did you deal with that?
What You'll See:	The candidate talked about dropping a singing class because they couldn't keep up with their classmates. We chose to include this replay, even though it's not a technical project, because it checked so many of the boxes. It was a signal-sending failure that turned into a success. It was difficult, and it was recent. If you're just entering tech, all of your stories don't have to be technical, as long as they send a clear, impressive, and positive signal about you.
Role:	New grad eng role at TikTok
Who:	*Interviewer*: Staff Software Engineer at LinkedIn *Candidate*: Senior at Carnegie Mellon University
Outcome:	The candidate got invited to the next round at TikTok but had already taken another job.

View Online:	bctci.co/behavioral-content-replay-4 @ 28:48 - end
The Question:	Can you tell me about a time when you had to make a decision between standards and delivery? What tradeoff did you have to make? And what was the outcome?
What You'll See:	The candidate chose a story that made it look like they didn't prioritize testing code.
Role:	SDE2 at Amazon
Who:	*Interviewer*: Software Engineer at Amazon *Candidate*: 8 years of experience
Outcome:	The candidate got the job at Amazon!

GENERATING YOUR STORIES

At this point, we've talked pretty thoroughly about *what* to say. Find good projects, make sure that they demonstrate the right level, and—while you're at it—try to match them to the signal. Easy, right?

Maybe not, but it does get easier with time. And preparation. And practice.

STORY GENERATION

Before walking into your interview, we recommend having at least three technical projects and five stories that you feel comfortable talking about in depth. We already talked about how to come up with these projects (pg 147), but what about these stories?

There is a strategy to brainstorming stories—two, in fact. We recommend you do both.

Our goal here is to balance quality *and* quantity. Having a few really exceptional stories is important, but you don't know what you'll *actually* be asked in the real interview. For that reason, we also want to come up with a lot of stories, so that you'll always have one to match the specific question.

Strategy #1: Category-Based Generation

Many behavioral questions can be grouped into a few basic categories:

- **Accomplishments & Challenges:** What are things you're most proud of? Where did you hit obstacles, and how did you overcome them?

- **Leadership, Influence & Decision-Making:** How did you drive alignment on your team or across teams? What decisions did you make, and how did you influence people to agree? When have you proposed a change or something new? Note that "leadership" doesn't necessarily mean "managed people." Even an intern can demonstrate leadership.

- **Conflicts & Collaboration:** When have you disagreed with teammates? Are there other conflicts you have faced? How did you address these?

- **Enjoyment & Learning:** What did you love? What did you learn, whether it's new technologies or new approaches?

- **Mistakes & Failures:** What mistakes did you make? When have you really struggled, or even failed?

Ideally, you're going to want one story from *each* job (or team, or section of your career).

Behavioral Category Matrix

For each job, fill out a matrix like this one, with just a few keywords per story. Don't fill in the full story—we'll do that later (pg 164). The idea here is to just have an idea of which story you might provide.

Access this spreadsheet at bctci.co/behavioral-content-resource-1

	TEAM 1	TEAM 2
Accomplishments & Challenge	API Re-design	Backwards Compatibility
Leadership, Influence, and Decision-Making	Best: API Re-design Backup: Documentation initiative	Integration Issues with Client
Conflicts & Collaboration	Security issue	Best: Backwards Compatibility Backup: Mobile client
Enjoyment & Learning	Analytics tools	Scalability
Mistakes & Failures	Production outage	Security issue

We'll warn you that this will be challenging; there are *a lot* of stories to come up with. In some cases, a single story might be the best option for two different categories. When this happens, that's okay! Put the best story in there, but try to add a backup too. Again: we want high-quality stories, but we also want a high quantity of stories.

Strategy #2: Signal-Based Generation (Strengths, Weakness, and Values)

Yes, yes, we know—asking about strengths and weaknesses is a bit of a snoozefest, if not outdated. However, remember all that stuff about signal? When candidates generate stories by *starting* from a signal, these stories usually do a pretty good job of demonstrating that signal.

There are three types of signals you should have coverage of. For each of the below, come up with a story—one per job, if possible—that shows this attribute.

1. Your strengths. Yes, your *actual* strengths. What are you really good at? How would people describe you? This might be things like initiative, influence, persistence, attention to detail, or being data-driven. These could—and probably should—be demonstrated through technical stories.

2. Your weaknesses. Yes, your actual weaknesses. Are you a bit impulsive? Too blunt? Poor attention to detail? Of course, you don't want to give anything *too* damning (e.g., lacking honesty), but you should have some genuine weaknesses. These stories will generally lend themselves to stories about mistakes and failures.[9]

3. The company's values. Many companies have their corporate values posted publicly, and their behavioral questions will often match these values. If you find stories that demonstrate the specific attributes they're evaluating, you'll be a step ahead.

Make a list of your strengths and weaknesses—and the company values—and put them into a matrix like this one.

Behavioral Signal Matrix

Don't worry. Your stories can overlap here. It doesn't have to be a *different* story for every single signal.

Access this spreadsheet at bctci.co/behavioral-content-resource-2

	TEAM 1	TEAM 2
Strength 1: Persistence	Mobile redesign	Integration Issues with Client
Strength 2: Data-Driven	Analytics tools	Backwards Compatibility
Strength 3: Influence	API Re-design	Security issue
Weakness 1: Blunt	Teammate feedback reaction	Load screen redesign
Weakness 2: Impulsive	Production outage	Mobile client
Value 1: Customer Driven	Mobile redesign	Backwards Compatibility
Value 2: Mentorship	Junior engineer/PIP	Integration Issues with Client
...		

If you've done the math (a few strengths + a few weaknesses + a few company values), you'll find that this adds up to probably 10+ stories.. per job. It's okay if some stories are in multiple categories, and that some stories are much better than others. That's to be expected.

CHOOSE YOUR STORIES AND PROJECTS

If you've filled out both of these grids, you'll now have your pick of *a lot* of stories. Great!

Choose at least five stories *plus* three projects to really practice. The stories will primarily be used when you're asked about a question like, "Tell me about a time when you faced a conflict with a teammate", while the projects will be used in very open-ended discussion, where you're just talking about the work that you've done. However, there is considerable overlap; a discussion might start off with an open discussion about a project, and then involve more specific follow-ups.

All those other stories? Don't forget about those too. Those will be used to fill in the gaps when one of your prepared stories don't quite match the question.

---

9 You might be worried that your stories will be *too* damning if it is a mistake caused by an actual weakness of yours. Be cautious about this, but don't panic about this. The biggest issue candidates face with stories about mistakes or failures is that the story sounds weak and lacks introspection. Many interviewers feel candidates who haven't made big mistakes haven't had big responsibilities—or that a refusal to offer a sufficiently large mistake means the candidate isn't forthcoming. A story involving a mistake attributed to an actual personal weakness can be incredibly powerful, when paired with acknowledgement of the weakness and a discussion of what you've learned and how you've improved.

LEVELING

While behavioral interviews may not matter as much as their technical counterparts, they're often used for leveling. Here are the main reasons that engineers get down-leveled based on their behavioral interviews, according to interviewing.io's data.

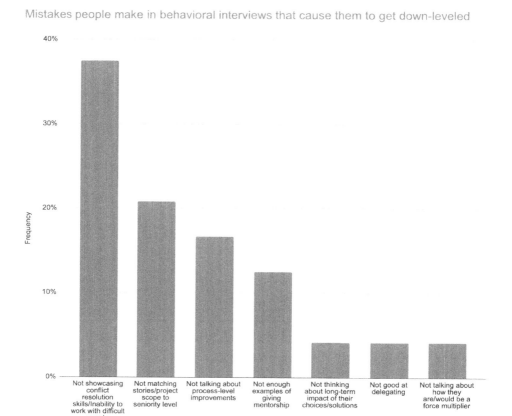

Mistakes people make in behavioral interviews that cause them to get down-leveled

With these mistakes in mind, make sure to pick projects that paint you and your contributions at a scope commensurate with the level you're targeting. This matters *especially* when you're targeting a level above the one you're at now. If that's the case, make sure that your story:

- Includes you suggesting architectural changes or making significant architectural contributions to the design of the project
- Includes you proactively pushing back on the scope of a project and successfully changing it (either to something smaller or bigger, depending on the circumstances). This could be a situation where building something that the business needs, as is, would take forever, but with a few small changes, it would still get you most of the way there but would take way less time.
- Even if this isn't a management position, highlight an example of you mentoring your peers, as above. The more senior you get, the more expectation there is that you'll be helping others on the team, even if you don't have a management title.

- Includes an example of you proactively communicating with non-engineering members of the team, whether it's product managers, salespeople, or other stakeholders.
- Includes at least one example of you proactively communicating with non-engineering members of the team, whether it's product managers, salespeople, or other stakeholders.

Especially if you're targeting your first management position, as much as you can, make sure that your story:

- Showcases your ability to lead. Remember that leadership is about much more than managing employees; it's about influence, driving decisions, mentorship, and more. So, even if you're not officially the leader, pick a story where you led by example or where you took the initiative.
- Showcases examples of you making improvements in your team's or company's process, for future projects.
- Includes some friction or conflict between you and other members of the team that you successfully resolved.
- Includes an example of when you successfully mentored your peers. If it's difficult to think of something, we recommend going back to code reviews you've done or thinking back to times when you were the domain expert on a specific piece of code. Depending on your relationship with your coworkers, you can also ask them to think of a time when you were helpful to them.
- Includes multiple examples of you proactively communicating with non-engineering members of the team, whether it's product managers, salespeople, or other stakeholders.

ASSESS YOUR PROJECT: A SELF-QUIZ

Got a project in mind? Great! Evaluate it with this self-quiz.

Individual Contributor Positions

If you're applying for a mid-to-senior role, then choosing the correct project matters much more. You should be targeting a score of at least 5 out of 7.

- [+1 Point] Can you clearly articulate the impact that you made, preferable with numbers?

  » [+1 Point] Did the project have well-defined metrics?

    - [+1 Point] Did you come up with the metrics?.

- [+1 Point] Did you make any meaningful architectural decisions as part of this project?
- [+1 Point] Did you advocate for putting in some kind of process or some changes that made future projects better?

  » [+1 Point] Were you able to actually implement said process?

- [+1 Point] Do you remember this project in enough detail, to the point where you'd be comfortable answering in depth if your interviewer asks about what you would have done if some constraints were different?

If you're applying for a junior role, where you likely don't have a ton of past projects to choose from, you should simply choose projects where you can 1) articulate the impact you made, preferably with metrics, and 2) you remember the project in enough detail. Everything else is extra credit.

Managerial Positions

If you're applying for your first managerial position, use the questions and points from above and also add the following. For the previous section, you want at least 5 out of 7. For this section, you want a score of at least 2 out of 3.

- [+1 Point] Were you instrumental in resolving conflict on your team?
- [+1 Point] Did you take on an unofficial leadership role as the project went on?
- [+1 Point] Can you demonstrate, through this project, that you're a force multiplier?

INTERVIEW REPLAYS

Here are some examples of candidates choosing a project or a story that wasn't entirely commensurate with the level they were targeting. All the interviews below were successful, but they didn't always hit all the notes for the candidate's desired level. Unlike the previous replays, we mostly won't be linking to a specific snippet because leveling concerns generally come from an overall impression of the candidate and not just one specific answer. Where we can pinpoint one moment in the interview, though, we will.

TARGETING A SENIOR ENGINEERING ROLE   INTERVIEW REPLAY

View Online:	bctci.co/behavioral-content-replay-5 @ 6:11-16:17
The Question:	Give me an example of a time when you were unable to meet a commitment to a team member.
What You'll See:	The candidate talked about a time when they forgot to run some important scripts for a customer because of a rough on-call schedule. While they did a good job of answering the question, they didn't choose a project that had the scope and impact you'd expect from a senior engineer.
Role:	Senior Software Engineer (company not specified)
Who:	*Interviewer*: Engineering Manager at Amazon *Candidate*: 12 years of experience
Outcome:	The candidate got offers from Salesforce, Google, Facebook and Airbnb, at the senior level.

TARGETING E5 AT META   INTERVIEW REPLAY

View Online:	bctci.co/behavioral-content-replay-6 @ 0:00 - end; feedback starts at 47:13
The Question:	We recommend listening to the whole interview.
What You'll See:	The candidate did well in this interview, but they didn't signal that they were at the E5 level. Specifically, they should have chosen stories that showed them as someone who's able to build relationships between teams (rather than primarily focusing on the work of one team) and figure out what needs to be done rather than just executing on what they were asked to do.
Role:	E4/E5 Infrastructure Security Engineer at Meta
Who:	*Interviewer*: Staff Software Engineer at Meta *Candidate*: 5 years of experience
Outcome:	The candidate got the job at Meta! (E4)

TARGETING A SENIOR MANAGEMENT ROLE INTERVIEW REPLAY

View Online: bctci.co/behavioral-content-replay-7 @ 0:00 - end; feedback starts at 1:03:17

The Question: We recommend listening to the whole interview

What You'll See: Though this interview went well, the candidate missed a few opportunities to position themselves as a manager of managers and to choose the largest-scope stories that show them as someone who manages several teams.

Role: Senior Engineering Manager at Google (L7 on the management track), Director of Engineering at Docusign

Who: *Interviewer*: Engineering Manager at Amazon
Candidate: Senior Engineering Manager at Twilio

Outcome: The candidate got an M1 offer from Meta (which is comparable to Google L6 on the management track, one down from what they were targeting).

ANOTHER EXAMPLE OF TARGETING E6 AT META INTERVIEW REPLAY

View Online: bctci.co/behavioral-content-replay-8 @ 0:00 - end; feedback starts at 46:27

The Question: We recommend listening to the whole interview, but the question that affected leveling the most was: Tell me about a project you're most proud of and why.

What You'll See: The candidate talked about how they got Shopify to invest $1M into Ruby-Gems.org. While it was a great story (and this candidate had a few other great stories as well), the *Interviewer*'s feedback was that for this particular question, which can be particularly telling to interviewers, it's important to pick a project that has 1) huge scope, 2) working cross-functionally, and 3) leading other engineers. The interviewer predicted that the candidate would likely get down-leveled to E5.

Role: E6 at Meta

Who: *Interviewer*: Formerly Senior Software Engineer at Meta, currently Engineering Manager at a large startup
Candidate: 14 years of experience

Outcome: The candidate got the job at Meta, albeit at E5.

## CHAPTER 17

COMMUNICATION: HOW TO SAY IT

> Successful behavioral interviews are all alike; every
> failed interview fails in its own way.
>
> Leo Tolstoy(ish)

Behavioral interviews are often seen as tests of your experiences and skills, but they're also tests of how well you communicate. In some cases, interviewers are explicitly evaluating this—can you explain complex ideas clearly? Can you tell a compelling story?

But, even when communication isn't the primary focus, it shapes how the interviewer interprets your answer. A poorly structured response can obscure the depth of your technical abilities or your contributions to a project. Conversely, a well-communicated answer can elevate even a simple story, helping the interviewer see the real signal behind your words.

Communication is the bridge between your experiences and your interviewer's understanding. It's not just about answering the question—it's about telling the right story in the right way to demonstrate the right things.

REMEMBER THE SIGNAL

While this chapter is about communication, we cannot cleanly separate communication from content. However, since we already talked at length about signal (pg 141), we won't rehash it. (But if you skipped over this, please go back and read it.)

However, we do want to call out that as you're thinking about how to communicate, the end goal is to communicate a *signal* to your interviewer about yourself—that you're smart, that you are persistent, that you are knowledgeable, and that, overall, you're a great engineer.

As you read about STAR, remember signal. Your *actions* should demonstrate the signal; the situation and task offer the context for this signal; and the result is proof that this signal is real and desirable.

THE STAR METHOD

Some classics never go out of style, and that goes for the classic STAR (Situation Task Action Result) framework. This framework helps you discuss your past work in a way that makes sense to interviewers who lack context about your project. It clearly articulates the problem (Situation), what you needed to do (Task), how you did it (Action), and what ultimately happened (Result).

WHY IT MATTERS

The STAR method is a formula for piquing the interviewer's interest by highlighting a problem and then demonstrating your awesomeness by showing how you solved it and the goodness that happened. It makes them think, "If this person can solve this problem, then they can help solve our company's problems too."

Let's look at this common interview question, that basically gives you free reign to tell your interviewer about how awesome you are:

Tell me about a time when you fixed a problem at work.

Here's one answer:

> Sure, I did some pretty significant optimizations to some backend code at work. To start, I used SQL Profiler to analyze query execution times and identified a query that was causing performance issues due to inefficient indexing. I revised the query to use proper joins and ensured that frequently accessed columns were indexed appropriately. Alongside this, I used pgAdmin to review the database schema and optimize table structures where necessary.
>
> Once the optimizations were implemented, I utilized our in-house testing framework to validate functionality and JMeter to perform load testing under simulated peak traffic conditions.

When I read that, it just feels like it's missing something. This candidate has literally told me what they did, with lots of keywords sprinkled throughout. And yet, when I read it, I feel like I neither understand nor really care. It's literally missing the *story*.

Let's try again:

> In a previous role, I observed that a backend feature responsible for serving high-traffic user data was experiencing noticeable slowdowns during peak usage periods. This feature was critical for delivering real-time information to thousands of users, and its inefficiency was beginning to impact the overall user experience.
>
> Although this wasn't directly assigned to me, I decided to investigate the issue, as it was a critical part of the user experience.
>
> I began by analyzing query performance using SQL Profiler, which revealed that a key database query was poorly optimized and relying on a full table scan. Diving deeper, I identified that the lack of appropriate indexing on certain columns was a significant bottleneck. I studied our existing database schema and implemented changes to optimize table structures and indexing strategies. Additionally, I rewrote the query to use more efficient joins and reduced redundant calculations. After making the updates, I rigorously tested the system using our internal testing framework to ensure functionality remained intact, and conducted load testing with JMeter to simulate peak traffic conditions.
>
> This demonstrated that the optimizations reduced query execution time by nearly 50%. The feature's response time improved noticeably, leading to smoother user experiences. The changes not only resolved the immediate performance issues but also encouraged a broader initiative within the team to audit and optimize other critical queries.

Yes, the second example tells a story, but it's a particular *type* of story. The story neatly outlines four pieces (for your convenience, each paragraph delineates one section): the Situation, the Task, the Action, and the Result.

In doing so, it teaches the interviewer not only what they did, but also why it mattered. Communicating those things clearly is really what the STAR method is all about.

SITUATION

What It Is

The *situation* sets the context of the problem and outlines just enough information for your interviewer to understand the issue and its importance without leaving them overwhelmed with details. It helps them understand, *"What was the problem and why does it matter?"*

Think about how you'd describe your work project to a friend. You wouldn't start throwing around buzzwords. Instead, you'd probably explain the context and why it matters. So do that in interviews as well!

Let's fill in the blanks for the above using a recent project we worked on at interviewing.io, through the lens of one of our engineers. Let's pretend the interviewer asked us to tell them about a challenging project.

> I'm the technical lead at interviewing.io, which is an anonymous mock interview platform. Candidates pay us for mock interviews, and strong candidates can also be referred out to companies. So, having great and well-calibrated interviewers is critical.
>
> Originally, we were doing manual quality control. New interviewers would do two trial interviews, and then our system would match them randomly with candidates. Our ops team would periodically manually cull underperforming interviewers.
>
> The manual quality control of course didn't scale well as we grew.

Now, we've effectively set the stage! Our interviewer knows what the company does and what the project's goals were in the context of the business.

Unfortunately, many candidates leave out this stage-setting entirely, or provide too much information, and it's one of the biggest failure modes for behavioral interviews.[1] The goal of the *situation* part is to provide enough information that the rest of your story makes sense.

If you work on a product that's universally known, you might be able to leave out the description of the product, but you will likely still need some additional context to understand the problem. Explain what your team's purpose is and how that fits into what the company does, as a whole—but only to the extent necessary to understand the problem you faced.

---

1   Incidentally, many resumes would benefit from an explanation of the "situation". If you work at a company not everyone has heard of, we strongly recommend including a few sentences on your resume explaining, in very simple terms, what the company does, and why what you worked on mattered for the business. Including this information puts all your bullet points in context. The people reading your resume are humans, too, and they appreciate being able to understand what you were working on and why.

Excellent Situation Replays

▶ MOST COMPLEX PROJECT · INTERVIEW REPLAY

View Online:	bctci.co/behavioral-communication-replay-1 @ 20:46-end
The Question:	Tell me about the most complex project you've worked on.
What You'll See:	The candidate did an excellent job explaining what their startup did, their role in the project, and what made building it hard.
Role:	SDE2 at Amazon AWS
Who:	*Interviewer*: Senior Software Engineer at Amazon AWS *Candidate*: 19 years of experience
Outcome:	The candidate got the job at AWS!

▶ A FAILED PROJECT · INTERVIEW REPLAY

View Online:	bctci.co/behavioral-communication-replay-2 @ 14:25-18:05
The Question:	Tell me about a time where you worked diligently on a project, but it didn't produce the desired result.
What You'll See:	First, the candidate asked the interviewer if the example should be technical (this is a good habit to get into). They talked about rebuilding a game and clearly explained why it had to happen, why it mattered, and what went wrong.
Role:	Senior Software Engineer at Google, Amazon, or Meta
Who:	*Interviewer*: Engineering Manager at a FAANG+ company *Candidate*: 15 years of experience
Outcome:	The candidate interviewed at five companies and got all five offers. They ended up at Meta (E5).

▶ A TIGHT DEADLINE · INTERVIEW REPLAY

View Online:	bctci.co/behavioral-communication-replay-3 @ 2:47-19:00
The Question:	Tell me about a project you delivered under a tight deadline.
What You'll See:	The candidate hit some setbacks while working on a project to increase student usage of Deliveroo. They clearly explained the project, the cross-functional team they worked with, and how they dealt with setbacks.
Role:	E5 at Meta
Who:	*Interviewer*: Engineering Manager at Amazon *Candidate*: 8 years of experience
Outcome:	The candidate got the job at Meta!

Poor Situation Replays

▶ **MOST DIFFICULT ASPECT OF A PROJECT**   INTERVIEW REPLAY

View Online:	bctci.co/behavioral-communication-replay-4 @ 4:40-11:08
The Question:	Walk me through one of your most recent projects, and highlight the most difficult aspects.
What You'll See:	The candidate described automating market research with APIs and training an intern, but failed to provide crucial context about the product's purpose and business impact.
Role:	Software Engineer at Google (L3/L4)
Who:	*Interviewer*: Software Engineer at Google *Candidate*: 2 years of experience
Outcome:	The candidate did not get the job at Google.

▶ **REFUSING TO COMPROMISE STANDARDS**   INTERVIEW REPLAY

View Online:	bctci.co/behavioral-communication-replay-5 @ 4:18-13:32
The Question:	Tell me about a time when you refused to compromise your standards around quality.
What You'll See:	The candidate chose a story about automating unit tests but took a long time to come up with their answer and omitted key context, requiring the interviewer to probe for essential details.
Role:	E5 at Meta
Who:	*Interviewer*: Senior Engineering Manager at Amazon *Candidate*: 9 years of experience
Outcome:	The candidate got the job at Meta! (We confirmed that they practiced more between this mock interview and the real one.)

TASK

What It Is

Now that we've set the stage, it's time to state the actual solution and your role in it. It is easy for this to get confused with either the situation or the actions. Remember: The *situation describes* the problem and the *action* is the implementation details. The *task* is the piece that connects them. It is often very short—one or two sentences—and briefly outlines the goals, constraints, and/or the chosen solution.

> {Describe your solution to the problem you posed in the Situation portion above}
>
> *In order to solve this problem, we decided to [insert solution description here].*
>
> {If it makes sense to, you should also explain why you chose this solution, possibly over others.}
>
> *We thought this was a good solution because [insert reason here].*

Here's a continuation from the interviewing.io example we started above.

> I needed to work with our ops team to figure out exactly how to automate interviewer prioritization, build it, and roll it out smoothly. They also needed a dashboard which allowed override the prioritization as needed.

It is vital to your interview performance that the *task* part is clear. If your interviewer doesn't understand what your specific task was, everything else falls apart because your actions won't make a lot of sense.

Probably the biggest failure mode for describing the task or project is either glossing over the task *or* spending so much time explaining it that your interviewer loses track of the problem. There is nothing wrong with using the specific phrase, "My task was to …" to make it extremely clear to your interviewer.

Interview Replays

Excellent Task Replays

UNPOPULAR DECISION	INTERVIEW REPLAY

View Online:	bctci.co/behavioral-communication-replay-6 @ 3:03-6:25
The Question:	Tell me about a time you made an unpopular decision and how you handled the feedback that it was unpopular.
What You'll See:	The candidate clearly stated what the task was: implementing a webhook listener for a Docusign microservice. They explained what the original design was and why they disagreed with it.
Role:	Software Engineer at JPMorgan Chase
Who:	**Interviewer**: Staff Software Engineer at a FAANG+ company **Candidate**: 3 years of experience
Outcome:	The candidate got the job at JPMorgan Chase!

CURRENT ROLE AND PROJECT	INTERVIEW REPLAY

View Online:	bctci.co/behavioral-communication-replay-7 @ 15:25 -16:50
The Question:	Tell me about your current role and project.
What You'll See:	The candidate did a great job of concisely and systematically listing the three tasks that comprised their project and of setting up the Situation in the first few minutes.
Role:	Senior/Staff role at a FAANG+ company or mid-sized startup
Who:	*Interviewer*: Senior Manager at Amazon *Candidate*: 8 years of experience, Senior SWE at Google
Outcome:	The candidate landed a Principal Engineer role at a mid-sized startup!

Poor Task Replays

DISAGREEING WITH YOUR TEAM	INTERVIEW REPLAY

View Online:	bctci.co/behavioral-communication-replay-8 @ 10:25-20:08
The Question:	Tell me about a time when you didn't agree with a decision made by your team.
What You'll See:	The candidate's team was building a gun detection model for schools. The candidate did not go into enough technical detail to justify why their approach was superior to their teammate's. As a team leader, this reflected poorly on both their technical communication and leadership abilities.
Role:	E5 at Meta
Who:	*Interviewer*: Senior Software Engineer at Amazon and Meta *Candidate*: 15 years of experience
Outcome:	The candidate got the job at Meta!

▶ **NOVEL APPROACH TO A PROBLEM**	INTERVIEW REPLAY

View Online: bctci.co/behavioral-communication-replay-9 @ 6:19-end

The Question: Tell me about a time where you proposed a novel approach to a problem.

What You'll See: The candidate didn't use the STAR format and blended their Task and Action together, which made it hard for them to explain their solution and why it was novel.

Role: E5 at Meta or Snap

Who: *Interviewer*: Principal Software Engineer at Amazon
Candidate: 9 years of experience, Software Engineer at Pinterest

Outcome: The candidate got the job at Meta!

ACTION

What It Is

The Action is what you actually did; *how* you solved the problem as well as your individual contributions to the solution if you were working in a team.

> {Break down your actions into several components. This might be different phases of the project, different steps, different attempts, different challenges, etc. Usually about three pieces is a good goal.}

Let's look at the above, again through the lens of the interviewing.io AI Interviewer project. Here we'll write as if we're the lead engineer on the project.

> In the early stages of analysis and design, we identified the key inputs for prioritization:
>
> • Scores: How candidates rate this interviewer, plus how well calibrated the interviewer is
> • Utilization: How frequently are they being booked
>
> One of the things that made it tricky was that there were lots of edge cases, such as:
>
> • Making sure new interviewers get booked for their trial interviews, even though they don't have scores
> • Good interviewers sometimes not having an accurate score, even after two trial interviews
> • Allowing the ops team to override the algorithm as needed, based on their best judgment
>
> With all of this in mind, I implemented a custom prioritization algorithm that buckets interviewers by their score, and then sorts within those buckets based on utilization, while accounting for the special cases I just mentioned.
>
> This involved several complex MongoDB aggregations, functional JavaScript to map and transform data structures for efficient processing and also to transfer over the network to the client application.
>
> I also implemented asynchronous pre-caching of interview time slots as users arrive at the site; this reduced latency when users viewed the dashboard. Building this plus the appropriate cache-eviction routines used RabbitMQ for queueing and Redis as a key-value store.
>
> Finally, the ops team needed transparency into how the system was working and the ability to override it, so I built some internal observability tooling and reporting. This included porting our Metabase dashboard to our admin site (which relied on in-app data rather than SQL logic) and a colorized heatmap of how interviewers are prioritized in real time. This gave the ops team enough information to be able to override the machine when needed.

In a real interview, your interviewer may ask you follow-up questions which could dive into technical trade-offs, interpersonal challenges, or many other topics. The above example is meant to be illustrative but not meant to cover everything that would be discussed.

Interview Replays

Excellent Action Replays

TWO TEAMS IN CONFLICT INTERVIEW REPLAY

View Online:	bctci.co/behavioral-communication-replay-10 @ 16:10-20:41
The Question:	Tell me about a time when two teams couldn't agree on a path forward.
What You'll See:	The candidate discussed a conflict between two teams at Square. They broke up their answer into two buckets: short-term actions and long-term actions and explained both clearly, at the right level of detail.
Role:	L7 at Meta
Who:	*Interviewer*: Senior Staff Software Engineer at Meta *Candidate*: 18 years of experience, Staff Software Engineer at Airbnb
Outcome:	"I completely choked in my Meta interview. I've never had that happen before. I think I just wanted it too badly and got too nervous. A few months later I interviewed at Airbnb for a senior staff role (basically the same as L7 at Meta) and I'm here now!"

OPPORTUNITY TO DO SOMETHING BETTER INTERVIEW REPLAY

View Online:	bctci.co/behavioral-communication-replay-11 @ 8:50-18:00
The Question:	Tell me about a time when you were working on an initiative or goal and saw an opportunity to do something much bigger or better.
What You'll See:	The candidate effectively described automating copyright headers across repos, balancing technical details with team dynamics and showing good judgment in pushing for a long-term automated solution over a quick fix.
Role:	Infrastructure Engineer at OpenAI (L5-equivalent)
Who:	*Interviewer*: Engineering Manager at Amazon *Candidate*: 10 years of experience, Eng Manager at a FAANG+ company
Outcome:	"I ultimately did not receive an offer (the recruiter told me it was specifically my DS&A/programming round that cost me), but I did hear very positive feedback that both my system design rounds and cross-functional onsite rounds (the ones I prepped for in the replay) were highlights in the hiring panel discussion."

Poor Action Replays

WRONG RATIO OF TECHNICAL DETAILS TO PEOPLE DETAILS INTERVIEW REPLAY

View Online:	bctci.co/behavioral-communication-replay-12 @ 0:00-end
The Question:	Describe a major disagreement you had at work
What You'll See:	The candidate showed strong technical depth discussing hardware design tools they built, but struggled to address the interpersonal aspects of the behavioral question.
Role:	Staff-level individual contributor role
Who:	*Interviewer*: Senior Engineering Manager at a FAANG+ company *Candidate*: 18 years of experience

▶	**A RECENT PROJECT**	INTERVIEW REPLAY

View Online:	bctci.co/behavioral-communication-replay-13 @ 12:56-25:45
The Question:	Tell me about a recent project.
What You'll See:	The candidate talked about leading a project to automate the payments platform at a startup. Though the Situation and Task portions were good, the Action portion was missing entirely. At 14:45, the interviewer called that out. Listen to the rest of the interviewer's feedback, too, because the interviewer went on to explain how to apply the STAR method at 20:50.
Role:	Software Engineer at Google
Who:	*Interviewer*: Senior Software Engineer at FAANG+ *Candidate*: 3 years of experience
Outcome:	This was the first behavioral interview the candidate had ever done. After refining their stories, they were able to get the job at Google!

RESULT

What It Is

This is the part where you talk about what happened after you did the Task. Did it succeed or fail? How did you define success or failure? What happened next? How did you and the team grow from this experience? What was the overall impact on the business?

> For this project, we defined success as:
>
> - Better user experience — increase our average interviewer score by at least 10%.
> - New interviewers getting onboarded faster — we wanted to cut that down by at least 30%.
> - Reduce interviewer complaints about not getting matched down to zero.
> - Less ops time spent on manual quality control
>
> We're still tracking these metrics because the feature shipped fairly recently, but so far:
>
> - Average interviewer score is up by 12%
> - Onboarding time is TBD because not enough time has passed to measure it.
> - Interviewer complaints have decreased by over 90%.
> - Ops is spending no time on manual quality control
>
> All in all it's been a huge success.

Regardless of your seniority level, you should be prepared to be more introspective. What could you have done better, even if the project was a success? How did this experience change you for the better?

For more senior roles, you should be prepared to also discuss what you will do moving forward to make your whole team more effective next time. It's also important to show your grasp of business impact. What did you learn from this project that you can use to make not just your team, but the whole product, better?

Interview Replays

Excellent Result Replays

DEALING WITH FAILURE	INTERVIEW REPLAY

View Online: bctci.co/behavioral-communication-replay-14 @ 45:00 - 54:23

The Question: Tell me about a time when you failed.

What You'll See: This is a great example of a different kind of answer for the Result portion, because it's about personal growth rather than metrics. Talking about personal growth is ok in a behavioral interview, but when in doubt, ask your interviewer about what kind of answer they're looking for (which is exactly what this candidate did).

Role: E4/E5 at Meta

Who: *Interviewer*: Senior Software Engineer at Meta
Candidate: 2 years of experience

Outcome: The candidate got the job at Meta (E4)!

SEEING A BIGGER OPPORTUNITY THAN PLANNED	INTERVIEW REPLAY

View Online: bctci.co/behavioral-communication-replay-15 @ 21:35-29:14

The Question: Tell me about a time that you saw the opportunity to do something bigger than originally planned.

What You'll See: The candidate talked about moving from a monolith to a distributed architecture. Their whole answer is quite good, but the Result portion starts at 28:34. They covered what this move unlocked and quantified the performance improvement (over 10X in this case).

Role: L6 at Meta

Who: *Interviewer*: Senior Engineering Manager at Amazon
Candidate: 11 years of experience

Outcome: "I did not receive an offer from Meta after my onsite. In hindsight, I made a pretty glaring mistake in one of the system design interviews that I'm still kicking myself over."

Poor Result Replays

NO METRICS	INTERVIEW REPLAY

View Online: bctci.co/behavioral-communication-replay-16 @ 5:00 - 18:32

The Question: What's your proudest professional accomplishment?

What You'll See: The candidate failed because they didn't include metrics in their answer, but there were a few other issues— they didn't pick a story that was recent enough, and they didn't make their accomplishments sound impressive enough (even though they were quite impressive!).

Role: L5 at Google

Who: *Interviewer*: VP of Engineering at a large startup
Candidate: 14 years of experience

Outcome: The candidate got the job at Google!

| DISAGREEMENT WITH MANAGER | INTERVIEW REPLAY |

View Online:	bctci.co/behavioral-communication-replay-17 @ 11:58-30:34
The Question:	Tell me about a time that you disagreed with your manager.
What You'll See:	Despite strong content about implementing Smithy at Disney Streaming, the candidate strayed from STAR format and needed interviewer prompting to clarify their story. Though the project had real impact, their muddled delivery prevented them from effectively conveying its value.
Role:	E4/E5 at Meta
Who:	*Interviewer*: Senior Software Engineer at Microsoft *Candidate*: 12 years of experience
Outcome:	The candidate did not get the job at Meta.

PREPARING AND PRACTICING

When we discussed the Behavioral Signal Matrix (pg 149) and the Behavioral Category Matrix (pg 148), you selected (at least) five stories and three projects. Now it's time to practice these. Before you dive in and just *speak*, we recommend you stop and diagram your stories into—yes—another matrix.

BEHAVIORAL ANSWER MATRIX

For each project or story, fill in the cells below. For now at least, just use bullets / keywords. Don't write out the story word-for-word.

Access this spreadsheet at bctci.co/behavioral-communication-resource-1

	ANSWER 1	ANSWER 2
Situation	Inconsistent crashing, usually during peak hours. Couldn't repro in test.	Requests for dark mode. Hard b/c legacy codebase didn't support dynamic themes
Task	Fix bug ASAP. Added pressure from holiday season.	Make dark mode; ensure compatibility; time constraints
Action(s)	Analyze logs Rapid rearchitecture Bigger rebuild later	Reviewed codebase Create theme manage system Collab with QA +UX for testing framework
Result	Stable for future. Sales up 15% Improved automation for future	Launched on schedule 40% adoption Became basis for future work
Signals	Technical competence Finding compromises Prioritization	Thoroughness Technical competence Collaboration
Learnings/Improvements	Proactive testing	Consult earlier engineers earlier on

You might notice two things added: signal(s) and the learnings/improvements.

- **Signal:** What does this story or project say about you? Make a list of what possible signals might be demonstrated from each project. Depending on the specific question, you might tweak your response in a live interview to focus more on specific aspects. (pg 141 for more information on Signal).

- **Learnings/Improvements:** Because it's so common for interviewers to ask you either what did you learn or what would you change for next time, it's worth it to be prepared for these follow-ups.

If your interview is remote, you can consider having these notes in front of you during the interview. However, be careful that they are actually useful and don't become a distraction.

PRACTICING

For most people, just diagramming your answer with bullets will be sufficient. Writing out each word in the story is a waste of time *and* can lead to you getting too stuck on specific wording rather than adjusting based on the specific question.

Time Yourself

At a very minimum, practice your answers out loud—not just in your head. Once you talk out loud, you might discover that a project you thought was the perfect candidate for behavioral interviews doesn't actually work well.

Use a timer to ensure you don't speak too long (a good target is about three or four minutes per question).

Even better is to record yourself. This way, if you aren't sure how on earth you spoke for nine minutes, you can go through the recording and figure out where you went wrong.

Use a Practice Partner

Once you're ready to practice with a human, don't just run through stories, one after another, with your practice partner. That's not how it works in real interviews, right?

Instead, have your practice partner ask the questions *they* think they should ask. Some of them won't perfectly match any story you have. Yep, that's just how it goes in real interviews too.

Once they've asked the questions they know of, then go through the rest of your stories that you haven't used yet. It's a little artificial to do things that way, but it's better than *not* practicing a story.

As you practice these stories:

- **Allow your partner to interrupt you if needed.** Hopefully, your story shouldn't *need* interruption, but if it does, it does. Your partner should interrupt you to clarify details, ask why certain metrics were the right ones, and what you would have done if some crucial detail had actually turned out differently.
- **Encourage follow-up questions.** If your partner can think of follow-up questions, they should ask them. Your goal is to get practice for a real interview.
- **Ask your partner...**
  - » if they're convinced that the project would not have been possible without you
  - » if you provided enough supporting details
  - » if your answers were crisp
  - » if they're convinced that if you were in a similar circumstance in the future, that you would have done it better. If they say yes, ask them why, and make sure their answer is believable.
  - » What they learned about you

If your partner is comfortable with it, we encourage you to record these mock sessions as well. If nothing else, knowing how long you spoke for can be very valuable information.

MORE INTERVIEW REPLAYS

▶ More behavioral mock interviews at bctci.co/behavioral-communication-replay-bonus.

PRINCIPLES OF CODING INTERVIEWS

PART VI

Watch for these speech-bubble icons, which mean there is online content.

✦ **AI Interviewer:** Each problem can be tried online with the AI Interviewer.

▶ **Interview Replay:** Recordings of actual mock interviews.

🗋 **Snippet:** Material to copy/paste online, including email templates and code recipes.

🗗 **Resource:** Bonus chapters, worksheets, and other material.

PRINCIPLES OF CODING INTERVIEWS

This chart represents how we see the landscape of interview questions:

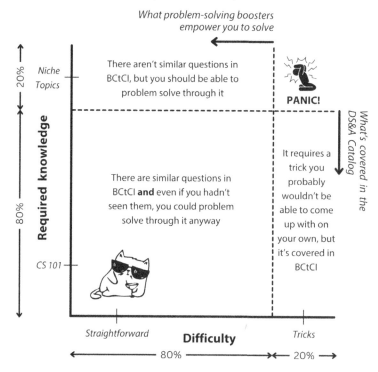

Figure 1. Landscape of Interview Questions, for someone who prepares with BCtCl.

Our goal with this book is twofold:

1. Teach you the 80% most common topics and ideas used in interview problems. That's what Part VII: The Catalog of Technical Topics, is all about. The remaining 20% are *niche topics*.

2. Teach you problem-solving strategies so you can figure out 80% of questions on your own, even if you haven't seen the idea before. This is what the *problem-solving boosters* (Chapter 24: Problem-Solving Boosters, pg 248) are for. The remaining 20% of questions rely on *tricks* (ideas that are really hard to come up with on your own if you haven't seen them before).[1]

Combining these two, after going through the book, you should be able to tackle all but 20% * 20% = 4% of questions, which are those based on niche topics *and* requiring tricks. But if that happens, you've been truly unlucky.

THE PRINCIPLES AND THE CATALOG

Besides solving problems, we want to help you practice effectively and know how to navigate an interview setting. This is covered in Part VI: Principles of Coding Interviews (pg 166). It includes:

- **Study Plan:** A detailed study plan for how to practice using this book's materials.
- **Universal Rubric:** How you're evaluated by interviewers.
- **Interview Checklist**: Breaking down each step you should take in a coding interview.
- **Big-O Analysis:** In-depth coverage of the "language" of technical interviews.
- **Problem-Solving Strategies:** Boundary thinking, trigger thinking, and problem-solving boosters.

The second part is a **Catalog** of data structures and algorithms topics. We've broken the technical topics into tiers, with Tier 1 being the highest priority.

- **Tier 1:** Essential topics from sets & maps to trees and graphs.
- **Tier 2:** Intermediate topics like heaps, sliding windows, and prefix sums.
- **Tier 3:** Niche (online-only) topics that didn't warrant a spot in the physical book because they don't come up that often (this is where we enter the niche 20% territory). The online-only chapters can be found at bctci.co/bonus.

Chapter 18: How to Practice (pg 170) should be your entry point to the rest of the book.

TOPICS, RECIPES, AND REUSABLE IDEAS

There are three related concepts you'll find as you peruse the Catalog: topics, reusable ideas, and recipes. Here's a quick definition to keep them straight:

- **Topic:** A chapter from the Catalog, like Binary Search.
- **Reusable Idea**: A coding idea that can typically be used across problems (and even across topics). They are tactical tips worth remembering, such as "pass indices, not strings in recursive code to avoid using extra space." You'll typically find them next to the first problem where they are used (look for the ♻ icon).
- **Coding Recipe:** A pseudo-code template related to a specific topic that can be used as a building block to solve similar problems with small tweaks.

Questions, comments, or bugs? Report bugs at bctci.co/bugs or geek out with the authors on Discord: bctci.co/discord.

---

1   Our mantra? If you encounter something once, it's a trick; if you encounter it repeatedly, it's a tool.

HOW TO PRACTICE

AI interviewer, replays, and more materials for this chapter at bctci.co/how-to-practice

> Plans are useless, but planning is indispensable.
>
> Dwight D. Eisenhower

In Managing Your Job Search (pg 82), we outlined a timeline that covers the entire job search: outreach, recruiter management and scheduling, studying, and doing actual interviews. In this chapter, we'll zoom in on the "studying" part.

We'll propose a study plan for coding interviews with two phases:

Phase 1:   Learn the topics from the Catalog.

Phase 2:   Interview simulation.

This plan focuses on how to practice coding interviews, but we will address how to study for other types of interviews, like system design, at the end of this chapter.

THE CATALOG OF TECHNICAL TOPICS

The Catalog Part of the book (pg 280) contains all the topics you may need for interviews, separated into three tiers.

- Tier 1 topics are foundational and typically should be covered before diving into harder topics.
- Tier 2 topics occur commonly in interviews but might require prerequisite knowledge.
- Tier 3 is all extra credit and is only for if you have time and want the extra breadth. You can find some of them online at bctci.co/bonus (with more to come!)

The question we tackle in this chapter is: How should you approach learning all these topics?

Let's start with the main tools you'll use to prepare for coding interviews.

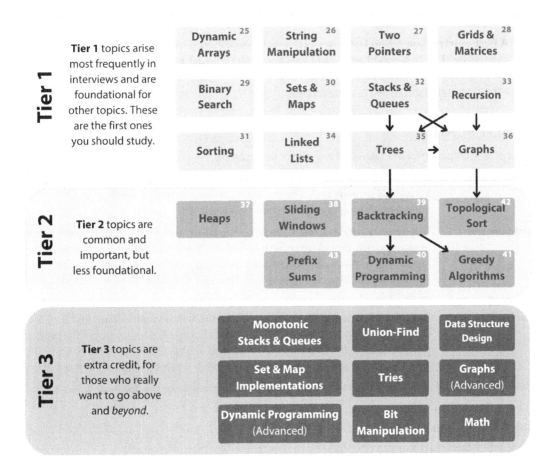

Figure 1. Catalog chapters. Topic prerequisites are indicated with arrows.

☑ STUDY TOOLS

Here are all the things you may need to prepare effectively:[1]

- **Learning Materials**: That includes this book and any other resources you find helpful to learn data structures and algorithms for interviews.

- **Practice Problems**: Many websites offer curated lists, but we find the best practice mimics an actual interview. To help with that, we created an AI Interviewer where you can practice the problems from the book: bctci.co/online.

- **Interview Checklist**: It's good to know the steps to follow in an interview. We explained our proposed *Interview Checklist* on page 190.

- **Cheat Sheet**: A place to collect crucial information personalized to what **you** struggle to remember. It could include tricky custom comparator syntax, code recipes, and actionable tips. Download our template at bctci.co/interview-cheat-sheet.

---

1 Even though we tried to provide every tool you need, you don't have to use *ours*. Any version of these tools should help your practice.

- **Mock Interviews**: Nothing reveals communication blind spots better than a mock interview. Whether you work with a professional coach or a study partner, the goal is to improve clarity, time management, and comfort in the interview setting. Don't overlook this powerful tool!
- **A Post-mortem Log & Bug List**: After each practice question, we recommend completing a post-mortem (pg 174) to pinpoint what went well and what could use improvement. Common mistakes will surface over time, which can be added to a *bug list* for heightened awareness. Check out templates at bctci.co/post-mortem and bctci.co/bug-list.

STUDY PLAN

Most people preparing for interviews fall into one of three camps:

Marathoners: This camp follows a consistent routine, often setting goals like "solve one question a day." This strategy builds strong habits and consistency over time, but it can take unnecessarily long to reach interview readiness.

List hunters: This group gravitates toward "magic question lists," believing that doing a curated list of questions will provide them with everything they need for interviews. While this can expose you to the most popular questions, it puts the emphasis on the wrong thing. It's more important to learn reusable techniques that improve your problem-solving skills.

Pattern matchers: This last camp attempts to categorize all questions into solution "patterns." The idea is that if they memorize the patterns, they'll be able to solve any question. The problem with this approach is that they use patterns as a substitute for *understanding*, so they get rusty quickly and struggle when faced with problems outside of familiar patterns.

Our study plan balances the best of all three camps while guarding you from the downsides:

- Consistent but effective practice.
- Curated questions contextualized in broader strategies.
- Code recipes that focus on understanding the concepts rather than memorizing.

We hope you like it!

PHASE 1: LEARN THE TOPICS

Before we even start

Before studying topics in our Catalog, we strongly encourage you to:

1. **Review Big O Analysis (pg 206)**: shakiness on this topic will have a downstream negative impact on your studying.
2. **Skim the remaining Principles chapters:** these chapters (How You Are Evaluated, Anatomy of a Coding Interview, Boundary Thinking, Trigger Thinking, and Problem-Solving Boosters) are all about how to apply the knowledge from the Catalog topics to interviews. You'll probably want to take a deeper dive *after* learning the basic Catalog topics, but skimming them now will give you a sense of the big picture and what you are building toward.
3. **Plan your study timeline in Managing Your Job Search (pg 78)**: it is foolish to wait until you're "interview ready" to start applying to companies. Don't get stuck in study purgatory. Once you get your foot in the door, we'll teach you how to slow down and speed up to accommodate your studying (pg 88).

Topic order

Now that you've done these preliminary steps, you can start learning topics from Figure 1. The book chapter order is a valid order for reviewing the topics, but you can start at any topic that either doesn't have arrows going into it, or you're confident in your skills with the incoming arrow topic.[2] Tier-1 topics are foundational and should typically be prioritized. Tier-2 topics occur commonly in interviews but might require pre-requisite knowledge. Tier 3 is all extra credit and is only for if you have time and want the extra breadth.

How many topics you study will depend on your overall job search timeline and how new these topics are to you. Try to learn as many topics as your timeline allows for—at least up through the end of Tier 2.

> ### "Why didn't you include topic <x> on this list?"
>
> Let's address this common objection right away. Our topic list is based on a careful analysis of question frequency and topic difficulty across interviewers on interviewing.io, who represent a non-trivial sample of FAANG+ engineers.
>
> That's not to say other topics don't show up—of course they do—but when they occur, you've encountered some bad luck. With the release of this book, you'll find three Tier-3 topics on this diagram. These topics were too niche to put in the book, but if you're shooting for every advantage you can get, they are available to learn as online-only resources available in the bonus section at bctci.co/bonus. More online-only materials will continue to be released for these extra-credit topics—you can check our update-to-date change log at bctci.co/changelog.
>
> For now, just know that learning past the Tier-2 topics has a steep drop in the return on your time invested. Manage your time wisely, and don't make the classic mistake of practicing too much at the expense of outreach.

How to learn a topic

Each chapter in the book has practice problems we recommend attempting as you read. After you have made it through a chapter and completed the chapter questions, we will consider the topic "learned" (but probably not quite mastered). From that point on, it's important to periodically practice questions from that topic so we don't get rusty. That's where *interleaved practice* comes in.

Interleaved Practice

Some people prefer to practice one topic at a time until they master it before moving on to the next one. The issue with this approach is that (1) this eliminates the step in a real interview of "figuring out the topic," and (2) you'll start to get rusty with the earlier topics.

We recommend splitting your study sessions into two types:

- **Learning a topic:** This is where you read a chapter and do the corresponding problems. Dedicated practice as you go through a chapter for the first time is encouraged to solidify the concepts.
- **Interleaved practice:** This is where you practice interview problems picked randomly from all the topics you have learned so far. As you learn more topics, the variety of questions during interleaved practice will grow, getting closer to the real interview setting, and you'll keep revisiting older topics, making sure you don't get rusty.[3]

---

2 Yes, we've arranged your learnings in topological order. How clever of us. ☺

3 Watch out! Anecdotally, interleaved practice tends to **feel harder** (and even less productive) than working through one topic at a time because it doesn't let you get comfortable with a single topic before moving on to the next. It's still worth it.

While focusing on one topic at a time *feels* more efficient, we have some decent evidence to support the idea of *interleaved* practice as a superior study method.[4]

We have built our AI interviewer at <u>bctci.co/ai</u> with interleaved practice in mind. It allows you to select the topics you have already learned, and then it will select a random question from those topics for you. It probably makes sense to use this randomized "shuffle mode" once you've learned 4–5 topics (we don't recommend adding topics you haven't learned yet).

How to do a practice problem effectively

> At some point, the learning stops and the pain begins.
>
> S. Rao Kosaraju, inventor of Kosaraju's algorithm[5]

You can do all the problems in the book online at bctci.co.[6] Whether you are doing a problem from the book or interleaved practice, this is our advice to practice effectively during this phase:

- **Don't fixate on time spent per question.** Time management matters, but not in this phase. We never recommend spending more than one hour per problem, but don't worry if you use a full hour on a problem—we'll work on speed in Phase 2.
- **Focus on the idea, not the code.** Stuck with a bug? Use an AI chatbot to help you find it (and explain it). This isn't the time to get hung up on the little things.
- **Feel free to skip extra-credit sections.** These sections start with 'Extra Credit' and can be seen as Tier-3 subtopics within more basic topics.
- **Don't neglect post-mortems.**

Post-mortems: How & Why

If you're like most people, once you're done with an interview question, you move on to the next one. This is a missed opportunity. Finishing a question is where the long-term learning *starts*. We can maximize the value of practicing each question if we take a few minutes to fill out a post-mortem log reflecting on how we did.

The most important post-mortem questions are:

- What could I have done differently?
- What mistakes do I keep making, and how can I adjust my workflow to address them?
- Is there anything I should add to my cheat sheet?

Post-mortems are tempting to skip because they take effort. Vague answers like "I should debug faster" or "I'm bad at graphs" won't lead to improvement. You have to actually dig deep to identify *actionable* takeaways.

Doing post-mortems isn't reserved for problems you did poorly on, either. Whether you solved the problem or not, reviewing your approach can reveal missed solutions and possible optimizations. Whatever you do, don't skip your post-mortem! See example on page 631.

---

4   The studies and experiments are described in detail in the book, Make it Stick: The Science of Successful Learning. Though the exact mechanism is not well understood, interleaving likely forces you to think more critically since you can't predict the type of question you'll face next. This holds across various fields like music, sports, language, art, and design.

5   This has been attributed to S. Rao Kosaraju (who invented an algorithm for finding strongly connected components in directed graphs) and is a popular saying at Johns Hopkins University.

6   You can find any problem using the short link: <u>bctci.co/problem-name</u>

PHASE 2: INTERVIEW SIMULATION

We can't overstate this point: the biggest mistake that we see candidates make when preparing for interviews is grinding away at online problems alone for extended periods of time. Yes, learning the material is critical, and some time spent grinding alone is necessary, but it is not sufficient. So, at some point, when you've learned a good chunk of topics in Phase 1, it is time to move to Phase 2: interview simulation (you can still continue to learn new topics, but you need to balance the two phases).

Interviewing requires a different approach in how you communicate, code, and test your solution. Simply solving problems isn't enough. Therefore, in Phase 2, we want to keep doing interleaved practice, but this time, we want to practice under conditions as close as possible to the real thing.

How do you simulate the interview setting when you do a practice problem?

- Practice following the **Interview Checklist** (pg 190) that you will use on a real interview. Make sure to go through all the steps to internalize them.
- Manage time as if you were in an interview. That means you should aim to solve the question in 45 minutes.
- During post-mortems, evaluate yourself as an interviewer would, in terms of every category in the **Universal Rubric** (pg 170): problem-solving, coding, verification, and communication (more on communication in a second).[7] Reflect on the kind of *signal* you would have given an interviewer.

Of course, the most distinctive aspect of the interview setting is *doing the problem in front of someone*. This is why Phase 2 is split into *solo practice* and *mock interviews*.

\#   The beginning of Phase 2 is the best time to review the Principles chapters (pg 166) more in-depth.

Mock interviews

A mock interview means practicing with someone acting as the interviewer. As we saw in *Mindset and the Numbers Game*, there's a "tipping point" at five interviews—once you get five interviews under your belt, you're anywhere from 1.5X to almost 2X as likely to pass your next interview (pg 40).

Whether you do your mocks with a professional interviewer, a study partner,[8] or a friend who is an engineer, get in those reps!

The trick is making sure that each mock interview is with a competent engineer who is willing to stay engaged, attentive, and willing to give you critical feedback without coddling you. That means your mom doesn't count.[9]

Mock interviews are the best way to improve your communication skills (pg 186). They also help you get rid of coding jitters, identify your personal blind spots, and get a sense of what it's most important for you to work on.

Solo practice

Of course, it's not realistic to spend all your time doing mock interviews, so most of your study time will probably still be on your own. What matters is following the outlined steps to simulate the interview setting as you do interleaved practice.

---

7   In Chapter 19: How You Are Evaluated (pg 180), we give examples of the types of questions interviewers fill out after an interview.

8   Switching sides and acting as the interviewer for your study partner can also be a really insightful experience.

9   Unless of course your mom is an engineer who won't hold back the punches, in which case, rock on mom. Rock on.

If speed is your weakness (it often is), start using a timer to monitor how long it takes you to (1) design the algorithm, and (2) implement it. These two measurements will help dictate what areas to focus on (problem solving vs. coding). See our suggestions on improving speed on page 186.

As you become more skilled, you can increase the difficulty by:

- Including hard problems in your interleaved practice.
- Limiting the time to 30 minutes (or two problems in an hour). This will test your speed.
- Running the code at the end, with the goal that it works on the first try. This will test your verification skills (pg 184).

Furthermore, you can still work on the communication aspect during solo practice.

- Try recording yourself solving problems.
- Try working with an AI chatbot (our AI Interviewer or any AI tool of your choice) and chatting with it as if it were a real interviewer.

Realistically, most candidates will get a job learning all the topics and doing everything in this study plan. That's a good thing! We just want to make sure you always know what to work on to keep improving.[10]

STUDY PLAN TIPS

Now that you understand the plan, here is a concise list of tips.

SCHEDULING AND TIME MANAGEMENT TIPS

- **No cramming!** A plan that requires you to cram many hours of studying into a single-day session is ineffective. To enhance retention, spread your practice over shorter, more frequent sessions—like one hour daily. While it's easier said than done, most people realize that cramming hampers retention.
- **Plan for your worst week.** To create a sustainable study plan, base it on what you can accomplish during your worst weeks, not ideal weeks. Assuming that there will be no hiccups is unrealistic and will make it hard to sustain your study plan. The less demanding the plan, the longer you'll stick with it.
- **Plan with your willpower in mind.** Plan your practice at the time of day when your willpower is strongest. If you're exhausted at the end of the day, you're less likely to follow through on practicing at that time. The best time will be individual to you.
- **Schedule time to practice.** "If it's not in your calendar, it doesn't exist." You're not likely to stumble your way into studying interview questions. It takes intentionality and forethought. Treat it as a mandatory meeting with yourself to help build a self-reinforcing habit.
- **Try speedsolving.** If you're short on time on a given day but still want to get some practice in, skip coding and spend 10–15 minutes per problem focusing on designing the algorithm.
- **Schedule the inputs, not the outcomes.** It's tempting to put things like "Learn dynamic programming" or "Solve five questions" in a time slot, but we can't control these outcomes. The only thing we control is the time scheduled for them. Instead of focusing on an uncontrollable outcome like those above, we recommend focusing on controllable inputs such as, "Spend an hour learning about dynamic programming" and "Do an hour of interview question practice." It's easier to achieve, avoids frustration, and still helps you move forward.

---

10   What about *after* you get the job? We recommend doing a practice problem from time to time so you don't get rusty. We call this the *maintenance phase*, and it helps you stay competitive in case anything happens with your current job. However, you don't need to start immediately—you definitely earned a break.

- **Declare an endpoint.** Like diets and financial budgets, practice plans are easier to stick to when you know when they will end. Practice plans longer than four months are usually abandoned, so we recommend a two to three month duration for most people. This ties into your overall job search timeline (pg 78).

EFFECTIVE STUDY TIPS FOR PRACTICE

- **Use active learning.** Active learning is when you take part in the action. Every problem in the book can be *read*, but it can also be *attempted*, and the latter is way more important. Even things like rereading and highlighting are not as effective. Don't just read this book, do this book!
- **Embrace deliberate practice.** Instead of repeating questions or grinding even more problems, use each problem to deliberately identify and refine weak points with the help of your *cheat sheet*, *bug list*, and *post-mortem logs* (pg 171).
- **Seek challenge over question counts.** Harder problems often give more "bang for your buck." Don't just stick with medium-difficulty questions because someone online said that "they are most likely to be asked." The exact question difficulty doesn't matter as much as constantly challenging yourself and learning something from it. Just stick to a one-hour maximum timebox, even for hard problems, so you don't waste too much time on any single question.
- **Leverage AI chatbots (wisely).** You can ask for hints, confirm you're on the right track, verify solution approaches, or get test cases. Just remember their limitations.
- **Suffering is optional.** Engineers often face a kind of hazing when preparing for interviews, being told they're bad coders if they can't solve problems on their own. This is nonsense. You learn by understanding the solution. It isn't based on the number of hours you spent not understanding it. Give it an honest effort, but timebox yourself to one hour, and then move on.
- **Generate multiple interview solutions.** Even if you find an optimal approach immediately, push yourself to find other valid solutions. Instead of just trying to find any solution, reframe success as finding all valid solutions to a problem.
- **Respect time limits.** Spend up to 20 minutes designing the algorithm and up to one hour total. If you can't finish either portion in time, consult a hint or solution and do a thorough post-mortem.

HOW TO PRACTICE SYSTEM DESIGN

System design interviews are a different type of interview altogether. While they don't tend to require first-hand experience with distributed systems, they do require a breadth of knowledge about them, and it would be impossible to cover it in the book.

Thankfully, some great resources already exist on this topic. We heartily recommend reading Designing Data-Intensive Applications (Martin Kleppmann and Chris Riccomini) and checking out interviewing.io's senior engineering guide on designing distributed systems (bctci.co/system-design). Retention plays a larger role in these interviews, so be sure you're reading, understanding, and retaining the information you study.

As for studying, your two main tools are (1) mock interviews with senior engineers and (2) mock interviews with an AI chatbot. While our AI Interviewer handles coding interviews, it doesn't do system design. Any standard AI chatbot can help you perform a mock interview with a prompt similar to the following (just be aware of their limitations):

> As a senior/staff engineer, you are conducting a system design interview.

> Your task is to guide the candidate through a popular system design question in a step-by-step manner. Follow the structure below for the interview:

1. Question Selection: Choose a popular system design question to ask.

2. Requirements: Discuss both functional and non-functional requirements.

3. High-Level Design: Guide the candidate to create a high-level design.

4. Detailed Design: Go into more detailed components such as data flows, APIs, storage, etc.

5. Scaling Considerations: Address scalability and performance optimization.

6. Conclusion: Summarize the design and provide feedback or suggestions for improvement.

Please start by selecting a popular system design question to ask.

CHOOSING A PROGRAMMING LANGUAGE

Most Big Tech companies let you choose which language to interview in. You should pick one upfront and do all your practice in that language, which is not necessarily the one you know best. So, which one?

Our best advice is to optimize for two things:

Optimization 1:   The language that you're most comfortable in. If you're not sure, ask yourself which language you can easily do the following in, without having to look anything up:

- Instantiate a hash table and find a key in it.

- Know whether strings in your language of choice are immutable or not.

- Sort using a custom comparator.

Optimization 2:   The language that makes it easiest for you to use common interview data structures (e.g., hash sets/maps, binary trees, heaps, etc).

For many people, that language will be Python. If that's your weapon of choice, one word of caution (and this warning holds for JavaScript as well). Some interviewers may expect you that if you choose one of these languages, you'll be very well-versed in idiomatic syntax, even if your code works otherwise. We don't agree with this approach, but we've seen it enough that we'd be remiss if we didn't call it out.[11]

One final word of warning about Python. Because it's so readable and because it's so easy to access and use common data structures, with many of the implementation details completely abstracted away, some Python engineers get complacent about time and space complexity. Not all interviewees have this bias, but we've seen some interviewers who tend to come down harder on Python users about how their actual code works under the hood.[12] Though we advise everyone to build a solid understanding of big O analysis, if your language of choice hides low-level details like pointers or memory allocation, make extra sure that big O isn't your Achilles heel.

---

11   The code in this book is in Python. However, we avoid Python-specific syntax like *list comprehensions* because we want to make this book readable for everyone. This means that our Python is not the most idiomatic, because it wouldn't translate well to other languages. If you code in Python, write better code than ours!

12   In one particularly poignant example, an interviewer on the IO platform was drinking a glass of water while his candidate muddled through traversing an array of integers in Python. At some point, the candidate assured the interviewer that checking if an element was in the array took constant time... at which point you can hear the glass breaking. We asked the interviewer what happened, and he told us he crushed it in a rage, not at the candidate, per se, but at Python for abstracting so much from the end user that they no longer had a feel for how anything worked (you can learn how arrays work under the hood in Chapter 25: Dynamic Arrays (pg 282).

STRESS DURING INTERVIEWS AND THE LIMITATIONS OF MORE PRACTICE   INTERVIEW REPLAY

View Online: https://bctci.co/how-to-practice-replay-1 @ 57:30 - end

The Question: How do I deal with stress during my Google coding interview?

What You'll See: The audio quality in this interview isn't great, but the interviewer was exceptional and gave great advice.

The interviewee confidently worked from the brute force to the optimal solution. They then struggled to implement the code, overly worried about making a mistake.

Who: *Interviewer*: Software Engineer at FAANG+
Candidate: College student

SHOULD YOU SWITCH TO PYTHON FOR YOUR CODING INTERVIEWS?   INTERVIEW REPLAY

View Online: https://bctci.co/how-to-practice-replay-2 @ 7:06 - 9:57

The Question: Is it okay to interview in Python?

What You'll See: The interviewer walked the candidate through some of the pros and cons of using Python as their main language.

Who: *Interviewer*: Software Engineer at AWS
Candidate: College student

ONLINE RESOURCES

Online resources for this chapter include:

- Interview replays that show specific mistakes people make with coding problems

Go online at bctci.co/how-to-practice.

## CHAPTER 19

HOW YOU ARE EVALUATED

AI interviewer, replays, and more materials for this chapter at bctci.co/how-you-are-evaluated

Max Howell, the creator of the popular Homebrew package manager, infamously tweeted after interviewing at Google:

Max Howell ✔ 🔲 @mxcl · Jun 10, 2015   · · ·
Google: 90% of our engineers use the software you wrote (Homebrew), but you can't invert a binary tree on a whiteboard so f⬛ ⬛ off.

If you take one thing away from this incident, it's probably that coding interviews are broken. But if you were to take away two things, it might be that to succeed in coding interviews, we must understand what's expected of us and how our performance is evaluated.[1] In this chapter, we will introduce a *Universal Rubric* with the four categories you'll find on most Big Tech interview rubrics.

For each category, we will provide examples of real *rubric questions* that interviewers fill out after an interview, so you can see exactly what they are looking for.

In this chapter, we'll examine these questions and give you *actionable advice* on how to send the right *signal* to your interviewers. In the next chapter, we will apply what we learn from the Universal Rubric to design a step-by-step *Interview Checklist* that you can follow during an interview to hit all the important points.

SIGNAL

In the behavioral chapters, we talked about signal (pg 141); that comes into play here, too—at least, with a good interviewer.

Signal is about the *why*. In theory, interviewers shouldn't be judging you on binary metrics like "Is your code correct? Is it complete? Is it optimal?" Even if the items in their rubric are phrased as yes/no questions like these, they should be looking at the *why*. If your code isn't correct, why? Is it that...

- You tackled a more complex algorithm than other candidates?
- You confused `.add()` and `.append()`?
- You were horribly confused about the approach as you were coding it?

---

1   Check out the back cover of this book for an easter egg that concludes this story nicely. ☺

Each of these reasons has different implications, and a good interviewer will look at *what the reason means*. A focus on signal is what offers greater forgiveness on more challenging problems and, conversely, higher standards on easier problems.

But, of course, not all interviewers are good. Most interviewers implicitly understand signal to some extent, but the degree to which they really analyze the signal—the *why*—varies.

THE UNIVERSAL RUBRIC

We don't recommend focusing your job search on a single "dream" company—you're better off casting a wide net. Thus, we do not want to tailor our advice too much to a single company. Instead, we extracted four categories of an interview rubric relevant to Big Tech companies: Problem Solving, Coding, Verification, and Communication.

PROBLEM SOLVING

What many employers don't like to say, but is useful to understand, is that the problem-solving portion of a coding interview is meant to be an intelligence test. Yes, yes, there are many types of intelligence, and it's obviously not an *actual* IQ test, but this is the simplest way to understand what interviewers are looking for. Your ability to solve this problem—by using your brain, not the internet—is meant to evaluate, "Are you smart?"

This is why already *knowing* the algorithm isn't terribly impressive to the interviewer and doesn't earn you bonus points. Your interviewer doesn't want you to *know* how to do this; they want to see if you can figure it out. It is truly about the journey, not the destination—at least, with an effective interviewer.

This category is about demonstrating that you're smart—this is the *signal* interviewers are looking for. More specifically, it's about exploring multiple solutions, identifying obstacles, evaluating tradeoffs, and working to improve your algorithm. Along the way, you might also demonstrate an appropriate knowledge of computer science fundamentals, like Big O analysis and data structures.

Rubric Questions:

- How much difficulty did they have finding an algorithm and optimizing it, relative to the difficulty of the problem?
- How much help did they need, relative to other candidates?
- Did they discuss tradeoffs in terms of the time and space complexity?
- Did they use appropriate data structures and algorithms to solve the problem?

Question difficulty and interviewer assistance vary from interview to interview, so it's difficult to say that you're "expected" to solve the question optimally without assistance; for a very challenging question, even exceptional candidates might need some help. Similarly, we can't say that solving the problem optimally without assistance is "sufficient"; if it takes you a long time to solve an easy problem, this might result in a low score—even if you did so entirely independently.

The truth is somewhat reminiscent of the old joke:

> Two hikers see a bear in the woods. The first hiker is resigned to his fate as bear food, while the second changes into his sneakers. The first hiker says, "Why bother? You can't outrun a bear!" His friend responds, "I don't have to outrun the bear. I just have to outrun you."

Interviewers will often compare your performance on a question to other candidates they've asked the same question to. You don't necessarily need to solve the problem optimally or without help; you just need to do *better* than most other candidates.

How do you solve it better? That is the essence of this part of the book and the next:

- Master big O analysis (Chapter 21: Big O Analysis, pg 206).
- Use boundary thinking and trigger thinking (Chapter 22: Boundary Thinking, pg 230 and Chapter 23: Trigger Thinking, pg 242).
- Learn general problem-solving strategies (Chapter 24: Problem-Solving Boosters, pg 248).
- Learn as many topics from the Catalog of Technical Topics (pg 280) as possible to add to the tools in your toolbelt.
- Learn *reusable ideas* (look for the ♻ icon) placed throughout the Catalog, which capture ideas that can be consistently deployed across a wide number of problems.
- And, finally, yes, some amount of *grinding* problems is necessary. See Chapter 18: How to Practice (pg 170) for how to do it effectively.

CODING

Coding in interviews is quite different from "normal" coding. This category is about coding well under time pressure, in a barebones environment, and without being able to look things up on the fly. It is all about code structure, knowledge of your programming language, and clean code. There is no universal style guide you must adhere to—you just don't want to be told that you write Python like it is Java (or, worse, have no consistent style[2] across your code).

Rubric Questions:

- Could they translate their ideas into correct code?
- Did they overcomplicate the logic?
- Did they demonstrate good coding hygiene (clear variable names, abstracting relevant code into reusable helper functions instead of copy/pasting, consistent and reasonable style, etc.)?
- Is the code well organized and idiomatic to the language used?
- Did they demonstrate internalized software engineering principles?

Here is our main coding advice *tailored to the interview setting*.

How to code faster

- **Use short but meaningful variable names.** While whiteboard interviews are less common than they used to be, avoiding long variable names like `group_id_to_max_height_map` can still save us a bit of time, even on an editor. On the other hand, we are still evaluated on code clarity, so we should avoid ambiguous names like `map` or `m`.[3] The Goldilocks zone may be something like `max_height_map`.
- **Punt on tricky expressions.** If you get stuck on a technical detail, like the exit condition in a while loop, the exact range of a for loop, the base case of a recursive algorithm, or how to handle an edge case, you can leave a TODO and return to it once you have everything else in place. The additional context may help you get it right.
- **Keep error handling simple.** For interviews, we can often get away with returning an invalid value like `-1` instead of raising an exception, for the sake of time. You can ask the interviewer if that is OK.

---

2   For example, it's a red flag when someone writes variables both as `max_width` and `minWidth`.

3   Idiomatic exceptions in your language should be fine. Interviewers aren't likely to mark you down for using `i` and `j` in your loops, for instance.

- **Do not bother validating that the input will be what the interviewer/prompt said.** For instance, if we are told that the input will be a positive number and a square matrix, we generally do not need to check for the cases where the number is negative or the matrix has different dimensions. You can always mention that you *would* do it outside of an interview or ask the interviewer if they want you to do it. A great compromise here, particularly if your code won't be executed, is calling a helper function like check_inputs(), which you don't fill in. This demonstrates the signal to your interviewer that you are a person who thinks about input validation, without having to spend time doing it.

- **Don't optimize on the first pass**. It is easy to have planned out an algorithm that you know works, but when you decide to start coding it, get sidetracked with minor optimizations (e.g., early exits). We recommend first that you get your code working with the algorithm you planned, then do a pass to make improvements.

- **Keep comments to a minimum.** Documentation is generally not expected in interviews, so it may not be a good use of time. Use comments if they help you, but the interviewer should already understand what you're doing from your explanation of your solution.

How to write clear code

- **Follow universal good coding practices.** E.g., avoid copy-pasting repetitive code that can be factored into a function, avoid mutable global variables, try to reduce side effects, follow a consistent style, and so on.

- **Write idiomatic code**, which means following the conventions and mannerisms of the language. For instance, some languages have a custom of using snake_case for variable names, while others use camelCase. Non-idiomatic code can be correct but gives the impression of an inexperienced coder, so we recommend researching what is considered idiomatic in your language of choice, especially if it is not your main language. During your practice, asking an AI chatbot to suggest more idiomatic ways of writing your code is a good way to learn language-specific quirks quickly.[4]

Non-idiomatic Python

```
1 arr1 = []
2 arr2 = []
3 for i in range(10):
4   arr1.append(0)
5   arr2.append(i)
```

Idiomatic Python

```
1 arr1 = [0]*10
2 arr2 = [i for i in range(10)]
```

- **Consider using composite data types (like 'structs' or classes) to represent data** for code clarity. If you won't be executing your code, you may not need to write up the whole class definition.

Using basic types

```
1 def dist(x1, y1, x2, y2):
2   return math.sqrt((x2 - x1)**2 +
3                     (y2 - y1)**2)
```

Using a class

```
1 def dist(p1, p2):
2   return math.sqrt((p2.x - p1.x)**2 +
3                     (p2.y - p1.y)**2)
```

- **Use sensible defaults.** The initial conditions of an algorithm can significantly impact its implementation. For example, in maximization problems, we can often initialize the result to 0, while in minimization problems, we can initialize it to infinity. These safe defaults minimize the need for edge case adjustments.

---

4 You'll notice we don't follow our own advice in some parts of this book. That is because we want to make this book readable for everyone. Idiomatic Python uses language-specific features, like *list comprehensions*, that don't translate well to other languages. If you code in Python, write better code than ours!

- **Get familiar with recipes.** Throughout this book, we capture reusable pseudocode snippets into "recipes." Following these recipes can facilitate a cleaner and speedier implementation. You can add useful recipes (including your own) to your personal cheat sheet for quick reference.

- **Make stuff up.** If your language does not have a common method or library, like heaps, that exists in most other languages, you can ask your interviewer if it is okay to pretend it exists. If you can't remember if you were supposed to use `.append()` or `.add()`, just pick one and move on; your intent is clear. Memorization isn't the point, and most companies don't actually have you run your code. That said, try to keep this to a minimum. There is a difference between forgetting a method and just not knowing your programming language.

- **Stick with conventional libraries.** Related to the above, while you may need a library when your language doesn't have one, you should stick to common libraries. With languages like Python, where there is a library for everything, remember that you're expected to solve the question yourself—not import a library that solves it for you.[5][6]

CANDIDATE MODULARIZES A HELPER FUNCTION AND USES TYPE HINTS	INTERVIEW REPLAY

View Online:	bctci.co/rubric-replay-1 @ 10:42 - 11:30
The Question:	Given a grid and a starting point, floodfill the matrix as far as the boundaries will allow you to.
What You'll See:	Modularizing specific logic into different methods keeps code clean and easy to reason about.
Who:	*Interviewer*: Senior Software Engineer at FAANG+ *Candidate*: 12 years exp.

VERIFICATION

Strong verification signals come from two places during the interview: (1) At the beginning, when we do *requirement gathering* (asking good clarifying questions, considering edge cases before diving into coding, etc.), and (2) at the end, when we check the correctness of our code with test cases and examples. Candidates who don't verify the requirements properly at the beginning often end up misunderstanding the question or adding "hotfixes" to their solutions because they didn't carefully consider potential edge cases.

Rubric Questions:

- Did they ask good clarifying questions (that weren't already answered in the question description or examples)?
- Did they proactively consider edge cases?
- Did they test their code or provide a good argument for its correctness?
- Were they able to spot and fix any bugs?

We have a lot to say about how to boost your Verification signal in an interview, but most of the advice is in our Interview Checklist. See both the Ask Clarifying Questions step (pg 193) and Verify the Solution step (pg 202) for in-depth advice.

---

5   The exact line on what is considered okay will likely vary between interviewers. Almost any interviewer is likely to be okay with you using a built-in sorting library—assuming the question isn't "Implement a sorting algorithm from scratch"—but many interviewers will object to you using the built-in `bisect` module in Python when the difficult part of the question is implementing a binary search. When in doubt, ask your interviewer.

6   Another reason to be cautious of relying on extra libraries is that your interviewer may not be familiar with the library you want to use. Most people will be familiar with a library like `defaultdict`, which is part of the standard library, but you may lose interviewers if you start relying on `sortedcontainers`.

COMMUNICATION

While technical interviews might seem entirely focused on problem solving and coding, most rubrics include a communication category. Coding interviews offer—or, at the very least, appear to offer—a unique window into what it's like to collaborate with you.

As we saw in Chapter 4: What Interviewers Won't Tell You (pg 32), thinking out loud is essential in technical interviews, but beyond a baseline, communication may not significantly impact outcomes—at least for roles below Staff. Here are the things your interviewer is keeping in mind when deciding if you have reached that baseline.

> **Are you nervous about not knowing what to say?** In the Interview Checklist (pg 190), we give suggestions and examples of what to say at each step, which should eliminate most of the guesswork. You don't need to memorize any lines, though! Just the gist of the main points to hit at each step.
>
> Besides, it's good to remember that your interviewer is just an engineer who has been on the other side of the table as well, probably many times.

Rubric Questions:

- Were they able to clearly communicate their thoughts, even when the conversation got technical?
- Were they able to answer technical questions?
- Were they open to feedback?
- If they were confused, were they able to articulate why?

Here are some actionable tips to improve your communication signal:

- Whatever you do, be sure to **keep your interviewer in the loop**. From the interviewer's perspective, it can be frustrating when the candidate seems to be lost in thought, and it is not clear what they are thinking. However, that does *not* mean you have to be constantly talking out loud, which is a common misconception. For instance, if you need a couple of minutes to think in silence about the problem, that is totally fine—just politely tell the interviewer this so they know *why* you are silent (often, the interviewer will welcome the chance to focus on writing down notes).
- Use computer science terminology to **showcase your depth of knowledge**. The goal is to give the interviewer positive signal without going off on tangents. For instance, "I'll use a hash map" can become "I'll use a hash map because it provides amortized constant-time lookups." The two sentences are almost the same, but the latter showcases more technical depth without deviating too far from the main thread of the conversation.
- Related to the above, be sure to use the **Name-and-Justify** technique (pg 199).
- Illustrating points with examples in the shared editor can make them easier to follow. See our **advice on drawing** examples in an editor (pg 192).
- Good communication is not only about what you say to the interviewer but also about being a **responsive listener**. That means paying attention to their comments, considering the implications, and being willing to pivot based on their inputs. If you're focused on a specific way of solving the problem, it's easy to keep thinking about your solution when an interviewer suggests—or even subtly hints at—an alternative approach. Don't do this! **Follow their lead.**
- **Writing things down** can avoid miscommunication. For instance, we recommend writing down the big O analysis (pg 206).
- **Don't argue** with your interviewer. Even if you're right, it won't help your score.

Mock interviews can be vital in identifying communication issues and breaking bad communication habits. In our experience, it's hard to improve communication while practicing alone. It's easier for another person to notice gaps in your communication style. Alternatively, you can record yourself and then watch the replay. Are you being too quiet or too rambly? Are you just reading code out loud instead of explaining the point? After just a single recording, most people walk away with concrete ideas for how to improve.

▶ **SILENCE IS OKAY—JUST COMMUNICATE WITH YOUR INTERVIEWER!**   INTERVIEW REPLAY

View Online:	bctci.co/rubric-replay-2 @ 28:15 - 29:15
The Question:	Given a directed acyclic graph of tasks, determine task dependencies.
What You'll See:	The candidate said they needed a minute to think silently and then walked the interviewer through a solid plan.
Who:	*Interviewer*: Principal Software Engineer at Amazon *Candidate*: Junior engineer

---

▶ **VISUAL EXAMPLES MAKE YOUR EXPLANATIONS LESS CONFUSING**   INTERVIEW REPLAY

View Online:	bctci.co/rubric-replay-3 @ 2:20 - 6:30
The Question:	Given a set of words, determine the longest chain of words in that set that can be made out of those words with specified properties.
What You'll See:	The candidate's verbal-only explanation was confusing. Using examples and visuals (pseudocode or drawings) would have been clearer and less error-prone.
Who:	*Interviewer*: Senior Software Engineer at Google *Candidate*: 8 years exp.

WHAT ABOUT SPEED?

How 'speed' is factored in an interview rubric is a complex question. What interviewers often describe as being "slow" is usually about a deficit in one of the rubric categories we already mentioned.

'Speed' is sometimes a rubric category by itself, but a good interviewer is not literally timing how many minutes it takes you to get to an optimal answer. If you take longer to arrive at an optimal answer because you and your interviewer were discussing complex issues around memory utilization, that is a very different signal than if it took you equally long because you struggled to optimize the brute force solution.

Of course, not all interviewers are good—and there's a lot of gray area (interviewers who sort of understand signal but don't always think about things in the right way). For that reason, it can still be useful to think about how to improve your speed, both in ways that *actually* show better signal to good interviewers and in ways that will leave a more positive impression with the bad (or bad-ish) interviewers.

Here is a list of considerations, broken down by potential bottlenecks, to help improve speed:

Problem Solving Issues:

- Are you frequently unable to come up with solutions to questions? See our suggestions on page 181.

Coding Issues:

- Are you being too verbose with code? See our advice on how to code faster (pg 182).

- Does it take you a long time to code your ideas? Our advice is to build your own cheat sheet of recipes and reusable ideas from Chapter 18: How to Practice (pg 170) and then use it during your practice sessions. Include in your cheat sheet the tasks that stall you often so that you can keep revisiting them and get faster over time. With practice, programming tasks like "do a DFS through a grid" become second nature.

Verification Issues:

- Does your code have too many bugs? Throughout the book, we emphasize coding conventions to minimize bugs like off-by-one errors. See, e.g., the 'Index Manipulation Advice' section in Two Pointers (pg 296), the 'Implementation Advice' section in Recursion (pg 396), and the 'How To Slide a Window' section in Sliding Windows (pg 513).

- Do you struggle to find bugs when they do slip in? In the Interview Checklist, we have tips on how to better verify your solutions (pg 202).

- Do you spend too much time working through examples to validate your code? See 'How to Test Manually' (pg 203).

Communication Issues:

- Are you spending too much time on the small talk at the beginning? You can't brush it off, but you shouldn't needlessly drag it out.

- Are you misreading the question and then having to go back and read it again? It's important to take your time to understand the question, so slow down when reading it—you cannot solve a problem that you do not understand! Skimming might save you time in the short term, but it could cost you the interview if you misread something.

- Is your interviewer confused when you describe your solution? Are you too long-winded in your explanations? Use examples to illustrate points. See our advice on drawing examples effectively in an editor (pg 192).

- Are you spending too much time on pseudocode? We don't recommend writing detailed or formal pseudocode. Instead, if you write pseudocode, keep it high level. We call our preferred flavor of pseudocode "indented English": It's like normal English, but using indentation for code blocks to outline the code skeleton (pg 198).

- Are you just a slow typer? Many candidates think they need to type faster, but unless you are hunting and pecking at the keyboard, this shouldn't be your focus. Fast typers have a *slight* advantage, but this is *almost never* the real issue—100+ words per minute isn't as big of an advantage as it sounds.

Attempting to rush interview steps to save time typically backfires. Expert marksmen have a saying: "Slow is smooth. Smooth is fast." Practice moving smoothly through the steps in the Interview Checklist, and speed will follow.

▶ INDENTED ENGLISH MAKES YOU FASTER!		INTERVIEW REPLAY
View Online:	bctci.co/rubric-replay-4 @ 56:00 - 57:50	
The Question:	Given an elevation map, determine the final destination of water droplets in a given array.	
What You'll See:	Running out of time on the second question pushed the candidate to explain their solution in "indented English." They quickly described a solution and gave the interviewer a strong positive signal.	
Who:	*Interviewer*: Software Engineer at FAANG+ *Candidate*: 9 years exp.	

▶ ARGUMENTS AGAINST TRADITIONAL PSEUDOCODING IN AN INTERVIEW   INTERVIEW REPLAY

View Online:	bctci.co/rubric-replay-5 @ 5:22 - 22:59
The Question:	Merge two lists into a single sorted list.
What You'll See:	The candidate perfectly illustrates their thought process with a mix of traditional pseudocode and some 'indented English,' but they spend almost 20 minutes just this step!
Who:	*Interviewer*: Software Engineer at Google *Candidate*: 3 years exp.
Outcome:	The candidate got a job at Meta!

WHAT ABOUT CULTURAL VALUES?

Every company says they want employees that showcase the company's values, but not all of them have a dedicated rubric category for it in coding interviews (or give much weight to it, if they do). Cultural values are mostly evaluated in behavioral interviews (pg 136). Still, a few value-related questions may creep into coding interview rubrics.

From Netflix's Culture Memo to Apple's fanboy favoritism, the truth is that each company asks the same question to varying degrees: do you value the same things the company values, and would you do well at that particular company? At Amazon, your technical interview scores may be incredible, but you won't get the job unless you also score well on their "Leadership Principles." In contrast, Google says it's important that you are "Googley," but mostly just wants you to be enthusiastic about the job and technically brilliant.

In any case, signaling that you're a good fit is a good idea. In general, most companies want to make sure that you are:

- **Independent and resourceful.** In an interview, that means coming up with your own ways of getting unstuck rather than asking for a hint (see our advice on how to ask for help on page 274).
- **Collaborative.** See our tip above about being a responsive listener.
- **Friendly and enthusiastic.** Don't brush off the small talk at the start of the interview (but also do not spend too much time). Remember the interviewer's name—you can write it down if it helps!
- **Asking thoughtful engineering-specific questions.** You want to end the interview on a good note. Our thoughts on good end-of-interview questions are on page 75.
- **Not a jerk.** Even companies that don't highly prioritize cultural values still tend to have a "no jerks" rule. Be kind, courteous, and respectful. If you're condescending to your interviewer, you aren't likely to pass.

Besides those general traits, values change from company to company, so research the specifics of the company you are interviewing for.[7]

WHAT MATTERS MOST?

We have learned about the four key categories of how you're judged in an interview, but they are not all weighted equally. For instance, it is rare to pass a technical interview if you can't provide an efficient solution. From a technical perspective, when you're in a coding interview, the majority of what matters is that your code works and has the asymptotic complexity expected by the interviewer. That's it. Everything else, like micro-optimizations, typing speed, how idiomatic your code is, or your closing questions, is unimportant in comparison.

---

7   If you haven't seen them yet, interviewing.io has a curated list of company-specific guides for this exact reason: https://interviewing.io/topics#companies

How does the rubric change for senior engineers?

Some companies expect more from senior engineers because they have more experience. Other companies argue the opposite; senior engineers have been out of school (and algorithms classes) for longer, so they'll be rustier with DS&A but better at system design. Many companies, however, don't outline different expectations either way.

As a general rule, companies will expect the same level of performance in the problem-solving aspects, regardless of experience. The expectations on translating your algorithm into correct code will also be about the same—typically. However, companies might be less forgiving of poor style or a lack of knowledge in certain areas (e.g., writing unit tests) for senior engineers. They will also have a higher bar for communication for Staff-level (and above) engineers.

A CONTROVERSIAL INTERVIEWER GIVES SUGGESTIONS[8]   INTERVIEW REPLAY

View Online:	bctci.co/rubric-replay-6 @ 49:30 - 1:02:00
The Question:	You are given a nested object of dictionaries/hashmaps, arrays/lists, and primitives/non-containers. Return the value at the end of a given path.
What You'll See:	An interviewer with a lot of opinions.
Who:	*Interviewer*: Software Engineer at Google *Candidate*: 6 years exp.

ONLINE RESOURCES

Online resources for this chapter include:

- Interview replays that show specific mistakes people make with coding problems

Try online at bctci.co/how-you-are-evaluated.

---

8 Ok, this interview was spicier than a jalapeño eating contest on a summer day. We admit that this particular interviewer has a lot of "hot takes" which we completely disagree with. For instance, Google interviewers taking a break to "read the newspaper" during an interview is neither tolerated or common, Python uses 'pass-by-assignment' (not by reference), and despite popular belief, neither Gayle or any of the rest of us authors "created" the current coding interview style at FAANG companies. Still, the interviewer does a good job explaining the basic steps of a coding interview, and emphasizing the importance of generating multiple solutions before coding. If nothing else, we suspect you'll find it humorous. The next chapter illustrates our recommended steps to follow in an interview.

CHAPTER 20

ANATOMY OF A CODING INTERVIEW

AI interviewer, replays, and more materials for this chapter at bctci.co/anatomy

> Tactics without strategy is the noise before defeat.
>
> Sun Tzu

THE INTERVIEW CHECKLIST

Some coding interview resources cover tactics but fail to provide a strategy. What's the difference? *Tactics* are the algorithms and data structures we use to solve problems, while *strategy* is the higher-level thought process to determine which tactics to use. People often assume that if they learn all the data structures and algorithms, they'll be able to solve any problem, but this line of thinking is incomplete. It's equally important to know which one to use.

We frame our strategy in terms of an *Interview Checklist*—a clear, ordered list of steps we should do during the interview, and we can mentally "check off" as we do. These steps will help you solve the problem *and* send positive signal to the interview in terms of problem-solving, coding, communication, and verification (see the *Universal Rubric* (pg 181).

The interview checklist still applies to the online assessment setting and when practicing questions by yourself. The main difference is that we do not need to worry about communication in these settings.

Figure 1 summarizes the steps in our interview checklist.

OPENING CHAT

Usually, we don't jump straight into the question. The opening chat is mostly up to the individual interviewer, so follow their lead. There are usually introductions, perhaps followed by some short questions about your past work or projects. We don't want to stretch this time too long, because we want more time for the technical portions. This portion will probably be just a few minutes, but—again—follow your interviewer's lead. See Behavioral Interviews on page 136.

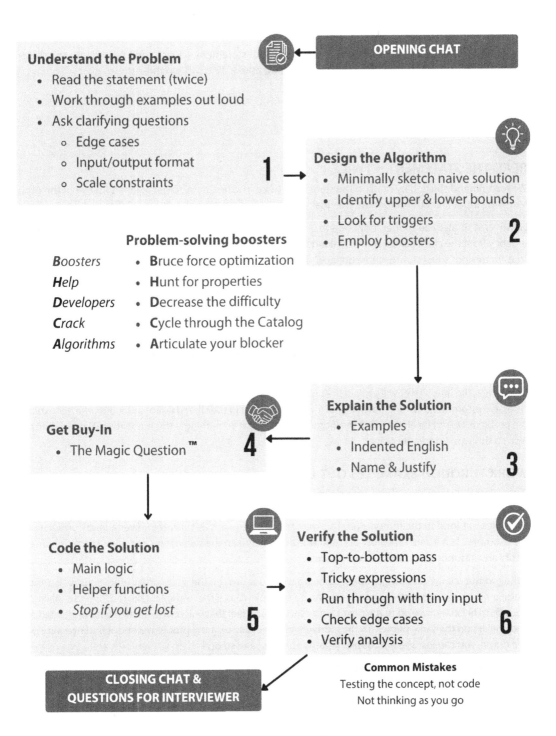

Figure 1. Interview checklist.

STEP 1: UNDERSTAND THE PROBLEM

The real interview begins when they give you a problem statement, usually copy-pasted into the shared editor. Our first goal will be to *fully digest* what is being asked. We do this in three steps:

- Read the statement—twice.
- Work through examples out loud.
- Ask clarifying questions.

READ THE STATEMENT—TWICE

We recommend starting by reading the statement *twice*. The first time, to get a general sense of the problem—the input and output formats, the goal, and the main constraints.

However, a single read is often not enough. At this point in the interview, candidates often feel a sense of urgency from the clock ticking down, making it easy to miss critical information. A little detail, like missing a "not" or mixing "subset" with "subsequence," can derail your interview. You would be shocked at how often this happens!

Besides, the wording may be ambiguous, and it's important to recognize all the ambiguous parts so you can clarify them with the interviewer. Some interviewers ask questions with purposefully ambiguous parts to test how you deal with ambiguity.

Thus, the second pass is to make sure you did not miss anything. Slow down and parse the text carefully—like a lawyer carefully analyzing a contract for loopholes. **Do not skip the second pass.**

Sometimes, the interviewer will explain the problem out loud instead of giving you a written prompt. In those cases, we recommend writing down all the important tidbits in the shared editor as the interviewer explains the problem. Do not be afraid to ask the interviewer to repeat something—this is not an oral comprehension test, so this won't dock you points.

WORK THROUGH EXAMPLES OUT LOUD

Right after the statement, there are usually one or more examples, which will be our next focus. We use the examples to double-check our understanding of the problem. Our recommendation is to explain the examples out loud to the interviewer. This may seem redundant, as the interviewer already understands the examples, but it starts the flow of communication between the two of you and gives them a chance to clarify any misunderstandings you may have.

If the prompt comes with no examples, come up with your own on the spot—many questions with difficult wordings are simple to understand after seeing an example. Also, if the examples take too long to explain, feel free not to finish—move on to the next step as soon as you feel that you have solidified your understanding and you are on the same page with the interviewer. For instance, if the problem is about finding every path in a graph, you can just show a couple of paths and say, "and so on."

Working through examples manually can also be a problem-solving technique in itself. See the *DIY technique* (pg 254).

Drawing advice

When working through an example, a drawing can often make what is happening more clear. However, we don't want our drawings to slow us down, so it is important to make effective drawings:

FANCY DRAWINGS	EFFECTIVE DRAWINGS

<pre>[3, 5, 9, 2, 10, 8, 12, 1]
  ^   ^
 	
	|
	 left right</pre>
		<pre>3 5 9 2 10 8 12 1
		1
		            r</pre>

<pre>   2
      /   \
     5   8
    / \   / \
   3   9 10   12
               \
                1</pre>
	<pre> 2
	        5 8
	     3 9 10 12
	                          1</pre>

This is a topic best learned by example, so we made a no-frills video that walks through how to draw things like graphs and matrices effectively on an editor: <u>bctci.co/drawing-advice</u>. We also give drawing advice for specific topics throughout the Catalog part of the book.

▶ WALKING THROUGH EXAMPLES HELPS YOU CLARIFY THE QUESTION   INTERVIEW REPLAY

View Online:	<u>bctci.co/anatomy-replay-1</u> @ 55:50 - 56:30
The Question:	Given a list of cards, find the highest N straight flush if any.
What You'll See:	The interviewer explained how and why it is a good idea to come up with your own examples when first playing with the problem.
Who:	*Interviewer*: Software Engineer at Google *Candidate*: 4 years exp.
Outcome	The candidate got the job at Google!

ASK CLARIFYING QUESTIONS

> People do not wish to appear foolish; to avoid
> the appearance of foolishness, they are willing to
> remain actually fools.
>
> Alice Walker

Now that we have extracted all the relevant information from the prompt, it is time for us to fill in the gaps. Problem statements are often *intentionally* ambiguous because interviewers want to evaluate your *requirement-gathering* skills. It's like the interviewer is roleplaying as a client, commissioning you a job (solving the coding interview), but the client may not know exactly what they want. That means you need to identify gaps that may be missing or open to interpretation and work with the interviewer to clarify them. Asking good clarifying questions demonstrates both verification and communication skills, so it is an easy way to make a good impression early in the interview! However, be mindful not to waste too much time and avoid asking questions already answered in the prompt.

There are three main types of clarifying questions:

- Edge cases.

- Input and output format.
- Scale constraints.

Edge cases

Consider the following problem:

Implement a split(s, c) method, which receives a string s and a character c and splits s at each occurrence of c, returning an array of strings.

If you get a problem statement like this in an interview, the interviewer is likely testing your ability to clarify the requirements, as there are edge cases that are not covered in the statement:

1. If s is empty, should we return an empty list?
2. If s starts with c, should we return an empty string at the beginning of the list?
3. If s ends with c, should we return an empty string at the end of the list?
4. If there are two consecutive occurrences of c, should we add an empty string?

Sometimes, the statement does not cover the edge cases, but they can be deduced from the examples. For instance, which of the edge cases above are addressed in the following example?[1]

▶ **Example:** s = "/home/./..//Documents/", c = '/'
  Output: ["", "home", ".", "..", "", "Documents", ""]

Confirming with the interviewer how to address all the edge cases is still a good idea, as the examples could be misleading. For instance, all the examples for a problem may consist of a sorted input with unique elements, when in reality, the input may not be sorted or contain duplicates.

Common edge cases that you can ask about, depending on the nature of the input, include:

- Integers:

  » Negative or zero values.
  » Very large numbers (which, in most languages, could result in integer overflow if you add or multiply them together).

- Arrays and strings:

  » Empty arrays and strings.
  » Duplicated elements.
  » Inputs that are too small to return a valid solution (e.g., if the problem says to choose k input elements, what if the input has fewer than k elements?)
  » Non-letter or non-ASCII characters in a string.

- Multi-dimensional arrays and strings:

  » Grids with a different number of rows and columns.
  » Different string lengths in an array of strings.

- Other:

  » Null/'None' values or pointers.

You can also ask clarifying questions about what is allowed in the output. For instance,

---

1 Answer: it covers edge cases #2, #3, and #4. We'll see a full solution to this in Solution 26.1: String Split (pg 291).

whether the output elements need to be different or you can reuse the same one multiple times.

Try to think of as many edge cases as possible!

Input and output format

Consider this problem:

Given a list of k playing cards, return the five cards that make the best poker hand.

On top of multiple edge cases that we could ask about (how many can you come up with?), this is an example where the input and output types are underspecified. There are many ways to represent a poker hand or even a single card. For instance, a card like the seven of hearts could be represented as the string "H7", as a numeric code, or as an 'object' with suit and rank fields (for which we would also need to choose types). There is no objectively correct way to represent the data, so you can make proposals, discuss different options, and try to cater to the interviewer's preference—the customer is always right.[2]

Don't assume you are allowed to modify the input—maybe the interviewer wants your function to not have side-effects. If you want to do this, it's best to check with them if you are allowed.

Scale constraints

Sometimes, questions will include constraints that tell you the maximum input size. If they don't, we can ask:

▶   "Are there any constraints on how big the input could be? I want to ensure that my solution can scale to all expected inputs."

See page 235 on why we might want to ask this question.

VAGUE QUESTIONS ARE OFTEN INTENTIONAL!		INTERVIEW REPLAY
View Online:	bctci.co/anatomy-replay-2 @ 1:02:00 - 1:03:05	
The Question:	Design a class Quack, which is a combination of both a queue and stack.	
What You'll See:	The interviewer had **intentionally** left parts of the question vague in the hope that the candidate would ask clarifying questions.	
Who:	*Interviewer*: Staff Software Engineer at FAANG+ *Candidate*: 3 years exp.	
Outcome:	The candidate got a job at Meta!	

STEP 2. DESIGN THE ALGORITHM

This step is the main problem-solving part of the interview, where we come up with the algorithm that we will implement. We break it down into four steps:[3]

1.   Minimally sketch the naive solution.
2.   Identify upper and lower bounds.
3.   Look for *triggers*.
4.   Employ *problem-solving boosters*.

---

2   As a general rule, if you get to define your own types, composite types will earn you more code cleanliness 'points.'

3   If you ever forget these steps, remember MIKE's advice: (1) **M**inimally sketch the naive solution, (2) **I**dentify bounds, (3) **K**eywords (triggers), and (4) **E**mploy boosters.

Solutions: "optimal" vs. "right for the interviewer" vs. "right for you"

A common misconception in coding interviews is that we must aim to code the most **optimal** solution. However:

- Your interviewer may have selected a problem where the optimal solution is far too complex for an interview.

- Your interviewer may be expecting a different solution. They may not even know the most optimal one.

So, what you probably need is not necessarily the optimal solution, but the solution that is **right for the interviewer**.

Another way to look at it is that the best solution is the one that you can code. If you are deciding between:

- A solution you're confident you can code, even if it is slightly suboptimal.

- A complex solution that might be hard to finish in time without bugs but is optimal.

The best thing may be to discuss the trade-off with the interviewer and ask them if they have a preference. Ultimately, in this game, the interviewer is always "right." But if they don't, the suboptimal solution may be the one that is **right for you**.

MINIMALLY SKETCH THE NAIVE SOLUTION

We recommend always starting with an idea for a naive solution.[4] This is the simplest code you can imagine that will solve the problem, and it sets a baseline for what you have to beat.

If it doesn't waste too much time, we may even sketch it. If we do, the sketch should be so high-level that we can think of it as "indented English:" normal English but with indentation for code blocks. For instance, consider this variation of the classic 3-sum problem (Problem 24.1: 3-Sum, pg 251):

Given a list of numbers, return whether it contains three numbers that are all different and add up to 0.

Our sketch could be:

```
Algo 1: Brute force
n: the length of the array
T: O(n^3)
S: O(1)
for each number x
  for each number y after x
    for each number z after y
      if they are different and x + y + z is 0
        return true
return false
```

The sketch (or even just a plain sentence giving the high-level idea) has multiple benefits:

- It gets the ball rolling in terms of exploring the solution space.

- It helps confirm with the interviewer that you are solving the right problem (in our example, the interviewer may interject and say, "Actually, you need to return the elements, not just true or false").

---

4 In this book, we use the terms "naive solution" and "brute force" interchangeably to mean the simplest possible solution, without worrying about whether the time or space complexity is (potentially) abysmal. In other contexts, "brute force" is more formally defined as "an algorithm that does an exhaustive search through all possible solutions," but that is generally the simplest possible solution anyway.

- It sets an *upper bound* for the time complexity we need to beat (see "Naive Upper Bound" on page 234).
- It is the starting point for the **BRUTE FORCE OPTIMIZATION** *booster* (pg 250).

We do not need to code the naive solution to get any of those benefits, so don't waste precious time on it.

\#   Throughout the course of the interview, we may consider multiple algorithms. It's a good habit to write down the time and space complexity for each one, as we did in our sketch above.

The next two replays help illustrate the importance of not overlooking the brute-force solution.

BRUTE FORCE OR OPTIMIZE IMMEDIATELY?   INTERVIEW REPLAY

View Online:	bctci.co/anatomy-replay-3 @ 1:22:15 - 1:22:54
The Question:	Should I keep trying to find an optimal answer when I'm stuck or spend time coding the brute force?
What You'll See:	The interviewer explained why it almost always makes sense to start with brute force if you don't immediately know how to optimize.
Who:	*Interviewer*: Senior Software Engineer at FAANG+ *Candidate*: 3 years exp.

SKIPPING THE BRUTE FORCE IS DANGEROUS   INTERVIEW REPLAY

View Online:	bctci.co/anatomy-replay-4 @ review written feedback
The Question:	Why do you suggest spending time on the brute force?
What You'll See:	The interviewer emphasized starting with the brute force solution. Skipping it can lead to over-engineering.
Who:	*Interviewer*: Software Engineer at Meta *Candidate*: 3 years exp.

IDENTIFY UPPER AND LOWER BOUNDS

Now that we have a good grasp of what we have to solve, it's time to start making progress towards a solution. An incredibly common way to fail an interview is to choose the wrong approach and not realize it until you have wasted too much time, so it's often wise not to commit to a solution too quickly. For example, you think a problem is a graph question when, in reality, the optimal approach is to use a union–find data structure.

To mitigate this, this step is about **narrowing the range of approaches we should consider**. We do this in terms of the big O analysis: using the techniques in Chapter 22: Boundary Thinking (pg 230), we establish a *lower bound* and an *upper bound* for the runtime of the optimal solution. This way, we do not need to waste any time considering approaches that are slower than the upper bound or faster than the lower bound.

This is like if an architect got commissioned to design a school and asked two questions before starting: (1) what is the minimum number of floors needed to have enough classrooms for all the students? and (2) What is the maximum number of floors the city allows? These two questions narrow down the range of designs the architect needs to consider.

At first, it may seem odd to discuss big O analysis this early in the interview, but people who excel at algorithms instinctively consider complexity analysis every step of the way. Thus, doing so sends positive signal to the interviewer.

LOOK FOR TRIGGERS

At this point, we set some bounds for the solution space we should consider. The next step is to look for *triggers* that point to a specific approach. Triggers are not an exact science—they are based on the observation that certain keywords, constraints, and question topics are often solved with a specific technique, so they *trigger* us to try them. By being familiar with these triggers, we can sometimes navigate straight to the right solution. Chapter 23: Trigger Thinking (pg 242) will cover everything about triggers.

This is like a carpenter being hired to create an outdoor table and automatically narrowing down the choice of wood to the one or two options that usually handle the outdoor elements the best.

Even though triggers can be very useful, we do not need to discuss triggers with the interviewer or write them down—it may signal to them that we are over-relying on memorization rather than problem-solving.

EMPLOY BOOSTERS

Hopefully, triggers were enough to identify the correct algorithm or data structure we should use. However, since triggers are not an exact science, we may not have arrived at the right idea yet, especially for hard problems. This is where the more "free-form" problem-solving begins. In Chapter 24: Problem-Solving Boosters (pg 248), we discuss our top problem-solving strategies, which we call *boosters*, roughly in the order that you should consider them:

1. Brute force optimization.
2. Hunt for properties.
3. Decrease the difficulty.
4. Cycle through the Catalog.
5. Articulate your blocker.

We have a mnemonic to remember the initials of the five boosters in order: ***BOOSTERS HELP DEVELOPERS CRACK ALGORITHMS***.

Having a strategy for what to do when you are stuck is a powerful way to stay calm under pressure.

▶	DISCUSSING TIME & SPACE COMPLEXITIES BEFORE CODING SAVES TIME	INTERVIEW REPLAY
View Online:	bctci.co/anatomy-replay-5 @ 53:45 - 57:45	
The Question:	Given an integer n, return the largest number that is less than or equal to n with monotone increasing digits.	
What You'll See:	The interviewer stressed the importance of describing your approach before coding. They also had a hot take on pseudocoding.	
Who:	*Interviewer*: Machine Learning Engineer at Meta *Candidate*: College student	

STEP 3. EXPLAIN THE SOLUTION

Whatever solutions we come up with, we must keep the interviewer in the loop. There is usually a back-and-forth between designing the algorithm and explaining our ideas to the interviewer, so this step usually happens concurrently with Step 2.

Explaining the solution is not only for the interviewer's benefit:

- It is critical to your communication score.
- It will help you figure out how to structure the code better when you get to it.

Here are three techniques used by good communicators:

1. We can complement our explanation with 'indented English,' similar to the brute force solution (if we sketched it). Again, keep it high-level to save time. E.g.:

```
Algo 2: Using a set              Algo 3: binary search
T: O(n^2)                        T: O(n^2)
S: O(n) extra space              S: O(1) extra space (modifies input)
put all values in a hash set     sort the input array
for each number x                for each number x
  for each number y after x        for each number y after x
    z = -(x+y)                       z = -(x+y)
    if x,y,z are different and       if x,y,z are different and
       z is in the set                  binary_search(z) is true
      return true                      return true
return false                     return false
```

2. Use examples to illustrate ideas. You can use the given ones or your own.

3. Use the **name-and-justify technique**.

Don't forget to include the time and space analysis when explaining algorithms to your interviewer!

NAME-AND-JUSTIFY TECHNIQUE

Whenever you choose an algorithm, data structure, or technique, it is important to *name* it and *justify* why you chose it. Imagine a candidate who misses either of these:

You say...	Your interviewer thinks...
GOOD EXAMPLE - NAME AND JUSTIFY	
"I'm thinking of using a <u>heap</u> because it allows me to <u>retrieve the next smallest element in the dataset efficiently</u>."	I understand what you're doing and why you're doing it.
BAD EXAMPLE - NAMING WITHOUT A JUSTIFICATION	
"I'll use a <u>heap</u> instead of storing things in a list."	Ok, but do you know why a heap is appropriate, or are you just guessing?
BAD EXAMPLE - JUSTIFYING WITHOUT A NAME	
"I'll use a data structure to <u>track the smallest element efficiently</u>."	Do you mean a min-heap? Do you know it's called a min-heap?

Even for a brute force solution, naming and justifying what you're doing is helpful: "I will start sketching a <u>brute force</u> solution to <u>have a working baseline and then try to improve it</u>."

This also extends to individual decisions about your algorithm. E.g., in a breadth-first search algorithm, you might say, "To avoid an infinite loop, I will track visited nodes in <u>a set</u> because it has <u>amortized constant time lookup</u>."

Naming the high-level idea and justifying it demonstrates a solid understanding of the CS principle and clear communication skills.

▶	**ARGUMENTS FOR PSEUDOCODING IN AN INTERVIEW**	INTERVIEW REPLAY

View Online:	bctci.co/anatomy-replay-6 @ 1:05:02 - 1:06:32
The Question:	Given two strings, determine the number of copies of the first string you'd need to make the second string.
What You'll See:	The interviewer showed how writing pseudocode makes you faster because it communicates your solution more effectively to the interviewer (he advocated specifically for indented English, though he didn't call it that).
Who:	*Interviewer*: Software Engineer at Amazon *Candidate*: 2 years exp.

STEP 4. GET BUY-IN

At this point, we should have a solution that we already explained to the interviewer.

Do not—we repeat—do *not* start coding yet. It is important to ensure our interviewer understands what we're trying to do *and* is on board with it by getting them to "buy-in."

We get buy-in with the **The Magic Question**™.

THE MAGIC QUESTION™

Coding requires *consent*. Before transitioning into coding, you should explicitly ask your interviewer if they want you to code:

> I would like to use <X algorithm> with <Y time> and <Z space> to solve the problem. Should I code this now, or should I keep thinking?

Why is this a magic question? Consider scenarios where:

- You propose what you believe is the optimal answer, but a better solution exists—and your interviewer prefers you to code the optimal answer.[5]
- You propose a solution that appears to work, but has a flaw.
- Your interviewer got distracted, or you're not sure if they followed the explanation of the solution you're proposing.

In these scenarios, we want to give the interviewer a chance to correct you before you waste time on a solution that they don't want to see you code. The Magic Question™ should not come across as asking for a hint since, at this point, we have already showcased our problem-solving skills and improved upon the naive solution. Additionally, you're *not* asking, "Is this optimal?" You're asking whether your interviewer wants you to code this algorithm right now.[6]

This question is the final confirmation you need before diving into the code. Don't skip it!

\#   Notice that The Magic Question™ includes time and space complexity. This means we must analyze our proposed solution *before* starting to code.

---

5   It might seem like an interviewer would only want you to code the optimal answer, but this isn't necessarily the case. An interviewer might have you code something less optimal early-on to evaluate your coding skills early, and then have you continue to optimize after.

6   Psst, interviewers: don't let the candidate code if you don't want them to! Yes, we're instructing candidates to check with you first, but you should be managing this process too.

STEP 5. CODE THE SOLUTION

At this point, we have buy-in for our solution and we just need to translate it into actual code.

Our main advice is to **write top-down, not bottom-up.** Structure your code as a single function with the overall logic (there should be no "loose" code). Write the main logic first, using yet-to-be-written helper methods for smaller, self-contained bits of code that get in the way of the main algorithm. We suggest this order because the main logic is what the interviewer wants to see the most, and until you finish the main logic, there is always a chance you may need to change course and use different helper functions. For example, the first pieces of code you might write might look something like the next example—with none of these functions filled in!

```
1   def invert(expression):
2     if not expression:
3       return -1
4     min = get_min(expression)
5     max = get_max(expression)
6     count = 0
7     for v in range(min, max):
8       count += search(expression, v)
9     return count
```

Refer to the Coding section of the Universal Rubric (pg 182) for all our coding tips tailored to the interview setting.

If you really understand what you're coding, this should generally be pretty easy. If you find yourself struggling, this is typically because you don't *actually* understand what you're doing. The worst thing you can do is try to "power through" just to keep making progress; that's like driving around and hoping you stumbled on your desired destination, rather than looking up directions. If you're struggling or getting confused while you're coding, **stop** and go back to your example. Figure out what you're trying to do—how exactly your algorithm works—and then come back to coding.

Do I need to talk out loud while I code?

We've seen people literally read the code aloud as they type it—don't do that! It is not effective communication or useful for the interviewer. If you can, you should describe what you're about to do after each logical step. For example:

- "First, we will loop through the matrix, searching for the first occurrence of a one."

<code>

- "Now, we need to start the depth-first search if the located one isn't in our visited set"

<code>

Communicating like this can be helpful to you and the interviewer.

However, don't stress yourself out over how—or even if—you talk while you're coding. Most interviewers are fine with complete silence if you've clearly explained the algorithm before you start coding and then you code it without getting stuck. You're only likely to get in trouble with silence when your interviewer doesn't know what you're thinking or if you're stuck.

If you stop coding, it can be a concern for an interviewer because they don't know why. As a rule of thumb, if you aren't coding, describe what you're thinking. Don't be afraid to ask the interviewer for a minute to think quietly if you need it!

STEP 6. VERIFY THE SOLUTION

After we finish coding, it may seem like we are done, but verification is quite important as it is usually weighted in the rubric (pg 184). *Before* saying you're done, we should verify the solution:

1. Read the solution **top to bottom**, walking through the approach at a high level. Does the logic make sense? Do not plug in an example at this point, particularly if you are not allowed to run the code (manual testing is very slow). Often, bugs can be caught by simply running through the logic.

2. Focus on **tricky expressions**: common places bugs might pop up. Look at your code and think, "*if* I didn't know what this code did, but I knew there was a bug, where would it most likely be?" For example:

    » Any math, such as a calculation like (i * j) / 2. Mentally check that it is what you expect in a couple of cases.

    » Atypical array index calculations. Double-check a line like arr[i + 2]. You probably wrote that for a reason, but it's also very easy for that to go wrong. You can think: "*If* there was an input that made it go out of bounds, what would it be?"

    » Starting and terminating conditions of loops and recursion.

    » Null inputs and out-of-bound errors.

3. **Run through the code with a tiny input**: Yes, *tiny*; this is really important, particularly if you aren't able to execute your code. Manually running through an array with even five or six elements can take a while. But a tiny example will find almost all the same bugs, so use that.

4. **Check edge cases:** You already did a quick double-checking with some edge cases in step 2, but now you want to re-run your code with these edge cases, such as single-element arrays. Again—if you are doing manual testing, keep your examples small.

Should you code unit tests?

Regardless of whether you're offered the ability to execute your code, you can suggest writing unit tests. Proactively suggesting tests without prompting is a positive signal in an interview. Not all interviewers will want you to do this, so we suggest offering it as a **potential next step** and seeing what they say. They may agree or stop you (e.g., so they can ask a follow-up question).

HOW TO TEST MANUALLY

Testing by hand is a different beast than running unit tests. It means walking through your code, line by line, explaining (mostly to yourself, but in part to your interviewer) what's happening.

Very often, candidates make one of two mistakes in this process.

Mistake #1: Testing the concept, not the code

Some candidates test their concept or algorithm rather than their code. This was obvious back in the white-board days. Candidates would say they were testing their "code," and yet they were not even looking at it. Make sure you are actually running through your code, line by line, and *doing* each calculation or step. Yes, plug in those numbers, test that if-statement logic, and so on.

Mistake #2: Not Thinking As You Go

Often, candidates blindly execute their code and wait until the end to ask: Did I get the right answer? At best, this half works—but even then, it's an inefficient bug-finding process.

It's actually more efficient to think as you go along. At each line, briefly think: Is this the right result? E.g., if you are recursing on the left half of the array, is that what you're supposed to do and are your indices where you'd expect them to be?

This identifies bugs earlier and where they originated, so you can fix them better. It can also expose bugs that do not cause an inaccurate result for your specific input.

FIXING BUGS

I found a bug! Now what? Deep breath. Your code will probably have bugs. While that's not ideal, it's also the norm. What matters is how you address it. The important part is to avoid **hotfixes** and the **death spiral**.

Some candidates, in a rush to make their code perfect, make quick fixes as soon as they find an issue. If they notice that the code returns 1 when it should be returning 2, they immediately change the return statement to `return x + 1`. This is what's called a *hotfix*.

The problem with applying hotfixes is twofold. First, even if they make the right changes, they're coding without thinking things through, which will send the wrong signal to the interviewer. Second, often the hotfix *isn't* correct, and they've just introduced a new bug—which, often, they address through another hotfix. Soon, their code is convoluted and littered with hotfixes, and likely more buggy than it was to start with. This is the *death spiral*.

The alternative? When you find a bug, think about the *actual* cause. Where did the bug originate from? And what is the best way to fix it? Then, once you know the actual cause and the best fix, fix the bug.

VERIFICATION #1: THINK THROUGH TRICKY EDGE CASES BEFORE CODING		INTERVIEW REPLAY
View Online:	bctci.co/anatomy-replay-8 @ 58:00 - 59:10	
The Question:	Given a binary tree and a list of nodes to delete, return the root of each new subtree that is created after deleting the nodes	
What You'll See:	The candidate arrived at an approach that worked for the happy path using the **provided** example but didn't work in all cases. They spent the interview making 'hotfixes' to their solution.	
Who:	*Interviewer*: Software Engineer at Google	
	Candidate: College student	

▶ VERIFICATION #2: DEBUG QUICKLY AND SHOW YOUR THOUGHT PROCESS   INTERVIEW REPLAY

View Online:	bctci.co/anatomy-replay-9 @ 20:40 - 23:05
The Question:	Given a positive integer, n, return the minimum number of steps to get to 1, assuming we can repeatedly either (a) subtract 1, (b) divide by two if evenly divisible, or (c) divide by three if evenly divisible.
What You'll See:	This whole interview is excellent, but the candidate's fast verification skills are worth seeing. Their methodical approach to checking their solution, finding their bug, and fixing it perfectly displays verification in action. Overall, a very beautiful interview.
Who:	*Interviewer*: Software Engineer at Facebook *Candidate*: 1 year exp.
Outcome:	The candidate got the job at Meta!

VERIFY YOUR ANALYSIS TOO

We should have analyzed our approach way before starting to code and mentioned it in The Magic Question™. However, your actual implementation may have diverged from your original analysis. It could be that you didn't factor in some low-level detail that wouldn't come up in a high-level description, like the fact that *slicing* in Python takes linear time.

Thus, conclude by confirming that your time and space analysis is still correct. Clearly state—preferably in writing—your solution's final time and space complexity.

Can you optimize after coding?

In some cases, you might code a suboptimal algorithm, even a brute-force one. This doesn't necessarily mean you did anything wrong—your interviewer might have even said "Yes," when you asked The Magic Question™ (pg 200). Interviewers sometimes do this for a variety of reasons:

- They want to get coding out of the way early on so you have more time for optimizing.
- The optimal answer is too complicated to code.
- The optimal answer is really short because it involves some neat trick. They prefer to analyze *coding signal* through the brute-force solution which has more room for functions and structure.

In those cases, you'll go back to Step 2: Design the Algorithm (pg 195), and continue to optimize. You might not code your eventual optimal answer at all. Effectively, your interviewer flipped the coding and problem-solving pieces: you code the obvious answer, and then come back to the problem solving.

AFTER THE QUESTION

After you finish the question, the interview may go in a number of different directions:

- You may get a follow-up question.
- You may get an entirely different question.
- There are no new questions, and the interviewer wraps up with a bit of chitchat.

If you get an extension to the first question, you should try to extend your current solution without re-doing all the checklist steps. If it's similar enough, you may be able to copy-paste parts of your code and tweak them. However, **do not erase or overwrite what you did for the first question**. Write a horizontal line in the editor and work on the new question below the line. This way, in the end, even if you do not finish the second question, you will at least have the solution to the first one.

If you get an entirely new question, don't forget to reset and do the entire checklist again. Depending on how much time you have left, you may have to try to rush through them. Also, keep in mind that you are not always expected to finish the second question. The interviewer may just want to see how far you get in order to keep observing your technical skills until the end of the allotted time.

What if I know beforehand that I'll get two questions?

We might know this either because our recruiter or interviewer told us or because the company is known for it. First, it is a good idea to confirm it upfront by asking:

"Can you confirm that there will be two questions in this interview? I'd like to budget my time appropriately"[7]

Then, you may have to compress some checklist steps:

- Don't write any pseudocode, even 'indented English.'
- Don't worry about your communication score as much. Focus on getting through questions faster.
- Brush over the verification a bit. You may need to skim through some of the manual verification

.

If there are no new questions, the interviewer is very likely to ask if you have questions for them. See "Good Questions from Candidates" on page 75 about how to leave a lasting positive impression.

KEY TAKEAWAYS

Every company is different, so it is always a good idea to ask your recruiter what to expect beforehand. Your interview may deviate from the checklist, but if you practice these steps (see Chapter 18: How to Practice, pg 170), you should be able to move more swiftly through interviews while scoring well in the *Universal Rubric* categories (pg 181).

As a final reminder, this checklist is for an *algorithms and data structures interview*. Other interview types, like a system design interview or a front-end interview, have different goals and priorities.

⬚ ONLINE RESOURCES

Online resources for this chapter include:

- Interview replays that show specific mistakes people make with coding problems

Go online at bctci.co/anatomy.

---

7   Even if there is a single question, remember that speed is a factor in how you are evaluated (pg 186). You shouldn't just start chilling because you think you have time to kill—move as fast as you can!

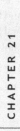
BIG O ANALYSIS

AI interviewer, replays, and more materials for this chapter at bctci.co/big-o-analysis

> He took nothing for granted. He began a tradition of starting from scratch, assuming that the players were blank slates who carried over no knowledge from the year before… He started with [...] "this is a football."
>
> David Maraniss, on Vince Lombardi

▶ *Prerequisites: None*

What a Football Coach Can Teach You About Interviewing Better

In his Vince Lombardi biography,[1] David Maraniss tells the story of the famous football coach. Lombardi had some unusual conventions when coaching his teams into some of the best players the world has ever seen—he started from scratch.

Remember that these athletes were professional players, and most had been playing the game in one way or another since they were in diapers. Yet Lombardi insisted on starting from the beginning and walking his athletes through every part of the game, including how to hold a football correctly, how to fall if they were being tackled, and even how to tie their shoes to avoid tripping. Lombardi recognized that improvement had more to do with being *brilliant at the basics* rather than a focus on complicated plays.

DS&A interviews are like a "game" where the goal is to find optimal answers. To be good at it, we need to understand a few foundational concepts thoroughly, especially big O analysis. Big O is how we measure optimality, so, without it, you can't develop a good sense of what the interviewers are looking for.

Big O analysis shouldn't just be an afterthought after coding your solution. Great candidates tie it into every aspect of the interview: how they design their code, evaluate trade offs, find optimizations, and even how they communicate with the interviewer. Understanding it well will already pay off in the next chapter, Boundary Thinking, where we will see how to use big O analysis to narrow down possible algorithms to optimal solutions.

So, before diving into fancy algorithms and data structures, let's get brilliant at the basics—bifg O analysis.

---

1 When Pride Still Mattered: A Life of Vince Lombardi.

What Is Big O, Anyways?

Imagine you find yourself in an interview, considering two ways of solving a coding problem. How do you choose one? The answer—in interviews and on the job—is often based on big O analysis. Big O analysis is how we measure the efficiency of our code. We estimate this against two key metrics: time and space.

- **Time Complexity:** How does the runtime of our code scale as the *input size* grows?
- **Space Complexity:** How does the amount of memory used by our code scale as the *input size* grows?

In big O analysis, time and space are measured with funny expressions like $O(n)$ and $O(n^2)$, pronounced "big Oh of n" and "big Oh of n squared". The equations inside the parentheses express how time and space increase relative to the input size, which is usually denoted with the variable n. A runtime of $O(n)$ would mean that our program's execution time scales linearly—doubling the input size will roughly double the execution time.[2]

\#   Big O is not an expression for how long code *actually takes*, as much as it is for how code *scales* as the input size increases. This is a really important point, but if you don't understand this just yet, that's okay.

One way to figure out how the runtime of our code scales would be to run it with various input sizes, measure how long it takes each time, chart the measurements, and try to notice a trend in the inputs plotted. The beauty of big O is that we don't need to execute our code to figure out how it scales; we can just look at the code. It may seem fuzzy at first, but it is truly convenient:

- Big O analysis is **not affected by the execution environment**. Actual measurements in units like milliseconds are hard to replicate since the time it takes to run a program depends on many factors, such as your computer's hardware or whether your OS is busy multi-tasking. Big O analysis is not affected by a computer being twice as slow as another (these are called *constant factors*—pg 209).
- You don't even need to have written the code. To evaluate code by the literal time it takes to run, you have to code it first. Big O, however, allows us to **analyze the efficiency by just thinking about our approach**. That saves us a lot of development time.
- If you try running your code with various inputs, you might not realize that the code performs poorly for other inputs you didn't think of trying. When we use big O, we focus on *worst-case analysis* (pg 215), meaning that **it applies to any possible input**.
- Big O **focuses on how your code scales**, which is when efficiency really matters. When looking at specific measurements, you could easily miss the trend for inputs bigger than the ones you measured. The difference between a slow and a fast algorithm is mostly irrelevant on small inputs. For instance, if your code to merge two sorted arrays only runs on arrays with 100 elements, it probably doesn't matter a ton how you write it (within reason!). However, when your arrays contain millions of elements, the difference between $O(n)$ and $O(n^2)$ will be night and day.

In short, big O analysis is powerful because it gives a broad picture of the algorithm's scaling behavior in a way that is easy to calculate and communicate.

---

2 Yes, yes. We know it's a bit more complicated than this. It could be, for example, that the program always starts off with a 900 ms initialization sequence, and then, when n = 1000, it takes 100 ms to run the rest. Doubling the input to n = 2000 may lead to a runtime of 1100 ms—a mere 10% increase in this case. (However, note that as n gets really big—which is when we start **really** caring about runtime—this 900 ms initialization makes very little difference and it will start looking a lot more like actually doubling the time.) Please forgive our slight inaccuracy and handwaviness for the sake of simplicity.

THE RULES OF BIG O

In this chapter, we will learn about big O expressions and how to manipulate them. We expect that the reader has already seen terms like O(n) before, but may be fuzzy on what they mean exactly and how to use them correctly.

One myth to dispel upfront is that big O analysis requires some kind of advanced math. Sure, exponential functions, logarithms, and even factorials come up in algorithm analysis, but we mostly just need to know what they mean (we will discuss each with just the right level of depth). When it comes to actual math manipulation, we'll mostly just use **the two rules of big O** later in the section—a fun and handwavy kind of math that allows us to focus on the big picture rather than the exact numbers and details. Some candidates are thrown off by the mathematical definition of big O based on asymptotic limits, but we can safely skip it in the interview context.

We'll start with the basic concepts. Although we typically hear about big O in the context of algorithms, it actually exists independently of algorithms.[3] At its core, it's a way of *classifying and grouping functions based on their approximate rate of growth*. By functions, we mean something like f(n) = 3n + 2 (we are not talking about code functions yet!), and, by approximate, we mean that we ignore *constant factors* (we'll expand on this with Rule 1). A big O term like O(n) is called a 'complexity class' and represents a class of functions that all have the same approximate growth rate.

For instance, O(n) represents the class of all functions that grow linearly. Examples of functions in the O(n) class are f(n) = n, f(n) = n + 1, f(n) = 2n, and f(n) = 3n + 2. Examples of functions that are *not* in the O(n) class are f(n) = n², f(n) = n²/2, and f(n) = n² + n. Those functions grow faster than linearly, and they belong to their own class called O(n²).

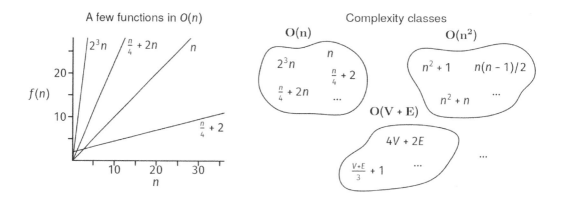

Figure 1.

O(n) and O(n²) are just two examples of complexity classes. In reality, there are infinitely many of them, and you never know what you could encounter in algorithm analysis. It could be a funky-looking complexity like O(√n * log n), or perhaps a multi-variable one like O(V + E).

To be interview-ready, the main question we need to know how to answer is, "Given a function, f(n), which complexity class does it belong to?"

We answer it in two steps:

---

3   For instance, it is correct and useful to say things like, "A string with n characters has O(n²) substrings." It's not about code—it's about how one thing (number of substrings) scales as a function of another thing (number of characters).

1. We wrap $f(n)$ inside big O so it reads like $f(n) = O(f(n))$.[4]
2. We apply **the two rules of big O** to simplify the complexity class.

Let's look at the simplification rules.

RULE 1: REMOVE ADDITIVE AND MULTIPLICATIVE CONSTANTS

Additive and multiplicative constants are called *constant factors*. Imagine we have $f(n) = 3n + 5n + 3^2$.
The first rule is easy to apply:

```
f(n)      = O(3n + 5n + 3²)        (wrapping inside big O
          = O(8n + 9)             (simplifying)
          = O(8n + 9)             (removing the additive constant
          = O(n)                  (removing the multiplicative constant)
```

Here are some nuances about Rule 1:

- When we drop additive constants, that includes negative ones: $n - 1 = O(n)$.
- Similarly, we drop multiplicative constants like $n/2 = 0.5n = O(n)$.
- In contrast, we cannot drop the 2 in the exponent in n^2. It is not an *additive* or *multiplicative* constant, which can be seen by rewriting n^2 as $n*n$.
- We broke down the steps for illustration purposes, but, with practice, we can start skipping steps.

RULE 2: REMOVE NON-DOMINANT ADDITIVE TERMS.

By *dominant term*, we mean the term that is the biggest for any value of n **after some point**. For example, n^2 is bigger than n for any value of n, so n^2 *dominates* n. Similarly, n is bigger than $\min(n^2, 10)$ for any n bigger than 10, so n dominates $\min(n^2, 10)$.[5]

Here is an example of applying Rule 2 for $f(n) = n^2 + n * (2n + 2)$:

```
f(n)      = O(n² + n * (2n + 2))   (wrapping inside big O)
          = O(n² + 2n² + 2n)       (simplifying)
          = O(n² + n² + n)         (removing the multiplicative constants
          = O(n²)                  (removing non-dominant terms
```

In our example, the *dominant* term, n^2, is not unique. In such cases, we only keep one of them. Alternatively, we could simplify $n^2 + n^2$ to $2n^2$ and apply Rule 1, and we would get the same result.

Note that you cannot apply Rule 2 for multiplicative terms: $O(n^2 * n) = O(n * n * n) = O(n^3)$, not $O(n^2)$.

What's dominant and why?

To recognize the dominant term in an expression, it helps to be familiar with the **hierarchy of class complexities**. The following table shows the most common ones (with a single input variable) ordered from slowest to fastest growth. In the context of algorithm scaling, those would be from "best" to "worst":

---

4 When we write an expression like $3n = O(n)$, note that on the left side of the '=' we have a function and on the right side we have a class of functions. It means that the function 3n *is* **in** the class of functions $O(n)$. Out loud, we can read it as "3n is in $O(n)$" or "3n is $O(n)$".

5 The function $\min(x, y)$ is defined as x or y, whichever is smallest.

COMPLEXITY CLASS	NOTATION	DESCRIPTION	EXAMPLES OF FUNCTIONS IN THE CLASS
Constant	O(1)	The growth rate does not depend on the input.[6]	18, 3 * 3 * 3 10! min(n, 10)
Logarithmic	O(log n)	Very slow growth rate. When the input doubles, the value only increases by a constant.	$\log_2(n)$ $\log_3(n)$ $6*\log_2(2n+1)$
Linear	O(n)	When the input doubles, the value at most doubles.	n n/10 3n + 5 $n + \log_2(n)$
Linearithmic	O(n log n)	Slightly faster growth than linear. When the input doubles, the value grows by a bit more than double.	$7n * 3\log_2(n)$ $n * \log_2(n) + n$
Quadratic	O(n²)	When the input doubles, the value at most quadruples.	n(n-1)/2 1 + 2 + 3 + ... + n
Cubic	O(n³)	When the input doubles, the value grows at most eight-fold.	$n^3 + n^2*\log_2(n)$
Exponential (with base 2)	O(2ⁿ)	Extremely fast growth rate. When the input grows by one, the value can double.	2^n $2^{(n+1)}$ $2^n + n^2$
Exponential (with base 3)	O(3ⁿ)	Extremely fast growth rate. When the input grows by one, the value can triple.	3^n $3^{(n+4)}$ $3^n + 2^n$
Factorial	O(n!)	Even faster growth rate. When the input grows by one, the value gets multiplied by a factor that increases each time.	n! + n! 1 * 2 * 3 * ... * n

Table 1. Common complexity classes.

This seems like a lot to memorize, but most of it is pretty straightforward. You probably already know, for example, O(n) grows faster than O(log n); it follows then that O(n * n) grows faster than O(n log n) (we'll talk more about logarithms on page 219).

One that might be less obvious is why O(n!) grows faster than O(2ⁿ) and O(3ⁿ). To see this, consider that 2 * 2 * 2 * 2 * 2 is less than 5 * 4 * 3 * 2 * 1. That is, a bunch of equal numbers multiplied together n times is going to be smaller (eventually) than the product of n numbers that keep getting bigger.

Notes:

- "Polynomial time complexity" is an umbrella term referring to classes in the form O(nᶜ), where c is a constant. For example, O(n), O(n²) and O(n²·¹). These are not, however, the same class.[7]
- "Exponential time complexity" is an umbrella term referring to classes in the form O(cⁿ), where c is a constant and c > 1. For example, O(2ⁿ) and O(3ⁿ). These are also not equivalent.

---

6   Even though we learned in Rule 1 to get rid of constants, the constant complexity class is the exception as it is denoted by O(1). It contains all functions where the value does not depend on the input, like f(n) = 5. It also contains functions where the value is below some constant for any input, like f(n) = min(n, 10). This function is never bigger than 10, so min(n, 10) = O(1).

7   Among polynomial time complexities, O(n) (i.e., O(n¹)), O(n²), and O(n³) have their own names: linear, quadratic, and cubic. After that, we just say, "n to the fourth," "n to the fifth," etc. We can also say "n to the power of c."

- Any exponential time complexity grows faster than every polynomial time complexity. Yes, even $O(1.1^n)$ grows faster than $O(10^n)$, for sufficiently large n.[8]
- Factorial grows faster than every exponential time complexity.

The following plot visualizes the time complexities.

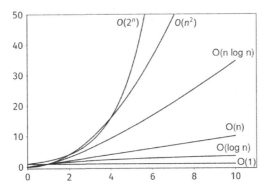

Figure 2. Plot of functions 1, $\log_2(n)$, n, n $*$ $\log_2(n)$, n^2, and 2^n up to n $=$ 10.[9]

As n gets larger, a function from a worse complexity class always ends up above one from a better complexity class. For instance, even if we graphed $f(n)$ $=$ 5n (which would make a steep straight line), the $O(n$ $\log$ $n)$ line would still eventually beat it.

BIG O SIMPLIFICATION PROBLEM SET

The following quiz drills down the issue of finding the dominant term. It's more advanced than what you would find in an interview, but worth practicing to ensure you fully grasp the material!

Simplify the following big O expressions by finding the dominant term:

(a) $O(\sqrt{n} + n)$

(b) $O(n^3 + 3^n)$

(c) $O(2^n + 2^{n+1})$

(d) $O(2^n + 2^{n+n})$

(e) $O(2^n + 3^n)$

(f) $O(10^n + n!)$

BIG O SIMPLIFICATION ANSWERS

(a) $\sqrt{n}$ can be rewritten as $n^{0.5}$, and n can be rewritten as n^1, so n has a larger exponent than $\sqrt{n}$. Thus, n dominates $\sqrt{n}$, and we can simplify the expression to $O(n)$.

(b) Exponential functions always grow faster than polynomial ones, so 3^n is the dominating term and we can simplify the expression to $O(3^n)$.

(c) If we rewrite 2^{n+1} as 2 $*$ 2^n, we can see that it is just 2^n multiplied by a constant. As such, neither term dominates the other. We can simplify the expression to $O(2^n)$.

---

8 Interestingly, n doesn't even have to get that big for 1.1^n > n^{10}. They cross at n $=$ 685.

9 The functions only go up to n $=$ 10. The bigger the scale, the most pronounced the difference between complexity classes.

(d) 2^{n+n} is $2 * 2 * \ldots * 2$ (2n times). By grouping pairs of 2s (of which there are n),we can rewrite it as $(2 * 2)^n = 4^n$. 4^n dominates 2^n, so we can simplify the expression to 4^n.

(e) We can simplify the expression to $O(3^n)$. When comparing exponential functions with the same exponent (e.g., 2^n vs 3^n), the higher base dominates. If the exponent is different (e.g., 2^{2n} vs 3^n), then the higher base may not dominate.

(f) As we mentioned, factorials grow faster than any exponential function. Thus, we can simplify the expression to $O(n!)$.

Congratulations, you learned the two rules of big O!

Big O with multiple variables

As we will see, functions with multiple inputs come up often in algorithm analysis. Thankfully, we still use the same two rules. For instance:

- $f(a, b) = 3a + b/2 + 1 = O(a + b)$, and
- $f(a, b) = a*b^2 + a*b = O(a*b^2)$ because b^2 dominates b, so $a*b^2$ dominates $a*b$.

The one thing to remember is not to assume that the two variables have the same value. For example, even if you have $f(a, b) = a! + b$, you cannot simplify it to $O(a!)$; you need to say $O(a! + b)$ because b could be the dominant term when b is much larger than a.

RUNTIME ANALYSIS WITH BIG O

It's time to apply what we learned about big O to algorithms and data structures. We'll start with runtime analysis. Much like a mathematical function, an algorithm takes an input and computes an output. What we care about is how long that computation takes as a function of the *input size*, and big O notation will help us with that.

Let's say a computer is running a program. The CPU goes instruction by instruction, executing each in order. Some instructions require more CPU cycles than others, but for big O analysis, we can ignore this; since constants go away with big O, what matters is the number of instructions that the program has to execute, not the type.

By that same logic, it does not matter either which language the program is coded in. Sure, Python is slower than C, but it is still safe to assume that each basic instruction in any popular language becomes a constant number of low-level instructions, and that's enough for big O. That's why the language you choose in interviews doesn't matter! It is also why it is fine to discuss algorithm analysis using *pseudo-code* (text that looks like code but is not in any particular language).

So, if we agree that what matters is counting how many instructions are executed, how do we go about counting them? The first thing to do is look for loops in the code, like for and while loops. Loops add the ability to run a block of code several times depending on the input, which can affect the time complexity.

Let's look at two examples. Assuming that arr is an array with n integers, what's the runtime of the following two snippets?

```
1  def has_even_length(arr):
2    is_even = true
3    for elem in arr:
4      is_even = !is_even
5    return is_even
```

```
1  def sum_of_products(arr):
2    prod_sum = 0
3    for elem1 in arr:
4      for elem2 in arr:
5        prod_sum += elem1 * elem2
6    return prod_sum
```

The function has_even_length() has a simple loop that does n iterations. The bits outside the loop take $O(1)$ time, so the number of instructions executed is $O(n)$.

In the case of sum_of_products(), there are two *nested* loops. That means that for each of the n iterations of the first loop, we do n iterations of the second loop. The total number of iterations is n*n, which takes $O(n^2)$ time.

LOOP ANALYSIS PROBLEM SET

Let's learn by example. If n is the size of an array of integers, arr, what is the time complexity of the following snippets?

```
1  (a) def sum_first_half(arr):
2          sum = 0
3          for i in range(len(arr) // 2):
4              sum += arr[i]
5          return sum
```

```
1  (b) def sum_first_ten(arr):
2          sum = 0
3          for i in range(10):
4              if i >= len(arr):
5                  break
6              sum += arr[i]
7          return sum
```

```
1  (c) def sum_and_product_1(arr):
2          sum, prod = 0, 1
3          for elem in arr:
4              sum += elem
5              prod *= elem
6          return sum, prod
```

```
1  (d) def sum_and_product_2(arr):
2          sum, prod = 0, 1
3          for elem in arr:
4              sum += elem
5          for elem in arr:
6              prod *= elem
7          return sum, prod
```

```
1  (e) def sum_of_products_2(arr):
2          prod_sum = 0
3          n = len(arr)
4          for i in range(n):
5              for j in range(i + 1, n):
6                  prod_sum += arr[i] * arr[j]
7          return prod_sum
```

LOOP ANALYSIS ANSWERS

(a) sum_first_half() has a loop that does n/2 iterations (rounded down). Remember what Rule 1 of big O says about multiplicative constants? It doesn't matter if there are n iterations or 0.5n iterations; the complexity is still $O(n)$.

(b) In sum_first_ten(), if n ≤ 10, the loop visits every element. But, no matter how big n is, the loop never does more than 10 iterations, and that's what matters for big O analysis. Since the number of instructions executed is bounded by a constant for any input size, this snippet runs in $O(1)$ time.

(c) The analysis for sum_and_product_1() is analogous to the analysis of has_even_length(): they both have a simple loop that does n iterations. It doesn't matter that one has more instructions per iteration than the other. As long as there are no *nested loops*, it's just a different multiplicative constant factor and we ignore it. Therefore, the number of instructions is $O(n)$.

(d) sum_and_product_2() has two loops, but they are *sequential* (first one, then the other). For sequential loops, we can find the total number of instructions by adding the number of iterations of each: $O(n) + O(n) = O(n)$.

(e) In sum_of_products_2(), we visit all pairs of indices (i, j) where i < j. This nested loop pattern comes up whenever we need to visit each pair of *distinct* indices once. The runtime analysis is interesting because the number of iterations in the inner loop decreases at every iteration of the outer loop. The runtime is clearly at most $O(n^2)$, but is it less than that? Although the inner loop sometimes does as few as one or two iterations, the answer is no—it is still $O(n^2)$. One way to see it is to visualize the iterations like below. We can see that sum_of_products_2() does roughly half as many iterations as sum_of_products()—and that's just a constant factor.[10]

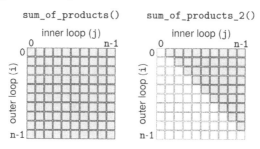

Figure 3. There is one row for each iteration of the outer loop and one column for each iteration of the inner loop. The shaded squares correspond to pairs of indices visited by the algorithm.

▶ **RELYING ON "LOOP COUNTING" IS DANGEROUS**   INTERVIEW REPLAY

View Online:	bctci.co/big-o-replay-1 @ 50:44 - 1:01:55
The Question:	Given a binary grid, find all unique shapes in the grid.
What You'll See:	This candidate made the common mistake of counting loops to figure out time complexity. This approach fails about as often as it works and is usually a gross oversimplification.
Who:	*Interviewer*: Software Engineer at Amazon *Candidate*: 8 years exp.

The time complexity of built-in methods

To be effective programmers, we often leverage the *built-in methods* provided by the language, such as len() and sorted() in Python. Most languages also have a standard library with commonly used methods and data structures. For example, in C++, anything in the std namespace, like std::string, is from the standard library.

Built-in and standard-library methods take time and space, and you need to count them as part of your algorithm, even if you didn't write the code.

In the previous snippets, we've been using the built-in method len() that returns the length of a list/array. To analyze those methods, we need to know that len() takes $O(1)$ time.[11]

\#   If you don't know the time or space used by a built-in method, ask yourself, "If I implemented this, how would I do it?" and analyze based on that. If you are not sure during practice, you can look it up. In an interview, make your best guess. You can say, "Assuming that this method takes <X> time, then the time complexity of my algorithm is <Y>." You'll probably be right, but even if you're wrong, your interviewer

---

10 This pattern extends to three or more nested loops: visiting all triplets of indices (i, j, k) where i < j < k takes $O(n^3)$ time. Generally speaking, for any constant m, an array of length n has $O(n^m)$ subsets of m elements.

11 If you thought that len() takes $O(n)$ time, see Chapter 25: Dynamic Arrays (pg 282). We'll walk through a full implementation of dynamic arrays (the equivalent of Python lists).

probably won't care too much as long as your reasoning was solid—and they might not even know themselves.

WORST-CASE, AVERAGE-CASE, AND BEST-CASE ANALYSIS

One term you will hear thrown around often is "worst-case analysis." It's good to know what it refers to, why we focus so much on it, and the alternatives.

Let's analyze one more snippet:

```
1   def has_negatives(arr):
2     for elem in arr:
3       if elem < 0:
4         return True
5     return False
```

At first sight, has_negatives() looks like some of the loops in the previous problem set. What sets it apart is that the loop has an *early exit condition*. If arr has no zeroes, the loop does n iterations and takes O(n) time. However, if the first element in arr is 0, the loop does only 1 iteration regardless of how big arr is, taking only O(1) time. What do we do when we get different time complexities, for the same code, depending on the input?

We can express this as follows:

- Worst-case runtime: the *maximum* number of steps taken by the algorithm for an input of size n.
- Best-case runtime: the *minimum* number of steps taken by the algorithm for an input of size n.

For certain algorithms, it can also be useful to express a third idea:

- Average-case runtime: the *average* number of steps taken by the algorithm for any input of size n.

For has_negatives(), the worst-case runtime is O(n), the best-case runtime is O(1), and the average-case runtime depends on how likely negative values are in the input.

The good news is that, in an interview, **you are typically only expected to give the worst-case analysis**. Sure, it is good if we get a "lucky" input and our code runs faster than in the worst case, but the worst case is considered our baseline and also needs to be fast.

Let's take the example of programming an algorithm for the enemy AI in a video game. If your code has good best-case and even average-case performance but takes a long time in specific scenarios, the game may lag from time to time, making for a not-so-fun experience for the player.

More broadly, engineering with the worst-case scenario in mind is a sound practice. An e-commerce website needs to be able to handle Black Friday traffic, even if that worst-case scenario occurs only once a year.

In the Dynamic Arrays chapter, we'll see another type of analysis that comes up in the analysis of data structures: amortized time (pg 285).

Big O, Big Theta (Θ), and Big Omega (Ω)

If you studied big O in school, or read a serious algorithms textbook, you might be wondering how big theta (Θ) factors into all this. That's where we (and the whole industry) get a bit sloppy.

See, somewhere along the way, professionals adopted big O and messed things up a bit. According to its actual definition, big O is about *upper bounds*. So n^2 is—technically—in $O(n^3)$ and even in $O(n!)$. Those complexities dominate n^2, so they are upper bounds for n^2.

Despite the official definition, **in practice, in the industry, big O is only used to give the smallest possible upper bound.** If your code does n simple iterations and you say the runtime is $O(n^2)$, while technically correct, the most likely outcome is that you'll confuse your interviewer. They might even think that it's *you* who doesn't understand big O.

We have a word to describe the "smallest upper bound" class complexity for a function: we say that $O(n)$ is the *tight* upper bound for n because it is the smallest one containing n. In contrast, $O(n^2)$ is an upper bound of n, but it's not tight.

So, what about big theta (Θ) and big omega (Ω)? The *official* definitions are that:

- Big O expresses an upper bound. It's sort of a "less than or equal to" between complexity classes.
- Big Ω (omega) expresses a lower bound. We can say that n^2 is $\Omega(\log n)$ or even $\Omega(1)$. It communicates "greater than or equal to."
- Big Θ (theta) means both big O *and* big Ω. For instance, $n^2 = O(n^2)$ and $n^2 = \Omega(n^2)$, so $n^2 = \Theta(n^2)$.

So, the way we use big O for "tight upper bounds" is closer to the definition of big Θ. We call this out here in case you've come across this in an algorithms textbook and think we're doing it wrong. *We are.* But, so is everyone else.

\# The default, hidden assumption in coding interviews is that we are trying to find a tight upper bound (essentially big Θ, even though we use big O) on the worst-case analysis. That's true for both time and space.

With all this out of the way, we won't see big Θ or big Ω again for the rest of the book. We'll also assume that we are always asking for the worst-case analysis.

IS WORST-CASE/AVERAGE-CASE/BEST-CASE ANALYSIS THE SAME AS BIG O/Θ/Ω?

This is a common misconception, but no. We can technically use big O/Θ/Ω to give upper/tight/lower bounds for each type of case analysis. Big O/Θ/Ω describe whether the runtime (for some input) is ≤, =, or ≥ some value, whereas worst/average/best case describe the runtime for less favorable vs. more favorable input.

Imagine a function with 3 nested loops that does n iterations in the best case, n^2 iterations in the average case, and n^3 iterations in the worst case. All of the following are correct statements:

	Exact bound	Upper bounds (using the official definition of big O)	Lower bounds
Best-case analysis	$\Theta(n)$	$O(n), O(n^2)$	$\Omega(n), \Omega(1)$
Average-case analysis	$\Theta(n^2)$	$O(n^2), O(n^3)$	$\Omega(n^2), \Omega(n)$
Worst-case analysis	$\Theta(n^3)$	$O(n^3), O(n^4)$	$\Omega(n^3), \Omega(n^2)$

In interviews we focus on finding a tight upper bound on the worst-case analysis, which is why big O is often equated with worst-case analysis. However, the other combinations are sometimes useful too. For instance, on page 364, we talk about a *lower bound* for the worst-case analysis of sorting algorithms.

A GOOD START: IDENTIFY THE INPUT VARIABLES

A common mistake interviewees make is not being clear about what the variable(s) represent in the big O notation. You cannot say, "This algorithm runs in $O(n)$ time," before telling the interviewer what n is. Likewise, you cannot say, "This algorithm runs in linear time," without specifying what the linear dependency is on. Even better, write it down.

Even if it may seem obvious in some cases, it's a good habit to always be clear about the variables in the big O analysis. If the input is an array, `arr`, we might write down our time and space analysis next to the code like this:

```
Algo 1: binary search
n: the length of arr
T: O(...)
S: O(...)
<code>
```

Here are a few examples of the variables we might use depending on the input type, written down as we would in an interview:

Input: a string, s

We often use the letter n for the size of simple inputs like an array of numbers or the length of a string (but we can use a different variable too).

```
n: the length of s
```

Input: two strings, s1 and s2, of different lengths

While it is common to use n and m, those get easily mixed up; not only do they sound similar, but we use n so much in big O expressions that candidates end up describing loops—even through a different variable—as $O(n)$. It is better to use variables tied to the strings' names.

```
n1: the length of s1
n2: the length of s2
```

\# The general advice is to use variable names that reflect what they represent. (This applies not only to the variables for the analysis but also to naming variables in code!)

Even if the input consists of two strings or arrays with different sizes, if there is some relationship between their lengths, the big O analysis may end up with only one variable after simplifying. For example:

```
n1: the length of arr1
n2: the length of arr2
T: O(n1 + n2) = O(n1) (because n1 >= n2)
S: O(...)
```

Notice how we showed the time complexity before and after simplifying n2 away. This shows the interviewer that you didn't simply forget about n2.

Input: two strings, s1 and s2, of the same length

Since they have the same length, it is OK to use only one variable.

```
n: the length of s1 == the length of s2
```

\# When the input contains multiple strings or arrays, it is an excellent *clarifying question* for the interviewer to ask if they have the same length.

Input: an array, arr, of strings of different lengths

This is tricky since it looks like we might need a variable for the length of each string. A typical approach here is to analyze the algorithm assuming that all the strings are as long as the longest one. Then, only two variables are needed:

```
n: the number of strings in arr
k: the maximum length of any string in arr
```

This may be a pessimistic assumption, but we know for sure that we will get an upper bound, so it is in line with big O analysis. It's also possible to use a variable for "the sum of lengths of all the strings" instead. Deciding which makes more sense depends on the problem (we'll see examples of both).

Input: a two-dimensional matrix, mat
```
R: number of rows in mat
C: number of columns in mat
```

Many candidates use n and m for matrix dimensions, but R and C are clearer (and reduce mistakes) as they tie to the concepts of rows and columns.

Input: a square two-dimensional matrix mat
```
n: number of rows in mat == number of columns in mat
```

Since the number of rows and columns is the same, it is common to use n for both, but be careful—there is potential for confusion. Consider a simple algorithm with a nested loop that visits every cell in the matrix once. Since we usually associate $O(n)$ with linear complexity and the algorithm is linear on the input size, candidate sometimes (incorrectly) describe the runtime as $O(n)$. The mistake is that the matrix size is n^2, not n.

Notice how, when using words like 'linear' or 'quadratic' to describe our runtime, it can be critical to specify what the dependency is on: we can say "The runtime is linear on the matrix size," or "The runtime is quadratic on n." Both are correct!

Input: a number n

The only case where you do *not* need to define the variable is when the input (or one of the inputs) is a number. We can just use it directly in the big O notation. For example, we'll see a $O(\sqrt{n})$-time algorithm for finding whether a number n is prime (Chapter 24: List Of Divisors, pg 253). The input itself appears in the analysis.

> While we use n often as a variable in runtime, we also urge caution on this. A lot of candidates make mistakes because they define n to be one thing (e.g., the length of an array of strings), but then accidentally use it in another way (e.g., the length of a specific string). Beware of this mistake. If there is any ambiguity about what n might mean, it may be safest to just not use n at all for this problem.

Implicit inputs

A function's runtime may depend on the size of variables that are not direct inputs to the function, like global variables. In such cases, we also need a variable for the size of the global variable. We could write something like:
```
n: the size of the global array 'arr'
```

Global variables do not come up often in interviews, but data structure operations that depend on the amount of data stored in the data structure do. For example, consider the push() method on a heap. The input is the element to insert, but we analyze it in terms of the number of elements in the heap. We would write:
```
n: the size of the heap
```

Whether inputs are implicit or explicit, defining the variables you use in your analysis goes a long way.

LOGARITHMS IN BIG O ANALYSIS

We pulled logarithms into their own section because most candidates tend to be particularly rusty about them, and the way they are treated in big O analysis is quite different from how you learned about them in math class anyway.

The logarithm that comes up most often in algorithm analysis is the base-2 logarithm, denoted by $\log_2(n)$. Mathematically, $\log_2(n) = a$ means that $2^a = n$, but there is an alternative way to think about it which is much more relevant to algorithm analysis:

We can think of $\log_2(n)$ as **the number of times we have to halve n to reach 1**:

- $\log_2(1) = 0$ because n is already 1.
- $\log_2(2) = 1$ because $2/2 = 1$.
- $\log_2(4) = 2$ because we need to halve 4 twice to get to 1.
- $\log_2(12)$ is somewhere between 3 and 4 because $\log_2(8) = 3$ and $\log_2(16) = 4$.

The base-two logarithm comes up in algorithms and data structures that employ the concept of *halving*:

- Binary search is a classic search algorithm for sorted lists that, at each step, *halves* the search range. After at most $\log_2(n)$ steps, only one element remains in the range.
- In a balanced binary tree (), the descendants of each node are *split roughly evenly* between the left and the right subtree, so it has logarithmic height.
- Merge sort (pg 362) is a divide-and-conquer algorithm that *splits the array to sort in half*, sorts each half recursively, and finally merges the two sorted halves into a single sorted list. The maximum recursion depth is $\log_2(n)$, and we will later see that logarithms appear in its runtime complexity as a result (pg 404).

More on each of those soon!

Although less common in algorithm analysis, the same idea also applies to other logarithm bases. E.g., $\log_3(n)$ is the number of times we need to divide n by 3 to get to 1. Thus, $\log_3(27) = 3$ because $27/3 = 9, 9/3 = 3$, and $3/3 = 1$.

Exponential = very fast, logarithmic = very slow

Logarithms are essentially the opposite of exponential functions: $\log_2(n)$ is the number x such that $2^x = n$. So, $\log_2(16)$ is 4 because $2^4 = 16$.

If exponentials grow very fast, logarithms grow very slowly. Very. That's the number one thing to remember about them. It is not far-fetched to say that $\log_2(n)$ is essentially a constant for any practical input size: when n is one trillion, $\log_2(n)$ is barely 40.

Thus, it may seem like interviewers shouldn't care between, say, a $O(n)$-time algorithm and a $O(n \log n)$-time algorithm. However, even if it's true that this difference isn't meaningful in the real world, interviewing isn't about doing what's best in the real world; it's about showing your problem-solving skills, largely by finding ways to reduce this metric called big O. As we said in the beginning, this is a game and this is how we score points.

What about the base of the logarithm?

In math class, you might have been taught that, unless a base is specified, we assume that $\log(n)$ means $\log_{10}(n)$. You might also notice that we—by which we mean the authors and programmers as a whole—usually drop the base for logs, *even while we're talking about halving operations*. Does that mean that we are assuming $\log(n)$ means $\log_2(n)$?

The answer isn't yes or no—it's that *it doesn't matter*. For mathy reasons you don't need to worry about, $\log_2(n)$ and $\log_{10}(n)$ are only off by a constant factor. Specifically:

$$\log_2(n) = \log_{10}(n)/\log_{10}(2) \approx 0.301*\log_{10}(n)$$

That is, $\log_{10}(n)$ grows slower than $\log_2(n)$, but only by a constant factor (0.301) which goes away in big O notation. Thus, instead of writing $O(\log_2(n))$ or $O(\log_{10}(n))$, we just write $O(\log n)$.

LOGARITHMS PROBLEM SET

The following problem set shows some of the more advanced manipulations of logarithms.

Find the complexity class for the following functions:

(a) $\log_{10}(n)$

(b) $2^n * \log_2(n)$

(c) $n + \log_2(n)$

(d) $\log_2(n^2)$

(e) $(\log_2(n))^2$

In the below problems, assume n is the number of elements in an array, `arr`. What is the time complexity of the following snippets?

```
(f) def sum_power_of_2_indices(arr):
        i = 2
        res = 0
        while i < len(arr):
            res += arr[i]
            i *= 2
        return res
```

```
(g) def weighted_sum(arr):
        i = len(arr)
        res = 0
        while i > 0:
            for j in range(i):
                res += arr[j]
            i = i // 2
        return j
```

LOGARITHMS ANSWERS

(a) As mentioned, the base of the logarithm does not matter, so $\log_{10}(n) = O(\log n)$.

(b) Even though 2^n grows much faster than $\log_2(n)$, we cannot simplify further as they are multiplicative terms. The complexity is $O(2^n * \log n)$.

(c) The dominant term is n, so this is $O(n)$ (not to be confused with its similar-looking multiplicative cousin $O(n \log n)$).

(d) One manipulation that we can do with logarithms is "pulling the exponent out": $\log_2(n^2) = 2*\log_2(n)$. In other words, it takes twice as many halvings to reach 1 starting from n^2 as from n. For instance, $\log_2(4) = 2$ and $\log_2(16) = 4$. By applying this, we see that $\log_2(n^2) = 2*\log_2(n) = O(\log n)$.

(e) We can rewrite this as $\log_2(n) * \log_2(n)$. Since there are no constants or additive terms, we cannot simplify further. We can leave it as $O((\log n)^2)$. Sometimes, this complexity is also written as $O(\log^2 n)$.

(f) This snippet adds up the elements in `arr` at the indices which are powers of two. The number of iterations of the while loop is the number of times you can double a number starting at 2 before you reach n. Counting *repeated doublings* is like counting halvings but in the opposite direction, so the complexity is $O(\log n)$.

(g) In this snippet, i halves at each iteration of the while loop, so the loop does 0(log n) iterations. The inner loop is interesting. The first time, it does n iterations, then floor(n/2), then floor(n/4), and so on. To know the total number of inner-loop iterations, we need to find the sum n + n/2 + n/4 + ..., where we can factor n out and rewrite as n * (1 + 1/2 + 1/4 + ...). The bit inside the parentheses is a well-known geometric series that starts with 1, 1.5, 1.75, 1.875, 1.9375, and never quite reaches 2. So, the runtime of this algorithm is 0(2n) = 0(n).

Figure 4. In the sum 1 + 1/2 + 1/4 + ..., each term adds half of the remaining amount to reach two, so it never quite gets to two.[12]

RECURSIVE FUNCTIONS IN BIG O ANALYSIS

Knowing how to analyze recursive algorithms is an important aspect of mastering big O. However, we have stayed away from recursion in our examples so far because we want to first introduce the topic. We will learn to analyze recursive functions in the Recursion chapter (pg 206).

SPACE ANALYSIS

Congratulations! You've learned about time complexity. We haven't talked much about space complexity yet for two reasons:

1. Once you understand time complexity, space complexity is simple to understand by comparison. It uses the same rules of big O analysis but tends to be more straightforward.

2. Time complexity is generally more important. As computer memory became more available over time, we shifted our focus in the industry to care much more about time than space, which also translated to interviews. For most problems, the goal will likely be to optimize time complexity first and space second.

A natural question is, "What counts as 'using memory'?"

In short, when you initialize a variable, you use memory to hold its value.[13] The amount of memory depends on the variable's type:

- **Primitive types** are the basic types built into the language, like 32-bit or 64-bit integers, real numbers (also known as floating-point numbers), characters, booleans, and pointers/references (i.e., memory addresses). All of them take no more than a few bytes of memory. The exact representation and size may change between languages and systems, but the point is that they all take 0(1) space.[14]

- **Composite types** are types with multiple fields, like classes or 'structs', and they can be user-defined. The space taken by an instance of a struct (or object) is the sum of the space of each field. For instance, if you have a Point object with two fields, an x coordinate and a y coordinate, the struct takes 0(1) + 0(1) = 0(1) space.

- **Collection types** include types that contain a variable number of elements, like arrays, strings, sets, and maps. Collections of primitive types take space proportional to the number of elements. For instance, an array with n numbers takes 0(n) space, a string with n characters takes 0(n) space, and so on.

---

12 This illustration is a bit like Zeno's arrow paradox, where each term in the sum 1/2 + 1/4 + 1/8 + ... halves the remaining amount to reach 1, but never quite gets to 1.

13 There's another type of memory usage we'll see in the Recursion chapter: the *call stack* (pg 392).

14 Python is a bit of an exception, as integers are not limited to using 32 or 64 bits as in most other languages. Instead, they can theoretically grow indefinitely, but integers beyond 64 bits are not needed for most practical applications. So, even in Python, we assume that integers take 0(1) space unless indicated otherwise.

We can combine the different types, like a collection of structs or a struct with a collection as a field. For instance, a struct with two integer arrays, one with length n and the other with length n^2, takes $O(n + n^2)$ = $O(n^2)$ space.

One case of particular interest is 'recursive structs', such as binary trees. A struct is recursive if at least one of the fields is a pointer/reference to another struct of the same type. The space used by a recursive data structure is the sum of the space of all the structs reachable through the pointers. We'll cover the analysis in detail in future chapters.

Input space vs extra space

When it comes to analyzing your code's space complexity, distinguishing between **input memory** and **extra memory** is helpful. Input memory is the memory taken by our function's inputs. Those inputs existed before our function was called, meaning that the memory for them was allocated somewhere outside the function. Extra memory is memory allocated by our function itself.

> Extra memory is the most important type to analyze since our code is directly responsible for it. In interviews, we typically talk about the extra space, not the input space. When we are asked about the space complexity of an algorithm, we are referring to the extra memory, and we don't include the input.

We can write something like this:

```
n: the length of arr
T: ...
S: O(1) extra space¹⁵
```

SPACE COMPLEXITY PROBLEM SET

Let's practice the concepts of space analysis with a quiz. If s is a string with n letters, what is the extra space complexity of the following snippets? For simplicity, assume that s can use only the 26 lowercase letters from 'a' to 'z'.

```
1  (a) def empty_grid(s):
2          mat = []
3          for i in range(len(s)):
4              mat.append([])
5              for j in range(len(s)):
6                  mat[i].append(0)
```

```
1  (b) def empty_lists(s):
2          arr = []
3          for i in range(len(s) // 2):
4              arr.append([])
```

```
5  (c) def letter_set(s):
6          my_set = set()
7          for c in s:
8              my_set.add(c)
```

```
1  (d) def letters_to_indices(s):
2          m = {}
3          for i, c in enumerate(s):
4              if c not in m:
5                  m[c] = []
6                  m[c].append(i)
```

---

15   We recommend writing "extra space" to make it clear we are not including the input space. This way, the interviewer won't get confused thinking we think the input space is $O(1)$ too.

```
1  (e) class Foo:                          1  (f) def all_substrings(s):
2          def __init__(self, val, next):  2          arr = []
3              self.val = val               3          for i in range(len(s)):
4              self.next = next             4              for j in range(i + 1, len(s)):
5                                           5                  arr.append(s[i:j])
6          def linked_foos(s):
7          curr = Foo('x', None)
8          for c in s:
9            if c != 'x':
10               curr = Foo(val, curr)
```

SPACE COMPLEXITY ANSWERS

(a) We create a matrix as a list of n lists. When we have a collection of collections, we need to add the length of all the nested collections. Thus, the space is $O(n * n) = O(n^2)$.

(b) We create an array containing floor(n/2) empty lists. Since the lists are empty, it may seem like they do not take any space. However, an empty list takes $O(1)$ space, since it is usually represented internally as a pointer to the first element. The pointer may be 'null' for empty lists, but a null pointer still takes $O(1)$ space. Thus, the extra space is $O(n/2 * 1) = O(n)$.

(c) We create a set of all characters in s. At first, it might seem that since we add n times to a collection, we are using $O(n)$ extra space. However, the distinguishing feature of sets is that they do not contain duplicates. Since there are only 26 letters, the size of the set will be at most 26, which is only $O(1)$ space.

(d) We create a map from each letter to the list of indices where we can find that letter in s. Like sets, maps cannot contain duplicate letters, so the map contains at most $26 = O(1)$ keys. However, we have a list for each key, and we do a total of n appends to those lists, so the map takes $O(n)$ space.

(e) We initialize a recursive struct, so the vital question is how many instances of the struct we create. We can see that it depends on how many letters 'x' there are in s. But remember, we care about worst-case analysis. Thus, we should assume that s contains no 'x's. In that case, we create a total of n + 1 nodes. Each node takes $O(1)$ space, so the total space is $O((n + 1) * 1) = O(n)$.

(f) This one is tricky. We can do this in two ways. The first way is to realize that we have an $O(n^2)$-time nested loop, and each iteration creates a substring with a maximum length of n. Therefore, we are using at most $O(n^3)$ space. Another way is to look how big the final contents of arr will be. We add every substring of s into arr, and there are $O(n^2)$ substrings (pg 533). Each substring has a maximum length n, so the space complexity will be $O(n^2 * n) = O(n^3)$. Technically, we haven't shown that $O(n^3)$ is tight, since we only said that the *max* length is n, but this would probably be sufficient for an interview.[16]

SPACE PITFALLS

Let's analyze one more round of code snippets, but this time, each question will highlight an interesting point about space analysis and—probably more relevant to you—cover one of the points that commonly trips candidates up.

The space complexity of copies

If s is a string of length n, what is the space complexity of this code?

---

16 We *could* prove that the $O(n^3)$ bound is tight. Let X be the set of all substrings that start in the first n/4 indices and end in the last n/4 indices. Each of these will have length at least n/2. Since there are n/4 beginnings and n/4 endings, there are $n/4 * n/4 = n^2/16$ such substrings. Since each string has length of at least n/2, the total number of characters contained is at least $n^2/16 * n/2 = n^3/32 = O(n^3)$. Thus, we found a **subset** of substrings that takes $O(n^3)$ space, so the set of **all** substrings also takes **at least** $O(n^3)$ space. Thus, $O(n^3)$ is tight!

```
1  def repeated_str(s):
2    strs = []
3    for i in range(len(s)):
4      strs.append(s)
```

We append n strings of length n to `strs`, so it looks like the space complexity should be $O(n^2)$. However, in Python, it is $O(n)$. Can you see why? There is a difference between *copying* a variable and just *referencing* it. In Python, `strs.append(s)` just appends a reference of s (i.e., a pointer to the address of s in memory), which takes just $O(1)$ space.

Copies can happen when using the assignment operator (=), but they may not be apparent because there is no consistent syntax between languages. Here are some examples:

	Copy of a string s.	Making a **reference** of a string s.
Python	s2 = s[:]	s2 = s
C / C++	s2 = s;	s2 = &s;
Go	s2 = s	s2 = s[:]
Javascript	s2 = s.splice()	s2 = s

For every language, there is a way to copy and a way to reference a variable, and mixing them up can derail an interview:

- If you intend to make a reference but make a copy instead, your code will use more space than needed and your space analysis may be wrong.
- If you need a copy but make a reference, your algorithm may be incorrect because you are unintentionally modifying the same variable instead of separate copies.

It is a common problem in interviews when candidates might not be using their primary language and there are discrepancies between how each language works! Familiarize yourself with when copies happen in the language you use in interviews.

Copies can also happen when passing parameters to a function. Parameters can be passed by *value* (copy) or by *reference* (no copy). Again, there is no consistency between languages. In a language like C++, the default is passing by value, while in Python, the default is passing by reference.

As an exercise, you can rewrite `repeated_str()` in your language of choice in a way that makes copies and in a way that doesn't.

▶ **PYTHON SLICES CAN GET EXPENSIVE!**	INTERVIEW REPLAY

View Online:	bctci.co/big-o-replay-2 @15:51 - 16:31
The Question:	What is the time and space complexity associated with slicing a string in Python?
What You'll See:	The candidate is unaware that Python slices take linear time and space. They incorrectly believe it is just an iterator with $O(1)$ guarantees.
Who:	*Interviewer*: Senior Software Engineer at Meta *Candidate*: 8 years exp.

The space complexity of built-in methods

If arr is an array of integers of length n, what is the extra space complexity of this code?

```
1   def smallest(arr):
2     if len(arr) == 0:
3       return -1
4     arr.sort()
5     return arr[0]
```

As we mentioned on page 214, we need to factor in the time and space used by built-in methods.

It might seem like smallest() only uses O(1) extra space because we are not declaring any new variables. In Python, the arr.sort() method modifies arr **in place**—it doesn't return anything. However, the important question is: how much *extra* space does arr.sort() use internally? As we'll see on page 369, this is language-specific, but in the case of Python, it takes O(n) extra space.

Thus, the extra space of smallest() is O(n).

As an aside, smallest() modifies the input, which some interviewers don't allow. Sometimes, modifying the input can be convenient (or even a sneaky way of using less extra space), but you should consult with your interviewer first if you are allowed to.

The space complexity of integers

If k is a positive integer, what's the time complexity of this code?

```
1   def list_of_digits(k):
2     digits = []
3     while k > 0:
4       digits.append(k % 10)
5       k = k / 10
```

This function creates an array with one element per digit of k. For instance, if k is 980, we create an array [0, 8, 9]. So, what's the final length of the array?

Thus far, we've been treating the space used by an integer as O(1). But, what if our number got really, *really* big? In some languages, our integers have a max size (like 32 or 64 bits) and, if you try to represent a number that does not fit in that number of bits, you get what is called an *integer overflow* error. For those languages, each integer takes O(1) space.

Python works differently. Integers are *unbounded* by default, meaning that they never overflow. More bits are internally allocated as necessary to represent any integer. That is **not** constant space. So, if we have a super big integer, k, how many bits do we need? One way to think about it is that, each time we add one bit to the representation, we can represent twice as many values. With 1 bit, we can represent 2 values. With 2 bits, we can represent 4 values, and so on. This is the *repeated doubling* pattern we saw in the logarithms section (pg 219). The fact that the range doubles for each bit means that we need O(log k) bits to represent a value k.

That means, that, *technically*, an integer k in Python takes O(log k) space. However, the default assumption is that we are not working with hugh numbers and each integer takes O(1) space. After all, 64 bits is enough to represent numbers in the billions of billions, which is enough for the vast majority of coding problems.

So, returning to list_of_digits(), we can approach it in two ways:

- We can assume that numbers take O(1) space, which means that the array will contain O(1) digits.
- We can say that a number k has $\log_{10}(k)$ = O(log k) digits, so the array will contain O(log k) elements.

Your interviewer could be looking for either, so this may be an interesting point to discuss with them, especially if you use Python and/or the problem is directly related to the magnitude of the number.

See Problem 43.3: Exclusive Product (pg 615) for a related concern: even if the input numbers are small, depending on how we operate with them, we could get integer overflow/non-constant-size integers.

SPACE VS TIME COMPLEXITY

Given the choice, do you optimize for time complexity or space complexity? Typically, we prioritize the time complexity and let space complexity "break the tie" between otherwise equally time-efficient algorithms. But, you can always check with your interviewer; maybe they want you to play by different rules.

Note that the time complexity is always equal or bigger than the extra space complexity. That is, while there are plenty of algorithms with $O(n^2)$ time and $O(n)$ extra space, it doesn't make sense have an algorithm with $O(n)$ time and $O(n^2)$ extra space. The reason for this is simple: it takes $O(n^2)$ time to initialize $O(n^2)$ space. If our algorithm uses a lot of space, it will also use as much time.

This is perhaps part of why we prioritize time complexity over space complexity; as long as our algorithm is time-efficient, it really can't be all that space-inefficient.

EXTRA CREDIT: NP-COMPLETE PROBLEMS

Usually, we think of exponential-time algorithms as really inefficient and something to avoid. However, for some problems, no polynomial-time algorithm exists, and we *need* an exponential-time algorithm or worse.

Sometimes, it is easy to see if that's the case. For instance, Problem 39.2: Subset Enumeration (pg 551) asks us to output an array of length $O(2^n)$, which automatically means that we can't do better than $O(2^n)$ time.

If an interviewer asks a question like this, **they are looking for an exponential-time algorithm**. We will tackle this type of problem in Chapter 39: Backtracking (pg 540). In this section, we will discuss a class of problems which also require exponential time, but for which it is far from obvious that they do: *NP-complete* problems.

Without defining them formally, **NP-complete problems**[17] [18] are problems for which the output size is *not* exponential, but nevertheless, no one knows any better-than-exponential algorithms for them. Basically, brute force is about as good as we know how to do—and computer scientists have good reason to believe that no polynomial-time algorithm exists. To understand where the name "NP-complete" comes from or why computer scientists believe that they are so hard, we would have to talk about the famous "P vs NP" question. We encourage the reader to read into this fascinating topic, but in this book, we will stick to what is applicable to interviews.

When it comes to interviews, what matters is knowing what to do if you get asked an NP-complete problem. The hard part is identifying that a problem is NP-complete in the first place since they often look "innocent," meaning that it *feels like* an efficient algorithm could exist. To make this point, let's look at one of the most commonly asked NP-complete problems.

In the **traveling salesperson problem** (known as TSP), you are given an undirected graph in which every node represents a city and every node is connected to every other node. Each edge has a length representing the travel distance between the two cities at the endpoints. What is the shortest path that goes through all the cities and ends at the starting city?

---

17   To be rigorous, we should mention that when we talk about NP-complete problems, we are also referring to FNP-complete problems. For instance, the version of TSP in this section is not technically NP-complete, it is FNP-complete. This distinction is usually ignored outside of theoretical computer science, so we also ignore it here.

18   Another term you may see is "NP-hard." Without getting into the technical definition, colloquially, we say a problem is NP-hard if it's at least as hard as NP-complete problems, but possibly more. So, every NP-complete problem is NP-hard, but not the other way around. For instance, Chapter 39: Subset Enumeration (pg 551) is NP-hard but not NP-complete.

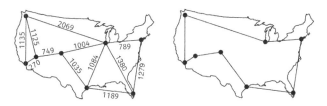

Figure 5. Example of TSP input (not all edges are shown) and solution.

A typical candidate will see the words "graph" and "shortest path," and conclude that the solution must be to use an algorithm typically associated with shortest paths, like breadth-first search (pg 475) or Dijkstra's algorithm. Or they will think it must be related to sorting and attempt to sort the cities by distance from the first city. Or they'll come up with a Greedy algorithm (pg 206) and use a loop to find the nearest remaining city at each step. However, no matter what they come up with, for some graphs, the output path will not be the shortest one.

Candidates insist on finding an efficient solution for an NP-complete problem like TSP because it feels like there should be a better solution and spin their wheels without making progress. In truth, brute-forcing through all n! permutations of city orders is about as good as we can do for this problem (see pg 555).[19]

When asking such a question, the interviewer aims to see if the candidate can recognize the problem as NP-complete and not waste time trying to find a solution that is both efficient *and* optimal. That is why identifying NP-complete problems is a valuable skill. Once you identify it, your interviewer and you can discuss whether to settle for a brute-force solution or use an efficient approach that gets a suboptimal path (like a Greedy algorithm).

Identifying NP-complete problems

If NP-complete problems can look innocent like TSP, how can we identify them? Thankfully, there are only a handful of famous NP-complete problems a candidate could be expected to know. It is worth familiarizing yourself with some of them, so we listed some of the main ones below. For now, the goal is not to be able to code a solution, but just to recognize an NP-complete problem when it's given to you.

- **Traveling salesperson problem** (see above).
- **Longest path problem:** find the longest path in a graph from a given start node to a given end node without repeating any nodes. This problem is a prime example of an innocent-looking NP-complete problem: if we change "longest" to "shortest," the problem is no longer NP-complete! The problem is NP-complete even if the edges do not have lengths.[20]
- **Hamiltonian path problem:** given a graph, find whether there is a path that visits every node without repeating any node. Again, if we change a detail in the statement, the problem is not NP-complete anymore. If we make the problem about visiting every edge without repeating any edge, then there is a linear-time algorithm (this version is known as the Eulerian path problem).

---

19 There is a dynamic programming algorithm to find the best path for TSP in $O(2^n * n^2)$ time. That is significantly faster than $O(n!)$, but the point is that it is still exponential.

20 The song "Find the Longest Path" by Daniel J. Barrett is dedicated to this problem. You can hear it on Youtube at https://www.youtube.com/watch?v=a3ww0gwEszo.

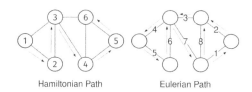

Figure 6. Hamiltonian path is NP-complete, but Eulerian path is not.

- **Graph coloring problem:** given a graph, assign a "color" to each node so that adjacent nodes have different colors. The goal is to find the smallest number of colors needed. In particular, determining if a graph can be colored with just 3 colors is NP-complete, but determining if it can be colored with just 2 is not.[21]

Figure 7. A graph that can be colored with 2 colors.

- **The knapsack problem:** given a list of n items, each with a size and a value, determine the maximum value we can get from items that fit in a knapsack of capacity k. That is, we need to pick the subset of items with maximum value under the constraint that their sizes add up to at most k. See Chapter 39: IKEA Shopping (pg 557), which is a version of the knapsack problem.[22]
- **Subset sum problem** (pg 542): given a list of integers, find whether there is a subset of the integers that adds up to exactly 0.

Notice how many of these problems are graph problems? This is helpful to know, so next time you are stuck on a graph problem that you just can't seem to optimize, consider the possibility of it being an NP-complete problem with no simple solution. If you are not familiar with graphs yet, you can revisit this list after going through Graphs and Backtracking.

The final point about recognizing NP-complete problems is that, sometimes, a problem that does not look exactly like one of the famous NP-complete problems may be one in disguise. Thus, it is also good to be able to identify when a problem is actually one of the popular NP-complete problems that you know. Here are a couple of example problems that are TSP in disguise:

- **Problem:** Given a grid consisting of characters `'.'`, `'x'`, and `'c'`, where `'.'` represents a walkable cell, `'x'` represents a wall, and `'c'` represents a coin, find the shortest path through adjacent cells in the matrix that collect every coin without passing through any cell marked with `'x'`.[23]
- **Problem:** A 3D printer needs to extrude ink at a list of points in the print bed, each with x and y coordinates. Find the shortest distance the printer nozzle must travel from a given starting position to reach every point.

---

21 This problem is famous because of the "4-color theorem": with just four colors, you can color the regions in any map in a way such that no two adjacent regions have the same color. You can think of a map as a graph with one node per region and edges connecting adjacent regions. For graphs that can be created from a map, the 4-color theorem tells us that the answer to the graph coloring problem is at most 4. However, not all graphs can be created from maps.

22 There exists a dynamic programming algorithm for the knapsack problem that runs in $O(n*k)$ time, where n is the number of items and k is the knapsack capacity. This does not contradict the fact that the knapsack problem is NP-complete because of the k in the runtime. The runtime is polynomial on k but exponential on the size of the space needed to write down the number k, as it can be written down using $\log_2(k)$ bits. Problems like this—exponential on the input size but polynomial on the input value—are called weakly NP-complete.

23 This is similar to Problem 39.11: Escape with All Clues (pg 559).

If a candidate were asked one of these questions in an interview, an ideal response would be to recognize that it is a variant of TSP and thus as hard as TSP. The candidate can use this fact to ask the interviewer if they prefer a slow, 'brute force' algorithm, or an algorithm that finds suboptimal solutions. In Chapter 39: Backtracking (pg 540), we will show the techniques to implement brute-force algorithms that you can use to solve NP-complete problems.

NP-complete problems are less common in interviews, but it's good to know that not every problem has a clean and efficient solution. Sometimes, brute force is the correct approach, and even when it isn't, there is value in starting from there when we are stuck in order to help get the ball rolling.

KEY TAKEAWAYS

Even though we won't do it for every problem in the book due to space constraints, one advice that's easy to adopt is writing the analysis down next to your code, clearly labeling the variables in the analysis and the time and *extra* space. Something like:

```
Algo 1: binary search
n: the length of arr
T: O(...)
S: O(...) extra space
```

It's expected that you will give the most simplified big O expression. For this, see "The Rules of Big O" on page 208.

With practice, you can even fill in the time and space complexity before coding the algorithm, if you already have a general idea of the structure of the code. That's because analyzing iterative code often comes down to analyzing the structure of nested loops (just don't forget to factor in built-in methods and operations). Analyzing recursive algorithms is a whole other story that we'll see in the Recursion chapter.

The rest of the book will weave big O analysis into all our discussions. This should give you an idea of how you should talk about it in interviews as well.

Even though there are infinite class complexities, the runtime of algorithms tends to fall into one of the class complexities that we introduced in Table 1 (pg 210): $O(1)$, $O(\log n)$, $O(n)$, $O(n \log n)$, $O(n^2)$, $O(n^3)$, $O(2^n)$, and $O(n!)$. Algorithms with the same runtime complexity sometimes have similar patterns and themes, so classifying algorithms becomes more intuitive once we have analyzed a few. As an example, we saw how nested loops tend to lead to polynomial complexities (though not always).

This is why we generally **don't recommend memorizing the time and space complexity of well-known algorithms**. Except for a few tricky exceptions (like merge sort and quicksort), with a bit of practice, it becomes easy to deduce the complexity of algorithms on the spot if you have an idea of how they work.

⤢ ONLINE RESOURCES

Online resources for this chapter include:

- Interview replays that show specific mistakes people make with Big O Analysis

Go online at bctci.co/big-o-analysis.

## CHAPTER 22

BOUNDARY THINKING

AI interviewer, replays, and more materials for this chapter at bctci.co/boundary-thinking

▶ *Prerequisites: Big O Analysis*

Often, the most challenging part of a coding interview is not the coding, but rather figuring out what to code—that is, the algorithm. There are no apparent steps to follow, and the possibilities to consider seem endless. In this chapter and the next, Trigger Thinking, we'll introduce a framework to organize our thoughts and narrow down the options to explore.

Boundary thinking is about establishing lower and upper bounds for the time complexity of the solution. As we'll see, this can help us narrow down on the best algorithm we should use.

A **lower bound** for a problem is the best runtime we could theoretically have to solve this problem.[1] For instance, if a problem has a lower bound of $O(n^2)$,[2] it means that we can't solve it in $O(n)$ time or anything faster than $O(n^2)$. Knowing a lower bound for a problem is useful because it can prevent us from making unnecessary optimizations.[3] However, it doesn't mean that the lower bound is actually achievable—only that we can't do better than it.

Conversely, an **upper bound** is the worst possible runtime of algorithms we should consider. While it is always possible to make a slower algorithm, there are upper bounds to the runtimes the interviewers are looking for. Again, if we can find an upper bound, we can avoid wasting time implementing an algorithm that is too slow to pass the interview.

In this chapter, we'll see how to establish lower and upper bounds at the start of an interview.

We suggest contemplating these bounds *before* trying to generate solutions. This allows us to narrow possible solutions down to a more manageable shortlist.

> If you've waited until *after* you've written code to give any thought to your time and space complexity, you've already missed the point of the interview. You should use big O analysis to decide what to code in the first place. You might not know the exact time complexity before writing the code, but you should be able to estimate it.

---

1   This is also called the Best Conceivable Runtime (BCR) in Cracking the Coding Interview. We changed the term here because we'll also be talking about upper bounds.

2   The technically correct notation would be to use $\Omega(n^2)$ (big omega) for lower bounds. However, we'll stick to the way those terms are used in industry and just say "the lower bound is $O(n^2)$." See page 215 for more details.

3   For example, if the first step in our algorithm takes $O(n)$ time and the lower bound for the problem is $O(n)$, then there is little value in optimizing the first step. It will not improve the big O analysis.

A Motivating Example

Let's use a problem to demonstrate what can happen if you skip the boundary thinking step. Think through how you might solve the problem below.

✦ **PROBLEM 22.1   TUNNEL DEPTH**

We are given an nxn binary matrix, `tunnel_network`, representing a tunnel network that archeologists have excavated. The ground level is above the first row. The first row is at *depth 0*, and each subsequent row is deeper underground.

- 1's represent excavated tunnel pathways in the network.
- 0's represent earth that has not been excavated yet.

The tunnel starts at the top-left and top-right corners (the cells (0, 0) and (0, n - 1) are always 1's) and consists of a single connected network. That is, this is not a valid input because there is a 1 that is not reachable:

```
tunnel_network = [
  [1,0,0,1],
  [1,1,1,1],
  [0,0,0,0],
  [1,0,0,0],
]
```

Write a function that returns the maximum tunnel depth.

▶ **Example:** `tunnel_network = [`
```
  [1,0,0,0,1], # depth 0
  [1,1,1,0,1], # depth 1
  [1,0,1,0,1], # depth 2
  [1,1,1,1,1], # depth 3
  [0,0,0,0,0]  # depth 4
]
```
Output: 3

▶ **Example:** `tunnel_network = [`
```
  [1,1,0,0,0,1], # 0
  [0,1,0,0,0,1], # 1
  [1,1,0,0,0,1], # 2
  [1,0,0,0,0,1], # 3
  [1,1,0,0,0,1], # 4
  [0,1,1,1,1,1], # 5
]
```
Output: 5

SOLUTION 22.1   TUNNEL DEPTH

Imagine we ask this question to two different engineers:

- Alex is an intermediate engineer who has done many coding questions and is relatively confident in their abilities.
- Jamie, another engineer, has done significantly fewer coding questions and is less confident in their abilities.

Let's see how each engineer tackles this problem.

Alex's algorithm: graph traversal

Alex has seen many problems similar to this one. They immediately recognize it as a graph problem, visualizing the 1's in the grid as vertices and edges connecting vertices next to each other horizontally or vertically. They confirm with the interviewer that diagonals are not allowed.

Alex codes a DFS (depth-first search) starting at the top-left corner. The DFS traverses the entire graph—since it is connected—while tracking the maximum depth found at any node. At the end, they return the maximum depth.

- **Time complexity:** $O(n^2)$, since the grid could be filled with ones.
- **Space complexity:** $O(n^2)$ to track already visited nodes.

Alex finishes the code and analysis quickly, confident they crushed the question.

Jamie's algorithm: Iterate through the matrix

Jamie does not jump to the graph solution. First, they confirm that we can't have a 1 without a path of 1's above it (a logical assumption, since you can't excavate a piece without having gotten there by excavating). Then, they recognize that the answer can be found simply by iterating through the matrix and recording the deepest 1 seen. They even suggest starting from the bottom and iterating backward through the matrix. This way, we can terminate our search early upon the first occurrence of a one.

- **Time complexity**: $O(n^2)$. In the worst case, we still need to iterate through every row to find a 1.
- **Space complexity**: $O(1)$. We need no data structures!

Who had the better solution?

While both reach the same time complexity, Jamie's solution minimized the space complexity.

Alex's breadth of experience with coding questions *hurt* his performance because they could only think of one approach to the problem. We could say that Alex had *tunnel* vision (see what we did there?) In contrast, Jamie kept it simple and, as a result, didn't end up with an overengineered solution.

We'll later revisit this problem to see how boundary thinking could have helped Alex and Jamie.

RUNTIME LOWER BOUNDS

We'll start by talking about single-input problems. We'll extend the thought process to problems with multiple inputs later.

There are two main types of lower bounds: *output-size* lower bounds and *task-based* lower bounds.[4]

OUTPUT-SIZE LOWER BOUND

This one is straightforward: **the output size is a lower bound for the runtime**. That is, with a sequential algorithm, we can't output an array of size $O(n)$, in less than $O(n)$ time. That's how long it takes just to write it.

Imagine a variant of the classic 2-sum problem (pg 295) where we are given an array of integers of length n and an integer k. The goal is to return all pairs of integers in the array that add up to k. We can ask: *what's the worst case for the output size?* Consider an input where the array has all 0's and k = 0. For this input, we need to output every pair of indices, of which there are $O(n^2)$ (pg 213). Therefore, we'll need $O(n^2)$ time in the worst case. A faster algorithm is *impossible*.[5]

If the output is just a number or boolean, we unfortunately do not get any useful output-size lower bound. In many problems, the output size is linear on the input size, which allows us to rule out sub-linear options. Sometimes, the output size may even be higher than linear. That's when it is the most constraining.

---

4   In "Extra Credit: NP-Complete Problems" (pg 226), we saw a third type of lower bound: if we identify that a problem is NP-complete, we can rule out any subexponential-time algorithms.

5   There's an advanced concept known as *output-sensitive analysis*, where we analyze algorithms based not only on the input size, but also on the output size. For instance, for this problem, an algorithm that takes $O(n + p)$ time, where p is the number of output pairs, could be considered better than an algorithm that always takes $O(n^2)$ time regardless of whether p is 0 or $O(n^2)$. Output-sensitive analysis is not really used in interviews.

TASK-BASED LOWER BOUND

Sometimes, it is *obvious* that, no matter how we approach the problem, there's a 'task' that needs to happen, and we can use that to establish a lower bound.

The 'task' could be having to check every value in the input. Consider a variant of 2-sum where we only need to output a boolean, indicating whether a pair of values add up to k or not. The **output-size** lower bound is $O(1)$, but it is obvious that, in the worst case, we'll need to check every integer in the array. The **task-based** lower bound is $O(n)$.

Having to check every input element is very common, and it allows us to discard sublinear solutions like $O(\log n)$ or $O(1)$ for most problems. However, be careful. Sometimes, it may *seem like* we have to visit every element in the input when it isn't truly necessary. For instance, we might be missing a clever way to do binary search.

The 'task' could be something else. Imagine a problem where we have a list of n student IDs and grades, and we have to return the IDs of all the students with grade 'A', sorted by ID. The **output-size** lower bound is $O(n)$ since every student could have an 'A'. However, we also need to sort. Barring some information about the nature of the IDs, we can't beat $O(n \log n)$ time. If we could, then we could sort an array in better than $O(n \log n)$ time, which is not possible in general (see page 361 for a discussion on comparison sorts vs specialized sorts). The **task-based** lower bound is $O(n \log n)$, where the 'task' is sorting.

Again, be careful—just because you find a solution for a certain problem that uses sorting, it doesn't mean that a solution without sorting doesn't exist.

\#   The main purpose of the task-based lower bound is to rule out sublinear solutions. You can ask, "Is it necessary to use every element in the input?"

CHOOSING BETWEEN BOUNDS

What happens if the output-size lower bound is $O(n^2)$ and the task-based lower bound is $O(n)$? Which one is the "right" lower bound? The answer is simple: the *greater* of the two. After all, if we know we can't beat $O(n^2)$, saying we can't beat $O(n)$ is obvious.

Similarly, if we have two *upper* bounds, say $O(n!)$ and $O(n^2)$, we'll choose the *lesser* of the two: $O(n^2)$. We always want the most constraining one.

\#   Just because we find a lower bound of $O(<X>)$, it doesn't mean it is possible to find an algorithm with runtime $O(<X>)$. However, it is worth looking for one, since there is no immediate reason why it is impossible.

RUNTIME UPPER BOUNDS

Like a lower bound, an upper bound allows us to filter out certain solutions from consideration. Occasionally, problems helpfully state the upper bound that you need to beat. One might explicitly say, "Identify a solution with a runtime better than O(time complexity)."

However, we usually need to find one ourselves. Let's examine the two main ways of establishing upper bounds.

NAIVE UPPER BOUND

Think about the most obvious solution that comes to mind and solves the problem. We call this the *naive solution*. Whatever its runtime is, it is an upper bound for time complexities we should consider. We call this the **naive upper bound**.[6]

Besides establishing an upper bound, coming up with a naive solution can also be the starting point of more optimized solutions (see "Booster 1: *BRUTE FORCE OPTIMIZATION*" on page 250).

TLE UPPER BOUND

Have you ever done an online programming assessment where, after solving the question and painstakingly ironing out all the edge cases, you submitted your code just to get a dreaded Time Limit Exceeded (TLE) rejection? This message indicates that your solution was too slow and was unable to pass the largest test cases for the problem.

Let's run a little hypothetical scenario. Imagine that an *online judge* for an assessment platform has the following parameters:

- The online judge runs for 1 second for each test before timing out and returning a TLE error.
- The online judge runs on a 2 GHz processor ($2 * 10^9$ CPU cycles per second).
- We submit different solutions to this online judge, with time complexities ranging from $O(n!)$ to $O(1)$.

The question is: for each time complexity, at what point will we run into a TLE error?

Of course, as we discussed on page 206, time complexities are only about *scaling* behavior. The actual number of CPU cycles needed by the algorithm largely depends on the *constant factors* hidden by big O. Let's add one more assumption:

- If our algorithm scales like $O(f(n))$, then it needs between $10 * f(n)$ (low end) and $1000 * f(n)$ (high end) CPU cycles.

This is a somewhat reasonable range for simple algorithms. A language like Python may be closer to the high end, while a language like C may be closer to the low end.

Time Complexity	Max n (low end)	Max n (high end)
$O(n!)$	11	9
$O(2^n)$	27	20
$O(n^3)$	584	125
$O(n^2)$	14,142	1,414
$O(n \log n)$	8,677,239	118,649
$O(n)$	200,000,000	2,000,000
$O(\log n)$	Super high	Super high
$O(1)$	Infinite	Infinite

Table 1. When we will hit TLE based on the time complexity.

At this point, you may be wondering, *what does any of this have to do with boundary thinking?*

Do you know that scene in *The Karate Kid* where the protagonist, Daniel, who had been asked by Mr. Miyagi to "sand the floor" and do other repetitive chores for weeks, suddenly realizes he has been learning karate

---

6   Don't overcomplicate it. Experienced interviewees can struggle to come up with a "dumb" solution because they are used to skipping directly to more optimal ones.

moves all along? If you're wondering what the hypothetical scenario was for, that's what happened here, too. You now know metaphorical karate for coding interviews, and we Miyagi'd you. Give us a second to explain.

Often, coding problems specify **input-size constraints**. It usually looks something like this at the end of the description:

▸   Constraints: $1 \le n \le 1000$

Without even looking at the question, we can examine the input-size constraints to infer two things:

- Time complexities that are definitely too high.
- Time complexities that the interviewer or online judge is likely looking for.

For instance, if the maximum input size is 500, we definitely cannot use exponential-time algorithms. In contrast, if a problem states that the maximum input size is 20, in most cases, that is *tacit permission* to use exponential-time algorithms. Think of it this way: in an online assessment, if the goal of the problem setter was to check if you can find the optimal solution, which happens to take $O(n)$ time, they would add test cases large enough to ensure $O(n^2)$-time and worse solutions would time out (assuming plausible constant factors).

We can use Table 1 to estimate the thresholds. Let n be the input size.

- Constraint: $n < 10$. The problem setter is likely looking for a factorial solution.
- Constraint: $n < 20$. The problem setter is likely looking for an exponential solution.
- Constraint: $n < 500$. The problem setter is likely looking for a cubic solution. Anything higher can be ruled out.
- Constraint: $n < 10,000$. The problem setter is likely looking for a quadratic solution. Anything higher can be ruled out.
- If the input size can be bigger than $10,000$, we can rule out quadratic or worse solutions.

We call these **TLE upper bounds**. They are not hard rules but useful heuristics.

TLE upper bounds work even in in-person interviews where you are not expected to run the code. If the statement includes input-size constraints, you can make similar inferences—the thresholds are just more fuzzy. At least, you can discuss the implications of the maximum input size with the interviewer.

> ### Should you ask the interviewer for the maximum input size?
>
> If we are not given input-size constraints in an interview, we can ask the interviewer. Our goal is to gain information about the sought time complexity, so if the naive upper bound already matches the lower bound, we probably don't need to ask.
>
> If we ask, we don't want to come across as asking for a hint. Instead, we want to frame it as part of our diligent requirement-gathering phase (pg 193) and use it to showcase our understanding of big O analysis. We can say:
>
> "Are there any constraints on how big the input could be? I want to ensure that my solution can scale to all expected inputs."
>
> Let's say an interviewer answers "one million" as the maximum input size. We can tell them, "Based on this requirement, I can rule out any algorithm with a quadratic or worse complexity, as those would take an unpractical amount of time to run."
>
> If the interviewer doesn't know—that's fine; we just won't be able to establish a TLE upper bound. Be cautious that an interviewer may throw out a very large number without realizing that even the optimal algorithm would take an eternity on a supercomputer. The value they give cannot be trusted as much as the constraints in an online assessment.

USING THE BOUNDS

After identifying upper and lower bounds, you'll be in one of two scenarios:

a) **Your upper and lower boundaries are identical.** You can narrow your search to algorithms with that time complexity. Like Sherlock Holmes' famous line of reasoning, *"When you have eliminated the impossible, whatever remains, however improbable, must be the truth."*

b) **Your upper bound is higher than your lower bound.** You have to consider solutions that could be anywhere in the range.

Tunnel Depth Revisited

Let's go back to Problem 22.1: Tunnel Depth (pg 231) and try to apply boundary thinking.

- **Runtime upper bound:** Counterintuitively, if you consciously chose to start with a naive solution, you'd likely find Jamie's solution of iterating through the entire matrix. The **naive** upper bound is $O(n^2)$. We weren't given any maximum input sizes, so we don't have a **TLE** upper bound.

- **Runtime lower bound:** the **output-size** lower bound is $O(1)$ since the output is just a number. The interesting boundary here is our **task-based** lower bound. We can ask, "In the worst case, must we visit (nearly) every element in the matrix to find the answer?" Our intuition may be "yes," but if we are not completely sure, we should default to the known lower bound of $O(1)$.

Now comes the fun part. Our upper bound is $O(n^2)$, and our lower bound is $O(1)$. We need to consider runtimes in that range. We can look at common runtimes in that range and see what algorithms we can come up with that fit in that complexity.

- $O(1)$ (the lower bound): A constant-time solution seems highly unlikely. Constant time answers usually involve a math equation.

- $O(\log n)$: This complexity is usually associated with binary search on linear ranges, but we have a grid.

- $O(n)$: Scanning through a single row or column already takes $O(n)$ time, so finding the maximum depth in this much time seems really challenging.

- $O(n \log n)$: This complexity is associated with sorting, certain data structures like heaps, and divide-and-conquer algorithms. However, it's still only enough to explore a tiny fraction of the tunnel, which can have up to n^2 1's.

- $O(n^2)$ (the upper bound): Perhaps the naive solution is the best we can do.

Given this landscape, it makes sense to target an $O(n \log n)$ runtime—we already have an $O(n^2)$ solution, and the smaller complexities seem far-fetched.

Since the grid has size $O(n^2)$, both Alex's and Jamie's solutions take linear time on the grid size. What *sublinear-time* techniques do we know of?

Optimal Answer

You get a gold star if you thought of leveraging binary search. Before even asking *how* binary search could be useful, we identified it as a potential approach based on boundary thinking.

With this promising idea to try a binary search, we can identify a solution—the key is to binary search over the depth. We can look at the middle row and ask, "Is there a 1 in this row?" If yes, we can skip searching the upper half of the grid. If the answer is "no," then we can skip searching the lower half instead. We repeat this until we close in on the deepest row with a 1 (this is an example of the *guess-and-check technique*, pg 338).

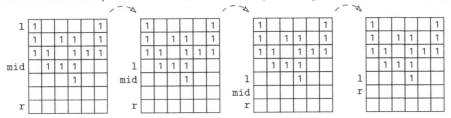

Figure 1. Binary search steps to close in on the final row with 1's.

What's the time complexity now? We perform a binary search over the rows, which means we perform $O(\log n)$ iterations. In each iteration, we scan a row to see if there is a 1, which takes $O(n)$ time. When we add it all up, the time complexity matches our identified target complexity: $O(n \log n)$.

BOUNDARY THINKING PROBLEM SET

For each of the following problems, try to find a runtime lower bound and a runtime upper bound.

- For the lower bound, take the maximum between the **output-size** lower bound and the **task-based** lower bound (if applicable).
- For the upper bound, take the minimum between the **naive** upper bound and the **TLE** upper bound (if applicable).

You don't need to code anything or even know how to solve the problems yet. Just focus on identifying the bounds.

QUESTION 1   CONSECUTIVE LETTERS

Given a string, s, with n lowercase English letters, return the longest sequence of consecutive letters in the alphabet such that all the letters appear in the string.

▶ **Example:** s = "onion"
  Output: "no"
▶ **Example:** s = "axdxbxc"
  Output: "abcd"
  Constraints: n ≤ 100,000

QUESTION 2   SORTED TERNARY ARRAY

Given an array, arr, of length n, return an array with the same elements but in sorted order. The array only contains 0's, 1's, and 2's.

▶ **Example:** arr = [2, 2, 0, 2, 1]
  Output: [0, 1, 2, 2, 2]
  Constraints: n ≤ 100,000

QUESTION 3   VALLEY ARRAY MIN

Given a *valley array*, arr, of length n, return the smallest value. A *valley array* is an array of unique integers that first decreases and then increases (like a valley).

▶ **Example:** [8, 5, 2, 7, 13, 14, 19, 21]
  Output: 2

SUBSETS

Given a positive integer, n, return an array with every possible subset of the numbers from 1 to n as a nested array. The order of the subarrays or the elements in each subarray doesn't matter.

▸ **Example:** n = 3
   Output: [[], [1], [2], [3], [1, 2], [1, 3], [2, 3], [1, 2, 3]]
   Constraints: $1 < n \le 15$

QUESTION 5   **SUBARRAYS**

Given an array, arr, with n unique integers, return an array with every unique subarray.

▸ **Example:** arr = [8, 2, 4]
   Output: [[8], [2], [4], [8, 2], [2, 4], [8, 2, 4]]
   Constraints: $1 < n \le 300$

QUESTION 6   **SUM-K SUBARRAYS**

Given an array, arr, with n unique integers, and an integer k, return the number of subarrays with sum exactly k.

▸ **Example:** arr = [2, 2, 4, -2], k = 4
   Output: 3. The subarrays with sum 4 are [2, 2], [4], and [2, 4, -2].
   Constraints: $1 < n \le 10^6$

QUESTION 7   **SUM OVER 100**

Given an array, arr, of n positive integers, return whether their sum is 100 or more.
   Constraints: $1 < n \le 10^6$

QUESTION 8   **SUDOKU**

You are given a 9x9 grid representing a Sudoku puzzle.[7] Your goal is to solve the Sudoku.

QUESTION 9   **CONNECTED POINTS**

Given n points in the plane where each point consists of coordinates (x_i, y_i), find the shortest path in the plane that goes through every point.
   Constraints: $2 < n \le 10$

PROBLEM SET SOLUTIONS

ANSWER 1   CONSECUTIVE LETTERS

- **Output-size lower bound:** $O(1)$. The longest possible output would be every letter in the alphabet (26).
- **Task-based lower bound:** $O(n)$ because we may need to check every character in the string to make sure we can't extend the sequence.
- **Naive upper bound:** $O(n \log n)$. We can sort the letters and then look through the sorted list to find the longest sequence.
- **TLE upper bound:** Subquadratic (anything less than $O(n^2)$). With an input size of 100,000, a quadratic algorithm would probably be too slow.

---

7   You can try to establish the bounds without knowing the Sudoku rules, but they are explained on page 319.

- **Conclusion:** Since we already know a $O(n \log n)$-time algorithm (the naive one), we should focus our energy on trying to improve the runtime to $O(n)$ (the best conceivable runtime for this problem).

ANSWER 2   SORTED TERNARY ARRAY

- **Output-size lower bound:** $O(n)$.
- **Task-based lower bound:** $O(n)$ to read every index. It may seem that the task-based lower bound is $O(n \log n)$ because we need to sort an array. However, for the special case of an array having only three different values, we can sort it in $O(n)$ time, so the comparison sort lower bound (pg 364) doesn't apply.
- **Naive upper bound:** $O(n \log n)$. The naive solution is to use the built-in sort function.
- **TLE upper bound:** Subquadratic.
- **Conclusion:** Since we already know a $O(n \log n)$-time algorithm, we should focus our energy on trying to improve the runtime to $O(n)$ (the lower bound).[8]

ANSWER 3   VALLEY ARRAY MIN

- **Output-size lower bound:** $O(1)$.
- **Task-based lower bound:** $O(1)$. It may seem that the task-based lower bound is $O(n)$ since the minimum could be anywhere. However, that doesn't mean we always need to check every element.
- **Naive upper bound:** $O(n)$ to iterate through the array.
- **TLE upper bound:** None. We are not given any input-size constraints.
- **Conclusion:** We should look for solutions in the range from $O(1)$ to $O(n)$.[9]

ANSWER 4   SUBSETS

- **Output-size lower bound:** $O(2^n * n)$. A set with n elements has 2^n subsets, each with $O(n)$ elements (pg 555).
- **Task-based lower bound:** None.
- **Naive upper bound:** $O(2^n * n)$. The naive algorithm is to generate all subsets with backtracking. This takes $O(2^n * n)$ time (pg 555).
- **TLE upper bound:** Exponential. A maximum input size of 15 is tacit permission to use an exponential algorithm (maybe even factorial).
- **Conclusion:** We have matching upper and lower bounds. The naive backtracking solution is the best we can do for this problem.

ANSWER 5   SUBARRAYS

- **Output-size lower bound:** $O(n^3)$. There are $O(n^2)$ subarrays, and their combined length is $O(n^3)$ (pg 222).
- **Task-based lower bound:** $O(n)$ because we need to read every number.
- **Naive upper bound:** $O(n^3)$. We can solve this problem with 3 nested loops.
- **TLE upper bound:** Cubic. A maximum input size of 300 is tacit permission to use a cubic algorithm.

---

8 See Problem 27.16: Dutch Flag Problem (pg 308) for a linear-time solution.

9 See Problem 29.3: Valley Bottom (pg 333) for a logarithmic-time solution.

- **Conclusion:** The more restrictive lower bound is $O(n^3)$. Since the lower bound and upper bounds match, the naive solution is optimal for this problem.

ANSWER 6   SUM-K SUBARRAYS

- **Output-size lower bound:** $O(1)$.
- **Task-based lower bound:** $O(n)$ because we need to read every number.
- **Naive upper bound:** $O(n^3)$. We can solve this problem with 3 nested loops.
- **TLE upper bound:** $O(n \ \log \ n)$. A maximum input size of $1,000,000$ makes quadratic algorithms most likely too expensive. Something like $O(n \ * \ (\log \ n)^2)$ would be fine, too—logarithmic factors have too small of an impact for TLE upper bounds. After all, $\log_2(1,000,000) \approx 20$.
- **Conclusion:** The naive solution is too slow for this problem, so we need to find something better. We should focus on solutions in the range between linear and linearithmic runtime.

ANSWER 7   SUM OVER 100

- **Output-size lower bound:** $O(1)$.
- **Task-based lower bound:** It may seem that the task-based lower bound is $O(n)$ since we need to add up the elements in the array, but is that really true? Since all numbers are positive, if the array length is 100 or more, the sum is guaranteed to be at least 100. Thus, we only need to iterate through input arrays with a length of less than 100. At most, we need to do $100 \ = \ O(1)$ iterations.
- **Naive upper bound:** $O(n)$ to add up all the elements.
- **TLE upper bound:** Linearithmic. Quadratic would be too much for an input size of one million.
- **Conclusion:** Thinking about the task-based lower bound has led us to an $O(1)$-time algorithm (the best we could hope for): if $\text{len(arr)} \geq 100$, return true; otherwise, return $\text{sum(arr)} \geq 100$.

ANSWER 8   SUDOKU

Since a Sudoku has $9x9 \ = \ O(1)$ cells, any algorithm for it technically takes $O(1)$ time—the way the problem is stated, there is no input size to scale on. Big O analysis is not very useful in this case. Instead, we should focus on minimizing the constant factors.

ANSWER 9   CONNECTED POINTS

- **Output-size lower bound:** $O(1)$.
- **Task-based lower bound:** $O(n)$, since we need to at least know where all the points are.
- **Naive upper bound:** $O(n! \ * \ n)$ to consider all possible orderings of points with backtracking (pg 555).
- **TLE upper bound:** Factorial. A maximum input size of 10 is tacit permission to use a factorial algorithm.
- **Conclusion:** The overall lower bound is $O(n)$, so there is a huge gap between lower and upper bounds. However, this is a bit of a trick question, as this is a version of TSP, an NP-complete problem (pg 545). That means that no polynomial-time algorithm is known—the *de facto* lower bound is exponential. Even if we didn't identify that the problem is NP-complete, a maximum input size of 10 reveals the intentions of the problem setter. A small input size is a *trigger* for backtracking (more on triggers in the next chapter).

In an interview, you probably don't have time to be as systematic as in this problem set, but you can try during practice and see what kind of useful insights you gain that you were missing before.

BOUNDARY THINKING WITH MULTIPLE VARIABLES

So far, we have discussed how this works with single-input questions, but sometimes, we will be given more than one input. Consider Problem 31.6: First K (pg 372):

Given an array of n unique integers, `arr`, return the k smallest numbers, in any order. Assume that $0 < k < n$.

▶ **Example:** `arr = [15, 4, 13, 8, 10, 5, 2, 20, 3, 9, 11, 27]`, `k = 5`
   `Output: [4, 3, 2, 5, 8]`

Notice we have two inputs. Given both variables, let's identify our upper and lower bounds.

Runtime upper bound: A naive solution would be to sort the array and then access the first k elements. The **naive** upper bound is $O(n \log n)$. We are not given any constraints, so the **TLE** upper bound is unknown.

Runtime lower bound: The **output-size** lower bound is $O(k)$; the **task-based** lower bound is $O(n)$ because we'd need to check every element just to find the largest one, let alone the k smallest ones.

So, we should be willing to consider algorithms that fall in the range between $O(n)$ and $O(n \log n)$. For instance, $O(n + k \log n)$ is in this range—a complexity often associated with heaps. This leads us to a valid solution: we can solve this problem in $O(n + k \log n)$ time with heaps.

The optimal solution for this problem is actually $O(n)$, matching our lower bound. It is based on the *quick-select* algorithm (pg 378).

We don't need to consider a complexity like $O(k \log n)$ because, for certain values of k like $k = 1$, it would be below our $O(n)$ lower bound. Such a runtime is impossible.

KEY TAKEAWAYS

If we are stuck in an interview, it's important to extract every drop of information from the statement. In our experience, one way great candidates do this intuitively is with *boundary thinking*. In this chapter, we tried to articulate this thought process so you can start applying it too.

We can use a mix of **output-size** lower bounds, **task-based** lower bounds, **naive** upper bounds, and **TLE** upper bounds to narrow down the time complexities we should consider. In turn, those time complexities can hint at what algorithms to try.

Our discussion has centered on improving the time complexity and not the space because interviews heavily skew toward caring about that. In principle, boundary thinking also applies to space, but you're unlikely to have time in an interview to go through boundary thinking for the space complexity.

⤢ **ONLINE RESOURCES**

Online resources for this chapter include:

- A chance to try the problem in this chapter in AI Interviewer
- Separate full code solutions for the problems in this chapter in multiple programming languages

Try online at bctci.co/boundary-thinking.

## CHAPTER 23

TRIGGER THINKING

AI interviewer, replays, and more materials for this chapter at bctci.co/trigger-thinking

In 2018, Sean Lee was a junior at the University of British Columbia. Just back to school from his second FAANG internship, he started receiving a lot of attention from his peers about how he had passed his FAANG interviews when the questions were historically challenging. Happy to help but not wanting to repeat himself, Sean decided to record a small talk on the subject so that he could have all the information in one place.

To his surprise, Sean's talk, titled *"How to Get a Job at the Big 4 - Amazon, Facebook, Google & Microsoft"*[1] went viral, receiving over 1.5 million views. His talk had a message delivered in the right way at the right time, on the cusp of the 2020 hiring spree. It summarized the best strategy the internet had devised for passing technical interviews—do as many problems as possible until you've developed an intuition for how to solve new problems well. Let's call this the **Problem-Grind Mindset**.

The Problem-Grind Mindset

The Problem-Grind Mindset posits that candidates are bad at interview problems simply because they need to practice more. Sean drew a large circle on a whiteboard to represent a candidate's current 'knowledge map' of questions. The empty circle demonstrates that a candidate's map starts blank, but after doing one problem after another, they can add little "dots" to their map and, over time, eventually start to fill the circle.

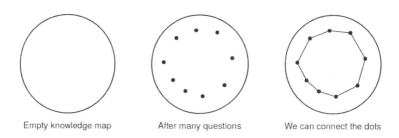

| Empty knowledge map | After many questions | We can connect the dots |

Figure 1. Growing our knowledge map through practice questions.

"Some people will be better at this than others, but no matter who you are, once you have enough of these dots, it becomes trivial to connect them." - Sean Lee

Similar to how people can game their SAT scores with consistent practice, Sean proposed that getting good at coding interviews requires more practice than the average candidate tends to put in.

---

1 Watch the original video at bctci.co/seans-story.

Sean goes on to say, *"If you're a student right now and want to be a software engineer [at a big tech company], you've got to start training!"* He points out that an interviewer can *"limit you to 45 minutes [in the interview], but they can't limit how much you prepare in advance."*

Sean's point was that we should have prior experience with past problems to develop intuitions about how to solve *new* problems—the previous problems build our "map" and give us something to work from.[2]

Should We Apply The Problem-Grind Mindset To Our Study Strategies?

Kind of. This approach to studying for coding interviews works, but it has two distinct disadvantages.

Time is the obvious first problem. In the How To Practice chapter, we talked about how to make the most out of each problem (e.g., by doing *post-mortems*, avoiding problem topics before you've learned the basics of those topics, etc.), which naturally means we'll get to fewer problems. Ideally, we still want to build a question map as complete as someone who did many more problems, and we can do this by making connections faster with better study prep.

The more insidious issue is **overconfidence** bred from pattern memorization. Focusing too much on problems that are similar to one another can lead to a false sense of security, and you may end up getting the rug pulled out from under you when you are given a problem that doesn't match a pattern. That's why it is good to also rely on more advanced techniques like *boundary thinking* (pg 230) and *problem-solving boosters* (pg 248).

We know what you're thinking: *"What is a better way to do it if more problems aren't the answer?"*

There is a saying, *"Experience is something you don't get until just after you need it."* We agree we should learn from experience, but no one said it has to be *our own* experience. We can kickstart our learning from the question maps built by those who have done hundreds of problems already.

USING TRIGGERS

The Problem-Grind Mindset suggests that problem *quantity* is what leads to intuitions about what to do in any problem. These intuitions stem from pieces of information in the problems themselves, which we will call *triggers*. The more triggers you have in your map, the easier it is to relate new problems to techniques you know.

By learning the triggers directly, we don't have to rely as much on problem quantity. We call this **trigger thinking**.

Trigger thinking is a shortcut to optimal answers in coding interviews. If you see a particular trigger in a problem, it indicates that a specific technique, data structure, or algorithm could be useful. That is, triggers are little hints embedded in the problems themselves.

TRIGGER EXAMPLES

At this point, you're probably asking, "Where are these hints in problems, and how can I identify them?" You should look for triggers everywhere: the description, the input and output types, the constraints, the examples, and even based on your initial naive solution. Here are some examples.

---

2 While Sean didn't invent this idea of building a question map, he was onto something. He has gone on to work at every "Big Four" company on his list.

TRIGGER	SHOULD CAUSE US TO CONSIDER TRYING...
The *input* is a *tree*.	Try DFS or BFS.
The *output* is a *subarray*.	Try a sliding window.
The problem has a *constraint* requiring us to find an *in-place* solution.	Try the two-pointer technique.
The problem *description* mentions *dependencies*.	Try topological sort.
The *description* contains a *self-referential* definition.	Try recursion.
The *input examples* are *sorted*. You ask a clarifying question to see if this is always the case, and the interviewer confirms.	Try binary search.
The *bottleneck* in your approach is *sorting*.	Try heaps or specialized sorts.
The problem has a *trigger* for *greedy algorithms*, but the greedy approach doesn't work.	Try closely related techniques such as backtracking and dynamic programming.

Table 1. A list of example trigger scenarios and what each trigger suggests we try next.

At the end of each chapter in the Catalog part of the book, we include a list of common triggers for the corresponding topic. You can find them all in one place in the **Trigger Catalog** online at bctci.co/trigger-catalog.

It's recommended that you take note of triggers that *you* often miss and those that you find particularly helpful. Analyzing triggers should be a natural part of your practice post-mortems.

Should you memorize triggers?

While you *could* load these triggers into flashcards and start attempting to memorize them, you'd be missing the point if you did. Much like the big O analysis of algorithms and data structures, instead of memorizing triggers, the triggers for a given technique should become intuitive once you understand that technique.

What we are actually advocating for is making "scan for triggers" an explicit step in your problem-solving workflow. Instead of "What problems do I know that are similar to this one?" it is more effective and comprehensive to ask, "What triggers does this problem have?"

TRIGGER THINKING PROBLEM SET

Try to identify triggers in the problems below and guess the data structure or algorithm you should try as a result. While you likely haven't gone through all the DS&A Catalog topics yet and may not know all these triggers, this will give you an idea of what to look for. You don't need to code anything yet at this point.

| QUESTION 1 | **1. LARGEST CONNECTED AREA** |

Given a binary grid, grid, determine the largest area of connected 1's. Two 1's are connected if they are next to each other vertically or horizontally (not diagonally).

▸ **Example:** grid = [[0, 0, 1, 1],
                        [0, 1, 0, 0],
                        [1, 1, 0, 0]]

  Output: 3. The clump of 1s in the top bottom-left corner has size 3 (diagonals don't count).

QUESTION 2 **2. CONSECUTIVE ONES AFTER FLIP**

Given a binary array, arr, return the maximum number of consecutive 1's in the array if you can flip at most one 0 to a 1.

▶ **Example:** arr = [1, 1, 0, 0, 1, 1, 0, 1]
   Output: 4. We can flip the 0 at index 6, which leads to four consecutive 1s.

QUESTION 3   **3. POWER SET**

The *power set* of a set S is the set of every subset of S. Given a list of unique integers, return its power set. Return each subset as a list. The order of the elements doesn't matter.

▶ **Example:** [1, 2, 3]
   Output: [[], [1], [2], [3], [1, 2], [1, 3], [2, 3], [1, 2, 3]]. The subsets
            include the empty list, three lists with a single element, all two-
            element lists, and the full list.

QUESTION 4   **4. GRID PATHS**

Given a binary grid, grid, find all possible paths from the top-left corner to the bottom-right corner that don't go through any 1's and return the number. You can only go down or right.

▶ **Example:** grid = [[0, 1, 1],
                        [0, 0, 0],
                        [0, 0, 0]]
   Output: 3. The three paths are:
            - D, D, R, R
            - D, R, D, R
            - D, R, R, D

QUESTION 5   **5. SORT TERNARY LIST**

Given a list containing only 0's, 1's, and 2's, sort the list in place using only O(1) extra space.

▶ **Example:** nums = [2, 0, 1, 2, 0]
   Output: nums = [0, 0, 1, 2, 2] (modified in place)

QUESTION 6   **6. SERIAL SUBSEQUENCE**

Given an array of positive numbers, find the length of the longest sequence of consecutive integers such that all the integers are in the array.

▶ **Example:** nums = [8, 6, 5, 2, 102, 100, 101, 4, 3, 4]
   Output: 5. We can find 2, 3, 4, 5, 6 in the array.
Constraints: len(nums) < 10^6

PROBLEM SET SOLUTIONS

ANSWER 1   **1. LARGEST CONNECTED AREA**

The *input* is a *grid graph* (pg 482), which suggests DFS or BFS.

ANSWER 2   **2. CONSECUTIVE ONES AFTER FLIP**

Even if the problem does not say *subarray* explicitly, the *output* is effectively the length of a subarray, which is a trigger for sliding windows (pg 511).

ANSWER 3   3. POWER SET

This one has two triggers:

1. *'Subset'* is a keyword trigger for backtracking (pg 555).
2. Even though the statement doesn't explicitly say 'enumeration,' the problem is asking us to list all possible subsets, so this is an enumeration problem (pg 542)—another trigger for backtracking.

We could have also concluded that backtracking is the right approach via boundary thinking (pg 232).

ANSWER 4   4. GRID PATHS

This one can send us in a few directions:

1. 'Path' is a keyword trigger for graph DFS or BFS.
2. "Find all" is a trigger for backtracking.
3. It's the counting variant of an enumeration-like problem. This is a trigger for dynamic programming.

Dynamic programming turns out to be the right approach for this problem (see Chapter 40: Count 0-Sum Paths, pg 577). It is a common technique for *counting problems* (pg 542) where backtracking would be too slow according to our boundary thinking.

ANSWER 5   5. SORT TERNARY LIST

As shown in Table 1, "in-place" is a trigger for using a two-pointer approach.

ANSWER 6   6. SERIAL SUBSEQUENCE

'Subsequence' is a trigger for backtracking (and dynamic programming) because there is an exponential number of subsequences. However, the input-size constraint makes backtracking unfeasible.

The fact that the subsequence we are looking for has consecutive numbers is a trigger for sorting. Indeed, this problem can be solved by sorting the input first. However, there is also a linear-time, hash-set-based solution for which there are no clear triggers. This shows that triggers won't always point you to the optimal solution.

COMBINING BOUNDARY THINKING AND TRIGGER THINKING

We have now learned two ways of narrowing in on the correct approach. While each strategy can be used individually, we can combine them to create a more robust system for tackling problems.

1. Start with boundary thinking to establish upper and lower bounds.
2. Then, identify triggers and consider the relevant techniques that fit within our established boundaries.

This way, you can filter out triggers that are likely to lead you in a bad direction. For instance, if the problem has a trigger for backtracking, but the upper bound is linear, we ignore that trigger.

Let's apply this to the problem of merging two sorted arrays into a single sorted array.

1. The **output-size** lower bound is linear.
2. The trigger that stands out the most is that the *input is sorted*, which is a strong trigger for binary search. However, since logarithmic times are ruled out, binary search is less attractive. We shouldn't immediately rule it out, though! Binary search could be a step in a broader algorithm.
3. Sorted inputs and two-array inputs are triggers for two-pointers. This is the best approach for this problem which you can see Problem 27.6: Merge Two Sorted Arrays (pg 300).

TRIGGER LIMITATIONS

Triggers are a powerful problem-solving shortcut, but they have some limitations.

NOT A SILVER BULLET

As we have seen, triggers are highly fallible. Some candidates new to interview prep tend to anchor too strongly to this trigger-based approach. Do not abandon all critical thinking and spend the whole interview trying to force a particular solution based on a trigger. It could be a red herring. If you've given a technique an appropriate amount of thought and can't figure out how to apply it, take a step back and try a different approach.

Just as solving many questions isn't a guarantee of a good interview performance, learning a bunch of triggers isn't the panacea some online courses make them out to be.

NOT EXHAUSTIVE

Our Trigger Catalog (bctci.co/trigger-catalog) is not exhaustive. The list of all possible triggers for coding problems is too long to be useful in interviews. We have tried to list the most relevant ones.

As mentioned, take note of triggers that *you* find particularly helpful. You can add them to your cheat sheet.

MULTIPLE TRIGGERS PER PROBLEM AND MULTIPLE TOPICS PER TRIGGER

Sometimes, a question has more than one trigger. If multiple triggers are present, we should explore all catalog topics associated with each trigger—don't just stick with the first one you see!

It is also possible a trigger can be associated with more than one topic. E.g., the 'median' keyword is a trigger for both quickselect and heaps. We should consider both.

KEY TAKEAWAYS

Our stance, echoed throughout the book, aligns with Sean Lee's sentiment. Practice *is* a prerequisite for doing well in interviews because we need to build our knowledge map. Learning triggers along the way is a way to fill your knowledge map faster and connect the dots.

We made 'look for triggers' an explicit step in our *interview checklist* (pg 198). However, triggers are fallible, and we shouldn't use them to circumvent the point of interviews: demonstrating critical thinking. Let's not turn off our brains in an interview because we think we've spotted a trigger.

## CHAPTER 24

PROBLEM-SOLVING BOOSTERS

AI interviewer, replays, and more materials for this chapter at bctci.co/boosters

▶ *Prerequisites: Big O Analysis*

Does getting asked a question you've never seen before scare you? You're in good company. No matter how many questions we go through, there can always be a tricky idea in a new problem that stumps us.

This chapter introduces our top problem-solving techniques tailored to the interview setting, which we call *problem-solving boosters*. We've organized them in a *framework* so you know which ones to use and when. This framework can serve as a reliable fallback plan for when you inevitably get stuck—whether in an interview or during practice—and give you the extra boost you need to crack the solution. We tried to keep things simple, so that you can follow it in a high-pressure situation.

Some notes about this chapter:

- If we illustrate a booster on a problem, it doesn't mean other boosters are not helpful for that problem.
- Our goal isn't to 'wow' you with slick solutions—quite the opposite. We want to illustrate a problem-solving thought process that feels relatable and replicable.
- We use problems from many different topics later in the book you may not know yet. **On a first read, it may be best to skim it to get an idea of the high-level ideas**. You can revisit this chapter after you've gone through the Catalog chapters.
- We don't give coding solutions for most problems in this chapter directly in the book, as we are focusing on the problem-solving aspect. They can be found online at bctci.co/boosters.

You'll see these boosters in action throughout the rest of the book!

THE BOOSTER FRAMEWORK

Picture yourself staring at a coding problem, completely stuck. By this point, you've already established a *naive solution*, applied *boundary thinking* (pg 230) and *trigger thinking* (pg 242), but the solution still eludes you—it's time to turn to boosters.

The first booster you should consider is ***BRUTE FORCE OPTIMIZATION (#1)***. This is where we take the naive (i.e., brute force) solution, and try to optimize it. This booster covers the most common strategies for speeding up existing code.

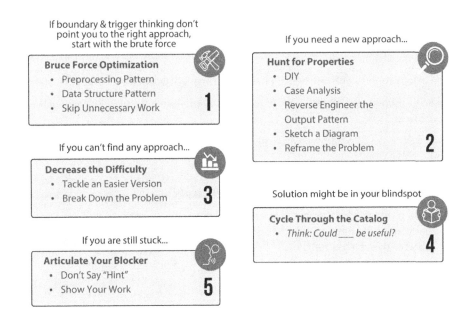

Figure 1. The booster framework.

For harder problems, it is often not obvious how to optimize the naive solution—we might need a different approach altogether. Often, the breakthrough comes from uncovering some "hidden" observation or property not explicitly mentioned in the statement. The second booster, *HUNT FOR PROPERTIES (#2)*, covers techniques for finding these properties.

If we can't find any useful property, the problem might simply be too complex to tackle directly. When this happens, we should start with an easier problem that gradually builds toward the original one. The next booster, *DECREASE THE DIFFICULTY (#3)*, is about picking an easier problem so we can start making progress.

If boosters 1–3 fail, the solution is probably in your blind spot—something you'd never consider for this problem based on the *triggers* you know and problems you've seen before. This is a bit of a last-ditch effort, but the next booster, *CYCLE THROUGH THE CATALOG (#4)*, is to literally cycle through every DS&A topic you know and consider *how* each one could potentially be useful.

Your final resource in the interview setting is the interviewer itself. The final booster, *ARTICULATE YOUR BLOCKER (#5)*, is about how to get help from the interviewer effectively. It's what we say when we're stuck without appearing to give up or outright asking for a hint.

We can use the following mnemonic device to remember the initials of the five boosters in order: *BOOSTERS HELP DEVELOPERS CRACK ALGORITHMS*.

Should boosters be tried in order?

Kind of. They are roughly ordered based on the expected pay off relative to the time invested.

- *BRUTE FORCE OPTIMIZATION (#1)* is straightforward to try if you've already considered the brute force solution (e.g., in order to establish the *naive upper bound* (pg 234).

- *DECREASE THE DIFFICULTY (#3)* can be more time consuming than the first two because we'll effectively have to solve two problems, the easier one and the original one.

- *CYCLE THROUGH THE CATALOG (#4)* may be needed if the solution really is in our blind spot, but it's toward the end because it's the least targeted approach, so it could take too much time.

- We reach for booster *ARTICULATE YOUR BLOCKER (#5)* when we want a hint—although we won't actually frame it that way.

Often, making progress with one booster means we can pivot to a different one. For instance:

- Finding a property with Booster 2 may enable us to optimize our code with some of the techniques from Booster 1.

- If we use Booster 3 to start with an easier problem, we can then use Boosters 1 and 2 on the easier problem.

BOOSTER 1: BRUTE FORCE OPTIMIZATION

We suggest starting with this booster because, at this point in the interview, you should have already thought about a naive solution and analyzed it (pg 196).

This first booster consists of:

1. taking the naive solution
2. identifying the bottlenecks
3. and looking for possible optimizations.

> If boundary & trigger thinking don't point you to the right approach, start with the brute force
>
> **Bruce Force Optimization**
> - Preprocessing Pattern
> - Data Structure Pattern
> - Skip Unnecessary Work
>
> **1**

The *bottlenecks* of a program are the steps with the highest time complexity. We focus on the bottlenecks because we *must* speed them up to improve the overall time complexity. If your algorithm has two steps, the first with $O(n^2)$ and the second with $O(n)$, optimizing the second step will not reduce your time complexity at all.

We'll look at three types of optimizations:

- Can you pull work out of the bottleneck into a *PREPROCESSING* step?
- Is there a *DATA STRUCTURE* designed to address the type of work done in the bottleneck?
- Is the bottleneck wasting time on stuff that is ultimately *UNNECESSARY WORK*?

BRUTE FORCE OPTIMIZATION: PREPROCESSING PATTERN

Imagine someone asked you to find a specific card, like the 5 of diamonds, in an unsorted deck of cards. That will take you $O(n)$ time, and there's no way around it. If they asked you to perform tasks like this repeatedly, you'd probably sort the deck first. Sure, it's a bunch of upfront work, but in the end it saves you time. That's *PREPROCESSING*.

The idea is to store useful information in a convenient format before we get to the bottleneck, and then use that information during the bottleneck to speed it up. We call this the **PREPROCESSING PATTERN**, and it is everywhere once you know to look for it.

Preprocessing Pattern: Examples from the Book[1]

- The *linear scan tradeoff* discussed in Sets & Maps (pg 346). Say the naive solution to a problem does n linear searches over an array of length n, resulting in $O(n^2)$ total runtime. If we first store the array elements in a hash set, we can often turn the linear-time searches into constant-time set lookups, at the cost of extra space for the set.

---

1 These are examples from material we haven't covered yet, so these may not make total sense to you at this point. Feel free to revisit this at a later point.

- Problem 36.5: Reachability Queries (pg 468). By precomputing a map from nodes to connected components with DFS, we can then find if two nodes are in the same connected component in constant time.

- The 'range sum queries' recipe in the Prefix Sums chapter (pg 612). By precomputing a *prefix sum array* in $O(n)$ time and space, we can compute subarray sums in $O(1)$ time. Without preprocessing, this would take $O(n)$ time.

When is preprocessing worth it? Whenever it (a) is less than the original algorithm's time complexity and (b) reduces the original algorithm's time complexity. That is, if our algorithm is $O(n^2)$, and doing $O(n \log n)$ preprocessing work can reduce the rest of it to $O(n)$, that's a win.

Preprocessing often increases space usage. Typically, that's worth it; interviewers tend to focus more on time complexity than space complexity.

A classic application of the **PREPROCESSING PATTERN** is the 3-sum problem:

✦ **PROBLEM 24.1**   **3-SUM**

Given an array of integers, arr, and a number w, return whether there are 3 integers in arr that add up to w. We cannot use the value at the same index more than once.

▸ **Example:** arr = [4, 4, 5, -6, -4, 0], w = 4
  Output: True. The triplet (4, 4, -4) adds up to 4.
▸ **Example:** arr = [5, 0, 1], w = 5
  Output: False. We cannot use the 0 twice.

SOLUTION 24.1   3-SUM

The naive solution involves a triple nested loop. In 'indented English':

```
1    for index i
2      for index j > i
3        for index k > j
4          if elements i, j, and k add to w
5            return true
6    return false
```

This takes $O(n^3)$ time, where n is the length of arr. To speed up the most inner loop, we notice that after fixing i and j, there's only one possible value that works for arr[k]: arr[i] + arr[j] - w. In a *PREPRO-CESSING STEP*, we can store all values in arr in a hash set. Then, we can replace the most inner loop for a $O(1)$-time set look up.

We need a way to ensure that we don't reuse arr[i] or arr[j] when we check for arr[i] + arr[j] - w in the hash set. One way to handle this is to use a *hash map* instead of a *hash set*, and map each value to the array of indices where it appears. This way, we can skip indices i and j.

This solution reduces the time from $O(n^3)$ to $O(n^2)$ but increases the extra space from $O(1)$ to $O(n)$.

BRUTE FORCE OPTIMIZATION: DATA STRUCTURE PATTERN

Many bottlenecks come from having to do some calculation inside a loop. In those situations, ask yourself,

▸   Do I know of any data structure which makes this type of operation faster?

Every data structure is designed to speed up certain operations. For example, hash maps are designed to make lookups really fast, whereas queues are designed to allow adding and removing from different ends.

Every data structure is designed to speed up a particular type of operation. The more data structures we know—and triggers for when to use them—the broader set of algorithms we can optimize.

The difference between the **PREPROCESSING PATTERN** and this one is that data structures can also be updated inside the bottleneck. That means we can do more things than just dumping all the input elements in a data structure and then querying it from the bottleneck.

Data Structure Pattern: Examples from the Book

- Efficient sliding window algorithms usually maintain information about the window in some data structure, and update the data structure as the window moves. See, e.g., Chapter 38: Unique Best Seller Streak (pg 516). The exact data structure used depends on the type of information we care about.

- Heaps can be used to track the k largest numbers in a dataset as we add numbers to the dataset (pg 501). Heaps can even track the median value (pg 505).

- The union–find data structure can keep track of connected components in a graph as we add edges to it (Figure 3 in bctci.co/union-find).

BRUTE FORCE OPTIMIZATION: SKIP UNNECESSARY WORK PATTERN

By definition, a brute-force search is not very targeted. Sometimes, we can *SKIP UNNECESSARY WORK* by ruling out suboptimal or unfeasible options. Ask yourself,

▶ Of all the options considered by the brute-force search, is there any part of the search range that we can *SKIP*?

For example, consider Problem 39.6: Jumping Numbers (pg 557). A *jumping number* is one where every two consecutive digits differ by one, such as 2343. The problem asks us to find every jumping number smaller than some value n. The naive solution is to take every number from 1 to n and check if it is a jumping number. However, most numbers are not jumping numbers, so this does a lot of unnecessary work we might be able to *SKIP*. We'll see how to use backtracking to generate *only* the jumping numbers up to n instead of every number (pg 560).

Skip Unnecessary Work Pattern: Examples from the Book

- Binary search is a classic example of converting a linear search into a $O(\log n)$-time search by skipping unnecessary parts of the search range.

- The *guess-and-check technique* (pg 338) is a way of applying binary search to maximization and minimization problems. For instance, we used it for the Tunnel Depth problem (pg 236)—instead of checking the entire mine, we used binary search to *SKIP* most rows.

- *Pruning* in backtracking is an optimization where we "prune" (i.e., skip) branches of the decision tree when we know for sure that it won't lead to a valid solution (pg 545).

- *Memoization* in dynamic programming is a way of *SKIPPING* repeated work (pg 571).

Consider the following problem:

✦ **PROBLEM 24.2**   **COUNT SUBSTRINGS WITHOUT LETTER**

Given a string, s, count the number of non-empty substrings of s that do not contain the letter 'a'.

▸ **Example:** "bcadefa"
  Output: 9. The 9 substrings without 'a' are: "b", "c", "bc", "d", "e", "f",
               "de", "ef", and "def".

SOLUTION 24.2   COUNT SUBSTRINGS WITHOUT LETTER

The naive approach is to iterate through all substrings of s, of which there are $O(n^2)$, and, for each one, check if it has any a's. If we look at the example, doesn't it *feel like* it's unnecessary to check most substrings? A string like "abababa" has 28 substrings, but only 3 do not have any a's. That's our clue that we may be able to *SKIP* some work.

A better idea for this problem is to split s by each occurrence of 'a' (Chapter 26: String Split, pg 291):

    sections = split(s, 'a')

From a string like "bcadefa" we would get 3 sections, "bc", "def", and "". Then, we can count how many substrings there are in each section. In this way, we will count only the *valid* substrings. For each section, counting substrings by iterating through them is *also* unnecessary work. That is because there is a nifty formula for the number of substrings of length k: $k*(k+1)/2$ (pg 533). Math formulas often offer shortcuts to *SKIP* work. This formula is the kind of useful 'property' that we'll talk about in the next booster.

BOOSTER 2: HUNT FOR PROPERTIES

This booster spans a number of techniques, but they are all focused on finding that key property that unlocks a new approach or optimization.[2]

Consider the following classic problem:

✦ **PROBLEM 24.3**   **LIST OF DIVISORS**

Find all divisors of an integer n ≥ 1.

▸ **Example:** n = 40
  Output: 1, 2, 4, 5, 8, 10, 20, 40

SOLUTION 24.3   LIST OF DIVISORS

A naive algorithm would iterate through all positive numbers smaller than or equal to n, testing each one to see if it divides n evenly. This takes $O(n)$ time.

To improve this, we need to start looking for properties about the problem—or about divisors in general—that we can use in an algorithm.

Looking for properties is a bit like a climber feeling the rock above their head in search of a good hold they can grip to keep making progress—we are not sure of what we will find, so we should take note of every promising idea even if some of them do not pan out in the end.

Some general properties we may vaguely remember about divisors are:

Property 1:   They are somehow related to prime numbers.

---

2   As someone who has come up with many coding questions, including for this book, I (Nil) can offer some insight into how questions are created. Some come from actual work problems, with the context stripped away. But some start from an interesting property, like, "an array has (n+1)*n/2 subarrays." Then, we come up with problems, like Problem 24.2: Count Substrings Without Letter (pg 252), where the solution is to use that property. We make problems harder by (1) using more niche properties, or (2) obscuring the right property. For instance, in Problem 24.2, we added an extra step (splitting by a's) before the property could be used. So, when we say '*HUNT FOR PROPERTIES*', we are often looking for something that has been **intentionally** hidden.

Property 2:   Most numbers do not have that many divisors (prime numbers are the *prime* example of this, as their only divisors are 1 and themselves).

Property 3:   Most divisors tend to be smallish.

Those properties are not immediately useful, but they are like threads that we can explore. For instance, #2 suggests that looking through all numbers up to n may be unnecessary, so we should look for ways to *SKIP UNNECESSARY WORK*. Thinking in this direction, we may realize one more property that was hinted at by property #3:

Property 4:   There cannot be any divisors between n/2 and n. E.g., there are no divisors of 40 between 20 and 40.

When we find a property, we need to explore the implications for algorithm design. Property #4 means we can skip the top half of the search range. This roughly cuts the runtime in half, which is good, but does not move the needle in big O terms. The runtime is still $O(n/2) = O(n)$. We need to find a "stronger" property.

The actual property we need to crack this problem is this:

Property 5:   If d is a divisor of n, then so is n/d. E.g., if 5 is a divisor of 40, then $40/5 = 8$ is also a divisor of 40.

Now, let's consider how to "exploit" it in an algorithm. The idea is that whenever we find a divisor d, we can also get n/d "for free" (without having to search for it). If we do this, for every pair of divisors d and d' such that d x d' = n, we only need to find the smaller of the two. Since $\sqrt{n} * \sqrt{n} = n$, any divisor greater than $\sqrt{n}$ will be found as the larger pair of a divisor smaller than $\sqrt{n}$, so we can stop searching for divisors when we reach $\sqrt{n}$. For instance, $\sqrt{40} = 6.32...$, so we can stop searching at 6, and we will find the larger divisors (8, 10, 20, 40) from the smaller ones (1, 2, 4, 5). The new runtime is $O(\sqrt{n})$.

PROPERTY HUNTING STRATEGIES

The rest of this section goes over techniques for how to discover properties and use them.

- The starting point for hunting for properties should always be the *DIY (DO IT YOURSELF)* technique: try solving the problem by hand and observe the shortcuts your brain naturally comes up with.

- One way to make it easier to find properties is to first classify inputs into different cases. This way, instead of finding a property that applies to every input, we just need to find one that helps in each case. We call this a *CASE ANALYSIS*.

- Sometimes, the key property is a "hidden formula" that we need to deduce. In such cases, it can be helpful to manually compute the output for the first several smallest inputs, and then try to *REVERSE ENGINEER THE PATTERN*.

- Some patterns and relationships become more clear when the problem is visualized in the right way. That's why sometimes *SKETCHING A DIAGRAM* can help in our hunt.

- At times, two problems may fundamentally ask for the same thing, but the property needed to solve them is more apparent in one than the other. Thus, to find properties, sometimes we'll need to *REFRAME THE PROBLEM* into a different but equivalent problem and then search for properties there.

This list is not necessarily exhaustive, but it hits the major ideas we think you should consider.

HUNT FOR PROPERTIES: DIY (DO IT YOURSELF)

Give your closest non-coding friend a stack of sorted playing cards and ask them to pull out the 9 of diamonds. In all likelihood, they will not flip though one card at a time until they find it. More likely, they will flip through large chunks until they go too far, and then reverse a bit, until they narrow it down—effectively reinventing binary search.

This works so reliably because humans are, well, kind of lazy. We don't want to do silly manual work if we can skip it, so we find shortcuts when we can. The *DIY* technique is all about essentially *freeing your mind* to find these shortcuts:

Step 1:   **Create a non-trivial example:** one that's large enough that the answer is not immediately obvious, but without being too cumbersome.

Step 2:   **Solve it by hand:** Do not think about algorithms and data structures, or worry about how you're solving it. Just get the output.

Step 3:   **Reverse engineer:** Reverse engineer your thought process. What sort of shortcuts did you accidentally use?

Creating good examples

The problem statement may or may not come with examples. However, even when it does, examples provided by the interviewer are designed to clarify the question, not to help you solve it.

> #### What makes a good example?
>
> A *good* example can actually be very helpful in solving the problem. An ideal example is:
>
> - Sufficiently large, but not excessive large
> - Generic (that is, it avoids special cases)
>
> If the example provided to you doesn't meet these criteria, create a new one that does.

For instance, if you're asked to find all pairs of values within an array which sum to some number k, the array `[5, 3, 1]` is too small to be useful. The array `[1, 2, 3, 6, 9, 10, 11, 13, 15, 20, 25, 30]` is too large; it would be pretty time consuming to walk through this manually. This is why you want an example that is *LARGE, BUT NOT TOO LARGE.*

There's another issue though with that example: it involves a special case (three, in fact). The problem doesn't specify a sorted array, nor does it specify unique values, nor that the array has all positive integers. It would be a real shame to create an algorithm that accidentally hinges on details that aren't actually true.

Therefore, it is important to ensure your input is as *GENERIC* as possible. If you aren't told that the input is sorted, don't use sorted input.

Try the *DIY* technique for the following problem:

✦ **PROBLEM 24.4**   **SUB PERMUTATIONS**

Given two strings, s1 and s2, count how many permutations of s1 are substrings in s2. A *permutation* of a string s is a string with the same letters of s, in any order. Assume that n1 ≤ n2, where n1 is the length of s1 and n2 is the length of s2.

▸ **Example:** s1 = "bat", s2 = "tabbathat"
  Output: 2. The permutations are "tab" and "bat".

▸ **Example:** s1 = "a", s2 = "aa"
  Output: 1. Permutation "a" is counted once even though it appears multiple times.

SOLUTION 24.4   SUB PERMUTATIONS

When candidates are asked this question, they typically come up with the same brute force algorithm: create all permutations of s1 and search for each one in s2. It's *extremely* slow, as there are n1! permutations, but it's a starting point.

Often, candidates get stuck here. Stop and give the *DIY* approach a try, starting from *STEP 1: CREATE A NON-TRIVIAL EXAMPLE.*

The interviewer's examples were trivial, so let's create a better one. We want one that's a bit larger, and avoids edge cases that could make it simpler. This means, in this case, to be sure our example includes duplicate letters and overlapping permutations.

```
s1 = "aabbc", s2 = "ababacbabaabaaccbabacbab"
```

Now onto *STEP 2: SOLVE IT BY HAND.* Go on then, do it.

After discussing this problem with hundreds of people, we have never once seen a candidate actually generate all the permutations of s1; they come up with this algorithm, sometimes even insisting that you *must* generate all the permutations, but they never do it themselves.

Instead, what they do is typically some variant of: check the first n1 characters of s2, then slide that over by one character, and then another character, and so on. They've intuited a *sliding window* algorithm.

The key property we implicitly relied on is: "permutations grow exponentially while subarrays grow linearly, so we should iterate over substrings rather than over permutations."

STEP 3: REVERSE ENGINEER, then is pretty straightforward. We just need to formalize the details of the sliding window.[3]

Being software engineers has given us some wonderful tools to solve problems. But, as they say: "When your only tool is a hammer, everything looks like a nail." Our knowledge of data structures and algorithms can distract us from more intuitive ways of tackling problems. Sometimes it's good to use computer science principles, and sometimes it's best to forget them for a moment.

HUNT FOR PROPERTIES: CASE ANALYSIS

If we can't find any helpful property, it may help to first classify inputs into different cases. Then, we can focus on searching for a property for a specific case, instead of finding a property that applies to every input.

One way to figure out the cases is with a variation of the *DIY TECHNIQUE*: instead of trying a single non-trivial input, we try a bunch of inputs and see which ones have similarities. Try it on the following problem:

✦ **PROBLEM 24.5**   **MAGIC BALLS**

A magician has R red balls, G green balls, and B blue balls. The balls are magic because when two of them touch, they transform into a single ball:

1. Two balls of the same color become one ball of that color.
2. Two balls of different colors become a ball of the third color.

If the magician starts with at least one ball and starts transforming balls until there is a single ball left, what are the possible colors of the final ball? Return a string with a character for each possible color ('R', 'G', and 'B').

▶ **Example:** R = 4, G = 0, B = 0

---

3 An optimal algorithm for this problem would take O(n²) time. It would use a similar idea as Problem 38.15: Shortest With All Letters (pg 528).

> **Output:** "R". We only have red balls, so combining them can only result in more red balls.

▶ **Example:** R = 2, G = 1, B = 0
  Output: "BG". See Figure 2.

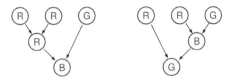

Figure 2. With two red balls and one green ball, we can end up with a blue ball or a green ball.

SOLUTION 24.5   MAGIC BALLS

Try to work out the solution manually for a bunch of input settings until you figure out a pattern. Start with cases with 2 balls, then 3, and so on. Try it before continuing reading!

Eventually, we should come up with a *CASE ANALYSIS* similar to this:

Case 1:   All the balls have the same color.

Case 2:   There are balls of every color.

Case 3:   There are only balls of two colors.

Figuring out what to do case by case is more manageable than tackling the general case.

Case 1:   All the balls have the same color (say, R). Then, we will end up with a ball of that color (R).

Case 2:   There are balls of every color.

    Case 2.a: If there is exactly one ball of each color. We can end up with any color based on the order in which we combine them.

    Case 2.b: If there are one or more balls for each color. We can get to Case 2.a by combining balls of the same color until there is only one of each. Thus, we can make any color.

Case 3:   There are only balls of two colors (say, R and G).

    Case 3.a: If there is exactly one ball of each color. Then, we can only make the third color (B).

    Case 3.b: If there are at least two balls of each color. Then, we can get to Case 2, so we can end up with any color.

    Case 3.c: There is exactly one ball of one color (G) and two balls of the other color (R). Then, like in Example 2, we can make the two colors for which we don't have 2 balls (G and B).

    Case 3.d: There is exactly one ball of one color (G) and more than two balls of the other color (R). We can get to case 3.c by repeatedly merging red balls, so we can get G and B. However, there is no way to get R: no matter what we do, we will always end up with red as one of the final two balls.

This is a *CASE ANALYSIS*: we come up with a bunch of cases such that every input falls in one of them, and then figure out how to solve each case. Once we have the *CASE ANALYSIS*, we can convert it into code with conditional statements. The final runtime should be O(1).

HUNT FOR PROPERTIES: REVERSE ENGINEER THE OUTPUT PATTERN

Sometimes, the key property to crack a problem is a "hidden formula" that we need to deduce. In such cases, it can be useful to manually find the output for the first few smallest inputs (similar to what we suggested for figuring out the cases for the *CASE ANALYSIS*), and then try to find some pattern in the output that can be extrapolated to larger inputs.

✦✦   **PROBLEM 24.6**   **HIRING AND TRAINING**

Your startup company starts with a single recruiter, and your goal is to grow it to *exactly* n recruiters, for some given n > 1. Each day, you can do one of two things:

HIRE   Hire new employees. You send each recruiter to hire one new employee (you don't send employees that have not been trained as recruiters yet).

TRAIN   Train all the new hires to become recruiters themselves (you can't train only a few of them).

How many days do you need to get to n recruiters?

Constraint: you must not hire more than n people.

▸ **Example:** n = 3
    Output: 3. On the first two days, you can send your recruiter to hire one
             new employee. On the third day, you train both of them to become
             recruiters.

▸ **Example:** n = 12
    Output: 7. We can follow the actions shown below:

	DAY 1	DAY 2	DAY 3	DAY 4	DAY 5	DAY 6	DAY 7
Action	Hire	Train	Hire	Train	Hire	Hire	Train
Recruiters	1	2	2	4	4	4	12
New hires	1	0	2	0	4	8	0

SOLUTION 24.6   HIRING AND TRAINING

A naive solution would be to try every possible sequence of actions with backtracking. We could then apply *BRUTE FORCE OPTIMIZATION (#1)* to try to optimize it with something like dynamic programming. However, here we will focus on a different approach.

If we try the *DIY* technique, we'll find it hard to turn our thought process into an algorithm because it seems that we have to do something different for each value of n. Instead, we can compute the output for the first few values of n and then try to deduce the pattern. See if you can spot it:

N	1	2	3	4	5	6	7	8	9
Output	0	2	3	4	5	5	7	6	6
Actions: (H)ire (T)rain	—	HT	HHT	HHHT or HTHT	HHHHT	HTHHT or HHTHT	HHHH-HHT	HTHTHT	HHTHHT

Some patterns begin to emerge, but they become more clear with more data points:

N	10	11	12	13
Output	7	11	7	13
Actions: (H)ire (T)rain	HTHHHHT or HHHHTHT	HHHHHHHHHHT	HTHTHHT or HTHHTHT or HHTHTHT	HHHHHHHHHHHHT

The pattern suggests a property:

Property 1: If n is *prime*, we need to hire n-1 times and then train on the last day.

Note that the problem does not have any triggers for prime numbers; it's only through looking at the *output patterns* that we noticed they play a role.

Be careful, though; patterns do not necessarily extrapolate to larger inputs. Ask yourself, "is this true for every prime?" In this case, we can assure ourselves that it is: if n is prime and we train more than 1 recruiter, we can't stop at exactly n new hires.

By reflecting on that logic, we can reach another property:

Property 2: If we get to a point where we have k recruiters, we can only reach numbers of recruiters multiple of k.

Next, we need to turn this property into an algorithmic idea:

Property 3: We should never train on days when the number of employees is not a divisor of n.

As we mentioned in Problem 24.3: List Of Divisors (pg 253), most numbers do not have that many divisors, so this property drastically reduces the number of options to consider. It enables us to ***SKIP UNNECESSARY WORK***. From this point, we could use this property to improve our naive backtracking solution or, even better, use it in a dynamic programming algorithm.[4]

HUNT FOR PROPERTIES: SKETCH A DIAGRAM

A common refrain is that "a picture is worth a thousand words," and we agree! In Anatomy of a Coding Interview, we talked about how drawing examples can help us understand the input (pg 192). Sketching a diagram can *also* help us find properties—some patterns and relationships become more clear when the problem is visualized in the right way.

Sketch a Diagram: Examples from the Book

- In backtracking algorithms, it often helps to visualize the *decision tree* (pg 543).
- In problems about intervals, it's easier to look for useful properties by actually drawing them. See, for instance, Problem 41.1: Most Non-Overlapping Intervals (pg 590).
- Problems involving geometric elements often require geometric properties. See for instance Problem 31.2: Nested Circles (pg 370).

We recommend grabbing pen and paper before looking at the following problems.

4 There is even a greedy algorithm for this problem, which is to train every time the number of employees reaches a divisor of n. However, to understand why that works we'd need even more advanced properties!

✦✛ **PROBLEM 24.7**   **INTERVAL XOR**

Given two intervals, a = $[a_s, a_e]$, b = $[b_s, b_e]$ with $a_s < a_e$ and $b_s < b_e$, return a list of intervals representing a xor b, defined as the sections of a that are not in b and the sections of b that are not in a. The output intervals should be sorted from left to right, non-overlapping, and not sharing an endpoint.

▸ **Example:** a = [5, 15], b = [10, 30]
  Output: [[5, 10], [15, 30]]. a and b overlap in the interval [10, 15]. It would not be correct to return [[15, 30], [5, 10]] because the intervals are not ordered from left to right.

▸ **Example:** a = [15, 30], b = [5, 15]
  Output: [[5, 30]]. It would not be correct to return [[5, 15], [15, 30]] because the two intervals share an endpoint and can be consolidated.

▸ **Example:** a = [5, 15], b = [5, 15]
  Output: [].

SOLUTION 24.7   INTERVAL XOR

This problem is not conceptually hard—it just has an extensive and annoying *CASE ANALYSIS*. There is one property that makes the *CASE ANALYSIS* simpler:

Property 1:   a xor b is the same as b xor a.

How can we exploit this property? It means we can reorder the intervals if it helps eliminate some cases. For instance, we can focus on the case where $a_s \le b_s$. If $a_s > b_s$, we can swap a and b without affecting the final solution. There are still many cases—eight to be exact! A *diagram* is the best way to catalogue them and be sure we didn't forget any:

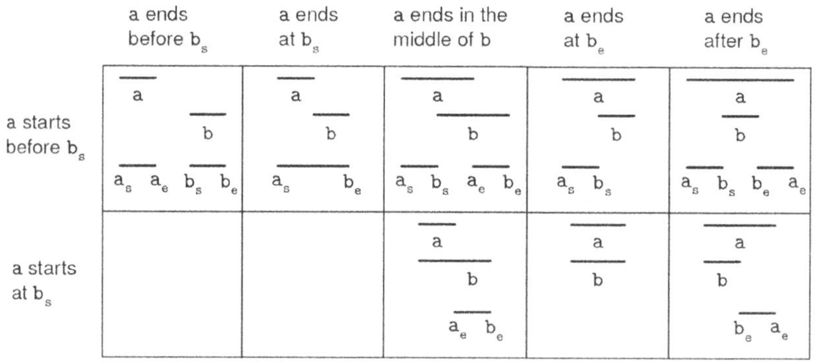

Figure 3. *CASE ANALYSIS* for Problem 7.

It should now be easier to go from the diagram to a coded solution.

Problem 24.7 shows that the techniques we are discussing are not mutually exclusive. We *SKETCHED A DIAGRAM* to help complete the *CASE ANALYSIS*.

✦✛ **PROBLEM 24.8**   **MATRIX ROTATION**

Given a square nxn matrix, mat, rotate it 90 degrees clockwise *in place*, using O(1) extra space.

▸ **Example:** mat = [[25, 15],
                    [10, 30]]
  Output: mat = [[10, 25],

```
                          [30, 15]]
```
We should not create a new matrix.

► **Example:** mat = [[1, 2, 3],
                      [4, 5, 6],
                      [7, 8, 9]]

  Output: mat = [[7, 4, 1],
                     [8, 5, 2],
                     [9, 6, 3]]

SOLUTION 24.8   MATRIX ROTATION

The challenge for this problem is how to do the index manipulation correctly, since we cannot just move one element at a time in place without overwriting some of the values. If we play with a couple of examples, we should arrive at the idea of doing 4-way swaps:

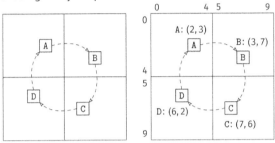

Figure 4.

The diagram on the left is more abstract, just showing 4 arbitrary elements, A, B, C, and D, that need to be swapped at once because A goes in the place of B, B goes in the place of C, and so on; the diagram on the right grounds the idea with some actual coordinates for A, B, C, and D in a 10x10 example.

One property that is easy to see in the diagram is:

Property 1:   We need to do a 4-way swap for every element in the top-left quadrant (though we need to be careful with cells in the middle row or column for matrices with odd dimensions).

So, we can iterate over the coordinates of in the top-left quadrant, and call each element there A. The challenging part is figuring out the coordinates of the corresponding B, C, and D.

We need to find some property that we can use about B, C, and D. If we call (r, c) the row and column of A in the matrix, we can draw the row and column offsets that we know for B, C, and D based on symmetry, and then use those offsets to compute the ones we need:

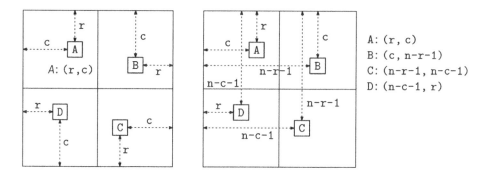

Figure 5.

The diagram helps us visualize the **property** that if B has r columns to its right, then it must have n-r-1 columns to its left, and similarly for the other coordinates:

A = mat[r][c], B = mat[c][n-r-1], C = mat[n-r-1][n-c-1], D = mat[n-c-1][r]

Solution 28.8: Matrix Operations (pg 325) shows a different *PROPERTY* which leads us to an alternative solution for this problem without 4-way swaps.

✦ ┃ PROBLEM 24.9 ┃   **COMPANY LAUNCHES**

A VC firm is analyzing n companies that launched in 1992. We are given two arrays of length n, launches and ads. The i-th company launched on day launches[i] (which is a number between 1 and 366) and had an ad spending of ads[i] (in dollars). We say a launch *overshadows* another launch if (1) it happened earlier and (2) it had more ad spending. Find the indices (starting at 0) of all the launches that were overshadowed by exactly one other launch. You can assume that all dates are different and all ad spendings are different.

▶ **Example:** dates = [12, 5, 2, 11, 4, 8, 3, 1, 10]
           ads   = [11, 4, 2, 5, 9, 7, 6, 3, 1]
           Indices: 0 1 2   3 4 5 6 7   8
   Output: [2, 5]
   Explanation:
           launch 2 is only overshadowed by launch 7
           launch 5 is only overshadowed by launch 4

SOLUTION 24.9   COMPANY LAUNCHES

We have two values for each launch (day and spending), so we can visualize each launch as a point in the plane, where one dimension is the launch day and the other is the ad dollars:

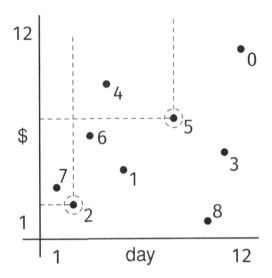

Figure 6. Example for Problem 9. Each point corresponds to a launch. The number next to the point is the input index. Launches overshadowed by exactly one other company are circled.

With this visualization, we can think about the problem in geometric terms and find geometric properties:

Property 1:   A launch overshadows another if it is to the left and above it in the plane.

Property 2:   The launches not overshadowed by anyone are those along the top-left 'frontier.' (7, 6, 4, and 0 in the example.)[5]

Property 3:   We are trying to find all the points with exactly one other point above and to the left.

This visualization can help us come up with a solution. Try to play with different point arrangements and see what you come up with.

We can use what is known as a 'sweep-line algorithm': imagine a vertical line sweeping the plane left to right, representing the passing of time. When the line reaches a point p, the corresponding launch can only be overshadowed by points that the line has already "swept." If p has the second-highest spending so far, we can add it to the result.

---

5   This is known as the 'pareto frontier.'

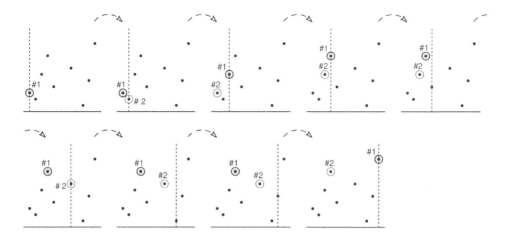

Figure 7. Line-sweep algorithm. We track the largest and second largest spending (y-axis) among the swept points. When a point is the second highest so far at the time it is swept, we add it to the result.

Here is the algorithm in indented English:

```
sort launches by date
initialize highest and second highest spendings to -1
for each launch from earliest to latest
  update highest and second highest spendings seen so far
  if the launch has the second-highest spending
    add its index to the result
```

For problems where input elements consist of two numeric values, you can view the elements as points in the plane and think about what that means geometrically. It's a way of **reframing the problem** into a more geometric version.

Try to do most drawings in the shared editor so the interviewer can follow along. However, for diagrams that are tricky to sketch in that format, you can keep pen and paper near you and ask the interviewer if it is OK to use it.

HUNT FOR PROPERTIES: REFRAME THE PROBLEM

At times, two problems may fundamentally ask for the same thing, but the property needed to solve them is more apparent in one than the other. So, if we find a way to *REFRAME THE PROBLEM*, we should consider if the reframed version is somehow easier. For instance, it could be a problem we are already familiar with.[6]

How do you know when to reframe a problem? Useful reframes often come from *triggers*. For instance, if a problem is not about graphs but mentions something about connections, you may be able to reframe it as a graph problem and use a connectivity algorithm like DFS. In fact, reframing problems as graph problems is so common that we have a section dedicated to it ("Graph Modeling" on page 485).

Reframe the Problem: Examples from the Book

- See the Graph Modeling section about how to reframe problems as graph problems (pg 485).

---

6   An amusing aspect of computer science is that an algorithm that may feel awkward to explain or code in one setting may fit like a glove in a different but equivalent setting.

- See the reusable idea: 'Reframe Balanced Parentheses As Plot Heights' (pg 386).

- Problems asking you to find the optimal way of modifying the input to achieve some goal can often be reframed in a way that eliminates the modification aspect. See Problem 38.9: Ad Campaign Boost (pg 522).

- Problems about *simulating a sequence of operations* can often be reframed so that you don't strictly need to follow the order and think about the final result directly. See Chapter 31: Delete Operations (pg 370).

We'll use reframes to find the key properties in the next two problems.

PROBLEM 24.10   MOST ONES WITH K FLIPS

Given a binary array, arr, what is the most consecutive 1's you can get if you flip at most k bits?

▶ **Example:** arr = [0, 1, 0, 1], k = 1
  Solution: 3. We should flip the second 0.

SOLUTION 24.10   MOST ONES WITH K FLIPS

It is hard to think about optimization *and* modification at the same time. The key idea here is to realize that the problem is equivalent to: "Find the longest subarray with at most k 0's." The length of this subarray is the answer to the original problem because we can flip the k 0's in it. The reframed problem is easier because it says nothing about modification.

This reframed problem can be solved with a sliding window solution. See Problem 38.9: Ad Campaign Boost (pg 522), which is very similar.[7]

REUSABLE IDEA: TRANSFORM THE INPUT

> Often, transforming the input in a preprocessing step is not strictly necessary, but it can simplify the logic of the final solution. If it retains the same time and space complexities, it can be worth doing to simplify your life and reduce the risk of bugs.

Next, we'll show how sometimes even a hard problem can be reframed into an easy one.

PROBLEM 24.11   MULTIPLAYER VIDEO GAME

A group of n friends is playing a videogame with the following rules:

- Each player starts at some unique (x, y) integer coordinates in the videogame map.
- Players cannot move.
- A player can shoot and eliminate another player if they have the same x coordinate or y coordinate and no other player is between them (eliminated or not). Players cannot shoot in directions not aligned with the x-axis or the y-axis.
- Players can shoot more than once.
- Two players cannot shoot simultaneously.
- Once a player is eliminated, they cannot shoot anymore.

The game starts, and players shoot each other until no remaining player can shoot anyone else. Find the order of shots that minimizes the final number of players standing, and return that number.

---

7 Problem 38.9: Ad Campaign Boost (pg 522) and Chapter 38: Ad Campaign Boost (pg 522) use similar reframes.

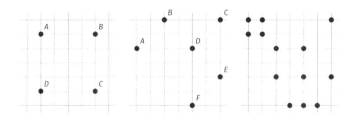

Figure 8. Examples 1, 2, and 3 of the multiplayer video game problem.

▶ **Example:** Figure 8, left.
  Output: 1. If (1) A shoots B, (2) D shoots C, and (3) D shoots A, the only player remaining will be D, so the answer is 1. There are other ways we could get down to 1 player.

▶ **Example:** Figure 8, center.
  Output: 2. C can shoot B and E, and D can shoot A and F, so we can get down to 2 players. No matter who shoots who, there is no way to have only one player left, so the answer is 2.

▶ **Example:** Figure 8, right.
  Output: 1.

SOLUTION 24.11   MULTIPLAYER VIDEO GAME

A naive solution for this problem would be to consider all the possible orders in which players could shoot each other, which would quickly grow exponentially.

We'll model this as a graph problem. We can construct a graph where each player is a node, and there is an edge between two players if they can shoot each other. Then, we can *REFRAME THE PROBLEM* as follows:

"We are given a graph G with n nodes. At any given step, we can remove any node with at least one neighbor. What is the smallest final number of nodes that we can get?"

Figure 9. Examples 1, 2, and 3 reframed as graphs.

After the reframing, the following **property** becomes much more evident:

Property 1:   There will be *at least* one node remaining for each connected component.

So, the answer will be at least the number of connected components.

The remaining question is whether every connected component can be 'reduced' to a single node. If you play with some examples (see the *DIY TECHNIQUE* on pg 254), you should find that there always seems to be an order that makes it possible, which is correct. In an interview, that is likely all you need, but for those of you who are not convinced, here is a proof:

Given a connected component, take any node, v. It doesn't matter which one. Start removing nodes one by one, always picking a node furthest away from v (breaking ties arbitrarily). Every node other than v can be removed because they have at least one neighbor closer to v, which means their neighbor has not been removed yet. In the end, you will only have v left.

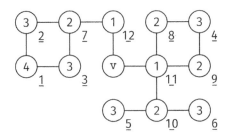

Figure 10. Graph for Example 3, with a node labeled v and the other nodes labeled with the distance from v. The underscored numbers denote a valid removal order (from furthest to closest to v) that will leave only v at the end.

In the end, the problem can be *REFRAMED* again as "count the number of connected components in a graph," a basic graph problem (pg 465). Counting connected components is something that we can do with graph traversal algorithms like DFS and BFS—we just need to construct the graph first.

The takeaway is twofold:

1. Many problems can be reframed as graphs, and
2. Once we reframe a problem as a graph problem, we can consider whether standard graph algorithms like DFS and BFS could be useful.[8]

For instance, imagine a follow-up that asked us for the order in which players should be eliminated to get to the minimum number of possible players. We have seen that we can find a valid order based on distances, which is something we can get with a BFS (pg 474), so a BFS could be used for this follow-up.

BOOSTER 3: DECREASE THE DIFFICULTY

If the problem is too hard to tackle with boosters 1 and 2, our advice is to start with an easier problem first. Think of a pianist trying to learn Rimsky-Korsakov's *Flight of the Bumblebee*. Musicians do two things:

1. They make the piece easier by playing it at a slower tempo first
2. They break down the piece into smaller sections and learn one at a time.

If you can't find any approach...

Decrease the Difficulty
- Tackle an Easier Version
- Break Down the Problem

3

It turns out that these two concepts also apply to solving coding interviews. They are the two ways in which we can *DECREASE THE DIFFICULTY*.

---

8 We expand on this process in the Graph Modeling section (pg 485).

DECREASE THE DIFFICULTY: START WITH AN EASIER VERSION

The idea of this technique is to tweak the problem to make it easier so we can make some progress. We solve the easier version with the hope of using our solution as a starting point for the solution to the original problem or, at least, to gain some insight.[9]

This technique is similar to *REFRAME THE PROBLEM*, except that now we are not finding a different but equivalent statement, but rather an easier (non-equivalent) version. For instance, for Problem 24.9: Company Launches (pg 262) we could have started by finding launches not overshadowed by any other launch (as opposed to launches overshadowed by exactly 1 launch). That's not equivalent—it is easier. E.g., in Figure 7 (pg 264), we'd only need to keep track of the largest spending, instead of the two largest ones. But it would have probably been a good starting point.

Here are some ways to tweak a problem:

- If the statement has some parameter, start with some small constant value for it, like the smallest non-trivial value. E.g., try 2-sum before 3-sum (pg 251).
- Drop some of the requirements. For instance, if a problem requires an in-place solution, try to first solve the version using extra memory.
- If the input graph is weighted, start with an unweighted one.
- If negative numbers make the problem tricky, focus on solving inputs with positive numbers only first.
- If duplicates make the problem tricky, start with the case where all elements are unique.

Decrease the Difficulty: Examples from the Book

- In Problem 30.9: Product of Alphabetical Sums (pg 355), we *TACKLE AN EASIER VERSION* by pretending the inputs are integers instead of strings.

- In Problem 36.11: Graph Hangout (pg 478), we first tackle a version with 2 friends before tackling the version with 3 friends.

We'll solve the following problem by tackling an easier version.

✦✦ **PROBLEM 24.12**   **TREE DIAMETER**

You are given the root root of a binary tree (using the typical Node class, as shown on page 431. Find the *diameter* of the tree. The diameter is the maximum distance between any two nodes.

---

9   Starting an interview by providing a naive solution is similar—we are making it easier (by ignoring the efficiency requirements) in order to gain insights (like an upper bound on the time complexity). In this booster, we want to focus on efficient algorithms, but we may simplify the problem another way.

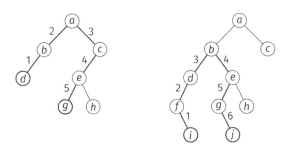

Figure 11. Examples 1 and 2 of the tree diameter problem. The numbers on the edges show (one of) the longest path(s).

▶ **Example:** Figure 11, left.
  Output: 5. Nodes d and g are at distance 5 (and so are d and h).
▶ **Example:** Figure 11, right.
  Output: 6. Nodes i and j are the farthest apart.

SOLUTION 24.12   TREE DIAMETER

We'll illustrate our thought process for tackling this problem. We'll skip Booster 1 (***BRUTE FORCE OPTIMIZATION***) and start from Booster 2 (***HUNT FOR PROPERTIES***).

Thought 1:	I'll start by brainstorming possible properties that could be useful. For each idea, I'll then assess whether it is true by looking for counterexamples.
Hunch 1:	the endpoints of the longest path must have the highest depth of any nodes.
	Assessment: False. Example 1 is a counterexample of this, as node d does not have the highest depth.
Hunch 2:	the longest path must go through the root.
	Assessment: False. Example 2 is a counterexample of this.
Hunch 3:	The longest path may not be unique.
	Assessment: True. Example 1 is an example.
Thought 2:	So far, I haven't found a helpful property (#3 is true but doesn't have a clear application). This is a tree problem, so let's think about common techniques for tree problems. A typical strategy is to compute, at each node, information about its subtrees (pg 436). What information about subtrees could be useful for this particular problem? Clearly, it's related to the height, but subtree height alone is not enough. Let's park this thought for now.
Thought 3:	In figuring out what information to store at each node, I identified the obstacle making this problem challenging. For any given node, there are four cases for how it could overlap

with the longest path: from above to the left subtree, from above to the right subtree, from the left subtree to the right subtree, or not at all. I can *SKETCH A DIAGRAM*:

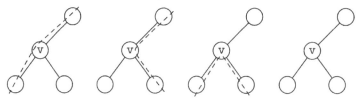

Figure 12. *CASE ANALYSIS* of the possible overlaps between the longest path and a given node v.

Not knowing which case each node falls into makes it hard to know what to compute about that node.

Thought 4:   Let's *TACKLE AN EASIER VERSION* by asking: "What is the length of the longest path in the tree that goes through the root?" Maybe if I can solve this, I can later generalize the solution to find the longest path overall.

Thought 5:   I know how to solve the easier version! I've seen this type of question before. It's the height of the left subtree of the root plus the height of the right subtree of the root—I just need to be careful in the edge cases where the root's children are missing.

Thought 6:   Going back to the original problem, the only case left is where the longest path does not go through the root. Let's capture the options in a *CASE ANALYSIS*:

Case a: The longest path goes through the root. I know how to solve this.

Case b: The longest path is fully contained in the left subtree.

Case c: The longest path is fully contained in the right subtree.

Since we are talking about subtrees, we can handle cases (b) and (c) recursively!

Thought 7:   I don't know how to identify if we are in case (a), as in Example 1, (b), as in Example 2, or (c). I can find the longest path for each case and return the maximum between the 3 options. I can write this down in 'indented English' to make sure I didn't forget anything:

```
compute the height of every subtree (preprocessing step)
option1 = height(left subtree)  + (1 if left subtree is not null)
+ height(right subtree) + (1 if right subtree is not null)
option2 = diameter(root.left)
option3 = diameter(root.right)
return max(option1, option2, option3)
```

Hopefully, no step in this train of thought felt like a "big jump." One key technique we used when faced with a *CASE ANALYSIS* that was too complex was to focus on one of the cases first. That is one way of decreasing the difficulty so that we can keep making progress. See page 430 for advice on implementing recursive binary tree algorithms.

DECREASE THE DIFFICULTY: BREAK DOWN THE PROBLEM

Sometimes, we get stuck on a problem because we try to do too much at once. Breaking the problem down into smaller pieces can help you make progress.

In a way, this is less "wasteful" than *TACKLING AN EASIER VERSION* because, even if the piece we tackle does not solve the whole problem, it can still be part of our final solution.

Break Down the Problem: Examples from the Book

- Some problems can be broken down into (1) finding valid starting bounds for binary search with *exponential search* (pg 338), and (2) doing binary search.

- See the reusable idea: 'Reusable idea: Linked List Reversal Break Down' (pg 421). It breaks down any problem about reversing parts of a linked list into four simple steps.

- See the reusable idea: 'Path Reconstruction' in Graphs (pg 470). We find paths between nodes, in two steps: (1) compute predecessors during DFS, and (2) follow a chain of predecessors.

- See the reusable idea: 'Solution Reconstruction' in Dynamic Programming (pg 583). It breaks down finding the optimal answer into (1) finding the value of the optimal answer, and (2) reconstructing the answer with that value.

- See 'Recipe 2: DAG problem recipe' in the Topological Sort chapter (pg 603). It breaks down how to approach most DAG (directed acyclic graph) problems in two steps: (1) find a topological order, (2) use the order in some way.

PROBLEM 24.13   **UNROOTED TREE DIAMETER**

Given the number of nodes, n > 0, and the edge list, edges, of an undirected graph. We know that the graph is a *tree*, meaning that it is connected and without any cycles (pg 467). Find the tree's *diameter*. The diameter is the maximum distance between any two nodes.

▸ **Example:** n = 8
            edges = [[0, 3], [2, 3], [1, 3], [4, 1], [1, 5], [1, 7], [7, 6]]
   Output: 4. Nodes 2 and 6 are at distance 4 (and so are 0 and 6).

SOLUTION 24.13   **UNROOTED TREE DIAMETER**

We have already seen how to solve this problem for rooted trees (Problem Problem 24.12 - pg 268), so we can break down this problem into two phases: (1) convert the unrooted tree into a rooted tree; (2) solve the problem on a rooted tree (note that the rooted tree may not be a *binary* tree anymore, but the same approach can be generalized to N-ary trees).

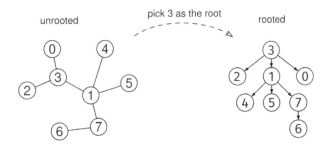

Figure 13. Turning the unrooted tree from the Example into a rooted tree by picking 3 as the root (we could pick any node).

Converting a free tree into a rooted tree is relatively easy to do with a graph traversal like DFS or BFS. We've broken down a hard problem into two easier steps.

Sure, there are more clever ways of solving this problem,[10] but why bother? Our algorithm is linear, which is already optimal. Play to your strengths!

✦ ⬛ PROBLEM 24.14   **LONGEST ALPHABET CHAIN**

You're given an array of lowercase letters, `arr`. Your task is to find the longest *alphabet chain* you can make with the input letters. An *alphabet chain* is a string where each letter is followed by the next letter in the alphabet, like `"def"`. An alphabet chain can wrap around from `'z'` to `'a'`, as in `"xyzab"`. You can reorder the input letters if necessary.

▶ **Example:** `arr = "acdf"`
  Output: `2. The longest chain is "cd".`

▶ **Example:** `arr = "aammzz"`
  Output: `2. The longest chain is "za".`

▶ **Example:** `"mnopqrstuvwxyzxxmnopxxabcdefghijklmnop"`
  Output: `30. The longest chain is "mnopqrstuvwxyzabcdefghijklmnop".`

SOLUTION 24.14   LONGEST ALPHABET CHAIN

When there is a lot going on in a problem, it is good to start by identifying all the complications that make a problem hard:

- Looping around from `'z'` to `'a'`.
- The same letter being used multiple times.
- Hard to know where to start the alphabetic chain.

We could remove any of the complications to make an **EASIER VERSION** of the problem. However, first we should brainstorm for **PROPERTIES** to help with these obstacles (even if some don't end up paying off).

Property 1:   The order of the letters in the input does not matter, but the frequencies of the letters seem important. A *frequency map* (pg 348) with the count of each letter could be useful.

Property 2:   If any letter is missing, duplicates do not matter: we could never cycle all the way back to a duplicated letter.

Property 3:   If every frequency is at least k, we can do k full loops, so the answer will be at least 26*k.

Property 4:   We could **REFRAME** this as a graph problem (graph modeling): if each input letter is a node and two nodes are connected when their letters are next to each other in the alphabet (or an `'a'` and a `'z'`), the problem is equivalent to finding the longest path in this graph.

Finally, it feels like we strike gold:

Property 5:   If the input is not missing any letters from the alphabet, we can do at least one full loop. We can decrease every frequency by 1, solve the smaller problem, and then add 26 to the resulting length. It doesn't matter where the chain for the smaller problem starts!

For instance, the frequency map for Example 3 is:

```
a b c d e f g h i j k l m n o p q r s t u v w x y z
1 1 1 1 1 1 1 1 1 1 1 1 3 3 3 3 1 1 1 1 1 1 5 1 1
```

That means that the solution is 26 plus the solution for an input with this frequency map:

---

10 A clever algorithm for this problem that does not involve rooting the tree first is to take an arbitrary node in the tree, u. Then, find the node (or one of the nodes) furthest from u, say, v, using BFS. Next, find a node furthest from v, say, w, with a second BFS. The distance between v and w is the diameter of the tree (you can find a proof that it works on https://codeforces.com/blog/entry/101271). Most people wouldn't come up with this trick in an interview—you either know it or you don't. This is the type of solution we don't want to emphasize in this book, especially in this chapter.

```
a b c d e f g h i j k l m n o p q r s t u v w x y z
0 0 0 0 0 0 0 0 0 0 0 2 2 2 2 0 0 0 0 0 0 0 4 0 0
```

This property gives us an idea to **BREAK DOWN** the problem into two phases that we can solve independently:

Phase 1:	Use Property #5 to reduce the problem to the case of at least one missing letter.
Phase 2:	Solve the case with at least one missing letter.

For Phase 1, we can find the lowest frequency, k, among all letters. If it is 0, we can proceed to phase 2 immediately. If not, we can reduce k from every frequency and move on to Phase (2). In the end, we will add 26*k to the result.[11]

For Phase 2, we can ignore frequencies (see Property #2). The only thing that matters is whether they are 0 or not. In other words, we can **REFRAME THE PROBLEM** as a sliding window problem: "Find the longest subarray of non-zeros in a 'circular' array (meaning that it wraps from the end to the start)."

This reframed problem is not hard, so you probably don't need it, but there is a nifty trick that is often useful for problems about circular arrays that makes it even easier: Take two copies of the array and concatenate them. This allows us to **REFRAME THE PROBLEM** again to: "Find the longest subarray of non-zeros in a (normal) array." This final problem should be trivial coding-wise! Here is the final 'indented English' solution:

```
Algo: two-phase breakdown
n: len of the input array
Time: O(n)
Space: O(26) = O(1)
initialize an array of length 26 with the letter frequencies
k = min in the array
subtract k from every element in the array
concatenate two copies of the array
m = len of longest subarray of non-zeros in the concatenated array
return 26*k + m
```

To recap, when **HUNTING FOR PROPERTIES**, we found Property #5, which allowed us to **BREAK DOWN THE PROBLEM** into two phases, each of which was easier to tackle by itself. If we hadn't found that property, we may have tried to start with an easier version first, like the one where there is at least one missing letter (which is our Phase 2). In the end, we may have ended up with a similar algorithm. This shows that there is no unique correct order of applying boosters.

♻ REUSABLE IDEA: LENGTH-26 ARRAY

When the input is a string of lowercase letters, we often can use an array of length 26 where index 0 corresponds to 'a', index 1 corresponds to 'b', and so on. This is more efficient than using a map data structure.

For instance, if we want to count how many times each letter appears in a string:

```
1   # We are told that s only contains lowercase letters.
2   def letter_counts(s):
3     counts = [0] * 26
4     for c in s:
5       index = ord(c) - ord('a')
6       counts[index] += 1
7     return counts
```

---

11 We could also see this as a **CASE ANALYSIS** where we can reduce Case (1) to Case (2).

If we want to support all ASCII characters, then we can use an array of length 128 instead (and *not* subtract ord('a')).

BOOSTER 4: CYCLE THROUGH THE CATALOG

Some of the most challenging problems are those where the best solution comes from the least expected place. Such problems often have triggers urging us to try some approach, but it's the wrong one.

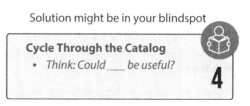

Solution might be in your blindspot

Cycle Through the Catalog
- *Think: Could ___ be useful?*

4

When the right algorithm or data structure to solve a problem is something you'd never consider, we say it's in your blind spot. It's not necessarily an obscure algorithm you don't know. Maybe you know it but you haven't made the connection of how it applies here (have we already mentioned how commonly graphs show up in seemingly unrelated problems?)

The only way to find something in your blind spot may be to systematically cycle through the topics of the Catalog (Figure 1 on pg 171), and, for each topic, spend a few seconds asking yourself:

Is there any way in which XYZ could be useful for this problem?

Do this even if the connection is not apparent—that is the whole point.

For instance, in Problem 22.1: Tunnel Depth (pg 231), both Alex and Jamie missed the optimal solution with binary search. They would have never considered binary search for a grid-based problem. However, if they asked themselves, "Even though there is no sorted array in this problem, is there any way a binary search could be used?" and then spent a minute entertaining the idea and exploring the implications, they may have found it.

Of course, doing this for every topic we know is very time-consuming, which is why this booster is second to last. But sometimes, it's what it takes to overcome a blind spot.

BOOSTER 5: ARTICULATE YOUR BLOCKER

Hints and coding interviews have a complicated relationship. Yes, they're normal. No, ideally you don't need one. Yes, you probably will. No, you shouldn't ask for one. Yes, you should expect that you might get one. See what I mean?

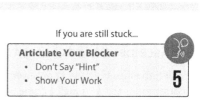

If you are still stuck...

Articulate Your Blocker
- Don't Say "Hint"
- Show Your Work

5

WHY YOU SHOULDN'T ASK FOR A HINT

- *Effective interviewers* aim to ask challenging questions, ones that really make the candidate think. They want to stretch the candidate—not too hard, but just hard enough—and see what the candidate can do (pg 181).
- *Effective interviewers* will be engaged and paying attention, jumping in when the candidate needs help but standing back when they believe the candidate can soon make progress independently. They will be kind and supportive, balancing creating a positive experience with extracting signal.
- *Effective interviewers* are doing their very best, based on the information they have. They might give you a hint, but don't want you to ask for one.

So why would an effective interviewer *offer* hints, but then not want you to ask for one?

As (hopefully) effective interviewers, we give hints when we feel it's the right time, and we might offer just a very small one—just enough to nudge you along, without giving too much away. Therefore, if we haven't given a hint, it's likely because we don't think it's in your best interest to get one. We've probably asked this question many times, and we may have a better idea than you do about your progress and what's just around the corner.

But then, you ask us for a hint, and we have to make a difficult choice:

- Do we decline "for your own good," possibly making you feel uncomfortable?
- Do we give you a nice big hint? You feel good because you made progress, but you didn't need it and now lost the opportunity to show us that you could have overcome this obstacle yourself.
- Or do we give you a tiny hint, but then you feel possibly bad because you just asked for something and it didn't even seem to help you?

None of these are good options. Asking for a hint—with an effective interviewer—is often a lose–lose.

What about ineffective interviewers?[12] Well, then, all bets are off and we really don't know how they'll react. Maybe they'll dislike you for "giving up" by asking for a hint. Maybe they'll give you points for making more progress, even if it was really due to a hint. Better to just ignore this and assume your interviewer is an effective one.

HINTING FOR A HINT IN A WIN-WIN WAY

Imagine you're stuck on Problem 24.14: Longest Alphabet Chain (pg 272). You suspect there's a linear solution and you are considering using a hashmap, but you can't quite make it work. Deciding to ask for help, you say:

> May I have a hint?

Your interviewer replies:

> Sure. You can do this in linear time.

Yikes! That wasn't helpful; it possibly counted as a hint against your problem-solving score and told you something you already intuited.

There is an alternative to asking for a hint—and in a way that is actually good for everyone. The key is to *show your work*.

As we explained, effective interviewers are paying attention and giving you the help that they think would benefit you in making progress, while still allowing ample room for independent problem solving. They have the benefit of having asked many candidates this question and understanding where you *really* are in the problem, but they're still operating on imperfect information. They don't know everything that's going on in your head.

What can you do, then? Give them more transparency into your current thought process.

Follow these steps:

Step 1:   *RECAP* your current approach to ensure the interviewer is on the same page.

Step 2:   Describe the *OBSTACLE*. You must be able to articulate a specific thing you are struggling with, not just a blank "I'm stuck." Help them help you.

Step 3:   *SHOW YOUR WORK* by mentioning what you have tried so far to overcome the obstacle. This shows that asking for a hint is not the first thing you try when you get stuck!

For example, for Problem 24.14, you could say:

---

12 Hey, it's not their fault. Being a great interviewer is a different skill from actually being a great engineer. And, on top of this, many companies don't train their interviewers effectively.

> I'm having trouble pinpointing where to start the chain. For instance, if a has the lowest frequency, I know I need to start at b, but if there are multiple letters with the smallest frequency, I'm unsure where to start. I could try starting at each letter, which would only be a constant factor slower because there are only 26 letters, but I think I'm missing a smarter approach.

Now, you've given the interviewer insight into your thought process and specific challenges. Trust them. If they aren't jumping in to help, great! It means that they believe that you can reach the next step yourself. If they do jump in to help, great! They knew what you were thinking and were able to maximize the value of the information they gave you.

Hints might not always sound like hints

The job of effective interviewers is to give you the smallest hint possible to unblock you. If you're struggling to figure out some step of the problem or piece of the optimization, they probably won't just tell you exactly what to do.

Instead, they might give a tiny little nudge. For the above problem, they might ask a tiny question like, "If there were only two letters with the lowest frequency, and they were a and c, what would be the best place to start?" This idea—or some idea it leads you to—might be all you need to make progress.

Hints could be even less. It could be as little as reminding you of a detail of a problem, asking you a follow-up question, or explicitly pointing out something clearly visible in the example. Pay attention to your interviewer, and think carefully about the things they say. Sure, sometimes they say things just to say stuff—or ask questions in the middle to assess something—but often, their words are designed to gently guide you in some way.

KEY TAKEAWAYS

To wrap up the chapter, we will give an example of an extra hard (and extra fun) problem and illustrate our thought process as we use multiple boosters.[13]

✦ **PROBLEM 24.15**   **SELF-DOUBLING SEQUENCE**

Consider the following infinite sequence, S:

    S: 0, 1, 1, 2, 1, 2, 2, 3, 1, 2, 2, 3, 2, 3, 3, 4, ...

The sequence S is constructed as follows:

- It starts with the number 0.
- We extend the sequence by repeatedly doing the following operation: (1) take a copy of the sequence so far, (2) add 1 to each number in the copy, and (3) concatenate the copy to the original sequence:

$$0 \rightarrow 0, 1 \rightarrow 0, 1, 1, 2 \rightarrow 0, 1, 1, 2, 1, 2, 2, 3 \rightarrow 0, 1, 1, 2, 1, 2, 2, 3, 1, 2, 2, 3, 2, 3, 3, 4 \rightarrow ...$$

Given $n \geq 0$, return $S(n)$, the n-th number in S (it starts at index 0).

▶ **Example:** n = 0
   Output: 0.
▶ **Example:** n = 10
   Output: 2.
   Constraints: $0 \leq n \leq 10^{10}$.

---

13 Problem 24.15: Self-Doubling Sequence (pg 276) could be considered a 'brain teaser.' We personally think brain teasers are not great for interviews, as they favor candidates who are good at riddles rather than candidates with a solid CS foundation. Unfortunately, some companies still use them.

SOLUTION 24.15   SELF-DOUBLING SEQUENCE

The naive solution is to construct the sequence up to the n-th term, but if we use *boundary thinking* (see "TLE Upper Bound" on page 234), we see that the constraint $n \leq 10^{18}$ implies that we need to do better than $O(n)$. The *triggers* (pg 242) for this problem are:

- Binary search because we need a sublinear solution.
- Recursion because S is defined in a self-referential way.
- 'Math' because we need to "crack the formula."

It is not clear how to apply any of those directly, so we'll employ boosters.

The first booster we will use for this problem is to *SKETCH A DIAGRAM*. We can visualize the copies within the sequence, as well as the starting and ending index of each copy:

$$0 \overset{0}{}$$

Copy 1: $1 \overset{1}{}$

Copy 2: $1 \overset{2}{}$ $2 \overset{3}{}$

Copy 3: $1 \overset{4}{}$ 2 2 $3 \overset{7}{}$

Copy 4: $1 \overset{8}{}$ 2 2 3 2 3 3 $4 \overset{15}{}$

Copy 5: $1 \overset{16}{}$ 2 2 3 2 3 3 4 2 3 3 4 3 4 4 $5 \overset{31}{}$

Figure 14. The sequence S with one copy per line. The first and last index of each copy is underscored on the top left of the corresponding elements.

This diagram shows some *PROPERTIES* that may be useful (even if it's not clear how yet):

Property 1:   Copy k has length 2^{k-1}.

Property 2:   Each copy starts at an index a power of 2. More precisely, copy k starts at index 2^{k-1} and ends at index $2^k - 1$.

The algorithmic application of property #2 is that, for any n, we can find the copy it belongs to in $O(\log n)$ time using *exponential search* (pg 338).

If finding the copy is easy, we can consider *BREAKING DOWN THE PROBLEM* into two steps:

Step 1:   Find the copy k that n belongs to.

Step 2:   Use k in some way to compute S(n).

Even if we haven't coded it yet, we feel confident we can do Step 1, so we should turn our attention to Step 2. From Figure 14, we can see that the first half of each copy overlaps with the previous copy, which suggests that we may have to do something different based on whether n is in the first half of the copy or the second half. We can do a *CASE ANALYSIS* and tackle each case individually.

Case 1:   If n is in the first half of the copy, then its value is the same as the value at the same position in the previous copy. E.g., S(8) = S(4) and S(9) = S(5).

Case 2:   If n is in the second half of the copy, then its value is the same as a value in the first half plus 1. For instance, S(12) = S(8) + 1 and S(13) = S(9) + 1. The offset between 12 and 8, or between 13 and 9, is 4, half the length of the copy.

In both cases, it seems that we can compute S(n) in terms of S(m) for some number m < n. The question then, is "Given n, what should m be?" We can find the mapping manually for a few inputs to *REVERSE ENGINEER THE PATTERN*. We can expand our previous diagram following the *CASE ANALYSIS*.

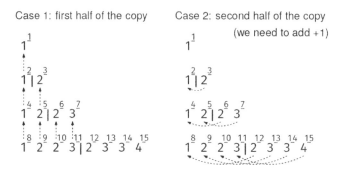

Figure 15. The index of each number in the sequence is shown on the top left of the number. For each number with index n, the arrow points to a number with a smaller index (m) such that we can compute S(n) from S(m).

Instead of giving a formula for S(n), we'll give a formula for S(k, i), where k is the copy of n, and i is the position of n within the copy, starting from 1 ($1 \leq i \leq 2^{k-1}$). *REFRAMING THE PROBLEM* this way does not change it—they are equivalent formulations—but it is a better fit for our *CASE ANALYSIS*.

Case 1:   If i is in the first half of the copy ($i \leq 2^{k-1}/2$): S(k, i) = S(k-1, i)

Case 2:   If i is in the second half of the copy: S(k, i) = S(k, i - $2^{k-1}/2$) + 1

Before implementing anything, we should analyze the number of steps of this recursive formula (i.e., the number of arrows we need to follow in Figure 15). In particular, is this sublinear? The analysis combines two properties:

Property 1:   Each copy is twice as long as the previous one, so k (the copy of n) grows logarithmically on n.

Property 2:   We need at most 2 steps of our recursive formula to get to the previous copy.

Combining these two facts, we get that we need to do at most O(2 log n) = O(log n) steps.

We can finally write the full 'indented English' algorithm:

```
Algo: recursive formula
Time: O(log n)
Extra space: O(log n) (for the call stack)

if n is 0, return 0
use exponential search to find k, the copy of n
compute i = n - 2^(k-1) + 1, the index of n in the copy
return f(k, i)

f(k, i):
  if k == 1: return 1
  first_half = i ≤ 2^(k-1)/2
  if first_half: return f(k-1, i)
  return f(k, i - 2^(k-1)/2) + 1
```

As you can see, we use a combination of boosters to tackle hard problems. But imagine that we could not figure it out, and decided to *ARTICULATE OUR BLOCKER*. After showing our work, the interviewer throws a question back at us: "How is S(n) related to the binary representation of n?" Can you figure out the property they are hinting at?

It turns out that there is a different approach to this problem. $S(n)$ is simply the number of 1's in the binary representation of n. For instance, $S(5) = 2$ because 5 in binary is 101, which has 2 1's. We prefer our recursive formula approach because it is more intuitive, but it shows that hard problems often become easy if you can find the right property. This property was probably in your blind spot because the problem does not have any triggers for 'bit manipulation'. Only a skilled problem solver who **CYCLED THROUGH THE CATALOG** and asked themselves "Is there any way bit manipulation may be useful here?" may have arrived at this property on their own.

> We realize this chapter is a lot to take in, and may require multiple passes. The topic of problem-solving strategies has essentially unlimited depth, and, even though we tried to narrow it down to the most effective strategies for interviews, each of those can still be used in many ways. Our advice is to keep the overall framework in mind (perhaps by adding Figure 1 (pg 249) to your *cheat sheet*), and revisit the techniques within it as you work through practice problems.

⬈ ONLINE RESOURCES

Online resources for this chapter include:

- A chance to try each problem in this chapter in AI Interviewer
- Full code solutions for every problem in the chapter in multiple programming languages

Try online at bctci.co/boosters.

CATALOG OF TECHNICAL TOPICS

PART VII

Watch for these speech-bubble icons, which mean there is online content.

✦ **AI Interviewer:** Each problem can be tried online with the AI Interviewer.

▶ **Interview Replay:** Recordings of actual mock interviews.

🗋 **Snippet:** Material to copy/paste online, including email templates and code recipes.

🗗 **Resource:** Bonus chapters, worksheets, and other material.

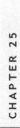

## CHAPTER 25

DYNAMIC ARRAYS

AI interviewer, replays, and more materials for this chapter at bctci.co/dynamic-arrays

▶ *Prerequisites: None*

We probably do not need to explain to you what an array is, but just so we are on the same page: an array is an ordered list of elements stored sequentially in memory, without gaps. Arrays are convenient because you can easily access any element by index in $O(1)$ time.[1] Most of the time, interview problem inputs are given as arrays (or strings, which are essentially arrays of characters).

Arrays come in two flavors: fixed-size arrays and dynamic arrays. With fixed-size arrays, we set the size upfront, and when they are full, they cannot accommodate more data. In contrast, dynamic arrays can expand or contract to accommodate a changing number of elements. High-level languages like Python and JavaScript typically come with dynamic arrays so that you do not need to worry about resizing.[2]

In this chapter, we will look at how dynamic arrays work under the hood. Understanding how the data structures you use daily work internally has multiple benefits:

- In some cases, it is directly relevant to passing the interview: you may get a *data structure design* question about providing or modifying the implementation of a well-known data structure.

- We are not just learning how to implement a particular data structure; we are learning reusable algorithmic techniques. The same ideas can be used for other problems.

- The big O analysis for the data structure operations becomes intuitive rather than something that's tedious to memorize.

DYNAMIC ARRAY IMPLEMENTATION

Let's implement a dynamic array from scratch, including the resizing logic. To make it interesting, we will phrase it as a *data structure design* question. You can attempt it online at bctci.co/implement-dynamic-array.

---

1 Since all the elements are next to each other, they have predictable memory addresses: in order to get the element at index i, we just need to know two things: the memory address of the first element and the size of each element. If the first element is stored at address A and each element takes up k bytes, then the second element is at address A+k, the third one is at address A+2k, and so on. To get the element at index i, we can go straight to memory address A + i*k. In other data structures like linked lists or binary trees it is not as straightforward to find where an element is actually placed in memory.

2 Some languages have fixed-sized arrays as a core part of the language and dynamic arrays as part of their standard library, like the ArrayList class in Java and the vector class in C++.

✦ **PROBLEM 25.1**   **IMPLEMENT DYNAMIC ARRAY**

Assume your programming language only supports fixed-size arrays. Implement a dynamic array data structure that supports the following:

```
Dynamic Array API:
    append(x):  adds element x to the end of the array.
    get(i):     returns the element at index i.
    set(i, x):  updates the preexisting element at index i to be x.
    size():     returns the number of elements in the array.
    pop_back(): removes the last element.
```

You should only declare arrays of a fixed size and not use built-in append() methods or equivalent. If you are coding in a strongly typed language, assume all elements are integers.

SOLUTION 25.1   IMPLEMENT DYNAMIC ARRAY

It's easy enough to store the elements in DynamicArray in an underlying fixed-size array. The challenging case is when this underlying fixed-size array is full. We can't grow it, so what can we do? Simple! Create a new, bigger array and copy all the elements over. We call this process *resizing*.

But how much do we grow it by? Growing it by one each time would get very expensive; every append() would take O(n) time since we'd have to copy all the elements over each time.

A better approach is to double the capacity, ending up with a half-empty fixed-size array after resizing. This hits a sweet spot where we rarely need to do expensive resizings while also not wasting too much space.

We can start with a capacity of 10 to give us some room to grow:[3]

```
1   class DynamicArray:
2     def __init__(self):
3       self.capacity = 10  # Number of slots in the underlying array.
4       self._size = 0      # Number of elements actually stored.
5       self.fixed_array = [None] * self.capacity
```

Notice how we have both a *size* and a *capacity*. Size refers to the actual number of elements, while capacity refers to the number of "slots" we have in our fixed-size array.

```
1   def get(self, i):
2     if i < 0 or i >= self._size:
3       raise IndexError('Index out of bounds')
4     return self.fixed_array[i]
5
6   def set(self, i, x):
7     if i < 0 or i >= self._size:
8       raise IndexError('Index out of bounds')
9     self.fixed_array[i] = x
10
11  def size(self):
12    return self._size
```

When checking if an index is within bounds, we compare it against the size, not the capacity. For instance, even if our capacity is 10, if we've only stored 3 elements, we don't let someone read or write index 7. Also

---

3 You can find our full DynamicArray implementation in various languages online under the solution for this problem: bctci.co/implement-dynamic-array

note that size() takes constant time (some candidates get mixed up and think you need to iterate through all the elements to find the size[4]).

The interesting stuff happens in append(). If we still have space in our fixed-size array, we put the new element in the next free slot. Otherwise, we first create a new fixed-size array with twice as much capacity and copy all existing elements into it.

```
1   def append(self, x):
2     if self._size == self.capacity:
3       self.resize(self.capacity * 2)
4     self.fixed_array[self._size] = x
5     self._size += 1
6
7   def resize(self, new_capacity):
8     new_fixed_size_arr = [None] * new_capacity
9     for i in range(self._size):
10      new_fixed_size_arr[i] = self.fixed_array[i]
11    self.fixed_array = new_fixed_size_arr
12    self.capacity = new_capacity
```

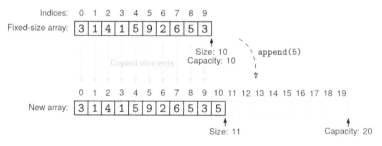

Figure 1. Appending to a dynamic array when no resize is needed.

Figure 2. Appending to a dynamic array when a resize is needed.

Finally, pop_back() removes the last element. When should we shrink the fixed-size array?

Option 1:   Never.

  • Not a good idea. This may lead to arrays that waste a lot of space.

Option 2:   Shrink if the array is <50% empty.

  » Also not a good idea. An append() which required resizing followed by a single pop_back() would trigger shrinking. We don't want to bounce between expanding and shrinking too often.

  • **Option 3:**   Shrink when the array is fairly empty, like 25% full.

---

4 This is true of some other data structures, like linked lists if you only have access to the first node, and "C-style" strings.

> » If we halve the capacity when the array is 25% full, the underlying array will be 50% full after the shrinking. This avoids excessive shrinking while not wasting too much space.[5]

```
1  def pop_back(self):
2    if self._size == 0:
3      raise IndexError('Pop from empty array')
4    self._size -= 1
5    if self._size / self.capacity < 0.25 and self.capacity > 10:
6      self.resize(self.capacity//2)
```

Conveniently, we do not need to explicitly "zero out" the popped element because, if we attempt to access its index after decreasing the size, we will get an 'Index out of bounds' error.[6]

This completes the implementation of dynamic arrays.

DYNAMIC ARRAY ANALYSIS

The get(), set(), and size() methods take constant time, as we don't do anything fancy.[7]

The worst case for append() is when we need to resize. This takes $O(n)$ time, where n is the number of elements. However, this happens very infrequently, so how do we factor this in to the big O analysis? We can say:

- Worst-case time: $O(n)$
- Amortized time: $O(1)$

What is Amortized Time?

When a program uses a data structure and performs a series of operations with it, what we care about is the worst-case runtime of the entire program, not of each individual data structure operation.

Imagine that we start with an empty DynamicArray and append elements to it until the size is some number n. Think about the resizes that happened to get to that point. Working backward from the last resize, the final resize copied at most n elements. The one before that, at most n/2. The one before that, at most n/4, and so on. Summing the number of copied elements across all resizes, we get $n + n/2 + n/4 + \ldots$ copies, all the way down to the starting capacity. As we saw on page 219, this sum is less than $2n = O(n)$.

This means that doing n consecutive appends on an empty dynamic array takes $O(n)$ time in total, so each append took—on average—$O(1)$ time. We say the **amortized runtime is $O(1)$ per operation**, where "amortized" means "average over the entire program."

Assuming that each operation takes the worst-case time is too pessimistic! Appending to dynamic arrays has poor worst-case performance but excellent amortized performance.

---

5 The choice to halve the capacity when the array is 25% full is largely arbitrary—we could have used other values like 15% or 35%. The way we set it up—doubling the capacity when it's 100% full and halving it when it is 25% full—the *utilization ratio* (size/capacity) after both growing and shrinking will be at 50%. 50% is far from both 25% and 100%, guaranteeing that another resize won't be needed again soon.

6 Historically, C compilers did not have the out-of-bounds check enabled by default, so, if you passed an index out of bounds, you could actually read or write completely unrelated variables that happened to be stored after the array in memory, leading to all kinds of unexpected behavior. Imagine a program is updating an array with random seat assignments for students and accidentally starts writing into an array containing student grades. Oops! Even worse, hackers have found ways to exploit this ability to read and write beyond arrays in what are called *buffer overflow* attacks.

7 When we say that these data structure operations take constant time, there is an implicit assumption that either (a) the elements in the data structure take constant space, like numbers or strings of constant length, or (b) we are not making a copy of those elements when we assign them in set() or return them in get(). Otherwise, we need to factor in the non-constant time necessary to copy the elements. This type of caveat applies to most data structures.

The analysis of pop_back() is similar: O(n) in the worst-case, but the amortized time per operation over the course of a program is still O(1).

Space Complexity

Dynamic arrays take the most space per element when the fixed-size array is as empty as possible. With our implementation, we shrink the array when it reaches below 25% capacity, so, in the worst case, we hold four times more space than we actually need. In other words, an array with n elements takes O(4n) = O(n) space.

> **PROBLEM 25.2**   **EXTRA DYNAMIC ARRAY OPERATIONS**

Add the following methods to the dynamic array data structure we implemented in Problem 1. For each method, provide the time analysis.

1. **Pop:** Add a pop(i) method, which removes the element at a specific index. Every element after that index should be *shifted left* by one index so that there are no gaps remaining in the fixed-size array. Return the element removed.

2. **Contains:** Implement a contains(x) method, which takes an element and returns whether the element appears in the array.

3. **Insert:** Implement an insert(i, x) method, which takes an index and an element and adds the element at that index, *shifting right* any preexisting elements at index i or greater.

4. **Remove:** Implement a remove(x) method, which takes in an element and removes the first instance of that element in the array. Return the index that the element was at or -1 if the element was not found.

SOLUTION 25.2   EXTRA DYNAMIC ARRAY OPERATIONS

1. Pop: There are two cases: if the index i is size - 1, we pop the *last* element of the array, so we are in the same scenario as in pop_back(). If we pop an element other than the last, we first need to shift all the elements after it one slot to the left to keep all the remaining elements contiguous. Then, we can call pop_back() to reduce the size and handle resizing if necessary.

```python
def pop(self, i):
    if i < 0 or i >= self._size:
        raise IndexError('Index out of bounds')
    saved_element = self.fixed_array[i]
    # Starting at index i, replace elements with their element to the right.
    for index in range(i, self._size - 1):
        self.fixed_array[index] = self.fixed_array[index + 1]
    self.pop_back()
    return saved_element
```

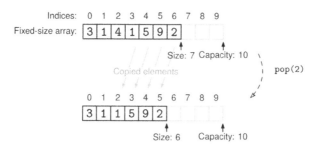

Figure 3. Shifting elements to the left during a pop() operation.

The worst case for pop() is when we pop from the front of the array, in which case we need to shift n-1 elements. Thus, pop() takes linear time in the worst case. Interviewees commonly believe that pop() is as fast as pop_back(), but that is **incorrect**. Unlike pop_back(), the amortized runtime of pop() is still $O(n)$: popping from the front n times in a row takes $O(n^2)$ total time.

\# If you find yourself needing to pop from *both* ends of an array, consider using a double-ended queue (pg 384), also called a deque, which supports both these operations in constant time.

2. Contains: Checking if a data structure contains an element is often useful. With an unordered array, the only way to do it is by looking at every index, which takes $O(n)$ time. If you need contains() to be fast, an unordered array is probably a bad idea. We'll see algorithms and data structures that make this operation faster.

3. Insert: This is the opposite of pop(): we need to shift elements past the insertion point to the right. In the worst case, if we insert at the beginning, we need to shift all the elements to the right, taking $O(n)$ time. Again, if you want to insert elements from both ends, a double-ended queue may be the right choice.

4. Remove: the difference between pop() and remove() is that one removes based on an index and the other based on a value. We can use the contains() method to find the index of the element, and then, if we find it, we can call pop() on its index. The worst case is $O(n)$.

KEY TAKEAWAYS

The following table shows the big-O analysis of dynamic arrays as we implemented them:

append(x)	O(1) (amortized)
get(i)	O(1)
set(i, x)	O(1)
size()	O(1)
pop_back()	O(1) (amortized)

Dynamic arrays are a building block for other data structures like stacks, heaps, and hash sets and maps (bctci.co/set-and-map-implementations). The key technique that we learned is **dynamic resizing** and how to analyze data structures with **amortized analysis**.

Covering the applications of dynamic arrays in a single chapter would be impossible. Instead, we'll use them throughout the rest of the book.

ONLINE RESOURCES

Online resources for this chapter include:

- A chance to try each problem in this chapter in AI Interviewer
- Full code solutions for every problem in this chapter in multiple programming languages

Try online at bctci.co/dynamic-arrays.

## CHAPTER 26

STRING MANIPULATION

AI interviewer, replays, and more materials for this chapter at bctci.co/string-manipulation

▶ *Prerequisites: None*

Strings come up so often in interviews that it is worth knowing how to work with them well. This chapter focuses on basic string manipulations that are sometimes needed as part of other algorithms.

But first, a bit of background. How do computers represent text?

ASCII AND UNICODE

Internally, characters are just short numeric codes. The character represented by each code is specified by a particular *encoding*, such as ASCII (American Standard Code for Information Interchange). In ASCII, each character—whether it is 'a', 'A', '2', or '?'—is represented by a unique 7-bit number.[1]

In a computer, a string like "Hello" encoded in ASCII is just an array of small numbers, [72, 101, 108, 108, 111], and thus has all the properties of arrays.

The main character encoding in use today is Unicode. ASCII was historically used due to its compactness, but with 7 bits, it can only represent 128 characters. Now that space is no longer the main concern, Unicode has emerged as an alternative with a broader range that is more suitable for handling characters from different languages and even emojis.

When you declare a string variable in a program, the encoding used could vary depending on the language, but you usually do not need to worry about it for coding interviews. Conveniently, Unicode is backward compatible with ASCII, which means that characters represented by ASCII, like letters and numbers, retain the same code in Unicode. For instance, 'a' is 97 in both ASCII and Unicode.

For coding interviews, we may need to transform a character to its number representation and backward. The syntax to do this varies from language to language. For instance, in Python, ord(c) returns the numerical code of character c, and chr(i) does the opposite: it returns the character that the numerical code i represents.

We can use these functions to manipulate characters as if they were numbers. For instance, imagine we want to implement a function, is_lowercase(c), that returns whether a character c is a lowercase English letter.

A useful fact about ASCII codes is that all the lowercase letters appear sequentially from 'a' to 'z', so we can check if c is in that range:

---

1   You can find the full ASCII table at https://en.wikipedia.org/wiki/ASCII.

```
1   def is_lowercase(c):
2     return ord(c) >= ord('a') and ord(c) <= ord('z')
```

We could have said 97 and 122 instead of ord('a') and ord('z'), but we do *not* need to memorize the ASCII code for 'a' and 'z'!

- In ASCII, lowercase letters appear sequentially (97–122), and so do uppercase letters (65–90) and digits (48–57). We can use this fact to check if a character falls into one of these categories. Just don't memorize any codes.
- Learn how to convert characters to their numeric representation and backward in your language of choice.

CHARACTER MANIPULATION PROBLEM SET

The following problems cover some common character manipulation operations.[2] For Python, try to solve them using only ord() and chr().

QUESTION 1

Implement a function is_alphanumeric(c) that returns whether a character c is a lowercase or uppercase English letter or a digit between '0' and '9'.

QUESTION 2

Implement a function to_uppercase(c) that converts a lowercase character c to uppercase. If c is not a lowercase character, the function does nothing.

PROBLEM SET SOLUTIONS

ANSWER 1

Just like lowercase English letters are contiguous in the ASCII table, so are uppercase letters and digits. Thus, we can check whether c is in any of these three ranges.

```
1   def is_uppercase(c):
2     return ord(c) >= ord('A') and ord(c) <= ord('Z')
3
4   def is_digit(c):
5     return ord(c) >= ord('0') and ord(c) <= ord('9')
6
7   def is_alphanumeric(c):
8     return is_lowercase(c) or is_uppercase(c) or is_digit(c)
```

ANSWER 2

If c is a lowercase letter, we can subtract the ASCII code of 'a' from the ASCII code of c to get a number between 0 and 25 representing the index of c in the alphabet. Then, if we add the ASCII code of 'A', we will get the code of the corresponding uppercase letter. Finally, we need to convert the code back to a string format with chr().

```
1   def to_uppercase(c):
```

---

2 These are excellent to practice, but aren't really **interview questions**. This problem set—along with a small handful of others in this book—do not have corresponding AI interviewer links, because they don't make sense to practice in an interview context. When no link exists, we suggest just trying the exercise in your favorite editor.

```
2    if not is_lowercase(c):
3      return c
4    return chr(ord(c) - ord('a') + ord('A'))
```

STRING MUTABILITY

A string is essentially an array of characters, but in some languages like Python, JavaScript, and Java (not C++), they are *immutable*. This means they don't allow any kind of modifications, like appending characters. For instance, if s is a Python string, s += 'a' actually creates a new string, which takes O(len(s)) time to copy all the characters. We generally want to avoid overusing the += syntax for Python strings, as it could become the runtime bottleneck.

The workaround for constructing strings character by character depends on the language. Some languages, like Java, offer a StringBuilder library.

In Python and JavaScript, the workaround is to add the characters one by one to a *dynamic array*, which supports O(1) amortized appends. When we are done, we can convert the array to a string with the built-in join method. The syntax is ''.join(my_array) in Python and my_array.join("") in JavaScript.

 REUSABLE IDEA: BUILDING STRINGS WITH DYNAMIC ARRAYS

> Check if strings are mutable in your language of choice.
>
> If you need to build a string character by character, and the strings in your language are immutable, put the characters in a dynamic array instead. When you are done, convert the array to a string with the built-in join method.

▶	**STRING MUTABILITY IS LANGUAGE-SPECIFIC. KNOW YOUR LANGUAGE**	INTERVIEW REPLAY

View Online:	bctci.co/string-replay-1 @ 34:30 - 36:00	
The Question:	Generate all valid strings up to a given length with a set of `allowed` characters.	
What You'll See:	The candidate wasn't familiar with string immutability, or that string concatenation takes linear time and space—they thought it was constant time.	
Who:	*Interviewer*: Senior Software Engineer at Google	
	Candidate: College student	

STRING MANIPULATION PROBLEM SET

✦ *Try these problems with AI Interviewer: bctci.co/string-problem-set-1*

Since strings usually represent text, we often need to perform special text-based manipulations, such as splitting a string into words. This type of basic string manipulation is sometimes needed as part of other problems.

\# Most languages provide character and string manipulation methods by default, so you may not need to implement them yourself if the interviewer allows you to use these built-in methods. Familiarize yourself with the built-in string methods in your language to save time in interviews.

Try to implement the following common string manipulation by hand, even if your language has a function to do it.

PROBLEM 26.1   **STRING SPLIT**

Without using a built-in string split method, implement a `split(s, c)` method, which receives a string s and a character c and splits s at each occurrence of c, returning a list of strings.

► **Example:** s = "split by space", c = ' '
  Output: ["split", "by", "space"]
► **Example:** s = "beekeeper needed", c = 'e'
  Output: ["b", "", "k", "", "p", "r n", "", "d", "d"]
► **Example:** s = "/home/./..//Documents/", c = '/'
  Output: ["", "home", ".", "..", "", "Documents", ""]
► **Example:** s = "", c = '?'
  Output: []

PROBLEM 26.2   **STRING JOIN**

Without using a built-in string join method, implement a `join(arr, s)` method, which receives an array of strings, arr, and a string, s, and returns a single string consisting of the strings in arr with s in between them.

► **Example:** arr = ["join", "by", "space"], s = " "
  Output: "join by space"
► **Example:** arr = ["b", "", "k", "", "p", "r n", "", "d", "d!!"], s = "ee"
  Output: "beeeekeeeepeer neeeedeed!!"

If strings in your language are immutable, assume that you have access to a function `array_to_string(arr)`, which takes an array of **individual** characters and returns a string with those characters in `O(len(arr))` time.

PROBLEM 26.3   **STRING MATCHING**

Implement an `index_of(s, t)` method, which returns the first index where string t appears in string s, or -1 if s does not contain t.

Assume that s has at most 10^5 characters and t has at most 100 characters.

✦ PROBLEM SET SOLUTIONS

SOLUTION 26.1   STRING SPLIT

We can figure out all the edge cases from the examples:

1. If s is empty, we should return an empty list.
2. If s starts with c, we should return an empty string at the beginning of the list.
3. If s ends with c, we should return an empty string at the end of the list.

We can process each character in s in order. We add them to a 'current word' array until we find c. Then, we add the current word to the result and start a new word.

```
1   def split(s, c):
2     if not s:
3       return []
4     res = []
5     current = []
6     for char in s:
7       if char == c:
```

```
 8      res.append(''.join(current))
 9      current = []
10    else:
11      current.append(char)
12    res.append(''.join(current))
13    return res
```

As mentioned, Python strings are immutable, so we want to avoid using the += operator. Instead, we build the current word as an array and then turn it into a string with ''.join(current).

With a dynamic array, we take O(1) amortized time per character, so split() takes O(len(s)) time in total.

SOLUTION 26.2   STRING JOIN

If n is the length of arr and k is the sum of the lengths of all the strings in arr, the length of the output is k + (n-1)*len(s). Thus, the **output-size** lower bound is O(k+n*len(s)). To achieve this lower bound, we should spend O(1) time per output character.

Since Python strings are immutable, we add the characters one by one to a dynamic array. The main loop alternates between appending a string in arr and s. At the end, we use the array_to_string() function provided in the statement.

```
1    def join(arr, s):
2      res = []
3      for i in range(len(arr)):
4        if i != 0:
5          for c in s:
6            res.append(c)
7        for c in arr[i]:
8          res.append(c)
9      return array_to_string(res)
```

SOLUTION 26.3   STRING MATCHING

This is a classic problem also known as "string searching." A naive approach checks for t at each index of s. This takes O(sn * tn) time, where sn is the size of s and tn is the size of t, which is good enough given the input size constraints.

There are at least two advanced algorithms to do it more efficiently: the KMP algorithm and the rolling hash algorithm. Both take O(sn) time, which is optimal. Of the two, we find the rolling hash one easier to learn, so we will show it when we talk about hashing (bctci.co/set-and-map-implementations).

▶ **EVEN "SIMPLE" STRING PROBLEMS CAN BE TOUGH IN A GOOGLE INTERVIEW**   INTERVIEW REPLAY

View Online:	bctci.co/string-replay-2 @ 4:15 - 42:17
The Question:	Generate a password of a given length.
What You'll See:	This Google-style problem is quirky. Even though it sounds like a standard data structures and algorithms problem, it isn't just about generating strings. You also have to consider what makes passwords good. You'll see the candidate struggle with this task.
Who:	*Interviewer*: Senior Software Engineer at FAANG+ *Candidate*: 4 years exp.
Real-life Outcome:	The candidate got the job at Google!

KEY TAKEAWAYS

We'll see *a lot* of strings in the rest of the book, so the goal of this chapter is to become comfortable with them. We won't have to implement operations like 'split' and 'join' by hand most of the time (we should default to using the built-in methods to save time instead), but it's good to have a general sense of how they work and their big O analysis.

Similarly, we won't be manipulating ASCII codes in most problems, but it can be useful when we need to treat characters as numbers (e.g., to use them as array indices, as in the reusable idea: length-26 array (pg 273).

One reusable idea that we'll often return to is how to build strings incrementally in languages with immutable strings. The workaround is to use a dynamic array (pg 290).

☑ ONLINE RESOURCES

Online resources for this chapter include:

- A chance to try each problem in this chapter in AI Interviewer
- Interview replays that show specific mistakes people make with string manipulation problems
- Full code solutions for every problem in the chapter in multiple programming languages

Try online at bctci.co/string-manipulation.

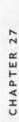
TWO POINTERS

AI interviewer, replays, and more materials for this chapter at bctci.co/two-pointers

▶ *Prerequisites: None*

The term 'pointer' in the two-pointers technique refers to a variable used as an array index, like i in arr[i]. That is, pointers 'point to' array elements.[1] A two-pointer algorithm is one that uses two such pointers, often dancing around each other in a carefully arranged choreography to achieve some goal.

Although many algorithms require two (or more) array indices, the term 'two pointers' is typically reserved for the types of movement patterns in the next section.[2] In the Linked Lists chapter, we'll see these types of movement patterns again, but there the pointers will be actual node address pointers/references rather than array indices.

MOVEMENT PATTERNS

The first decision when using the two-pointer technique is the direction of our pointers. There are three common movement patterns:

- **Inward pointers:** two pointers moving inward from both ends of an array until they meet at some point in between.[3]
- **Slow and fast pointers:** two pointers moving through an array from left to right, but one usually stays ahead of the other.
- **Parallel pointers:** two pointers moving through two different arrays.

We'll illustrate a simple case of each.

✦ **PROBLEM 27.1**   **PALINDROME CHECK**

Given a string s, return whether s is a *palindrome*. A palindrome is a string that reads the same forward and backward, like "level" or "naan."

SOLUTION 27.1   PALINDROME CHECK

This is a classic example of two inward pointers, which we call 1 (left) and r (right):

---

1 Depending on the context, 'pointer' is used differently than here. In languages like C and C++, 'pointer' is formally defined as a "memory address" data type.

2 Some techniques like binary search and sliding windows are also sometimes called 'two-pointers' techniques. There's no strict categorization.

3 Binary search is a special case of inward pointers, but 'two pointers' is more commonly associated with algorithms where the pointers move one position at a time.

```
1  def palindrome(s):
2    l, r = 0, len(s)-1
3    while l < r:
4      if s[l] != s[r]:
5        return False
6      l += 1
7      r -= 1
8    return True
```

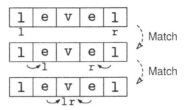

Figure 1.

✦ **PROBLEM 27.2** **SMALLER PREFIXES**

Given an array of integers, arr, where the length, n, is even, return whether the following condition holds for every k in the range $1 \leq k \leq n/2$: "the sum of the first k elements is smaller than the sum of the first 2k elements." If this condition is false for any k in the range, return false.

▶ **Example:** arr = [1, 2, 2, -1]
   Output: True. The prefix [1] has a smaller sum than the prefix [1, 2], and the prefix [1, 2] has a smaller sum than the prefix [1, 2, 2, -1]. The other prefixes have length > n/2.

▶ **Example:** arr = [1, 2, -2, 1, 3, 5]
   Output: False. The prefix [1, 2] has a larger sum than the prefix [1, 2, -2, 1].

SOLUTION 27.2   SMALLER PREFIXES

The naive solution would be to iterate over all values of k from 1 to n/2, and for each value, compute and compare the sums of the two prefixes. This would take $O(n^2)$ time. Instead, we can use a slow pointer, sp, and a fast pointer, fp, where fp moves twice as fast as sp.[4]

```
1  def smaller_prefixes(arr):
2    sp, fp = 0, 0
3    slow_sum, fast_sum = 0, 0
4    while fp < len(arr):
5      slow_sum += arr[sp]
6      fast_sum += arr[fp] + arr[fp+1]
7      if slow_sum >= fast_sum:
8        return False
9      sp += 1
10     fp += 2
11   return True
```

Figure 2.

\# Two pointers moving at different speeds through a data structure can accomplish many things in problems with arrays and strings but also appear in linked lists to detect cycles (Chapter 34: Linked-List Cycle Detection, pg 423)!

✦ **PROBLEM 27.3** **ARRAY INTERSECTION**

Given two sorted arrays of integers, arr1 and arr2, return a new array with the elements that appear in both arrays, in sorted order, *including duplicates* present in both arrays.

---

4 We could also call them fast and slow. While naming is subjective, we particularly dislike i and j as pointer names because they are easier to mix up than variables with purposeful names.

▶ **Example:** `arr1 = [1, 2, 3]`, `arr2 = [1, 3, 5]`
  Output: `[1, 3]`.

▶ **Example:** `arr1 = [1, 1, 1]`, `arr2 = [1, 1]`
  Output: `[1, 1]`.

SOLUTION 27.3   ARRAY INTERSECTION

We can use a pointer for each input array. If both point to the same value, we can add it to the output. The key detail to make sure we don't miss any element is that both arrays are sorted, so elements to the right of the pointers will be the same or larger. This means we can skip over the smallest element among the two pointers, as that element won't appear again in the other array.

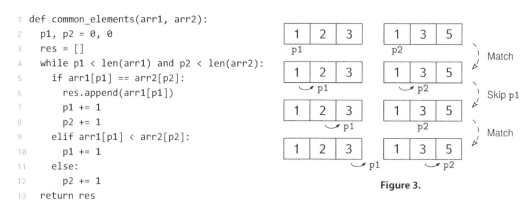

```
1  def common_elements(arr1, arr2):
2    p1, p2 = 0, 0
3    res = []
4    while p1 < len(arr1) and p2 < len(arr2):
5      if arr1[p1] == arr2[p2]:
6        res.append(arr1[p1])
7        p1 += 1
8        p2 += 1
9      elif arr1[p1] < arr2[p2]:
10        p1 += 1
11      else:
12        p2 += 1
13    return res
```

Figure 3.

We'll work with these basic movement patterns for the rest of the chapter.

INDEX MANIPULATION ADVICE

The biggest challenge with the two-pointer technique is that the implementation often requires *careful index manipulation*. For instance, off-by-one and out-of-bounds errors commonly get the best of candidates.[5] In this section, we'll focus on simplifying the mechanics of moving pointers.

We'll use this variant of the 'Palindrome Check' problem to illustrate our advice:

✦ **PROBLEM 27.4**   **PALINDROMIC SENTENCE**

Given a string s, return whether its letters form a palindrome ignoring punctuation, spaces, and casing.[6]

▶ **Example:** `s = "Bob wondered, 'Now, Bob?'"`
  Output: `true`

SOLUTION 27.4   PALINDROMIC SENTENCE

We use the 'inward pointers' movement pattern, as usual for palindrome problems. Here are two ways we could have coded the solution:

---

5 In many interviews, if your solution has minor bugs but is mostly correct, you can still pass. However, interviewers asking two-pointer questions are generally less forgiving of off-by-one errors, because instead of testing your DS&A knowledge, these questions test your attention to detail. So, take your time to try to avoid these mistakes.

6 As a general rule, for string inputs, it's always a good idea to ask a clarifying question about which characters are allowed. It is usually **not safe** to assume that the input will only contain lowercase letters.

Solution following our guidelines.

```
1  def palindromic_sentence(s):
2    l, r = 0, len(s)-1
3    while l < r:
4      if not s[l].isalpha():
5        l += 1
6      elif not s[r].isalpha():
7        r -= 1
8      else:
9        if s[l].lower() != s[r].
           lower():
10         return False
11       l += 1
12       r -= 1
13   return True
```

Solution with nested loops.

```
1  def palindromic_sentence(s):
2    l, r = 0, len(s)-1
3    while l < r:
4      while l < len(s) and not s[l].isalpha():
5        l += 1
6      while r >= 0 and not s[r].isalpha():
7        r -= 1
8      if l < r and s[l].lower() != s[r].lower():
9        return False
10     l += 1
11     r -= 1
12   return True
```

Here are the general guidelines to keep index manipulation simple we used in Solution 34.4 (they are for any two-pointer solution, not just for inward pointers). As usual, coding guidelines are not universal—it is fine to deviate from them on a case-by-case basis.

1. Avoid nested loops.

Have a single loop with a condition that ensures the pointers are in bounds. For instance, with inward pointers, if l and r are initialized to 0 and len(arr)-1 and the loop condition is l < r, both l and r are guaranteed to be within bounds at the beginning of each iteration.

The solution with nested loops for the 'Palindromic Sentence' problem introduces more chances for pointers to end up out of bounds.

2. Don't try to do multiple things in the same iteration.

We don't need to move both pointers at every iteration; it suffices to make a single step toward exiting the loop. The more things we change within one iteration, the easier it is to mess up.

3. Break down each iteration into a case analysis.[7]

List all the cases that you could find yourself on, depending on the values pointed at by the pointers.

For instance, in the 'Palindromic Sentence' problem, we can list three cases:

1. arr[l] is not a letter,
2. arr[r] is not a letter,
3. arr[l] and arr[r] are both letters.

It is often easier to reason about your code without shared code between the cases. In Solution 34.4, r -= 1 could be factored out of cases (2) and (3) to save one line, but it's easier to think about the cases independently (if you want, you can always factor out shared code once you are certain of the correctness of your solution).

4. Take a simple action for each case.

For each case, we just need to take a tiny step toward the solution. Here are common actions:

  a. **Skip** over an irrelevant element.

---

7 There is a parallel with the '***CASE ANALYSIS***' booster (pg 256): in the same way as breaking down a problem into cases helps with problem-solving, it's easier to get the index manipulation right in each two-pointer iteration by tackling one case at a time.

b. **Compare** the values pointed at by the two pointers and do something based on the result.

c. **Swap** the elements pointed at by the pointers.

d. **Write** the value at one pointer at the location of the other.

Make sure that **every action makes progress towards your termination condition** to avoid getting 'stuck' in an infinite loop. Usually, each case should move at least one pointer.

For instance, in the 'Palindromic Sentence' problem, if we are in cases (1) or (2), we can **skip** over the non-letter character. If we are in case (3), we must **compare** the letters and then move past them. In Solution 34.4, we avoid doing multiple things in the same iteration, like trying to skip over both s[1] and s[r]. We could, but it is simpler if we don't. We always advance at least one pointer, so the runtime is linear regardless.

▸ **TWO-POINTER PALINDROME QUESTION**   INTERVIEW REPLAY

View Online:	bctci.co/two-pointers-replay-1 @ 4:28-26:28
The Question:	Return true if the given string s is a palindrome; otherwise, return false.
What You'll See:	The candidate used an optimal two-pointer approach to solve the classic "validate a palindrome" question, with a robust set of test cases.
Who:	*Interviewer*: Staff Software Engineer at Meta *Candidate*: 3 years exp.

LOOP INVARIANTS

The key problem-solving question when using the two-pointer technique is:

▸ How do I know which cases to include in the case analysis and what operation to perform in each case?

Think about the following problem:

✦ **PROBLEM 27.5   REVERSE CASE MATCH**

Given a string, s, where half of the letters are lowercase and half uppercase, return whether the word formed by the lowercase letters is the same as the reverse of the word formed by the uppercase letters. (Assume that the length, n, is always even.)

▸ **Example:** s = "haDrRAHd"
  Output: true. Both spell 'hard'.
▸ **Example:** s = "harHrARDd"
  Output: false. The uppercase letters in reverse spell 'drah'.

SOLUTION 27.5   REVERSE CASE MATCH

We need to read two words, a left-to-right one and a right-to-left one, so we can use inward pointers.

Next, we need to figure out the **case analysis** and the actions to take in each case. Some people find it helpful to state a *loop invariant* upfront and use it to guide a clean implementation.[8] A loop invariant is a property that is true at the beginning of each iteration. For this problem, we can state this invariant:

▸ Lowercase letters to the left of 1 and uppercase letters to the right of r have already been matched to each other.

The invariant should be true at the beginning, so we can initialize 1 to 0 and r to len(s)-1. Each iteration needs to:

---

8 Thinking in terms of 'loop invariants' is not mandatory—some people find them more confusing than helpful, so feel free to ignore this advice if it doesn't help you.

1. maintain the loop invariant, and

2. progress toward the end of the loop.

This helps us think about how to design the case analysis and the actions to take:

- If l points to an uppercase letter, we can skip it.
- If r points to a lowercase letter, we can skip it.
- If l points to a lowercase letter and r to an uppercase letter, we see if they match.

Imagine we update our pointers in a way that maintains the invariant throughout every iteration, and eventually, we get to a point where either l or r finishes traversing the array. According to the invariant, we'll be in one of the following situations, depending on which variable reached the end:

- If l is at len(s): *All lowercase letters have already been matched.*
- If r is at -1: *All uppercase letters have already been matched.*

Since the statement guarantees there is the same number of uppercase and lowercase letters, we are done!

```
1  def reverse_case_match(s):
2      l, r = 0, len(s) - 1
3      while l < len(s) and r >= 0:
4          if not s[l].islower():
5              l += 1
6          elif not s[r].isupper():
7              r -= 1
8          else:
9              if s[l] != s[r].lower():
10                 return False
11             l += 1
12             r -= 1
13     return True
```

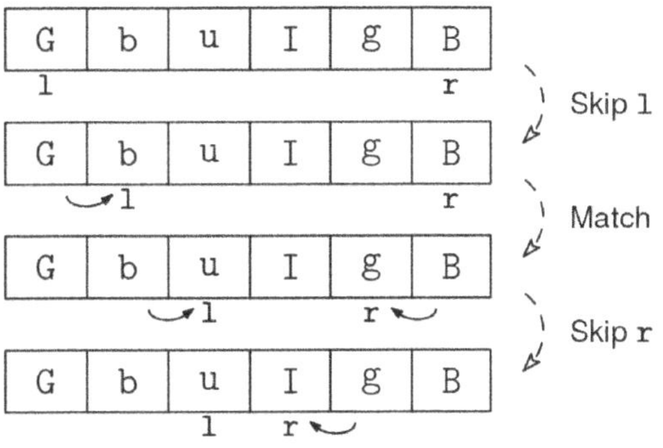

Figure 4.

An edge case that is easy to miss for this problem is that r can reach the beginning before l reaches the end, like for "BbbB". So, l < len(s) alone wouldn't be a valid 'while' condition.

> The point of invariants is that instead of asking, "How should I code this loop to solve the problem?" we narrow the scope down to, "How should I code one iteration to maintain the invariant (while making progress)?" The latter is much more tractable, so thinking in terms of invariants can make our lives easier.

VALIDATION & DRAWING ADVICE

After you finish typing a two-pointer algorithm, it is crucial to *validate* any edge cases related to index manipulation.

Being able to verify edge cases matters for every problem (it is part of the verification rubric, pg 184), but it may be weighted more heavily in two-pointer problems because they emphasize careful coding more than problem-solving.

Besides validating that our code works for the typical edge cases, like an empty array/string or an array/string with length 1, we recommend validating our solution by visualizing the pointer motion through a few small inputs.

It helps to actually move them around in your shared editor:

- Draw each pointer on a separate line. This way, you can conveniently move each pointer independently by adding or removing spaces from the beginning of the line.
- Use single-letter names for the variables.
- To avoid wasting time, do not bother with commas, brackets, or quotes.

Instead of		Try
`['h', 'i', ',', ' ', 'm', 'o', 'm', '!']`		`hi, mom!`
`^` `^`		`l`
`left` `right`		`r`

So, which inputs should you visualize? We recommend:

1. A short input (or set of inputs) that exercises every case in our case analysis.
2. A short input for each possible way to exit the loop.

In addition, pay close attention to what happens when you exit the loop. Is there any 'wrap-up work' we still need to do?

- When a pointer reaches the end, what happens with the other one?
- For two inward pointers, what happens when they meet?

For instance, in the 'Palindrome Check' problem, we recommend visualizing your pointers' motion with an odd length input (where the pointers meet in the middle) and an even length input (where the pointers cross over), ensuring that the code works for both.

Think about the following classic problem:[9]

✦ **PROBLEM 27.6**   **MERGE TWO SORTED ARRAYS**

Given two sorted arrays of integers, `arr1` and `arr2`, return a new array that contains all the elements in `arr1` and `arr2` in sorted order, including duplicates.

▶ **Example:** `arr1 = [1, 3, 4, 5]`, `arr2 = [2, 4, 4]`
  Output: `[1, 2, 3, 4, 4, 4, 5]`.
▶ **Example:** `arr1 = [-1]`, `arr2 = []`
  Output: `[-1]`

SOLUTION 27.6   MERGE TWO SORTED ARRAYS

This problem requires parallel pointers and can be approached similarly to Problem 27.3: Array Intersection (pg 295). However, unlike in Array Intersection, when a pointer reaches the end, we are *not* done. We still need to continue with the other pointer until the end of its array. Some candidates forget about this wrap-up work.

```
1   def merge(arr1, arr2):
2     p1, p2 = 0, 0
3     res = []
4     while p1 < len(arr1) and p2 < len(arr2):
5       if arr1[p1] < arr2[p2]:
6         res.append(arr1[p1])
7         p1 += 1
8       else:
9         res.append(arr2[p2])
10        p2 += 1
```

---

9 This two-pointer algorithm is part of the well known merge sort algorithm.

```
11      while p1 < len(arr1):
12        res.append(arr1[p1])
13        p1 += 1
14      while p2 < len(arr2):
15        res.append(arr2[p2])
16        p2 += 1
17      return res
```

MOVEMENT PATTERNS PROBLEM SET

✦ *Try these problems with AI Interviewer: bctci.co/two-pointers-problem-set-1*

PROBLEM 27.7 2-SUM

Given a sorted array of integers, return whether there are two *distinct* indices, i and j, such arr[i] + arr[j] = 0. Do not use more than O(1) extra space.[10]

▸ **Example:** arr = [-5, -2, -1, 1, 1, 10]
  Output: true. -1 + 1 = 0
▸ **Example:** arr = [-3, 0, 0, 1, 2]
  Output: true. 0 + 0 = 0
▸ **Example:** arr = [-5, -3, -1, 0, 2, 4, 6]
  Output: false

PROBLEM 27.8 3-WAY MERGE WITHOUT DUPLICATES

Given three sorted arrays, arr1, arr2, and arr3, return a new array with the elements of all three arrays, in sorted order, *without duplicates*.[11]

▸ **Example:** arr1 = [2, 3, 3, 4, 5, 7], arr2 = [3, 3, 9], arr3 = [3, 3, 9]
  Output: [2, 3, 4, 5, 7, 9]

PROBLEM 27.9 SORT VALLEY-SHAPED ARRAY

A *valley-shaped* array is an array of integers such that:

1. it can be split into a non-empty prefix and a non-empty suffix,
2. the prefix is sorted in decreasing order (duplicates allowed), and
3. the suffix is sorted in increasing order (duplicates allowed).

Given a valley-shaped array, arr, return a new array with the elements sorted.

▸ **Example:** arr = [8, 4, 2, 6]
  Output: [2, 4, 6, 8]
▸ **Example:** arr = [1, 2]
  Output: [1, 2]. The array is already sorted (the prefix is just [1]).
▸ **Example:** arr = [2, 2, 1, 1]
  Output: [1, 1, 2, 2]

---

10 The constraint of using O(1) extra space means we cannot use a hash-set-based solution. "O(1) extra space" is a common trigger for two pointers. Sorted arrays are mainly a trigger for binary search, but they can also be a trigger for inward pointers.

11 Despite the name, the 'two-pointer technique' sometimes involves more than two pointers. Two is just the most common case.

PROBLEM 27.10   **MISSING NUMBERS IN RANGE**

Given a sorted array of integers, arr, and two values indicating a range, [low, high], with low ≤ high, return a new array with all the numbers in the range that do not appear in arr.

▶ **Example:** arr = [6, 9, 12, 15, 18], low = 9, high = 13
   Output: [10, 11, 13]
▶ **Example:** arr = [], low = 9, high = 9
   Output: [9]
▶ **Example:** arr = [6, 7, 8, 9], low = 7, high = 8
   Output: []

PROBLEM 27.11   **INTERVAL INTERSECTION**

In this problem, we represent an *interval* as an array with two integers, [start, end], where start ≤ end. Both endpoints are considered part of the interval, which may consist of a singular point if start = end.

You are given two arrays of intervals, arr1 and arr2. For each array, the intervals are non-overlapping and sorted from left to right. Return a similarly non-overlapping, sorted array of intervals representing the *intersection* of the intervals in arr1 and arr2. An interval shouldn't start at the same value where another interval ends.

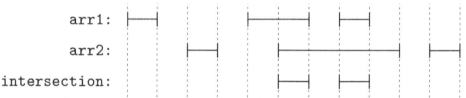

Figure 5. Example 1 for Problem 27.11: Interval Intersection (pg 302).

▶ **Example:** arr1 = [[0, 1], [4, 6], [7, 8]], arr2 = [[2, 3], [5, 9], [10, 11]]
   Output: [[5, 6], [7, 8]]
▶ **Example:** arr1 = [[2, 4], [5, 8]], arr2 = [[3, 3], [4, 7]]
   Output: [[3, 3], [4, 4], [5, 7]]. The array [[3, 3], [4, 4], [5, 6], [6, 7]]
            would not be correct because [5, 6] and [6, 7] can be combined.

✦ PROBLEM SET SOLUTIONS

SOLUTION 27.7   2-SUM

We need to find two numbers that are the opposite of each other, like -5 and 5. We have all the negative numbers at the beginning and all the positive numbers at the end, which suggests trying **inward pointers**. We can compare the first and the last numbers, which are the smallest (most negative) and the largest. If they add to more than 0, like if arr[l] is -5 and arr[r] is 10, the largest number (10) is too large: we will not find -10 anywhere in the array, so we can skip over 10 by decreasing r. In the opposite case, where the sum is negative, we can skip over the most negative number by increasing l.

```
1  def two_sum(arr):
2    l, r = 0, len(arr) - 1
3    while l < r:
4      if arr[l] + arr[r] > 0:
5        r -= 1
6      elif arr[l] + arr[r] < 0:
7        l += 1
8      else:
9        return True
10   return False
```

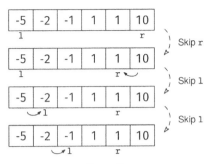

Figure 6.

♻ REUSABLE IDEA: SEARCHING WITH INWARD POINTERS

In problems where we have to find an index or pair of indices in a sorted array, we can often 'discard' the largest value based on the smallest one or vice versa. Such problems are a natural fit for inward pointers.

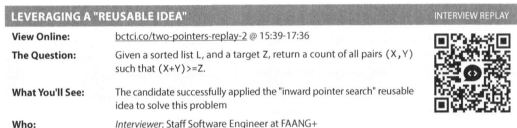

SOLUTION 27.8   3-WAY MERGE WITHOUT DUPLICATES

The strategy for this problem is similar to Problem 27.6: Merge Two Sorted Arrays (pg 300). However, it is good practice for index manipulation, as we have to manage three parallel pointers instead of two.

SOLUTION 27.9   SORT VALLEY-SHAPED ARRAY

The first obstacle in this problem is that the element that goes first in the output could be anywhere in the array. We *could* find it with binary search, but there is one key question we can ask when implementing the two-pointer technique:

▶   *"Of all the possible combinations of pointer directions, which one makes my life the easiest?"*

In this case, the largest element is the first one or the last one, so we know one of them must go at the end of the output array. This suggests that starting from the largest element and working backward is easier than trying to fill in the elements from left to right.

We can **REFRAME THE PROBLEM** as a variation of Problem 27.6: Merge Two Sorted Arrays (pg 300): each slope of the valley is one of the two "input" sorted arrays, and we can traverse them from largest to smallest element with two **inward pointers**, l and r. Our loop invariant can be:

▶   *Every number before L or after r in the input array is already in the correct place in the output array.*

If we maintain this invariant at every iteration while making progress, eventually, l and r will meet and point to the same element—the smallest one (or one of them). We add the smallest element as part of the 'wrap-up work.'

```
 1  def sort_valley_array(arr):
 2    if len(arr) == 0:
 3      return []
 4    l, r = 0, len(arr) - 1
 5    res = [0]*len(arr)
 6    i = len(arr) - 1
 7    while l < r:
 8      if arr[l] >= arr[r]:
 9        res[i] = arr[l]
10        l += 1
11        i -= 1
12      else:
13        res[i] = arr[r]
14        r -= 1
15        i -= 1
16    res[0] = arr[l]
17    return res
```

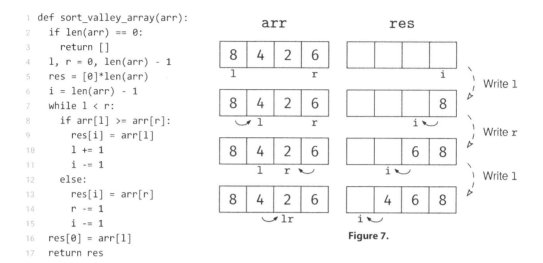

Figure 7.

SOLUTION 27.10   MISSING NUMBERS IN RANGE

We can use the *REFRAME THE PROBLEM* booster: imagine an array that goes arr2 = [low, low+1, low+2, ..., high]. Then, the problem becomes: "Given two sorted arrays, find all the elements that appear in arr2 but not arr1." This is similar to **parallel-pointer** problems we have seen before.

The key idea is that we don't need to materialize arr2. We can use a pointer that iterates over values, *not* indices, from low to high, *as if* it were traversing arr2.

SOLUTION 27.11   INTERVAL INTERSECTION

We use **parallel pointers**. We maintain the following invariant, which relates the pointers, p1 and p2, to the result array, res:

▸   *res contains the intersection of every interval in arr1 before p1 and every interval in arr2 before p2.*

At each iteration, our goal is to advance one of the pointers while preserving this invariant.

- The easy case is when arr1[p1] and arr[p2] do not overlap, as we can advance whichever pointer is earlier.
- If they overlap, we add their intersection to res and advance whichever pointer *ends* earlier.

For problems about intervals, we often need to work out the endpoint logic:

- How do we know if two intervals overlap?
- If they don't, how do we know which one is earlier?
- If they do, how do we compute the overlap?

To get these questions right, we recommend using the *CASE ANALYSIS* (pg 256) and *SKETCH A DIAGRAM* (pg 259) boosters. Code-wise, it can help to factor out some of the interval-specific logic to helper functions.

```
 1  # Assumes that int1 and int2 overlap.
 2  def intersection(int1, int2):
 3    overlap_start = max(int1[0], int2[0])
 4    overlap_end = min(int1[1], int2[1])
 5    return [overlap_start, overlap_end]
 6
 7  def interval_intersection(arr1, arr2):
 8    p1, p2 = 0, 0
 9    n1, n2 = len(arr1), len(arr2)
10    res = []
11    while p1 < n1 and p2 < n2:
12      int1, int2 = arr1[p1], arr2[p2]
13      if int1[1] < int2[0]:
14        p1 += 1
15      elif int2[1] < int1[0]:
16        p2 += 1
17      else:
18        res.append(intersection(int1, int2))
19        if int1[1] < int2[1]:
20          p1 += 1
21        else:
22          p2 += 1
23    return res
```

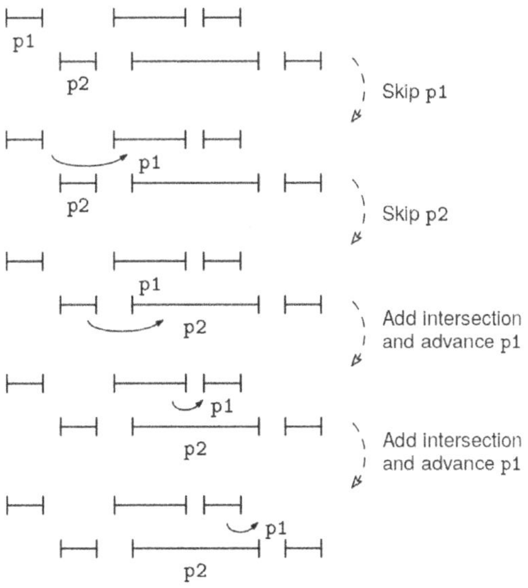

Figure 8.

IN-PLACE MODIFICATION

A recurrent theme of two-pointer problems is the need to modify the input in place[12] using only $O(1)$ extra space. Recall that extra space is space created by our function, not passed as input. In particular, the call stack counts as memory created by our function (pg 405), so we generally cannot use recursion since the call stack needs $O(\text{call depth})$ space.

Consider the classic problem of reversing an array:

✦⁑   PROBLEM 27.12   **ARRAY REVERSAL**

Reverse an array of letters, arr, in place using $O(1)$ extra space.[13]

SOLUTION 27.12   ARRAY REVERSAL

If we were reversing arr into a new array, we could use a simple backward loop. However, when doing things *in place*, we need to worry about writing over elements that we still need to move—we cannot simply write the first element to the final position because the element at the final position would get 'erased.' Instead, we can use **inward pointers** to swap the first and final elements.

---

12   For Python users: recall that Python strings are *immutable*, meaning that it is not possible to modify them in place. In Python, in-place algorithms are only possible when the input is a list. Other languages follow different rules for immutability. See 'Reusable Idea: Building Strings With Dynamic Arrays' on page 290.

13   Most programming languages provide a function that does this for you. You should default to using it *unless* the question is specifically about how to reverse a string.

```
1  def reverse(arr):
2    l, r = 0, len(arr) - 1
3    while l < r:
4      arr[l], arr[r] = arr[r], arr[l]
5      l += 1
6      r -= 1
```

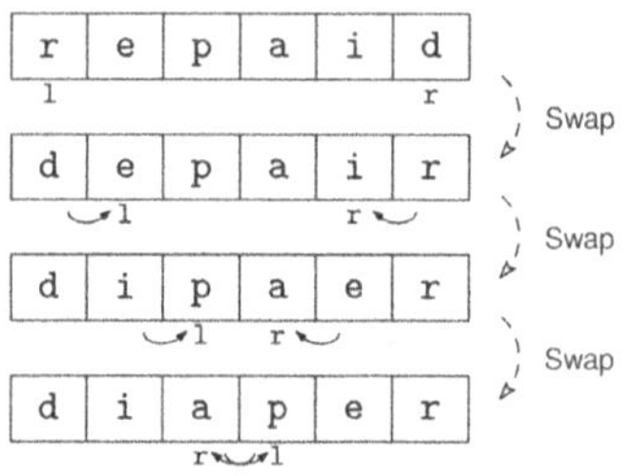

Figure 9.

Tip: Learn if there is a quick way to swap two elements in a single line in your language of choice, as this is a common operation for two-pointer algorithms. If it doesn't, consider defining a helper swap() function to keep your logic clean.

As mentioned, a key question to think about is:

▸   *"Of all the possible combinations of pointer directions, which one makes my life the easiest?"*

When we have a problem that requires us to modify the input in place, we can think about the best direction to read and the best direction to write:

▸   "If I start reading from the beginning of the array, where do I need to put the elements I encounter? What if I start reading from the end instead?"

▸   "If I start writing to the beginning of the array, where should I pull the elements from? What if I start writing from the end?"

There's often one configuration that makes things a lot easier than the rest. Think about the best read/write directions for the following problem:

✦✦   **PROBLEM 27.13**   **PARITY SORTING**

Given an array of integers, arr, modify it in place to put all even numbers before all odd numbers. The relative order between even numbers does not matter. Same for the odd numbers.

▸ **Example:** arr = [1, 2, 3, 4, 5]
   Output: [2, 4, 1, 3, 5]. There are other valid outputs, like [4, 2, 3, 1, 5].

▸ **Example:** arr = [5, 1, 3, 1, 5]
   Output: [5, 1, 3, 1, 5]. Since all numbers are odd, any ordering is valid.

SOLUTION 27.13   PARITY SORTING

For this problem:

· If we start reading from the left, we may encounter even or odd numbers. The even ones are already in the right place, while the odd ones must be moved to the end of the array.

· The opposite is true if we start reading from the right.

This leads us to the idea of using **inward pointers** with the following loop invariant:

Every number to the left of L is even, and every number to the right of r is odd.

If we maintain this invariant throughout the loop, when l and r meet or cross, the array will be in the desired order.

```
1  def sort_even(arr):
2    l, r = 0, len(arr)-1
3    while l < r:
4      if arr[l] % 2 == 0:
5        l += 1
6      elif arr[r] % 2 == 1:
7        r -= 1
8      else:
9        arr[l], arr[r] = arr[r], arr[l]
10       l += 1
11       r -= 1
```

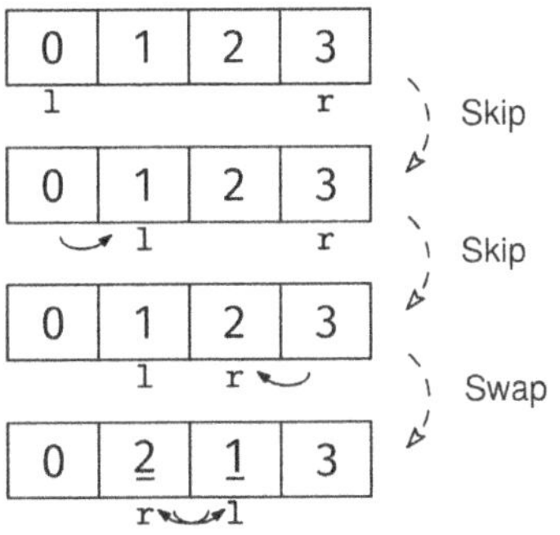

Figure 10.

SEEKER AND WRITER POINTERS

In-place modification problems can get tricky when we need to read the elements from left to right *and* write them from left to right.

For problems like this, we recommend using **fast and slow** pointers, except that each one has a specific role:

- The fast pointer is the *seeker*, looking for the next element to write.
- The slow pointer is the *writer*, staying at the position where the next element needs to be written.

We can update these pointers according to the following recipe:

RECIPE 1: SEEKER AND WRITER

```
seeker_writer_recipe(arr)
  seeker, writer = 0, 0
  while seeker < len(arr)
    if we need to keep arr[seeker]
      arr[writer] = arr[seeker]
      advance writer and seeker
    else
      only advance seeker
```

The classic example of this is removing duplicates in place:

PROBLEM 27.14   IN-PLACE DUPLICATE REMOVAL

Given a sorted array of integers, arr, remove duplicates in place while preserving the order, and return the number of unique elements. It doesn't matter what remains in arr beyond the unique elements.

▶ **Example:** arr = [1, 2, 2, 3, 3, 3, 5]
  Output: 4 (arr = [1, 2, 3, 5, 0, 0, 0]). The last 3 values could be
            anything; [1, 2, 3, 5, 1, 2, 3] would also be valid.

SOLUTION 27.14   IN-PLACE DUPLICATE REMOVAL

We can use Recipe 1: Seeker and Writer (pg 307) the **seeker** looks for the next unique element, while the **writer** stays at the first position that hasn't been written yet.

```
1  def remove_duplicates(arr):
2    s, w = 0, 0
3    while s < len(arr):
4      must_keep = s == 0 or arr[s] != arr[s-1]
5      if must_keep:
6        arr[w] = arr[s]
7        w += 1
8      s += 1
9    return w
```

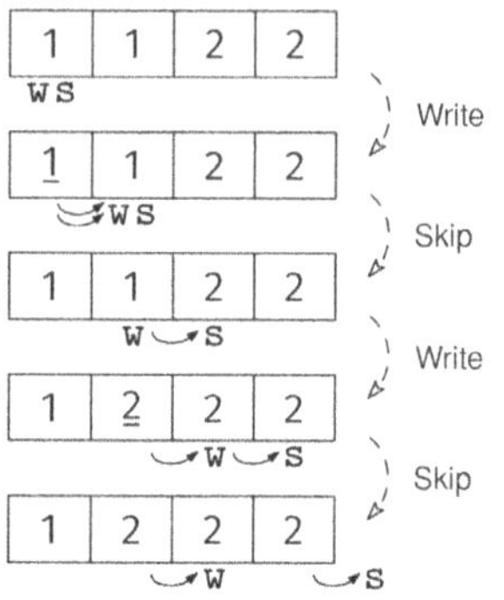

Figure 11. Seeker and writer pointers for Solution 27.14: In-Place Duplicate Removal (pg 307).

When the two pointers point to the same element, the assignment arr[w] = arr[s] has no effect because the element is already in the right position. That is fine—we still make progress by advancing both pointers.

IN-PLACE MODIFICATION PROBLEM SET

✦ *Try these problems with AI Interviewer: bctci.co/two-pointers-problem-set-2*

PROBLEM 27.15   **QUICKSORT PARTITION**

Given an array of integers, arr, and a number, pivot, modify arr in place using only O(1) extra space so that (1) every element smaller than the pivot appears before every element greater than or equal to the pivot, and (2) every element larger than the pivot appears after every element smaller than or equal to the pivot. The relative order of the elements smaller than or greater than the pivot does not matter.[14]

▶ **Example:** arr = [1, 7, 2, 3, 3, 5, 3], pivot = 4
   Output: [1, 3, 2, 3, 3, 7, 5]. Other orders, such as [3, 2, 1, 3, 3, 5, 7], would also be valid.

▶ **Example:** arr = [1, 7, 2, 3, 3, 5, 3], pivot = 3
   Output: [1, 2, 3, 3, 3, 7, 5]. Other orders, such as [2, 1, 3, 3, 3, 5, 7], would also be valid.

PROBLEM 27.16   **DUTCH FLAG PROBLEM**

Given an array consisting of letters 'R', 'W', and 'B', sort it in place to put all the 'R' before all the 'W' and all the 'W' before all the 'B'.[15]

▶ **Example:** arr = [R, W, B, B, W, R, W]
   Output: arr = [R, R, W, W, W, B, B]

PROBLEM 27.17   **PREFIX–SUFFIX SWAP**

We are given an array of letters, arr, with a length, n, which is a multiple of 3. The goal is to modify arr in place to move the prefix of length n/3 to the end and the suffix of length 2n/3 to the beginning.

---

14 This partition problem is a step in the quicksort algorithm. There is a harder version of this problem where we also need to preserve the relative order of the elements before and after the pivot. That version, which is used for the stable version of quicksort, requires 3 pointers and a careful case analysis. We don't include it because it's beyond what is expected for interviews.

15 This classic problem is known as the Dutch flag problem because the flag has three stripes colored red, white, and blue.

► **Example:** arr = [b, a, d, r, e, v, i, e, w]
  Output: arr = [r, e, v, i, e, w, b, a, d]. The prefix of length 3 is [b, a, d], which gets moved to the end. The order of the suffix, [r, e, v, i, e, w], is preserved.

PROBLEM 27.18 **SHIFT WORD TO BACK**

You are given an array of letters, arr, and a string, word. We know that word appears within arr as a *subsequence* (its letters appear in order, though not necessarily contiguously). Identify the earliest occurrence of word in arr (that is, the first subsequence from left to right that spells out word) and move all those letters, in order, to the end of arr. You must do this in place, using only O(1) extra space, and preserve the relative order of both the moved letters and the remaining letters.

► **Example:** arr = [s, e, e, k, e, r, a, n, d, w, r, i, t, e, r], word = "edit"
  Output: [s, e, k, e, r, a, n, w, r, e, r, e, d, i, t]
            The subsequence that needs to be moved is shown underscored:
            [s, e, e, k, e, r, a, n, d, w, r, i, t, e, r]
► **Example:** arr = [b, a, c, b], word = "ab"
  Output: [b, c, a, b]. We cannot move the first 'b' because we need to find 'a' first. [c, b, a, b] would be incorrect.
► **Example:** arr = [b, a, b, c], word = "b"
  Output: [a, b, c, b]. We must move the first 'b' to the end, not the second one. [b, a, c, b] would be incorrect.

✦ PROBLEM SET SOLUTIONS.

SOLUTION 27.15 QUICKSORT PARTITION

We can use **inward pointers** to place elements smaller than the pivot left to right and elements larger than the pivot right to left. The challenge is where to put elements equal to the pivot.

One way to approach this is to use the **break down the problem** booster and solve it in two steps:

1. Put all the elements ≤ pivot before all the elements > pivot (with a solution similar to Problem 13, 'Parity Sorting').
2. Now, take the section of the array with the elements ≤ pivot and use inward pointers again to put the elements < pivot before those = pivot.[16]

SOLUTION 27.16 DUTCH FLAG PROBLEM

This problem is essentially the same as Problem 27.15: Quicksort Partition (pg 308) if we think of W as the pivot, R as the smaller elements, and B as the larger elements. We *could* follow the same two-pass approach. However, there is a simpler way:

1. Walk through the array and count how many letters there are of each type.
2. Re-write the values in the array based on the counts.[17]

---

16 This could be considered a 'two-pass solution.' A common question we hear from candidates is whether it is OK to do a multi-pass solution or they should aim for a single-pass one. You can check if the interviewer has a preference, mentioning that it doesn't make a difference in the big O analysis. If they don't care, you can go for multiple passes if you are worried about messing up a single-pass solution.

17 This is a special case of the sorting algorithm known as *counting sort*, which works well in cases where the input range is small.

This solution leverages that the *input range* consists of only 3 values. When the input range is small, there often are simpler or more efficient solutions. We capture this as a **reusable idea** on page 349.

SOLUTION 27.17   PREFIX–SUFFIX SWAP

The challenge in this problem is that the prefix and suffix we need to swap have different lengths. We'll show three different ways of solving this problem.

1. Since swapping arrays of the same length is simpler, we can **break down the problem** into two steps, where we swap equal-length arrays at each step:

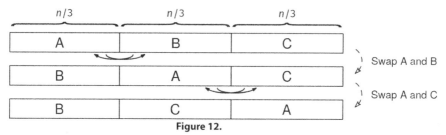

Figure 12.

2. We can do *3-way swaps* (similar to the 4-way swaps for matrix rotation, pg 261):

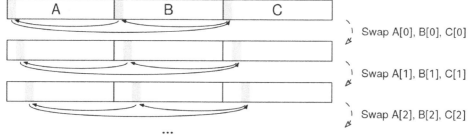

Figure 13.

3. Solutions 1 & 2 wouldn't work if the length of the prefix wasn't exactly $n/3$. There is a *trick* that allows you to reverse a *prefix of any length* in place.[18] Imagine we want to swap the prefix of the first k letters to the end. We do it in three steps:

a. Reverse arr in place (see Problem 27.12: Array Reversal (pg 305)). This puts the suffix before the prefix, but both are now reversed.

b. Reverse the final k letters of arr. This fixes the order of what was initially the prefix.

c. Reverse the first $n-k$ letters of arr. This fixes the order of what was initially the suffix.

For instance, if we have "outbreak" and we need to move "out" to the end, we can (a) reverse the whole thing to get "kaerbtuo", (b) reverse the final three letters to get kaerbout, and (c) reverse the first five letters to get breakout.

SOLUTION 27.18   SHIFT WORD TO BACK

To tackle this tricky in-place problem, it helps to realize that, even if we jumble the contents of arr, we can always read the word string. This means that we can **break down the problem** into two steps:

1. Write the letters *not* in the word subsequence at the beginning of the array.

2. Write word at the end.

---

18 Tricks like this are hard to come up with, but once you've seen them, you can add them to your toolset.

For (1), we can use Recipe 1: Seeker and Writer (pg 307). The seeker seeks the letters *not* in word (which are then written by the writer) and skips over the letters in word. We need a third pointer, i, to keep track of the next letter in word to seek.

For (2), if k is the length of word, when the seeker reaches the end, the writer will be k letters behind. At that point, we can write word in the final positions.

```python
def move_word(arr, word):
    seeker, writer = 0, 0
    i = 0
    while seeker < len(arr):
        if i < len(word) and arr[seeker] == word[i]:
            seeker += 1
            i += 1
        else:
            arr[writer] = arr[seeker]
            seeker += 1
            writer += 1
    for c in word:
        arr[writer] = c
        writer += 1
```

KEY TAKEAWAYS

The most common movement patterns are inward pointers, slow and fast pointers, and parallel pointers. We recommend starting two-pointer algorithms by asking,

> *"Of all the possible combinations of pointer directions, which one makes my life the easiest?"*

Our advice to nail the index manipulation is to **keep the logic simple** (pg 296), lean on **loop invariants** (pg 298), and **validate edge cases** after the fact (pg 299).

Recipe 1: Seeker and Writer (pg 307) can be helpful for in-place modification problems that read and write from the same side, which can be particularly tricky.

> **Two-pointer triggers:** The input consists of one or two arrays/strings/linked lists. We need to use $O(1)$ extra memory or modify the input in place. The input is sorted. The naive solution is $O(n^2)$, and we want to get to $O(n)$.
>
> **Keywords:** palindrome, reverse, swap, merge, partition.

ONLINE RESOURCES

Online resources for this chapter include:

- A chance to try each problem in this chapter in AI Interviewer
- Interview replays that show specific mistakes people make with two pointers problems
- Full code solutions for every problem in the chapter in multiple programming languages

Try online at bctci.co/two-pointers.

## CHAPTER 28

GRIDS & MATRICES

AI interviewer, replays, and more materials for this chapter at bctci.co/grids-and-matrices

▶ *Prerequisites: None*

This chapter discusses problems about *grids*, which are 2D arrays with nested arrays of equal length. Grid problems are popular because grids can represent many things, such as terrain maps, pixels on a screen, graphs,[1] and linear algebra matrices. Problems based on board games often use grids: for instance, a chess board can be represented as an 8x8 grid, while a Tic-tac-toe board can be represented as a 3x3 grid.

When specifying the dimensions of a grid, we write the number of rows first and then the number of columns. So, a 4x2 grid has four rows and two columns (four nested arrays of length two), whereas a 2x4 grid has two rows and four columns. Row and column indices start at zero. This means that the top-left cell of a 4x2 grid is grid[0][0], and the bottom-right cell is grid[3][1].

> Avoid using the variables x and y with grids. We've seen this lead to confusion and bugs because we tend to like writing grid[x][y] or matching x with the rows. However, in math notation, the x-axis actually corresponds to the *columns*, not the rows. It's just safer and more intuitive to use grid[r][c].

Grids are sometimes also called *matrices*, but we will stick to calling them 'grids' except in the specific context of linear algebra operations.

MOVING IN A GRID

Grid problems often require some notion of moving between cells, usually as a building block in larger algorithms.

Imagine a problem where a grid represents an *escape room*. Each cell can be either an obstacle (denoted by a 1) or a walkable space (denoted by a 0). A player in the escape room can move one space at a time—up,

---

1   Grids are a natural representation for *grid graphs*, where nodes form a rectangular layout, and edges connect adjacent nodes horizontally or vertically. Grid graphs will be discussed on page 482, building on this chapter.

down, left, or right. Given the grid, room, and a player's position, [r, c], what are the *immediately* available cells they can move to?

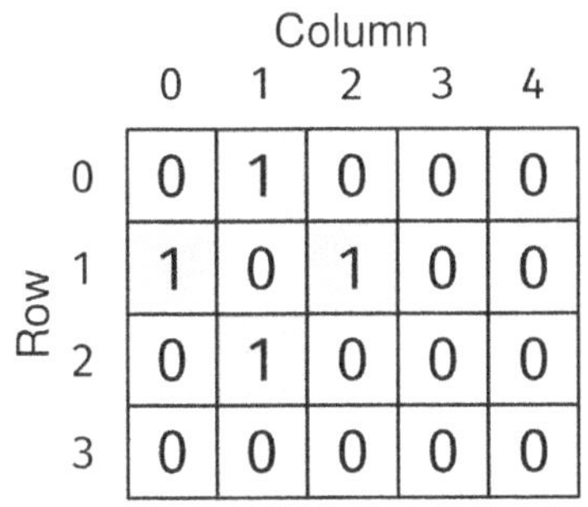

Figure 1.

For instance, if the escape room is like the grid in Figure 1 and the player is at [2, 3], they can move in all four directions. If they are at [0, 4], they can only go left (to [0, 3]) or down (to [1, 4])—going up or right leads out of bounds. And if they are at [1, 1], they cannot go anywhere—all directions are blocked by obstacles.

Candidates new to this type of problem often construct four separate conditional statements and check each direction with a conditional that looks like this:

```
1   # DON'T DO THIS
2   if r + 1 < len(room) and room[r + 1][c] != 1:
3     # Add [r + 1, c] to the solution
4   if r - 1 >= 0 and room[r - 1][c] != 1:
5     # Add [r - 1, c] to the solution
6   if c + 1 < len(room[0]) and room[r][c + 1] != 1:
7     # Add [r, c + 1] to the solution
8   if c - 1 >= 0 and room[r][c - 1] != 1:
9     # Add [r, c - 1] to the solution
```

Four conditional statements like this give us plenty of chances to mess up the row/column index math. Instead, we can use a **directions array** to generate the neighbor coordinates in all four directions:

```
1   def is_valid(room, r, c):
2     return 0 <= r < len(room) and 0 <= c < len(room[0]) and room[r][c] != 1
3
4   def valid_moves(room, r, c):
5     moves = []
6     directions = [[-1, 0], [1, 0], [0, -1], [0, 1]]
7     for dir_r, dir_c in directions:
8       new_r = r + dir_r
9       new_c = c + dir_c
10      if is_valid(room, new_r, new_c):
11        moves.append([new_r, new_c])
12    return moves
```

This code works by iterating through all directions, calculating the new row and column indices, and then calling is_valid() on them.[2] The is_valid() method performs the boundary and obstacle checks *in that order*. Swapping the order of these two checks is a common mistake that results in out-of-bounds errors.

---

2 Even though we use a for loop over the directions, the method still takes constant time since the number of directions is constant!

REUSABLE IDEA: DIRECTIONS ARRAY TO VISIT GRID NEIGHBORS

Navigating through a grid by checking neighbor cells is common in graphs, backtracking, and other topics. We can do this compactly with a `directions` array that contains all the possible offsets to add to the current position to generate its neighbors.

We can easily extend the `directions` array with additional directions (e.g., diagonals) depending on the problem.

 REUSABLE IDEA: FACTOR OUT VALIDATION TO A HELPER FUNCTION

When checking if a cell is valid, embedding the logic directly in your main algorithm can clutter the code. Instead, consider encapsulating the validation logic in a dedicated `is_valid()` function.

Beyond grid cells, this applies anywhere you must validate 'something' before using it.

Messing up the boundary conditions and accidentally going out of bounds is easy in an interview, as you will see in the next replay. These reusable ideas will prevent you from making these mistakes in an actual interview!

| ▶ **BOUNDARY CONDITION BLUNDER** | INTERVIEW REPLAY |

View Online:	bctci.co/grids-replay-1 @ 1:05:00 - 1:07:00
The Question:	Given a binary grid, find all unique shapes in the grid.
What You'll See:	The candidate messed up the boundary logic and had an index out-of-bounds issue.
Who:	*Interviewer*: Software Engineer at Amazon *Candidate*: 8 years exp.

MOVEMENT PROBLEM SET

✦ *Try these problems with AI Interviewer: bctci.co/grids-problem-set-1*

In this problem set, we'll look at some common variations of the **directions array** reusable idea.

PROBLEM 28.1   CHESS MOVES

This is how the King, the Knight, and the Queen move in chess:

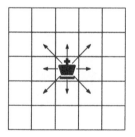
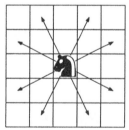
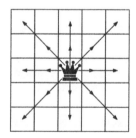

Figure 2.

The king can go to any adjacent cell, including diagonals. The knight 'jumps' one cell in one dimension and two in the other, even if there are pieces in between. The queen can move *any number* of cells in any direction, including diagonals, but cannot go through occupied cells.

We are given three things:

- board, an nxn binary grid, where n > 0, a 0 denotes an empty cell, and a 1 denotes an occupied cell (for this problem, it doesn't matter what piece is in it).
- piece, which is one of "king", "knight", or "queen".
- r and c, with 0 ≤ r < n and 0 ≤ c < n, which denote an unoccupied position in the board.

Return a list of all the *unoccupied* cells in board that can be reached by the given piece in one move, starting from [r, c]. The order of the output cells does not matter.

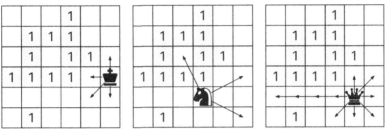

Figure 3. Examples for Problem 28.1 (the white cells are 0's).

▶ **Example:** board from Figure 3, piece = "king", r = 3, c = 5
  Output: [[2, 5], [3, 4], [4. 4], [4, 5]]
▶ **Example:** board from Figure 3, piece = "knight", r = 4, c = 3
  Output: [[2, 2], [3, 5], [5, 5]]
▶ **Example:** board from Figure 3, piece = "queen", r = 4, c = 4
  Output: [[3, 4], [3, 5], [4, 0], [4, 1], [4, 2], [4, 3], [4, 5], [5, 3], [5, 4], [5,5]]

| PROBLEM 28.2 | QUEEN'S REACH |

Continuing with the chess theme, imagine that a board has a number of queens in it and no other pieces. We are given an nxn binary grid, board, where n > 0, a 0 denotes an empty cell, and a 1 indicates a queen (the color of the queen doesn't matter). Return a binary board with the same dimensions, where a 0 denotes that a cell is safe, and a 1 denotes that a cell is not safe. We say a cell is *safe* if there isn't a queen in it and no queen on the board can reach it in a single move.

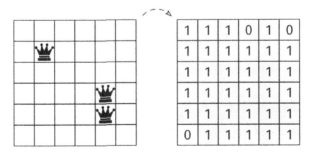

Figure 4. Example input (left) and output (right) for Problem 28.2 (the cells with queens in the input are 1's).

PROBLEM 28.3   **SPIRAL ORDER**

Given a positive and odd integer n, return an nxn grid of integers filled as follows: the grid should have every number from 0 to n^2-1 in *spiral order*, starting by going down from the center and turning clockwise.

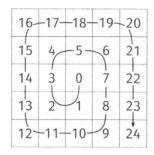

Figure 5. Example of spiral order for n = 5.

PROBLEM 28.4   **SNOWPRINTS**

We are tracking *Elsa*, an arctic fox, through a rectangular snowy field represented by a binary grid, field, where a 1 denotes snowprints and a 0 denotes no snowprints. We know that the fox crossed the field from left to right, so each column has exactly one 1. Between two consecutive columns, the row of the 1 may remain the same, go up by one, or go down by one. Above the field (above the first row), there is an icy river. Return how close the fox got to the river, in terms of the number of rows between it and the river. Assume that field has at least one row and one column.

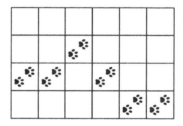

Figure 6. Example for Problem 28.4 (the cells with paws are 1's).

▸ **Example:** the field from Figure 6.
  Output: 1. The fox was the closest to the river in column 2.

✦ PROBLEM SET SOLUTIONS

SOLUTION 28.1   CHESS MOVES

For the king and knight, the logic is just like the escape room—we just need to modify the **directions array**. For the queen, we can use a loop to advance in each direction until we reach an occupied cell or the edge of the board. The is_valid() function is the same one we used for the escape room.

```
1   def queen_valid_moves(board, piece, r, c):
2     moves = []
3     king_directions = [
4       [-1, 0], [1, 0], [0, -1], [0, 1],    # Vertical and horizontal.
5       [-1, -1], [-1, 1], [1, -1], [1, 1]   # Diagonals.
```

```
 6       ]
 7       knight_directions = [[-2, 1], [-1, 2], [1, 2], [2, 1], [2, -1], [1, -2], [-1, -2],
 8                            [-2, -1]]
 9       if piece == "knight":
10         directions = knight_directions
11       else:  # King and queen.
12         directions = king_directions
13       for dir_r, dir_c in directions:
14         new_r, new_c = r + dir_r, c + dir_c
15         if piece == "queen":
16           while is_valid(board, new_r, new_c):
17             moves.append([new_r, new_c])
18             new_r += dir_r
19             new_c += dir_c
20         elif is_valid(board, new_r, new_c):
21           moves.append([new_r, new_c])
22       return moves
```

SOLUTION 28.2   QUEEN'S REACH

First, we need to be able to create an empty grid. This comes up frequently in interviews, so it's worth learning the most convenient way to do it in your language of choice.

We can iterate through the input grid to find each queen. When we do, we can use a **directions array** to mark all cells it can reach in the output array. The is_valid() function is still the same one we used for the escape room.

```
 1   def safe_cells(board):
 2     n = len(board)
 3     res = [[0] * n for _ in range(n)]
 4     for r in range(n):
 5       for c in range(n):
 6         if board[r][c] == 1:
 7           res[r][c] = 1
 8           mark_reachable_cells(board, r, c, res)
 9     return res
10
11   def mark_reachable_cells(board, r, c, res):
12     directions = [
13       [-1, 0], [1, 0], [0, -1], [0, 1],   # Vertical and horizontal.
14       [-1, -1], [-1, 1], [1, -1], [1, 1]  # Diagonals.
15     ]
16     for dir_r, dir_c in directions:
17       new_r, new_c = r + dir_r, c + dir_c
18       while is_valid(board, new_r, new_c):
19         res[new_r][new_c] = 1
20         new_r += dir_r
21         new_c += dir_c
```

Learn the easiest way to initialize an empty grid in your language of choice. For instance, in Python, we can do:[3]

---

3 Warning for Python users: [[0] * num_cols] * num_rows looks correct and shorter, but it leads to a subtle bug: all rows are the same underlying variable! That is, modifying a value in one row will modify all the rows, which is not what we want.

```
grid = [[0] * num_cols for _ in range(num_rows)]
```

Similarly, it's also important to know how to copy an existing grid. In Python, we can do:

```
grid_copy = [row.copy() for row in grid]
```

SOLUTION 28.3   SPIRAL ORDER

We can start by initializing an empty grid, and then fill in the numbers following the spiral order. To start, we need to find the center: $[(n - 1)/2, (n - 1)/2]$. From there, we can:

- Move by 1 → turn
- Move by 1 → turn
- Move by 2 → turn
- Move by 2 → turn
- Move by 3 → turn
- Move by 3 → turn

While it could be a bit annoying to implement, it is quite feasible.

However, there is a *trick* that makes it simpler to code: spiral from the end to the beginning. Whether we have a 1x1, 3x3, 5x5, or any odd nxn grid, we can observe that the end is always at the bottom-right corner, so we can start there. It's also easy to know when to turn: we turn whenever the next step would take us off the edge of the board or onto a cell that already has a number.

```
1   def is_valid(grid, r, c):
2     return 0 <= r < len(grid) and 0 <= c < len(grid[0]) and grid[r][c] == 0
3
4   def spiral(n):
5     val = n * n - 1
6     res = [[0] * n for _ in range(n)]
7     r, c = n - 1, n - 1
8     directions = [[-1, 0], [0, -1], [1, 0], [0, 1]]  # Counterclockwise
9     dir = 0  # Start going up
10    while val > 0:
11      res[r][c] = val
12      val -= 1
13      if not is_valid(res, r + directions[dir][0], c + directions[dir][1]):
14        dir = (dir + 1) % 4  # Change directions counterclockwise
15      r, c = r + directions[dir][0], c + directions[dir][1]
16    return res
```

♻ REUSABLE IDEA: HANDLE WRAPAROUNDS WITH MOD

For problems involving 'circular arrays,' where the last element wraps around to the first one, modular arithmetic can simplify indexing logic: the next element after index i is always (i + 1)%n, where n is the length of the array.

SOLUTION 28.4   SNOWPRINTS

Let R and C be the dimensions of the grid. A naive solution would be to iterate through the entire grid, which would take O(R*C) time. However, it is more efficient to trace the fox's steps. We can start by finding where the fox started along the first column, in O(R) time. Then, for each other column, we can find where the fox went next with a **directions array** that covers the three options. Since we only need to consider 3 cells per column, this takes O(C) time, for a total time of O(R+C).

```
1   def distance_to_river(field):
2     R, C = len(field), len(field[0])
3     def has_footprints(r, c):
4       return 0 <= r < R and 0 <= c < C and field[r][c] == 1
5     r, c = 0, 0
6     while field[r][c] != 1:
7       r += 1
8     closest = r
9     directions_row = [-1, 0, 1]
10    while c < C:
11      for dir_r in directions_row:
12        new_r, new_c = r + dir_r, c + 1
13        if has_footprints(new_r, new_c):
14          r, c = new_r, new_c
15          closest = min(closest, r)
16          break
17    return closest
```

Astute readers may realize that this problem is similar to Problem 22.1: Tunnel Depth (pg 231), just flipped upside down. The key difference is that here, there is a single 1 per column, so tracing the path of 1's from the first 1 only takes O(C) time instead of O(R*C).

The problems in this chapter generally don't involve much traditional problem-solving. Instead, their difficulty comes from having to recognize and apply unusual pointer movements that navigate through a grid in unfamiliar ways. Identifying these patterns on the spot can be especially challenging. Check out the next replay for another interesting problem where the candidate struggles to manipulate their pointers through the grid correctly.

TRICKY GRID MANIPULATIONS   INTERVIEW REPLAY

View Online:	bctci.co/grids-replay-2 @ 4:15 - end
The Question:	Given a grid, return a list of all elements in diagonal order.
What You'll See:	The candidate struggled to derive the pattern behind how the pointers must move to get the correct answer.
Who:	*Interviewer*: Machine Learning Engineer at Meta
	Candidate: College student

SUBGRID PROBLEM SET

✦ *Try these problems with AI Interviewer: bctci.co/grids-problem-set-2*

A *subgrid* is a grid inside another grid. In this section, we'll practice a few problems involving subgrids.

PROBLEM 28.5   VALID SUDOKU

Given a 9x9 grid, board, representing a Sudoku,[4] return true if the board does not have any conflicts and false otherwise. The board contains only numbers between 0 and 9 in each cell, with 0's denoting empty

---

4 For those who don't know the rules of Sudoku: the grid starts off with some cells pre-filled with numbers. The player is asked to fill in the empty cells with the numbers 1 through 9, such that there are no duplicates in the same row, column, or subgrid (the 3x3 sections shown with the thicker outline).

cells. A *conflict* is a duplicate number (other than 0) along a row, a column, or a 3x3 subgrid (shown with a thicker outline in Figure 7). For the purposes of this problem, it doesn't matter if the Sudoku has a valid solution or not—only whether it has a conflict in the already-filled cells.

```
5 0 0 | 0 0 0 | 0 0 6      5 0 0 | 0 0 0 | 0 0 6
0 0 9 | 0 5 0 | 3 0 0      0 0 9 | 0 5 0 | 3 0 0
0 3 0 | 0 0 2 | 0 0 0      0 3 0 | 0 0 2 | 0 0 0
8 0 0 | 7 0 0 | 0 0 9      8 0 0 | 7 0 0 | 0 0 9
0 0 2 | 0 0 0 | 8 0 0      0 0 2 | 0 0 0 | 8 0 0
4 0 0 | 0 0 6 | 0 0 3      4 0 0 | 0 0 6 | 0 0 3
0 0 0 | 3 0 0 | 0 4 0      0 0 0 | 3 0 0 | 0 4 0
0 0 3 | 0 8 0 | 2 0 0      0 0 3 | 0 8 0 | 7 0 0
9 0 0 | 0 0 0 | 0 0 7      9 0 0 | 0 0 0 | 0 0 7
```

Figure 7. Example of a Sudoku without conflicts (left) and a Sudoku with a conflict (right): the bottom-right 3x3 subgrid has a duplicate, 7.

PROBLEM 28.6   **SUBGRID MAXIMUMS**

Given a rectangular RxC grid of integers, grid, with R > 0 and C > 0, return a new grid with the same dimensions where each cell [r, c] contains the maximum in the subgrid with [r, c] in the top-left corner and [R-1, C-1] in the bottom-right corner.

▸ Example: grid = [[1, 5, 3],
                   [4,-1, 0],
                   [2, 0, 2]]
   Output: [[5, 5, 3],
                    [4, 2, 2],
                    [2, 2, 2]]

PROBLEM 28.7   **SUBGRID SUMS**

Given a rectangular RxC grid of integers, grid, with R > 0 and C > 0, return a new grid with the same dimensions where each cell [r, c] contains the sum of all the elements in the subgrid with [r, c] in the top-left corner and [R - 1, C - 1] in the bottom-right corner.

▸ Example: grid = [[-1, 2, 3],
                   [4, 0, 0],
                   [-2, 0, 9]]
   Output: [[15,14,12],
                    [11, 9, 9],
                    [7, 9, 9]]

✦ PROBLEM SET SOLUTIONS

SOLUTION 28.5   VALID SUDOKU

This question isn't terribly difficult, but it requires a decent amount of code. While there is a one-pass solution, let's **break down the problem** and handle each constraint as a separate subtask:

```
1   def is_valid(board):
2       return valid_rows(board) and valid_cols(board) and valid_subgrids(board)
```

Validating the rows: This is a straightforward nested loop that walks through each row, checking the cells in each for duplicates. We can use a set to efficiently track what numbers we've seen so far in the current row.

```
1   def valid_rows(board):
2     R, C = len(board), len(board[0])
3     for r in range(R):
4       seen = set()
5       for c in range(C):
6         if board[r][c] in seen:
7           return False
8         if board[r][c] != 0:
9           seen.add(board[r][c])
10    return True
```

Validating the columns: This is almost identical to the row validation, but iterating over the columns instead of the rows (omitted for brevity).[5]

Validating the subgrids: To keep the code clean, we can factor out the subgrid validation to a helper function that receives the top-left cell in a 3x3 subgrid. We can use a similar approach as a row validation, but with two nested loops instead of one long loop:

```
1   def valid_subgrid(board, r, c):
2     seen = set()
3     for new_r in range(r, r + 3):
4       for new_c in range(c, c + 3):
5         if board[new_r][new_c] in seen:
6           return False
7         if board[new_r][new_c] != 0:
8           seen.add(board[new_r][new_c])
9     return True
```

Finally, we need to pinpoint the coordinates of each top-left cell in a subgrid. It helps to know that there are 9 subgrids, and they are evenly spaced:[6]

```
1   def valid_subgrids(board):
2     for r in range(3):
3       for c in range(3):
4         if not valid_subgrid(board, r * 3, c * 3):
5           return False
6     return True
```

SOLUTION 28.6   SUBGRID MAXIMUMS

The naive solution computes the maximum for each individual cell by iterating through the corresponding subgrid. This takes $O(R*C)$ time per subgrid, resulting in a total runtime of $O((R*C)^2)$.

To improve this runtime, we should look for ways in which we can *reuse* the maximums that we have already computed to compute the maximums of additional cells. The key **property** is that the maximum of the

---

5   You *could* transpose the grid (pg 325) and then reuse the row validation code to validate the columns. This increases code reusability, but the trade off is that it takes more space or modifies the input (in Python, there's even a one-liner to transpose a grid: `[list(row) for row in zip(*grid)]`).

6   It is also possible to avoid looping through the rows, columns, and subgrids separately by initializing a hash set for each row, each column, and each subgrid. Then, in a single pass through the grid, we can add each value to the corresponding row, column, and subgrid sets. If we find that a value is already in a set before adding it, there is a conflict.

subgrid for a given cell [r, c], if not grid[r][c] itself, must be the same as the maximum of the cell below ([r + 1, c]) or the cell to the right ([r, c + 1]), assuming they are within bounds. That is:[7]

$$res[r][c] = max(grid[r][c], res[r + 1][c], res[r][c + 1])$$

To take advantage of this property, we must iterate backward through the grid:

```
1   def subgrid_maximums(grid):
2     R, C = len(grid), len(grid[0])
3     res = [row.copy() for row in grid]
4     for r in range(R - 1, -1, -1):
5       for c in range(C - 1, -1, -1):
6         if r + 1 < R:
7           res[r][c] = max(res[r][c], grid[r + 1][c])
8         if c + 1 < C:
9           res[r][c] = max(res[r][c], grid[r][c + 1])
10    return res
```

SOLUTION 28.7   SUBGRID SUMS

This is a harder version of Problem 28.6: Subgrid Maximums (pg 320). We could try a similar formula:

$$res[r][c] = grid[r][c] + res[r + 1][c] + res[r][c + 1]$$

However, this *doesn't work*. For instance, for a grid like:

```
[[0, 0],
 [0, 1]]
```

we should get:

```
[[1, 1],
 [1, 1]]
```

Instead, if we apply the formula backward through the grid, we'd get:

```
[[2, 1],
 [1, 1]]
```

Where did the 2 come from, if there's a single 1 in the entire grid?

The issue is that we are *double counting* the 1 at [0, 0]—once through the sum for the cell below and once through the sum for the cell to the right. The solution is to subtract the sum of elements that are double counted, which are those in the subgrid diagonal from [0, 0].

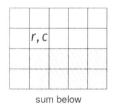 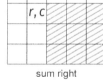 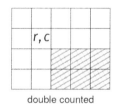

sum below   sum right   double counted

Figure 8.

```
1   def backward_sum(grid):
2     R, C = len(grid), len(grid[0])
3     res = [row.copy() for row in grid]
4     for r in range(R - 1, -1 , -1):
5       for c in range(C - 1, -1, -1):
```

---

7 This pattern, where we compute values for certain cells and then reuse them to compute values for others, is common in dynamic programming, so it's worthwhile to start familiarizing yourself with it.

```
6        if r + 1 < R:
7          res[r][c] += res[r + 1][c]
8        if c + 1 < C:
9          res[r][c] += res[r][c + 1]
10       if r + 1 < R and c + 1 < C:  # Subtract double-counted subgrid.
11         res[r][c] -= res[r + 1][c + 1]
12     return res
```

MATRIX MATH

A *matrix* is a grid of numbers. The terminology comes from linear algebra, where matrices are used extensively in fields like computer graphics, scientific computing, and machine learning. Thankfully, you don't need to know linear algebra or any of these topics for general SWE coding interviews—do not worry about memorizing matrix types, formulas, or things like what eigenvectors are or how the Cholesky Decomposition works.

Nonetheless, basic matrix operations sometimes come up in coding interviews because they involve interesting grid transformations, but they usually don't assume background knowledge.

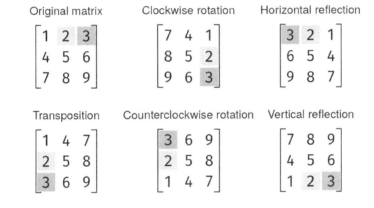

Figure 9. Matrix transposition, 90-degree rotations, and reflections.

- **Transposition**: The first row becomes the first column, the second row becomes the second column, and so on.
- **Rotation:** A transformation that turns the matrix 90 degrees, clockwise or counterclockwise.
- **Horizontal reflection**: The first column becomes the last column, the second column becomes the second last, and so on.
- **Vertical reflection**: The first row becomes the last row, the second row becomes the second last, and so on.

\# Tip: While using m and n as the number of rows and columns in a matrix is conventional, we recommend sticking to R and C (or similar) for interviews. Linguistically, m and n sound similar, and it can be difficult to discern differences between phrases like "n log m" and "m log n".

For addition and subtraction, the dimensions of the two matrices must match. For A + B, the result at each position (r, c) is A[r][c] + B[r][c], and similarly for A - B.

$$A \qquad B \qquad A + B \qquad\qquad A \qquad B \qquad A - B$$

$$\begin{bmatrix} 7 & 10 \\ 8 & 11 \\ 9 & 12 \end{bmatrix} + \begin{bmatrix} 1 & 2 \\ 4 & 5 \\ 7 & 8 \end{bmatrix} = \begin{bmatrix} 8 & 12 \\ 12 & 16 \\ 14 & 20 \end{bmatrix} \qquad \begin{bmatrix} 7 & 10 \\ 8 & 11 \\ 9 & 12 \end{bmatrix} - \begin{bmatrix} 1 & 2 \\ 4 & 5 \\ 7 & 8 \end{bmatrix} = \begin{bmatrix} 6 & 8 \\ 4 & 6 \\ 2 & 4 \end{bmatrix}$$

Figure 10. Matrix addition and subtraction between 3x2 matrices. In each case, the shaded output number comes from operating on the shaded input numbers.

Multiplication is a bit different: we can only multiply two matrices together if the number of *columns* in the first matrix is the same as the number of *rows* in the second matrix. The result is a new matrix where each element [r, c] is calculated as the *dot product* of row r in the first matrix and column c in the second matrix.[8] In addition, the order of the matrices matters in the multiplication—unlike number multiplication, A*B is not the same as B*A. Matrix multiplication between two nxn matrices takes $O(n^3)$ time, because each of the $O(n^2)$ dot products takes $O(n)$ time.[9]

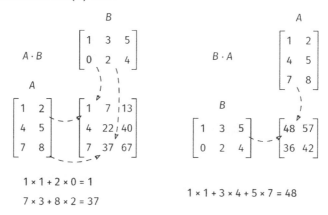

$$1 \times 1 + 2 \times 0 = 1$$
$$7 \times 3 + 8 \times 2 = 37$$

$$1 \times 1 + 3 \times 4 + 5 \times 7 = 48$$

Figure 11. Matrix multiplication between a 3x2 matrix (A) and a 2x3 matrix (B). A*B produces a 3x3 matrix, while B*A produces a 2x2 matrix. In this visualization, the second matrix is placed above the result matrix so that each column lines up with the corresponding column in the result.

✦ **PROBLEM 28.8**   **MATRIX OPERATIONS**

Implement a `Matrix` class that can be initialized with a square grid of floating point numbers. It must have methods for transposition, clockwise rotation, anticlockwise rotation, horizontal reflection, and vertical reflection. All the methods should take zero parameters, modify the matrix *in place*, using only O(1) extra space, and return nothing.

---

8   The dot product of two vectors (i.e., arrays of numbers) of the same length is a single number. To compute it, we multiply the two elements at index 0, the two elements at index 1, and so on, and add up all the products together.

9   There is a lot of interest in efficient matrix multiplication algorithms, both in theory and in practice, as it is a core operation in fields such as deep learning and computer graphics (matrices can describe affine transformations of space, which are important for things like rendering a 3D scene in a video game). For this reason, the hardware in GPUs is highly optimized for matrix multiplication. In the theoretical realm, in 1969, Volker Strassen came up with a clever divide-and-conquer algorithm that reduces the number of operations for square matrices from $O(n^3)$ to $O(n^{\log_2(7)}) \approx O(n^{2.8074})$. Since then, a long line of research has been progressively inching closer and closer to the output-size lower bound, $O(n^2)$, with the best current algorithms having an exponent between 2.3 and 2.4. Finding the best possible complexity is one of the biggest open problems in theoretical computer science.

SOLUTION 28.8   MATRIX OPERATIONS

We can initialize the class by making a copy of the input grid.

```
1  class Matrix:
2    def __init__(self, grid):
3      self.matrix = [row.copy() for row in grid]
```

Tracking rows and columns through a transposition example can help work out the logic. Essentially, the rows become columns, and the columns become rows. We can achieve it by swapping elements under the main diagonal with elements above it.

```
1  def transpose(self):
2    matrix = self.matrix
   for r in range(len(matrix)):
3      for c in range(r):
4        matrix[r][c], matrix[c][r] = matrix[c][r], matrix[r][c]
```

The limited range in the second loop makes it so we only iterate through the cells under the main diagonal. If we forget it, we will swap each pair of cells twice, leaving them in their original place!

Reflections are straightforward to implement:

```
1  def reflect_horizontally(self):
2    for row in self.matrix:
3      row.reverse()
4  def reflect_vertically(self):
5    self.matrix.reverse()
```

For rotations, we saw a 4-way swap solution on Problem 24.8: Matrix Rotation (pg 260). However, there is a *trick* that allows us to leverage the previous solutions: notice how both transpositions and rotations turn rows into columns and columns into rows. By transposing the matrix, we are close to achieving a rotation. We only need to follow it with a reflection:

```
1  def rotate_clockwise(self):
2    self.transpose()
3    self.reflect_horizontally()
4  def rotate_counterclockwise(self):
5    self.transpose()
6    self.reflect_vertically()
```

KEY TAKEAWAYS

The main goal of this chapter is to become comfortable working with multiple dimensions. The main reusable idea we learned is the **directions array** for moving in a grid. We will see further examples of grid-based problems in future chapters, such as Graphs, Backtracking, and Dynamic Programming.

☑ ONLINE RESOURCES

Online resources for this chapter include:

- A chance to try each problem in this chapter in AI Interviewer
- Interview replays that show specific mistakes people make with grids & matrices problems
- Full code solutions for every problem in the chapter in multiple programming languages

Try online at bctci.co/grids-and-matrices.

## CHAPTER 29

BINARY SEARCH

AI interviewer, replays, and more materials for this chapter at bctci.co/binary-search

▶ *Prerequisites: None*

When it comes to binary search, software engineers are split in half: One camp thinks it's too basic to be an interview question, and the other dreads it because they always mess up the index manipulation.

The first group overlooks the fact that binary search has many uses beyond the basic "find a value in a sorted array." Far from it, binary search has many non-obvious applications, which we'll cover in this chapter. For the second group, we'll provide a recipe focusing on simplicity and reusability across applications—even the unconventional ones we just foreshadowed.

BINARY SEARCH IS EASY TO MESS UP

Let's start with something simple—the classic binary search setting—and then build up to harder problems.

✦✦ **PROBLEM 29.1**   **SEARCH IN SORTED ARRAY**

Given a sorted array of integers, arr, and a target value, target, return the target's index if it exists in the array or -1 if it doesn't.

▶ **Example:** arr = [-2, 0, 3, 4, 7, 9, 11], target = 3
   Output: 2.

▶ **Example:** arr = [-2, 0, 3, 4, 7, 9, 11], target = 2
   Output: -1.

SOLUTION 29.1   SEARCH IN SORTED ARRAY

We assume most engineers are familiar with the basic premise of binary search: two pointers move inward from the ends of a sorted array, closing in on the target by checking if the midpoint is too small or too large.

Pop quiz! Here is an *attempted* solution, but it has a bug. Can you spot it?

```
1   def BUGGED_binary_search(arr, target): # DON'T USE IN INTERVIEWS!
2     l, r = 0, len(arr)
3     while l <= r:
4       mid = (l + r) // 2
5       if mid == target:
6         return mid
7       if target > mid:
8         r = mid+1
9       else:
10        l = mid-1
11    return -1
```

Check the solution in the footnote.[1] Regardless of what you found, the point is that it is easy to miss errors in a binary search implementation.

Here is one way to do it correctly:

```
1  def binary_search(arr, target):
2      n = len(arr)
3      if n == 0:
4          return -1
5      l, r = 0, n - 1
6      if arr[l] >= target or arr[r] < target:
7          if arr[l] == target:
8              return 0
9          return -1
10     while r - l > 1:
11         mid = (l + r) // 2
12         if arr[mid] < target:
13             l = mid
14         else:
15             r = mid
16     if arr[r] == target:
17         return r
18     return -1
```

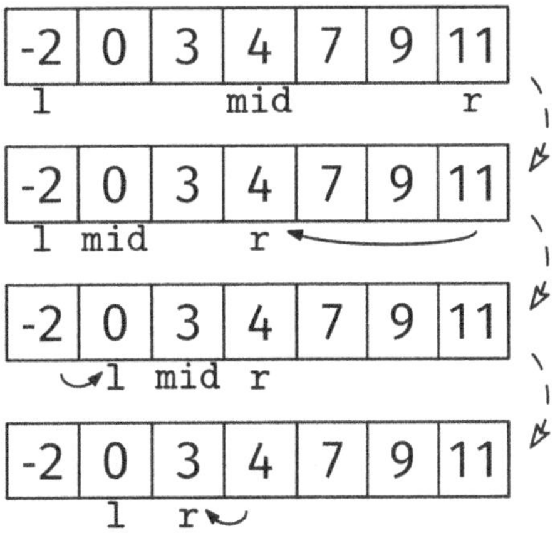

Figure 1. Binary search for target 3.

We'll punt on breaking down this solution until we talk about our transition-point recipe (pg 330).

BINARY SEARCH HAS SURPRISING APPLICATIONS

Imagine that your bike had gotten stolen, and your only chance of getting it back hinged on your ability to explain binary search to a police officer. That is the very situation Tom Whipple, a science journalist, found himself in.[2]

The rack from which the bike went missing was right under a security camera, but the police told him they didn't have the resources to watch many hours of footage just to identify when the bike was stolen. Tom explained that this wouldn't be necessary: they could skip ahead to the middle of the video and check if the bike was still there. If it was, the bike was stolen during the latter half; if not, it was stolen earlier. This could be repeated to quickly narrow down the time of the crime.

In the end, the thief was never caught—the footage was too grainy. Regardless, the story showcases an unconventional use of binary search. We can formalize it into an interview question:

✦ **PROBLEM 29.2**   **CCTV FOOTAGE**

You are given an API called is_stolen(t) which takes a timestamp as input and returns True if the bike is missing at that timestamp and False if it is still there. You're also given two timestamps, t1 and t2, representing when you parked the bike and when you found it missing. Return the timestamp when the

---

1 We were not completely honest—there isn't just one bug; there are closer to six, depending on how you count them. (1) r is initialized out of bounds, (2 & 3) we check mid instead of arr[mid] (twice!), (4) we update r when we should be updating l, (5) l should be set to mid+1, not mid-1, and (6) r should be set to mid-1, not mid+1.

2 https://www.thetimes.com/article/i-have-owned-11-bikes-this-is-how-they-were-stolen-d3r553gx3

bike was first missing, minimizing the number of API calls. Assume that 0 < t1 < t2, is_stolen(t1) is False, and is_stolen(t2) is True.

t1   t2

Figure 2.

SOLUTION 29.2   CCTV FOOTAGE

This problem is quite different from Problem 29.1: Search In Sorted Array (pg 326): it doesn't have an array input, and we don't have a target value. In fact, if we tried to use the same binary search code from earlier, we'd have to change almost every line in the algorithm before it would work correctly. That many tweaks make it easy to reintroduce bugs. Nonetheless, we can still use binary search because the range of possible answers can be broken down into two **regions**: (1) **before** the bike was stolen and (2) **after** it was stolen. We are searching for the **transition point** from 'before' to 'after:'

Figure 3.

Initially, we don't know where the transition point is, but we can binary search for it:

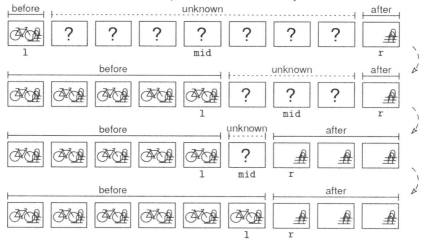

Figure 4.

```
 1   def is_before(val):
 2     return not is_stolen(val)
 3
 4   def find_bike(t1, t2):
 5     l, r = t1, t2
 6     while r - l > 1:
 7       mid = (l + r) // 2
 8       if is_before(mid):
 9         l = mid
10       else:
```

```
11        r = mid
12     return r
```

At the beginning, l is in the 'before' region, and r is in the 'after' region. From there, l never leaves the 'before' region and r never leaves the 'after' region, but they end up next to each other: at the end, l is the last 'before' and r is the first 'after.'

Here is the kicker: **every binary search solution can be reframed as finding a transition point.** For instance, Problem 29.1: Search In Sorted Array can be reframed as finding the "transition point" from elements smaller than `target` to elements greater than or equal to `target`.

If we learn a recipe for finding transition points, we'll be able to use it for every binary search problem. We don't need specialized recipes for various problem types.

TRANSITION-POINT RECIPE

In an important interview—with tensions mounting and anxiety running high—you are not working at total capacity. We joke that you are ~20% dumber than during practice. To counter this, it helps to have a recipe you know well for tricky algorithms like binary search. A good recipe should be easy to remember, have straightforward edge cases, and make it easy to avoid off-by-one errors.

🗐 RECIPE 1. TRANSITION-POINT RECIPE

```
transition_point_recipe()
  define is_before(val) to return whether val is 'before'
  initialize l and r to the first and last values in the range
  handle edge cases:
    - the range is empty
    - l is 'after'  (the whole range is 'after')
    - r is 'before' (the whole range is 'before')
  while l and r are not next to each other (r - l > 1)
    mid = (l + r) / 2
    if is_before(mid)
      l = mid
    else
      r = mid
  return l (the last 'before'), r (the first 'after'), or something else,
         depending on the problem
```

The point of the initialization and the initial edge cases is to get to a setting that looks like the first row of Figure 4: l *must* be in the 'before' region, and r *must* be in the 'after' region. The three edge cases are designed to ensure this.

Once we get to that point, the main `while` loop is *the same for every problem*—no tweaking needed!

The loop has the following **invariants**, which are guarantees that make our lives easier:

- From start to end, l is in the 'before' region, and r is in the 'after' region. They are never equal and never cross over.[3]
- The midpoint is always strictly between l and r (l < mid < r), which guarantees we always make progress (we don't need to worry about infinite loops).
- When we exit the loop, l and r are always next to each other.

---

3 If we were a little more willing to buck conventions, we'd rename from l and r to b and a, since they always map to 'before' and 'after' values. However, you might get odd looks from an interviewer if you do this!

Something that is typically tricky with binary search is the exit condition of the loop. Here, we keep going until l and r are next to each other (i.e., until the 'unknown' region in Figure 4 is empty), which happens when r - l is 1. That's why the condition says r - l > 1.[4]

Another tricky part is knowing what to return. With this recipe, we just need to reason about the transition point: do we need the final 'before' or the first 'after'?

We recommend starting by defining the is_before() function. Keep in mind that, for binary search to work, we must define it in such a way that the search range is *monotonic*: all the 'before' elements must appear before all the 'after' elements. That's why binary search doesn't work on unsorted arrays.

Revisiting Solution 29.1

Here is how we applied the recipe in Solution 29.1: we defined the 'before' region as the elements < target, and the 'after' region as the elements ≥ target.

In the initialization, we have the three edge cases from the recipe to ensure that l is 'before' and r is 'after':

```
1    if n == 0:
2      return -1
3    l, r = 0, n - 1
4    if arr[l] >= target or arr[r] < target:
5      if arr[l] == target:
6        return 0
7      return -1
```

The while loop is just like the recipe, except that we didn't factor out is_before() into a helper function:

```
1    while r - l > 1:
2      mid = (l + r) // 2
3      if arr[mid] < target:
4        l = mid
5      else:
6        r = mid
```

Finally, when we find the transition point, we consider what that means: l is at the largest value smaller than the target, and r is at the smallest value greater than or equal to the target. So, if the target is in the array at all, it must be at index r.

```
1    if arr[r] == target:
2      return r
3    return -1
```

What to do at the end depends on how we define the 'before' region. We could have also defined 'before' as "less than or equal to the target," in which case, at the end, we would have to check the element at l instead of r.

This recipe is a bit like a one-size-fits-all pair of socks. While more concise (but less reusable) implementations may exist for some problems, there is value in needing only one easy-to-remember recipe.

TRANSITION-POINT PROBLEM SET

For each of the following problems:

- **Reframe** it as finding a transition point by defining 'before' and 'after' regions.
- Find the location of l and r after finding the transition point for the given example input.

---

4 We could have also written this in other ways, like r > l + 1. One way to remember the formula for the number of elements between l and r, r-l-1, is that it looks like a sleepy cat.

- Identify what to return after finding the transition point.

You don't need to code anything yet—focus on the transition logic.

QUESTION 1   GIT COMMITS

Find the first commit that fails a test in a sequence of Git commits. We know the test was passing for every commit until it started failing at some point.

```
["pass", "pass", "pass", "pass", "fail", "fail", "fail"]
```

QUESTION 2   SQUARED TARGET

Given a sorted array of positive integers and a target value, find the largest number in the array that can be squared and still be less than or equal to the target, if any. Return the number (not its index).

```
[2, 3, 4, 5, 6, 7, 8, 11, 20, 21, 23, 25, 25], target = 36
```

QUESTION 3   FIRST NON-NEGATIVE

Return the index of the first non-negative integer in a sorted array (duplicates allowed), if any.

```
[-21, -15, -9, -5, -5, -1, -1, 0, 0, 4, 7, 12, 21]
```

4. First 'p':

Find the first word that begins with 'p' in an array of words in dictionary order, if any.

```
["apple", "banana", "peach", "strawberry"]
```

QUESTION 4   NEAREST ELEMENT

In a sorted array of integers (duplicates allowed), find the last occurrence of a given target value. If the target does not exist, return the index of the next closest value (it could be smaller or larger than the target).

```
[1, 3, 5, 6, 7, 7, 8, 11, 13, 21], target = 7
```

QUESTION 5   DECK CUT

You're given an array that contains each number from 1 to 52 once, representing a deck of playing cards. The deck started in order, but it was then "cut," meaning that a random number of cards was taken from the top (the front of the array) and moved as a block to the bottom (the back of the array). Determine the index where you must "cut" the deck again to return to sorted order (that is, the index with the 52).

```
[36, 37, 38, ..., 50, 51, 52, 1, 2, 3, ..., 33, 34, 35]
```

PROBLEM SET SOLUTIONS

In the solutions below, we circled which of the two pointers we should return at the end.

ANSWER 1   GIT COMMITS

```
        before: val == "pass"            after: val == "fail"
  ├──────────────────────────────┤├──────────────────────────┤
["pass", "pass", "pass", "pass", "fail", "fail", "fail"]
                            1        (r)
```

ANSWER 2   SQUARED TARGET

We should return arr[1], since the last number in the 'before' region is the largest number that still works.

```
   before: x² ≤ 36         after: x² > 36
[2, 3, 4, 5, 6, 7, 8, 11, 20, 21, 23, 25, 25]
                  (1) r
```

ANSWER 3   FIRST NON-NEGATIVE

```
         before: x < 0              after: x ≥ 0
[-21, -15, -9, -5, -5, -1, -1, 0, 0, 4, 7, 12, 21]
                           1  (r)
```

Including 0 in the 'before' region would be a mistake: if there are multiple zeros, 1 would point to the last one, but the goal is to return the first one.

First 'p': The 'before' region consists of words that start with a–o and the 'after' region consists of words that start with p–z. If there are words that start with 'p', the first one will be at index r.

```
   before: word[0] < 'p'      after: word[0] ≥ 'p'
["apple", "banana", "peach", "strawberry"]
              1         (r)
```

Including words that start with 'p' in the 'before' region would be incorrect: if we inserted another word starting with 'p,' like "pear," I would point to the last word starting with 'p' rather than the first one.

ANSWER 4   NEAREST ELEMENT

```
      before: x ≤ 7          after: x > 7
[1, 3, 5, 6, 7, 7, 8, 11, 13, 21]
               (1) r
```

Post-processing requires a bit of thought. If the target is in the array, it will be at 1. We can peek at arr[1] and return 1 if it is the target. Otherwise, we need to find the closest value to it, which could be at 1 or r. We return either 1 or r, based on whether arr[1] or arr[r] is closer.

ANSWER 5   DECK CUT

Trick question! This doesn't require binary search as the answer is always 52 - deck[0]. Still, we could find the transition point from 52 back to 1 with a binary search. The 'before' region would be numbers ≥ deck[0]. The 1 pointer would end up at the 52 and the r pointer at the 1. We would return 1.

VALIDATION & DRAWING ADVICE

Visualizing the binary search in an interview is helpful both for you and your interviewer. Instead of trying to verbally explain what you're doing, show them in the shared editor. Our suggestions are similar to the Two Pointers chapter (pg 296):

- Write each pointer (1, r, and m for the midpoint) on its own line so you can move them independently with ease.

- Writing indices on the top of the array makes it faster to do midpoint calculations.
- You can also draw the transition point between 'before' and 'after.'

Instead of   **Try**

```
[1, 2, 2, 3, 3, 4, 5, 8, 8]        0 1 2 3 4 5 6 7 8
 ^           ^           ^         [1 2 2 3 3 4|5 8 8]
left        mid        right       l
                                                   r
                                             m
                                   m = (0+8)/2
```

So, which inputs should you validate and visualize? Consider the following edge cases, when applicable:

- The range is empty.
- The range only has 'before' elements.
- The range only has 'after' elements.
- The target is not in the array.
- The target is in the array multiple times.

ANALYSIS

> But officer, it is O(log n)!

In the Big O analysis chapter, we defined $\log_2(n)$ as roughly the number of times we need to halve a number to reach 1. Binary search halves the search range at each step, so binary search converges in O(`log n`) iterations, where n is the size of the range (e.g., `t2 - t1` in Problem 29.2: CCTV Footage (pg 327).[5]

Some binary search implementations stop early when `arr[mid] == target`. For simplicity, our recipe doesn't have that, which means that it takes O(`log n`) time even in the best case. That's fine—we mainly care about the worst case.

Don't forget to factor in the time it takes to compute `is_before()` in the runtime calculation if it is not constant!

Finally, the extra space is O(`1`). Binary search can also be implemented recursively, in which case the extra space increases to O(`log n`) for the call stack.

BINARY SEARCH PROBLEM SET

✦✦ *Try these problems with AI Interviewer: bctci.co/binary-search-problem-set-1*

Let's tackle some problems that require creative approaches for using binary search. The transition-point recipe should prove useful!

> **PROBLEM 29.3**   **VALLEY BOTTOM**

A *valley-shaped* array is an array of integers such that:

- it can be split into a non-empty prefix and a non-empty suffix,
- the prefix is sorted in decreasing order,
- the suffix is sorted in increasing order,
- all the elements are unique.

---

5   See page 219 for why we "drop" the base of the logarithm in big O notation.

Given a valley-shaped array, arr, return the smallest value.

▸ **Example:** arr = [6, 5, 4, 7, 9]
   Output: 4

▸ **Example:** arr = [5, 6, 7]
   Output: 5. The prefix sorted in decreasing order is just [5].

▸ **Example:** arr = [7, 6, 5]
   Output: 5. The suffix sorted in increasing order is just [5].

PROBLEM 29.4   2-ARRAY 2-SUM

You are given two non-empty arrays of integers, sorted_arr and unsorted_arr. The first one is sorted, but the second is not. The goal is to find one element from each array with sum 0. If you can find them, return an array with their indices, starting with the element in sorted_arr. Otherwise, return [-1, -1]. Use O(1) *extra space* and do not modify the input.

▸ **Example:**   sorted_arr = [-5, -4, -1, 4, 6, 6, 7]
                  unsorted_arr = [-3, 7, 18, 4, 6]
   Output: [1, 3]. We can use -4 from the sorted array and 4 from the
                  unsorted array.

PROBLEM 29.5   TARGET COUNT DIVISIBLE BY K

Given a sorted array of integers, arr, a target value, target, and a positive integer, k, return whether the number of occurrences of the target in the array is a multiple of k.

▸ **Example:**   arr = [1, 2, 2, 2, 2, 2, 2, 3]
                       target = 2, k = 3
   Output: True. 2 occurs 6 times, which is a multiple of 3.

▸ **Example:**   arr = [1, 2, 2, 2, 2, 2, 2, 3]
                       target = 2, k = 4
   Output: False. 2 occurs 6 times, which is not a multiple of 4.

▸ **Example:**   arr = [1, 2, 2, 2, 2, 2, 2, 3]
                       target = 4, k = 3
   Output: True. 4 occurs 0 times, and 0 is a multiple of any number.

PROBLEM 29.6   RACE OVERTAKING

You are given two arrays of positive integers, p1 and p2, representing players in a racing game. The two arrays are sorted, non-empty, and have the same length, n. The i-th element of each array corresponds to where that player was on the track at the i-th second of the race. We know that:

1. player 1 started ahead (p1[0] > p2[0]),
2. player 2 overtook player 1 *once*, and
3. player 2 remained ahead until the end (p1[n - 1] < p2[n - 1]).

Assume the arrays have no duplicates, and that p1[i] != p2[i] for any index.

Return the index at which player 2 overtook player 1.

▸ **Example:**   p1 = [2, 4, 6, 8, 10],
                  p2 = [1, 3, 5, 9, 11]
   Output: 3

PROBLEM 29.7   SEARCH IN SORTED GRID

You're given a 2D grid of integers, grid, where each row is sorted (without duplicates), and the last value in each row is smaller than the first value in the following row. You are also given a target value, target. If the target is in the grid, return an array with its row and column indices. Otherwise, return [-1, -1].

▶ **Example:**   target = 4
```
                grid = [[1, 2, 4, 5],
                        [6, 7, 8, 9]]
```
    Output: [0, 2]. The number 4 is found in row 0 column 2.

▶ **Example:**   target = 3
```
                grid = [[1, 2, 4, 5],
                        [6, 7, 8, 9]]
```
    Output: [-1, -1]

PROBLEM 29.8   SEARCH IN HUGE ARRAY

We are trying to search for a target integer, target, in a sorted array of integers (duplicates allowed) that is too big to fit into memory. We can only access the array through an API, fetch(i), which returns the value at index i if i is within bounds or -1 otherwise. Using as few calls to the API as possible, return the index of the target, or -1 if it does not exist. If the target appears multiple times, return any of the indices. There is no API to get the array's length.

✦ PROBLEM SET SOLUTIONS

SOLUTION 29.3   VALLEY BOTTOM

This problem shows that binary search can be used even if the input array is not monotonically sorted.

Intuitively, we want to define the 'before' region as the descending prefix and the 'after' region as the ascending suffix. The tricky part is that an array like [6, 5, 4, 7, 9] can be formed in two ways:

- With a descending prefix [6, 5, 4] and an ascending suffix [7, 9].
- With a descending prefix [6, 5] and an ascending suffix [4, 7, 9].

We need a clear rule for how to define is_before(). For instance, if we want the 4 to be in the 'before' region, we can say that a number is in the 'before' region if (a) it is the first element, or (b) it's smaller than the previous element.

This definition is workable, but according to it, an array like [7, 6, 5] only contains 'before' elements; we need to check for that case during preprocessing.

The smallest value in the entire array will be either the last 'before' or the first 'after,' so we use binary search to move l and r to those elements and return the minimum of the two.

```
1   def valley_min_index(arr):
2     def is_before(i):
3       return i == 0 or arr[i] < arr[i-1]
4     l, r = 0, len(arr)-1
5     if is_before(r):
6       return arr[r]
7     while r - l > 1:
8       mid = (l + r) // 2
9       if is_before(mid):
10        l = mid
11      else:
```

```
12        r = mid
13    return min(arr[l], arr[r])
```

Interestingly, in the variation of this problem where we allow duplicates in the input, binary search does not work: if mid lands on a value that is the same as the previous one and the next one, we can't tell if we are in the descending prefix or the ascending suffix.[6]

SOLUTION 29.4   2-ARRAY 2-SUM

This problem, which is a variant of the classic 2-sum problem, shows binary search as a building block of a broader algorithm.

Let n1 be the length of the sorted array and n2 the length of the unsorted array. The "only $O(1)$ extra space" constraint means that we can't use a map-based solution, which would take $O(n1)$ or $O(n2)$ space.

Instead, we can iterate through the numbers in the unsorted array and, for each one, binary search for its inverse in the sorted array. The total runtime will be $O(n2 * \log n1)$.

```
1   def two_array_two_sum(sorted_arr, unsorted_arr):
2     for i, val in enumerate(unsorted_arr):
3       idx = binary_search(sorted_arr, -val)
4       if idx != -1:
5         return [idx, i]
6     return [-1, -1]
```

We omit the binary search step because it is the same as Solution 1.

SOLUTION 29.5   TARGET COUNT DIVISIBLE BY K

The key is to find the first *and* last occurrence of the target, first and last. If present, the number of occurrences of the target is last - first + 1. We can check if this number is multiple of k.

If the target is in the array, we can find first and last with a binary search for each:

*   one defining 'before' as '< target' and returning r,
*   one defining 'before' as '< target + 1' and returning l.

The runtime is $O(2*\log n) = O(\log n)$.

SOLUTION 29.6   RACE OVERTAKING

We say an index is 'before' if player 2 has not overtaken player 1 yet. That is:

```
1   def is_before(i):
2     return p1[i] > p2[i]
```

According to the statement, index 0 is 'before' and index n-1 is 'after,' so we don't need to worry about the initial edge cases. We just need to find the transition point and return r.

SOLUTION 29.7   SEARCH IN SORTED GRID

We could solve this problem in two steps:

1. Binary search over the rows to find a single row that may contain the target.
2. Binary search over the row.

---

6   In fact, for this variant, we cannot do better than $O(n)$ time. The array could consist of all 1's and a single 0, which could be anywhere and can only be found with a linear scan.

While this works, a **trick** that makes the implementation easier is to imagine that we "flatten" the grid into a single, long array with all the rows consecutively:

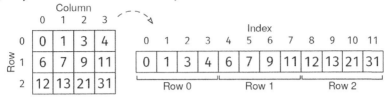

Figure 5.

This would be a sorted array with R*C elements. We can binary search over this 'flattened-grid' array without actually creating it. We'd start with l = 0 and r = R*C - 1. To define the is_before() function, we must map the 'flattened-grid array' index to the actual grid coordinates on the fly:

```
1   def is_before(grid, i, target):
2       num_cols = len(grid[0])
3       row, col = i // num_cols, i % num_cols
4       return grid[row][col] < target
```

Once we find the transition point, we have to map r back to grid coordinates to check if the target is there and return them.

REUSABLE IDEA: GRID FLATTENING

If we want to iterate or search through a grid with dimensions RxC as if it was a 'normal' array of length R*C, we can use the following mapping from grid coordinates to "flattened-grid array" coordinates:

$$[r, c] \rightarrow r * C + c$$

and the reverse mapping to go from "flattened-grid array" coordinates to grid coordinates:

$$i \rightarrow [i // C, i \% C]$$

For instance, cell [1, 2] in Figure 5 (the 9) becomes index 1 * 4 + 2 = 6, and, conversely, index 6 becomes cell [6 // 4, 6 % 4] = [1, 2].

SOLUTION 29.8   SEARCH IN HUGE ARRAY

Leveraging the **break down the problem** booster, we can break the problem into two. One problem is quickly finding the target in a huge array. Binary search is an obvious choice here, but it leads to the second problem: our left pointer can start at zero, but where do we start our right pointer without knowing the length of the array?

A silly way to solve this would be to keep trying one index after another until the API eventually returns -1. Instead, we can double our index at each step. If the length is n, we'll reach it in approximately $\log_2(n)$ steps. The rest of the problem is a straightforward application of the transition-point recipe.

```
1   def find_through_api(target):
2       def is_before(idx):
3           return fetch(idx) < target
4       l, r = 0, 1
5       # Step 1: Get the rightmost boundary
6       while fetch(r) != -1:
7           r *= 2
8       # Step 2: Binary search
9       # ...
```

The total runtime is $O(\log n)$, where n is the size of the huge array.

 REUSABLE IDEA: EXPONENTIAL SEARCH

Whenever we need to search for a value in a range, but the upper bound (or even lower bound) of the range is unknown, we can find it efficiently with repeated doubling.

This is often useful in the guess-and-check technique (e.g., Problem 29.10: Water Refilling, pg 340).

GUESS-AND-CHECK TECHNIQUE

Since I was unable to come up with any approach, I
knew the solution was going to be Binary Search.

Anonymous Leetcode User, 2023

As the stolen bike story illustrates, binary search is often used in problems where it is not an obvious choice. Now that we have a solid recipe for any binary search problem, we will discuss the **guess-and-check** technique, which allows us to use binary search on many optimization problems.

Recall that an optimization problem is one where you are asked to find some minimum or maximum value, subject to some constraint. For example, consider the following problem:

✦⁑ **PROBLEM 29.9**   **MIN-SUBARRAY-SUM SPLIT**

Given a non-empty array with n positive integers, arr, and a number k with $1 \le k \le n$, the goal is to split arr into k non-empty subarrays so that the largest sum across all subarrays is minimized. Return the largest sum across all k subarrays after making it as small as possible. Each subarray must contain at least one value.

▶ **Example:** arr = [10, 5, 8, 9, 11], k = 3
  Output: 17. There are six ways of splitting the array into three subarrays.
        The optimal split is: [10, 5], [8, 9], and [11]. The largest sum
        among the three subarrays is 17.

▶ **Example:** arr = [10, 10, 10, 10, 10], k = 2
  Output: 30.

SOLUTION 29.9   MIN-SUBARRAY-SUM SPLIT

This is an optimization problem because we have a goal and a constraint: we are trying to minimize the largest subarray sum, subject to having at most k subarrays. Without the constraint, we would just put every element in its own subarray.

A naive solution that tries every way of splitting the array into k subarrays would take exponential time.[7] There is a dynamic programming solution that takes $O(n*k)$ time (pg 574).

Here, we'll use a different approach. Given a value, max_sum, we can ask:

Is there a way to split arr into k subarrays such that every subarray has sum at most max_sum?

• For max_sum < max(arr), the answer is "no" (some numbers are too big to be in a subarray, even by themselves).

---

7 You need to choose k out of n-1 possible splitting points, so there are (n-1 choose k) options, which is $O((n-1)^k)$ = $O(n^k)$ for any constant value of k. If k is n/2, the number becomes exponential on n ($O(2^n/\sqrt{n})$ to be exact, but you don't need to worry about where that formula comes from). Once k gets larger than n/2, the number of possibilities starts decreases (if we are picking more than half the points, we can think about picking the points **not** to split at, of which there are fewer than n/2).

- For `max_sum == sum(arr)`, the answer is "yes" (any split will do).

We can **binary search** for the transition point where the answer goes from "no" to "yes" with our **transition point recipe**. The value x corresponding to the first "yes" is the *value* of the optimal solution.

To implement our `is_before(max_sum)` function, we need to be able to compute the answer to the question. Thankfully, it is much easier than the original problem: we can grow each subarray up until the point where its sum would exceed `max_sum`. At that point, we start a new subarray, and so on. If we need more than k subarrays, the answer is "no." Otherwise, the answer is "yes."

```
# "Is it impossible to split arr into k subarrays, each with sum <= max_sum?"
10  def is_before(arr, k, max_sum):
11    splits_required = get_splits_required(arr, max_sum)
12    return splits_required > k
13  # Returns the minimum number of subarrays with a given maximum sum.
14  # Assumes that max_sum >= max(arr).
1   def get_splits_required(arr, max_sum):
2     splits_required = 1
3     current_sum = 0
4     for num in arr:
5       if current_sum + num > max_sum:
6         splits_required += 1
7         current_sum = num  # Start a new subarray with the current number.
8       else:
9         current_sum += num
10    return splits_required
11
12  def min_subarray_sum_split(arr, k):
13    l, r = max(arr), sum(arr)  # Range for the maximum subarray sum.
14    if not is_before(arr, k, l):
15      return l
16    while r - l > 1:
17      mid = (l + r) // 2
18      if is_before(arr, k, mid):
19        l = mid
20      else:
21        r = mid
22    return r
```

Let S be the sum of `arr`. Binary search will take $O(\log S)$ steps to converge, and each `is_before()` check takes $O(n)$ time. The total runtime is $O(n \log S)$. Depending on whether $O(k)$ or $O(\log S)$ is larger, DP or binary search will be better. Neither dominates the other.

To recap, the **guess-and-check technique** involves narrowing in on the value of the optimal solution by **guessing** the midpoint and **checking** whether it's too high or too low. To start, we need lower and upper bounds for the value of the optimal solution (if the bounds are not obvious, exponential search can help).

For minimization problems (like Problem 29.9: Min-Subarray-Sum Split), there is often a transition point where smaller values do not satisfy the constraint, but larger values do. Conversely, for maximization problems, there is often a transition point where larger values do not satisfy the constraint, but smaller values do.

When should I use the guess-and-check technique?

We can try it when we have an optimization problem and finding the optimal value directly is challenging. Ask yourself:

"Is it easier to solve the yes/no version of the problem, where we just check if a given value (optimal or not) satisfies the constraint?"

Think of it like making a deal: You get to solve an easier problem (checking if a specific value satisfies the constraint), but you pay a 'logarithmic tax' in the runtime (to binary searching for the transition point).

We've seen the guess-and-check technique before, in the Boundary Thinking chapter with Problem 22.1: Tunnel Depth (pg 231). It is easier to binary search for the first depth where the tunnel doesn't reach than to try to compute the maximum depth directly.

▶ **BOUNDARY THINKING IN ACTION**[8]	INTERVIEW REPLAY

View Online:	bctci.co/binary-search-replay-1 @ 38:55 - end
The Question:	Return the maximum tunnel depth in a grid.
What You'll See:	The candidate chose a graph traversal after seeing the grid, and the interviewer and candidate discussed multiple solutions and how to avoid getting "tunnel" vision.
Who:	*Interviewer*: Software Engineer at Google *Candidate*: 7 years exp.

GUESS-AND-CHECK PROBLEM SET

✦ *Try these problems with AI Interviewer: bctci.co/binary-search-problem-set-2*

PROBLEM 29.10 **WATER REFILLING**

We have an empty container with a capacity of a gallons of water and another container with a capacity of b gallons. Return how many times you can pour the second container full of water into the first one without overflowing. Assume that a > b.

- Constraint: You are not allowed to use the division operation, but you can use still divide by powers of two with the right-shift operator, >>. Recall that x >> 1 is the same as x // 2.

▶ **Example:** a = 18, b = 5
  Output: 3. After pouring 5 gallons three times, the first container will be
            at 15, and 5 more gallons would make it overflow.

PROBLEM 29.11 **MIN PAGES PER DAY**

You have upcoming interviews and have selected specific chapters from BCtCI to read beforehand. Given an array, page_counts, where each element represents a chapter's page count, and the number of days, days, until your interview, determine the minimum number of pages you must read daily to finish on time. Assume that:

- You must read all the pages of a chapter before moving on to another one.[9]

---

8 I (Mike) am the interviewer in this particular interview. This question was the opener for the Boundary Thinking chapter and you can see a candidate make the same mistakes we discuss in that chapter and me walking through the boundary thinking mentality.

9 Hypothetically! It's fine to jump around chapters when reading *this actual book*.

- If you finish a chapter on a given day, you practice for the rest of the day and don't start the next chapter until the next day.
- len(page_counts) ≤ days.

▸ **Example:** page_counts = [20, 15, 17, 10], days = 14
  Output: 5. We can read 5 pages daily and finish all chapters. At a maximum
            of 5 pages per day, we spend:
               4 days on the first chapter.
               3 days on the second chapter.
               4 days on the third chapter (stopping when we finish early).
               2 days on the fourth chapter.
               In total, we spent 13 days reading 5 pages a day, which is the
               lowest amount we can read daily and still finish on time.

▸ **Example:** page_counts = [20, 15, 17, 10], days = 5
  Output: 17

PROBLEM 29.12   **TIDE AERIAL VIEW**

You are provided a series of aerial-view pictures of the same coastal region, taken a few minutes apart from each other around the time the tide rises. Each picture consists of an nxn binary grid, where 0 represents a part of the region above water, and 1 represents a part below water.

- The tide appears from the left side and rises toward the right, so, in each picture, for each row, all the 1's will be before all the 0's.
- Once a region is under water, it stays under water.

Determine which picture shows the most even balance between regions above and below water (i.e., where the number of 1's most closely equals the number of 0's). In the event of a tie, return the earliest picture.

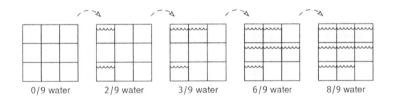

| 0/9 water | 2/9 water | 3/9 water | 6/9 water | 8/9 water |

Figure 6. Example input for Problem 9. The empty cells are 0's and the cells with water are 1's.

▸ **Example:** The pictures from Figure 6.
  Output: 2. The pictures at index 2 and 3 are equally far from having 50%
            water. We break the tie by picking the earlier one, 2.

✦ PROBLEM SET SOLUTIONS

SOLUTION 29.10   WATER REFILLING

Try to solve this problem manually for a = 182983 and b = 90. Use a calculator if you want, just do not use the division operation. Done? How did you do it? Try to *REVERSE-ENGINEER* your process and map it to an algorithmic technique.

What you *definitely* didn't do is check sequential multiples of 90 until you reached 182983. Most people make guesses in increasingly larger jumps until they find a guess that is too large. If we double the guess at each time, this is *exponential search* (pg 338). Then, they start searching between their closest guess below and above the answer, closing in on the number—something we can do with binary search. Despite the problem not having clear triggers for binary search, it's a natural fit for this thought process.

```
1   def num_refills(a, b):
2     # "Can we pour 'num_pours' times?"
3     def is_before(num_pours):
4       return num_pours * b <= a
5
6     # Exponential search (repeated doubling until we find an upper bound).
7     k = 1
8     while is_before(k * 2):
9       k *= 2
10
11    # Binary search between k and k*2
12    l, r = k, k * 2
13    while r-l > 1:
14      gap = r - l
15      half_gap = gap >> 1  # Bit shift instead of division
16      mid = l + half_gap
17      if is_before(mid):
18        l = mid
19      else:
20        r = mid
21    return l
```

SOLUTION 29.11   MIN PAGES PER DAY

For a given value `daily_limit`, we pose the question:

> Can I finish all the chapters in time reading at most `daily_limit` pages a day?

We can **guess and check** for the answer to this question.

Since we can only finish one chapter per day, the maximum answer is the longest chapter (20 pages in the example). The minimum is 1 page per day. We can binary search between these bounds and simulate reading the guessed amount of pages per day. If the guess allows us to finish within the given days, we try a smaller number. If it takes too many days, we try a larger number.

```
1   def days_to_finish(page_counts, daily_limit):
2     days = 0
3     for pages in page_counts:
4       days += math.ceil(pages / daily_limit)
5     return days
6
7   def is_before(page_counts, daily_limit, days):
8     return days_to_finish(page_counts, daily_limit) <= days
```

SOLUTION 29.12   TIDE AERIAL VIEW

We can binary search for the transition point where it goes from majority above water to majority underwater. The 'before' pictures are < 0.5 water, and the 'after' pictures are ≥ 0.5 water. The answer will be the last 'before' or the first 'after'.

However, if you constructed the `is_before()` function to just loop through the matrix, counting the number of cells underwater, you missed something! Besides doing a binary search across the range of pictures, we can speed up the count of underwater cells by *also* doing a binary search on each row: the rows are monotonic, with all 1's followed by all 0's.

```
1  def get_ones_in_row(arr, row):        1  def is_before(picture):
2    def is_before_row(v):               2    water = 0
3      return row[v] == 0                 3    for row in picture:
4    l, r = 0, len(row)                   4      water += get_ones_in_row(row)
5    while r - l > 1:                     5    total = len(pictures[0])**2
6      mid = (l + r) // 2                 6    return water/total < 0.5
7      if is_before_row(mid):
8        l = mid
9      else:
10       r = mid
11   return l
```

Checking the number of ones in a row takes O(log n) time. Checking the number of ones in an entire grid takes O(n log n) time. The total time is O(n log n log k), where k is the number of pictures.

BINARY SEARCH GONE WRONG		INTERVIEW REPLAY
View Online:	bctci.co/binary-search-replay-2 @ 2:45 - 26:07:00	
The Question:	Write an algorithm to compute the square root of a given non-negative number	
What You'll See:	The candidate struggled to implement a working version of binary search, and each change led to further problems with the algorithm.	
Who:	*Interviewer*: Software Engineer at Meta *Candidate*: 7 years exp.	

CONCLUSIONS

Binary Search triggers: The input is a sorted array/string. The brute force involves repeated linear scans. We are given an optimization problem that's hard to optimize directly.

Keywords: sorted, threshold, range, boundary, find, search, minimum/maximum, first/last, smallest/largest.

Binary search is often a step or a possible optimization in more complicated algorithms. Binary search is so common that it can (and will) be seen alongside almost every other Catalog topic, like Graphs (Problem 36.9: First Time All Connected, pg 469), Sliding Windows (Chapter 38: Longest Repeated Substring, pg 525), and Greedy Algorithms (Problem 41.6: Time Traveler Max Year, pg 595).

The key idea in this chapter is that we can reframe every binary search problem as finding a transition point. This way, we only need one recipe for every scenario—the transition-point recipe (pg 329)—and we can focus our energy on more complicated parts of the code.

At this point, you should be ready to start adding binary search problems to your practice rotation. You can find the problems in this chapter and additional problems in the companion AI interviewer.

ONLINE RESOURCES

Online resources for this chapter include:

- A chance to try each problem in this chapter in AI Interviewer
- Interview replays that show specific mistakes people make with binary search problems
- Full code solutions for every problem in the chapter in multiple programming languages

Try online at bctci.co/binary-search.

## CHAPTER 30

SETS & MAPS

AI interviewer, replays, and more materials for this chapter at bctci.co/sets-and-maps

> If you can copy-paste and use hash maps, you can
> solve any problem in computer science.
>
> Albert Einstein(ish)

▶ *Prerequisites: None*

Alright, you caught us. Einstein didn't say this, but there is a lot of truth to it. Hash sets and hash maps have many applications that are likely to be useful in your interviews, often as key pieces in broader algorithms. In this chapter, we will learn to recognize the many ways they can be used.

We can define these data structures as follows:

- A *set* data structure is a collection of elements with *no duplicates and no order.* That is, the sets {1, 3, 5} and {5, 1, 3} are equivalent, and {1, 3, 3, 5} is not a valid set at all.

- A *map*—also called a *dictionary*—is like a set where each element is called a *key* and has an associated *value*. For instance, {"aa": 1, "bb": 3, "aabb": 1} is a map with string keys, integer values, and three key–value pairs. Unlike keys, values can be repeated.

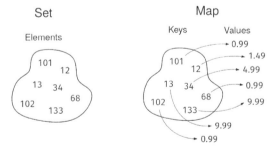

Figure 1. Example of a set and a map. The map *keys* could represent unique product IDs in a grocery store, and the map *values* could be their prices (more than one product may have the same price).

Sets and maps are *abstract data types.* They are concepts with defined behaviors, not a specific implementation. The most popular implementation, hash sets and hash maps, are based on *hash tables*, which we show how to build from scratch in the online-only chapter bctci.co/set-and-map-implementations.

The strength of hash sets and hash maps comes from their excellent asymptotic runtimes:

O(1) (WORST-CASE) SET AND MAP OPERATIONS				
Hash Sets	add(x)	remove(x)	contains(x)		size()
Hash Maps	add(k, v)	remove(k)	contains(x)	get(k)	size()

Table 1. Set and map operations, all with O(1) worst-case runtimes.

However, it is important to remember the caveats (see bctci.co/set-and-map-implementations for details):

- The runtimes for add() and remove() are **amortized** because of the dynamic resizing technique, which can make a single add() or remove() slow from time to time.

- All the runtimes, except size(), are **expected runtimes**, and that's assuming we are using a good hash function.

- A common mistake is forgetting that hashing a string takes time proportional to its length, so hash set and hash map operations do *not* take constant time for strings (unless the strings have a fixed maximum length).

In this chapter, we'll just say 'set' and 'map' instead of 'hash set' and 'hash map' since those are their most common implementations. There's also a tree-based implementation we'll mention on page 455.

COMMON TECHNIQUES

THE LINEAR SCAN TRADEOFF

The most common reason for using a set or map in interviews is to get constant-time lookups, thereby avoiding repeated linear scans over an array. This falls under the *PREPROCESSING PATTERN* we discussed in the Problem-Solving Boosters chapter (pg 248): we pay an upfront cost of O(n) time and space to build the map, and we unlock O(1)-time lookups. It often comes down to a tradeoff between time and space (linear scans are slower but only use O(1) space).

To spot when to use the linear scan tradeoff, look for nested loops in the brute force solution. Consider the following question:

✦✦ **PROBLEM 30.1**   **ACCOUNT SHARING DETECTION**

You've compiled a list of IP addresses of all the clients connected to your service and the username associated with each one. Assume all IPs are unique and username lengths are between 1 and 30. We say a username is being shared if it appears in two connections. If usernames are being shared, return an IP of any of them. Otherwise, return an empty string.

▸ **Example:** connections = [("203.0.113.10", "mike"), ("298.51.100.25", "bob"), ("292.0.2.5", "mike"), ("203.0.113.15", "bob2")]
   Output: "203.0.113.10". User "mike" is connected from that IP and "292.0.2.5", so "292.0.2.5" would also be a valid output.

▸ **Example:** connections = [("111.0.0.0", "mike"), ("111.0.0.1", "mike"), ("111.0.0.2", "bob"), ("111.0.0.3", "bob")]
   Output: "111.0.0.0". Any of the IPs would be a valid output, because all the IPs are being used by an account-sharing user.

   Example: connections = [("111.0.0.0", "mike"), ("111.0.0.1", "mike2"), ("111.0.0.2", "mike3"), ("111.0.0.3", "mike4")]
   Output: "". No usernames are shared.

SOLUTION 30.1   ACCOUNT SHARING DETECTION

The naive solution loops over every pair of IPs in a nested loop to check for repeated usernames:

```
for i in range(len(connections)):
  for j in range(i+1, len(connections)):
    ...
```

By controlling where we start the inner loop, we can avoid accessing each pair twice, but the time complexity is still quadratic. This is the perfect opportunity for the linear scan tradeoff:

```
1   def account_sharing(connections):
2     seen = set()
3     for ip, username in connections:
4       if username in seen:
5         return ip
6       seen.add(username)
7     return ""
```

This improves the runtime from $O(n^2)$ to $O(n)$ but worsens the extra space from $O(1)$ to $O(n)$.

\#   Interview Tip: When using a hash map in an interview, consider whether you can accomplish the same task with a set instead. In particular, when you have a map where the value is a boolean, you can typically use a set instead.[1] This does not affect the asymptotic analysis, but it is "more fitting" because there is no need for key–value pairs. Data from interviewing.io suggests candidates commonly get marked down for *not* doing this.

If the problem only asked us to return whether any account sharing is happening instead of finding the user doing it, we could have also solved it by creating a set with all the usernames and comparing the set size to the original size.

```
1   def account_sharing(connections):
2     usernames = set()
3     for _, username in connections:
4       usernames.add(username)
5     return len(usernames) == len(connections)
```

This works because adding a duplicate to a set has no effect. In the end, the set size will differ from the input size only if a duplicate username exists.

\#   If we add all the elements of an array into a set, the difference between their sizes is the number of duplicates in the array.

The linear scan tradeoff doesn't apply if the array is already sorted, because we can use binary search. In such cases, the tradeoff is between $O(\log n)$ time for binary search and $O(1)$ lookup time for sets/maps. Which one to use depends on the situation, but a binary search should be considered if (1) we care about the order, (2) duplicates are important, or (3) the input array is already sorted and we want to avoid using $O(n)$ time and space to build a set or map.

FREQUENCY MAPS

A set allows us to check whether something exists or not, but sometimes, we need to count how many times something appears. For this, we can use a *frequency map*, where we use a map to associate a count with each element. For example:

---

1   Go is an exception—it encourages using maps with boolean values because it does not provide a built-in set.

✦ **PROBLEM 30.2**   **MOST SHARED ACCOUNT**

You've compiled a list of IP addresses of all the clients connected to your service and the username associated with each one. Assume all IPs are unique and username lengths are between 1 and 30. We say a username is being shared if it appears in two (or more) connections. Return the most shared username. In case of a tie, return any of them.

▶ **Example:** `connections = [("203.0.113.10", "mike"), ("208.51.100.25", "bob"), ("202.0.2.5", "mike"), ("203.0.113.15", "bob2")]`

  Output: `"mike"`. User `"mike"` is connected twice, while other users are connected once.

SOLUTION 30.2   MOST SHARED ACCOUNT

We can use a map with usernames as keys and the number of IPs as values.

```
1   def most_shared_account(connections):
2     user_to_count = dict()
3     for _, user in connections:
4       if not user in user_to_count:
5         user_to_count[user] = 0
6       user_to_count[user] += 1
7     most_shared_user = None
8     for user, count in user_to_count.items():
9       if not most_shared_user or count > user_to_count[most_shared_user]:
10        most_shared_user = user
11    return most_shared_user
```

> To code fluently during your interview, make sure you know the most effective way to (a) iterate through the keys, (b) iterate through the values, and (c) iterate through the (key, value) pairs of a map in your language of choice.
>
> For instance, in Python, we can use `.items()` to iterate through (key, value) pairs.

We could also solve the problem in a single pass, keeping track of the most shared username as we add items to the frequency map. This results in less code, but it doesn't change the runtime or space complexity.[2]

 REUSABLE IDEA: FREQUENCY MAPS

> A *frequency map* is a map from elements to counts. It can be initialized in O(n) time and is useful in questions about duplicate detection, counting, and most frequent elements.

Optimizing the Set Away

Consider this variation of Problem 30.2: Most Shared Account:

✦ **PROBLEM 30.3**   **MOST FREQUENT OCTET**

You've compiled a list of IP addresses of all the clients connected to your service. Assume all IPs are unique and follow the IPv4 format, which consists of four 8-bit numbers (called octets) separated by dots. Return the most common first octet among the connections.

---

2 It's common for candidates to argue that doing this in a single pass will be fewer operations than two passes. It's not that simple. When we do it in a single pass, we're doing *more work* in that pass. In fact, it might even be (imperceptibly) slower because we're doing the max check on every IP address in `connections` rather than every *unique* IP address.

▶ **Example:** ips = ["203.0.113.10", "208.51.100.5", "202.0.2.5", "203.0.113.5"]
  Output: "203". 203 appears twice as the first octet.

SOLUTION 30.3   MOST FREQUENT OCTET

Coding-wise, nothing new here: this problem can be solved with a frequency map just like Problem 30.2: Most Shared Account (pg 348), but with the first octets of the IPs as keys. Where interviewees go wrong with this question is in the space analysis: many interviewees incorrectly say the extra space is O(n) because we add n elements to a hash map.

The size of a set/map is bounded by the number of *unique* keys we add, not the number of additions. In this case, there are only 256 8-bit numbers, so the extra space complexity is O(256) = O(1).

We could even use a fixed-size 256-element array and store the frequency of each octet in the corresponding index in the array. If n is large, that could improve the constant factors since we wouldn't need to do any hashing. However, it doesn't change the asymptotic analysis.

REUSABLE IDEA: LEVERAGE THE INPUT RANGE

> When the input range is small, leveraging it can lead to significantly more efficient solutions. For instance, when it comes to sorting, we may be able to use specialized algorithms like counting sort (pg 363). Similarly, the **difference array technique** in Prefix Sums (pg 624) works well for interval problems when the maximum value in the range is constrained—like 24 to represent the hours in a day.

COMMON BUGS AND MISCONCEPTIONS

Even if you understand the theory of hash sets and hash maps (we cover it in detail in bctci.co/set-and-map-implementations), there are a few 'gotchas' that trip people up when using them—especially if you switch languages just for interviews, as they can be language-dependant.

For this section, we strongly recommend opening an editor and creating a set/map with some mock data to test the behaviors.

The iteration order may not be deterministic

Most languages offer a way to iterate through all the elements in a set/map, but the order is usually not the insertion order. This is language-specific, but the iteration order is usually based on how elements are hashed (i.e., something close to random). In fact, the order may change just by adding/removing elements (because the hash table may need to be resized, changing the hashes of the elements—see bctci.co/set-and-map-implementations, Putting it All Together section). Even without changing the code at all, the iteration order may change between runs of the same program (hashing often involves randomness, and the random seed may change between runs).

Don't rely on the iteration order of a set/map unless your language of choice makes guarantees about it.[3]

A set or map cannot be updated while iterating through it

If you try to update a set/map while iterating through it, depending on the language, you could get an error or unexpected behavior.[4] Imagine we have a map from names to ages, and we want to delete every entry with age < 18. *Don't do this* (except to see what happens):

```
1   # DON'T DO THIS
```

---

3 C++ and Java make no guarantees. Starting from Python 3.7, Python guarantees that set/map iteration order matches insertion order. If you rely on this fact in an interview, mention it to the interviewer, as they may not be aware.

4 JavaScript handles this well: you can safely iterate over a set while deleting elements.

```
2    for name in names_to_ages:
3      if names_to_ages[name] < 18:
4        del names_to_ages[name]
```

As a workaround, we can save the keys to delete in a list first, and then iterate through the list while deleting from the map.

```
1    underage = []
2    for name in names_to_ages:
3      if names_to_ages[name] < 18:
4        underage.add(name)
5    for name in underage:
6      del names_to_ages[name]
```

Set and map keys cannot be modified

Some languages, like Python, won't let you use a variable with a *mutable* type, like an array, as keys in a set. See what happens if you try to have a map like sum_map = {[1, 2, 3]: 6}—you should get an error. Other languages will let you, but if you modify a variable that has been inserted as a key in a map, you may get unpredictable (i.e., buggy) results. For instance, if you

1. have a variable arr with value [1, 2, 3],

2. add it to a set s,

3. update arr[2] to 4, and

4. check if [1, 2, 4] is in s, you may get that it is not.

The problem is that if a set element changes, its hash also changes, but the element doesn't automatically move to the correct location in the hash table. If we attempt to look up the newly edited element ([1, 2, 4]), the hash set would check the position based on the new hash and miss it.

Since arrays are so common, this creates a problem for languages like Python: how do you use arrays as set/map keys if you need to? It's language-specific. In Python, there are a few ways: you can use a *tuple* instead of a list (with tuple(arr)), which is immutable, or you can serialize the array into a string (with ','.join(arr)), which is also immutable.

In contrast, modifying map *values* is generally fine since those are not hashed.

✦✧ **PROBLEM 30.4**   **MULTI-ACCOUNT CHEATING**

Our company runs an online game where the terms of service state that each person can only have one account. We have a list of usernames and the (unordered) list of IP addresses that they have ever connected from. We say two users are suspected of belonging to the same person if the list of IPs is the same. Return whether any two lists contain the exact same set of IPs. Assume that usernames are non-empty and each list has between 1 and 10 IPs.

▸ **Example:** users = [("mike", ["203.0.3.10", "208.51.0.5", "52.0.2.5"]),
               ("bob", ["111.0.0.10", "222.0.0.5", "222.0.0.8"]),
               ("bob2", ["222.0.0.5", "222.0.0.8", "111.0.0.10"])]
   Output: True. Users "bob" and "bob2" have the same IPs.

SOLUTION 30.4   MULTI-ACCOUNT CHEATING

Conceptually, we want to look for duplicates in the lists of IPs. However, arrays are mutable, so we can't use them as set elements in Python. We need to transform them into an immutable type first.

The lists could contain the same IPs but in a different order, so we sort them before transforming them into tuples. The sorted version of each list is like a *canonical representation* shared by all the lists with the same elements.[5]

```
1  def multi_account_cheating(users):
2    unique_lists = set()
3    for _, ips in users:
4      immutable_list = tuple(sorted(ips))
5      if immutable_list in unique_lists:
6        return True
7      unique_lists.add(immutable_list)
8    return False
```

REUSABLE IDEA: IMPOSE A CANONICAL ORDER

> If a problem deals with arrays and we want to treat two arrays as the same when they have the same elements regardless of the order (like [1, 2] and [2, 1]), we can sort them and compare (or hash) their sorted versions rather than comparing them directly.

Learn how to use arrays as set/map keys in your language of choice. If your language allows it, remember not to modify the elements of arrays that are set/map keys.

Not all types are hashable

We already saw that languages like Python don't allow mutable types as set/map keys. Sometimes, you may want to use some user-defined type as keys. This introduces a practical consideration: *your programming language needs to know how to hash the keys.* Most programming languages come with built-in methods for hashing common types like numbers and strings, but that doesn't work for custom types.

> *Learn how to use custom types as set/map keys in your language of choice.*
>
> For instance, in Python, you need to add __hash__() and __eq__() methods to a class to make it hashable. If the class consists of basic fields that Python already knows how to hash, the easiest way to implement __hash__() is to return the hash of a tuple of those elements. E.g.:
>
> ```
> 1  def named_point(self, x, y, name):
> 2    ...
> 3    def __hash__(self):
> 4      return hash((self.x, self.y, self.name))
> 5    ...
> ```
>
> Remember not to modify objects being used as keys.

If you need nearest-element searches...

As established, checking whether a hash set contains a number takes $O(1)$ time. If the number is missing, we may (incorrectly) think that hash sets are also useful for finding the nearest number to it (just like how binary search supports this type of "nearest-value searches," pg 331). That is not the case. In fact, "nearest-value search" is an *anti-trigger* for hash sets and maps. That is because of the nature of hash functions: two consecutive integers like 17 and 18 could end up in buckets very far apart (see bctci.co/set-and-map-implementations, Hash Functions section, for details).

---

5 In Python, we could have also used the built-in frozenset, which is an immutable version of a set, similarly to how a tuple is an immutable version of a list.

We are talking specifically about *hash-based* sets and maps. There are tree-based implementations of sets and maps, sometimes known as `TreeSet` and `TreeMap`, that **support nearest-value search**.[6] So, *if* we need nearest-key searches, we should consider those. The tradeoff is that all operations take $O(\log n)$ time instead of $O(1)$.

Since nearest-key searches are uncommon, hash-based sets and maps are usually used by default. In fact, some languages, like Python, do not have built-in tree-based sets and maps. So, if you need one, you can (1) use sorting and binary search if the data is static, or (2) ask the interviewer if you may assume that there is a TreeSet/TreeMap library.

APPLICATIONS

CHOOSING KEYS AND VALUES

To use a map in an algorithm, sometimes the hard part is identifying what to use as keys and values. We might need to create the keys and/or values ourselves by transforming the input or doing some computation (like imposing a canonical order, as we did in Solution 30.4: Multi-Account Cheating).

A common mistake interviewees make is using the wrong value type in a map. We'll see how that could happen with the following problem:

✦✦ **PROBLEM 30.5**   **DOMAIN RESOLVER**

You manage a shared web hosting server with multiple IP addresses, and where multiple domains can share the same IP address. Each domain can have multiple subdomains. Implement a class, `DomainResolver`, that supports three methods:

- `register_domain(ip, domain)`: associates a domain with an IP. You can assume that this function will be called at most once for a given domain.
- `register_subdomain(domain, subdomain)`: adds a subdomain to a domain. You can assume that the domain will have been previously registered. Different domains can have a subdomain with the same name.
- `has_subdomain(ip, domain, subdomain)`: returns whether there is a domain registered at that IP that has the given subdomain.

IPs, domains, and subdomains are strings.

▸ Example:

```
resolver = DomainResolver()
resolver.register_domain("192.168.1.1", "example.com")
resolver.register_domain("192.168.1.1", "example.org")
resolver.register_domain("192.168.1.2", "domain.com")
resolver.register_subdomain("example.com", "a")
resolver.register_subdomain("example.com", "b")
resolver.has_subdomain("192.168.1.1", "example.com", "a")  # Returns True
resolver.has_subdomain("192.168.1.1", "example.com", "c")  # Returns False
resolver.has_subdomain("127.0.0.1", "example.com", "a")    # Returns False
resolver.has_subdomain("192.168.1.1", "example.org", "a")  # Returns False
```

---

6   The most wellknown tree-based set and map implementations are AVL trees and red-black trees. They are tricky to implement, so that is generally not expected in coding interviews. Read more about them on page 449.

SOLUTION 30.5   DOMAIN RESOLVER

Interviewees can usually correctly identify that they should use a hash map with IPs as keys. However, for the value type, they may use an array of domains. This works, but can devolve into slow linear scans when an IP has many domains. An optimal solution stores the domains for each IP in a set. The same applies to subdomains.

```python
 1  class DomainResolver:
 2    def __init__(self):
 3      self.ip_to_domains = dict()
 4      self.domain_to_subdomains = dict()
 5
 6    def register_domain(self, ip, domain):
 7      if ip not in self.ip_to_domains:
 8        self.ip_to_domains[ip] = set()
 9      self.ip_to_domains[ip].add(domain)
10
11    def register_subdomain(self, domain, subdomain):
12      if domain not in self.domain_to_subdomains:
13        self.domain_to_subdomains[domain] = set()
14      self.domain_to_subdomains[domain].add(subdomain)
15
16    def has_subdomain(self, ip, domain, subdomain):
17      if ip not in self.ip_to_domains:
18        return False
19      if domain not in self.domain_to_subdomains:
20        return False
21      return subdomain in self.domain_to_subdomains[domain]
```

Interview Tip: Communicating the contents of your data structure clearly in an interview is crucial to avoid losing your interviewer and wasting time. When describing a map you plan to use in your algorithm, always sketch a quick example of the key and value.

For instance, in Solution 5, we could sketch the `ip_to_domains` map as follows:

> {
>
>   192.168.1.1: {example.com, example.org}
>
>   192.168.1.2: {domain.com}
>
> }

SETS AND MAPS PROBLEM SET

✦ *Try these problems with AI Interviewer: bctci.co/sets-and-maps-problem-set-1*

PROBLEM 30.6   **FIND ALL SQUARES**

Given an array of unique, positive integers, `arr`, return a list with all pairs of indices, `[i, j]`, such that `arr[i] == arr[j]`^{2}. You can return the pairs in any order.

▸ **Example:** arr = [4, 10, 3, 100, 5, 2, 10000]

> Output: [[5, 0], [1, 3], [3, 6]]. The 3 pairs of values that satisfy the
> constraint are (2, 4), (10, 100), and (100, 10000). We return [5,
> 0] because arr[5] is 2 and arr[0] is 4, and similarly for the other
> two pairs. Other orders like [[1, 3], [0, 5], [3, 6]] would also be
> valid.

▸ **Example:** arr = [1]
  Output: [[0, 0]]. 1 squared is 1.

PROBLEM 30.7   **WORD EXPANSION CLASS**

Implement a class, Checker, that receives a string s upon initialization. The class must support a method,
expands_into(s2), which takes another string and checks if s2 can be formed by adding exactly one letter
to s1 and reordering the letters. All letters in both strings are lowercase alphabetical characters.

▸ **Example:** checker = Checker("tea")
```
print(checker.expands_into("tea"))  # returns False
print(checker.expands_into("team")) # returns True
print(checker.expands_into("seam")) # returns False
```

▸ **Example:** checker = Checker("on")
```
print(checker.expands_into("nooo"))  # returns False
print(checker.expands_into("not"))   # returns True
print(checker.expands_into("now"))   # returns True
```

PROBLEM 30.8   **CHEATER DETECTION**

You are given an array, answers, with the answers of a multi-choice test. The list has k characters ('a', 'b',
'c', or 'd'), where k is the number of questions in the exam.

You are also given m, the number of desks per row in the classroom where the exam took place.

You are also given an array, students, of students' answers for the test. Each entry is a tuple [student_id,
desk, answers], where:

• Student IDs are unique positive integers.

• Desks are unique positive integers. Desks are arranged in rows of m desks, starting with desks 1 to m in
  the first row, m+1 to 2m in the second row, and so on. Not all desks may be occupied. E.g., there may be
  a student at desk 2 but none at desk 1.

• For each student, answers is an array of k characters ('a', 'b', 'c', or 'd').

Two students are considered *suspect* if they have made *identical mistakes* (matching correct scores are not
suspicious) and sit next to each other in the same row (we don't care about students in the front or behind
one another).

Return a list of all pairs of suspect students in any order (the order of the two students in a pair also doesn't
matter).

▸ **Example:** answers = ['a', 'b', 'c', 'c'], m = 5, students = [
```
            # student ID, desk, answers
            (4, 10, ['a', 'b', 'c', 'd']), (1, 6,  ['a', 'b', 'c', 'd']),
            (3, 8,  ['a', 'b', 'd', 'd']), (5, 11, ['a', 'b', 'c', 'd']),
            (9, 7,  ['a', 'b', 'c', 'd']), (6, 16, ['a', 'b', 'd', 'd']) ]
```
  Output: [[1, 9]]. Students 1 and 9 made the same mistakes and sit next to
  each other.

| PROBLEM 30.9 | **PRODUCT OF ALPHABETICAL SUMS** |

Given a list of lowercase strings, words, where each string has between 1 and 3 letters, determine if there exist three strings such that the product of their *alphabetical sum* is a given target value, target. The alphabetical sum of a string is the sum of the positions of its letters in the alphabet (e.g., the alphabetical sum of "abz" is $1 + 2 + 26 = 29$). Return true if such a triplet exists. The same string can be used more than once.

▶ **Example:** words = ["abc", "fg", "hij", "klm", "nop", "qrs", "vwx"]
                target = 1620
  Output: True. The triplet is "abc", "hij", "klm": 6 * 27 * 10 = 1620.
▶ **Example:** words = ["a", "b"], target = 2
  Output: True. The triplet is "a", "a", "b": 1 * 1 * 2 = 2.

| PROBLEM 30.10 | **ACTION LOG ANOMALIES** |

You are given an action log, log, from a tech support system. Each entry is a tuple [agent, action, ticket_number], where the ticket number is a positive integer, the agent is a string, and the action is "open" or "close". The log is sorted chronologically.

Your goal is to find all the tickets with *anomalies*, in any order. A ticket *doesn't* have anomalies if:

- It is opened and closed once, in that order.
- The opening and closing agent is the same.
- The agent didn't do any action for a different ticket between opening and closing the current ticket.

▶ **Example:** logs = [
                ["Dwight", "close", 2], ["Dwight", "open",   2],
                ["Drew",   "open", 32], ["Drew",   "close", 32],
                ["Drew",   "open", 32], ["Drew",   "close", 32],
                ["Susa",   "open", 7], ["Jo",   "close", 7],
                ["Susa",   "open", 33], ["Jo",   "open",   8],
                ["Jo",   "open", 36], ["Jo",   "close", 8],
                ["Susa",   "close", 33]]
  Output: [2, 32, 7, 8, 36].
                - 2 was closed before it was opened.
                - 32 was opened multiple times.
                - 7 was opened and closed by different agents.
                - 8 was opened and closed, but the agent did something in between.
                - 36 was not closed.

| PROBLEM 30.11 | **LARGEST SET INTERSECTION** |

You are given a non-empty array, sets, where each element is an array of unique integers representing a set. Return the index of the set that should be excluded to maximize the size of the intersection of the remaining sets. The *intersection* of a list of sets is the set of elements that appears in every set.

▶ **Example:** sets = [[1, 2, 3], [3, 2, 1], [1, 4, 5], [1, 2]]
  Output: 2. Excluding the third set (index 2) yields a set intersection of
                size 2: {1, 2}.
▶ **Example:** sets = [[1, 2], [3, 4], [5, 6]]
  Output: 0. The sets don't have any elements in common, so the intersection
                will be empty regardless of what set you exclude.
▶ **Example:** sets = [[1, 2], [3, 4, 5]]

> **Output:** 3. After excluding a set, there will be only one set left, so the
> intersection is the size of the set.
>
> ▶ **Example:** sets = [[1, 2, 3]]
> **Output:** 0. There is only one set, so after excluding it, the intersection is
> empty.

✦ PROBLEM SET SOLUTIONS

SOLUTION 30.6   FIND ALL SQUARES

If we just had to find the pairs, we could put all the numbers in a set, and, for each number arr[i], check
if arr[i]² is in the set. Since we also need the *indices*, we can use a map. The numbers are the keys—the
thing we need to search for—and the indices are the values—the thing we need to return when we find a
match (since input numbers are unique, we don't need to worry about map keys clashing).

```
1    def find_squared(arr):
2      # Create a map from number to its index (allow multiple indices per number)
3      num_to_indices = {}
4      for i, num in enumerate(arr):
5        if num not in num_to_indices:
6          num_to_indices[num] = []
7        num_to_indices[num].append(i)
8      res = []
9      # Iterate through each number and check if its square exists in the map
10     for i, num in enumerate(arr):
11       square = num ** 2
12       if square in num_to_indices:
13         for j in num_to_indices[square]:
14           res.append([i, j])
15     return res
```

\# A map from input elements to their indices in the input can often be useful when the problem asks to
output indices or requires knowing the indices.

SOLUTION 30.7   WORD EXPANSION CLASS

First, s can only be expanded into s2 if the length of s2 is one more than the length of s. If not, we can
return false immediately.

The next observation is that we don't care about the order of the letters, so we could sort the letters in both
s and s2 (that is, impose a canonical order) and use a two-pointer algorithm to check that every letter in s
is also in s2 (see parallel pointers, pg 294). Here, we will use a hash map to avoid sorting.

The fact we don't care about the order of the letters means a **frequency map** could be useful. More precisely,
the frequency map of s must match the frequency map of s2 for every letter except one, which must be
one less.

Here is the 'indented English' version of expands_into():

```
if len(s2) != len(s) + 1
  return false
initialize a map from letters to counts
for each letter in s2
  increase the count of the letter
```

```
  for each letter in s
    decrease the count of the letter
  return true if all the counts are 0 except one, which is 1
```

SOLUTION 30.8   CHEATER DETECTION

We could sort the students by desk position, which would put potentially suspect students next to each other. However, sorting takes $O(n \ \log \ n)$ time, where n is the number of students, and we can do this faster with a map.

The key (pun intended) to this problem is the desk numbers. For each student sitting at a desk, desk, we only care about at most two other students, those sitting at desk - 1 and desk + 1. If we map desks to students, we can easily find them in constant time. When populating this map, we can ignore students who got every answer right.

```
1   def suspect_students(answers, m, students):
2     def same_row(desk1, desk2):
3       return (desk1 - 1)//m == (desk2 - 1)//m
4     desk_to_index = {}
5     for i, [student_id, desk, student_answers] in enumerate(students):
6       if student_answers != answers:
7         desk_to_index[desk] = i
8     sus_pairs = []
9     for student_id, desk, answers in students:
10      other_desk = desk + 1
11      if same_row(desk, other_desk) and other_desk in desk_to_index:
12        other_student = students[desk_to_index[other_desk]]
13        if answers == other_student[2]:
14          sus_pairs.append([student_id, other_student[0]])
15    return sus_pairs
```

SOLUTION 30.9   PRODUCT OF ALPHABETICAL SUMS

Let's *TACKLE AN EASIER VERSION OF THE PROBLEM*. Pretend our input is not a list of strings but instead a list of integers. Now, we need to find three integers whose product is a given target—a variation of Problem 24.1: 3-Sum (pg 251).

The brute force algorithm has a cubic complexity, with nested loops slowing down our algorithm. We can follow the same $O(n^2)$ approach as for 3-sum:

- Put all the numbers in a set,
- Iterate through every pair of numbers in the input, a and b, and check if target/(a*b) is in the set.

Be careful not to use integer division and truncate target/(a*b) to a whole number when it is not. That could result in incorrectly returning true.

The runtime of this easier version of the problem would be $O(n^2)$. As an optimization, we could use preprocessing to filter out values that are not divisors of target, but that would not change the worst-case analysis.

As for the strings in the original problem? We can transform them into integers on the fly in constant time.

Observe that the alphabetical sums of the strings range from 1 to 3*26. That means there are only 78 unique sums in the input, regardless of how big the input is. We can *leverage the input range* and modify our 3-sum-based algorithm to loop over the *sums* instead of over the input strings:

```
1   def alphabetic_sum_product(words, target):
2     sums = set()
```

```
3      for word in words:
4        sums.add(alphabetical_sum(word))
5      for i in sums:
6        if target%i != 0:
7          continue
8        for j in sums:
9          k = target/(i*j)
10         if k in sums:
11           return True
12     return False
```

The runtime is $O(n)$ to compute the sums plus $O(78^2) = O(1)$ to search for the triplets.

SOLUTION 30.10   ACTION LOG ANOMALIES

We use a combination of sets and maps so that we can process each log in constant time:

- A map from opened tickets to the agent who opened them. This allows us to check that the closing agent is the same.

- A set of already-seen tickets. This allows us to not open or close a ticket more than once.

- A map from agents to the ticket they are currently working on. This allows us to mark that ticket as anomalous if they do some other action.

- A set for the solution, so that we don't count tickets more than once.

```
1   def find_anomalies(log):
2     opened = {}  # ticket -> agent who opened it
3     working_on = {}  # agent -> ticket they are working on
4     seen = set()  # tickets that were opened or closed
5     anomalies = set()
6     for agent, action, ticket in log:
7       if ticket in anomalies:
8         continue
9       if action == "open":
10        if ticket in seen:
11          anomalies.add(ticket)
12          continue
13        if agent in working_on:
14          # If agent is working on another ticket, that ticket is anomalous
15          anomalies.add(working_on[agent])
16        opened[ticket] = agent
17        working_on[agent] = ticket
18        seen.add(ticket)
19      else:
20        if ticket not in opened or opened[ticket] != agent:
21          anomalies.add(ticket)
22          continue
23        if agent not in working_on or working_on[agent] != ticket:
24          anomalies.add(ticket)
25          continue
26        del working_on[agent]
27        del opened[ticket]
28    # Any tickets still open are anomalous
29    anomalies.update(opened.keys())
30    return list(anomalies)
```

SOLUTION 30.11   LARGEST SET INTERSECTION

Let's start with an easier problem: computing the intersection of a (non-empty) list of sets. If the lists have n elements in total, this can be done in $O(n)$ time, assuming all the sets are hash sets:

```
1   def set_intersection(sets):
2     res = sets[0]
3     for i in range(1, len(sets)):
4       res = {elem for elem in sets[i] if elem in res}
5     return res
```

A naive solution would be to consider excluding the sets one by one and call `set_intersection()` for the remaining sets. This would take $O(k*n)$ time, where k is the number of sets.

We should *HUNT FOR PROPERTIES*. First, let's ignore the edge cases with only one or two sets—if there's only one set, the answer is 0, and if there are two, the answer is the largest of the two.

Looking at a set and determining if we should exclude it or not is hard. Sometimes, it helps to shift our focus: what if we think about the numbers instead of the sets? That is, for a specific number, x, what can we say about it? It isn't much of a leap to guess that its frequency might matter. Let's do a *CASE ANALYSIS* based on how many sets it appears in:

- If x appears in every set, it will be in the intersection regardless of our choice, so we don't need to factor such elements in when making our choice.
- If x appears in only one set, it won't be in the intersection regardless of our choice because we must include at least one set without it. Generalizing, any element missing from more than one set (i.e., appearing in k-2 or fewer sets) will not be in the intersection and can be ignored!
- This only leaves numbers that are missing from exactly one set, i.e., that appear k-1 times. If x is missing from exactly one set, x will only be in the intersection if we pick that set. These are the only elements we should base our choice on.

This means we want to pick the set with the fewest elements that appear in k-1 sets. We can turn this thought into an algorithm:

1. Create a **frequency map** from integers to the number of sets they appear in.
2. For each set, count how many elements it has with a frequency of k-1.
3. Return the index of the set with the smallest count.

There is also a prefix sum solution for this problem, which we will see on page 619.

Interview Tip: Your language may provide built-in set methods like intersection, union, and difference, but it's language-dependent. If it doesn't, they are not hard to implement by hand.

   For instance, in Python, instead of

   ```
   res = {elem for elem in sets[i] if elem in res}
   ```

   we could have done

   ```
   res = res.intersection(sets[i])
   ```

   or even

   ```
   res &= sets[i]
   ```

   In any case, the time complexity is the same.

THE HARDEST SET QUESTION GOOGLE ASKS   INTERVIEW REPLAY

View Online:	bctci.co/sets-and-maps-replay-1 @ 28:50 - end
The Question:	Given a list of sets, find the set that should be excluded to maximize the size of the intersection of the remaining sets.
What You'll See:	The candidate crushed the first binary search question but got stuck on a particularly challenging set question. At the end of the interview, the interviewer gives details on the Google interview process and what to do to improve your odds.
Who:	*Interviewer*: Software Engineer at Google *Candidate*: 10 years exp.
Outcome:	The candidate got the job at Google!

KEY TAKEAWAYS

It's important to get comfortable working with sets and maps. In particular, be aware of all the "gotchas" we listed in 'Common Bugs and Misconceptions.' Likewise, you should be comfortable with the big O complexity of their operations (pg 346). While they seem straightforward (all operations take basically $O(1)$ time), we listed some nuances to be aware of.

We touched on two common applications, the **linear scan tradeoff** and **frequency maps**. For less obvious applications, your first goal should be identifying the right keys (and possibly values) in the problem.

> **Set & map triggers:** There is some "key-like" concept in the problem. We are doing multiple linear scans in arrays. The input and/or output order is irrelevant in our algorithm. Linear-time target complexity. Sliding window problem.

> **Keywords:** frequency, unique, duplicate, grouping, union, intersection, anagram, caching.

ONLINE RESOURCES

Online resources for this chapter include:

- A chance to try each problem in this chapter in AI Interviewer
- Interview replays that show specific mistakes people make with sets & maps problems
- Full code solutions for every problem in the chapter in multiple programming languages

Try online at bctci.co/sets-and-maps.

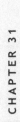

CHAPTER 31

SORTING

AI interviewer, replays, and more materials for this chapter at bctci.co/sorting

Bubble sort would be the wrong way to go.

Barack Obama[1]

▶ *Prerequisites: None*

In this chapter, we explore sorting algorithms and their applications to coding interviews. Sorting is typically used to arrange elements in a convenient order for iteration, such as processing events chronologically. It can be a preprocessing step in algorithms to enable tasks like binary search, two-pointer techniques, finding duplicates, and pinpointing medians or outliers.

COMPARISON SORTS VS SPECIALIZED SORTS

If you're like most candidates, you might be under the impression that sorting cannot be done in better than O(n log n) time. That's partially true. To address this confusion, it helps to classify sorting algorithms as *comparison sorts* and *specialized sorts*.

COMPARISON SORTS

When asked what's an efficient sorting algorithm, most engineers think of *merge sort* or *quicksort*. These are examples of *comparison sorts*.

Comparison sorts are "one-size-fits-all" algorithms: they can sort any type of data (even user-defined types) based on any sorting criterion. They do it by abstracting the logic of "what goes before what" into a *comparator function*—a mini-function that takes two elements and determines which one should go first. A comparison sort receives the comparator as a parameter and calls it to determine where to put the elements. The signature may look something like this:

```
sort(arr, cmp): sorts the elements in arr according to cmp()
```

where cmp() is a function that must satisfy the following signature (or something analogous):

```
cmp(x, y): returns -1 if x < y, 0 if x == y, 1 if x > y
```

Since merge sort and quicksort are already very well-known, we'll only cover them briefly. We'll see another efficient comparison sort, heapsort, in the Heaps chapter (pg 499).

---

1 During a Q&A at Google in 2007, Barack Obama was jokingly asked "What is the most efficient way to sort one million 32-bit integers?" and this was his response.

Merge Sort

Merge sort is a recursive algorithm[2]: it splits the input array down the middle, sorts each half recursively, and then merges the two halves into a single sorted list:

```
1  def mergesort(arr):
2    n = len(arr)
3    if n <= 1:
4      return arr
5    left = mergesort(arr[:n//2])
6    right = mergesort(arr[n//2:])
7    return merge(left, right)
```

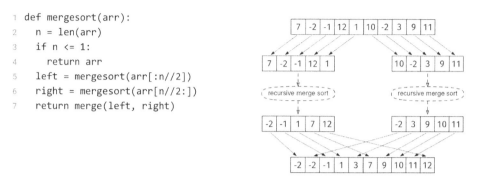

Figure 1. Merge sort. The recursive steps where each half is sorted are omitted.

We learned how to merge two sorted arrays in linear time in Problem 27.6: Merge Two Sorted Arrays (pg 300). The merge function we showed uses the < operator, but we could have used a custom cmp() function.

We'll get into the merge sort analysis when we talk about analyzing recursive algorithms (pg 404). For now, know that merge sort requires O(n log n) comparisons (i.e., calls to the provided cmp()).

Quicksort

Quicksort is also recursive: it picks a random element in the array as pivot and *partitions* the array into three parts: elements smaller than, equal to, and bigger than the pivot (according to the comparator function). The parts are sorted recursively and recombined. Unlike merge sort, we don't need to merge the sorted parts because of how the elements were partitioned—we simply concatenate them.

```
1   def quicksort(arr):
2     if len(arr) <= 1:
3       return arr
4     pivot = random.choice(arr)
5     smaller, equal, larger = [], [], []
6     for x in arr:
7       if x < pivot: smaller.append(x)
8       if x == pivot: equal.append(x)
9       if x > pivot: larger.append(x)
10    return quicksort(smaller) + equal + quicksort(larger)
```

---

2   If you are rusty with recursion, don't worry—it's not the focus of this chapter. We'll talk about it in Chapter 33: Recursion (pg 392).

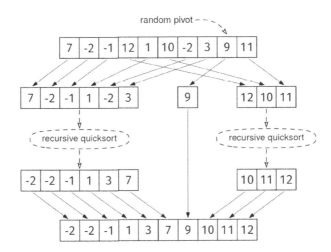

Figure 2. Quicksort. (Omitted: Recursive steps where the smaller and larger elements are sorted.)

This code shows the version with built-in <, >, == operators, but we could have also used a custom cmp() function. In the Two Pointers chapter (pg 308), we saw how to do the partition in place, which saves extra space. You can check with your interviewer to see if they prefer you to do it in place. If not, keep it simple and use smaller, equal, and larger arrays.

An interesting feature of quicksort is that the pivot is random. For any specific input, the runtime depends on how 'lucky' we get with the random pivot choices. Quicksort performs poorly if the partitions are unbalanced, with most elements on the same side of the pivot. If you have the worst possible luck, the runtime deteriorates to $O(n^2)$. However, as n grows, the probability of that happening becomes negligible. Contrary to popular belief, the worst-case number of comparisons is $O(n \ log \ n)$ with high probability, matching merge sort.

SPECIALIZED SORTS

Remember the reusable idea: leverage the input range (pg 349)? **Specialized sorts** are based on this idea. Instead of abstracting out the comparison logic with a comparator function, they are designed with specific types of inputs in mind and take advantage of special properties in those types. As specialized algorithms, they are often the best choice in the right context but cannot be used beyond that.

For instance, we could "sort" an array of zeros and ones in linear time by simply counting the zeros and ones in the array and then re-writing the current amounts back into the array. It's not very broadly applicable, but it would indeed sort this specific type of data. We already saw this 'counting' idea in Problem 27.16: Dutch Flag Problem (pg 308). The generalized algorithm is called *counting sort*, which we'll show here. Other popular ones are *bucket sort* (pg 371) and *radix sort* (which we think you're unlikely to need in interviews).

Counting Sort

Sorting n integers in increasing order with a comparison sort like merge sort takes $O(n \ log \ n)$ time. Counting sort is an alternative algorithm that takes $O(n \ + \ R)$ time and space, where R is the size of the input range: the largest value minus the smallest value. We should only use it when R is small relative to $O(n \ log \ n)$, which requires prior knowledge about what the integers are or what they represent. For instance, a good application would be sorting millions of people by age: the input range (~100)[3] is much smaller than the input size.[4]

Imagine we are sorting n integers with values from 0 to R. The idea of counting sort is to initialize an array of R+1 counters, one for each value in the range. For each value x in the array to be sorted, we increase the counter at index x. At the end, we iterate through the counters, reconstructing the array in sorted order based on the counts.[5]

```
1  def counting_sort(arr):
2      if not arr: return []
3      R = max(arr)
4      counts = [0] * (R + 1)
5      for x in arr:
6          counts[x] += 1
7      res = []
8      for x in range(R + 1):
9          while counts[x] > 0:
10             res.append(x)
11             counts[x] -= 1
12     return res
```

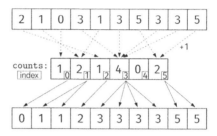

Figure 3. Counting sort. The dotted arrows increase the counter by one. The indices of the counts array are shown shaded.

If the range does not start at 0, we can subtract the smallest element from each number before mapping it to a counter. E.g., if the input range goes from 1000000 to 1000100, we only need 100 buckets; we can map 1000000 to bucket 0, and so on.

ANALYSIS

Comparison sorts have a proven lower bound: any comparison sort requires at least O(n log n) comparisons (i.e., calls to cmp()) to sort n elements. This classic result in computer science[6] means that any comparison sort takes at least O(T*n log n), where T is the time it takes to compare two elements.

Comparison sorts that achieve this asymptotically optimal runtime include merge sort, quicksort, and heapsort. This is why most programming languages leverage one of these algorithms for their built-in sorts. In contrast, bubble sort, selection sort, and insertion sort are three well-known but suboptimal comparison sorts, as they require O(n²) comparisons in the worst case.

When sorting simple types like integers or constant-length strings, the comparison time, T, is constant. However, this isn't always the case. For instance, comparing two strings of length k takes O(k) time, so sorting n strings with maximum length K takes O(K*n log n). It is a common mistake to forget this!

As shown by the counting sort analysis, specialized sorts are *not* subject to this O(n log n) lower bound.

> Since the built-in sort in programming languages is typically a comparison sort, and comparison sort algorithms have an O(n log n) runtime lower bound, we should add O(n log n) to our

---

3   We might want to play it extra safe here an pretend it goes up to 150 to guarantee a slot in the array for any possible number. Adding an extra 50 slots for padding is not costly.

4   Because age is a constant maximum, in many interview problems the sort drops from O(n+R) to O(n).

5   Here, we only show the simple case of counting sort for sorting integers. There's another version that can sort generic types based on a numeric key (like Person objects based on their age field) and is stable.

6   While not relevant to interviews, the proof is worth looking up, as it gives some insight into what it takes to prove that something **cannot** be done.

runtime whenever we invoke the built-in sort. We also need to factor in the time T it takes to do each comparison. If it is not constant, then the runtime increases to $O(T*n \log n)$.[7]

If you are looking for a linear-time solution, you can't use built-in sorts (or comparison sorts in general), which leaves you two options: (1) look for a non-sorting solution, or (2) try to apply a specialized sort like counting sort.

USING BUILT-IN SORT

The most common sorting-related questions from candidates are

- *Should I learn how to implement sorting from scratch?*
- *Do I need to know every sorting algorithm?*
- *When am I allowed to use the built-in sorting function, and is it better to use it?*

In interviews, we should default to using the language's provided built-in sort because it takes less of your interview time. You're unlikely to be asked to implement sorting from scratch, but just in case, it doesn't hurt to know the two most popular ones, merge sort and quicksort (as you can see earlier, they are just a few lines of code).

If you are unsure if you are allowed to use a built-in sort, you can always ask your interviewer.

CUSTOM COMPARATORS

To take full advantage of the built-in sorting function, we should know how to define custom comparators.

The exact signature of the comparator is language-dependent. It's also usually optional, with the < operator as default. That means that for basic types like numbers and strings, we usually don't need to provide our own comparator—unless we want to sort them in an order that is not the default.

How does your language sort strings?

Most languages sort arrays in what is called *lexicographic order*. This is the normal "dictionary order" extended to non-letter characters. The order of two strings is based on the ASCII/Unicode value of the first character, where they differ. If one is a prefix of the other, then the prefix goes first. In ASCII/Unicode, characters are sorted in this order: (1) Punctuation; (2) Digits; (3) Uppercase letters; (4) Lowercase letters.[8]

The following problem set will ensure that you know how to sort:

- In ascending and descending order.
- An array of strings by the character at a specific index.
- An array of nested arrays by the element at a specific index.
- An array of objects by a specific field.
- Sort by a field while breaking ties by another field.
- Sort by a field while breaking ties by the original index in the array.

---

7   By default, assume that built-in sort takes $O(n)$ extra space even when it is sorting in-place. It may be possible that some implementations improve that, but it's not a safe general assumption.

8   One perplexing behavior of JavaScript that has tripped many developers up is that, when sorting an array of numbers, the numbers are sorted based on the lexicographic order of their string representation. This means that 10 ("10") comes before 2 ("2")! To sort the numbers by *value*, we have to pass a custom comparator: `arr.sort((a, b) => a - b)`.

The solutions are very language-specific. We use Python here, but check how it works in your language of choice!

> We should become intimately familiar with the built-in sort since it can be critical on interview day! In particular, we should learn how to provide custom comparators for questions requiring a custom sorting logic. Many candidates overlook this, especially when they are interviewing in a different language than they are used to.

Python has a built-in `sorted()` function, which takes a list and returns a new list with the elements sorted. Python lists also have a `sort()` method, which modifies the list in place and does not return anything. We can choose either depending on whether we want to modify the input or not.

\# It might be clear from the problem whether it's okay to modify the input. But if you're not sure, just ask the interviewer.

Python's approach to custom comparators is a bit special. Comparator functions were deprecated in Python 3; instead, `sort()` and `sorted()` accept an optional `key()` function, which takes a single element and is applied to each element before sorting. Then, the elements are sorted according to their "keys." For instance, if you are given a list of people objects and you need to sort them by a particular attribute like age or height, you can do:

```
people.sort(key=lambda person: person.age)
```

or

```
people.sort(key=lambda person: person.height)
```

The in-line *lambda* function syntax is compact, but the key function could also be defined outside:

```
1  def get_height(person):
2    return person.height
3  people.sort(key=get_height)
```

▶ **FORGETTING CUSTOM COMPARATOR SYNTAX CAN TANK YOUR INTERVIEW**   INTERVIEW REPLAY

View Online:	bctci.co/sorting-replay-1 @ 40:30 - 43:20
The Question:	Given a list of non-negative integers nums, arrange them such that they form the largest possible number.
What You'll See:	The candidate realized they needed to use a custom comparator in the interview but completely forgot the syntax. The interviewer was laid back about it, and let the candidate look it up but warned that not all interviewers would.
Who:	*Interviewer*: Senior Software Engineer at Amazon *Candidate*: 8 years exp.
Outcome:	The candidate got the job at a FAANG+ company!

CUSTOM COMPARATORS PROBLEM SET

For each problem, define a custom comparator in your language. We recommend opening an editor and trying them out with our examples.[9]

---

9 These custom comparators could be a great addition to your customized interview cheat sheet.

View online materials for Beyond Cracking the Coding Interview at bctci.co

QUESTION 1   CASE-INSENSITIVE SORT

Given an array of strings, sort it *lexicographically* (the dictionary order) in descending order, ignoring case.

▸ **Example:** ["apple", "Banana", "3", "Cherry", "42", "GRAPE", "10"]
  Output: ["GRAPE", "Cherry", "Banana", "apple", "42", "3", "10"]

QUESTION 2   SORT BY ELEMENT AT INDEX

Given an array of intervals, where each interval consists of a start value and an end value, sort the intervals by the end value.

▸ **Example:** [[3,9], [1,4], [4,7], [2,3]]
  Output: [[2,3], [1,4], [4,7], [3,9]]

QUESTION 3   SORT BY FIELD

You are given an array, deck, of objects of the Card class, representing a deck of playing cards:

```
1   class Card:
2     def __init__(self, value, suit):
3       self.value = value # A number between 1 and 13.
4       self.suit = suit   # 'clubs', 'hearts', 'spades', or 'diamonds'
```

Sort the cards by *value* in ascending order. Aces are represented by the value 1, and Jacks, Queens, and Kings are represented by the values 11, 12, and 13, respectively. When the value is the same, break the tie with the *suit*, where Clubs < Hearts < Spades < Diamonds.

▸ **Example:** deck = [{8, 'hearts'}, {8, 'clubs'}, {3, 'clubs'}, {3, 'hearts'}]
  Output: [{3, 'clubs'}, {3, 'hearts'}, {8, 'clubs'}, {8, 'hearts'}]

QUESTION 4   NEW DECK ORDER

Given the same deck array, sort it in "new deck order," where the suits are separated in the order Hearts < Clubs < Diamonds < Spades, and each suit is sorted from Ace (low) to King (high).

▸ **Example:** deck = [{8, 'hearts'}, {8, 'clubs'}, {3, 'clubs'}, {3, 'hearts'}]
  Output: [{3, 'hearts'}, {8, 'hearts'}, {3, 'clubs'}, {8, 'clubs'}]

QUESTION 5   STABLE SORTING

Given the same deck array, sort it by value while preserving the relative order of the cards for each value. A sorting algorithm that breaks ties by the input order is called *stable*.

▸ **Example:** deck = [{9, 'clubs'}, {4, 'spades'}, {9, 'spades'}, {4, 'clubs'}]
  Output: [{4, 'spades'}, {4, 'clubs'}, {9, 'clubs'}, {9, 'spades'}]

✦ PROBLEM SET SOLUTIONS

ANSWER 1   CASE-INSENSITIVE SORT

In some languages, a parameter can be passed to sort in descending order rather than ascending order. In Python, it is the reverse parameter. We can combine it with the key() function to convert all the strings to lowercase. This way, sorting will be case-insensitive.

```
1   def descending_sort(strings):
2     return sorted(strings, key=lambda s: s.lower(), reverse=True)
```

ANSWER 2   SORT BY ELEMENT AT INDEX

Our key is the first index (second element) of each interval.

```
def sort_by_interval_end(intervals):
    return sorted(intervals, key=lambda interval: interval[1])
```

ANSWER 3   SORT BY FIELD

To handle ties with the key() function, we make the key a tuple with two fields: the card value first, and a numeric value for the suit second (we don't want to use the lexicographic order for the suit strings). Python compares tuples by the first element, breaking ties by the second element, and so on.

```
def sort_value_then_suit(deck):
    suit_map = {'clubs': 0, 'hearts': 1, 'spades': 2, 'diamonds': 3}
    return sorted(deck, key=lambda card: (card.value, suit_map[card.suit]))
```

Learn to control how to break ties while sorting. Using tuples is a common theme to handle tie-breaking in Python.

ANSWER 4   NEW DECK ORDER

We can get this order by changing our suit mapping and swapping the tuple fields from the previous question.

```
def new_deck_order(deck):
    suit_map = {'hearts': 0, 'clubs': 1, 'diamonds': 2, 'spades': 3}
    return sorted(deck, key=lambda card: (suit_map[card.suit], card.value))
```

ANSWER 5   STABLE SORTING

A sorting algorithm that breaks ties by the input order is called *stable*. We could use tuples (value, input index) as keys. However, it's not necessary—Python's sort is stable by default, i.e., it breaks ties according to the input order.

```
def stable_sort_by_value(deck):
    return sorted(deck, key=lambda card: card.value)
```

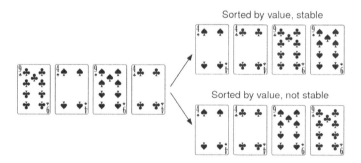

Figure 4.

CONCEPTS

IN-PLACE SORTING

Like Python's sort(), 'in-place' algorithms mutate the input directly rather than returning a new variable. You should check how to do in-place and not-in-place sorting in your language (like Python's sort() and sorted()), as both can be useful.

The term *"in-place"* is strongly associated with algorithms that use O(1) extra space, but that is **not** always the case. Most in-place sorting algorithms, like Python's built-in sort(), still take O(n) extra space.[10] If the rest of your code takes sublinear extra space, the built-in sort could be the space bottleneck.

STABLE SORTING

As mentioned in the custom comparator problem set, a sorting algorithm is considered *stable* if it preserves the original order of equal elements. For example, imagine you're sorting Person objects based on their age; two different objects might have equal age. If Bob and Alice are both 47 years old,[11] and Bob was before Alice in the original array, should Bob still be before Alice in the sorted array?

Most of the time, it doesn't matter if a sorting algorithm is stable or not. It only matters when the elements you are sorting have fields that you are not sorting on *and* you care about how you break ties. Perhaps the most common usage in interviews is when a problem says that you should break ties based on the original order in the input.

While most sorting algorithms are not stable by default, most language libraries provide stable sorts. Look into the details of your own language.

SORTING PROBLEM SET

✦ *Try these problems with AI Interviewer: bctci.co/sorting-problem-set-1*

PROBLEM 31.1   **SORTING BY FREQUENCY**

Given a string, word, consisting of lowercase letters only, return a sorted array with all the letters in word sorted from most frequent to least frequent. If two frequencies are the same, break the tie alphabetically.

---

10   Implementing merge sort in place using O(1) extra space is possible, but fairly tricky (you most likely don't need to know it for interviews). Even so, with a recursive implementation, you still need O(log n) extra space just for the call stack. Implementing quicksort in place using O(1) extra space (not counting the call stack) is easier (see Chapter 27: Quicksort Partition, pg 308).

11   Ron Rivest, Adi Shamir, and Leonard Adleman created the 'Alice' and 'Bob' characters in their 1978 paper "A Method for Obtaining Digital Signatures and Public-key Cryptosystems," making them 47 in 2025.

▸ **Example:** "supercalifragilisticexpialidocious"
  Output: ['i', 'a', 'c', 'l', 's', 'e', 'o', 'p', 'r', 'u', 'd', 'f', 'g', 't', 'x']

PROBLEM 31.2   NESTED CIRCLES

You are given a non-empty array of circles, circles, where each circle is specified by its center coordinates (x, y) and its radius r. Your task is to determine whether the circles are *nested*. For the circles to be considered nested, one of the following conditions must be met:

1. There is a single circle.
2. One circle completely surrounds all the others (without touching boundaries), and the other circles are themselves *nested* (this is a *recursive definition*).

Write a function that returns a boolean indicating whether the circles are nested.

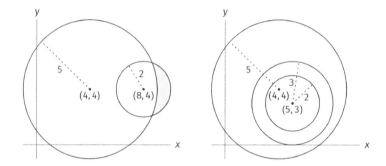

Figure 5. Example 1 (Left) and Example 2 (Right) for Problem 2.

▸ **Example:** circles = [((4, 4), 5),   # Circle with center (4, 4) and radius 5
                ((8, 4), 2)   # Circle with center (8, 4) and radius 2]
   Output: false. Neither circle is surrounded by the other. The shaded area of the second circle in Figure 5 is outside of the first circle.
▸ **Example:** circles = [((5, 3), 3), ((5, 3), 2), ((4, 4), 5)]
   Output: true. The third circle contains all the first and second circles, and the first circle contains the second circle.
▸ **Example:** circles = [((5, 3), 3)]
   Output: true.

PROBLEM 31.3   DELETE OPERATIONS

You're given an array of n integers, nums, and another array of at most n integers, operations, where each integer represents an *operation* to be performed on nums.

• If the operation number is k ≥ 0, the operation is "delete the number at index k in the *original* array if it has not been deleted yet. Otherwise, do nothing."
• If the operation number is -1, the operation is "delete the smallest number in nums that has not been deleted yet, breaking ties by smaller index."

Return the state of nums after applying all the operations. Every number in operations is guaranteed to be between -1 and n-1, included.

▸ **Example:** nums = [50, 30, 70, 20, 80], operations = [2, -1, 4, -1]

`Output: [50]`

- We delete index 2 **in the original array**, element 70: [50, 30, 20, 80]
- We delete 20, the smallest non-deleted number: [50, 30, 80]
- We delete index 4 **in the original array**, element 80: [50, 30]
- We delete 30, the smallest non-deleted number: [50]

PROBLEM 31.4   **SPREADSHEET**

Design a class called Spreadsheet with the following API. Spreadsheets have between 1 and 100 rows and columns. The values at each cell are integers.

```
Spreadsheet API:
  new(rows, cols): initializes a spreadsheet with the specified size and 0 in
    every cell.
  set(row, col, value): sets the cell at (row, col) to value.
  get(row, col): gets the value at (row, col).
  sort_columns_by_row(row): sorts all the columns based on the values in the
    given row. Sorting should be stable.
  sort_rows_by_column(col): sorts all the rows based on the values in the
    given column. Sorting should be stable.
```

Rows and columns start at 0. Assume that no rows or columns will be out of bounds.

▶ **Example:**

```
spreadsheet = Spreadsheet()
spreadsheet.new(3, 3)
spreadsheet.set(0, 0, 5)
spreadsheet.set(0, 1, 3)
spreadsheet.set(0, 2, 8)
spreadsheet.set(1, 0, 6)
spreadsheet.set(2, 1, 1)
spreadsheet.sort_columns_by_row(0)
spreadsheet.sort_rows_by_column(1)
spreadsheet.get(1, 1)  # Returns 5.
```

Figure 6.

PROBLEM 31.5   **SORT BY PUBLICATION YEAR**

You are given an array, books, of objects of the Book class:

```
1  class Book:
2    def __init__(self, title, author, page_count, genre, year_published):
3      self.title = title
4      self.author = author
5      self.page_count = page_count
6      self.genre = genre
7      self.year_published = year_published
```

Return the books sorted by publication year. It doesn't matter how you break ties.

▶ **Example:** books = [

```
Book("Shadow of Tomorrow", "Elliot Greyson", 350, "Science Fiction", 2020),
Book("Whispers in the Wind", "Lila Hart", 280, "Romance", 2018),
Book("Echoes of Eternity", "Mara Vance", 420, "Fantasy", 2018),
Book("Fragments of Dawn", "Cora Blake", 310, "Mystery", 2019),
```

```
  Book("Beneath the Starlit Sky", "Aria Monroe", 270, "Drama", 2020)
  ]
Output: [
  Book("Echoes of Eternity", "Mara Vance", 420, "Fantasy", 2018),
  Book("Whispers in the Wind", "Lila Hart", 280, "Romance", 2018),
  Book("Fragments of Dawn", "Cora Blake", 310, "Mystery", 2019),
  Book("Beneath the Starlit Sky", "Aria Monroe", 270, "Drama", 2020),
  Book("Shadow of Tomorrow", "Elliot Greyson", 350, "Science Fiction", 2020)
  ]
```

PROBLEM 31.6   **FIRST K**

Given an array of n unique integers, arr, return the k smallest numbers, in any order. Assume $0 < k < n$.

▸ **Example:** arr = [15, 4, 13, 8, 10, 5, 2, 20, 3, 9, 11, 27], k = 5
  Output: [4, 3, 2, 5, 8]

✦ PROBLEM SET SOLUTIONS

SOLUTION 31.1   SORTING BY FREQUENCY

We can leverage our **frequency map** reusable idea (pg 348) to build a map from each letter to its frequency. We can then convert the map to an array of (letter, frequency) tuples and sort the tuples based on the frequencies, breaking ties by the letter. In particular, we negate the frequencies so larger frequencies appear first.

```
1   def letter_occurrences(word):
2     letter_to_count = dict()
3     for c in word:
4       if c not in letter_to_count:
5         letter_to_count[c] = 0
6       letter_to_count[c] += 1
7     tuples = []
8     for letter, count in letter_to_count.items():
9       tuples.append((letter, count))
10    tuples.sort(key=lambda x: (-x[1], x[0]))
11    res = []
12    for letter, _ in tuples:
13      res.append(letter)
14    return res
```

If n is the length of word, it may seem that the algorithm takes $O(n \log n)$ time because of sorting. However, the frequency map only ever has 26 keys, so sorting it takes $O(26 \log 26) = O(1)$ time. The actual bottleneck is building the frequency map, which takes $O(n)$ time.

SOLUTION 31.2   NESTED CIRCLES

Drawing examples is usually the key to uncovering useful **properties** for geometric problems. After looking at some examples, we may realize that if we sort the circles must be nested from largest to smallest radius. Thus, if we sort them in that order, we only need to check that each circle contains the next one in the sorted order.

We need a way to check if a circle contains another. For now, let's compartmentalize this task and assume that we are given a function contains(c1, c2).

```
1   def are_circles_nested(circles):
```

```
2    circles.sort(key=lambda c: c[1], reverse=True)
3    for i in range(len(circles) - 1):
4      if not contains(circles[i], circles[i + 1]):
5        return False
6    return True
```

Now that we have the main function down, we can implement contains(c1, c2). The easy case is when c1 and c2 share the same center. In that case, all that matters is that radius(c1) > radius(c2).

In the general case, it seems hard to check if c1 contains every point in c2, since circles are made of infinitely many points! Can we narrow it down somehow? We should look for the point in c2 farthest away from c1. If that point is inside c1, we can safely say that the entirety of c2 is in c1 as well.

Figure 7 shows how to find the point p in the boundary of c2 that is the furthest from the center of c1:

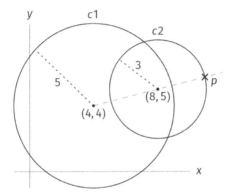

Figure 7. The point p in the boundary of c2 which is the furthest from c1 is on the same line as the center of c1 and the center of c2.

By looking at our drawing, we can see that the distance from the center of c1 to p is distance(center(c1), center(c2)) + radius(c2). We need to check that this distance is less than radius(c1).

```
1    def contains(c1, c2):
2      (x1, y1), r1 = c1
3      (x2, y2), r2 = c2
4      center_distance = sqrt((x1 - x2)**2 + (y1 - y2)**2)
5      return center_distance + r2 < r1
```

SOLUTION 31.3   DELETE OPERATIONS

The naive way to solve this problem would be to execute each operation individually, editing the array as necessary. However, repeatedly finding the minimum and popping elements from an array is slow.

A better way would be to track which elements should be deleted as we iterate through the operations but wait until the end to construct our final answer. We can **REFRAME THE PROBLEM** by asking, "What elements still exist in the array after all operations are completed?"

The tricky part is tracking the next smallest element that has yet to be deleted. When we need to keep track of the current smallest or largest element in an array, a natural solution might be to use a heap.

An alternative, *reusable idea* for repeatedly finding the smallest or largest element in an array is to sort a copy of the indices 0 to n-1 based on the values in the array. In our solution, sorted_indices is a list of indices from nums sorted by the values at those indices. We can iterate through this sorted list efficiently, skipping already-deleted indices by keeping track of them in a set.

```
                                    Indices
                              0   1   2   3   4
                  nums = [50, 30, 70, 20, 80]

        sorted_indices = [ 3 ,  1 ,  0 ,  2 ,  4 ]
```

Figure 8. Sorting array indices by array values.

```
1   def process_operations(nums, operations):
2     n = len(nums)
3     deleted = set()
4     sorted_indices = []
5     for i in range(n):
6       sorted_indices.append(i)
7     sorted_indices.sort(key=lambda i: nums[i])
8     smallest_idx = 0
9     for op in operations:
10      if 0 <= op < n:
11        deleted.add(op)
12      else:
13        # Skip until the next non-deleted smallest index.
14        while smallest_idx < n and sorted_indices[smallest_idx] in deleted:
15          smallest_idx += 1
16        if smallest_idx < n:
17          deleted.add(sorted_indices[smallest_idx])
18          smallest_idx += 1
19    res = []
20    for i in range(n):
21     if not i in deleted:
22       res.append(nums[i])
23    return res
```

♻ REUSABLE IDEA: SORT TO TRACK THE SMALLEST/LARGEST ELEMENTS

If we need to repeatedly find the smallest/largest elements of an array without modifying the array itself, we can sort the indices instead, and iterate through the indices.

If we do not have all the elements upfront, it tends to be more efficient to use a heap (see Problem 37.3: Top Songs Class, pg 501).

SOLUTION 31.4   SPREADSHEET

This solution combines custom sorts to tackle both row and column sorting, with a unique comparator depending on which method is called.

```
1   class Spreadsheet:
2     def __init__(self, rows, cols):
3       self.rows = rows
4       self.cols = cols
5       self.sheet = []
6       for _ in range(rows):
7         self.sheet.append([0] * cols)
8
9     def set(self, row, col, value):
10      self.sheet[row][col] = value
11
```

```
12    def get(self, row, col):
13      return self.sheet[row][col]
14
15    def sort_rows_by_column(self, col):
16      self.sheet.sort(key=lambda row: row[col])
17
18    def sort_columns_by_row(self, row):
19      columns_with_values = []
20      for col in range(self.cols):
21        columns_with_values.append((col, self.sheet[row][col]))
22      sorted_columns = sorted(columns_with_values, key=lambda x: x[1])
23      sorted_sheet = []
24      for r in range(self.rows):
25        new_row = []
26        for col, _ in sorted_columns:
27          new_row.append(self.sheet[r][col])
28        sorted_sheet.append(new_row)
29      self.sheet = sorted_sheet
```

SOLUTION 31.5   SORT BY PUBLICATION YEAR

This question is straightforward with the built-in sort—we just need the appropriate custom comparator. However, that would take O(n log n) time, where n is the number of books. If the range of publication years is relatively small compared to n, we can do better with a *specialized sort*. An online repository of books may have millions of books, while books haven't been around for that long.

If we just needed the list of publication years, we could use counting sort (pg 363). Since we need to sort whole objects, we'll use *bucket sort*, which is pretty similar: we create a bucket for each publication year, and we toss the books in the appropriate bucket. At the end, we walk along the buckets, collecting the books.

```
1    def bucket_sort(books):
2      if not books: return []
3      min_year = min(book.year_published for book in books)
4      max_year = max(book.year_published for book in books)
5      buckets = [[] for _ in range(max_year - min_year + 1)]
6      for book in books:
7        buckets[book.year_published - min_year].append(book)
8      res = []
9      for bucket in buckets:
10        for book in bucket:
11          res.append(book)
12      return res
```

SOLUTION 31.6   FIRST K

This question is trivial if we sort the input. After sorting, we can get the first k elements. However, sorting is 'overkill.' We don't need to sort the elements we return, let alone the rest.

To make things concrete, say we are looking for the k = 5 smallest elements. The first observation is that we only need to find the 5th smallest element. If we can do that, then we can do a single pass to get all the elements equal to or smaller than it. So, how do we find the 5th smallest element?

Quickselect is an algorithm similar to *quicksort* for this exact problem in O(n) expected worst-case time. It is based on the following property:

▸   After the quicksort partition step, the pivot is in the correct index.

Say we pick a random pivot, x and we do the quicksort partition step, splitting the remaining n-1 elements into the `smaller` and `larger` groups. We can do a *CASE ANALYSIS* to see where the 5th smallest element is:

1. If `smaller` contains 5 or more elements, the 5th smallest element is there, so we can search for it recursively.

2. If we get lucky and `smaller` contains exactly 4 elements, that means the pivot **is** the 5th smallest element, so we can return it directly!

3. In the remaining case (`smaller` has 3 or fewer elements), the 5th smallest element is in the `larger` group. More precisely, the 5th smallest element overall is the 5 - `len(smaller)` - 1 element in `larger` (-1 because of the pivot), so we can recursively search for that.

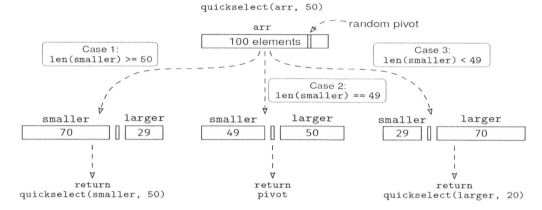

Figure 9. Case analysis of quickselect when searching for the 50th smallest element in an array with 100 elements.

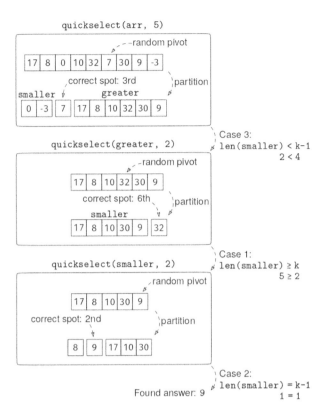

Figure 10. Quickselect example: finding the 5th smallest element in `arr`.

The implementation is similar to quicksort. In particular, the partition logic is the same (we just don't worry about duplicate pivots, since elements are unique[12]). The main difference is that we have a single recursion call depending on the case analysis, a bit like binary search.

```
1   def quickselect(arr, k):
2     if len(arr) == 1:
3       return arr[0]
4     pivot_index = random.randint(0, len(arr) - 1)
5     pivot = arr[pivot_index]
6     smaller, larger = [], []
7     for x in arr:
8       if x < pivot: smaller.append(x)
9       elif x > pivot: larger.append(x)
10    if k <= len(smaller):
11      return quickselect(smaller, k)
12    elif k == len(smaller) + 1:
13      return pivot
14    else:
15      return quickselect(larger, k - len(smaller) - 1)
16
17  def first_k(arr, k):
```

---

12 The algorithm can be adapted to the case where the array can have duplicates by adding an equal part to the partition, which may have length more than 1. We need to factor in the length of equal in the case analysis.

```
18     if len(arr) == 0: return []
19     kth_val = quickselect(arr, k)
20     return [x for x in arr if x <= kth_val]
```

The analysis is a bit tricky. The partition takes O(n) time, and, on average, we expect to decrease the search range by 25% at every recursive step (we won't include a proof here). That's enough for the worst-case runtime to be O(n) with high probability, which is an improvement over sorting.

Quickselect is not very common in interviews, but once you've seen it, it's not hard to implement, so you can add it to your bag of tricks!

We'll revisit this problem again in the Heaps chapter (pg 492). With a heap, we can slove this problem in O(n + k log n) time, which is better than sorting and as good as quickselect when k is constant.

KEY TAKEAWAYS

We saw a mix of comparison and specialized sorts:

	Time	Space	Type
Merge sort	O(n log n)	O(n)	Comparison sort
Quicksort	O(n log n)[13]	O(n)	Comparison sort
Counting sort	O(n + R)	O(n + R)	Integer sort
Bucket sort	O(n + R)	O(n + R)	Integer sort
Quickselect	O(n)[14]	O(n)	k-th smallest

Table 1. Algorithms and their runtimes, where n is the number of elements, and R is the size of the range of integers.

We also learned the concepts you need to speak fluently about sorting: comparison vs specialized sorts, in-place sorting, and stable sorting.

Our main practical advice is to be ready to use the built-in sort during interviews. We emphasized the use of custom comparators to sort any type of data according to any criteria.

⤤ ONLINE RESOURCES

Online resources for this chapter include:

- A chance to try each problem in this chapter in AI Interviewer
- Interview replays that show specific mistakes people make with sorting problems
- Full code solutions for every problem in the chapter in multiple programming languages

Try online at bctci.co/sorting.

---

13   With high probability.

14   With high probability.

## CHAPTER 32

STACKS & QUEUES

AI interviewer, replays, and more materials for this chapter at bctci.co/stacks-and-queues

▶ *Prerequisites: None*

This chapter covers the implementation of stacks and queues and their application in interviews. Stacks are a data structure that supports the *Last-in-First-out* (LIFO) access pattern, whereas Queues support the *First-in-First-out* (FIFO) access pattern. A stack is like a can of Pringles: the chip at the top of the can is the last one put in and the first one taken out.[1] A queue is like a line at the grocery store: the first person to arrive is the first one attended to.

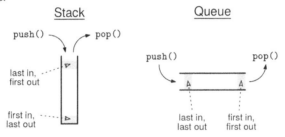

Figure 1.

Besides push() and pop(), stacks and queues often have a peek() method which returns the first element without removing it.[2] Stacks and queues can be implemented in such a way that all the operations take constant time:

Stack		Queue	
push(val)	O(1)	push(val)	O(1)
pop()	O(1)	pop()	O(1)
peek()	O(1)	peek()	O(1)
size()	O(1)	size()	O(1)

Table 1. Stack and queue operations and worst-case runtimes.

The main drawback of stacks and queues relative to dynamic arrays is that we can't access elements by index in O(1) time. Stacks and queues are more restrictive in the order in which we can access elements.

1　In the recursion chapter, we will talk about the *call stack*, the internal mechanism that makes recursion work (pg 392). In this chapter, we are talking about stack data structures that we declare as variables in our code.

2　Sometimes you'll hear "enqueue" and "dequeue" to push and pop from a Queue, but we use push and pop for consistency.

IMPLEMENTATION

STACKS

Stacks have at least two implementations: a dynamic-array-based one and a linked-list-based one. Here, we'll show the first one; for the linked-list-based one, see Problem 34.3: Linked-List-Based Stack (pg 418).

In the Dynamic Arrays chapter (pg 282), we showed how to implement a dynamic array and explained that Python lists (like [1, 2, 3]) are implemented as dynamic arrays. We also covered that appending to or removing from the end of a dynamic array takes O(1) amortized time (pg 285).

Implementing a stack with a dynamic array is straightforward. To write push(), simply append an element to the end of the array. To write pop(), remove from the end. Note that, in Python, index -1 can be used to access the last element in a list.

```
1    class Stack:
2      def __init__(self):
3        self.array = []
4
5      def push(self, value):
6        self.array.append(value)
7
8      def pop(self):
9        if self.is_empty():
10         raise IndexError("Stack is empty")
11        val = self.array[-1]
12        self.array.pop()
13        return val
14
15      def peek(self):
16        if self.is_empty():
17         raise IndexError("Stack is empty")
18        return self.array[-1]
19
20      def size(self):
21        return len(self.array)
```

Since this implementation is just a thin wrapper around a dynamic array, some programming languages (like Python) don't provide a dedicated stack library. In an interview, it is common to use a dynamic array directly in place of a stack—we simply call the variable stack.

QUEUES

Unlike stacks, **a** Python list (dynamic array) can't be leveraged efficiently to implement a queue because you can't pop or push efficiently from the front of a dynamic array. Overlooking this fact is a common mistake in interviews.

Instead, queues can be implemented efficiently using linked lists. We'll see how in Problem 34.4: Linked-List-Based Queue (pg 418).

If you don't need to implement a queue yourself, it is best to use a built-in library, so familiarize yourself with queues in your language. In this chapter, we will use a language-agnostic Queue API as defined at the beginning of the chapter.[3]

APPLICATIONS

Now that we've talked about how stacks and queues are implemented, let's see how they can be useful in interviews.

✦✦ PROBLEM 32.1 COMPRESS ARRAY

Given an array of integers, arr, a *compress operation* finds the first pair of consecutive equal numbers and combines them into their sum. If there are no consecutive equal numbers, the array is considered fully compressed. Your goal is to repeatedly compress the array until it is fully compressed.[4]

Figure 2. Compress operation.

▶ **Example:** arr = [8, 4, 2, 2, 2, 4]
   Output: [16, 2, 4]. The steps are [8, 4, 2, 2, 2, 4] -> [8, 4, 4, 2, 4] ->
                           [8, 8, 2, 4] -> [16, 2, 4]
▶ **Example:** arr = [4, 4, 4, 4]
   Output: [16]. The steps are [4, 4, 4, 4] -> [8, 4, 4] -> [8, 8] -> [16]
▶ **Example:** arr = [1, 2, 3, 4]
   Output: [1, 2, 3, 4]

SOLUTION 32.1   COMPRESS ARRAY

The compression order is important—if we merge pairs that are not the leftmost pair, we may end up with an incorrect result. For instance, in Example 1, we could have ended with [8, 4, 2, 8].

We can use a stack to add the array elements from *left to right*. Whenever we add a number, we see if it triggers any combinations. It could trigger a chain of combinations, which we handle with a nested loop:

```
1   def compress_array(arr):
2       stack = []
3       for num in arr:
4           while stack and stack[-1] == num:
5               num += stack.pop()
6           stack.append(num)
7       return stack
```

---

3 Python doesn't have a built-in Queue data structure, but you can use the deque (short for 'double-ended queue') from the collections module, which supports the same operations with the same runtimes. Instead of push() and pop(), they are called append() and popleft(). JavaScript has it worse, as there is no built-in Queue or equivalent as of 2024. If you need a queue in an interview, we recommend **pretending** (with the interviewer's approval) you have a queue API like the one described in this chapter. Explain to your interviewer you don't want to use a dynamic array because popping from the front takes linear time, and that it can be improved with a linked-list-based queue implementation. A reasonable interviewer won't ask you to implement a Queue from scratch in addition to solving the problem requiring it, but it is best to be able to (online assessments are a place where this may be required).

4 This problem is inspired by the game '2048' created by Gabriele Cirulli.

How would you modify the strategy for the following problem?

✦⁑ **PROBLEM 32.2**   **COMPRESS ARRAY BY K**

Given an array of integers, arr, and an integer k ≥ 2, a *k-compress operation* finds the first block of k consecutive equal numbers and combines them into their sum. If there are no k consecutive equal numbers, the array is considered fully k-compressed. Your goal is to repeatedly apply k-compress operations until the array is fully k-compressed.

▸ **Example:** arr = [1, 9, 9, 3, 3, 3, 4], k = 3
  Output: [1, 27, 4]
         The steps are [1, 9, 9, 3, 3, 3, 4] -> [1, 9, 9, 9, 4] -> [1, 27, 4]
▸ **Example:** arr = [8, 4, 2, 2], k = 2
  Output: [16]
▸ **Example:** arr = [4, 4, 4, 4], k = 5
  Output: [4, 4, 4, 4]

SOLUTION 32.2   COMPRESS ARRAY BY K

The parameter k makes the problem more challenging. Before, we only needed to care about two adjacent digits, but now we need to delay our combination until we have seen a number k times. A reusable idea when using data structures is storing *tuples* with extra fields that can help with bookkeeping. In this case, we can store the last seen number and its current count on the stack. For each array number, we first check if it is already on the top of the stack, and if it is, we don't add it again—we just update its count.

To keep the code cleaner, we factor out the processing of each new element in a helper function. The three cases are:

1. The number doesn't match the top of the stack.
2. The number matches the top of the stack, but there are not enough copies to trigger a merge.
3. We can merge, which may trigger more merges.

See the code that follows for an implementation.

```
1   def compress_array_k(arr, k):
2     stack = []
3     def merge(num):
4       if not stack or stack[-1][0] != num:
5         stack.append([num, 1])
6       elif stack[-1][1] < k-1:
7         stack[-1][1] += 1
8       else:
9         stack.pop()
10        merge(num * k)
11    for num in arr:
12      merge(num)
13    res = []
14    for num, count in stack:
15      for _ in range(count):
16        res.append(num)
17    return res
```

♻ **REUSABLE IDEA: PIGGYBACKING EXTRA INFO**

When storing elements in a data structure, it may help to store extra fields with information to help you process the element once you fetch it from the data structure. In Python, we can use tuples.

In Solution 32.2, the count piggybacks along with the number. For additional examples, see the 'node–height queue' recipe for trees, where the height piggybacks along with the node (pg 445), or Problem 37.2: K Most Played (pg 500), where the title of the song piggybacks in the heap along with the number of plays.

If you think about it, a *map* is just a *set* with extra info piggybacking along with each key.

✦ **PROBLEM 32.3**   **VIEWER COUNTER CLASS**

Streamers make money based on the number of views they receive while streaming. Implement a `Viewer-Counter` class that tracks the number of viewers within a configurable time window for a live stream event. Viewer types may be `"guest"`, `"follower"`, or `"subscriber"`.

> `ViewerCounter`:
> `__init__(window)`: establishes a window size ≥ 1.
> `join(t, v)`: registers that a viewer of type v joined at time t.
> `get_viewers(t, v)`: gets the viewer count of viewer type v within the time window of length 'window' ending at timestamp t: [t - window, t], with both endpoints included.

Both methods accept a timestamp t represented by an integer. It is guaranteed that each method call receives a time that is greater than or equal to any timestamp used in previous calls to either `join()` or `get_viewers()`.

▶ **Example:** `counter = ViewerCounter(10)`
             `counter.join(1, "subscriber")`
             `counter.join(1, "guest")`
             `counter.join(2, "follower")`
             `counter.join(2, "follower")`
             `counter.join(2, "follower")`
             `counter.join(3, "follower")`
             `counter.get_viewers(10, "subscriber"))` # The window is [0, 10].
             `Returns 1.`
             `counter.get_viewers(10, "guest"))`   # Returns 1.
             `counter.get_viewers(10, "follower"))`   # Returns 4.
             `counter.get_viewers(13, "follower"))`   # The window is [3, 13].
             `Returns 1.`

SOLUTION 32.3   VIEWER COUNTER CLASS

We need a mechanism to track when viewers 'fall out' of the window and are no longer relevant. The *first* to come *in* are also the *first* to go *out*, meaning we have a FIFO order, and a queue will likely be helpful.

We could store all the viewer types in a single queue, but since the `get_viewer()` method requires us to filter our answer based on the viewer type, a simpler approach is to store each type in a dedicated queue.

```
1   class ViewerCounter:
2     def __init__(self, window):
3       self.queues = {"guest": Queue(), "follower": Queue(), "subscriber": Queue()}
4       self.window = window
5     def join(self, t, v):
6       self.queues[v].put(t)
7     def get_viewers(self, t, v):
8       queue = self.queues[v]
9       while not queue.empty() and queue.peek() < t - self.window:
10        queue.pop()
```

```
11      return queue.size()
```

The description also mentions that multiple viewers can arrive at the same timestamp. That means that our queues may end up looking like [1, 2, 3, 3, 3, 3, 3, 3, 3, 3], which is wasteful in terms of space. We could save space by using the same piggybacking idea from the previous problem and storing [time-stamp, count] tuples. Then the same queue becomes [(1, 1), (2, 1), (3, 8)]. However, a plain queue is not enough for this: it requires being able to peek or push from both ends: one to remove the oldest viewers, as before, and one to update the count of the newest viewers. We would need a *double-ended queue*.

> A queue that supports push and pop from both ends is called a *double-ended queue*, or *deque*[5] for short, and is a common variation. It's possible to add the additional methods to a queue's linked-list-based implementation with O(1) time complexity.[6]

✦ ┃ **PROBLEM 32.4** **CURRENT URL**

You are implementing the *back arrow* functionality of a browser. You are given a non-empty array, actions, with the actions that the user has done so far. Each element in actions consists of two elements. The first is the action type, "go" or "back".

- When the action is "go", the second element is a URL string. The first action is always "go".
- When the action is "back", the second element is a number ≥ 1 with the number of times we want to go back. Going back once means returning to the previous URL we went to with a "go" action. If there are no previous URLs, going back stays at the current one.

Return the current URL the user is on after all actions are performed.

▸ **Example:** actions = [["go", "google.com"], ["go", "wikipedia.com"],
                          ["go", "amazon.com"], ["back", 4],
                          ["go", "youtube.com"], ["go", "netflix.com"],
                          ["back", 1]]
   Output: "youtube.com"

SOLUTION 32.4   CURRENT URL

The browser history can be modeled as a stack: going to a website pushes to the stack and returning pops from the stack.

```
1   def current_url(actions):
2     stack = []
3     for action, value in actions:
4       if action == "go":
5         stack.append(value)
6       else:
7         while len(stack) > 1 and value > 0:
8           stack.pop()
9           value -= 1
10    return stack[-1]
```

\# Right-to-left combinations/transformations and undo/redo actions are strong triggers for stacks.

---

5 Some people pronounce deque as "D.Q.", but the correct pronunciation is actually "deck".

6 Python's deque supports pushing and popping from both ends in O(1) time with append(), pop(), appendleft(), and popleft().

✦ **PROBLEM 32.5**   **CURRENT URL WITH FORWARD**

What if, in Problem 32.4, we add a third action, "forward" with the reverse functionality as "back"? Note that a "go" action removes the option to go forward. Going forward past the last page that we have gone to does nothing.

▶ **Example:** actions = [["go", "google.com"], ["go", "wikipedia.com"],
                  ["back", 1],   # Returns to google.com
                  ["forward", 1],   # Returns to wikipedia.com
                  ["back", 3],   # Returns to google.com
                  ["go", "netflix.com"],
                  ["forward", 3]]   # Stays on netflix.com
    Output: "netflix.com"

SOLUTION 32.5   CURRENT URL WITH FORWARD

We can use an extra stack to handle the forward action. Whenever we pop an element off the main stack, we push it onto the 'forward' stack. If we visit a new URL, we clear the 'forward' stack.

```
1   def current_url_followup(actions):
2     stack = []
3     forward_stack = []
4     for action, value in actions:
5       if action == "go":
6         stack.append(value)
7         forward_stack = []
8       elif action == "back":
9         while len(stack) > 1 and value > 0:
10          forward_stack.append(stack.pop())
11          value -= 1
12      else:
13        while forward_stack and value > 0:
14          stack.append(forward_stack.pop())
15          value -= 1
16    return stack[-1]
```

BALANCED PARENTHESES

Stacks are useful for problems about balanced parentheses. A string of ' (' and ') ' is *balanced* if each opening ' (' has a corresponding closing ') ', and the substring between them is also balanced. For instance:

- "(()())()" is balanced.
- ")(" is not balanced because there is a closing parenthesis before an opening one.
- "(()" is not balanced because one of the opening parentheses does not have a corresponding closing one.

Stacks are useful because parentheses match in a last-in, first-out fashion: if we have a string starting with "(()...", the closing parenthesis matches the second opening one, not the first one.

Figure 3. Corresponding opening/closing pairs.

Problems about balanced parentheses gravitate to the following questions:

- Checking if a string is balanced.
- Finding the longest balanced substring.
- Modifying a string to make it balanced.
- Breaking a string down into balanced substrings.
- Searching matching pairs, like the most nested pair or the furthest away pair.

Our main advice for this type of problem is to use the *REFRAME THE PROBLEM* booster:

 REUSABLE IDEA: REFRAME BALANCED PARENTHESES AS PLOT HEIGHTS

We can visualize a string of parentheses as a plot that starts at 0 and goes up for each opening parenthesis and down for each closing parenthesis:

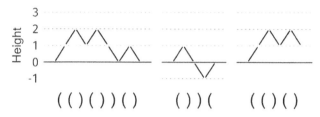

Figure 4. An example of a balanced string (left) and two unbalanced ones (center and right).

The plot for a balanced string creates a valid 'mountain range outline:'

1. it never goes below height 0, and

2. it ends at height 0.

Balanced parentheses questions are often easier to solve when reframed in terms of this plot.

The following code checks if a string of parentheses is balanced by checking that the plot never goes below 0 and ends at 0:

```
 1   def balanced(s):
 2     height = 0
 3     for c in s:
 4       if c == '(':
 5         height += 1
 6       else:
 7         height -= 1
 8         if height < 0:
 9           return False
10     return height == 0
```

This code is simple enough that we didn't need any data structure, but we'll see harder balanced parentheses problems later where stacks will be helpful.

As an example of how the mountain range visualization is useful, imagine you have a balanced string, and you want to find the parentheses that are most deeply nested in other parentheses. You would just need to find the highest point in the plot (peak in the mountain range). Here's another example:

✦ **PROBLEM 32.6   BALANCED PARTITION**

Given a balanced parentheses string, s, a *balanced partition* is a partition of s into substrings, each of which is itself balanced. Return the maximum possible number of substrings in a balanced partition.

▸ **Example:** s = "((()))(()())()(()(())"
  Output: 4. The balanced partition with the most substrings is "((()))", "(()
           ())", "()", "(()(()))".

SOLUTION 32.6   BALANCED PARTITION

If we think about this problem in terms of plot heights, we'll realize we should start a new substring every time the plot goes back to height 0:

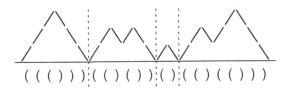

Figure 5.

```
1   def max_balanced_partition(s):
2     height = 0
3     res = 0
4     for c in s:
5       if c == '(':
6         height += 1
7       else:
8         height -= 1
9         if height == 0:
10          res += 1
11    return res
```

In Solution 32.6, we only need to track the plot's current height. Sometimes, we need to track extra information for each hanging open parenthesis. When that happens, the stack data structure is often the right choice.

For instance, a common variation is to mix different types of brackets, like [ ], { }, or < >. In those cases, a stack can be used to track the types of the hanging open brackets:

✦ | **PROBLEM 32.7**   **CUSTOM BRACKETS**

Given a string, s, and an array of strings, brackets, where each element consists of two characters, representing matching opening and closing brackets, return whether s is balanced according to those brackets:

- Characters not in brackets do not affect whether s is balanced.
- A pair of matching brackets of one type cannot surround only half of a matching pair of another type of brackets (see Example 3).
- Assume that brackets does not contain any repeated characters.

▸ **Example:** s = "((a+b)*[c-d]-{e/f})", brackets = ["()", "[]", "{}"]
  Output: True
▸ **Example:** s = "()[}", brackets = ["()", "[]", "{}"]
  Output: False
▸ **Example:** s = "([)]", brackets = ["()", "[]", "{}"]
  Output: False
▸ **Example:** s = "<div> hello :) </div>", brackets = ["<>", "()"]
  Output: False. The ')' does not have a matching '('.

▸ **Example:** s = ")))(()((", brackets = [")("]
  Output: True

SOLUTION 32.7   CUSTOM BRACKETS

We use a stack to track dangling brackets as we process s. To simplify our code, when we find an opening bracket, we put the corresponding closing bracket in the stack. So, if (and) are a bracket pair and we see (in the input, we'll put) in the stack. We ignore non-bracket characters.

```
1   def balanced_brackets(s, brackets):
2     open_to_close = dict()
3     close_set = set()
4     for pair in brackets:
5       open_to_close[pair[0]] = pair[1]
6       close_set.add(pair[1])
7     stack = []
8     for c in s:
9       if c in open_to_close:
10        stack.append(open_to_close[c])
11      elif c in close_set:
12        if not stack or stack[-1] != c:
13          return False
14        stack.pop()
15    return len(stack) == 0
```

Commonly missed stack and queue edge cases.

Candidates often handle the following edge cases incorrectly:

- **Empty stacks:** They pop or peek at a stack/queue that could be empty without checking if it's empty first.

- **Abandoned elements:** They implement a loop to process the input, which pushes and pops from a stack/queue, but they forget to handle the remaining elements in the stack/queue after the loop.

It's a good idea to double check these errors when you code.

We can capture this idea of tracking dangling brackets in a stack with a recipe:

RECIPE 1. DANGLING BRACKET STACK.

```
stack = []
for c in input s
  if c is an open bracket
    add it to the stack
  else if c is a closing bracket
    check that the stack is not empty
    try to match the top of the stack with the closing bracket
  else
    handle (or ignore) non-bracket elements
Check that there are no remaining unmatched parentheses in the stack
```

When using this stack recipe, there are two main questions:

1. What is the bracket-matching logic, and what information do we need to store on the stack to follow it?

2. How do we handle non-bracket input elements?

✦ **PROBLEM 32.8**	**LONGEST BALANCED SUBSEQUENCE**

Given a string of parentheses, s, return the longest balanced *subsequence*. A subsequence of s (not a subarray) is a string obtained by removing some of the letters in s. In other words, you have to delete the smallest number of characters necessary to make s balanced and return the resulting string.

▶ **Example:** s = "))(())(()"
   Output: "(())()". We removed the following characters: "~~))~~(())~~(~~()". We could
   				have also removed "~~))~~(())(~~(~~)".

▶ **Example:** s = "(()(()("
   Output: "()()". We removed the following characters: "~~(~~()~~(~~()~~(~~".

▶ **Example:** s = "())(()"
   Output: "()()". We removed the following characters: "()~~)~~(~~(~~)".

▶ **Example:** s = "("
   Output: ""

## SOLUTION 32.8	LONGEST BALANCED SUBSEQUENCE

Thinking of the mountain range visualization, we can characterize *invalid* parentheses as follows:

1. Closing parentheses that send the mountain outline 'underground.'
2. Opening parentheses that are left unmatched at the end.

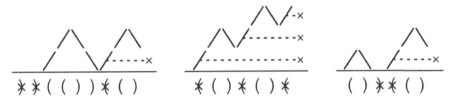

Figure 6. Finding invalid parentheses.

These invalid parentheses must be removed, so what we are left with after removing them is the longest balanced subsequence.

We can detect the first type as we build the mountain range. To find the second type, we can use a stack to track dangling opening parentheses. In the end, any parentheses still in the stack are unmatched and thus invalid.

Our algorithm does two passes: one to find the *positions* of the invalid parentheses, and another to reconstruct the final array skipping those positions.

▶ **A MEDIUM-LEVEL CALCULATOR-BASED QUESTION[7]**   INTERVIEW REPLAY

View Online:	bctci.co/stacks-and-queues-replay-1 @ 3:30 - 10:42
The Question:	Evaluate the value of an arithmetic expression in Reverse Polish Notation.
What You'll See:	The candidate realized that different operators have different priorities, which is a trigger to use a stack.
Who:	*Interviewer*: Senior Software Engineer at Amazon *Candidate*: 8 years exp.
Outcome:	The candidate got the job at a FAANG+ company!

▶ **A HARD CALCULATOR-BASED QUESTION[7]**   INTERVIEW REPLAY

View Online:	bctci.co/stacks-and-queues-replay-2 @ 4:04 - end
The Question:	Given a string s which contains a math expression, evaluate the expression and return its value.
What You'll See:	The candidate quickly identified that applying the correct order of operations is crucial to this problem and realized that controlling the order in which operations are processed with a stack would be optimal.
Who:	*Interviewer*: Staff Software Engineer at Uber *Candidate*: 18 years exp.

KEY TAKEAWAYS

Knowing how to implement a stack and a queue is helpful for data structure design questions.

- For stacks, a dynamic array implementation is probably the easiest choice.
- The easiest approach for queues (and double-ended queues, or deques) is to use a linked list. A common mistake to avoid is using an array to implement a queue.

In terms of applications, we saw that stacks are often useful for problems about balanced parentheses brackets (Recipe 1). We also saw a mountain range visualization to help with this type of problem. In the Tier-3 'Monotonic Stacks & Queues' chapter (bctci.co/monotonic-stacks-and-queues), we'll more advanced applications of stacks & queues.

The big O analysis of stacks and queues is simple: all operations take constant time.

> **Stack triggers.** Right-to-left combinations/transformations; undo/redo actions; balanced parenthesis. Brackets like [ ], ( ), { }, and < >.

---

7 Calculator-based questions are another common stack-based type of question. They are a little niche to get into in this book, but here is a great (free) resource for the die-hard enthusiasts. Just know it is a little overkill and definitely "Tier-3" material: bctci.co/advanced-stacks

ONLINE RESOURCES

Online resources for this chapter include:

- A chance to try each problem in this chapter in AI Interviewer
- Interview replays that show specific mistakes people make with stacks & queues problems
- Full code solutions for every problem in the chapter in multiple programming languages

Try online at bctci.co/stacks-and-queues.

## CHAPTER 33

RECURSION

AI interviewer, replays, and more materials for this chapter at bctci.co/recursion

▶ *Prerequisites: None*

A recursive[1] function is a function that calls itself until it reaches a base case. It looks something like:

```
1   function foo(input):
2     if input == BASE_CASE:
3       return DIRECT_ANSWER
4     else:
5       return foo(input.part1) + foo(input.part2)
```

While some questions focus strictly on recursion, recursion comes up more commonly in questions about trees, graphs, backtracking, and dynamic programming. A solid grasp on recursion is foundational and will pay off in the long run.

We assume that our readers are familiar with recursion, but we'll review its mechanics before giving interview-specific advice.

THE MECHANICS OF RECURSION

Here is a side-by-side comparison of iterative and recursive code for computing factorials. The *factorial* of a positive integer n, denoted by n!, is the product of all positive integers up to n.

```
1   def factorial_iter(n):
2     res = 1
3     for i in range(1, n+1):
4       res *= i
5     return res
```

```
1   def factorial_rec(n):
2     if n == 1:
3       return 1
4     return n * factorial_rec(n-1)
```

If we call factorial_rec(3), it will call factorial_rec(2), which will call factorial_rec(1), which won't call anything—it's the *base case*.

While both compute the same thing, internally, your computer does very different things when running one or the other. But before we even talk about recursive functions, we should talk about normal ones. How do function calls 'work,' anyway?

THE CALL STACK & STACK OVERFLOW

Imagine your computer running your code, churning out instruction after instruction in meticulous order. To keep track of what instruction comes next, your computer has an *instruction pointer*. Function calls make

---

1   The word 'recursion' comes from the Latin verb 'recurrere,' meaning "to run back" or "return." For an interactive recursion demo, see page 392.

your computer's job harder since, instead of executing the next instruction, it needs to jump to a completely different point in the code, execute the stuff there, and then resume from where it was previously.

To deal with this, when your computer executes a function call, like main() calling foo(), it stores where it was in main() so that it can return to that point after it finishes executing foo(). However, a single 'return address' is not enough because foo() could make another function call—we need to track the return addresses for all the nested function calls we executed.

Return addresses are stored in a special region of memory known as the *call stack*. When a function call is executed, the program adds a new *stack frame* at the top of the call stack. A stack frame is essentially a block of memory that holds information about the call, including the return address and things such as the parameters. When we return from a function, we 'pop' (remove) its frame from the top of the stack.

\# Yes, the program uses a stack in much the same way as we do in Stacks and Queues. The call stack, much like the data structure, works on a FIFO (first-in-first-out) principle.

As far as your computer is concerned, recursive function calls work like any other. That means that if we call factorial_rec(2), we will stack 2 frames.

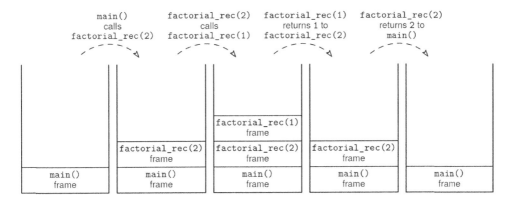

Figure 1. The call stack. The function at the bottom is the starting point of the program. Each other function in the stack was called by the function below it. After a function returns, its frame gets popped from the stack.

A *stack overflow error* occurs when the call stack gets too big. When your computer starts executing code, it reserves a fixed amount of memory for the call stack; if we run out, the program typically crashes as it cannot handle function calls properly anymore.[2]

The number of nested function calls you can make before hitting this limit depends on the programming language and the size of each frame, but the default for some languages may be lower than you would

---

2 Now you can understand the meaning of the *stack overflow* error that the famous programming Q&A website is named after. The fact that stack overflow errors can crash programs is one of the reasons why recursion is sometimes less preferred in production codebases.

expect: it may be in the thousands or tens of thousands. By default, Python has a limit of ~1000 stack frames, which is safe for non-recursive function calls but easy to trip up when using recursion.[3]

Try to avoid using recursion if you would need a call stack depth in the tens of thousands. If you can't avoid it in an interview setting, at least discuss the concern for stack overflow with the interviewer (partially to showcase your knowledge).

THE CALL TREE

The factorial_rec() function only calls itself at most once. What happens when a function calls itself multiple times? We'll illustrate this with the following problem:

✦✦ **PROBLEM 33.1**   **ROBOT INSTRUCTIONS**

We are given a string, seq, with a sequence of instructions for a robot. The string consists of characters 'L', 'R', and '2'. The letters 'L' and 'R' instruct the robot to move left or right. The character '2' (which never appears at the end of the string) means "perform all the instructions after this '2' twice, but skip the instruction immediately following the '2' during the second repetition." Output a string with the final list of left and right moves that the robot should do.

▸ **Example:** seq = "LL"
   Output: "LL"

▸ **Example:** seq = "2LR"
   Output: "LRR". The '2' indicates that
            we need to do "LR" first and
            then "R".

▸ **Example:** seq = "2L"
   Output: "L". The '2' indicates that we
            need to do "L" first and then
            "" (the empty string).

▸ **Example:** seq = "22LR"
   Output: "LRRLR". The first '2' indi-
            cates that we need to do "2LR"
            first and then "LR".

▸ **Example:** seq = "LL2R2L"
   Output: "LLRLL"

Figure 2.

SOLUTION 33.1   ROBOT INSTRUCTIONS

This is an example of a problem that is easier to do recursively than iteratively. We can simulate "do all the instructions after this one and then do them again" with two recursive calls (this solution has some inefficiencies that we'll address later on page 396):

```
1   def moves(seq):   # Inefficient version.
2       if len(seq) == 0:
```

---

3   As a little experiment, we recommend coding factorial_rec() in your language of choice and seeing how high n needs to be to trigger a stack overflow error. You may get an *integer overflow* error instead because factorials grow so quickly—if so, you can try computing the sum of the first n integers instead of the product. If you can't trigger a stack overflow, it may be because your compiler is performing *tail call optimization* under the hood, which is when the compiler is smart enough to find a way to reuse the same stack frame across all recursive calls. In general, you should not rely on the compiler being able to do this, as it depends on the language, the compiler, and the specific function. Also, for interviews, your interviewer may not know about it.

```
3        return ""
4     if seq[0] == '2':
5        return moves(seq[1:]) + moves(seq[2:])
6     else:
7        return seq[0] + moves(seq[1:])
```

As you can see, the recursive function may start multiple recursive calls. When that happens, it is useful to visualize the recursive calls as a *call tree*. For instance, here is the call tree when the input is "2LR":

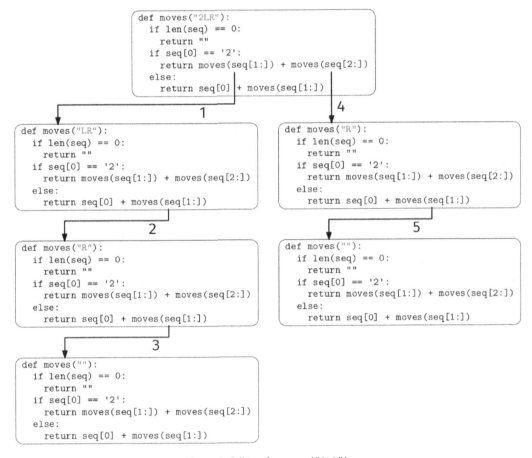

Figure 3. Call tree for moves("2LR").

The root is the original call to moves("2LR"), and each recursive call spawns a child node in the tree (if you are not familiar with this terminology, we'll cover it in the Trees chapter). The numbers indicate the order in which the calls are made.

Can you imagine what the call tree looks like for input "LL2R2L"? We can simplify the drawing by just labeling each node with the top-level call:

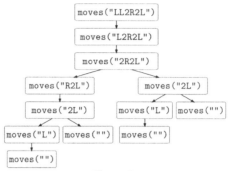

Figure 4.

How does the call stack differ from the call tree? The call stack captures the nested calls at a specific snapshot of time; the call tree captures every recursive call over the course of the algorithm. The call stack exists in the computer memory and makes recursion work. The call tree is just a concept we use to visualize recursive algorithms; it does not exist in memory.

IMPLEMENTATION ADVICE

COMMON MISTAKES

There are, of course, a wide variety of errors you can make with recursion, but a few of the most common are:

1. Forgotten or incorrect base case.
2. Not making progress.
3. Making unnecessary copies.
4. Merging recursive calls incorrectly.
5. Missing return.

Let's dive into each of these.

Mistake 1: Forgotten or Incorrect Base Cases

What would happen if we called our recursive factorial function, `factorial_rec()`, with 0? Mathematically, 0! = 1. However, we didn't define a base case for 0, so 0 would default to the recursive case. `factorial_rec(0)` would call `factorial_rec(-1)`, which would call `factorial_rec(-2)`, and so on, in an 'infinite loop' (unlike in iterative algorithms, infinite loops in recursion don't 'hang' the program—they hit stack overflow and crash it with a fatal error).

The rule of thumb is that **every valid input should be correctly classified as either base case or recursive case**. This may require adding extra cases beyond the usual "we reached the end of the input" and "we haven't reached the end of the input yet."

Mistake 2: Not Making Progress

Another basic check is that **every call in the recursive case should get closer to the base case.** Imagine that, in Solution 33.1, we coded moves() as follows:

```
1  def moves(seq):
2      if len(seq) == 0:
```

```
3        return ""
4    if seq[0] == '2':
5        return moves(seq[1:]) + moves(seq[2:])
6    if seq[0] in "LR":
7        return seq[0] + moves(seq[1:])
8    # Unknown instruction--try again.
9    return moves(seq)
```

The final case does not move us closer to the base case, so it would result in an infinite loop. Whenever you write a recursive call in your code, ask yourself: *is it making progress toward the base case?* It won't always be as obvious as our silly example!

Mistake 3: Making Unnecessary Copies

Many recursive implementations involve passing around arrays and strings. If you review our implementation of moves( ) in Solution 33.1, we did just that. In the process, we created two inefficiencies:

1. Every recursive call *creates a copy* of seq with one or two fewer characters (Python slicing makes copies).
2. Every string returned by the recursive calls is copied again when we do string concatenation (+).

We can fix (1) by passing our current index idx in seq rather than a string. We can fix (2) by appending all the characters into a single output array, res (we say an array instead of a string because, in Python, it's not possible to append to a string without making a copy, but we can convert the array to a string at the end).

To add these improvements, we need to create a helper function with the proper parameters:

```
1    def moves(seq):
2        res = []
3        moves_rec(seq, 0, res)
4        return ''.join(res)
5
6    # Adds to res the instructions for the robot starting from seq[idx]
7    def moves_rec(seq, idx, res):
8        if idx == len(seq):
9            # No instructions left
10           return
11       if seq[idx] == '2':
12           moves_rec(seq, idx+1, res)
13           moves_rec(seq, idx+2, res)
14       else:
15           res.append(seq[idx])
16           moves_rec(seq, idx+1, res)
```

Now, there is a single copy of seq and res throughout the entire algorithm.

♻ REUSABLE IDEA: PASS INDICES, NOT COPIES

By referencing positions within an original array or string using indices, we can eliminate the overhead of slicing and copying, improving time and space efficiency.

Avoiding copies does not only apply to recursion, but it can stack up quickly in recursive algorithms. It is very language dependent, so do some research on your language of choice about how to avoid them (we touched on this in "The space complexity of copies" on page 223).

Mistake 4: Merging Recursive Calls Incorrectly

When we make more than one recursive call, we need to combine the results somehow. In the 'Robot Instructions' problem, it is fairly clear that we need to concatenate the strings, but it won't always be straightforward.

Sometimes, when the recursive calls return numbers, it's not clear if we should add them or multiply them together.

Our advice is to work through a small example, drawing the call tree and what should be returned at each node.

Mistake 5: Missing Return

A more subtle class of mistakes revolves around **forgetting to "catch" the return value** or doing it incorrectly. What is wrong with the following snippets?

```
1  # BAD CODE
2  def binary_search(arr, target, l, r):
3    if l > r: return -1
4    mid = (l + r)//2
5    if arr[mid] == target:
6      return mid
7    elif arr[mid] > target:
8      binary_search(arr, target, l, mid - 1)
9    else:
10     binary_search(arr, target, mid + 1, r)
```

```
1  # BAD CODE
2  def moves(seq):
3    res = []
4    def moves_rec(pos):
5      if pos == len(seq):
6        return
7      if seq[pos] == '2':
8        moves_rec(pos+1)
9        moves_rec(pos+2)
10     else:
11       res.append(seq[pos])
12       moves_rec(pos+1)
13   return moves_rec(0)
```

Left: We forgot to "catch" the value of the recursive calls. Unless `target` happens to be precisely in the middle of the array, the function returns None.

Right: We forgot that `moves_rec()` stores the solution in `res` instead of returning it directly. As a result, `moves()` always returns None.

A recursive function standing alone on its own line without a return could indicate you forgot to catch the return value.[4]

IMPLEMENTATION CHOICES

In this section, we'll go over the typical things you need to consider when implementing a recursive solution. The goal is to be aware of the trade-offs and, when subjective, to find your preferred style and stick to it during practice. In later chapters, we'll give tailored advice for specific topics that use recursion, like trees, backtracking, and so on.

When to Use Helper Functions?

The function signature you are given may not be the most convenient for recursion, but that is not a big deal. You can design your own signature in a helper function. On line 6 on page 397, we did just that to avoid unnecessary copies.

Our preferred style in Python is to nest the helper functions inside the main function. For instance, in Solution 33.1, we don't need to pass `seq` and `res` as parameters, making it extra clear that we are not copying them:

```
1  def moves(seq):
2    res = []
3    def moves_rec(pos):
4      if pos == len(seq):
5        return
6      if seq[pos] == '2':
```

---

4 Recall that, in the 'How To Practice' chapter, we suggested keeping a 'bug list' with the mistakes that **you** commonly make (pg 172).

```
 7            moves_rec(pos+1)
 8            moves_rec(pos+2)
 9        else:
10            res.append(seq[pos])
11            moves_rec(pos+1)
12    moves_rec(0)
13    return ''.join(res)
```

Returning Values Directly Vs Updating a Variable

As a rule of thumb, if the output is just a numeric value, as in `factorial_rec()`, it's probably simpler to return it directly. If the output takes more than constant space, as in `moves()`, it's better to update the same variable throughout the call tree to avoid copies. This could be a variable passed by reference or a variable declared outside the recursive function but 'visible' from it (like `seq` and `req` in the previous snippet).[5]

Eager vs. Lazy Parameter Validation

Eager validation means that we validate the parameters *before* passing them to a recursive call, while lazy validation means that we validate them *after* the recursive call when we receive them as a base case. For instance, consider Problem 33.2:

✦ | **PROBLEM 33.2** | **NESTED ARRAY SUM**

A *nested array* is an array where each element is either:

1. An integer, or
2. A nested array (note that this is a recursive definition).

The *sum* of a nested array is defined recursively as the sum of all its elements.

Given a nested array, `arr`, return its sum.

► **Example:** arr = [1, [2, 3], [4, [5]], 6]
  Output: 21
► **Example:** arr = [[[[1]], 2]]
  Output: 3
► **Example:** arr = []
  Output: 0

Note: in Python, you can use `isinstance(x, int)` to check if x is an integer.

SOLUTION 33.2   NESTED ARRAY SUM

This problem is a good fit for recursion because we don't know upfront how many layers of nested arrays there are, which means that we can't just use a fixed number of loops (like we use two loops to iterate through the elements of a grid).

We have two ways for how to handle array elements that are integers.

Eager Checking

we check if `arr[i]` is a number before passing it to a recursive call.

Lazy Checking

pass `arr[i]` to a recursive call even if the element is a number, and catch it in a base case.

---

5 A common 'code cleanliness' advice is to avoid global variables. That's why we prefer scoping them to the outer function (or outer class in object-oriented languages).

```
1  def nested_array_sum_eager(arr):        1  def nested_array_sum_lazy(arr):
2    res = 0                               2    if isinstance(arr, int):
3    for elem in arr:                      3      return arr
4      if isinstance(elem, int):           4    res = 0
5        res += elem                       5    for elem in arr:
6      else:                               6      res += nested_array_sum_lazy(elem)
7        res += nested_array_sum_eager(elem)  7    return res
8    return res
```

Both lazy and eager approaches are correct (and have the same runtime)—the important point is that, depending on how we design the recursive case, we may need extra base cases to cover all the possibilities.

In general, we don't strongly prefer one over the other. When the code has multiple recursive calls, one advantage of lazy validation is that we only need to do it once at the beginning of the recursive function instead of once per recursive call.

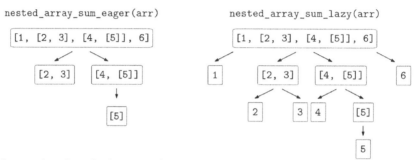

Figure 5. The call tree for the eager (left) and lazy (right) implementation for Example 1 in Problem 2. We just show the inputs at each node.

When should we even use recursion in the first place?

In general, we only use recursion for problems where it fits 'naturally,' like the ones in this chapter or the other 'recursion-first' chapters we mentioned (trees, graphs, backtracking, and memoization).[6] Depending on the programming language, we risk confusing an interviewer if we use a recursive approach to something easily handled iteratively, like searching the maximum in an array.

There is also the stack-overflow danger: we should probably avoid recursive algorithms when the potential depth is in the tens of thousands (or at least mention the concern to the interviewer).

Some algorithms are commonly coded both iteratively and recursively, like binary search, where stack overflow is not a concern. We implemented it iteratively in Binary Search (pg 327), but either approach is fine.

---

6 While certain problems are easier one way or the other, anything that can be coded recursively can be coded iteratively, and the other way around. This is not something you need to know for interviews, but a general way of converting recursive algorithms into iterative ones is to use a stack data structure to mimic what the recursion call stack does. Instead of calling a recursive function for each element, we push the parameters to a stack so we can get to them later in a LIFO order. This is not something you usually need to do in interviews, so our advice is to know this idea, but not fixate on it.

BIG O ANALYSIS

Analyzing recursive algorithms is often more difficult than iterative code because it's not about identifying loops and counting iterations. In fact, there are often no explicit loops, so we need to think about the call tree. There is one node per recursive call, so *the total amount of work done by the algorithm is the sum of the work done at each node.*

A great starting question is:

- How many nodes does the call tree have, as a function of the input size?

Consider this question for our 'Robot Instructions' problem: if the sequence has length n, how many nodes will the call tree have?

The answer is, "It depends." The tree will have fewer nodes for the sequence "LLL" than for the sequence "22L" (4 vs 7 nodes), even though both have length 3. Remember that we care about the *worst-case analysis*, i.e., the worst-case among all sequences of the same length. In our problem, this happens when the sequence contains lots of '2's, like in "22222R":

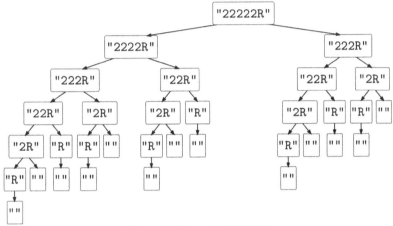

Figure 6. Call tree for "22222R".

To estimate the number of nodes in the tree, we can use the following formula:

> The maximum number of nodes in a tree with depth d and branching factor b (where $b \geq 2$) is $O(b^d)$. This is an upper bound—it may not be tight.

Where:

- The *depth* of the tree is the number of different levels.
- The *branching factor* of the tree is the maximum branching factor of any node.[7]

Why $O(b^d)$? The quick idea is that we start with one node at the root, then (up to) b nodes at the next level, then (up to) b^2 nodes at the next level (since each of the b nodes has up to b children), and so on—until the maximum level, d-1. This gives us $1 + b + b^2 + b^3 + \ldots + b^{d-1} \leq b^d$. (If you don't see how the left part is less than or equal to the right, see page 450.)

In many algorithms, the actual number of nodes ends up being less than this upper bound. For instance, for the 'Robot Instructions' problem, the maximum branching factor is b = 2, and the depth is d = n + 1, so the number of nodes is bounded by $O(2^{n+1})$, which we can simplify to $O(2 * 2^n) = O(2^n)$. However, this

---

7   We define these terms and more tree notation on page 430.

is *not tight* because, even in the worst case where the input has $n-1$ 2's, not all leaves in the call tree are at maximum depth (like in Figure 7). The number of nodes is closer to $O(1.618^n)$, but the math to derive the exact formula is beyond what you need for interviews.

THE BAD METHOD

Now that we have an upper bound on the total number of nodes in the call tree, we can return to the original problem: What's the total runtime of recursive algorithms?

> **The BAD method:** if we have a recursive algorithm and we know the maximum branching factor $b \geq 2$, the maximum depth d, and an upper bound $O(A)$ on the amount of *additional* work (not counting recursion) that happens at any particular node, then we can bound the total amount of work done by the algorithm by $O(b^d * A)$.

We use the acronym 'BAD' because it reminds us of the 3 variables that come up in the analysis, but also because this method can be "bad" in that it gives us a valid upper bound, but not necessarily the smallest one. It may not be tight if:

Reasons why the BAD method may not be tight	Example
• Not all leaves are at maximum depth	'Robot Instructions' problem
• Not all non-leaf nodes have the maximum branching factor	Permutation-based backtracking algorithms (pg 555)
• Not all nodes do the same amount of additional (non-recursive) work.	Merge sort (we'll analyze it shortly)

Even though the BAD method may not be tight, it is likely the level of analysis expected in interviews. If you think it is not tight for any of the listed reasons, mention it to the interviewer and explain why. You could say something like, "This is an upper bound, but I am not sure if it is tight because the amount of non-recursive work is not the same at every level."

\# Memorize the time complexity for well-known recursive algorithms like merge sort and quicksort. For anything else, there's the BAD method.

In the 'Robot Instructions' solution (the efficient one that doesn't make string copies, pg 397), the non-recursive work done at each node is just a couple of simple if statements and appending to an array, which takes (amortized) constant time. Thus, the BAD method tells us that the total amount of work is bounded by $O(2^n * 1) = O(2^n)$.

It helps to write things down clearly for the interviewer. You could write something like:

```
n: the length of seq
branching factor: 2
depth: n
additional work per node: O(1)
time: O(2^n * 1) = O(2^n)
space: O(2^n)
```

Try applying the concepts from this section in the following problem set:

PROBLEM SET

Imagine that you solved the 'robot instructions' problem in an interview, and the interviewer adds these follow-up questions. (You don't need to code anything at this point.)

QUESTION 1   BOUNDED TWOS

The interviewer tells us that the input sequence contains at most five instances of '2'. How does that change the runtime?

QUESTION 2   TRIPLE REPEAT

Consider a variation where the input sequence can also contain the character '3', which means "perform all the instructions after this '3' three times." How would you modify the algorithm? What would be the time complexity now?

QUESTION 3   STAR MULTIPLIER

Consider a variation where the input sequence can also contain the character '*', which means "do the 'R' instruction n times, where n is the length of the **input** sequence." How would you modify the algorithm? What would be the time complexity now?

ANSWERS

ANSWER 1   BOUNDED TWOS

With this restriction, nodes at only five levels of the tree can split into two children. This means that the number of leaves is at most $2^5 = 32$, which is a constant. So, the total amount of nodes is $O(32 * n) = O(n)$. Since the additional work per node is $O(1)$, $O(n)$ is also the runtime complexity.

ANSWER 2   TRIPLE REPEAT

We would add one more if statement for the '3' case, which would call the function recursively three times. With this change, the maximum branching factor is now 3, so, per the BAD method, the time complexity is $O(3^n * 1) = O(3^n)$.

ANSWER 3   STAR MULTIPLIER

We would add one more if statement for the '*' case, which would append 'R' to res n times. The nodes in the call tree corresponding to '*' do $O(n)$ additional work, so, per the BAD method, the time complexity is $O(2^n * n)$.

MERGE SORT ANALYSIS

At first glance, it might seem like the BAD method doesn't work for merge sort. After all, we know merge sort is $O(n \log n)$, not something that looks like $O(b^d * A)$. Then again, it'd be a bit troubling if it just *didn't work* for this algorithm — so let's give it a shot.

Recall that merge sort splits the input array down the middle, sorts each half recursively, and then merges the two halves into a single sorted list (pg 362).

To use the BAD method, let's identify the 3 variables:

- **Branching factor:** 2, because we branch left and right.
- **Depth:** $\log_2(n)$. At each recursive call, the size of the input is *halved*. So, if n is the length of the input array, the depth is the number of halvings it takes to reach 1, which is the definition of $\log_2(n)$.
- **Additional work:** The node that does the most non-recursive work is the root, as it needs to merge two arrays of length n/2 each, which takes $O(n)$ time.

Using the equation $O(b^d * A)$, we get $O(2^{\log_2(n)} * n)$. Since $2^{\log_2(n)} = n$, we get $O(n * n) = O(n^2)$.

The BAD method gave us a valid upper bound, but it is *not* tight. It would be correct if every node in the call tree did $O(n)$ additional work, but that is a gross overestimation. After all, the leaves and nodes near the leaves have to merge very small arrays, and most nodes are near the leaves. We have a few nodes doing a lot of additional work and many nodes doing very little:

- One node (the root) has to merge arrays of length n/2,
- Two nodes have to merge arrays of length n/4,
- Four nodes have to merge arrays of length n/8,
- and so on.

If we add up the lengths of the arrays from all the nodes, level by level, we get:

$$n + 2*n/2 + 4*n/4 + 8*n/8 + \ldots + n*n/n = n + n + n + n + \ldots + n$$

---

8 You got me (Mike). I'm the interviewer in this interview, though it was years before writing this book.

That is, all the nodes across each level do O(n) work combined, and there are O(log n) levels, so the total work is O(n log n):

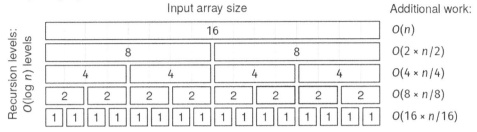

Figure 7.

This analysis is beyond what is expected in interviews. Since merge sort is a well-known algorithm, it is worth just memorizing that its runtime is O(n log n).

The concepts we learned, such as the call tree, the branching factor, the height, and the BAD method, make it easy to analyze recursive algorithms. As with everything, more advanced methods exist for analyzing recursive algorithms, such as the 'master theorem.' We find that these advanced methods are not expected in interviews (many interviewers do not know them themselves), so we do not recommend learning them.

SPACE ANALYSIS

We usually analyze the extra space used by our code based on the space our variables take. However, our programs create another type of memory that we often don't think about: the call stack.

The call stack counts as extra space created by your function, so we need to include it in the space analysis. The space used implicitly by the call stack (not including variables that you define yourself) is O(maximum call depth). That is, what matters is the maximum *nested* calls, not the overall number of calls (i.e., not the number of nodes in the call tree).

You don't need to worry about the space taken by the call stack for non-recursive functions—even if you call a function many times, you are doing a constant number of nested calls at most, so the call stack takes O(1) extra space. In contrast, in recursive functions, the number of nested calls usually depends on the input, so the extra space used by the call stack is typically not constant.

Quiz: If k is a number and arr is a list with n integers, what is the extra-space complexity of the following snippet?

```
1  def reverse_in_place(arr):
2    reverse_rec(arr, 0, len(arr)-1)
3    def reverse_rec(arr, i, j):
4      if i >= j:
5        return
6      arr[i], arr[j] = arr[j], arr[i]
7      reverse_rec(arr, i+1, j-1)
```

Answer: reverse_in_place() modifies the input array in place, so you may think it uses only O(1) *extra* space. However, it calls a recursive function with roughly n/2 nested calls, so that's the number of return addresses we need to store in the call stack. This takes O(n) space. Furthermore, if n could be large, we risk hitting stack overflow, so we'd favor an iterative implementation.

RECURRENCE RELATIONS

A *recurrence relation* is a function defined in terms of itself with smaller inputs. The classic examples are factorials, which we've already seen, and Fibonacci numbers, F_n, which are defined as follows for any $n \geq 0$:

```
F₀ = 1
F₁ = 1
For n > 1, Fₙ = Fₙ₋₁ + Fₙ₋₂
```

Sometimes the best way to approach a problem is to (1) find a recurrence relation that computes the solution and (2) code it up. Here's an example:

✤✤ **PROBLEM 33.3**   **POWERS MOD M**

Given two integers, $a > 1$ and $p \geq 0$, the basic recurrence relation for powers is:

```
a0 = 1
For p > 0,   ap = a * ap-1
```

We also have an integer $m > 1$, and we want to compute a^p % m. Recall that, when it comes to the modulo operation, we can apply it at each step without affecting the result:

```
a0 % m = 1
For p > 0, ap % m = (a * (ap-1 % m)) % m
```

Return a^p % m while avoiding storing intermediate values much larger than m.

▸ **Example:** a = 2, p = 5, m = 100
  Output: 32

▸ **Example:** a = 2, p = 5, m = 30
  Output: 2

♺ **REUSABLE IDEA: APPLYING MODULO AT EACH STEP**

> Some problems involve math operations that could result in really large integers that overflow in some languages. As a workaround, many questions ask to return the solution modulo some large prime (we'll use 10^9+7 in this book).
>
> When we see that, we should apply the modulo at each step rather than at the very end, to avoid overflow/ working with really large numbers. The neat property of modulo is that, if an operation only involves sums, subtractions, and multiplications (but *not* divisions), applying it at each step does not change the final output.
>
> E.g., (10 + 3 + 10 + 6) % 5 is 4, and so is (10 % 5) + (3 % 5) + (10 % 5) + (6 % 5).
>
> Division is the exception: dividing first and then applying modulo yields different results than applying modulo first and then dividing: (12 / 3) % 5 != (12 % 5) / 3.

SOLUTION 33.3   POWERS MOD M

We could code up the recurrence relation in the statement. Since we go from p to p-1, it would take O(p) time to reach the base case.

However, a *trick* to speed it up is to use an alternative but equivalent recurrence relation that can be computed more efficiently. The key property is that, if p is even, $a^p = a^{p/2} * a^{p/2}$. For instance, $2^{10} = 2^5 * 2^5 = 32 * 32 = 1024$. This property is great because it allows us to compute a^p in terms of a to a smaller exponent, but we can halve the exponent rather than decrease it one by one. We get the following recurrence relation:

```
a0 = 1
For even p > 0, ap = ap/2 * ap/2
For odd p > 0, ap = a * ap-1
```

That is, we compute 2^{10} as 2^5 * 2^5, 2^5 as 2 * 2^4, 2^4 as 2^2 * 2^2, and 2^2 as 2^1 * 2^1. When coding it, we apply the modulo at each step that can create numbers larger than m:

```
1  def power(a, p, m):
2    if p == 0:
3      return 1
4    if p % 2 == 0:
5      half = power(a, p // 2, m)
6      return (half * half) % m
7    return (a * power(a, p - 1, m)) % m
```

The branching factor of the call tree is 1, so the BAD method doesn't apply—the number of nodes is simply the depth. We halve p at most every two recursive calls, so the number of nodes is $O(\log p)$. Since we do $O(1)$ additional work at each node, the total runtime is $O(\log p)$.

MEMOIZATION

A key optimization when computing recurrence relations is **avoiding recomputing the same value twice**. This is important when the recurrence relation has more than one recursive term, as in Fibonacci. The solution is known as *caching* or *memoization*: we store the terms we computed so far in a map, and then check if they are already computed before using recursion:

Without **memoization: exponential runtime.**

```
1  def fib(n):
2    if n <= 1:
3      return 1
4    return fib(n-1) + fib(n-2)
```

With **memoization: linear runtime.**

```
1  def fib(n):
2    memo = {}
3    def fib_rec(i):
4      if i <= 1:
5        return 1
6      if i in memo:
7        return memo[i]
8      memo[i] = fib_rec(i-1) + fib_rec(i-2)
9      return memo[i]
10   return fib_rec(n)
```

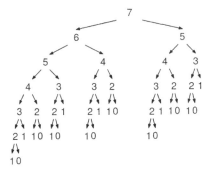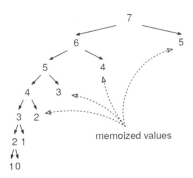

Figure 8. Call tree for Fibonacci without memoization (left) and with it (right).

While the call tree without memoization has exponential size ($O(2^n)$ per the BAD method[9]), we can see that the call tree on the right only has two nodes per level, so the runtime is $O(2n) = O(n)$.

---

9 The runtime is closer to $O(1.618^n)$ — but this involves math you don't need to know and your interviewer probably won't know either.

Memoization is the core technique behind dynamic programming, which we will discuss in Chapter 40: Dynamic Programming (pg 566).

RECURRENCE RELATIONS PROBLEM SET

Find recurrence relations for the following problems. You don't need to code them up.

QUESTION 4   **4TILING A 1XN FLOOR**

Given n > 1, find the number of different ways to cover a 1xn floor with 1x1 and 2x1 tiles.

▸ **Example:** n = 4
  Output: 5. The floor can be tiled as:

Figure 9.

QUESTION 5   **5TILING A 3XN FLOOR**

Given n ≥ 3, find the number of different ways to cover a 3xn floor with 3x1 and 1x3 tiles.

▸ **Example:** n = 6
  Output: 6. The floor can be tiled as:

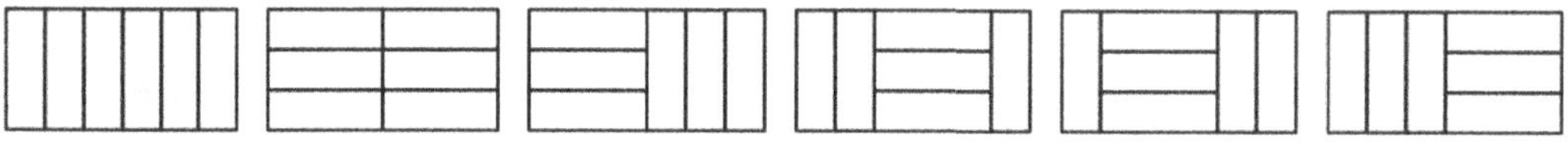

Figure 10.

PROBLEM SET SOLUTIONS

ANSWER 4   TILING A 1XN FLOOR

Let's call our recurrence relation tilings(n). If n is 1, we can only use a 1x1 tile, so tilings(1) = 1. For larger floors, we have two ways to cover the leftmost tile. If we put a 1x1 tile, we need to cover n - 1 remaining tiles, but if we put a 2x1 tile, we need to cover n - 2 remaining tiles. The recurrence relation ends up being the same as Fibonacci:

```
tilings(0) = 1
tilings(1) = 1
For n > 1, tilings(n) = tilings(n - 1) + tilings(n - 2)
```

ANSWER 5   TILING A 3XN FLOOR

Again, it helps to focus on what happens with the leftmost column. If we put a vertical tile, we have n - 1 columns remaining. If we put a horizontal tile, we'll have to put 2 more horizontal tiles under it, and we'll have n - 3 columns left. We end up with a recurrence like:

```
tilings(0) = 1
tilings(1) = 1
tilings(2) = 0
For n > 2, tilings(n) = tilings(n - 1) + tilings(n - 3)
```

Try using recurrence relations to solve the following interview question:

✦ **PROBLEM 33.4** **LEGO CASTLE**

You're building an n-story 2D Lego castle following these instructions:

- A 1-story castle is just a 1x1 block.
- An n-story castle is made with two (n-1)-story castles, side by side, one unit apart, with a row of blocks above them connecting them:

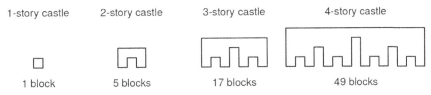

Figure 11.

Given n > 0, return the number of 1x1 blocks in an n-story castle.

SOLUTION 33.4 LEGO CASTLE

We're trying to find a formula, blocks(n), which returns the number of blocks needed for an n-story castle:

- blocks(1) = 1, and
- for n > 1, blocks(n) can probably be obtained from blocks(n - 1) somehow.

We can use the **break down the problem** booster and introduce another function, roof(n), representing the number of blocks in the top row of an n-story castle. This makes the recurrence relation for blocks(n) straightforward:

blocks(n) = 2 * blocks(n - 1) + roof(n)

Next, we need to tackle roof(n). We can again use a recurrence relation:

- roof(1) = 1
- for n > 1, roof(n) = 2 * roof(n - 1) + 1

Finally, we can translate the recurrence relations into code:

```
def blocks(n):
    if n == 1: return 1
    return blocks(n-1)*2 + roof(n)

def roof(n):
    if n == 1: return 1
    return roof(n-1)*2 + 1
```

Can you analyze the time complexity? We can visualize the call tree:

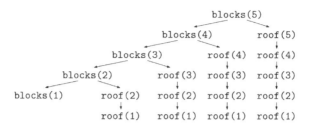

Figure 12.

- roof(n) takes O(n) time, since each recursive call decreases n by 1.
- blocks(n) calls roof(n) and blocks(n-1), which calls roof(n-1) and blocks(n-2), which calls roof(n-2) and blocks(n-3), and so on. The time complexity ends up being $O(n) + O(n-1) + O(n-2) + \ldots + O(1) = O(n^2)$.

We can improve the time complexity to O(n) by *memoizing* the repeated calls to roof().

```
1   def blocks(n):
2     memo = dict()
3     def roof(n):
4       if n == 1:
5         return 1
6       if n in memo:
7         return memo[n]
8       memo[n] = roof(n-1)*2 + 1
9       return memo[n]
10    def blocks_rec(n):
11      if n == 1:
12        return 1
13      return blocks_rec(n-1)*2 + roof(n)
14    return blocks_rec(n)
```

DIVIDE AND CONQUER

Divide-and-conquer is a type of recursive algorithm where:

- We *divide* the input into *disjoint* parts.
- We solve each part recursively.
- We combine the solution to each part into the final solution.

The classic divide-and-conquer algorithms are merge sort and quicksort. There are not that many interview questions where divide and conquer is the go-to approach, so don't worry too much about it. To get a taste, we'll give here one example of a problem that can be tackled with divide and conquer.

✦✦ **PROBLEM 33.5**   **LAMINAL ARRAYS**

We are given an array, arr, whose length is a power of 2. We determine if an array is *laminal* as follows:

- The array arr is laminal.
- Each half of a laminal array is laminal.
- A subarray of arr with a single element is laminal.

Find the laminal subarray in arr with maximum sum and return its sum.

▶ **Example:** arr = [3, -9, 2, 4, -1, 5, 5, -4]
  Output: 6. The laminal arrays are:
            [3, -9, 2, 4, -1, 5, 5, -4],
            [3, -9, 2, 4], [-1, 5, 5, -4]
            [3, -9], [2, 4], [-1, 5], [5, -4],
            [3], [-9], [2], [4], [-1], [5], [5], [-4]
The one with the maximum sum is [2, 4].

▶ **Example:** arr = [1]
  Output: 1.

▶ **Example:** arr = [-1, -2]
  Output: -1.

SOLUTION 33.5   LAMINAL ARRAYS

The self-referential nature of the 'laminal' definition makes this problem a good fit for recursion. Furthermore, the fact that the elements from the first half of arr are not in any of the same laminal subarrays as the elements from the second half allows us to employ a divide-and-conquer strategy:

- Find the max-sum laminal subarray in the first half of arr,
- Find the max-sum laminal subarray in the second half of arr,
- Return the max-sum array between those and arr itself.

```
 1   def max_laminal_sum(arr):
 2     # Returns the max sum for a subliminal array in arr[l:r].
 3     def max_laminal_sum_rec(l, r):
 4       if r - l == 1:
 5         return arr[l]
 6       mid = (l + r) // 2
 7       option1 = max_laminal_sum_rec(l, mid)
 8       option2 = max_laminal_sum_rec(mid, r)
 9       option3 = sum(arr)
10       return max(option1, option2, option3)
11     return max_laminal_sum_rec(0, len(arr))
```

Like merge sort, the call tree has $O(\log n)$ depth, branching factor 2, and $O(n)$ additional work at the root (for sum(arr)), which halves at each depth. The runtime is $O(n \log n)$ (as shown in Figure 7).

We can further optimize it by returning the sum of each half so that we don't need to make the expensive sum(arr) call:

```
 1   def max_laminal_sum(arr):
 2     # Returns the max sum for a subliminal array in arr[l:r] and the sum of arr[l:r].
 3     def max_laminal_sum_rec(l, r):
 4       if r - l == 1:
 5         return arr[l], arr[l]
 6       mid = (l + r) // 2
 7       option1, left_sum = max_laminal_sum_rec(l, mid)
 8       option2, right_sum = max_laminal_sum_rec(mid, r)
 9       option3 = left_sum + right_sum
10       return max(option1, option2, option3), option3
11     res, _ = max_laminal_sum_rec(0, len(arr))
12     return res
```

Now that all the nodes do the same amount of additional work, the BAD method gives a tight upper bound: $O(b^d * A) = O(2^{\log_2 n} * 1) = O(n)$.

KEY TAKEAWAYS

Nailing recursion starts with internalizing concepts like the *call stack* and the *call tree*; these will help you understand future recursion-focused topics, like backtracking and dynamic programming (which we already hinted at when we talked about *memoization*).

Big O analysis of recursive algorithms is a common source of confusion for candidates, so we proposed the BAD method, which should satisfy all but the most math-inclined interviewers.

Recursion triggers

- The input data is a recursive data structure or has a recursive or "nesting" nature (e.g., a binary tree or an array where each element can itself be an array).

- The problem statement includes a self-referential definition (e.g., Fibonacci or Problem 33.5: Laminal Arrays, pg 410).

- You find yourself wanting to write a number of nested loops that depend on the input.

- Merge sort or quicksort related.

Keywords: nested, quicksort, merge sort

ONLINE RESOURCES

Online resources for this chapter include:

- A chance to try each problem in this chapter in AI Interviewer
- Interview replays that show specific mistakes people make with recursion problems
- Full code solutions for every problem in the chapter in multiple programming languages

Try online at bctci.co/recursion.

## CHAPTER 34

LINKED LISTS

AI interviewer, replays, and more materials for this chapter at bctci.co/linked-lists

> Let's just say, I know a guy who knows a guy... who
> knows another guy.
>
> Saul Goodman

▶ *Prerequisites: None*

A linked list is a data structure consisting of an ordered sequence of nodes. There are two main types:

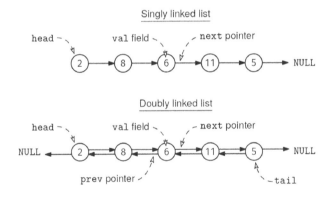

Figure 1.

Nodes are objects of a Node class/data type:

```python
# Singly linked list node.
class Node:
    def __init__(self, val):
        self.val = val
        self.next = None
```

```python
# Doubly linked list node.
class Node:
    def __init__(self, val):
        self.val = val
        self.next = None
        self.prev = None
```

The **singly linked list** node has a single 'link' (i.e., reference or pointer) to the next node, meaning we can only traverse the list forward. The **doubly linked list** node also has a link to the previous node, allowing us to travel the list forward and backward.

The *head* of a linked list is the start of the chain and is the only node we keep track of directly. From it, we can sequentially access the other nodes until we reach a node whose next link is null (None in Python). That's the last node, which is sometimes called the *tail*.

WHY NOT JUST USE A DYNAMIC ARRAY?

Dynamic arrays are wonderful. They store the elements contiguously in memory, which means that each index has a predictable memory address and can be accessed in O(1) time. They also allow appending and removing elements at the end in O(1) amortized time.

Nonetheless, they have their downside: if we want to add an element at the start, or between two elements, we have to shift all the elements after it down.

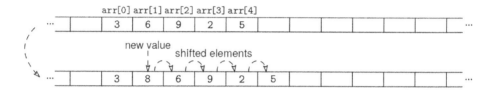

Figure 2. Inserting an element at index 1 to an array. The array is stored sequentially somewhere in memory.

With linked lists, we have a next pointer at each node, which can point anywhere in memory. That means that we can insert an element at any index without moving existing elements. We just need to update the next pointer of its predecessor:

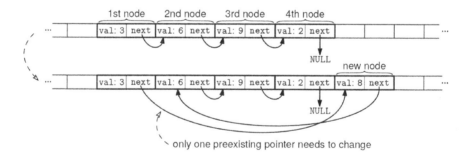

Figure 3. Inserting a linked list node at 'index' 1.

MANIPULATING LINKED LISTS

To warm up, let's see how we could do some basic manipulations with a **singly linked** list. We could create a list with two nodes as follows:

```
1   head = Node(1)
2   head.next = Node(2)
```

The list 'looks' like 1 -> 2. Imagine we want to add a new value, 3, at the end. We could do:

```
1   new = Node(3)
```

```
2    head.next.next = new
```

This code relies on the fact that the list had two elements. To make it more generic, we could use a while loop to reach the end of the linked list:

```
1    def add_to_end(head, val):
2      cur = head
3      while cur.next:
4        cur = cur.next
5      cur.next = Node(val)
```

In Python, we can use an object like `cur.next` directly as a boolean condition. It evaluates to false if the object is null (None). It is equivalent to `cur.next != None`.

Note: this code assumes that head is not None. Otherwise, `cur.next` would try to read the next field of a null pointer, a runtime error!

\# Every time you have a node variable, and you access one of its fields (like `.next`), ask yourself: *"Am I 100% sure that this variable cannot be null at this point?"* If not, add a null check.

Our list now looks like 1 -> 2 -> 3. If we want to 'delete' the latest node that we added, we set the next pointer of the second node to null:

```
1    head.next.next = None
```

This makes it so the third node is no longer accessible.[1]

Next, imagine we want to add a new value, 4, after the first node, so the list looks like 1 -> 4 -> 2. To append a node *between* two existing nodes, we can do:

```
1    new = Node(4)
2    new.next = head.next
3    head.next = new
```

\# Careful! A common mistake in linked lists is messing up the order of operations and **losing track of a node reference**. Before updating who the head points to, we must ensure the new successor points to the previous successor. Otherwise, we would lose the only pointer to the previous successor, making it unreachable.

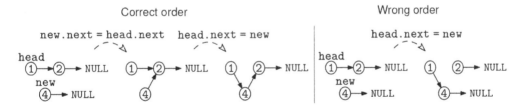

Figure 4. Correct vs wrong order of pointer updates. The wrong order leaves node 2 unreachable.

Finally, imagine we want to add a new node, 5, as the first node. We would do:

```
1    new = Node(5)
2    new.next = head
3    head = new
```

---

1   In languages with garbage collection, like Python, the program runtime will realize that the node is no longer accessible from anywhere and release its memory. In languages with manual memory management, like C/C++, we should free the memory of the node manually. Otherwise, the memory will remain occupied but unreachable until the program stops running. This is called a *memory leak*.

DESIGN

Building singly linked and doubly linked lists from scratch is an effective way to understand how they work. We can think of these as data structure design questions.

✦✦   **PROBLEM 34.1**   **SINGLY LINKED LIST DESIGN**

Implement a SinglyLinkedList class with the following methods. Reuse the Node class definition earlier in the chapter. The size() method should take O(1) time.

```
SinglyLinkedList:
  init():        Initializes an empty list.
  push_front(v): Adds a node with value v at the beginning of the list.
  pop_front():   Removes the node at the beginning of the list and returns
                 its value. If the list is empty, returns None.
  push_back(v):  Adds a node with value v at the end of the list.
  pop_back():    Removes the node at the end of the list and returns its
                 value. If the list is empty, returns None.
  size():        Returns the number of nodes in the list.
  contains(v):   Return the first node with value v, if any, or null
                 otherwise.
```

SOLUTION 34.1   SINGLY LINKED LIST DESIGN

Our class has two fields: the head of the list and a node counter so that we don't need to iterate through the list to find the size.

```
 1   class SinglyLinkedList:
 2     def __init__(self):
 3       self.head = None
 4       self._size = 0
 5     def size(self):
 6       return self._size
```

Adding to and removing from the front of the list is similar to the warmup manipulations.[2]

```
 1   def push_front(self, val):
 2     new = Node(val)
 3     new.next = self.head
 4     self.head = new
 5     self._size += 1
 6
 7   def pop_front(self):
 8     if not self.head:
 9       return None
10     val = self.head.val
11     self.head = self.head.next
12     self._size -= 1
13     return val
```

Adding a new node to the end requires traversing the list to the last node.

```
 1   def push_back(self, val):
 2     new = Node(val)
```

---

2   In languages with manual memory management, like C, when we remove a node, we need to release the memory used by the node. Otherwise, we would introduce a *memory leak*. For instance, in pop_front(), we would need to delete the old head node. In languages with garbage collection, like Python, the runtime will do it for us.

```
3      self._size += 1
4      if not self.head:
5        self.head = new
6        return
7      cur = self.head
8      while cur.next:
9        cur = cur.next
10     cur.next = new
```

It is possible to optimize this method to O(1) time by adding a tail field to our class that always points to the last node. Then, we could skip the traversal. The only downside is that we need to remember to update this extra pointer whenever the tail changes.

Removing the last node requires traversing the list and stopping at the second-to-last node so we can update its next pointer.

```
1    def pop_back(self):
2      if not self.head:
3        return None
4      self._size -= 1
5      if not self.head.next:
6        val = self.head.val
7        self.head = None
8        return val
9      cur = self.head
10     while cur.next and cur.next.next:
11       cur = cur.next
12     val = cur.next.val
13     cur.next = None
14     return val
```

Accessing multiple levels of pointers, like cur.next.next, should raise your alert level, as it's easy to mistakenly access a field of a null pointer. It's worth pausing to ask: *"Am I 100% sure that cur.next cannot be null at this point?"* This is why we check that cur.next is not null before checking if cur.next.next is.

Finally, the contains method traverses the list to check for a given value.

```
1    def contains(self, val):
2      cur = self.head
3      while cur:
4        if cur.val == val:
5          return cur
6        cur = cur.next
7      return None
```

✦ ┃ PROBLEM 34.2 ┃ **DOUBLY LINKED LIST DESIGN**

Implement a DoublyLinkedList class with the same methods as in Problem 1. The push_back(), pop_back(), push_front(), and pop_front() methods should all take O(1) time.

SOLUTION 34.2   DOUBLY LINKED LIST DESIGN

This solution can be found online. It requires extra care to handle prev pointers, as well as maintaining a tail pointer to make pop_back() and push_back() efficient.

ANALYSIS

From this design, we can understand the complexities associated with singly and doubly linked lists.

SPACE	O(N)
push_front(v)	O(1)
pop_front()	O(1)
push_back(v)	O(n) (O(1) with a tail pointer)
pop_back()	O(n) in singly linked lists (O(1) in doubly linked lists with a tail pointer).[3]
contains(v)	O(n)
size()	O(1)

Table 1. Linked list analysis.

RECURSIVE VS ITERATIVE

Our solutions so far have been iterative. We generally favor iterative traversals for linked lists because they take O(1) space, whereas recursive solutions require O(n) space for the call stack (pg 392). Practically speaking, recursion can make the code shorter, but it's also often harder to debug. If you use recursion, make sure to analyze the space correctly, and bring up the potential issue of stack overflow (pg 393).

DATA STRUCTURE DESIGN PROBLEM SET

✦ *Try these problems with AI Interviewer: bctci.co/linked-lists-problem-set-1*

PROBLEM 34.3   LINKED-LIST-BASED STACK

Implement a Stack class like the one on page 379 using a singly linked list. It should support push(), pop(), peek(), size(), and empty(), all in O(1) time.

PROBLEM 34.4   LINKED-LIST-BASED QUEUE

Implement a Queue class like the one on page 379 using a singly linked list. It should support push(), pop(), peek(), size(), and empty(), all in O(1) time.

PROBLEM SET SOLUTIONS.

SOLUTION 34.3   LINKED-LIST-BASED STACK

We can use the front of the linked list as the top of the stack. push() becomes push_front() and pop() becomes pop_front(). Both take constant time.

SOLUTION 34.4   LINKED-LIST-BASED QUEUE

Like in the previous solution, we can still pop from the front of the linked list with pop_front(). However, we must push to the opposite end with push_back(). For push() to be efficient, we need to keep a pointer to the tail of the list.

---

3 In singly linked lists, the pop_back() method cannot take advantage of the tail pointer because we can't go to the second-to-last node from tail without the prev pointer.

```
1   class Node:
2     def __init__(self, val):
3       self.val = val
4       self.next = None
5
6   class Queue:
7     def __init__(self):
8       self.head = None
9       self.tail = None
10      self._size = 0
11
12    def empty(self):
13      return not self.head
14
15    def size(self):
16      return self._size
17
18    def push(self, val):
19      new = Node(val)
20      if self.tail:
21        self.tail.next = new
22      self.tail = new
23      if not self.head:
24        self.head = new
25      self._size += 1
26
27    def pop(self):
28      if self.empty():
29        raise IndexError("empty queue")
30      val = self.head.val
31      self.head = self.head.next
32      if not self.head:
33        self.tail = None
34      self._size -= 1
35      return val
```

REUSABLE TECHNIQUES

In this section, we'll look at problems where the input is a linked list, and we need to do something with it. We'll see three techniques that make this type of problem easier.

DUMMY NODES

A common edge case in linked lists that requires special handling is when the head is null. To 'eliminate' this edge case, we can start by creating a 'dummy node' that is not part of the real list and attaching it to the front. Then, we do whatever we had to do to the list with the new dummy head.

REUSABLE IDEA: DUMMY NODE

Adding a dummy node at the head simplifies edge cases by reducing null checks—just don't forget that the real head is dummy.next!

✦✦ **PROBLEM 34.5**   **LINKED-LIST COPY**

Given the head, head, of a singly linked list, return a **new** list with the same values. The list may be empty.

SOLUTION 34.5   LINKED-LIST COPY

This question isn't particularly difficult, but it shows how we can use a dummy node to eliminate the null head check and copy the head node the same way as all the rest.

No Dummy Node

```
 1  def copy_list(head):
 2    if not head:
 3      return None
 4    new_head = Node(head.val)
 5    cur_new = new_head
 6    cur_old = head.next
 7    while cur_old:
 8      cur_new.next = Node(cur_old.val)
 9      cur_new = cur_new.next
10      cur_old = cur_old.next
11    return new_head
```

With Dummy Node

```
 1  def copy_list(head):
 2    dummy = Node(0)
 3    cur_new = dummy
 4    cur_old = head
 5    while cur_old:
 6      cur_new.next = Node(cur_old.val)
 7      cur_new = cur_new.next
 8      cur_old = cur_old.next
 9    return dummy.next
```

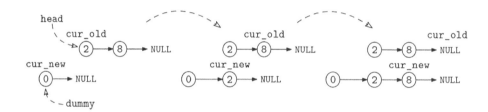

Figure 5. Solution 5 with dummy node.

REVERSAL PROBLEMS

Reversing a linked list, or parts of it, is a common theme in linked-list problems. We'll start with the simplest version of the problem (Problem 34.6) and later show how to reuse it to solve more complicated ones.

✦✦ **PROBLEM 34.6**   **LINKED-LIST REVERSAL**

Given the head, head, of a singly linked list, reverse the nodes *in place* and return the new head of the list. The list may be empty.

SOLUTION 34.6   LINKED-LIST REVERSAL

We can reverse one edge at a time. We iterate through the list with two pointers: cur, which points to the current node we are reversing, and prev, which points to the previous node in the original list. At each iteration, we need to

1. Store the pointer of cur.next so it doesn't become unreachable,[4]

2. flip cur.next to point to prev, and

---

4 We call the pointer nxt because next is a built-in function in Python. If you get mixed up, consider consistently using nxt in the node class too (e.g., head.nxt).

3. advance prev and cur.

At the end, prev is the new head.

```
1  def reverse_list(head):
2      prev = None
3      cur = head
4      while cur:
5          nxt = cur.next
6          cur.next = prev
7          prev = cur
8          cur = nxt
9      return prev
```

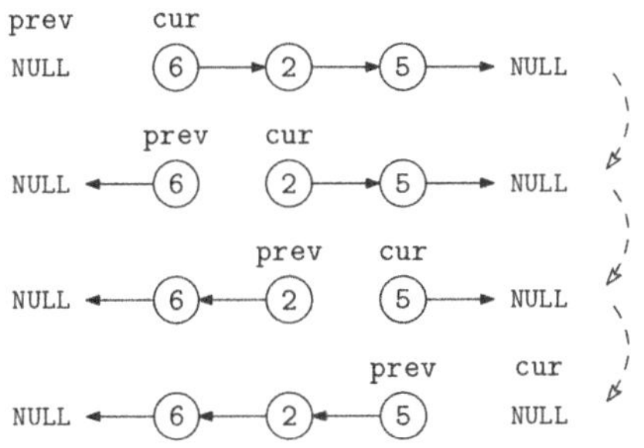

Figure 6. Reversing a linked list.

Now, imagine you are given a harder reversal problem:

✦ PROBLEM 34.7   SUBLIST REVERSAL

Given the head, head, of a singly linked list, and two indices, left and right, with $0 \leq$ left $<$ right, reverse all nodes between the two indices *in place* and return the new head of the list. If left is beyond the last index, do not modify the list. If only right is beyond the last index, reverse everything up to the last node.

▶ **Example:** linked list = 1 -> 2 -> 3 -> 4 -> 5 -> None, left = 1, right = 3
  Output: 1 -> 4 -> 3 -> 2 -> 5 -> None
             The first node (index 0) and last node (index 4) stay the same.
▶ **Example:** linked list = 1 -> 2 -> 3 -> 4 -> 5 -> None, left = 2, right = 7
  Output: 1 -> 2 -> 5 -> 4 -> 3 -> None
             All nodes starting at index 2 are reversed because index 7 is beyond
             the last index.
▶ **Example:** linked list = 1 -> 2 -> None, left = 5, right = 6
  Output: 1 -> 2 -> None
             left is out of bounds, so we leave the list untouched.

SOLUTION 34.7   SUBLIST REVERSAL

We could try to generalize Solution 34.6, but it's easy to lose track of all the pointers involved. Instead, we can use the following reusable idea:

REUSABLE IDEA: LINKED LIST REVERSAL BREAK DOWN

If a problem asks to reverse only a part of a linked list, we can use the *BREAK DOWN THE PROBLEM* booster and do it in steps:

1. Find the bounds of the section that need to be reversed.

2. Break that section out of the linked list without losing the before/after parts of the list.

3. Reverse the section (as in Solution 34.6).

4. Reattach the section.

Each of these steps should be easier to tackle. Using a dummy head will simplify the cases where the real head is part of the section being reversed.

Linked list questions might ask you to reverse a prefix, a suffix, every group of k nodes, or a number of variations. This idea can be used for all of them.

Let's apply the reusable idea to Problem 7.

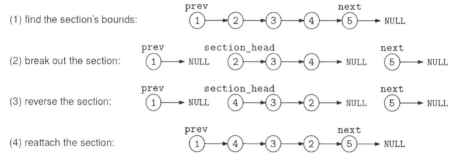

Figure 7. Steps to reverse the section from left = 1 to right = 3.

```
 1   def node_at_index(head, index):
 2     # Returns the node at the specified zero-based index.
 3     # Returns None if index is out of bounds.
 4     # Implementation can be seen online...
 5
 6   def reverse_section(head, left, right):
 7     dummy = Node(0)
 8     dummy.next = head
 9
10     # Step 1: find the nodes BEFORE and AFTER the section.
11     if left == 0:
12       prev = dummy
13     else:
14       prev = node_at_index(head, left - 1)
15     if not prev or not prev.next:
16       # Nothing to reverse.
17       return head
18     nxt = node_at_index(head, right + 1)  # May be None.
19
20     # Step 2: break out the section.
21     section_head = prev.next
22     prev.next = None
23     section_tail = section_head
24     while section_tail.next != nxt:
25       section_tail = section_tail.next
26     section_tail.next = None
27
28     # Step 3: reverse section -> same as the reverse a linked list solution.
29     old_section_head = section_head
30     new_section_head = reverse_list(section_head)
31
32     # Step 4: reattach the section.
33     prev.next = new_section_head
34     old_section_head.next = nxt
35     return dummy.next
```

SLOW AND FAST POINTERS

Imagine that your friend and you planned to meet at a pond. Upon getting there, you realize the pond is much bigger than you thought—almost like a lake!—and your friend is nowhere in sight. They could be anywhere around the pond. You could start walking around it, but if they are doing the same, you may never meet each other. And if you stay put and they do the same, that won't work either. The key to eventually finding each other, you realize, is for the two of you to go around the pond at different speeds. You get a bike from the nearby bike rental and start cycling around the pond, hoping they didn't have the same idea.

This scenario mirrors Floyd's 'tortoise and hare' algorithm for the cycle detection problem. Try to solve it first:

✦ **PROBLEM 34.8**   **LINKED-LIST CYCLE DETECTION**

You are given the head of a singly linked list, head, that may or may not contain a cycle. A *cycle* happens when the next pointer of a node is a node that is already in the linked list (this is generally not allowed in valid linked lists). Return whether the list has a cycle. Assume each list has at least one node.

SOLUTION 34.8   LINKED-LIST CYCLE DETECTION

Notice that we can't simply iterate through the linked list until we reach None. If there is a cycle, we would be in an infinite loop. We *could* detect a cycle by tracking all visited nodes in a hash map, but that would take linear space.

Floyd's 'tortoise and hare' algorithm finds a cycle in linear time and constant extra space. The key is to use two pointers, slow and fast. Both start at head, but when slow advances one node, fast advances two. If there is a cycle, both slow and fast will end in the cycle, and, at each iteration, the gap between them decreases by one. Eventually, fast will catch up to slow. In other words: if fast reaches None, there is no cycle. But if fast equals slow, there is a cycle.

```
1   def has_cycle(head):
2       slow, fast = head, head
3       while fast and fast.next:
4           slow = slow.next
5           fast = fast.next.next
6           if slow == fast:
7               return True
8       return False
```

The two most common variations to the cycle detection problem are finding the cycle's start node and the cycle's length. Finding the start is the hard part. If we can find the start, we can easily find the length as well: keep one pointer at the start of the cycle, and go around the cycle with another pointer, counting steps until both meet again.

To find where the cycle starts, the straightforward solution uses a hash table. However, there is a **trick** to find where the cycle starts using O(1) extra space. You start with the normal cycle detection algorithm (Solution 34.8) until fast and slow meet. Then, you start advancing two pointers at the same speed: p1 from head, and p2 from the meeting point. Surprisingly, these two pointers are guaranteed to meet, and the meeting position will be the start of the cycle.

WHY DOES THE TRICK WORK?

Let D be the distance from the head to the start of the cycle, and L the length of the cycle (initially, we don't know either of those values). The following figure shows why the trick works when L = D and when L > D. The case L < D is similar but more complicated. We won't show it here since our goal is just to get some intuition of why it works.

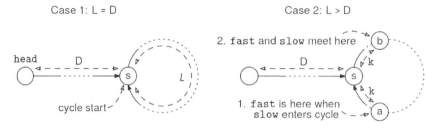

Figure 8.

If L = D, in the time slow gets to the start of the cycle, fast will have time to go exactly once around the cycle. They will meet at the start of the cycle, s. In the second stage, p1 will take D steps from the head to s and p2 will take L = D steps from s back to s, so they will meet again there.

If L > D, in the time slow gets to the start of the cycle, fast won't have completed the cycle yet. Let's say it is k steps before s (node a in Figure 8). In the time slow made D steps, fast made D + L - k steps, so 2D = D + L - k, or D = L - k. After k more iterations, slow and fast will meet k step after s (node b in Figure 8). In the second stage, p1 starts D steps away from s, and p2 starts L - k = D steps away from s, so they will meet there.

Slow and fast pointers come up often in linked list questions. Reach for this technique whenever a linked list problem asks you to do something with O(1) extra space or in only one pass.

| ▶ | **A DIFFICULT LINKED LIST QUESTION USING ALL OUR IDEAS** | INTERVIEW REPLAY |

View Online:	bctci.co/linked-lists-replay-1 @ 17:30 - 39:42
The Question:	Given two linked lists, split the list in half, reverse that half, and then weave it in between each element in the first half.
What You'll See:	The candidate struggled with a difficult linked list question that required a combination of reversing and weaving two separate lists together. The interviewer ultimately passed the candidate even with bugs in their solution but suggested *BREAKING DOWN THE PROBLEM* into steps next time to make it easier.
Who:	*Interviewer*: Senior Software Engineer at Meta *Candidate*: 8 years exp.

PROBLEM SET

✦✦ *Try these problems with AI Interviewer: bctci.co/linked-lists-problem-set-2.*

| **PROBLEM 34.9** | **DOUBLY LINKED LIST TO ARRAY** |

Given a non-null node, node, from a doubly linked list, which might or might not be the head, return an array with the values in the list, from head to tail.

▶ **Example:**
```
                              node
                               v
         None <-> 1 <-> 2 <-> 3 <-> 4 <-> None
```
   Output: [1, 2, 3, 4]
▶ **Example:**
```
                   node
                    v
         None <-> 1 <-> 2 <-> 3 <-> 4 <-> None
```
   Output: [1, 2, 3, 4]

PROBLEM 34.10   LINKED-LIST MIDPOINT

Given the head of a non-empty singly linked list, head, return the value in the middle of the linked list. If there is an even number of nodes, return the left middle node. Can you do it without computing the length of the list first?

▶ **Example:** 10 -> 20 -> 30 -> None
   Output: 20
▶ **Example:** 10 -> 20 -> 30 -> 40 -> None
   Output: 20

PROBLEM 34.11   REMOVE KTH NODE FROM THE END

Given the head of a singly linked list, head, and a number k, remove the k-th node *from the end* of the list. Assume k is smaller than or equal to the list's size. Can you do it without computing the length of the list first?

▶ **Example:** 1 -> 2 -> 3 -> 4 -> None, k = 2
   Output: 1 -> 2 -> 4 -> None
▶ **Example:** 1 -> 2 -> 3 -> 4 -> None, k = 4
   Output: 2 -> 3 -> 4 -> None

PROBLEM 34.12   LINKED-LIST ZIP

Given the heads of two singly linked lists, head1 and head2, merge them together by alternating one node from each. If lists are not the same size, append any remaining elements to the end. Modify the lists *in place* without creating new nodes. Return the new head.

▶ **Example:** 1 -> 3 -> 5 -> None,
              2 -> 4 -> 6 -> None
   Output: 1 -> 2 -> 3 -> 4 -> 5 -> 6 -> None
▶ **Example:** 1 -> 2 -> 3 -> 4 -> None,
              8 -> 7 -> None
   Output: 1-> 8 -> 2 -> 7 -> 3 -> 4 -> None

PROBLEM 34.13   DUPLICATE REMOVAL IN SORTED LINKED LIST

Given the head of a linked list with **sorted** integer values, head, remove duplicates *in place*.

▶ **Example:** 1 -> 1 -> 1 -> 3 -> 5 -> 5 -> None
   Output: 1 -> 3 -> 5 -> None

PROBLEM 34.14   LINKED LIST BLOCK REVERSAL

Given the head of a linked list, head, and a number k > 0, reverse blocks of k nodes of the linked list. If the last block has size less than k, do not reverse it.

▶ **Example:** `1 -> 2 -> 3 -> 4 -> None, k = 2`
   Output: `2 -> 1 -> 4 -> 3 -> None`
▶ **Example:** `1 -> 2 -> 3 -> 4 -> 5 -> None, k = 3`
   Output: `3 -> 2 -> 1 -> 4 -> 5 -> None`

We don't reverse the final block because it only has two elements.

✦⁺ PROBLEM SET SOLUTIONS

SOLUTION 34.9   DOUBLY LINKED LIST TO ARRAY

We can traverse prev pointers from node until we reach the head. Then, we can add each node's value in order into a result array as we traverse the list forward.

```
1  def convert_to_array(self, node):
2    cur = node
3    while cur.prev:
4      cur = cur.prev
5    res = []
6    while cur:
7      res.append(cur.val)
8      cur = cur.next
9    return res
```

SOLUTION 34.10   LINKED-LIST MIDPOINT

The straightforward approach involves traversing the linked list once to count the nodes, and then doing a second pass to stop at half of that.

A classic trick is to use **slow and fast pointers**. If slow moves once for each time fast moves twice, slow will be in the middle by the time fast gets to the end.

```
1  def get_middle(head):
2    slow, fast = head, head
3    while fast and fast.next:
4      slow = slow.next
5      fast = fast.next.next
6    return slow
```

Both approaches take O(n) time and O(1) space.

SOLUTION 34.11   REMOVE KTH NODE FROM THE END

We could do it in two passes: first, compute the length of the list, n. Then, walk n-k steps from the head and remove the element at that index.

The solution without computing the length uses two pointers, fast and slow. The idea is to start by moving the fast pointer k nodes into the list. Then, both pointers move *at the same pace*, maintaining a gap of length k between them. When fast reaches the end, slow is at the node to remove.

Since we might have to remove the head of the list (when k == n), we can simplify the logic using a **dummy node**.

```
1  def remove_kth_node(head, k):
2    if not head:
3      return None
4    dummy = Node(0)
5    dummy.next = head
```

```
6     fast = dummy
7     slow = dummy
8
9     for _ in range(k):
10      fast = fast.next
11
12    while fast and fast.next:
13      fast = fast.next
14      slow = slow.next
15
16    slow.next = slow.next.next
17    return dummy.next
```

Both solutions take O(n) time and O(1) space.

SOLUTION 34.12 LINKED-LIST ZIP

This question may feel familiar—it is similar to Problem 27.6: Merge Two Sorted Arrays (pg 300). We use two pointers, one for each list.

```
1   def merge(head1, head2):
2     dummy = Node(0)
3     cur = dummy
4
5     p1, p2 = head1, head2
6     while p1 and p2:
7       cur.next = p1
8       cur = cur.next
9       p1 = p1.next
10      cur.next = p2
11      p2 = p2.next
12      cur = cur.next
13
14    if p1:
15      cur.next = p1
16    else:
17      cur.next = p2
18    return dummy.next
```

SOLUTION 34.13 DUPLICATE REMOVAL IN SORTED LINKED LIST

If the list were not sorted, we could use a hash set to keep track of repeated elements. However, since the list is sorted, we can skip over repeated elements as we go:

```
1   def remove_duplicates(head):
2     cur = head
3     while cur and cur.next:
4       if cur.val == cur.next.val:
5         cur.next = cur.next.next
6       else:
7         cur = cur.next
8     return head
```

We could also modify the values of the nodes instead of the pointers. That way, we could reuse the 'seeker and writer pointers' solution from Solution 27.14: In-Place Duplicate Removal (pg 307). However, you should check with the interviewer if modifying the values is allowed.

Both approaches take O(n) time and O(1) extra space.

SOLUTION 34.14   LINKED LIST BLOCK REVERSAL

This is an advanced reversal problem, so we can use our **Linked List Reversal Break Down** reusable idea (pg 421).

1. Find the bounds of the first block to reverse. We can use a **dummy** node to act as the prev pointer of the first block. For the next pointer, we can advance k steps from the head.

2. Break the block out from the rest of the list.

3. Reverse the block with the standard block reversal routine (Solution 6).

4. Reattach the reversed block between prev and next.

5. Repeat the process starting from next instead of head.

The runtime will be O(n) and the space O(1).

PROJECTING CONFIDENCE IN YOUR DS&A KNOWLEDGE	INTERVIEW REPLAY

View Online:	bctci.co/linked-lists-replay-2 @ 50:15 - end
The Question:	Design a cache with get, set, and evict-item functionality.
What You'll See:	In Python, OrderedDict leverages a doubly linked list under the hood. The candidate knew this and used it to solve a particularly difficult question. At the end, the interviewer discussed the importance of showing projecting confidence about DS&A knowledge and how to do so without sounding arrogant.
Who:	*Interviewer*: Software Engineer at Google *Candidate*: 7 years exp.

KEY TAKEAWAYS

Linked-list triggers: The input is a linked list. We need O(1) access to both the beginning and the end of a data structure while maintaining insertion order. Data structure design questions.

Like dynamic arrays, linked lists are linear data structures, each with its pros and cons.

Dynamic Array	**Linked List**
• Direct access to any element by index: O(1)	• Linear traversal to access elements.
• Front insertions and removals: O(n)	• Front insertions and removals: O(1)
• Back insertions and removals: O(1) (amortized).	• Back insertions and removals: O(1) (with a doubly linked list).

Table 2. Dynamic array vs. linked list analysis.

For instance, the ability to do constant-time updates on both ends makes linked lists the ideal basis for implementing queues and deques.

Two-pointer and linked-list problems are often similar. It isn't uncommon to see the type of questions we saw in the Two Pointers chapter, but with a linked list instead of an array. These types of questions tend to require the same two-pointer movement patterns we learned (pg 294), but not having constant access to any index makes them more challenging. We might need to borrow from the toolset of reusable techniques we learned for linked lists, including **dummy nodes**, how to **break down reversal problems**, and Floyd's **cycle detection** algorithm.

For instance, imagine you were asked to determine if a singly linked list is palindromic. With an array, we would use **inward pointers** (pg 294), but it's not so easy with a singly linked list because we can't walk backward from the end. Instead, we can find the midpoint with **slow and fast pointers** (like in Problem 34.10: Linked-List Midpoint, pg 425), reverse the second half (with our **Linked List Reversal Break Down** reusable idea), and, finally, emulate the inward pointers by walking through the first half and the reversed second half with **parallel pointers**.

In the coming chapters, we'll explore non-linear data structures like trees and graphs.

ONLINE RESOURCES

Online resources for this chapter include:

- A chance to try each problem in this chapter in AI Interviewer
- Interview replays that show specific mistakes people make with linked lists problems
- Full code solutions for every problem in the chapter in multiple programming languages

Try online at bctci.co/linked-lists.

## CHAPTER 35

TREES

AI interviewer, replays, and more materials for this chapter at bctci.co/trees

▶ *Prerequisites: Stacks & Queues, Recursion*

Figure 1. A Pythagorean tree, a geometric representation of a *perfect binary tree*.

Trees are everywhere in computer science. They have many significant applications, like SQL databases (which use B-trees), code representation in compilers (abstract syntax trees), and version control systems like Git. Their unique properties—see the Big O Analysis section—make them the ideal backbone of other data structures, like heaps, union–find, and tries. Perhaps more relevant to your specific needs, binary tree problems rank among the most common in interviews.

Let's go over a bit of terminology:

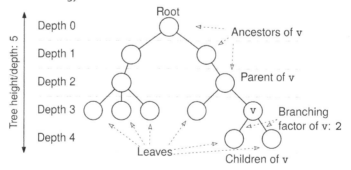

Figure 2. Tree terminology.

- Trees consist of *nodes*. Nodes can have *children*, which are other nodes branching out from it.
- We draw trees growing downward.[1] The *root* node is the one at the top, and it is the only node without a *parent*.

---

1 Some people say that "real" trees grow upward instead of downward, but that is inaccurate. Even when the nodes contain floating-point numbers, we still draw them downward.

- A *leaf* is a node with no children.
- The *branching factor* of a node is the number of children.
- The *depth, height,* or *level* of a node is the number of *ancestors* of that node. The root is at depth/height/ level 0, its children are at depth/height/level 1, and so on.[2]
- The *depth* or *height* of the entire tree is the maximum depth among all nodes plus one, or 0 if there are no nodes.[3] In Figure 2, the deepest leaves are at depth 4, so the tree's depth/height is 5.

The first thing we'll do is map those concepts to actual code. A tree is implemented as a *recursive data structure*, meaning that the Node class has pointers to other Node objects:[4]

```
1 class Node:
2   def __init__(self, val, left=None, right=None):
3     self.val = val
4     self.left = left
5     self.right = right
```

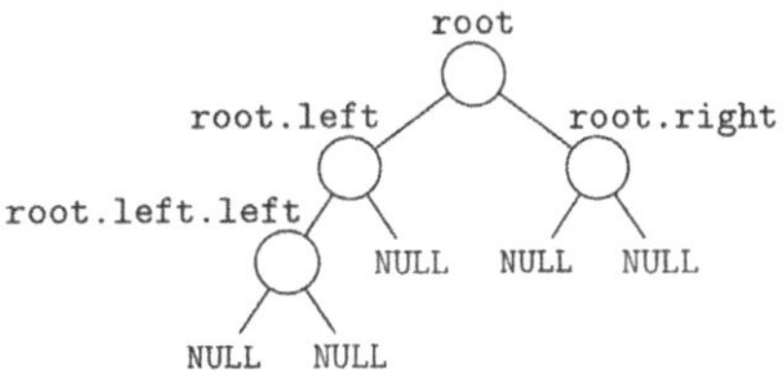

Figure 3. We usually won't draw the missing nodes.

This class represents a binary tree node, where nodes have a left and a right child, which could be missing (we also call missing nodes 'null', or None in Python). In a binary tree problem, we are usually given the node corresponding to the root, and we have to reach other nodes by following the left and right pointers. Nodes may have other fields depending on the problem.

Try to code the following problems, which will help you get comfortable with trees and internalize the terminology.

WARMUP PROBLEM SET (PART 1)

Given a pointer to a specific node in a tree, node, that might be null, and might or might not be the root, implement the following functions:

a. Return whether it is a leaf.[5]
b. Return the values of its children as an array of length at most 2.
c. Return the values of its grandchildren as an array of length at most 4.
d. Return the size of the node's *subtree*. A node's subtree includes itself *and* all of its *descendants*.
e. Return the height of its subtree.

PROBLEM SET SOLUTIONS (PART 1)

To check if node is a leaf, we check that both children are null. Importantly, before accessing node.left or node.right, we need to check that node itself is not null. Forgetting this check is a common mistake.

---

2 We should note that 'depth,' 'height,' and 'level' may be defined slightly differently in different sources (such as the root starting at height 1 instead of 0). If they come up in an interview, it's a great clarifying question for the interviewer. To keep things simple, in this book, we define depth, height, and level equally.

3 Why plus one? To distinguish an empty tree (height 0) and a node with just the root (height 1). The definitions we use are consistent with array indices in the following sense: the indices in an array of size is n range from 0 to n-1, while the node heights in a tree of heigh h range from 0 to h-1.

4 You can find the equivalent class/data type in other languages when you try our problems with the AI Interviewer.

5 A node can be the root and a leaf at the same time.

```
1  def is_leaf(node):
2    if not node:  # Checks if node is null.
3      return False
4    return not node.left and not node.right
```

Questions (b) and (c) require careful handling to avoid accessing a field of a missing node.

```
1  def children_values(node):
2    if not node:
3      return []
4    values = []
5    if node.left:
6      values.append(node.left.val)
7    if node.right:
8      values.append(node.right.val)
9    return values
10 def grandchildren_values(node):
11   if not node:
12     return []
13   values = []
14   for child in [node.left, node.right]:
15     if child and child.left:
16       values.append(child.left.val)
17     if child and child.right:
18       values.append(child.right.val)
19   return values
```

The size and height of the subtree can be computed recursively: if we count the nodes in the left subtree and the right subtree, we can add them up to get the total (+1 for node itself). For heights, what matters is the maximum height of the subtrees, not the sum. For instance, if the left subtree has a height of 5 and the right subtree has a height of 3, we can deduce that the total height is 6.

```
1  def subtree_size(node):
2    if not node:
3      return 0
4    left_size = subtree_size(node.left)
5    right_size = subtree_size(node.right)
6    return left_size + right_size + 1  # + 1 for 'node'.
7  def subtree_height(node):
8    if not node:
9      return 0
10   left_height = subtree_height(node.left)
11   right_height = subtree_height(node.right)
12   return max(left_height, right_height) + 1  # + 1 for 'node'.
```

WARMUP PROBLEM SET (PART 2)

If the problem asked us to find the node's *parent* instead of its children, we would be stuck: in the standard Node type, there is no way to go up the tree.[6] Consider an alternative definition of the node class that also includes a pointer to the parent:

```
1  class Node:
2    def __init__(self, id, parent, left, right):
3      self.id = id  # A unique integer id.
```

---

6 This is analogous to not being able to go backward in a singy-linked list.

```
4        self.parent = parent
5        self.left = left
6        self.right = right
```

Given a *non-null* node in the tree, node, which might or might not be the root, implement the following functions:

a. Return whether it is the *root*.

b. Return the IDs of all of its *ancestors* as an array, in any order.

c. Return the *depth* of the node.

d. Given two *non-null* nodes from the same tree, node1 and node2, return the ID of their *lowest common ancestor*. The lowest common ancestor (or LCA) of two nodes is the deepest node in the tree which is a *non-strict* ancestor of both. 'Non-strict' means that a node is considered its own ancestor. For instance, in Figure 4, LCA(j, f) = f.

e. Given two *non-null* nodes from the same tree, return the *distance* between them. The sequence of edges between two nodes is called a *path*, and the number of edges in the path is the distance between the two nodes. Note that, in a binary tree, the path between any two nodes is unique.

Depth

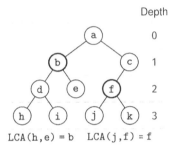

LCA(h,e) = b   LCA(j,f) = f

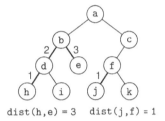

dist(h,e) = 3   dist(j,f) = 1

Figure 4.   **Figure 5.**

PROBLEM SET SOLUTIONS (PART 2)

The root is the only node without a parent:

```
1  def is_root(node):
2    return not node.parent
```

To find the ancestors and the depth of a node, we have to traverse parent pointers up to the root. We can do it recursively or iteratively—for instance, this is the iterative approach:

```
1  def ancestor_ids(node):          1  def depth(node):
2    ids = []                        2    res = 0
3    while node.parent:              3    while node.parent:
4      node = node.parent            4      node = node.parent
5      ids.append(node.id)           5      res += 1
6    return ids                      6    return res
```

The lowest-common ancestor (LCA) is the point in the two nodes' lists of non-strict ancestors (counting each node as its own ancestor) where the IDs start to match. They must match at some point, as all the nodes share at least one non-strict ancestor, the root.

We can find the LCA using O(1) space using a two-pointer-style solution:

1. We keep a 'pointer' starting on each node.

2. We find the depth of the two nodes. If one of the pointers is deeper than the other, we "catch up" its pointer to the height of the other.

3. After both pointers are at the same depth, we check, depth by depth, if their ancestor at that depth is the same.

```
1   def LCA(node1, node2):
2     depth1 = depth(node1)
3     depth2 = depth(node2)
4     while depth1 > depth2:
5       node1 = node1.parent
6       depth1 -= 1
7     while depth2 > depth1:
8       node2 = node2.parent
9       depth2 -= 1
10    while node1.id != node2.id:
11      node1 = node1.parent
12      node2 = node2.parent
13    return node1.id
```

The LCA is also useful for finding the distance between two nodes because the path between the two nodes goes through it. We can add the distance from each node to the LCA to get the node-to-node distance.

```
1   def distance(node1, node2):
2     lca_id = LCA(node1, node2)
3     dist = 0
4     while node1.id != lca_id:
5       dist += 1
6       node1 = node1.parent
7     while node2.id != lca_id:
8       dist += 1
9       node2 = node2.parent
10    return dist
```

We could also do it in a single pass by keeping track of the distance as we walk to the LCA.

ADVICE FOR WORKING WITH TREES

HANDLING MISSING NODES

As mentioned, trying to read a field from a null node is a common error in interviews. In recursive algorithms, we can handle null nodes eagerly or lazily:[7]

1. **Eager strategy:** we never call the recursive function with a null node. We must check that the node exists *before passing it* to a recursive call.

2. **Lazy strategy:** we don't check if nodes are null before calling the recursive function. Instead, we check if the node is missing with a conditional statement at the *beginning* of the function.

Here is the tree size solution again, comparing the two strategies:

---

7   We already touched on eager and lazy parameter validation in the Recursion chapter (pg 399).

Eager strategy

```
1  # Cannot be called with None.
2  def size(node):
3    res = 0
4    if node.left:
5      res += size(node.left)
6    if node.right:
7      res += size(node.right)
8    return res + 1
```

Lazy strategy

```
1  # Can be called with None.
2  def size(node):
3    if not node:
4      return 0
5    return size(node.left) + size(node.
         right) + 1
```

Both strategies are equally valid, so our advice is to pick a convention and stick to it during practice. We will stick to the lazy strategy in this chapter because there is a single 'null check' per function, and it is always at the beginning, so it tends to be a bit shorter.

DRAWING TREES

As we discussed in the Anatomy of a Coding Interview (pg 192) drawing examples is an important aspect of *communication* and—if done correctly—*speed*. Our main advice for drawing trees is to not bother drawing the edges and give plenty of space at the beginning, as the number of nodes can double at each level.

DEPTH-FIRST SEARCH

Many algorithms involve some kind of *traversal* to visit every element in a data structure. Traversing a linear data structure like an array is simple—you mostly just go forward or backward. But with trees, traversals get more interesting. There are two main types of tree traversals: *depth-first search* (DFS), which this section is about, and *breadth-first search* (BFS), which we'll cover next.[8]

PREORDER, INORDER, AND POSTORDER TRAVERSALS

Think of a tree not as a collection of nodes and edges, but as three things: a root, a left subtree, and a right subtree. In a DFS traversal, we go *deep* into the left subtree, visiting every node there. When we are fully done with it, we do the same with the right subtree (some candidates get confused by what "visit" means—the following snippets just print the nodes' values, but it could be anything, depending on the problem).

We have specialized names for DFS on a tree depending on when we visit each node relative to its subtrees:

3. Preorder traversal: the root <u>pre</u>cedes the subtrees.

4. Inorder traversal: the root is <u>in</u> between the subtrees.[9]

5. Postorder traversal: the root goes after the subtrees.

---

8 Graphs also have equivalent DFS and BFS traversals (pg 489).

9 "Inorder" also reflects that if the tree is a binary search tree, then the inorder traversal visits the node from smallest to largest value.

The traversals are defined recursively, meaning that, in a preorder traversal, each subtree is itself visited following a preorder traversal, and similarly with inorder and postorder traversals.

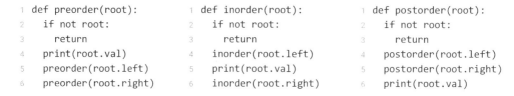

```
1  def preorder(root):        1  def inorder(root):          1  def postorder(root):
2    if not root:             2    if not root:               2    if not root:
3      return                 3      return                   3      return
4    print(root.val)          4    inorder(root.left)         4    postorder(root.left)
5    preorder(root.left)      5    print(root.val)            5    postorder(root.right)
6    preorder(root.right)     6    inorder(root.right)        6    print(root.val)
```

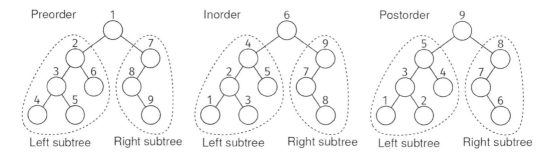

Figure 6. Each node is labeled with the visit order.

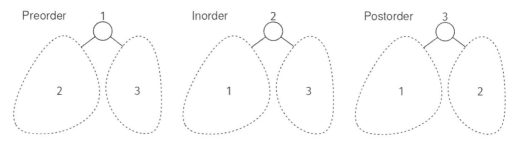

Figure 7. The order of the root relative to the subtrees.[10]

DFS-BASED ALGORITHMS

Many binary tree problems can be solved with a DFS traversal. The main question to ask when implementing a DFS-based solution is:

▸   What information needs to flow through the tree, and in which direction?

In a given problem, we may have information that flows in multiple directions—some up the tree, some down the tree, and some that sidesteps the recursive flow entirely:

DIRECTION	HOW TO PASS THE INFORMATION?	EXAMPLES OF INFORMATION THAT CAN FLOW IN THIS DIRECTION
Down the tree from parents to their children.	In the **parameters** of the recursive function.	A value we are looking for, or the current node's depth.

---

10   A common misconception is that postorder traversal is the reverse of preorder traversal. That's not true, as shown in Figures 6 and 7. Each traversal has its own reversed order.

View online materials for Beyond Cracking the Coding Interview at bctci.co

Up the tree from children to their parents.	In the return value of the recursive function.	Information about the subtree, like the size (Problem 1.d.), the height (Problem 1.e.), or the sum.
Sidestepping the recursive flow in "global" state.[11]	In variables visible from every recursive call.	An array where we store node values.

Table 1. Directions of information flow.

In code, the three options look something like this:

```
1  def visit(node, info_passed_down):
2    if base_case:
3      return info_to_pass_up
4    ... = visit(node.left, info_to_pass_down)
5    ... = visit(node.right, info_to_pass_down)
6    global_state = info_stored_globally
7    return info_to_pass_up
```

Global state is not strictly necessary—you can always pass a variable down *and* up the tree with the other two approaches we mentioned (or, alternatively, pass a *reference* to the variable down the tree). However, conceptually, sometimes it is cleaner to keep state outside of the recursive flow altogether.

Usually, we won't need all three directions in the same problem, but the solution to the following problem illustrates all three:

✦ **PROBLEM 35.1**   **ALIGNED CHAIN**

Given a binary tree, we say a node is *aligned* if its value is the same as its depth. Return the length of the longest descendant chain of aligned nodes. The chain does not need to start at the root.

▶ **Example:** The tree in Figure 8.
  Output: 3. The longest chain of aligned nodes is 1 -> 2 -> 3.

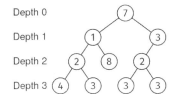

Figure 8. A tree where the aligned nodes are shaded.

SOLUTION 35.1   ALIGNED CHAIN

For this problem, we pass information as in Figure 9:

- We pass the current depth down the tree (a node doesn't know its own depth by itself).
- We pass the longest aligned chain starting at each node up the tree. This way, if a node is aligned, it can extend the longest chain in its children.

---

11 We call it 'global', but the variables do not need to be visible to the whole program—which is frowned upon—only to the recursive function. You can still encapsulate it in a class or, as we will do in Python, in an outer function. We talked about this in the Recursion chapter (pg 398).

- We track the longest chain seen so far using global state.[12]

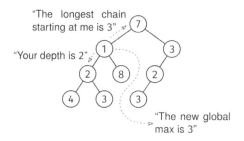

Figure 9.

```
1   def longest_aligned_chain(root):
2     res = 0
3     def visit(node, depth):  # Inner recursive function.
4       nonlocal res  # To make res visible inside visit().
5       if not node:
6         return 0
7       left_chain = visit(node.left, depth + 1)
8       right_chain = visit(node.right, depth + 1)
9       current_chain = 0
10      if node.val == depth:
11        current_chain = 1 + max(left_chain, right_chain)
12        res = max(res, current_chain)
13      return current_chain
14    visit(root, 0)  # Trigger DFS, which updates the 'global' res.
15    return res
```

Implementing recursive tree algorithms usually comes down to knowing what information to pass in what direction and how to translate that flow into code. The following problem set will help you practice this.

DFS PROBLEM SET

✦ *Try these problems with AI Interviewer: bctci.co/trees-problem-set-1*

PROBLEM 35.2   **HIDDEN MESSAGE**

The self-proclaimed 'cryptography expert' in your friend group has devised their own schema to hide messages in binary trees. Each node has a text field with exactly two characters. The first character is either 'b', 'i', or 'a'. The second character is part of the hidden message. To decode the message, you have to read the hidden-message characters in the following order:

- If the first character in a node is 'b', the node goes before its left subtree, and the left subtree goes before the right subtree.
- If it is 'a', the node goes after its right subtree, and the right subtree goes after the left subtree.
- If it is 'i', the node goes after its left subtree and before its right subtree.

---

12 In the Python solution, the nonlocal keyword indicates that res is not a new variable in visit(), but the same res variable from the outer function. The keyword is only necessary when assigning to the variable. If we were, for instance, appending to a nonlocal array, we wouldn't need it.

Given the root of the binary tree, return the hidden message as a string.[13]

▶ **Example:** The tree in Figure 10.
  Output: "nice_try!"

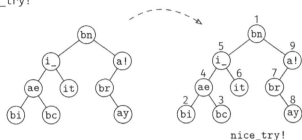

Figure 10. A tree with a hidden message (left) and the order of the nodes (right).

PROBLEM 35.3   **ALIGNED PATH**

Given the root of a binary tree, we say a node is *aligned* if its value is the same as its depth (as in Problem 35.1). Return the length of the longest *path* of aligned nodes (a path can start and end at any node—it's not restricted to a descendant chain).

▶ **Example:** The tree in Figure 8.
  Output: 3. There are two paths of aligned nodes with maximum length:
           1 -> 2 -> 3 and 3 -> 2 -> 3.

PROBLEM 35.4   **TREE LAYOUT**

You are given the root of a non-empty binary tree. We lay out the tree on a grid as follows:

1. We put the root at (r, c) = (0, 0).
2. We recursively lay out the left subtree one unit below the root (increasing r by one).
3. We recursively lay out the right subtree one unit to the root's right (increasing c by one).

For instance, the left child of the root goes on (1, 0) and the right child goes on (0, 1).

Two nodes are *stacked* if they are laid on the same (r, c) coordinates. Return the maximum number of nodes stacked on the same coordinate.

▶ **Example:** The tree in Figure 11.
  Output: 2

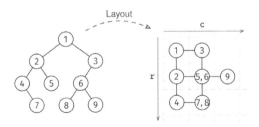

Figure 11. A tree where the maximum number of stacked nodes in the layout is 2.

---

13 The authors of this book are not liable for any outcomes caused by using this encryption scheme.

PROBLEM 35.5   **TRIANGLE COUNT**

Given the root of a binary tree, return the number of *triangles*. A triangle is a set of three distinct nodes, a, b, and c, where:

1. a is the lowest common ancestor of b and c,
2. b and c have the same depth,
3. the path from a to b only consists of left children, and
4. the path from a to c only consists of right children.

▸ **Example:** The tree in Figure 12.
  Output: 4

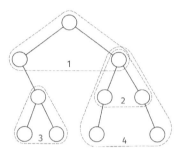

Figure 12. A tree with four triangles.

PROBLEM 35.6   **INVERT A BINARY TREE**

Given a binary tree, invert it by modifying the `left` and `right` pointers (do not modify the values in the nodes or create new nodes). The left subtree of the root should become the right subtree inverted, and the right subtree of the root should become the left subtree inverted. Return the root of the tree after modifying it.

▸ **Example:** Tree in Figure 13 (left).
  Output: Tree in Figure 13 (right).

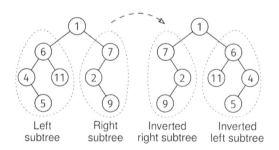

| Left subtree | Right subtree | Inverted right subtree | Inverted left subtree |

Figure 13.

PROBLEM 35.7   **EVALUATE EXPRESSION TREE**

We are given the root of a tree representing an arithmetic expression. It has the following type:

```
1    class Node:
2      def __init__(self, kind, num, children):
3        self.kind = kind          # One of "sum", "product", "max", "min", or "num".
```

```
4        self.num = num           # Only valid when kind is "num".
5        self.children = children  # Only valid when kind is not "num".
```

There are two types of nodes, depending on the value of kind:

- 'Number' nodes have "num" as the kind and have no children.
- 'Operation' nodes do not have "num" as the kind and have one or more children. There are no null children.

This is not a binary tree, as nodes can have **more than two children**. We call this an *N-ary tree*.

Implement an evaluate() function which evaluates the tree according to the following rules:

- The value of a numeric node is its num field, which is an integer.
- The value of an operation node depends on its kind: it is the sum, product, max, or min of the children's values (the product of a single value is itself).[14]

▶ **Example:** The tree in Figure 14.
  Output: 12

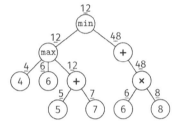

Figure 14. An expression tree. The evaluation of each node is underscored above the node.

✦ PROBLEM SET SOLUTIONS

SOLUTION 35.2   HIDDEN MESSAGE

We use preorder, inorder, or postorder on a node-by-node basis, depending on the first character of each node. We append the letters one by one to a "global" (function-scoped) list. We use a list (i.e., dynamic array) instead of a string because, in Python, it's not possible to append to a string in $O(1)$ time.

```
1   def hidden_message(root):
2     message = []
3     def visit(node):
4       if not node:
5         return
6       if node.text[0] == 'b':
7         message.append(node.text[1])
8         visit(node.left)
9         visit(node.right)
10      elif node.text[0] == 'i':
11        visit(node.left)
12        message.append(nodet[1])
13        visit(node.right)
14      else:
```

---

14 This problem is inspired by *abstract syntax trees* in compilers. For instance, an expression like 3*(2+4) becomes a tree with * (product) as the root, and two children: one child is a node with the number 3 and the other is a subtree with + as the root and 2 and 4 as children.

```
15          visit(node.left)
16          visit(node.right)
17          message.append(node.text[1])
18      visit(root)
19      return ''.join(message)
```

SOLUTION 35.3   ALIGNED PATH

A useful property in problems about finding paths in binary trees is that *a path has a single node with mini-mum depth*.

This allows us to use the **break down the problem** booster in problems about finding paths:

1. Find the node with minimum depth (closest to the root) in the path.
2. Construct the path as two descendant chains in the left subtree and the right subtree.

For this problem, how do we characterize the node with minimum depth in the optimal path? First, it has to be aligned. Among aligned nodes, we want to find one with long aligned chains on both subtrees. To be precise, we want to maximize the sum of their lengths.

If you analyze the information that we need at each node, it's the same as in Figure 9. The only difference with Solution 35.1 is how to update res:

```
1    res = max(res, 1 + left_chain + right_chain).
```

REUSABLE IDEA: FINDING THE NODE IN THE PATH WITH MINIMUM DEPTH

> A useful property in problems about finding paths in binary trees is that a path has a single node with minimum depth.
>
> Finding this node is often easier than finding the endpoints because there are only n candidates as opposed to $O(n^2)$ possible pairs of endpoints. If you can find this node, it's then usually easy to find the rest of the path.
>
> For instance, this property would have helped us solve Problem 24.12: Tree diameter (pg 268).

SOLUTION 35.4   TREE LAYOUT

Let's analyze the flow of information we need for this problem:

- Each node needs to know its coordinates in the grid, so we can pass them **down the tree**.
- We use a **frequency map** (pg 348) to map coordinates to the number of nodes at that coordinate. This map is **"global" state**—it's not part of the recursive flow.

```
1    def most_stacked(root):
2      pos_to_count = dict()
3      def visit(node, r, c):
4        if not node:
5          return
6        if (r, c) not in pos_to_count:
7          pos_to_count[(r, c)] = 0
8        pos_to_count[(r, c)] += 1
9        visit(node.left, r + 1, c)
10       visit(node.right, r, c + 1)
11     visit(root, 0, 0)
12     return max(pos_to_count.values())
```

The runtime and extra space are $O(n)$, where n is the number of nodes.

SOLUTION 35.5   TRIANGLE COUNT

We don't want to count triangles one by one; this would be too inefficient. Instead, we can find, for each node u, the number of triangles with u at the top. For this, we need to:

- Pass two things **up the tree**: left_side, the number of consecutive left descendants, and right_side, the number of consecutive right descendants.
- Compute the triangles with u at the top as min(left_side, right_side).
- Add the count to a running total, which can be stored as **"global" state**.

The runtime is O(n), where n is the number of nodes, and the extra space is O(1).

SOLUTION 35.6   INVERT A BINARY TREE

This problem asks us to modify the binary tree, which is less common. Since the definition of 'inverted' is recursive, we can handle it recursively: we swap the root's children and then invert each subtree.

```
1   def invert(root):
2     if not root:
3       return None
4     root.left, root.right = invert(root.right), invert(root.left)
5     return root
```

Congratulations. You have now learned how to invert a binary tree. Was it as difficult as it is made out to be?[15]

SOLUTION 35.7   EVALUATE EXPRESSION TREE

This problem introduces the notion of N-ary trees. Working with them is not much different than working with binary trees. All the same concepts still apply—we just need to iterate over the children.

To tackle this problem, we can walk through the tree. At each node, look at the kind. If it is an operation, apply that operation to the *results* of its children (not the values of the children themselves). Then, return the evaluation **up the tree**.

```
1   def evaluate(root):
2     if root.kind == "num":
3       return root.num
4     children_evals = []
5     for child in root.children:
6       children_evals.append(evaluate(child))
7     if root.kind == "sum":
8       return sum(children_evals)
9     if root.kind == "product":
10      return product(children_evals)
11    if root.kind == "max":
12      return max(children_evals)
13    if root.kind == "min":
14      return min(children_evals)
15    raise ValueError("Invalid node kind")
```

In Python, sum(), max(), and min() are built-in functions, so we would only need to provide our own product() helper function.

---

15 Here is the history behind this meme in case you're unfamiliar with it. Also check out the back cover for a fun inside joke: https://www.quora.com/Whats-the-logic-behind-Google-rejecting-Max-Howell-the-author-of-Homebrew-for-not-being-able-to-invert-a-binary-tree

View Online:	bctci.co/trees-replay-1 @ 17:19 - 36:12
The Question:	Given the root of a Binary Search Tree (BST), convert it to a greater tree such that every key of the original BST is changed to the original key plus the sum of all keys greater than the original key.
What You'll See:	The candidate wrote an algorithm / pseudocode to effectively take in feedback from the interviewer	*Interviewer* and candidate ran through different inputs to see what worke and what didn't
Who:	*Interviewer*: Senior Software Engineer at Microsoft *Candidate*: 10 years exp.
Outcome:	The candidate got the job at Amazon!

BREADTH-FIRST SEARCH

LEVEL-ORDER TRAVERSAL

In a BFS traversal, we visit the nodes level by level. It is fundamentally different from DFS, as we jump between nodes from the left and right subtrees—we are no longer following the recursive structure of the tree.

In the context of trees, BFS is also known as *level-order traversal*. To implement a level-order traversal, we use a queue. When we visit the root, we add its children to the end of the queue. Then, as we extract nodes from the front of the queue, we keep adding their children to the back. This ensures that nodes are visited level by level:[16]

```
1  def level_order(root):
2    Q = Queue()
3    Q.add(root)
4    while not Q.empty():
5      node = Q.pop()
6      if not node:
7        continue
8      print(node.val)
9      Q.add(node.left)
10     Q.add(node.right)
```

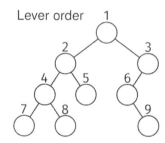

Figure 15.

---

16 For iterative algorithms, we also follow a lazy convention for handling missing nodes: (1) we check for null nodes first thing after taking them out of the queue; (2) we add nodes to the queue without checking if they are null.

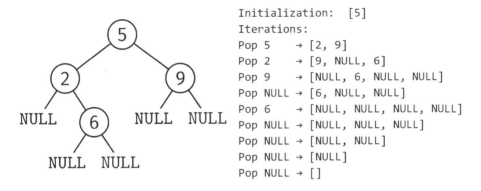

```
Initialization:  [5]
Iterations:
Pop 5     → [2, 9]
Pop 2     → [9, NULL, 6]
Pop 9     → [NULL, 6, NULL, NULL]
Pop NULL  → [6, NULL, NULL]
Pop 6     → [NULL, NULL, NULL, NULL]
Pop NULL  → [NULL, NULL, NULL]
Pop NULL  → [NULL, NULL]
Pop NULL  → [NULL]
Pop NULL  → []
```

Figure 16. Evolution of the level-order traversal queue.

Do **not** use a dynamic array (e.g., a Python list) for the queue because removing from the front of a dynamic array takes linear time. This is a common mistake.[17]

BFS-BASED ALGORITHMS

In problems that require level-order traversals, it is often useful to track the level of the nodes. We can do this with a simple change: in the queue, instead of putting only nodes, we put (node, depth) tuples:

📋 RECIPE 1. NODE–DEPTH QUEUE RECIPE FOR LEVEL-ORDER TRAVERSAL.

```
def node_depth_queue_recipe(root):
  Q = Queue()
  Q.add((root, 0))
  while not Q.empty():
    node, depth = Q.pop()
    if not node:
      continue
    # Do something with node and depth.
    Q.add((node.left, depth+1))
    Q.add((node.right, depth+1))
```

This is an example of the **piggybacking extra info** reusable idea (pg 382)—the depth piggybacks along with the node.

This recipe can be adapted to solve most problems requiring level-order traversals. Try it on the following problem set.

BFS PROBLEM SET

✦ *Try these problems with AI Interviewer: bctci.co/trees-problem-set-2*

---

17 Python doesn't have a built-in Queue data structure, but you can use the deque (double-ended queue) from the collections module, which supports the same operations with the same runtimes. Instead of push() and pop(), they are called append() and popleft(). For clarity, in this chapter, we will use the language-agnostic Queue API that we defined in the Stacks & Queues chapter (pg 379). See there for more details.

PROBLEM 35.8   LEFT VIEW

Given the root of a binary tree, return its *left view*. The left view is an array with the value of the first node on each layer, ordered from top to bottom.

▶ **Example:** The tree in Figure 17.
  Output: [5, 2, 6, 1]

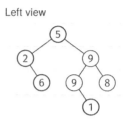

Left view

Figure 17. The nodes in the left view are shaded.

PROBLEM 35.9   MOST PROLIFIC LEVEL

Given the root of a binary tree, return the most prolific level. The *prolificness* of a level is the average number of children over all the nodes in that level. Return -1 if the tree is empty.

▶ **Example:** The tree in Figure 18.
  Output: 1. The most prolific level is 1, with a prolificness of 2.

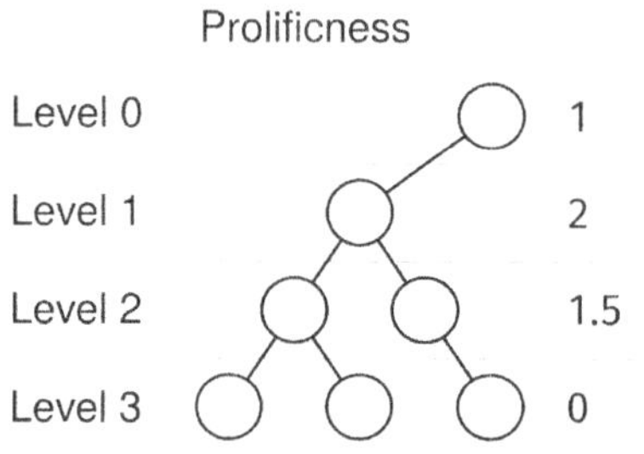

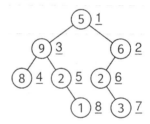

Prolificness

Level 0	1
Level 1	2
Level 2	1.5
Level 3	0

Figure 18. A tree and the prolificness at each level.

PROBLEM 35.10   ZIG-ZAG ORDER

Given a binary tree, return the values of all its nodes in *zig-zag* order. This is similar to a level-order traversal but alternating the direction of the nodes at each level. Nodes at even depth are ordered left to right, and nodes at odd depth are ordered right to left.

▶ **Example:** The tree in Figure 19.
  Output: [5, 6, 9, 8, 2, 2, 3, 1]

Zig-zag order

Figure 19. The underscored numbers show the zig-zag order.

PROBLEM 35.11   MOST PROTECTED NODE

Given the root of a non-empty binary tree, return the highest protection level of any node. The *protection level* of a node is the minimum of four values:

- The number of ancestors.
- The length of the longest chain of descendants.
- The number of nodes on the same level to its left.
- The number of nodes on the same level to its right.

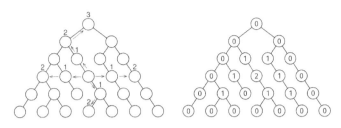

▶ **Example:** The tree in Figure 20.

Output: 2

Figure 20. Left: the protection level of the shaded node is min(3, 2, 2, 2) = 2. **Right:** each node is labeled with its protection level (not the value of the val field).

✦ PROBLEM SET SOLUTIONS

SOLUTION 35.8 LEFT VIEW

We use the Node–Depth Queue recipe to identify the first node at each depth.

```
1   def left_view(root):
2     if not root:
3       return []
4     Q = Queue()
5     Q.add((root, 0))
6     res = [root.val]
7     current_depth = 0
8     while not Q.empty():
9       node, depth = Q.pop()
10      if not node:
11        continue
12      if depth == current_depth + 1:
13        res.append(node.val)
14        current_depth += 1
15      Q.add((node.left, depth+1))
16      Q.add((node.right, depth+1))
17    return res
```

SOLUTION 35.9 MOST PROLIFIC LEVEL

The key property for this problem is that the prolificness of level i is the number of nodes at level i+1 divided by the number of nodes at level i. Using the node-depth queue recipe, we can easily determine the number of nodes at each depth. Then, we just need to compute the prolificness at each level.

```
1   def level_counts(root):
2     Q = Queue()
3     Q.add((root, 0))
4     level_count = defaultdict(int)
5     while not Q.empty():
6       node, depth = Q.pop()
7       if not node:
8         continue
9       level_count[depth] += 1
10      Q.add((node.left, depth + 1))
11      Q.add((node.right, depth + 1))
```

```
12      return level_count
13  def most_prolific_level(root):
14      level_count = level_counts(root)
15      res = -1
16      max_prolificness = -1  # Less than any valid prolificness.
17      for level in level_count:
18        if level + 1 not in level_count:
19          continue
20        prolificness = level_count[level + 1] / level_count[level]
21        if prolificness > max_prolificness:
22          max_prolificness = prolificness
23          res = level
24      return res
```

SOLUTION 35.10   ZIG-ZAG ORDER

We use Node–Depth Queue recipe, but we put the nodes at each level in a per-level array. For odd levels, we reverse this array before appending the nodes to the solution.

```
1   def zig_zag_order(root):
2     res = []
3     Q = Queue()
4     Q.add((root, 0))
5     cur_level = []
6     cur_depth = 0
7     while not Q.empty():
8       node, depth = Q.pop()
9       if not node:
10        continue
11      if depth > cur_depth:
12        if cur_depth % 2 == 0:
13          res += cur_level
14        else:
15          res += cur_level[::-1]  # Reverse order.
16        cur_level = []
17        cur_depth = depth
18      cur_level.append(node)
19      Q.add((node.left, depth+1))
20      Q.add((node.right, depth+1))
21    if cur_depth % 2 == 0:    # Add the last level.
22      res += cur_level
23    else:
24      res += cur_level[::-1]
25    return res
```

SOLUTION 35.11   MOST PROTECTED NODE

At each node, we need to know the number of nodes above, to the left, to the right, and below. We can use a combination of techniques we have already seen:

- The number of nodes above a node is just its depth, which we get "for free" with the Node–Depth Queue recipe.
- To count the nodes left and right of each node, we can adapt the Node–Depth Queue recipe to find the index of each node within its level.

- Finally, to find the longest chain of descendants at each node, it makes more sense to use a DFS-based traversal that passes subtree heights **up the tree** (as in Problem 1.e).

We can use a global map from each node to its protection level. Whenever we find the number of nodes in one direction for a node, we update its protection level in the map with the `min()` operation. At the end, we return the maximum value in the map.

BREADTH-FIRST SEARCH IN ACTION		INTERVIEW REPLAY
View Online:	bctci.co/trees-replay-2 @ 2:23 - 18:50	
The Question:	Given the root of a binary tree, return the zigzag level order traversal of its nodes' values.	
What You'll See:	The candidate quickly identified breadth-first search as an acceptable solution to the problem and coded it quickly and correctly.	
Who:	*Interviewer*: Principal Engineering Manager at Microsoft *Candidate*: 1 year exp.	

BIG O ANALYSIS

We analyze tree algorithms in terms of two variables: n, the number of nodes, and h, the height of the tree.

When analyzing the runtime, you should ask yourself what your algorithm does:

1. Does it follow one path from top to bottom? In this case, the runtime is based on the height. Assuming it does a constant amount of work at each node, the runtime will be O(h).

2. Does it visit each node *once*? In this case, the runtime is based on the number of nodes. If we spend O(1) time on each node, the runtime will be linear.

3. Something else? Generally speaking, we can analyze any tree algorithms as the product of two things: the number of nodes visited and the time spent at each node (not counting recursive work).[18]

Most tree problems can be solved by visiting each node once and doing a constant amount of work per node. If your algorithm is revisiting nodes more than once or twice, consider that your algorithm may not be optimal.

BALANCED TREES

The worst case for the height of a tree is the number of nodes, n, which occurs when all the nodes are in a long chain with only one child (similar to a linked list). However, we often work with *balanced* trees.

A binary tree is balanced if, for every node, the left and right subtrees contain roughly the same number of nodes (it doesn't need to be exactly the same). Balanced trees have O(log n) height: whenever we go from a node to one of its children, the size of the subtree roughly halves. After O(log n) halvings, we reach a leaf (recall that $\log_2(n)$ is the number of halvings it takes to go from n to 1).

The exact meaning of "roughly" depends on the type of balanced tree. Examples of balanced tree types include *perfect trees*, *complete trees* (see next section), *red-black trees*, and *AVL trees*, which all have O(log n) height.

Multiple data structures store data in balanced trees because every node is O(log n) steps away from the root:

- **Heaps** are based on *complete* binary trees.

---

18 This analysis is similar to the BAD method (pg 402), except that we don't need to estimate the number of nodes as b^d (the branching factor to the depth). We just use n for the number of nodes in the input tree.

- **Tree-based sets and maps** use *self-balancing BSTs*.
- The **union–find** data structure is based on a set of n-ary trees with amortized height even less than $O(\log n)$ (bctci.co/union-find).[19]

Perfect and Complete Trees

A *perfect binary tree* is a tree where every level has the maximum number of nodes. That is:

1. all the leaves are at the same depth, and
2. all the non-leaf nodes (also called internal nodes) have two children.

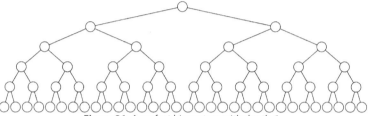

Figure 21. A perfect binary tree with depth 6.

A perfect binary tree has one node at depth 0 (the root), two nodes at depth 1, four nodes at depth 2, and so on. A perfect binary tree with depth $d \geq 1$ has $1 + 2 + 4 + 8 + \ldots + 2^{d-1}$ nodes. This brings us to another famous equality about the sum of powers of two: for any $d \geq 1$,

$$1 + 2 + 4 + 8 + \ldots + 2^{d-1} = 2^d - 1$$

In words, it says that the sum of the first $d-1$ powers of two is just one short of the next power of two. This can be visualized as follows:

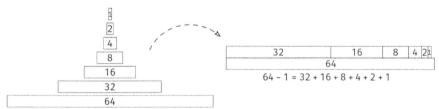

Figure 22. The sum $32 + 16 + \ldots + 1$ falls one short of 64.[20]

Translated to perfect binary trees, this means that *each level has as many nodes as all the previous levels plus one*. For example, the tree in Figure 21 has a depth of 6 and $2^6-1 = 63$ nodes, with 32 being leaf nodes and 31 being non-leaf nodes.

In big O terms, a perfect binary tree with depth d has both $O(2^d)$ nodes, as well as $O(2^d)$ leaves specifically. That is exponential on the depth: when the depth grows by one, the number of nodes essentially doubles.[21]

Looking at it from the opposite direction, we are saying that **the height is logarithmic on the number of nodes**: a perfect binary tree with n nodes has $\log_2(n+1)$ height, the minimum possible for a binary tree.

Perfect trees are quite special because the number of nodes must be one less than a power of 2. This means that, in the vast majority of cases, there is no way to rearrange or balance a tree to make it "perfect."

---

19 It is not possible for binary trees to have height less than $O(\log n)$, but it is possible for N-ary trees.

20 This is the same idea that we saw on Figure 4 of the Big O chapter (pg 221).

21 More generally, trees with than $b \geq 2$ children per node have $O(b^d)$ nodes. The bigger b is, the larger the fraction of nodes that are leaves.

A *complete binary tree* is a tree where all the levels except the last one have the maximum number of nodes; the last level may not be full, but all the nodes are aligned to the left. Complete binary trees are only slightly taller than perfect trees, with a height of floor($\log_2(n)+1$).

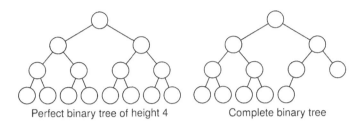

| Perfect binary tree of height 4 | Complete binary tree |

Figure 23.

Perfect and complete binary trees are balanced, but most balanced trees are neither perfect nor complete.

SPACE ANALYSIS

Imagine a typical recursive tree algorithm that visits every node once, does some constant-time work, and does not store any extra data structures. As mentioned, the runtime will be $O(n)$.

The space used by our recursive algorithm comes from the size of the *call stack*, i.e., the number of nested recursive calls, h. Therefore, the space is $O(n)$ for unbalanced trees and $O(h) = O(\log n)$ for balanced trees.

With recursive algorithms on unbalanced trees, we also need to worry about **stack overflow** (pg 393). In a live interview, you can discuss the concern with the interviewer. You can say, "The statement says that the tree is balanced, so I can use a recursive algorithm without worrying about stack overflow." Alternatively, you can ask, "Do we know the maximum height of the tree? I am concerned about stack overflow." For online assessments, most of the time, test cases are designed to allow recursive solutions, so you'll probably be fine with a recursive algorithm.

If you are still worried about stack overflow and you see that you can use BFS, go for it. It's probably not worth trying to learn how to do DFS iteratively, as it's more involved.[22]

BINARY SEARCH TREES

In most cases in interviews, we aren't just working with a binary tree; we're working with a binary *search* tree (BST). A binary tree is a BST if, for *every*[23] node:

- All the values on its **left** subtree are *less than or equal* to the node's value.
- All the values on its **right** subtree are *greater than or equal* to the node's value.

An inorder traversal on a BST goes through the nodes in order, which can be useful in some problems.

---

22 It is possible, but less common, to do recursive algorithms like preorder, inorder, and postorder traversals iteratively using a stack data structure instead of the call stack. You can find the implementations at nilmamano.com/blog/iterativetreetraversal.html.

23 It is not sufficient to merely have left ≤ node ≤ right. It must be true for *every* value on the left and *every* value on the right.

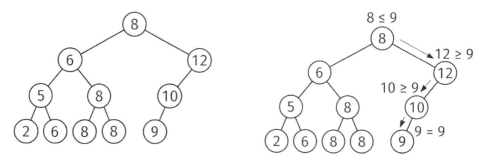

Figure 24. An example of a BST. The inorder traversal for this BST is: 2, 5, 6, 6, 8, 8, 8, 8, 9, 10, 12.

Figure 25. Search in a BST for the value 9.

Binary search trees are given that name because trying to find a value in a binary search tree is a bit like doing a binary search:

- In binary search, we compare the target to the middle element and then discard the left or right half of the array.
- In a binary search tree, we compare the target to the root and then discard the left or right subtree.

If the tree is balanced, then we can find any value in $O(\log\ n)$ time.[24]

BST PROBLEM SET

✦ *Try these problems with AI Interviewer: bctci.co/trees-problem-set-3*

Solve the following problems and analyze the runtime and space.

PROBLEM 35.12   BST SEARCH

Given the root of a binary search tree and a value, `target`, find if the tree contains the value.

▸ **Example:** The tree in Figure 24, target = 7
  Output: False

PROBLEM 35.13   BST NEAREST VALUE

Given the root of a non-empty binary search tree and a value, `target`, find the closest value to `target` in the tree. In case of a tie, return the smallest option.

▸ **Example:** The tree in Figure 24, target = 7
  Output: 6

PROBLEM 35.14   BST VALIDATION

Given the root of a binary tree, check if it is a binary search tree.

▸ **Example:** The tree in Figure 24
  Output: true

PROBLEM 35.15   BST DUPLICATE DETECTION

Given the root of a binary search tree, find whether it contains any repeated value.

---

24 This is why tree-based implementations of maps and sets like AVL trees or red-black trees take logarithmic time per operation.

▶ **Example:** The tree in Figure 24
  Output: true

BST KTH ELEMENT

Given the root of a binary search tree with n nodes, find the k-th smallest element (0-indexed), where $0 \le k \le n-1$.

▶ **Example:** The tree in Figure 24, k = 8
  Output: 9

BST MERGE INTO ARRAY

Given the roots of two binary search trees, return an array with all the elements from both in sorted order.

▶ **Example:** Two trees like the tree in Figure 24
  Output: [2, 2, 5, 5, 6, 6, 6, 6, 8, 8, 8, 8, 8, 8, 8, 8, 9, 9, 10, 10, 12,
          12]

✦ PROBLEM SET SOLUTIONS

SOLUTION 35.12 BST SEARCH

We implement the BST analogous of binary search over a sorted array. We can do it iteratively or recursively. Here is the iterative version:

```
1  def find(root, target):
2    cur_node = root
3    while cur_node:
4      if cur_node.val == target:
5        return True
6      elif cur_node.val > target:
7        cur_node = cur_node.left
8      else:
9        cur_node = cur_node.right
10   return False
```

The runtime is O(h), and the extra space is O(1) since this is an iterative solution.

SOLUTION 35.13 BST NEAREST VALUE

We need to use the following property:

▶   The node with the closest value to the target in BST lies on the search path you would take to find the target itself, even if the target is not present in the tree.

Say the target is 6, and the root's value is 5. The root is a *lower bound* for the target. Next, we go to the right child of the root. If its value is 8, that becomes an *upper bound* for the target. The nodes along the search path form bounds around the target, narrowing down on it. Any node outside the path would be further away from the target than the bounds we already found.

The implementation follows the same search path as Solution 35.12, but tracking the nearest value above *and* below the target. In the end, we return the closest of the two.

```
1  def find_closest(root, target):
2    cur_node = root
3    next_above, next_below = math.inf, -math.inf
4    while cur_node:
```

```
5      if cur_node.val == target:
6        return cur_node.val
7      elif cur_node.val > target:
8        next_above = cur_node.val
9        cur_node = cur_node.left
10     else:
11       next_below = cur_node.val
12       cur_node = cur_node.right
13   if next_above - target < target - next_below:
14     return next_above
15   return next_below
```

SOLUTION 35.14   BST VALIDATION

We can think about this problem in two different ways:

1. At each node, pass the subtree's max and min **up the tree**. We can use those to check the BST definition directly: at each node, we check that max(left subtree) ≤ node ≤ min(right subtree).

2. Alternatively, we can do an inorder traversal and check that each value is greater than or equal to the
   previous one. We can store the previous value in the traversal as **"global" state**, so that we can compare
   it with the current value.

Here is the second approach:

```
1    def is_bst(root):
2      prev_value = -math.inf
3      res = True
4      def visit(node):
5        nonlocal prev_value, res
6        if not node or not res:
7          return
8        visit(node.left)
9        if node.val < prev_value:
10         res = False
11       else:
12         prev_value = node.val
13       visit(node.right)
14     visit(root)
15     return res
```

In either case, since we are visiting every node recursively, the runtime is O(n), and the space is O(h).

SOLUTION 35.15   BST DUPLICATE DETECTION

We can follow the same two approaches as in the previous problem:

1. Pass subtree maximums and minimums from up the tree. There is a duplicate if, for some node, node
   == max(left subtree) or node == min(right subtree).

2. Do an inorder traversal, and check if two consecutive values are the same.

SOLUTION 35.16   BST KTH ELEMENT

We can do an inorder traversal and stop after k steps. We can keep the number of steps so far as **"global"**
state.

SOLUTION 35.17   BST MERGE INTO ARRAY

We can use the 'break down the problem' booster to solve this in two steps:

1. Use inorder traversal to extract the sorted array of values from each tree.
2. Reuse the solution for Problem 27.6: Merge Two Sorted Arrays, pg 300.

The runtime and extra space will both be O(n1 + n2), where n1 and n2 are the sizes of the two trees.[25]

SELF-BALANCING BSTS

We mentioned that sets and maps also have a tree-based implementation. The idea is to store the elements in a balanced BST. This way, values can be searched as in Solution 35.12 and Solution 35.13, and all values are relatively close to the root.

A *self-balancing BST* is a BST-based data structure that supports the following operations:

- You can insert and remove elements in O(log n) time.
- You can search for a given value or its **nearest value** in O(log n) time.

Nearest-value searches are the main feature that hash-based data structures do not support.

Self-balancing BSTs use a balancing algorithm to ensure the BST stays balanced as we insert and remove values. The tree does not need to stay as strictly balanced as a perfect tree or a complete tree. *Red-black trees* and *AVL trees* are self-balancing BSTs with different balancing algorithms.

- The height of a red-black tree is at most $2*\log_2(n+1)$ = O(log n).
- The height of an AVL tree is at most $1.44*\log_2(n)$ = O(log n).

> #### When should I use a TreeSet or TreeMap?
>
> Tree-based sets and maps are useful when we need to do *nearest-value searches on dynamic data*. If the data is static, we can just sort it and use binary search.
>
> Some languages provide tree-based sets and maps, and some don't. If your language of choice doesn't, tell your interviewer, then ask if you can assume that you have a TreeSet/TreeMap class. Typically, they'll let you assume you have one, as building your own self-balancing BST is fairly involved.

▶	**CONSISTENT VARIABLE NAMES PREVENT MISTAKES**	INTERVIEW REPLAY

View Online:	bctci.co/trees-replay-3 @ 38:13 - 54:28
The Question:	Given the root of a binary tree, return the max path sum of any non-empty path.
What You'll See:	The candidate confused their variable names in a depth-first search, mistakenly typing root.left rather than cur.left.
Who:	*Interviewer*: Software Engineer at AWS *Candidate*: 6 years exp.

---

25 It is also possible to write a single-pass solution that moves two **parallel pointers** (pg 294) through the two trees, each following an inorder traversal.

KEY TAKEAWAYS

Mastering tree problems starts with knowing the terminology, such as the types of traversals, balanced trees, and BSTs. We've seen two main types of solutions:

- For recursive algorithms, which are more common, the main question to think about is:

    » What information needs to flow through the tree, and in which direction?

    You should become comfortable with the mechanics of passing information **down the tree**, **up the tree**, and as **global state** (Table 1, pg 437).

- For iterative algorithms, we saw the **Node–Depth Queue recipe** (pg 447) to iterate through nodes in level order while tracking their depth.

During your practice, we recommend using a consistent strategy to handle missing nodes (pg 434).

When it comes to the analysis, don't forget to factor in if the tree is balanced, particularly in the space complexity of recursive algorithms.

ONLINE RESOURCES

Online resources for this chapter include:

- A chance to try each problem in this chapter in AI Interviewer
- Interview replays that show specific mistakes people make with trees problems
- Full code solutions for every problem in the chapter in multiple programming languages

Try online at bctci.co/trees.

## CHAPTER 36

GRAPHS

AI interviewer, replays, and more materials for this chapter at bctci.co/graphs

> Graphs are, like, really really important. More than you think. Even if you already think they're important, it's probably more than you think.
>
> Steve Yegge, from his popular blog post 'How to get that job at Google.' [1]

▶ *Prerequisites: Stacks & Queues, Recursion*

We agree, but why? For one, graphs come up in interviews *a lot*. Okay, but why do interviewers love these questions so much? Essentially, graphs hit this intersection between *useful* and *challenging*; a perfect storm for interviews.

1. Whereas people argue that binary trees and linked lists aren't really used in the real world, they can't argue that for graphs. Graphs are how we represent "things with pairwise relationships."

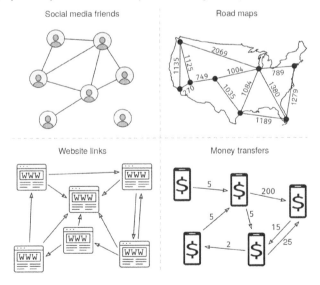

Figure 1. Some examples of graph applications.

---

1 https://steve-yegge.blogspot.com/2008/03/get-that-job-at-google.html

2. There are lots of challenging problems related to graphs, some of which explicitly mention graphs and some of which you need to figure out that it's a graph.

Graphs may be the topic with the most jargon. Graphs can be *directed* or *undirected*. Figure 2 shows the terminology for undirected graphs:

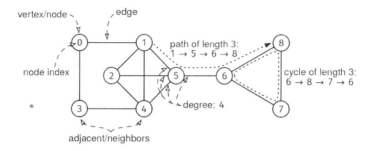

Figure 2. Terminology for undirected graphs.

- Graphs are made of *nodes* and *edges* (we can use *node* and *vertex* interchangeably).
- Two nodes are *adjacent* or *neighbors* if there is an edge between them.
- Two nodes connected by an edge are called the *endpoints* of the edge.
- There is a *path* between two nodes if it is possible to go from one to the other by moving along edges.
- A *cycle* is a sequence of edges starting and ending at the same node.
- We generally use V for the number of vertices and E for the number of edges.
- The *degree* of a node is the number of neighbors. Degrees can range from 0 to V-1.

The terminology for directed graphs is similar, with some differences:

- Edges have a direction, shown with an arrow. Edges have a *source* node and a *destination* node. We can have both (a, b) and (b, a) as different edges.
- Nodes have *incoming edges* and *outgoing edges*. The neighbors of a node are only those reachable with outgoing edges.
- The number of incoming edges into a node is called the *indegree*, and similarly for the *outdegree*.
- Paths and cycles must respect the edge directions.

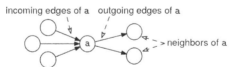

Figure 3. Terminology for directed graphs. The node a has indegree 3 and outdegree 2.

Graphs can also be *weighted* or *unweighted*. In weighted graphs, each edge has an associate value or 'weight.' Figure 1 shows the four combinations between directed/undirected and weighted/unweighted.

In this chapter, we'll work mostly with unweighted graphs, the most common type in interviews. If the type of graph is not clear from the statement, this is a great clarifying question.

REPRESENTING A GRAPH

Like sets and maps, graphs are an abstract data type that can have multiple implementations.[2] The two most common ones are the *adjacency list* and *adjacency matrix*. Of the two, the adjacency list representation is by far the most commonly used for interviews.

ADJACENCY LIST

We can think of the adjacency list data structure as a map from each node to the list of its neighbors. A common assumption used in interviews is that nodes are identified by indices from 0 to V-1, where V is the number of nodes. This means that we can store the V lists of neighbors in an array of length V instead of an actual map:

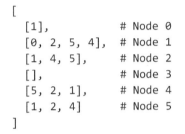

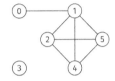

Figure 4. Graph represented by the adjacency list to the left.

Throughout this chapter, we will call graph the outer array, which makes graph[node] the list of neighbors of node, where node is an identifier between 0 and V-1. The neighbors are in no particular order.

The adjacency list data structure can be used for both directed and undirected graphs. In a directed graph, if there is an edge from node1 to node2, node2 appears in the list of neighbors of node1, graph[node1], but not the other way around.

The outer array has one entry per node, so its length is O(V). The inner arrays *combined* have a total length of O(E) because each edge appears once (for directed graphs) or twice (for undirected graphs). Thus, the space complexity is O(V+E).

Adjacency List Problem Set. Given the adjacency list, graph, of an undirected graph, code the following basic graph operations and analyze their runtime in terms of V and E:

1. Return the number of nodes in the graph.
2. Return the number of edges in the graph.
3. Return the degree of a node node, where 0 ≤ node < V.
4. Print all the neighbors of node node, where 0 ≤ node < V.

How would these operations change for a directed graph?

Solutions.

The adjacency list representation makes each of these operations straightforward.

1. The number of nodes, V, is the length of the outer list.
2. To compute the number of edges, E, observe that each edge (a, b) will be represented twice in the neighbor lists: one in a's list and one in b's list. Therefore, we add up the size of all the lists and divide by two. For a directed graph, we don't have this double-counting issue, so we should *not* halve the count in num_edges().

---

2 In fact, a lot of what we think of as concrete data structures—binary trees, stacks, etc.—are *technically* abstract data types. However, we almost always think about a specific implementation of them. With graphs though, we actually do sometimes implement them in other ways.

3. The degree of a node is the length of the node's neighbor list.

4. To print the neighbors of a node, we iterate through its neighbor list.

```
1   def num_nodes(graph):   # O(1)
2     return len(graph)
3   def num_edges(graph):   # O(V + E)
4     count = 0
5     for node in range(len(graph)):
6       count += len(graph[node])
7     return count // 2   # Halved because we counted each edge from both endpoints.
8   def degree(graph, node):   # O(1)
9     return len(graph[node])
10  def print_neighbors(graph, node):   # O(degree(node))
11    for nbr in graph[node]:
12      print(nbr)
```

Transforming from Edge List to Adjacency List

In interviews, graphs are commonly not given as an adjacency list as input. Instead, they are given as the number of nodes, V, and a list of edges in no particular order, where each edge is a pair of node indices.

For example, the graph in Figure 4 could be given as:

V = 6, edges = [[0, 1], [1, 2], [4, 5], [2, 4], [1, 5], [1, 4], [2, 5]]

The edge list format is not too useful. For instance, finding the neighbors of a node requires O(E) time instead of O(degree(node)). Thus, the first step in many graph questions is transforming an edge list to an adjacency list. **Learn how to do this quickly in your language of choice.**

We'll often skip this step in the book and start from the adjacency list because it is always the same.

 REUSABLE IDEA: EDGE LIST TO ADJACENCY LIST

> For *directed* graphs, each edge [node1, node2] in edge_list represents an edge from node1 to node2. Thus, we would add node2 to the adjacency list of node1, but not the other way around.
>
> ```
> 1   def build_adjacency_list(V, edge_list):
> 2     graph = [[] for _ in range(V)]
> 3     for node1, node2 in edge_list:
> 4       graph[node1].append(node2)
> 5       graph[node2].append(node1)
> 6   return graph
> ```

One variation worth mentioning is that, sometimes, the nodes are identified by something other than identifiers from 0 to V-1, like strings. In those cases, we can turn graph into a map from node names to neighbor arrays. The big O analysis will be the same, but we need to factor in the time for hashing and comparing the nodes.

An additional operation that is sometimes useful is quickly checking if two nodes are adjacent. With a standard adjacency list, we would need to iterate through the list of neighbors of one to see if the other is in it:

```
1   def adjacent(graph, node1, node2):   # O(degree(node1))
2     for nbr in graph[node1]:
3       if nbr == node2: return True
4     return False
```

If this operation ever becomes our bottleneck, we can turn graph into an array of *sets* rather than an array of arrays. Then, we can do a set membership check in O(1) (expected) time.

✦✦ **PROBLEM 36.1**   **ADJACENCY LIST VALIDATION**

Given an adjacency list, graph, write a function that returns whether graph is a *valid* undirected graph, meaning that:

1. Every node is between 0 and V-1.

2. There are no *self-loops*: edges connecting a node to itself.

3. There are no *parallel edges*: two edges connecting the same two nodes.[3]

4. If node1 appears in graph[node2], then node2 also appears in graph[node1].

SOLUTION 36.1   ADJACENCY LIST VALIDATION

We can check the first three conditions in a single pass through the adjacency list. To detect parallel edges, we use a set of already seen neighbors.

For the final condition, we can keep track of all the edges we have found *once* in a set. When we see them a second time, we remove them from the set. For instance, if we find 7 in the list of neighbors of 3, we add [3, 7] to the set. Then, when we find 3 in the list of neighbors of 7, we remove it. At the end, the set must be empty.

```
1   def validate(graph):
2     V = len(graph)
3     for node in range(V):
4       seen = set()
5       for nbr in graph[node]:
6         if nbr < 0 or nbr >= V: return False   # Invalid node index.
7         if nbr == node: return False            # Self-loop.
8         if nbr in seen: return False            # Parallel edge.
9         seen.add(nbr)
10      edges = set()
11      for node1 in range(V):
12        for node2 in graph[node1]:
13          edge = (min(node1, node2), max(node1, node2))
14          if edge in edges:
15            edges.remove(edge)
16          else:
17            edges.add(edge)
18      return len(edges) == 0
```

ADJACENCY MATRIX

In this representation, we use a VxV boolean matrix, where matrix[i][j] is true if there is an edge from node i to node j. In an undirected graph, the matrix will be symmetric across the diagonal.

---

3 Self-loops and parallel edges make sense on some problems, but, by default, we assume that graphs do not have them. This could be a good clarifying question.

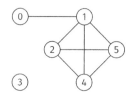

Figure 5. Graph represented by the adjacency matrix to the left

The matrix takes $O(V^2)$ space. The adjacency matrix representation shines when the graph is *dense*, meaning that each node has many neighbors. For instance, if a node has every other node as a neighbor, it is more compact to store n booleans than n-1 integers (as in the adjacency list). Thus, for dense enough graphs, where $E = O(V^2)$, the space usage of the adjacency matrix has better constant factors than the adjacency list. However, in non-dense or *sparse* graphs, $O(V^2)$ space is suboptimal.

In interviews, use an adjacency list except in the rare case where you know that the graph is dense and you care about optimizing the constant factors of the space complexity.[4]

One advantage of the adjacency matrix over the adjacency list is that we can check if two nodes, a and b, are neighbors in $O(1)$ time—we simply check if `matrix[a][b]` is true. However, as mentioned, we can achieve the same with an adjacency list if we turn the inner lists into sets.

BIG O ANALYSIS OF GRAPHS

Similar to how we analyze grid problems in terms of two parameters, rows and cols, we analyze graph algorithms in terms of V, the number of nodes, and E, the number of edges.

The following table summarizes the basic operations we can do with the adjacency list:

Space usage	O(V+E)
Count nodes	O(1)
Count edges	O(V)
Node degree	O(1)
Iterate through neighbors of a node	O(degree(node))
Find if two nodes are adjacent	O(degree(node1)) (can be optimized to O(1))
Initialize from edge list and node count	O(V+E)
Validate adjacency list (no self-loops, no parallel edges, no missing directions)	O(V+E)

Table 1. Adjacency list operations in a graph with V nodes and E edges.

Graph trivia: What's the maximum number of edges in a graph?

It depends if the graph is directed or not.

In a directed graph, each node could have an outgoing edge to every other node, resulting in $V*(V-1) = O(V^2)$ edges.

In an undirected graph, the maximum number of edges is half of that, as we can't have edges going to and from the same pairs of nodes: $V*(V-1)/2 = O(V^2)$.

---

4 To learn more about alternative representations, you can go to the interviewing.io learning center: https://interviewing. io/graphs-interview-questions.

For instance, a directed graph with 4 nodes may have as many as 4*3 = 12 edges, and an undirected graph with 4 nodes may have as many as 6 edges. When a graph has the maximum number of edges, it's called a *complete* graph.

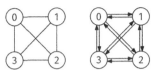

Figure 6. Directed and undirected complete graphs with 4 edges.

If we don't allow parallel edges (which we usually don't), E is always bounded by $O(V^2)$, but this might not be tight, so, *generally speaking, we don't want to simplify $O(E)$ to $O(V^2)$*.

For instance, we don't want to say, "Each inner array in the adjacency list could have V-1 elements, so the adjacency list takes $O(V^2)$ space." This is correct in the upper-bound sense, but it is more useful to say it is $O(V+E)$.

There exist *special cases* where we are given additional information about the graph (or we infer it from the statement) which allows us to simplify V or E away. This is analogous to how if we had a grid algorithm with a runtime of $O(\text{rows} + \text{cols})$ and we were told the grid is a square grid, we could simplify the analysis to $O(\text{rows})$.

Our general recommendation is to always **analyze graph algorithms in terms of both** V **and** E. Only once you have the formula in terms of V and E, consider if you can simplify it further, but that is not as important. E.g., you can write:

▸ T: O(V+E) = O(E) because the graph is connected.

Here are some common graph types that allow simplifications:

GRAPH TYPE	RANGE OF EDGE COUNT	EXAMPLE OF SIMPLIFICATION
All undirected graphs	$0 \le E \le V*(V-1)/2$	$O(V+E)$ cannot be simplified.[5]
Complete graphs	$E = V*(V-1)/2$	$O(V+E) = O(V+V^2) = O(V^2)$
Connected graphs	$V-1 \le E \le V*(V-1)/2$	$O(V+E) = O(E)$
Acyclic graphs (a.k.a. forests)	$0 \le E \le V-1$	$O(V+E) = O(V)$
Trees (connected and acyclic)	$E = V-1$	$O(V+E) = O(V)$
Graphs with maximum degree k, where k is a constant	$0 \le E \le V*K/2$	$O(V+E) = O(V+k*V) = O(V)$

DRAWING GRAPHS IN AN EDITOR

Drawing graphs in an editor can be tricky to do quickly. If possible, keep node indices/names to a single digit/letter (like S and T instead of `start` and `target`), and draw the nodes in a 'grid' layout where vertical and horizontal alignment represents edges. For undirected graphs, the same thought as for binary trees (pg 435) can help us save time here: don't draw the edges. For directed graphs, you at least need to indicate the directions of the edges:

---

5 A common mistake is simplifying $O(V+E)$ to $O(E)$ because some people incorrectly assume that there must be more edges than nodes. This is true for connected graphs, but not graphs in general (a graph could have any number of nodes and no edges; it would just be a boring graph).

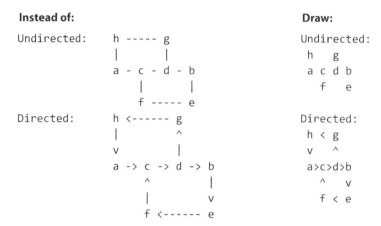

The idea is to not waste time with 'ASCII art.' However, the grid layout only allows a maximum degree of four. If you need more, you could always list the full adjacency list.

CONNECTIVITY PROBLEMS AND DFS

The first major class of graph problems is *connectivity* problems. These problems are all about which nodes can reach other nodes. Here are the main connectivity questions we can ask about undirected graphs:

- Is the graph connected? A graph is *connected* if there is a path from every node to every other node.
- How many connected components are there? A *connected component* is a maximal subset of nodes where every node can reach every other node.[6]
- Given two nodes, are they in the same connected component?

Depth-first search, commonly shortened to DFS, is a recursive graph traversal algorithm that allows us to answer this type of connectivity questions. We already talked about DFS traversals on binary trees (pg 435), and we'll now extend the same idea to graphs.

In trees, we start at the root and recursively visit each child. Similarly, in graphs, we can start at any node and recursively visit each neighbor. The crucial difference is that graphs can have cycles, which means that if we visit a chain of neighbors and end up at a previous node in the chain, we may start an infinite loop. We didn't need to worry about that for trees because trees do not have loops.

The workaround to avoid infinite loops is to keep track of already visited nodes in a visited set and avoid re-visiting nodes that are already in the set:

---

6 We'll focus on finding connected components in undirected graphs. For directed graphs, a maximal subgraphs where every node can reach every other node is called a *strongly connected component*. There are algorithms for finding strongly connected components, like Kosaraju's algorithm, that we don't cover in this book because it is a bit too niche for interviews.

RECIPE 1. GRAPH DFS.

```
def graph_DFS(graph, start):
  visited = {start}
  def visit(node):
    # Do something with node.
    for nbr in graph[node]:
      if not nbr in visited:
        visited.add(nbr)
        visit(nbr)
  visit(start)
```

Tree DFS (with eager null checking).

```
1  def tree_DFS(root):
2    def visit(node):
3      # Do something with node.
4      if root.left:
5        visit(root.left)
6      if root.right:
7        visit(root.right)
8    if root:
9      visit(root)
```

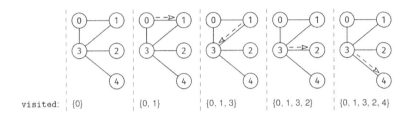

visited: {0}   {0, 1}   {0, 1, 3}   {0, 1, 3, 2}   {0, 1, 3, 2, 4}

Figure 7. DFS traversal starting from 0.

If we start DFS from a given node, start, it will visit every node reachable from start and add them to the visited set. This allows us to answer connectivity questions:

- To check if a graph is connected, we can do a DFS from *any* node and check at the end if the size of the visited set is V.
- To check if node1 and node2 are in the same connected component, we can do a DFS from node1 and check if node2 is in visited.

DFS can be used to find if two nodes are connected, but not the shortest path between them. It searches *deep*—going from one neighbor, to its neighbor, and so on. DFS could take the "scenic route" and go through thousands of nodes to get from A to B when there was an edge (A, B) all along.

Does it matter in which order we visit the neighbors?

Usually, no. The set of visited nodes will be the same regardless, just in a different order. It could matter in specific problems that are order-sensitive.

This is a bit like visiting the left child first or the right child first in a binary tree. In many problems, like computing the tree height or size, it doesn't matter. In others, like computing an inorder traversal, it does.

A reusable recipe that often helps with connectivity problems is launching a DFS for each connected component. We can do this to compute things such as the number of connected components. We reuse the visited set across all the DFS runs so we don't launch two DFS on the same connected component.

```
1  def count_connected_components(graph):
2      count = 0
3      visited = set()
4      for node in range(len(graph)):
5          if node not in visited:
6              visited.add(node)
7              visit(node)
8              count += 1
9      return count
```

RECIPE 2. CONNECTED-COMPONENT LOOP

```
connected_component_loop(graph):
    visited = shared set across all c.c.
    for node in graph:
        if node not visited yet:
            # Found a new c.c.
            # Visit all nodes in the c.c.
            visit(node)
```

IMPLEMENTATION CHOICES

Since nodes have indices between 0 and V-1, it is also common to use an array of booleans of length n instead of a visited set. There are some trade-offs between the two:

- The array has better constant factors than the set (which requires hashing).
- The array always uses O(V) space, while the final size of the set is proportional to the number of visited nodes (i.e., the size of the connected component), which could be smaller.

We'll stick to the set because it is a bit easier to code (in Python), and getting the number of visited nodes with len(visited) is sometimes helpful.

There is an iterative version of DFS, but it is a bit convoluted, so we don't recommend learning it. If you need iterative algorithms for a connectivity problem, you can always use the BFS algorithm we will learn next.[7]

DFS ANALYSIS

DFS visits every node reachable from the starting node and iterates over their edges. The worst case is when the whole graph is connected, making the runtime O(V+E).

When we use the 'Connected-component loop' recipe to launch a DFS from every connected component, the runtime is still O(V+E): O(V) for the outer loop and O(V+E) combined for each DFS launched, which will visit every node and iterate over every edge. Since each DFS traverses a separate connected component, we won't revisit nodes.

The extra space is O(V) for the visited set in the worst case, plus O(V+E) if we count the adjacency list.

CONNECTIVITY PROBLEM SET

✦ *Try these problems with AI Interviewer: bctci.co/graphs-problem-set-1*

PROBLEM 36.2   GRAPH PATH

Given the adjacency list of an undirected graph, graph, and two distinct nodes, node1 and node2, return a simple path from node1 to node2. A *simple path* does not repeat any nodes. Return an empty array if there is no path from node1 to node2.

---

7 Contrary to popular belief, replacing the queue data structure in a graph BFS does not result in a DFS: https://11011110. github.io/blog/2013/12/17/stack-based-graph-traversal.html. It results in a traversal that visits the nodes in a different order than DFS and BFS.

```
graph = [
    [1],              # Node 0
    [0, 2, 5, 4],     # Node 1
    [1, 4, 5],        # Node 2
    [],               # Node 3
    [5, 2, 1],        # Node 4
    [1, 2, 4]         # Node 5
]
```

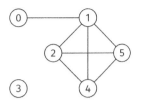

Figure 8.

▶ **Example:** graph from Figure 8, node1 = 0, node2 = 4
Output: [0, 1, 4]. There are other valid answers, like [0, 1, 2, 5, 4].

▶ **Example:** graph from Figure 8, node1 = 0, node2 = 3
Output: []. There is no path to node 3.

PROBLEM 36.3   TREE CHECK

Given a non-empty adjacency list of an undirected graph, graph, return whether it is a *tree*. A graph is a tree if it is *acyclic* and *connected*.[8]

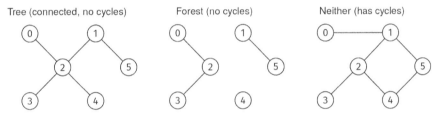

Figure 9. A tree, a forest, and a graph with cycles. A tree is connected and has no cycles. A forest has no cycles (a tree is also a forest).

▶ **Example:** graph from Figure 9 (left)
Output: True.

▶ **Example:** graph from Figure 9 (center)
Output: False. It is not connected.

▶ **Example:** graph from Figure 9 (right)
Output: False. It is not acyclic.

PROBLEM 36.4   SPANNING TREE

Given the adjacency list of an undirected, *connected* graph, graph, return a set of edges forming a *spanning tree*. A spanning tree is a subset of edges that connects (i.e., "spans") every node and has no cycles.[9]

▶ **Example:** graph from Figure 9 (right)
Output: [[0, 1], [1, 2], [2, 3], [2, 4], [4, 5]]. There are other valid answers.

---

8 The difference between the trees in this chapter and the trees in the 'Tree Basics' chapter is that here we don't have a hierarchical structure, so sometimes we call these trees *free* trees or *unrooted* trees.

9 In the Union–Find chapter (bctci.co/union-find), we'll talk about *minimum spanning trees*, which is the spanning tree minimizing the sum of edge weights in weighted graphs. In this problem, the graph is unweighted, so we just want to find **any** spanning tree.

PROBLEM 36.5	REACHABILITY QUERIES

Given the adjacency list of an undirected graph, graph, as well as an array, queries, of length k, where queries[i] is a pair of node indices, return a boolean array of length k where the i-th element indicates if the nodes in queries[i] are in the same connected component.

▶ **Example:** graph from Figure 8, queries: [[0, 4], [0, 3]]
   Output: [True, False]. The True corresponds to query [0, 4] and the False to query [0, 3].
            Assume that V < 10^5 and k < 10^5.

PROBLEM 36.6	STRONGLY CONNECTED GRAPH

Given the adjacency list of a non-empty *directed* graph, graph, return whether it is *strongly connected*. A directed graph is strongly connected if every node can reach every other node (in a directed graph, it is possible that node1 can reach node2 but not the other way around).

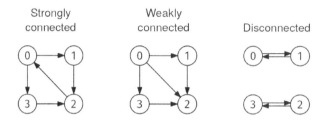

Figure 10. Strongly connected, weakly connected, and disconnected directed graphs. A directed graph is *weakly connected* if it would be connected if edges didn't have directions.

▶ **Example:** graph from Figure 10 (left)
   Output: True.

▶ **Example:** graph from Figure 10 (center)
   Output: False. Node 2 cannot reach node 0, among others.

▶ **Example:** graph from Figure 10 (right)
   Output: False. Node 0 cannot reach node 3, among others.

PROBLEM 36.7	HILLIEST CONNECTED COMPONENT

We're given the adjacency list, graph, of a non-empty, undirected graph with V nodes and an array, heights, of length V, where heights[i] is a floating-point number representing the *height* of node i. The *elevation gain* of an edge is the absolute difference of the heights of its endpoints. The *hilliness* of a connected component is the average elevation gain of the edges in it, or 0 if it has a single node. The *hilliest* connected component is the one with maximum hilliness.

Find the hilliest connected component and return its hilliness.

▶ **Example:** graph from Figure 11
        heights = [4, 1, 3, 2]
    Output: 2.

The graph has a single connected
component, which is the hilliest by
default. The edge elevation gains are
3 for [0, 1], 2 for [1, 2], 1 for [2,
3], and 2 for [3, 0]. The average is
2.

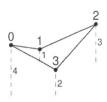

Figure 11. A graph with node heights. The numbers
above the nodes are the node indices, and the
numbers below are the heights.

PROBLEM 36.8   HIGHEST AVERAGE ELEVATION GAIN

Given V, the number of nodes in a graph, and an array, edges, where edges[i] is a triplet [node1, node2, elevation_gain] representing an edge and an associated elevation gain, find the connected component with the highest average elevation gain and return that average.

▶ **Example:** V = 4, edges = [[0, 1, 3], [1, 2, 2], [2, 3, 1], [3, 0, 2]]
    Output: 2. The elevation gains of the edges are the same as in Figure 11.

PROBLEM 36.9   FIRST TIME ALL CONNECTED

We are given V ≥ 2, the number of computers in a data center. The computers are identified with indices from 0 to V-1. We are also given a list, cables, of length E where each element is a pair [x, y], with 0 ≤ x,y < V and x ≠ y, indicating that we should connect the computers with indices x and y with a cable. If we add the cables in the order of the list, at what point will all the computers be connected (meaning that there is a path of cables between every pair of computers)? Return the index of the cable in cables after which all the computers are connected or -1 if that never happens.

▶ **Example:** V = 4
        cables = [[0, 2], [1, 3],
                  [1, 0], [1, 2]]
    Output: 2. The computers become all
            connected with the cables at
            indices 0, 1, and 2.
    Assume that V < 10^5 and E < 10^5.

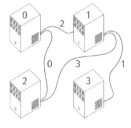

Figure 12. Example 1 of Problem 36.9, with the
cables labeled by appearance order.

✦ PROBLEM SET SOLUTIONS

SOLUTION 36.2   GRAPH PATH

We can start a DFS from node2. If node1 can be reached, we'll visit it at some point. During the DFS, we'll track the predecessors of each node in a map, which is the node we visited it from. We can then follow a **chain of predecessors** from node1 to node2 to find the path.

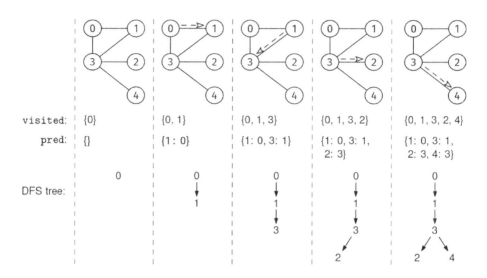

Figure 13. Tracking predecessors during DFS.

♻ REUSABLE IDEA: PATH RECONSTRUCTION

In DFS when we mark a node as visited, we can also track their *predecessor* in the DFS. The mapping from each node to its predecessor defines a 'DFS visit tree' rooted at the starting node. The predecessor of each node is the parent in this DFS tree (the starting node has no predecessor). Given any node, node, reachable from the starting node, start, we can follow a **chain of predecessors** to find a path from node to start.

Every chain of predecessors leads to the starting node, so we can keep going until we reach start:

```
1  path = [node]
2  while path[len(path) - 1] != start:
3    path.append(predecessors[path[len(path) - 1]])
```

Path reconstruction also works for BFS, in which case it doesn't just find any path, it finds the **shortest path**.

Since we are already tracking predecessors in the predecessors map, the visited set is redundant. A node can be considered visited if it is a key in predecessors.

```
1  def path(graph, node1, node2):
2    predecessors = {node2: None}  # The starting node doesn't have a predecessor.
3
4    def visit(node):
5      for nbr in graph[node]:
6        if nbr not in predecessors:
7          predecessors[nbr] = node
8          visit(nbr)
9    visit(node2)
10   if node1 not in predecessors:
11     return [] # node1 and node2 are disconnected.
12   path = [node1]
13   while path[len(path) - 1] != node2:
14     path.append(predecessors[path[len(path) - 1]])
15   return path
```

SOLUTION 36.3   TREE CHECK

We can *BREAK DOWN THE PROBLEM* into checking if the graph is connected and acyclic. Checking if it is connected is easy: we can start a DFS from any node and check that the size of the visited set is V. To determine if the graph is acyclic, every time we visit a node, node, and we iterate through one of its neighbors, nbr, there are three cases:

1. nbr is not visited yet. We can visit it normally.
2. nbr is in visited, and it is *not* the node we arrived to node from (the predecessor of node). This indicates a cycle.
3. nbr is in visited but it is the predecessor of node. Predecessors are always in the visited set, but that doesn't mean there is a cycle. We can ignore it.

In the implementation below, we use a "nonlocal" variable, found_cycle, which can be seen from all recursive calls. See page 437 for a discussion on nonlocal variables.

```
 1   def is_tree(graph):
 2     predecessors = {0: None}  # Start from node 0 (the starting node doesn't matter).
 3     found_cycle = False
 4
 5     def visit(node):
 6       nonlocal found_cycle
 7       if found_cycle:
 8         return
 9       for nbr in graph[node]:
10         if nbr not in predecessors:
11           predecessors[nbr] = node
12           visit(nbr)
13         elif nbr != predecessors[node]:
14           found_cycle = True
15
16     visit(0)
17     connected = len(predecessors) == len(graph)
18     return not found_cycle and connected
```

A simpler way to check if a connected graph is a tree is by leveraging this property: a tree has exactly V - 1 edges. To see why this is true, imagine that we start with an empty graph and start adding edges, one at a time, without creating cycles. Initially, the empty graph has V connected components. Each time we add an edge without forming a cycle, we connect two nodes in different connected components, reducing the number of connected components by one. After adding V - 1 edges without creating any cycles, only one connected component remains. We cannot add any more edges or we would create a cycle.

SOLUTION 36.4   SPANNING TREE

If the graph is connected, DFS will visit every node once, so the DFS visit tree (Figure 13) is a spanning tree. Thus, we just need to compute the predecessors map as usual and return an array with one edge per entry in the predecessors map.

SOLUTION 36.5   REACHABILITY QUERIES

We could do a DFS for each query. However, if the number of queries is potentially large, a more efficient approach is to precompute a map from each node to a connected component identifier. We can use the 'Connected-component loop' recipe (pg 466). Whenever we start a DFS through a new connected component, we increase the connected-component identifier.

```
 1   def connected_component_queries(graph, queries):
```

```
2    node_to_cc = {}
3
4    def visit(node, cc_id):
5      if node in node_to_cc:
6        return
7      node_to_cc[node] = cc_id
8      for nbr in graph[node]:
9        visit(nbr, cc_id)
10   cc_id = 0
11   for node in range(len(graph)):
12     if node not in node_to_cc:
13       visit(node, cc_id)
14       cc_id += 1
15
16   res = []
17   for node1, node2 in queries:
18     res.append(node_to_cc[node1] == node_to_cc[node2])
19   return res
```

SOLUTION 36.6   STRONGLY CONNECTED GRAPH

For directed graphs, it is not enough to check if a specific node can reach every node. For instance, in Figure 10 (center), node 0 can reach every node, but the graph is not strongly connected.

A naive solution is to do a DFS from every node. There is a *trick* that allows us to solve this problem efficiently: let u be any node in a directed graph. The graph is strongly connected if and only if (1) u can reach every node, and (2) every node can reach u. Why? On the one hand, if either condition is missing, the graph is not strongly connected because at least one node can't reach u or be reached from u. On the other hand, if the two conditions hold, you can go from any node to any other node. For instance, if you want to go from node1 to node2, you can go from node1 to u and from u to node2.

This trick gives us two conditions that we can check in linear time.

- We pick any node, say the one with index 0.
- To check if node 0 can reach every node, we do a normal DFS from it.
- To check if every node can reach node 0, we reverse the directions of all the edges in the adjacency list and do a DFS on the reversed graph. If there is a path from node 0 to node 7 in the reversed graph, that means that there is a path from 7 to 0 in the original graph.

We omit the visit() implementation since it is a standard DFS. You can find this and all the full solutions online.

```
1    def strongly_connected(graph):
2      V = len(graph)
3      visited = set()
4      visit(graph, visited, 0)
5      if len(visited) < V:
6        return False
7
8      reverse_graph = [[] for _ in range(V)]
9      for node in range(V):
10       for nbr in graph[node]:
11         reverse_graph[nbr].append(node)
12
13     reverse_visited = set()
```

```
14    visit(reverse_graph, reverse_visited, 0)
15    return len(reverse_visited) == V
```

SOLUTION 36.7   HILLIEST CONNECTED COMPONENT

This problem introduces the concept of *node weights*, which we have to use to compute the *hilliness* of each connected component. We use the **BREAK DOWN THE PROBLEM** booster and solve it in two steps:

1. Label each node with a connected component ID. We can use the 'Connected-component loop' recipe (pg 466) for this, as in Problem 4.

2. Compute the hilliness of each connected component. When computing averages, it is often easiest to focus on computing the numerator (the sum of elevation gains) and denominator (the number of edges) separately and dividing at the very end.

```
1    def max_hilliness(graph, heights):
2      node_to_cc = label_nodes_with_cc_ids(graph) # Same as Problem 4.
3      V = len(graph)
4      cc_to_elevation_gain_sum = {}
5      cc_to_num_edges = {}
6      for node in range(V):
7        cc = node_to_cc[node]
8        if cc not in cc_to_num_edges:
9          cc_to_elevation_gain_sum[cc] = 0
10         cc_to_num_edges[cc] = 0
11       for nbr in graph[node]:
12         if nbr > node:
13           cc_to_num_edges[cc] += 1
14           cc_to_elevation_gain_sum[cc] += abs(heights[node] - heights[nbr])
15     res = 0
16     for cc in cc_to_num_edges:
17       res = max(res, cc_to_elevation_gain_sum[cc] / cc_to_num_edges[cc])
```

We could have also solved the problem in a single pass, computing each connected component's hilliness as we traverse it.

♻ REUSABLE IDEA: COMPUTING AVERAGES

When computing averages, it is often easiest to focus on computing the numerator and denominator separately and dividing at the very end.

SOLUTION 36.8   HIGHEST AVERAGE ELEVATION GAIN

This is a weighted graph, where the edge weights represent elevation gains. We can **BREAK DOWN THE PROBLEM** into three steps:

1. Build the adjacency list. For graphs with edge weights, the adjacency list is a bit different: instead of a list of neighbors, we have a list of (neighbor, weight) tuples.

2. Use the 'Connected-component loop' recipe (pg 466) to label each node with a connected component ID, as in Problem 4.

3. Compute the hilliness of each connected component. This would be similar to Problem 6, but using edge weights instead of node weights.

SOLUTION 36.9   FIRST TIME ALL CONNECTED

A naive solution would be to add the edges one by one in order, and do a DFS after each one to check if the graph is connected. This would take O(E*(V+E)) time.

A better solution is to use the **guess-and-check technique** from the Binary Search chapter (pg 338). The goal is to find the **transition point** in the list of cables where the graph goes from disconnected to connected.

- Before adding any cables, the graph is clearly not connected, so we are before the transition point.
- After adding all the cables, the graph may be connected or not. We can check if it is in a preprocessing step. If it is not, we can return -1, if it is, then we are after the transition point.

We can binary search for the transition point using the **transition-point recipe** (pg 329). To check if the graph is connected with a given prefix of the cables, we do a DFS from any node with only edges for those cables.

```
1   def first_time_all_connected(V, cables):
2     def visit(graph, visited, node):
3       for nbr in graph[node]:
4         if nbr not in visited:
5           visited.add(nbr)
6           visit(graph, visited, nbr)
7
8     def is_before(cable_index):
9       graph = [[] for _ in range(V)]
10      for i in range(cable_index + 1):
11        node1, node2 = cables[i]
12        graph[node1].append(node2)
13        graph[node2].append(node1)
14      visited = {0}
15      visit(graph, visited, 0)
16      return len(visited) < V
17    l, r = 0, len(cables) - 1
18    if is_before(r):
19      return -1
20    while r - l > 1:
21      mid = l + (r - l) // 2
22      if is_before(mid):
23        l = mid
24      else:
25        r = mid
26    return r
```

The runtime now becomes O((V+E) log E). In the Union–Find chapter, we'll see an even faster solution to this problem (bctci.co/union-find).

DISTANCE PROBLEMS AND BFS

The second major class of graph problems is *distance-related* problems. These problems go beyond whether a node can reach another node. The main distance questions are:

- What is the shortest path between two nodes?
- What is the *distance* between two nodes? The distance between two nodes is the length of the shortest path between them. For nodes in different connected components, we say that the distance between them is infinite.

Breadth-first search (BFS) is an iterative graph traversal that allows us to answer **both connectivity questions (like DFS) and distance questions**. Whereas DFS goes down long-winded paths and only tells you which nodes are reachable from a starting node, BFS expands away from the starting node like the ripples of a stone cast on a lake. It searches outward from the starting node in layers, visiting all of its immediate neighbors before going to its neighbors' neighbors. *BFS computes the distance from the starting node to every reachable node.*

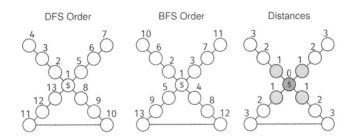

Figure 14. DFS vs BFS visit order. BFS visits nodes in order by distance from the starting node, while DFS doesn't.

We already talked about BFS traversals on binary trees (also called 'level-order traversal' in the context of trees, pg 444), and we'll now extend the same idea to graphs. Just as in a tree BFS, when we visit a node in a graph BFS, we put the children in a **queue** of nodes to visit. We start with only the starting node in the queue, and when we visit a node (i.e., pop it out of the queue), we push its neighbors to the back of the queue.

To deal with cycles and avoid revisiting nodes, we only add nodes to the queue if they are not visited yet. Furthermore, we must avoid adding nodes to the queue that are already in the queue waiting to be visited. This keeps the queue size bounded by $O(V)$ rather than $O(V^2)$.

When we visit a node, node and find a neighbor, nbr, that is not visited yet and not in the queue yet, the shortest path from start to nbr goes through node, and we can compute distance(start, nbr) as distance(start, node) + 1. We can store distances in a map as we traverse the graph.

Similar to DFS, we need some data structure to keep track of already-visited or already-enqueued nodes. Rather than having a visited set and a distances map, we can consolidate the two: with just the distances map, we can say that a node is already visited or queued if it is a key in distances.

RECIPE 3. GRAPH BFS.[10]

```
def graph_BFS(graph, start):
    Q = Queue()
    Q.push(start)
    distances = {start: 0}
    while not Q.empty():
        node = Q.pop()
        for nbr in graph[node]:
            if nbr not in distances:
                distances[nbr] =
distances[node] + 1
                Q.push(nbr)
    # Do something with distances.
```

Tree BFS

```
1  def tree_BFS(root):
2      Q = Queue()
3      Q.push(root)
4      while not Q.empty():
5          node = Q.pop()
6          if not node:
7              continue
8          # Do something with node.
9          Q.push(node.left)
10         Q.push(node.right)
```

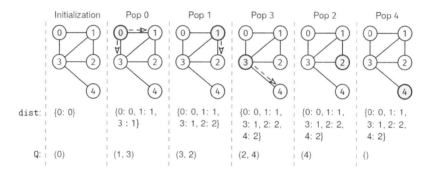

Figure 15. BFS iterations. The arrows show newly discovered unvisited neighbors from the current node. Nodes already visited or enqueued are shaded.

In Problem 36.4, we used the predecessors in a DFS tree to build a spanning tree. If we do the same with a BFS, the predecessors form a tree that not only reaches every node in the connected component of the starting node, but also is a *shortest-path tree*. The shortest path tree encapsulates the shortest paths from the start node to every other node. The BFS/shortest-path tree combined with the **path reconstruction** reusable idea (pg 470) allows us to find shortest paths efficiently.

However, BFS has an important limitation. *BFS only finds shortest paths in unweighted graphs.* In the weighted version of the problem, each edge has an associated weight or *length* and the shortest path between two nodes is the one minimizing the sum of edge lengths. For weighted shortest paths, we need to reach for a different algorithm, depending on the type of graph (see Table 3 on pg 489).

---

10 Python doesn't have a buit-in Queue data structure, but you can use the deque ('Doubly Ended Queue') from the collections module, which supports the same operations with the same runtimes. Instead of push() and pop(), they are called append() and popleft(). In this chapter, we will use the language-agnostic Queue API that we defined in the Stacks & Queues chapter (pg 379). See there for more details. Reminder: do **not** use a dynamic array for a queue because popping from the beginning of a dynamic array is O(n), not O(1).

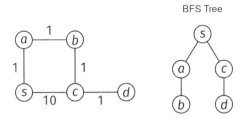

Figure 16. BFS doesn't work on weighted graphs: there is a path from s to d with length 4, but if we do a BFS from s, we'll find c as the predecessor of d, yielding a path s -> c -> d of length 11.

BFS ANALYSIS

Like DFS, BFS takes O(V+E) time and uses O(V) space for the queue and the distances map (not counting the adjacency list). This makes it a good alternative to DFS when we (or the interviewer) prefer an iterative algorithm. As a bonus, we don't need to worry about stack overflow.

Don't make these common BFS mistakes!

- Don't use a dynamic array for the queue. It increases the BFS runtime from O(V+E) to O(V²+E).

- Don't enqueue unvisited nodes more than once. The extra space complexity (not counting the adjacency list itself) increases from O(V) to O(E).

- Don't use BFS to find shortest paths in a weighted graph—it doesn't work. It is not possible to find shortest paths in O(V+E) time in weighted graphs (see Table 3, pg 489).

DISTANCE PROBLEM SET

Warmup Questions

As a warmup before getting to interview questions, imagine you have an undirected graph. Without coding, describe how you would use BFS to compute the following distances, and analyze the runtime and space in each case:

1. The distance from node1 to node2.
2. The distance from a start node to every other node.
3. The distance from every node to a specific goal node.
4. The distance from every node to every node.

How do your answers change if the graph is directed?

Warmup Solution Sets

1. We would start a BFS at node1 and stop as soon as we reach node2. In the worst case, the runtime is O(V+E).
2. We would start a BFS from start.
3. Since the graph is undirected, we can do a BFS starting from goal. The distance from goal to the other nodes is the same as the distance from the other nodes to goal.
4. We have to do a BFS from every node. The runtime is O(V*(V+E)).

If the graph is directed, (1), (2), and (4) do not change. For (3), we can use the trick of reversing edge directions before doing the BFS. For instance, say we want to find the distance from every node to a specific node u. Imagine the shortest path from a node w to u has length 3. Then, if we reverse the directions of all the edges, there will be a path of length 3 from u to w.

Use BFS to solve the following problems.[11]

✦ *Try these problems with AI Interviewer: bctci.co/graphs-problem-set-2*

PROBLEM 36.10   **SHORTEST-PATH QUERIES**

Given the adjacency list of an undirected graph, graph, a node index, start, and an array, queries, where each element is a node index, return an array with the same length as queries, where the i-th element is an array with the shortest path from start to queries[i]. If there is no path from start to queries[i], return an empty array for the i-th element.

▶ **Example:** graph from Figure 8, start = 0, queries = [1, 0, 3, 4]
   Output: [[0, 1], [0], [], [0, 1, 4]]. Node 3 cannot be reached from node 0.

> Assume that $V < 10^5$, $E < 10^5$, and len(queries) $< 10^5$, where V and E are the number of nodes and edges in the graph, respectively.

PROBLEM 36.11   **GRAPH HANGOUT**

Three friends want to meet. They live in nodes in a connected, undirected graph. Given the adjacency list, graph, and the nodes where they start, node1, node2, and node3, what's the minimum number of edges they need to traverse in total between the three to meet at *any* node in the graph?

▶ **Example:** graph in Figure 17 (the numbered nodes are where the 3 friends start).
   Output: 9.
   Each friend can get to the middle node by traversing 3 edges. The next clos-est meeting point is at one of the starting nodes, where the other two friends have to traverse 5 edges each.

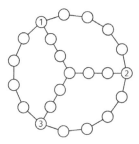

Figure 17.

✦ **PROBLEM SET SOLUTIONS**

SOLUTION 36.10   SHORTEST-PATH QUERIES

Doing a BFS for every query would be expensive. Instead, we can build a BFS tree rooted at start and use the **path reconstruction** reusable idea (pg 470) to find the shortest path for each query. Since the reconstructed paths following predecessor pointers end at start rather than start there, we need to reverse them at the end.

```
1   def shortest_path_queries(graph, start, queries):
2       Q = Queue()
```

---

11   As mentioned, BFS can also be used for connectivity problems, so if you want extra practice, you can solve all the problems in the DFS problem set with BFS.

```
3      Q.push(start)
4      distances = {start: 0}
5      predecessors = {start: None}
6      while not Q.empty():
7        node = Q.pop()
8        for nbr in graph[node]:
9          if nbr not in distances:
10            distances[nbr] = distances[node] + 1
11            predecessors[nbr] = node
12            Q.push(nbr)
13      res = []
14      for node in queries:
15        if node not in distances:
16          res.append([])
17        else:
18          path = [node]
19          while path[len(path) - 1] != start:
20            path.append(predecessors[path[len(path) - 1]])
21          path.reverse()
22          res.append(path)
23      return res
```

The runtime is $O(V+E)$ for the BFS and $O(\text{path length})$ for each query, which is optimal.

The `predecessors` map in BFS represents a *shortest-path tree*. This tree can be used to reconstruct the shortest paths between the starting node and every other node.

SOLUTION 36.11   GRAPH HANGOUT

Let's **start with an easier version**. What if there are only two friends? In that case, they should meet at any node along the shortest path between them. It doesn't matter which—that is just a matter of who walks more. We could do a BFS from node1 and return the distance to node2 (or the other way around).

Since there are three friends, the closest node to all of them may not be in the shortest path between two of the friends, as shown in Figure 17. Instead, we can compute a 'score' for each node, adding up the distances it would take to each friend to get there. We need the minimum score. To get the scores, we can do a BFS from each friend's location and add up the `distances` maps.

```
1    def walking_distance_to_coffee(graph, node1, node2, node3):
2      distances1 = bfs(graph, node1)   # Standard BFS (Recipe 3).
3      distances2 = bfs(graph, node2)
4      distances3 = bfs(graph, node3)
5      res = math.inf
6      for i in range(len(graph)):
7        res = min(res, distances1[i] + distances2[i] + distances3[i])
8      return res
```

MULTISOURCE BFS

By default, BFS computes the distances from one node to every other node. There are problems where there is a special subset of nodes, and we want to find the distance from every node to its closest node in the special subset. For instance:

PROBLEM 36.12 DAYS UNTIL ALL INFECTED

Some computers in a network have been infected by a virus. We are given the adjacency list of an undirected graph, `graph`, representing the computer network, and an array, `infected`, with the indices of the infected nodes. Every day, the virus spreads to all computers directly connected to an infected neighbor computer. How many days will it take to infect all computers?

▶ **Example:** `graph in Figure 18 (left)`.
  Output: 3.

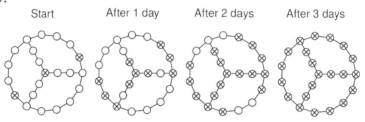

Figure 18.

SOLUTION 36.12 DAYS UNTIL ALL INFECTED

A naive solution would be to do a BFS from every infected node (similar to Problem 36.11: Graph Hangout, pg 478). Then, we can look for the node that is the furthest away from *any* infected node. The runtime would be O((V+E)*k), where k is the number of infected nodes. In the worst case, this becomes O((V+E)*V).

To improve the algorithm, note that all we need for this problem is the distance from every node to its closest infected node. Given those distances, it is easy to find the maximum.

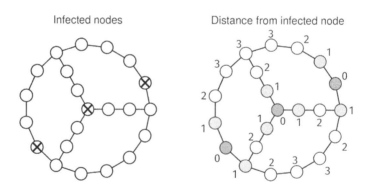

Figure 19.

A variation of BFS called *multisource BFS* accepts multiple starting nodes and can find the distance from every node to its closest starting node in O(V+E) time.[12] Multisource BFS is like a BFS except that, at the beginning, we add all starting nodes to the queue and set their distances to 0. From there, the main BFS loop works as

---

12 Not to be confused with *bidirectional BFS*—a variant of BFS where you want to find the distance or shortest path between two specific nodes, node1 and node2. We don't cover bidirectional BFS because it doesn't change the O(V+E) time complexity, but it has better constant factors. Similar to multisource BFS, the idea of bidirectional BFS is to initialize the queue with both node1 and node2, and grow the set of visited nodes from both nodes at the same time. We also need to mark whether each node was visited from node1 or node2. The search ends when we encounter the first edge [u, w] that connects a node visited from node1 and a node visited from node2. The shortest path from node1 to node2 goes from node1 to u, takes the edge [u, w], and then goes from w to node2.

usual, this time expanding from all starting nodes at the same pace. The visit order will be from closest to furthest from any starting node.

RECIPE 4. MULTISOURCE BFS.

```
def multisource_BFS(graph, sources):
  Q = Queue()
  distances = {}
  for start in sources:
    Q.push(start)
    distances[start] = 0
  while not Q.empty(): # Normal BFS loop.
    node = Q.pop()
    for nbr in graph[node]:
      if nbr not in distances:
        distances[nbr] = distances[node] + 1
        Q.push(nbr)
  # Do something with distances.
```

The time and space complexity of multisource BFS is the same as a normal BFS because all the sources share the same visited set, so every node is still visited only once.

Returning to Problem 36.12, we can use multisource BFS with the infected nodes as sources. This will give us the distance from each node to its closest infected node. We should return the maximum distance.

```
1  def all_infected(graph, infected):
2    distances = ...  # Multisource BFS with infected nodes as sources.
3    return max(distances)
```

REUSABLE IDEA: MULTISOURCE BFS

In O(V+E) time, we can find the distance from every node to its closest node in a designated subset with multisource BFS. It's like a normal BFS except for the initialization: we start by putting all the designated nodes in the queue and setting their distances to 0.

A REALISTIC INTERVIEW-LEVEL GRAPH QUESTION		INTERVIEW REPLAY
View Online:	bctci.co/graphs-replay-1 @ 57:00 - end	
The Question:	Given a list of conversion rates of various currencies and a list of queries, determine the conversion amounts for the queries.	
What You'll See:	The candidate realized that this was a graph problem and built a graph of exchange rates to get the correct outputs. They communicated effectively with the interviewer and gradually built up a solution.	
Who:	*Interviewer*: Software Engineer at Microsoft *Candidate*: 1 year exp.	
Outcome:	The candidate got the job at AWS!	

GRID GRAPHS

A grid can be seen as a graph where each cell is a node and its neighbors are its adjacent cells (above, below, left, and right). If the dimensions of the grid are RxC, the graph has up to RxC nodes with a maximum degree of 4.[13]

This grid could be something like a binary matrix, where 1 represents an accessible cell (a node) and a 0 represents a blocked cell. We might ask a question like: "Is there a path from cell A to cell B if we can move to adjacent cells (above, below, left, and right) but not cross through any blocked cells?

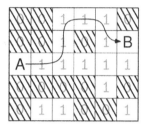

Figure 20. A grid graph represented as a boolean matrix and a path in the graph through '1' cells.

To solve problems like this, we can do a DFS or a BFS on the grid graph. In fact, graph problems with grid inputs are relatively common.

Unlike when the input is an edge list, *we do not need to create the adjacency list as a first step*. We can just iterate through the adjacent cells of a node directly with the reusable idea 'Directions Array To Visit Grid Neighbors' we saw in the Grids & Matrices chapter (pg 314). In the visited set, we store (r, c) tuples.[14]

📋 RECIPE 5. GRID DFS.

```
def grid_dfs(grid, start_r, start_c):
  # Returns if (r, c) is in bounds, not visited, and "walkable."
  def is_valid(r, c):
    ...
  directions = [(-1, 0), (1, 0), (0, 1), (0, -1)]
  visited = {(start_r, start_c)}
  def visit(r, c):
    # Do something with (r, c).
    for dir_r, dir_c in directions:
      nbr_r, nbr_c = r + dir_r, c + dir_c
      if is_valid(nbr_r, nbr_c):
        visited.add((nbr_r, nbr_c))
        visit(nbr_r, nbr_c)
  visit(start_r, start_c)
```

---

13 Depending on the problem, the maximum degree could be eight (if we include diagonally adjacent), two (right and below), or some other possibility.

14 The visited set could also be a boolean grid with rows x cols dimensions. In some languages, that may be more convenient than a map with tuples. Another common variation is modifying the input grid itself to mark already-visited cells.

RECIPE 6. GRID BFS.[15]

```
def grid_bfs(grid, start_r, start_c):
  # Returns if (r, c) is in bounds, not in distances, and "walkable."
  def is_valid(r, c):
    ...
  directions = [(-1, 0), (1, 0), (0, 1), (0, -1)]
  Q = Queue()
  Q.push((start_r, start_c))
  distances = {(start_r, start_c): 0}
  while not Q.empty():
    r, c = Q.pop()
    for dir_r, dir_c in directions:
      nbr_r, nbr_c = r + dir_r, c + dir_c
      if is_valid(nbr_r, nbr_c):
        distances[(nbr_r, nbr_c)] = distances[(r, c)] + 1
        Q.push((nbr_r, nbr_c))
  # Do something with distances.
```

When we use a graph algorithm in a grid, we *analyze it in terms of the grid dimensions*, not V and E. The number of nodes is O(R*C) and the number of edges is O(4*R*C) = O(R*C). This means that DFS and BFS on a grid take at most linear (O(R*C)) time.

GRID GRAPHS PROBLEM SET

✦ *Try these problems with AI Interviewer: bctci.co/graphs-problem-set-3*

Solve and analyze the following problems:

| PROBLEM 36.13 | **COUNT GRID ISLANDS**

In this classic problem, you are given a binary grid, grid, where 0 represents water and 1 represents solid ground. The goal is to count the number of *islands* in the grid, where an island is a four-directionally contiguous land region.

▸ **Example:** grid = [[0, 0, 1, 0],
                        [1, 1, 0, 1],
                        [0, 0, 1, 1]]
   Output: 3.
▸ **Example:** grid = [[]]
   Output: 0.

| PROBLEM 36.14 | **MULTI-EXIT MAZE**

A few friends are trapped on a maze represented by a grid of letters:

- 'X' represents a wall.
- 'O' represents an exit. There may be multiple exits.
- '.' represents walkable space.

---

15 The distances map could also be an integer grid with rows x cols dimensions with each value initialized to -1, meaning that the distance is unknown yet. See, e.g., Solution 14.

Given the grid, maze, return a grid with the same dimensions. Each cell (r, c) should contain the minimum number of steps needed to go from position (r, c) in the maze to the closest exit. If (r, c) is a wall in the maze, return -1 at that position. It is guaranteed that every walkable cell can reach an exit.

▶ Example: maze = ...X.O   Output: [[1, 2, 3, -1, 1, 0],
                   OX.X..   [0, -1, 4, -1, 2, 1],
                   ...X..   [1, 2, 3, -1, 3, 2],
                   .X....   [2, -1, 4, 5, 4, 3],
                   XOX.XX   [-1, 0, -1, 6, -1, -1]]

PROBLEM 36.15 RGB DISTANCES

The *taxicab distance* between two cells (r1, c1) and (r2, c2) in a grid is defined as abs(r1-r2) + abs(c1-c2). Given a grid of characters, screen, representing a screen with rows x cols pixels, where each element is one of 'R', 'G', or 'B', return a grid, output, with the same dimensions, where:

- If screen[i][j] = 'R', output[i][j] is the taxicab distance from screen[i][j] to the closest 'G'.

- If screen[i][j] = 'G', output[i][j] is the taxicab distance from screen[i][j] to the closest 'B'.

- If screen[i][j] = 'B', output[i][j] is the taxicab distance from screen[i][j] to the closest 'R'.

It is guaranteed that the screen contains at least one 'R', one 'G', and one 'B'.

▶ Example: Output: 2 1 1 2 1 **1**
   screen = RRRGRB   **1** 1 1 3 1 2
            BGRGRR   2 1 1 4 1 2
            RRRGRR   1 1 1 1 1 1
            RGRRRR   1 **2** 1 1 3 4
            GBGRGG   G cells have a gray background, and **B** cells have a
                                     black background.

✦ PROBLEM SET SOLUTIONS

SOLUTION 36.13   COUNT GRID ISLANDS

This problem is just counting connected components. We solve it by combining Recipe 2, the connected-component loop, and a grid DFS/BFS.

```
1   def count_islands(grid):
2     R, C = len(grid), len(grid[0])
3     count = 0
4     visited = set()
5     for r in range(R):
6       for c in range(C):
7         if grid[r][c] == 1 and (r, c) not in visited:
8           visited.add((r, c))
9           dfs(grid, visited, r, c)  # Normal grid DFS (Recipe 5).
10          count += 1
11    return count
```

SOLUTION 36.14   MULTI-EXIT MAZE

A naive solution would be to start a BFS from every walkable cell. Instead, we can start a BFS from all the exit nodes at the same time with a **multisource BFS on a grid**. In this case, the set of 'sources' are the exits of the maze. This will give us the distances from walkable cells to their closest exit cell. When looking for the neighbors of a cell, we need to make sure to skip walls.

```
 1   def exit_distances(maze):
 2     R, C = len(maze), len(maze[0])
 3     directions = [(-1, 0), (1, 0), (0, 1), (0, -1)]
 4     distances = [[-1] * C for _ in range(R)]
 5     Q = Queue()
 6     for r in range(R):
 7       for c in range(C):
 8         if maze[r][c] == 'O':
 9           distances[r][c] = 0
10           Q.push((r, c))
11     while not Q.empty():
12       r, c = Q.pop()
13       for dir_r, dir_c in directions:
14         nbr_r, nbr_c = r + dir_r, c + dir_c
15         if (0 <= nbr_r < R and 0 <= nbr_c < C and
16             maze[nbr_r][nbr_c] != 'X' and distances[nbr_r][nbr_c] == -1):
17           distances[nbr_r][nbr_c] = distances[r][c] + 1
18           Q.push((nbr_r, nbr_c))
19     return distances
```

SOLUTION 36.15   RGB DISTANCES

We can do a multisource BFS with all the G's as sources to find, for each R, the closest G. We can repeat the same for the other two colors.

\#   BFS distances on a grid without obstacles are *taxicab distances*, also known as *Manhattan distances*. Thus, those terms are triggers for BFS.

INTERVIEWER ADVICE ON THE BEST ROI WHEN STUDYING PROBLEMS		INTERVIEW REPLAY
View Online:	bctci.co/graphs-replay-2 @ 55:53 - 1:04:00	
The Question:	Given a color represented by a number and a matrix of 1s and 0s, "floodfill" the matrix with the color given a starting location.	
What You'll See:	The interviewer showed how to write code more cleanly and listed data structures and algorithms that the candidate should focus on to get the best return on their investment	
Who:	*Interviewer*: Senior Software Engineer at FAANG+ *Candidate*: College student	

GRAPH MODELING

Ever experienced the Baader-Meinhof Phenomenon, where once you notice something (e.g., particular type of car, or the number 23 [16]), you start seeing it everywhere? That's how we feel about graphs. Even when a

---

16   Jim Carrey starred in a movie about this: https://www.imdb.com/title/tt0481369/.

problem doesn't scream 'graph'—no edge lists, grids, or nodes—graphs have a way of appearing, hidden in plain sight.

Such problems often touch on the themes of reachability or distance in some non-obvious way, and we can solve them with DFS or BFS *if* we can first figure out what the nodes and edges should be. We call this 'graph modeling' because we take an input that is not a graph and turn it into one so that we can use graph algorithms.

Graph modeling is a textbook example of the **REFRAME THE PROBLEM** booster, and we already saw an example of graph modeling for Problem 24.11: Multiplayer Video Game (pg 265). Graph modeling extends to other graph algorithms we haven't seen yet, like topological sort.

Graph Modeling Steps

- Figure out how to model the problem as a connectivity or distance problem.
- Build a graph (usually an adjacency list) from the given input.
- Implement a graph algorithm (usually DFS or BFS).

GRAPH MODELING PROBLEM SET

✦ *Try these problems with AI Interviewer: bctci.co/graphs-problem-set-4*

PROBLEM 36.16   **THE FLOOR IS LAVA**

We are given an array, `furniture`, where each element consists of four integer coordinates, [`x_min`, `y_min`, `x_max`, `y_max`], indicating the boundary of a rectangular piece of furniture. The furniture pieces are non-overlapping (they can share an edge or a corner). We are playing the game 'the floor is lava,' where we have to reach from the first piece of furniture to the last one without touching the floor, only jumping on furniture. If we can jump at most a distance of d, where d is an integer, can we win?

Recall that `distance((`x_1`, `y_1`), (`x_2`, `y_2`))` $= \sqrt{((x_1 - x_2)^2 + (y_1 - y_2)^2)}$.

▶ Example:
  the furniture from Fig. 19
  d = 5
  Output: true
▶ Example:
    the furniture from Fig. 19

    d = 4
  Output: false

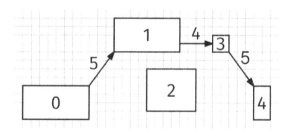

Figure 21. The arrows show a way to jump from furniture 0 to furniture 4 where each jump is at most distance 5.

PROBLEM 36.17   **WORD LADDER GAME VARIATION**

Two friends are playing a game. The first one says a word. Then, the other friend has to form another word by adding or removing a letter. The first friend then needs to find a *new* word (repetitions are not allowed) by doing the *opposite* operation (addition or removal). The game goes on, with each friend finding a new word and alternating additions and removals.[17] These are two examples of games:

    leap, lap, slap, sap, soap, sop, shop, hop
    car, care, are, fare, far, fart, art, cart

However, these are not valid games:

    bounce, ounce, once (we removed a letter twice in a row)
    hung, hug, hung (we repeated a word)
    car, race (we reordered the letters)
    vibes, vibess (vibess is not a real word)

Given two words (strings), word1 and word2, and a list of valid words, words, which contains word1 and word2, return whether it is possible to start the game at word1 and get to word2 using only words from words.

✦ PROBLEM SET SOLUTIONS

SOLUTION 36.16   THE FLOOR IS LAVA

To solve this problem, we need to pick up on the fact that it is about *things with pairwise relationships*. The 'things' are furniture pieces, and the 'relationship' is being at most distance d apart. This defines a graph, and the question becomes a standard reachability problem in that graph.

To build the graph, we need to be able to compute the distance between two pieces of furniture. There are two cases: if they overlap partially on either coordinate, we can jump in an axis-aligned direction. Otherwise, we need to jump diagonally. To know if two rectangles overlap along the x coordinate, think of each rectangle as a segment, [x_min, x_max]. Then, we just need a formula for whether two segments overlap.

```
 1   def segment_distance(min1, max1, min2, max2):
 2     return max(0, max(min1, min2) - min(max1, max2))
 3
 4   def distance(furniture1, furniture2):
 5     x_min1, y_min1, x_max1, y_max1 = furniture1
 6     x_min2, y_min2, x_max2, y_max2 = furniture2
 7     x_gap = segment_distance(x_min1, x_max1, x_min2, x_max2)
 8     y_gap = segment_distance(y_min1, y_max1, y_min2, y_max2)
 9     if x_gap == 0:
10       return y_gap
11     elif y_gap == 0:
12       return x_gap
13     else:
14       return math.sqrt(x_gap**2 + y_gap**2)
15
16   def can_reach(furniture, d):
17     V = len(furniture)
18     graph = [[] for _ in range(V)]
19     for i in range(V):
20       for j in range(i+1, V):
21         if distance(furniture[i], furniture[j]) <= d:
22           graph[i].append(j)
23           graph[j].append(i)
24     visited = {0}
25     def visit(node): ...   # Standard DFS (Recipe 1).
```

---

17 This is a variation of the 'word ladder' game invented by Lewis Carroll.

```
26   visit(0)
27   return V-1 in visited
```

SOLUTION 36.17   WORD LADDER GAME VARIATION

The first step of graph modeling is figuring out how to model the problem as a connectivity or distance problem.

We can make a graph where the words in words are the nodes, and the goal is to find a path from word1 to word2. The hard part is modeling the edges. Two words should be connected if they can follow each other in the game. It is tempting to add an edge between two words if it is possible to make one by adding or removing a letter from the other. However, in that graph, bounce -> ounce -> once would be a valid path, which is not allowed.

The key property for this problem is that the *first* choice determines the valid word lengths. If the starting word has length 1 and we start by adding a letter, the valid lengths are 1 and 1+1. Conversely, if we start by removing a letter, the valid lengths are 1 and 1-1. Thus, we need to do two connectivity checks: one using only words/nodes of length 1 and 1-1, and the other using only words/nodes of length 1 and 1+

▶	**GRAPHS BY ANY OTHER NAME WOULD TRAVERSE AS SWEET**	INTERVIEW REPLAY

View Online:	bctci.co/graphs-replay-3 @ 9:24 - 1:05:34
The Question:	Given a tree-like structure with offices, roads, and cars that drive to each with limited seating, return the minimum fuel required for a given number of representatives to reach a destination headquarters.
What You'll See:	The candidate quickly realized that the edge list provided can be converted into an adjacency list and that the problem can be solved with a customized depth-first-search.
Who:	*Interviewer*: Software Engineer at AWS *Candidate*: 10 years exp.

KEY TAKEAWAYS

In this chapter, we covered the two most common graph algorithms, DFS and BFS.

When to use DFS vs BFS

- For distance questions, you must use BFS.
- For connectivity questions, you can choose your favorite (or ask the interviewer what they prefer). Both visit every node reachable from the starting node in $O(V+E)$ time and $O(V)$ extra space (not counting constructing the adjacency list).

If you have a specific reason to prefer iterative over recursive code, use BFS.

- If you are worried about stack overflow for very large graphs.
- If you want an easy way to return from the middle of the traversal.

The following table shows all the graph algorithms you typically need for interviews. After DFS and BFS, the most important graph algorithm to learn is topological sort. The others only come up in niche graph problems.

ALGORITHM	TOPIC	GRAPH TYPES	IMPLEMENTATION	TIME	SPACE
DFS	Connectivity	Unweighted	Recursive	`O(V+E)`	`O(V)`
BFS	Connectivity & distance	Unweighted	Queue	`O(V+E)`	`O(V)`
Topological sort	Multi-purpose	DAGs	Modified DFS	`O(V+E)`	`O(V)`
Dijkstra's algorithm	Distance	Weighted (positive or 0 lengths only)	Priority queue	`O(V + E log E)`	`O(V)`[18]
Bellman–Ford algorithm	Distance	Weighted (any lengths)	Nested loop	`O(V*E)`	`O(V)`
One minimum spanning tree algorithm[19]	Minimum Spanning Tree	Weighted, undirected	Union–find	`O(V + E log E)`	`O(V)`

Table 2. Most relevant graph algorithms to interviews.

When finding distances or shortest paths in a graph, it is important to choose the right algorithm. The following table summarizes how to choose an algorithm for finding distances based on the type of graph. As a general principle, the more types of graphs an algorithm can handle, the bigger the runtime required.

ALGORITHM	WORKS ON
BFS	Unweighted graphs
Topological sort	Directed graphs with any weights but no cycles
Dijkstra's algorithm	Graphs with non-negative weights
Bellman–Ford	Graphs with any weights but no negative-weight cycles

Table 3. Comparison of graph single-source shortest-path algorithms.

Graph Triggers. The input is an edge list or a grid. The topic is related to connectivity, reachability, or distance. Problems involving pairwise relationships between input elements. Geometric problems.

Keywords: path, source, destination, goal, steps, travel, maze, points.

---

18 One of the popular versions, known as "lazy Dijkstra," takes `O(V+E)` extra space. Lazy Dijkstra may be the best version to learn for interviews, since it is simpler, well known, and the worse space complexity is probably not a deal breaker.

19 There are at least a couple of well-known minimum spanning tree algorithms with the same runtime analysis, including Prim's algorithm and Kruskal's algorithm (found in the online-only Union—Find chapter, bctci.co/union-find). For interviews, knowing one should be enough.

ONLINE RESOURCES

Online resources for this chapter include:

- A chance to try each problem in this chapter in AI Interviewer
- Interview replays that show specific mistakes people make with graphs problems
- Full code solutions for every problem in the chapter in multiple programming languages

Try online at bctci.co/graphs.

## CHAPTER 37

HEAPS

AI interviewer, replays, and more materials for this chapter at bctci.co/heaps

> I fell in love with a max-heap, but they only kept
> track of my greatest flaws.
>
> A sentimental binary search tree

▶ *Prerequisites: None*

Heaps are an elegant data structure—simple enough to feel like something you might have come up with on your own, but useful and flexible enough to be a favorite in coding interviews. So, what are they, and why are they useful?

Binary heaps, which we'll simply call heaps, are the most common implementation of the *priority queue* abstract data structure. If stacks are LIFO (last-in-first-out) and queues are FIFO (first-in-first-out), priority queues are "AIPO": anytime-in-priority-out. This is versatile because we get to define the priority of elements depending on the problem.

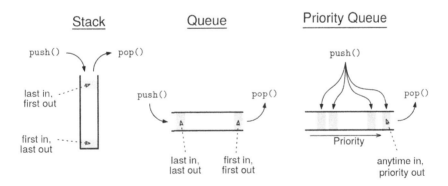

Figure 1.

This is a typical priority queue API:

```
initialize(priority_comparator): sets method to compare element priorities.
push(elem): adds an element to the priority queue.
pop(): removes and returns the highest-priority element.
top(): returns the highest-priority element without removing it.
size(): returns the number of elements in the priority queue.
```

where `priority_comparator()` is a *comparator function* that must satisfy the following signature (or something analogous):[1]

priority_comparator(x, y): returns true if x has higher priority than y, false otherwise

When the elements are numbers, the most common comparators are < (to prioritize smaller numbers elements) and > (to prioritize larger numbers). For the priority logic to make sense, this function must be:

- **Transitive:** if A has higher priority than B, and B has higher priority than C, then A should have higher priority than C.
- **Antisymmetric:** if A and B are different and `priority_comparator(A, B)` is true, then `priority_comparator(B, A)` must be false.

Heaps are the most popular priority queue implementation because they are relatively simple while achieving logarithmic runtimes:

Space complexity	O(n)
initialize(priority_comparator)	O(1)
push(elem)	O(log n) (amortized)[2]
pop()	O(log n) (amortized)
top()	O(1)
size()	O(1)
heapify(priority_comparator, arr)	O(n)

Table 1. Heap operations and runtimes with n elements.[3]

- When we use < to compare elements, the smallest element has the highest priority, so we call the heap a *min-heap*.
- Conversely, if we use >, we call it a *max-heap*.

As you can see, heaps have an extra operation not in the priority queue API: `heapify()`. This operation constructs a heap with all the elements in an array faster than pushing elements one by one.

\# Check out the API for heaps/priority queues in your language of choice. It may differ from the one shown here.

In this chapter, we will show you how to build your own heap, efficiently implement these operations, and use heaps to solve problems.

Consider Problem 31.6: First K (pg 372): given an array of integers, `arr`, and a number k, return the smallest k integers in any order.

▸ **Example:** arr = [1, 4, 2, 8, 10, 5, 2, 1, 3, 9, 11, 11, 27], k = 5
  Output: [1, 3, 2, 2, 1]

---

1 This is analogous to how we can pass a custom comparator function to comparison sorts (pg 361).

2 The amortized times are for the dynamic-array based implementation described in this chapter. See page 285 for a definition of amortized times.

3 The time and space assumes that each element takes O(1) space. If elements take more than O(1) space that may increase the space usage. We also need to factor in how long it takes to compare two elements. When comparing elements like strings, the time for push(), pop(), and heapify() increase to by a factor of O(s), where s is the length of the longest string.

We can trivially solve this problem by sorting and returning the first k elements. Sorting takes $O(n * \log n)$ time and $O(n)$ space.[4]

```
1   def first_k(arr, k):
2     arr.sort()
3     return arr[:k]
```

An alternative solution is to use heaps. We could dump the array into a **min-heap** and pop the k smallest numbers:

```
1   def first_k(arr, k):
2     min_heap = Heap(priority_comparator=lambda x, y: x < y, heap=arr)
3     res = []
4     for i in range(k):
5       res.append(min_heap.pop())
6     return res
```

Building the heap with heapify takes $O(n)$ time, and popping elements takes $k * O(\log n)$ time, resulting in $O(n + k \log n)$ time—an improvement compared to our sorting solution![5]

> **When should I implement my own heap vs using the built-in one?**
>
> Implementing a Heap data structure could be its own problem, so unless the problem asks for it, most of the time, interviewers will let you use the built-in one.
>
> However, some languages don't have a built-in heap implementation. If your language of choice doesn't have a Heap class, tell your interviewer, then ask if you can assume that you have a Heap class with an API like the one in Table 1. Typically, they'll let you.

Like in the case of dynamic arrays, it is valuable to know the techniques used to implement heaps. Now that we've seen a motivating example, let's learn to implement heaps from scratch.

IMPLEMENTATION

The implementation of heaps is a funny thing. We say they are *priority queues* (with push() and pop(), etc.), we visualize them as *binary trees*, and, as we'll see, we typically implement them with *dynamic arrays*!

THE HEAP PROPERTY

Heaps are *binary trees*[6] with two special properties:

1. They are *complete*: a complete tree is complete if all the levels except the last one have the maximum number of nodes; the last level may not be full, but all the nodes are aligned to the left. In particular, complete trees are balanced, which means that they have a **logarithmic height** (we talked about complete trees on page 450).

---

4   Even if we used in-place sorting (which would modify the input—potentially not allowed), most built-in sorts use $O(n)$ extra space internally.

5   But not as efficient as the quickselect solution we saw on page 372, which takes $O(n)$ time. However, the heap solution returns the first k elements in order, while quickselect doesn't. Also, if we use a built-in heap, the heap solution is much easier to implement.

6   When we say that they're binary trees, we're referring to the *abstract data type*, not the concrete data structure. We are conceptually thinking about them as binary trees, but we'll typically store the data in an array (pg 496).

2. The *heap property*: **every node has higher or equal priority than its children**.

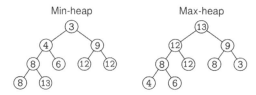

Figure 2. Min-heap and max-heap with the same elements. In the min-heap, every node is ≤ than
its children. In the max-heap, every node is ≥ than its children.

For the same set of elements, there can be multiple complete trees that satisfy the min-heap or max-heap
property.

> **What's the difference between the heap property and the binary search tree property?**
>
> In a heap, the root is smaller (for a min-heap) or larger (for a max-heap) than *both* of its children. In
> a binary search tree, the root is in between the children: it is larger than the left child and smaller
> than the right child.

For concreteness, we'll discuss how to implement a min-heap of integers, i.e., a heap where we use < as the
comparator. However, remember that the comparator could be flipped to get a max-heap instead.

TOP, PUSH, AND POP

The heap property makes accessing the smallest element in a min-heap trivial: it is always the root. The
top() method returns the root without removing it from the heap.

When we insert an element into the heap with push(), we must maintain both properties. To keep the
'complete tree' property, we start by putting the new element in the next available leaf in the tree (we'll see
how to find this node when we talk about the array-based implementation). However, this insertion can
break the heap property because the new element may be smaller than its parent. To fix it, we "bubble up"
the new element by repeatedly swapping it with its parent until the heap property is restored.

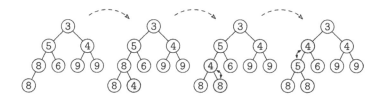

Figure 3. Bubbling up the new value after calling push(4).

When we pop() the smallest element in the heap, which is at the top, we need to figure out what to do with
the empty root. To fix it while keeping the 'complete tree' property, we move the rightmost node in the last
level to the root. After that, we "bubble it down" from the root by repeatedly swapping it with the smallest
of its two children until the heap property is restored (the smallest child will be a valid parent of the other
child once it becomes its parent).

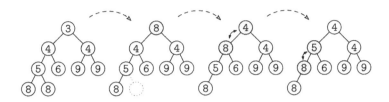

Figure 4. Bubbling down after popping the 3 with pop(). When bubbling 8 down, both children have the same value, 4, so we can make either of them the root.

Bubbling nodes up and down in the push() and pop() operations takes time proportional to the height of the tree in the worst case. That's why it is important for the tree to be balanced and have logarithmic height.

WARMUP PROBLEM SET

Imagine you have a min-heap with 12 nodes.

1. What is the maximum possible number of swaps needed to bubble up the newly inserted leaf after a push()?
2. What is the minimum possible number of swaps needed to bubble up the newly inserted leaf after a push()?
3. What is the maximum possible number of swaps needed to bubble down the new root after a pop()?
4. What is the minimum possible number of swaps needed to bubble down the new root after a pop()?

PROBLEM SET SOLUTIONS

1. The worst case for push() is when we push a number smaller than every number in the min-heap, as it will need to bubble up to the root. Thus, we may need 3 swaps (to go from height 3 to height 0).
2. If we push a number larger than every number in the min-heap, we won't need to do any swaps.
3. The worst case for pop() is when the last leaf is the largest element in the min-heap, as it will need to bubble down all the way from the root to a leaf. Depending on the path it goes down, we may need 2 or 3 swaps.
4. The best case for pop() is when all the elements in the heap are equal, in which case we don't need to do any swap.

HEAPIFY

Rather than adding elements to a heap individually, the heapify() method uses 'bubble down' operations to quickly transform a complete tree without the heap property into a proper heap.

All heapify does is bubble down all the non-leaf nodes in the tree, one by one, from bottom to top (the order within a level doesn't matter). This works because:

- Leaves satisfy the heap property (any single-node tree is trivially a heap).
- As we go from bottom to top, when we process each node u, the left and child subtrees of u already have the heap property, and, if we bubble down u, the whole subtree rooted at u will also have it.
- At the end, the whole tree will have the heap property.

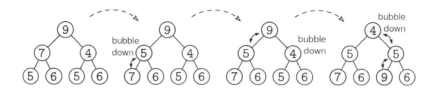

Figure 5. Heapify steps for a min-heap. The first tree is the initial state, which doesn't yet have the min-heap property. The next three trees show the evolution after bubbling down the three non-leaf nodes (7, 4, and 9), starting with the nodes at depth 1 and then the node at depth 0.

In the worst case, each node will get bubbled down all the way to a leaf. Thus, each node needs to move down $O(\log n)$ levels, so one might reasonably expect this to take $O(n \log n)$ time. This is correct in the 'upper bound' sense, but it is not tight: the total time is actually $O(n)$.

The intuition for why that is the case is that most nodes are in the deeper levels of the tree, where they don't need to travel a lot to get to the bottom—leaves alone make up at least half of the nodes in a complete tree.

PROOF THAT HEAPIFY TAKES O(N) TIME

The bottleneck for heapify is swapping values to bubble down nodes. We can show that, when we heapify a perfect binary tree, we need to do fewer than n 'bubble-down swaps', where n is the number of nodes, which makes the whole thing take $O(n)$ time.

We'll start with a tree with a single level and see what happens as we grow it level by level.

- If the height is 1 (there is only the root), no swaps are needed. The number of swaps (0) is less than the number of nodes (1).

- Every time we add a new level of leaves, every pre-existing node needs at most one extra swap to be bubbled down, while the new leaves do not need to be swapped as they are already at the bottom. Since a perfect binary tree has more leaves than internal nodes (by one, to be exact, pg 450), we are adding more nodes than required swaps.

Thus, as we add any number of levels, the number of required swaps never catches up to the number of nodes.

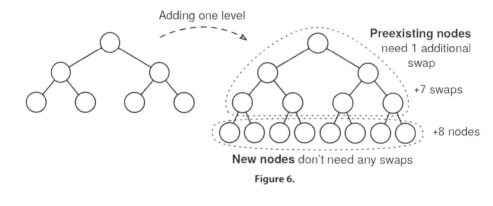

Adding one level

Preexisting nodes need 1 additional swap

+7 swaps

+8 nodes

New nodes don't need any swaps

Figure 6.

ARRAY-BASED IMPLEMENTATION

Based on all the binary tree diagrams we've seen, it would be reasonable to assume that we implement heaps like we do binary trees, with a Node class and `left` and `right` children. It would also be wrong (or at least less ideal).

A heap isn't just any kind of binary tree; it's a *complete* binary tree. What this means is that nodes are filled in in a predictable manner—top to bottom, left to right, with no gaps. As a result, we can throw the node values into an array and know where a node's `left` or `right` child is with a bit of simple (okay, fine, tedious) math.

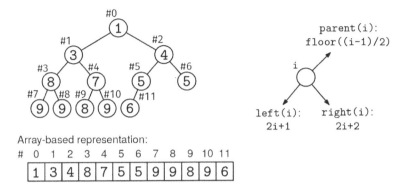

Figure 7. Left: Mapping from heap nodes to array indices. **Right:** Formulas to find the indices of the parent and children of a node based on its index, i, in the array.

The formulas in Figure 7 allow us to traverse the tree as we usually would with `left`, `right`, and `parent` pointers. In particular, left children are always at odd indices and right children are at even indices.

✦ **PROBLEM 37.1**   **IMPLEMENT A HEAP**

Assume your language does not support a heap or priority queue. Implement a Heap class from scratch with:

- A constructor that receives an optional list of elements to be heapified, and
- Operations `size()`, `top()`, `push(elem)`, and `pop()`.

You can either make it a min-heap or make it generic by receiving a comparator function in the constructor.

SOLUTION 37.1   IMPLEMENT A HEAP

First, we will construct helper functions that take a node's index and calculate the index of our left, right, and parent, like in Figure 7:

```
1  def parent(idx):
2    if idx == 0:
3      return -1  # The root has no parent.
4    return (idx - 1) // 2
5
6  def left_child(idx):
7    return 2 * idx + 1
8
9  def right_child(idx):
10    return 2 * idx + 2
```

The constructor receives an optional custom comparator to determine priority, which we set to < by default. If we receive an array of elements to heapify, we call `heapify()` immediately (which we'll see later). Otherwise, we initialize our array empty.

```
1  class Heap:
2    # If higher_priority(x, y) is True, x has higher priority than y.
3    def __init__(self, higher_priority=lambda x, y: x < y, heap=None):
4      self.heap = []
```

```
5      if heap is not None:
6        self.heap = heap
7      self.heap = heap if heap is not None else []
8      self.higher_priority = higher_priority
9      if heap:
10       self.heapify()
11
12   def size(self):
13     return len(self.heap)
```

The top() method is trivial since we just have to return the root, but don't forget to check that the heap contains at least one element.

```
1   def top(self):
2     if not self.heap:
3       return None
4     return self.heap[0]
```

For push(), we add the element to the bottom of the tree in the next available slot and then bubble it up. Adding to the next available tree slot in our array implementation just means appending it to the array.[7]

```
1   def push(self, elem):
2     self.heap.append(elem)
3     self.bubble_up(len(self.heap)-1)
```

Bubble up and bubble down can be implemented iteratively or recursively; we chose the recursive implementation because it is a bit more concise. The bubble-up logic involves a base case to stop at the root and a general case checking if the node has higher priority than its parent, in which case we need to continue bubbling up.

```
1   def bubble_up(self, idx):
2     if idx == 0:
3       return  # The root cannot be bubbled up.
4     parent_idx = parent(idx)
5     if self.higher_priority(self.heap[idx], self.heap[parent_idx]):
6       self.heap[idx], self.heap[parent_idx] = self.heap[parent_idx], self.heap[idx]
7       self.bubble_up(parent_idx)
```

For pop(), we save the root element in a temporary variable and copy the last element into the root position. We shrink the array by 1,[8] bubble down the new root, and return the saved element.

```
1   def pop(self):
2     if not self.heap: return None
3     top = self.heap[0]
4     if len(self.heap) == 1:
5       self.heap = []
6       return top
7     self.heap[0] = self.heap[-1]
8     self.heap.pop()
9     self.bubble_down(0)
10    return top
```

Bubble down is similar to bubble up, but with the extra complication that we can't just swap the node with either child. We need to swap it with the highest-priority child or we will break the heap property.

---

7 Remember that appending to a dynamic array takes O(1) amortized time.

8 Don't be confused by self.heap.pop()—it is not a recursive call to our heap's pop() method, we are just removing the last element in the array, which happens to have the same method name in Python.

```
1    def bubble_down(self, idx):
2      l_i, r_i = left_child(idx), right_child(idx)
3      is_leaf = l_i >= len(self.heap)
4      if is_leaf: return  # Leaves cannot be bubbled down.
5      child_i = l_i  # Index for the highest priority child.
6
7      if r_i < len(self.heap) and self.higher_priority(self.heap[r_i], self.heap[l_i]):
8        child_i = r_i
9
10     if self.higher_priority(self.heap[child_i], self.heap[idx]):
11       self.heap[idx], self.heap[child_i] = self.heap[child_i], self.heap[idx]
12       self.bubble_down(child_i)
```

Finally, we have heapify(), where we need to bubble up all internal nodes. In a complete tree, at least half the nodes are leaves, so we can start bubbling from the middle of the array:

```
1    def heapify(self):
2      for idx in range(len(self.heap)//2, -1, -1):
3        self.bubble_down(idx)
```

Now that we've learned how heaps are built, we can explore the diverse set of scenarios in which they are helpful.

APPLICATIONS

Heaps are used in some famous algorithms:

- Heapsort for sorting, as seen later in this chapter.
- Dijkstra's algorithm for shortest paths in graphs.
- Prim's algorithm for minimum spanning trees.

In this section, we'll see the most common heap techniques used in interviews.

SORTING VS HEAPS

Problem 31.6: First K (pg 372) shows that heaps have a natural connection to sorting.

In fact, we can use a heap to sort an array. *Heapsort* is a comparison-based sorting algorithm as efficient as merge sort and quicksort. It is like the 'First K' solution, but it pops every element instead of the first k. We heapify the array in linear time and then repeatedly pop elements in sorted order in O(n log n) time.

```
1    def heapsort(arr):
2      min_heap = Heap(priority_comparator=lambda x, y: x < y, heap=arr)
```

```
3    res = []
4    for _ in range(len(arr)):
5      res.append(min_heap.pop())
6    return res
```

Some problems can be solved with both sorting and heaps. In the Sorting chapter, we saw Problem 31.3: Delete Operations (pg 370), which required us to repeatedly "delete the smallest number in an array that has not yet been deleted." We used sorting to determine the sequence for deleting the numbers, but we could have just as easily tracked them in a min-heap.

When to use sorting vs heaps?

If you have a sorting solution, consider if a heap can be used to optimize it. Heaps may be best when you don't need every element sorted, as in "smallest k"/"largest k" type problems.

Heaps also tend to work better with *dynamic* data, such as 'data structure design' questions where we don't have all the elements to sort upfront (dynamic data is a *trigger* for data structures in general). We can use a heap to keep track of the smallest/largest element in an evolving collection.

PROBLEM SET

✦ *Try these problems with AI Interviewer: bctci.co/heaps-problem-set-1*

Consider the following setting: after studying hard, you've made it to the final round of on-site interviews at Spotify.[9] In each round, the interviewer pulls their inputs for questions from actual song metadata, including popular song names, total plays of each song (in millions), etc. With this metadata, the interviewer presents you with a novel question at each round.

PROBLEM 37.2   K MOST PLAYED

You are given a list of (title, plays) tuples where the first element is the name of a song, and the second is the number of times the song has been played. You are also given a positive integer k. Return the k most played songs from the list, in any order.

- If the list has fewer than k songs, return all of them.
- Break ties in any way you want.
- You can assume that song titles have a length of at most 50.

Can you solve it using only O(k) *extra space*?

▸ Example:
```
songs = [["All the Single Brackets", 132],
         ["Oops! I Broke Prod Again", 274],
         ["Coding In The Deep", 146],
         ["Boolean Rhapsody", 193],
         ["Here Comes The Bug", 291],
         ["All About That Base Case", 291]]
k = 3
```
  Output: ["All About That Base Case", "Here Comes The Bug", "Oops! I Broke Prod Again"]. Any order of these (excellent) songs would be valid.

---

9 This problem set is **not** indicative of the real Spotify interview process.

SOLUTION 37.2 K MOST PLAYED

This problem is similar to the 'First K' problem we introduced at the start of the chapter, with just a few tweaks. First, we need the largest elements, not the smallest.

We also need to return the titles, not the plays. Heaps are easy to use when you only store the priorities themselves. However, sometimes we have "things" that have priorities, and we want to find the "thing" with the highest priority (like the song with the most plays). We handle this by storing (`title`, `plays`) tuples in the heap and using a *custom comparator* to prioritize based on the plays.[10] You won't have access to our heap implementation in your interviews, so learn how to do this in your programming language.

To satisfy the O(k) extra-space constraint, we use a common **space-saving technique: limiting the heap size**. Since we only need to output k elements at the end, we can restrict the heap size to k. We iterate through the input elements, maintaining the top k so far in a heap. However, there is a challenge: how do we know if a new input element is part of the largest k or not? A max-heap only gives you the maximum, but we need to know the minimum among the largest k elements. The solution is to switch to a min-heap of the largest k elements. For each new element, we check if the next element is *larger* than the smallest one in the heap. Only when it's larger do we replace the smallest element.

```
1  def k_most_played(songs, k):
2    min_heap = Heap(higher_priority=lambda x, y: x[1] < y[1])
3    for song in songs:                      # O(n) iterations
4      if min_heap.size() < k:
5        min_heap.push(song)                 # O(log k)
6      elif min_heap.top()[1] < song[1]:
7        min_heap.pop()                      # O(log k)
8        min_heap.push(song)                 # O(log k)
9    return min_heap.heap.copy()             # O(k)
```

♻ REUSABLE IDEA: HEAP SIZE RESTRICTION

Depending on the problem, restricting the size of the heap to the size of the output can save space and even time.

For a 'largest k' problem, you can use either a max-heap or a restricted-size min-heap.

1. Max-heap: dump all elements in the max-heap with heapify and pop the largest k. This takes O(n + (k log n)) time and O(n) space.

2. Min-heap: add the elements one by one to a min-heap of the k largest elements so far. This takes O(n log k) time and O(k) space.

There is an interesting trade-off between the time and space of the two solutions.

✦ PROBLEM 37.3 TOP SONGS CLASS

Implement a TopSongs class that receives an integer k > 0 during initialization and has two methods:

- `register_plays(title, plays)` indicates that a song was played a given number of times. It returns nothing. The method is never called with the same title twice.
- `top_k()` returns the (up to) k registered song titles with the most plays, in any order, and breaking ties arbitrarily.

Analyze the space and runtime of each operation in terms of the number of songs registered so far. The goal is to minimize the total runtime assuming we will make the same number of operations of each type and that k will be relatively small compared to the number of songs.

---

10 This idea is the 'Piggybacking Extra Info' reusable idea we saw on page 382.

▸ **Example:** s = TopSongs(3)

```
s.register_plays("Boolean Rhapsody", 193)
s.register_plays("Coding In The Deep", 146)
s.top_k()  # Returns ["Coding In The Deep", "Boolean Rhapsody"]
s.register_plays("All About That Base Case", 291)
s.register_plays("Here Comes The Bug", 223)
s.register_plays("Oops! I Broke Prod Again", 274)
s.register_plays("All the Single Brackets", 132)
s.top_k()  # Returns ["All About That Base Case",
                      "Here Comes The Bug",
                      "Oops! I Broke Prod Again"]
```

SOLUTION 37.3   TOP SONGS CLASS

In this problem, the data is *dynamic*, meaning our top k values fluctuate as we add new plays. Dynamic data is a *trigger* for using data structures–in this case, heaps–rather than sorting algorithms.

Even though the problem asks for the k songs with the largest play counts, a max-heap solution would be suboptimal:

1. registering a song would take $O(\log n)$ time. Since we get songs one by one, we cannot use heapify.
2. for top_k(), we would have to pop the largest k elements and re-add them again, which would take $O(k * \log n)$ time.

The **size restriction** idea works better here. We can use a min-heap to store the k songs with the largest play counts so far.

1. registering a new song takes $O(\log k)$ time.
2. We can return the top k songs in $O(k)$ time by simply returning all the songs in the min-heap.

```
1    class TopSongs:
2      def __init__(self, k):
3        self.k = k
4        self.min_heap = Heap(higher_priority=lambda x, y: x[1] < y[1])
5
6      def register_plays(self, title, plays):
7        if self.min_heap.size() < self.k:
8          self.min_heap.push((title, plays))
9        elif plays > self.min_heap.top()[1]:
10         self.min_heap.pop()
11         self.min_heap.push((title, plays))
12
13     def top_k(self):
14       top_songs = []
15       for title, _ in self.min_heap.heap:
16         top_songs.append(title)
17       return top_songs
```

✦ **PROBLEM 37.4   TOP SONGS CLASS WITH UPDATES**

Implement a TopSongs class as in the previous problem, with the only change that we can call regis-ter_plays() with the same song title multiple times, meaning that we should *add* the new plays to the total number of plays for that song. How would this affect your design?

▸ **Example:** s = TopSongs(3)

```
    s.register_plays("Boolean Rhapsody", 100)
    s.register_plays("Boolean Rhapsody", 193)   # Boolean Rhapsody's
                                                          total is 293.
    s.register_plays("Coding In The Deep", 75)
    s.register_plays("Coding In The Deep", 75)             # 150 plays.
    s.register_plays("All About That Base Case", 200)
    s.register_plays("All About That Base Case", 90)   # 290 plays.
    s.register_plays("All About That Base Case", 1)    # 291 plays.
    s.register_plays("Here Comes The Bug", 223)
    s.register_plays("Oops! I Broke Prod Again", 274)
    s.register_plays("All the Single Brackets", 132)
    s.top_k()   # Returns ["All About That Base Case",
                "Boolean Rhapsody", "Oops! I Broke Prod Again"]
```

SOLUTION 37.4   TOP SONGS CLASS WITH UPDATES

Updating play counts for songs already in the heap is not possible with our implementation.[11]

Tracking the maximum while handling updates can be done with a self-balancing binary search tree. However, since self-balancing BSTs are generally less available in most programming languages and harder to implement manually than heaps, we'll show a max-heap solution.

A simpler alternative to updating elements already in the set is known as *lazy deletion*:[12] When we get an update for an existing song in the max-heap, we insert a new element without deleting the old one. For example, if we get a call,

```
    s.register_plays("Boolean Rhapsody", 100)
```

We push (`"Boolean Rhapsody", 100`) to a max-heap. Then, if we get another call,

```
    s.register_plays("Boolean Rhapsody", 193)
```

We push (`"Boolean Rhapsody", 293`) to the max-heap without deleting the old element. The added complication is that, when we pop elements, we need to check if they are *valid* (like (`"Boolean Rhapsody", 293`)) or *stale* (like (`"Boolean Rhapsody", 100`)).

To detect stale elements, we can maintain a map from each song title to the valid (i.e., latest) value.

```
 1   class TopSongs:
 2     def __init__(self, k):
 3       self.k = k
 4       self.max_heap = Heap(higher_priority=lambda x, y: x[1] > y[1])
 5       self.total_plays = {}
 6
 7     def register_plays(self, title, plays):
 8       new_total_plays = plays
 9       if title in self.total_plays:
10         new_total_plays += self.total_plays[title]
```

---

11 Some Heap implementations, instead of using a comparator function, expect explicit priorities for each element. That is, the signature for push() is push(elem, priority). Such heaps sometimes provide a method update_priority(elem, new_priority) which modifies the priority of an element already in the heap in O(log n) time. Implementing this operation requires maintaining a hash map from each element to its index in the heap. This map allows us to find elem in constant time, but we need to remember to update the map whenever we bubble elements up or down. When changing an element's priority, we risk breaking the heap property, so we must bubble it up or down based on whether the new priority is higher or lower. You can check if this operation is available in your language of choice. In most languages (like Python), it is not.

12 This is the approach used in *Lazy Dijkstra*, an easier implementation of Dijkstra's algorithm.

```
11      self.total_plays[title] = new_total_plays
12      self.max_heap.push((title, new_total_plays))
13
14    def top_k(self):
15      top_songs = []
16      while len(top_songs) < self.k and self.max_heap.size() > 0:
17        title, plays = self.max_heap.pop()
18        if self.total_plays[title] == plays:  # Not stale.
19          top_songs.append(title)
20      # Restore the max-heap:
21      for title in top_songs:
22        self.max_heap.push((title, self.total_plays[title]))
23      return top_songs
```

The downside of lazy deletion is that the size of the heap is now proportional to the number of regis-ter_plays() calls rather than the number of *distinct* songs.

The size restriction optimization does not work with lazy deletions—we cannot restrict the heap size to k while also allowing duplicates, or we might end up with fewer than k distinct songs in it.

So far, we've focused on problems with clear triggers that point to heaps. Let's see one where it is less evident that heaps are helpful.

✦ PROBLEM 37.5   POPULAR SONGS CLASS

Implement a PopularSongs class that has two methods:

- register_plays(title, plays) indicates that a song was played a given number of times. It returns nothing. The method is never called with the same title twice.

- is_popular(title) returns whether the given song is popular. A song is *popular* if its play count is strictly higher than the median play count (the median of a collection of integers with odd size is the middle element in sorted order; if the size is even, the median is the average of the two middle elements).

▸ **Example:**
```
p = PopularSongs()
        p.register_plays("Boolean Rhapsody", 193)
        p.is_popular("Boolean Rhapsody")                    # False
        p.register_plays("Coding In The Deep", 140)
        p.register_plays("All the Single Brackets", 132)
        p.is_popular("Boolean Rhapsody")                    # True
        p.is_popular("Coding In The Deep")                  # False
        p.is_popular("All the Single Brackets")             # False
        p.register_plays("All About That Base Case", 291)
        p.register_plays("Oops! I Broke Prod Again", 274)
        p.register_plays("Here Comes The Bug", 223)
        p.is_popular("Boolean Rhapsody")                    # False
        p.is_popular("Here Comes The Bug")                  # True
```

SOLUTION 37.5   POPULAR SONGS CLASS

The is_popular() method can be **reframed** as, "Is the current song's play count greater than the median?"[13]

---

13 If a list of numbers has odd length, the median is the middle element. If the length is even, the median is the average of the two middle elements.

If we just need to find the median of a list of numbers once, we can sort them list and check the middle element or even use quickselect (Solution 31.6: First K, pg 375). However, here we need to track the median of *dynamic* data. As mentioned, dynamic data is a *trigger* for using data structures, so is there a way we could use a heap for this?

The "trick"—which would be tough to come up with in an interview—is to put **the lower half of songs in a max-heap and the upper half in a min-heap**. This allows us to determine the median of all play counts in constant time by checking the top song of the heaps.

- If we have an *even* number of songs, each heap will contain n/2 songs, and the middle two elements will be the tops of the heaps. The median is the average of the tops.
- If we have an *odd* number of elements, the median is the top of whichever heap is bigger.

We can force the upper half's min-heap to always be the bigger one by **restricting its size** to be equal to or one larger than the lower half's max-heap.

We also need a map to keep track of the play counts of each song.

```
class PopularSongs:
  def __init__(self):
    # Max-heap for the lower half.
    self.lower_max_heap = Heap(higher_priority=lambda x, y: x > y)
    # Min-heap for the upper half.
    self.upper_min_heap = Heap()
    self.play_counts = {}

  def register_plays(self, title, plays):
    self.play_counts[title] = plays
    if self.upper_min_heap.size() == 0 or plays >= self.upper_min_heap.top():
      self.upper_min_heap.push(plays)
    else:
      self.lower_max_heap.push(plays)
    # Distribute elements if they are off by more than one.
    if self.lower_max_heap.size() > self.upper_min_heap.size():
      self.upper_min_heap.push(self.lower_max_heap.pop())
    elif self.upper_min_heap.size() > self.lower_max_heap.size() + 1:
      self.lower_max_heap.push(self.upper_min_heap.pop())

  def is_popular(self, title):
    if title not in self.play_counts:
      return False
    if self.lower_max_heap.size() == self.upper_min_heap.size():
      median = (self.upper_min_heap.top() + self.lower_max_heap.top()) / 2
    else:
      median = self.upper_min_heap.top()
    return self.play_counts[title] > median
```

♺ REUSABLE IDEA: TWO-HEAP MEDIAN TRACKING

Tracking the median in a dynamic dataset is possible by keeping the lower half in a max-heap and the upper half in a min-heap.

Each addition takes $O(\log n)$ time, and returning the median takes $O(1)$ time.

✦✦ **PROBLEM 37.6**   **MOST LISTENED ACROSS GENRES**

You are given an array, genres, of length m, where each element is an array of songs from a given genre. Each song consists of a [title, plays] pair.

- Each list is non-empty and *already sorted* from most to least played songs.
- There are n songs in total, and each song appears in at most one list.

You are also given a positive integer k. Return the titles of the top k most-listened songs across all genres, in order from most to least listened. It doesn't matter how you break ties.

▸ **Example:** genres = [
```
    [["Coding In The Deep", 123], ["Someone Like GNU", 97],
     ["Hello World", 98]], # Pop
    [["Ring Of Firewalls", 217]], # Country
    [["Boolean Rhapsody", 184], ["Merge Together", 119],
     ["Hey Queue", 102]] # Rock
  ]
  k = 5
```
   Output: ["Ring Of Firewalls", "Boolean Rhapsody", "Coding In The Deep",
             "Merge Together", "Hey Queue"]

SOLUTION 37.6   MOST LISTENED ACROSS GENRES

A first solution might be to dump all songs from every list into a max-heap, prioritizing by play count. Using heapify, the time complexity would be O(n + k log n).

We could also *restrict the size* of the heap to a maximum of k elements, reducing the extra space to O(k) but increasing the runtime to O(n log k). Can we improve further?

Recall the merging logic from Problem 27.6: Merge Two Sorted Arrays (pg 300), where merging two sorted arrays takes time proportional to their combined size. Here, we can apply the same idea, but with m arrays, requiring m pointers instead of just two, and stopping after k steps. At each step, we need to find the pointer pointing to the song with the most plays. Are your spidey senses tingling? Tracking the largest element is a trigger for a max-heap!

We start by initializing the max-heap with a pointer for each genre list, which starts at zero and represents the top song in each list. Each entry added to the heap consists of the song's play count (as the priority), the genre index, and the song index within that genre.

We repeat this process k times:

1. We pop the song with the highest play count from the max-heap and add it to our top k results.
2. We increment the pointer for that genre.
3. We add the next song for that genre to the max-heap.

```
1  def top_k_across_genres(genres, k):
2    initial_elems = []  # (plays, genre_index, song_index) tuples.
3    for genre_index, song_list in enumerate(genres):
4      plays = song_list[0][1]
5      initial_elems.append((plays, genre_index, 0))
6    max_heap = Heap(higher_priority=lambda x, y: x[0] > y[0], heap=initial_elems)
7    top_k = []
8    while len(top_k) < k and max_heap.size() > 0:
9      plays, genre_index, song_index = max_heap.pop()
```

```
10    song_name = genres[genre_index][song_index][0]
11    top_k.append(song_name)
12    song_index += 1
13    if song_index < len(genres[genre_index]):
14      plays = genres[genre_index][song_index][1]
15      max_heap.push((plays, genre_index, song_index))
16  return top_k
```

The heap has size O(m). The runtime is now O(m + k log m).

REUSABLE IDEA: M-WAY MERGE

> We can efficiently merge m sorted lists into a single sorted list by tracking m pointers in a heap pointing to the first non-added element from each list.

PROBLEM 37.7   **MAKE PLAYLIST**

Imagine your picky friends give you a list of song–artist tuples to create a playlist. Your task is to reorder the songs so that no two songs by the same artist are played back-to-back. If it's not possible, return an empty list.

▶ **Example:** songs = [["Coding In The Deep", "A Dell"],
                        ["Hello World", "A Dell"],
                        ["Someone Like GNU", "A Dell"],
                        ["Make You Read My Logs", "A Dell"],
                        ["Hey Queue", "The Bugs"],
                        ["Here Comes the Bug", "The Bugs"],
                        ["Merge Together", "The Bugs"],
                        ["Dirty Data", "Michael JSON"],
                        ["Man in the Middle Attack", "Michael JSON"],
                        ["Ring Of Firewall", "Johnny Cache"]]
   Output: ["Coding In The Deep", "Hey Queue", "Hello World", "Dirty Data",
            "Someone Like GNU", "Here Comes the Bug", "Make You Read My Logs",
            "Man in the Middle Attack", "Merge Together", "Boolean Rhapsody"]
There are other possible configurations.

SOLUTION 37.7   MAKE PLAYLIST

This question asks us to distribute songs so that two songs by the same artist never play back-to-back. Naively trying all permutations would be expensive.

If you had to solve this by hand, how would you do it? Try the **DIY** approach with the following input:

```
songs = [["Coding In The Deep", "A Dell"],
         ["Hello World", "A Dell"],
         ["Someone Like GNU", "A Dell"],
         ["Make You Read My Logs", "A Dell"],
         ["Hey Queue", "The Bugs"]]
```

After just a glance, you probably realized this wasn't possible. Why? Because we just have too many songs by 'A Dell'—if a single artist makes up more than half the songs (more than ceiling(n/2), to be exact), we won't find a playlist order that works. On the other hand, if we had 3 songs by 'A Dell' and 2 by 'The Bugs', it could work. The key is to put the most popular artist first.

We can come up with a strategy: we'll fill the playlist from left to right, always putting a song from the artist with the most remaining songs that's not the same as the last artist. We can use a max-heap to quickly find the artist with the most songs. Each heap entity can be a tuple (artist, songs) prioritized based on the number of songs.[14]

```
1   def make_playlist(songs):
2     # Group songs by artist.
3     artist_to_songs = {}
4     for song, artist in songs:
5       if artist not in artist_to_songs:
6         artist_to_songs[artist] = []
7       artist_to_songs[artist].append(song)
8
9     heap = Heap(higher_priority=lambda a, b: len(a[1]) > len(b[1]))
10    for artist, songs_list in artist_to_songs.items():
11      heap.push((artist, songs_list))
12
13    res = []
14    last_artist = None
15    while heap.size() > 0:
16      artist, song_list = heap.pop()
17      if artist != last_artist:
18        res.append(song_list.pop())
19        last_artist = artist
20        if song_list:  # If the artist has more songs, re-add it.
21          heap.push((artist, song_list))
22      else:
23        # We need to find a different artist.
24        if heap.size() == 0:
25          return []  # No valid solution.
26        artist2, song_list2 = heap.pop()
27        res.append(song_list2.pop())
28        last_artist = artist2
29        # Re-add the artists we popped.
30        if song_list2:
31          heap.push((artist2, song_list2))
32        heap.push((artist, song_list))
33
34    return res
```

Just when you thought you were done with the long onsite, the last interviewer decides to give you one final, very mathy problem.

✦✦ PROBLEM 37.8   SUM OF FIRST K PRIME POWERS

Given a non-empty array, primes, of *distinct prime* numbers, and a positive number k, return the sum of the first k numbers that are a positive power of a number in primes. If the answer is larger than 10^9+7, return it modulo 10^9+7.

▸ **Example:** primes = [2], k = 1.

---

14 While we wanted to show the heap solution, there is a solution for this problem that doesn't require a heap. It's more efficient, but also harder to prove that it works. It starts by putting all the songs by the most popular artist at even indices 0, 2, 4, ... After it is done with the most popular artist, it continues filling the even indices other artists one by one (in no particular order). When we run out of even indices, we wrap around and continue with odd indices. As long as the most popular artist has at most ceiling(n/2) songs, this will work.

Output: 2. The first positive power of 2 is $2^1 = 2$.

▸ **Example:** primes = [5], k = 3.
  Output: 155. The first 3 positive powers of 5 are 5, 25, and 125.

▸ **Example:** primes = [2, 3], k = 7.
  Output: 69. The first 7 numbers that are a positive power of 2 or 3 are 2, 3, 4, 8, 9, 16, and 27.

SOLUTION 37.8   SUM OF FIRST K PRIME POWERS

To solve this problem, it is helpful to realize the following property: the positive powers of a prime number (like 2, 4, 8, 16, ...) do not overlap with the positive powers of another prime (like 3, 9, 27, ...). Put another way, you can't multiply one prime together a bunch of times and get another prime multiplied together (i.e., 3^x will never equal 7^y unless x and y are zero).[15]

To get the n smallest numbers, we can put the numbers in primes in a min-heap. When we extract the smallest number, say, p, we can add the next power of p, p^2, to the min-heap. More generally, if we pop p^i from the min-heap, we add p^{i+1} to it. This ensures we get the n smallest powers among all the primes.

To avoid working with very large numbers, we apply the modulo operator at each step that could create numbers larger than 10^9+7 (see the reusable idea 'Applying Modulo At Each Step', pg 406).

```
 1   def sum_of_powers(primes, n):
 2       m = 10**9 + 7
 3       # Initialize the heap with the first power of each prime.
 4       # Each element is a tuple (power, base)
 5       elems = [(p, p) for p in primes]
 6       min_heap = Heap(higher_priority=lambda x, y: x[0] < y[0], heap=elems)
 7       res = 0
 8       for _ in range(n):
 9           power, base = min_heap.pop()
10           res = (res + power) % m
11           min_heap.push(((power * base) % m, base))
12       return res
```

Let n be the length of primes. Creating the heap with heapify takes $O(n)$ time, and each iteration takes $O(\log n)$ time, so the total time is $O(n + k \log n)$.

KEY TAKEAWAYS

Heaps are strongly linked to sorting problems and are commonly used to optimize naive sorting solutions. They particularly shine with *dynamic* data. We learned reusable ideas like

- Restricting the heap size is a common optimization to save time and space,
- Piggybacking extra info in the heap beyond a simple integer can make bookkeeping easier,
- Tracking the largest, smallest, or median element in dynamic data with min-heaps and max-heaps,
- Lazy deletion as a practical alternative to updating the priorities of heap elements,
- Merging m sorted lists with a heap of pointers.

---

15 More mathematically: if p1 and p2 are primes, $p1^a \neq p2^b$ for any powers a and b > 0. This follows from the Fundamental Theorem of Arithmetic, which states that prime decompositions of numbers are unique. Even if you do not know this theorem by name, you probably intuitively understand it.

Heap triggers: The data is **dynamic**, like in 'data structure design' questions where the answer changes over time; top-k type problems; the naive solution uses sorting; the goal is to optimize the extra space.

Keywords: top/bottom, minimum/maximum, largest/smallest, median.

▶ **THOROUGH REQUIREMENT GATHERING IS GOOD, BUT BE QUICK ABOUT IT**   INTERVIEW REPLAY

View Online:	bctci.co/heaps-replay-2 @ 5:10 - 43:00
The Question:	Write an efficient program for printing the k closest points to a target point.
What You'll See:	The candidate did a good job identifying requirements, running through examples, explaining brute force, pseudocoding, and optimizing. The problem solving was solid, and the time management was all this candidate was missing.
Who:	*Interviewer*: Software Engineer at Microsoft *Candidate*: 5 years exp.
Outcome:	The candidate got the job at Meta!

⧉ **ONLINE RESOURCES**

Online resources for this chapter include:

- A chance to try each problem in this chapter in AI Interviewer
- Interview replays that show specific mistakes people make with heaps problems
- Full code solutions for every problem in the chapter in multiple programming languages

Try online at bctci.co/heaps.

## CHAPTER 38

SLIDING WINDOWS

AI interviewer, replays, and more materials for this chapter at bctci.co/sliding-windows

▶ *Prerequisites: None*

In this chapter, we will use the sliding window technique to tackle problems about finding or counting subarrays.[1]

We will use the following setting for problems throughout this chapter: a bookstore is looking at the number of book sales. The sales for each day are stored in an array of non-negative integers called sales. We say a *good day* is a day with at least 10 sales, while a *bad day* is a day with fewer than 10 sales. An interviewer could ask questions such as the following:

- Find the most sales in any 7-day period (Problem 1).
- Find the most consecutive days with no bad days (Problem 5).
- Find the longest period of time with at most 3 bad days (Problem 8).
- Find the shortest period of time with more than 20 sales, if any (Problem 14).
- Count the number of subarrays of sales with at most 10 bad days (Problem 18).
- Count the number of subarrays of sales with exactly 10 bad days (Problem 19).
- Count the number of subarrays of sales with at least 10 bad days (Problem 20).

All these questions receive an array as input, sales. The first four ask us to find a subarray, while the last three ask us to count subarrays, making them ideal candidates for the sliding window technique. In this chapter, we will cover variants of the sliding window technique to tackle each of the mentioned problems and more.

The basic idea of a sliding window is to consider a subarray (the "window"), marked by left (l) and right (r) pointers. We move or "slide" the window to the right by increasing the l and r pointers, all while computing some value about the current window.[2][3]

---

1 Beyond DS&A, the term 'sliding window' is also used in network protocols like TCP (https://en.wikipedia.org/wiki/Transmission_Control_Protocol) and in machine learning architectures like convolutional neural networks (https://en.wikipedia.org/wiki/Convolutional_neural_network).

2 A sliding window is a special case of the two-pointer technique. Like in the Two Pointers chapter, we use the terms "pointer" and "index" interchangeably.

3 Sliding windows are usually not useful for problems about subsequences because they don't have a good way of dealing with "skipping" elements. Subsequence problems are more commonly tackled with other techniques that we will see later, like dynamic programming or backtracking.

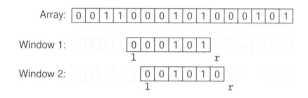

Figure 1. Window 1 is a subarray from l = 4 (included) to r = 10 (excluded). We can slide it and get Window 2 by increasing l and r.

THE ELEMENTS OF A SLIDING WINDOW PROBLEM

Problems where sliding windows may be useful tend to involve the following:

- You have to find a subarray of an input array.
- This subarray must satisfy some *constraint*, which separates the subarrays into *valid* and *invalid*. Examples of constraints:

  » The length must be k (for some given value k).
  » The sum must be at least / at most / exactly k.
  » It must contain or not contain specific elements.
  » It must not contain repeated elements.

- There is usually an *objective* that makes some subarrays "better" than others. For example:

  » Maximize/minimize the length of the window.
  » Maximize/minimize the sum of the elements in the window.
  » Maximize/minimize the number of distinct elements in the window.

- Less commonly, if there is no objective, the goal may be to count the number of valid subarrays.

For instance, in the first bookstore problem, the constraint is "the length of the subarray must be 7," and the objective is to maximize the sum. In the last one, the constraint is "at least 10 bad days," and there is no objective since it is a counting problem. Can you identify the constraints and objectives for the other bookstore problems?

BRUTE FORCE BASELINE

Most sliding window problems can be solved with a brute force algorithm that checks every subarray one by one. If the subarray is valid, then we check if it's the best one so far.

The brute force solution is *correct*, but we'd ideally like a more optimized solution. Before diving into *how* to do this, it can be useful to consider what our upper bound, lower bound, and target runtimes might be (see the Boundary Thinking chapter).

- Upper bound: $O(n^3)$ will be the most common brute force upper bound across sliding window problems, where n is the length of the input array. There are $O(n^2)$ subarrays to search through. For each of those, checking whether it is valid and the best so far in a naive way could take $O(n)$ time.
- Lower bound: if we don't look at every element in the input, we won't even know what some substrings look like, so $O(n)$ is the natural lower bound.
- Target: the sliding window technique often allows us to reach a linear runtime, so we should aim for that.

HOW TO SLIDE A WINDOW

To make things easy to remember, we follow some conventions for initializing and updating all sliding windows in this chapter:

1. The window goes from the element at index l **(inclusive)** to the element at index r **(exclusive)**. This means:

   » the window is empty when l == r,

   » r points to the first element after the window (if any), and

   » the length of the window is r - l.

2. We always initialize l and r to 0, meaning the window starts empty.

3. We *grow* the window by incrementing r. We can only grow it when r < len(arr).

4. We *shrink* the window by incrementing l. We can only shrink it when l < r.

5. We always have 0 ≤ l ≤ r ≤ len(arr).

Consistency enables us to predict what our possible off-by-one errors are likely to be. For instance, r - l always means "the size of the window," and l == r always means "the window is empty," without worrying about off-by-one errors.[4]

ANALYZING SLIDING WINDOWS

Every sliding window consists of a main loop, where, at each iteration, we either grow or shrink the window, or both. Since r never decreases and runs from 0 to n, our window can only grow n times. By this same token, the window can only shrink (by increasing l) n times. This means that any properly implemented sliding window does at most O(2n) = O(n) iterations. To get the total runtime, we need to multiply the number of iterations, O(n), by the time per iteration.

> As long as each iteration grows or shrinks the window (or both), a sliding window algorithm takes O(n*T) time, where n is the size of the array we are sliding over and T is the time per iteration.

Typically, we will be unlikely to reduce the *number* of iterations—we must reach the end of the array—so we should focus on reducing T: the time per iteration. We should try to get it down to constant time.

In terms of space analysis, remember that the window is not materialized, it is just identified by the two pointers. So, the space analysis will depend on what other information about the window we need to store.

FIXED-LENGTH WINDOWS

In fixed-length window problems, we have to find a subarray under the constraint that it has a given length. Such problems, which are fairly common, are on the easier side because there are not many subarrays to consider: for a value k in the range 1 ≤ k ≤ n, an array only has n-k+1 = O(n) subarrays of length k—a lot fewer than O(n²). Recall the first opening problem:

✦ | **PROBLEM 38.1** **MOST WEEKLY SALES**

Given an array, sales, find the most sales in any 7-day period.

▸ **Example:** sales = [0, 3, 7, 12, 10, 5, 0, 1, 0, 15, 12, 11, 1]

---

4 Our convention is that l is inclusive and r is exclusive, but this is merely our convention. If you prefer to consider r as inclusive, this is equally correct, but be sure to update the little details like the size of the window (which would now be r - l + 1). Whatever you do, be explicit about your convention and make sure the little details match.

Output: 44. The 7-day period with the most sales is [5, 0, 1, 0, 15, 12, 11]

▸ **Example:** sales = [0, 3, 7, 12]
  Output: 0. There is no 7-day period.

SOLUTION 38.1   MOST WEEKLY SALES

The fact that we are only looking for windows of length 7 gives us a simple strategy for when to grow and shrink the window:

1. Grow the window until it has length 7.

2. Grow and shrink at the same time so that the length stays at 7.

Here is a full solution:

```
1   def most_weekly_sales(sales):
2       l, r = 0, 0
3       window_sum = 0
4       cur_max = 0
5       while r < len(sales):
6           window_sum += sales[r]
7           r += 1
8           if r - l == 7:
9               cur_max = max(cur_max, window_sum)
10              window_sum -= sales[l]
11              l += 1
12      return cur_max
```

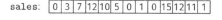

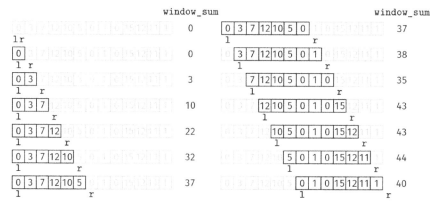

Figure 2. The sliding window of most_weekly_sales().

On top of our window pointers, l and r, we have:

*   window_sum: the sum of elements in the window, which corresponds to the objective we have to maximize. The key is to update it whenever the window grows or shrinks and not compute it from scratch at each iteration.

*   cur_max: where we keep the current maximum we have seen so far.

Each iteration starts by growing the window, which involves two things: updating window_sum to reflect that sales[r] is now in the window, and increasing r. The order of these operations matters!

After growing the window, we check if it is valid, meaning the window length (r - 1) is 7. If it is valid, we check if it is the best one seen so far and update cur_max accordingly.

If the window has a length of 7, we end the iteration by shrinking it so that when we grow it in the next iteration, it will have the right size again. Like growing, shrinking consists of two actions: updating window_sum and increasing 1.

The algorithm ends when the window can no longer grow (r == len(sales)).

We can put these ideas together in a general recipe for fixed-length window problems:

RECIPE 1. FIXED-LENGTH WINDOW RECIPE.

```
fixed_length_window(arr, k):
  initialize:
  - l and r to 0 (empty window)
  - data structures to track window info
  - cur_best to 0
  while we can grow the window (r < len(arr))
    grow the window (update data structures and increase r)
    if the window has the correct length (r - 1 == k)
      update cur_best if needed
      shrink the window (update data structures and increase l)
  return cur_best
```

By "data structures," we mean any information about the window that we need to maintain as we slide it in order to evaluate each window quickly. The data structures that we need change from problem to problem, and they could range from nothing at all to things like sets and maps. In the following problem set, you will have to consider what information to store about the window and how to update it efficiently.

\#   Maintaining information about the window as it slides is a key idea in designing efficient sliding windows.

▶ NESTED LOOPS ARE TOO SLOW FOR SLIDING WINDOW QUESTIONS   INTERVIEW REPLAY

View Online:	bctci.co/sliding-windows-replay-1 @ 10:36 - 47:30
The Question:	Given an array of positive numbers and a positive number k, find the maximum sum of any contiguous subarray of size k.
What You'll See:	The candidate struggled to identify the problem as a sliding window problem and coded the brute force instead of an optimal answer.
Who:	*Interviewer*: Software Engineer at FAANG+ *Candidate*: College student

---

FIXED-LENGTH WINDOWS PROBLEM SET

✦ *Try these problems with AI Interviewer: bctci.co/sliding-windows-problem-set-1*

We will continue with the bookstore setting. In addition to the sales array, we have an array of strings, best_seller, with the title of the most sold book for each day.

   Constraints:

   sales and best_seller have a length of at most 10^6.
   Each book title in best_seller has a length of at most 100.

PROBLEM 38.2   MOST SALES IN K DAYS

Given the array sales and a number k with $1 \leq k \leq$ len(sales), find the most sales in any k-day period. Return the first day of that period (days start at 0). If there are multiple k-day periods with the most sales, return the first day of the first one.

▶ **Example:** sales = [8, 1, 3, 7], k = 2
  Output: 2. The subarray of length 2 with maximum sum is [3, 7], which starts at index 2.

PROBLEM 38.3   UNIQUE BEST SELLER STREAK

Given the array best_seller and a number k with $1 \leq k \leq$ len(sales), return whether there is any k-day period where each day has a *different* best-selling title.

▶ **Example:** best_seller = ["book3", "book1", "book3", "book3", "book2", "book3", "book4", "book3"], k = 3
  Output: True. There is a 3-day period without a repeated value: ["book2", "book3", "book4"].

▶ **Example:** best_seller = ["book3", "book1", "book3", "book3", "book2", "book3", "book4", "book3"], k = 4
  Output: False. There are no 4-day periods without a repeated value.

PROBLEM 38.4   ENDURING BEST SELLER STREAK

Given the array best_seller and a number k with $1 \leq k \leq$ len(sales), return whether there is any k-day period where every day has the *same* best-selling title.

▶ **Example:** best_seller = ["book3", "book1", "book3", "book3", "book2"], k = 3
  Output: False.

▶ **Example:** best_seller = ["book3", "book1", "book3", "book3", "book2"], k = 2
  Output: True.

✦ PROBLEM SET SOLUTIONS

SOLUTION 38.2   MOST SALES IN K DAYS

We can reuse our solution to the previous problem, tweaking it slightly: replacing 7 with k and tracking the position of the best window in addition to its sum.

SOLUTION 38.3   UNIQUE BEST SELLER STREAK

In this problem, we need to check each window of length k for duplicate titles. Checking for duplicates in an array can be done in linear time using a hash map, assuming we can hash each element in constant time (recall that 'checking for duplicates' is a trigger for hash sets and maps).

As mentioned, efficient sliding window algorithms usually *maintain* information about the window. In this case, the information we need is a **frequency map** (the reusable idea from pg 348): a hash map from the titles in the window to the number of times that they appear in the window. So, for a window like ["book3", "book1", "book3"], the map would be {"book3": 2, "book1": 1}. We can update this map in $O(1)$ time whenever the window grows or shrinks.

We remove book titles from the map if their count goes back down to 0. This way, the size of the map always represents the number of unique keys (book titles) in the window, and the window satisfies the constraint if the map size is k. The extra space of our solution is O(k).[5]

```
1   def has_unique_k_days(best_seller, k):
2     l, r = 0, 0
3     window_counts = {}
4     while r < len(best_seller):
5       if not best_seller[r] in window_counts:
6         window_counts[best_seller[r]] = 0
7       window_counts[best_seller[r]] += 1
8       r += 1
9       if r - l == k:
10        if len(window_counts) == k:
11          return True
12        window_counts[best_seller[l]] -= 1
13        if window_counts[best_seller[l]] == 0:
14          del window_counts[best_seller[l]]
15        l += 1
16    return False
```

\# Frequency maps are often useful in sliding window problems.

SOLUTION 38.4   ENDURING BEST SELLER STREAK

This problem can be solved exactly the same way as the previous one, just by changing the window validity condition from len(window_counts) == k to len(window_counts) == 1. However, this solution requires O(k) extra space for the frequency map. Can you think of a constant-space solution? We'll see one in the next section about the next type of sliding windows: resetting windows.

RESETTING WINDOWS

We call the next type of sliding window "resetting windows." It is for problems where a bigger window is usually better, but a *single* element in the array can make the whole window invalid. Our approach will be simple: *grow the window if we can, and otherwise reset it to empty past the problematic element.*

Recall the second opening bookstore problem:

✦   **PROBLEM 38.5**   LONGEST GOOD DAY STREAK

Given an array, sales, find the most consecutive days with no *bad* days (fewer than 10 sales).

▸ **Example:** sales = [0, 14, 7, 12, 10, 20]
   Output: 3. The subarray [12, 10, 20] has no bad days.

SOLUTION 38.5   LONGEST GOOD DAY STREAK

This is a resetting window problem because if we encounter a bad day, whatever window we have so far needs to be discarded. This gives us a simple strategy for when to grow and shrink the window:

1. If the next day is *good*, grow the window.

2. If the next day is *bad*, skip it and reset the window.

---

5 Don't forget that when storing strings in a map, the space complexity of the map is not just the number of strings, as we also need to factor in the length of the strings. For this problem, we said that all the titles would have length at most 100, so the space complexity is O(100 * k) = O(k).

```
1  def max_no_bad_days(sales):
2    l, r = 0, 0
3    cur_max = 0
4    while r < len(sales):
5      can_grow = sales[r] >= 10
6      if can_grow:
7        r += 1
8        cur_max = max(cur_max, r - 1)
9      else:
10       l = r+1
11       r = r+1
12   return cur_max
```

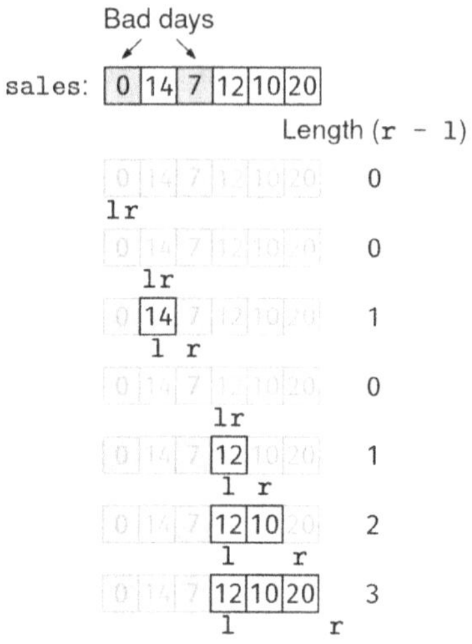

Figure 3. Illustration of the sliding window for max_no_bad_days().

Unlike in the fixed-length window case, a resetting window stays valid throughout the algorithm. We also introduced a can_grow variable to decide whether to *grow* or *reset*.[6] When sales[r] is a bad day, we reset the window by moving both l and r past the problematic element.

Once the window cannot grow anymore (r == len(sales)), we stop, as we surely won't find a bigger window by shrinking it.

We can put these ideas together in a general recipe for resetting window problems.

RECIPE 2. RESETTING WINDOW RECIPE.

```
resetting_window(arr):
  initialize:
  - l and r to 0 (empty window)
  - data structures to track window info
  - cur_best to 0
  while we can grow the window (r < len(arr))
    if the window is still valid with one more element
      grow the window (update data structures and increase r)
      update cur_best if needed
    else
      reset window and data structures past the problematic element
  return cur_best
```

Now that we have seen two types of sliding windows, it is worth mentioning that problems can fit the criteria for more than one window type.

Recall Problem 38.4: "Given the array best_seller and a number k with $1 \le k \le$ len(sales), return whether there is any k-day period where every day has the *same* best-selling title." We can solve it with a fixed-length window like we saw, or with a resetting window:

---

6 You could skip declaring the variable can_grow and put the condition directly in the if statement, but the name "can_grow" makes it clear what the if/else cases correspond to, so it is extra easy for the interviewer to follow.

We grow the window when it is (a) empty or (b) the next title is the same as every element in the window. We reset the window when the next element is different from the ones in the window. In that case, rather than skipping over the element that is different; we start growing a new window from that new element.

```
1   def has_enduring_best_seller_streak(best_seller, k):
2     l, r = 0, 0
3     cur_max = 0
4     while r < len(best_seller):
5       can_grow = l == r or best_seller[l] == best_seller[r]
6       if can_grow:
7         r += 1
8         if r - l == k:
9           return True
10      else:
11        l = r
12    return False
```

This solution improves the extra space to O(1).

RESETTING WINDOWS PROBLEM SET

✦ *Try these problems with AI Interviewer: bctci.co/sliding-windows-problem-set-2*

PROBLEM 38.6   MAX SUBARRAY SUM

Given a non-empty array arr of integers (which can be negative), find the non-empty subarray with the maximum sum and return its sum.

▸ **Example:** arr = [1, 2, 3, -2, 1]
  Output: 6. The subarray with the maximum sum is [1, 2, 3].
▸ **Example:** arr = [1, 2, 3, -2, 7]
  Output: 11. The subarray with the maximum sum is the whole array.
▸ **Example:** arr = [1, 2, 3, -8, 7]
  Output: 7. The subarray with the maximum sum is [7].
▸ **Example:** arr = [-2, -3, -4]
  Output: -2. The subarray cannot be empty.

PROBLEM 38.7   LONGEST ALTERNATING SEQUENCE

Given the array sales, find the longest sequence of days alternating between good days (at least 10 sales) and bad days (fewer than 10 sales).

▸ **Example:** sales = [8, 9, 20, 0, 9]
  Output: 3. The only good day is day 2, so the subarray [9, 20, 0] alternates from bad to good to bad.
▸ **Example:** arr = [0, 0, 0]
  Output: 1. Every day is bad, so we cannot find any pair of consecutive days that alternate.

✦ PROBLEM SET SOLUTIONS

SOLUTION 38.6   MAX SUBARRAY SUM

This is such a classic problem that the resetting window algorithm for it has its own name: *Kadane's algorithm*.

Let's consider the logic for when to grow and shrink our window. If we encounter a positive number, we definitely want to grow the window, as it makes the window sum bigger. If we encounter a negative number, should we keep it and keep growing (as in Example 2), or should we reset the window *past* it (as in Example 3)? The answer depends on the sum of the window elements so far:

- If our current window plus the negative element is still positive, it is worth keeping the current window even with the negative element.

- If the negative element makes the window sum negative, it is not worth keeping; we should reset it.[7]

```
1    def max_subarray_sum(arr):
2      max_val = max(arr)
3      if max_val <= 0: # Edge case without positive values.
4        return max_val
5      l, r = 0, 0
6      window_sum = 0
7      cur_max = 0
8      while r < len(arr):
9        can_grow = window_sum + arr[r] >= 0
10       if can_grow:
11         window_sum += arr[r]
12         r += 1
13         cur_max = max(cur_max, window_sum)
14       else:
15         window_sum = 0
16         l = r+1
17         r = r+1
18     return cur_max
```

SOLUTION 38.7   LONGEST ALTERNATING SEQUENCE

This is a resetting window problem because if we find two consecutive days that are both good or both bad, the whole window becomes invalid and we need to reset it (starting from the second of the two consecutive elements of the same type). We can grow the window when (a) it is empty or (b) the next element does not break the "chain" of alternating days (`(sales[r - 1] < 10) != (sales[r] < 10)`).

MAXIMUM WINDOWS

We are going to tackle general *maximization* problems (maximum length, maximum sum, etc.) with what we call maximum windows. *Maximum windows grow when they can and shrink when they must.* They are similar to resetting windows, but when we encounter an element that makes the window invalid, we don't discard the whole window and reset it. Instead, we shrink it element by element (by increasing l) until it becomes valid again.

---

7 In both cases, we need to increment r. You can see in our implementation that we could factor out that increment outside of the if/else cases and save a line of code. However, as we mentioned on page 297, when trying to come up with a valid solution, it is easier to think about each case independently first—shared code between the cases can make it harder to reason about the correctness of your code. If you have time, once you are sure your code is correct, you can do a 'clean-up' pass to tidy up the code.

Recall the third opening bookstore problem:

✦ **PROBLEM 38.8**   **MAXIMUM WITH AT MOST 3 BAD DAYS**

Given an array `sales`, find the most consecutive days with at most 3 bad days (fewer than 10 sales).

▸ **Example:** `sales = [0, 14, 7, 9, 0, 20, 10, 0, 10]`
  Output: 6. There are two 6-day periods with at most 3 bad days,
           `[14, 7, 9, 0, 20, 10]` and `[9, 0, 20, 10, 0, 10]`.

SOLUTION 38.8   MAXIMUM WITH AT MOST 3 BAD DAYS

We can follow this strategy for when to grow and shrink the window:

1. If the next day is *good* or the window contains fewer than 3 bad days, grow the window.

2. Otherwise, shrink it.

Here is a full solution:

```
 1  def max_at_most_3_bad_days(sales):
 2    l, r = 0, 0
 3    window_bad_days = 0
 4    cur_max = 0
 5    while r < len(sales):
 6      can_grow = sales[r] >= 10 or window_bad_days < 3
 7      if can_grow:
 8        if sales[r] < 10:
 9          window_bad_days += 1
10        r += 1
11        cur_max = max(cur_max, r - l)
12      else:
13        if sales[l] < 10:
14          window_bad_days -= 1
15        l += 1
16    return cur_max
```

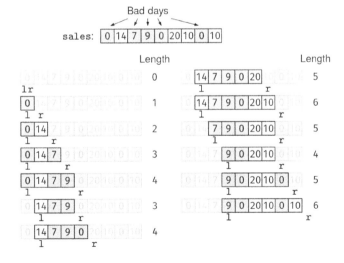

Figure 4. Sliding window for `max_at_most_3_bad_days()`.

Many elements of the solution should look similar to the resetting window recipe, like the can_grow variable. The only new part is what happens when we cannot grow the window. We remove *only* the first element in the window (sales[1]).

Here is a recipe for maximum windows. Note how, before shrinking the window, we need to check the case where the window is empty (1 == r)—an empty window cannot be shrunk! For many problems, an empty window is always valid, so we can omit this check (for example, in this problem, an empty window is always valid because it has 0 bad days).

🗐 RECIPE 3. MAXIMUM WINDOW RECIPE.

```
maximum_window(arr):
  initialize:
  - l and r to 0 (empty window)
  - data structures to track window info
  - cur_best to 0
  while we can grow the window (r < len(arr))
    if the window would still be valid with one more element
      grow the window (update data structures and increase r)
      update cur_best if needed
    else if the window is empty
      advance both l and r
    else
      shrink the window (update data structures and increase l)
  return cur_best
```

MAXIMUM WINDOWS PROBLEM SET

✦ *Try these problems with AI Interviewer: bctci.co/sliding-windows-problem-set-3*

Follow the maximum window recipe to tackle the following questions.

PROBLEM 38.9   AD CAMPAIGN BOOST

Imagine that our little bookstore has an array, projected_sales, with the projected number of sales per day in the future. We are trying to pick k days for an advertising campaign, which we expect to boost the sales on those specific days by at least 20. If we pick the days for the advertising campaign correctly, what is the maximum number of consecutive *good* days in a row we can get? (Recall that a good day is a day with at least 10 sales.)

▸ **Example:** projected_sales = [5, 0, 20, 0, 5], k = 2
  Output: 3. The only good day is day 2. We can boost days 0 and 1, days 1
            and 3, or days 3 and 4. For instance, if we boost days 0 and 1, the
            projected sales become [25, 20, 20, 0, 5], with 3 consecutive good
            days.

▸ **Example:** arr = [0, 10, 0, 10], k = 1
  Output: 3. We can boost day 2; boosting day 0 is suboptimal.

PROBLEM 38.10   AD CAMPAIGN WITH SMALL BOOSTS

In the previous problem, what would change if the boost from the advertising campaign was only 5 books instead of 20? You cannot boost the same day more than once. What is the maximum number of consecutive *good* days in a row we can get?

▸ **Example:** `projected_sales = [8, 4, 8], k = 3`
  Output: `1.` We can boost all 3 days, resulting in `[13, 9, 13]` projected
            sales. The max consecutive good days is 1.
▸ **Example:** `projected_sales = [10, 5, 8], k = 1`
  Output: `2.` We should boost day 1, resulting in `[10, 10, 8]` projected sales.

PROBLEM 38.11   **BOOSTING DAYS MULTIPLE TIMES**

In Problem 38.9, what would change if the boost from the advertising campaign was only 1 book instead of 20, but *you can boost the same day more than once*? What is the maximum number of consecutive *good* days in a row we can get?

▸ **Example:** `projected_sales = [5, 5, 15, 0, 10], k = 12`
  Output: `3.` We can reach 3 consecutive good ways in two ways: boosting days 0
            and 1, so both reach 10 sales, or boosting day 3.
▸ **Example:** `projected_sales = [5, 5, 15, 0, 10], k = 15`
  Output: `4.` We can boost days 1 and 3.

PROBLEM 38.12   **LONGEST PERIOD AT-MOST K DISTINCT**

Given an array of strings, `best_seller`, that lists the title of the most sold book for each day, and a number k ≥ 1, find the maximum consecutive days with at most k *distinct* best-selling books.

▸ **Example:** `projected_sales = ["book1", "book1", "book2", "book1", "book3",`
            `"book1"], k = 2`
  Output: `4.` The subarray `["book1", "book1", "book2", "book1"]` contains only 2
            distinct titles.
  Constraints: `best_seller` has a length of at most 10^6, and each book title in
            `best_seller` has a length of at most 100.

✢ PROBLEM SET SOLUTIONS

SOLUTION 38.9   AD CAMPAIGN BOOST

This problem introduces a new dimension: we need to make choices that "modify" the window that we are sliding over. This seems complicated at first since there could be many choices.

A naive solution would be to consider all possible sets of k days we could pick, but that would be very inefficient.[8] The key for this type of problem is usually to use the **REFRAME THE PROBLEM** booster. We want to find a way to *reframe it in a way that eliminates the choice aspect*. For our problem, instead of *choosing* k days to turn from bad to good, we can look for the longest window with *at most* k bad days because we can pick those bad days and turn them into good days.

With this reframing, the question becomes just like Problem 38.8, which we solved previously, but with a generic limit of k bad days instead of 3.

\# When a problem asks you to choose k elements to change (or flip, remove, etc.), the problem can often be reframed in terms of finding a window with at most k elements that need to be changed.

---

8 If k is a constant, the number of subsets of size k, denoted (n choose k), is $O(n^k)$. The worst case is when k is n/2, as (n choose n/2) = $O(2^n/\sqrt{n})$. Once k gets larger than n/2, the number of possibilities starts decreasing. For instance, there are only n subsets of size n-1.

SOLUTION 38.10   AD CAMPAIGN WITH SMALL BOOSTS

We can *REFRAME THE PROBLEM* as: "find the longest window with at most k values between 5 and 9 and 0 values less than 5." Then, it becomes a standard maximum window problem.

SOLUTION 38.11   BOOSTING DAYS MULTIPLE TIMES

First, we never want to boost a day beyond 10 projected sales, since we only care about the day being 'good.' The 'cost' of turning a day with x sales into a good day is max(10-x, 0). Thus, we can *REFRAME THE PROBLEM* as: "Find the longest window where the sum of max(10-x, 0) over each element x in the window is at most k." Then, it becomes a standard maximum window problem.

```
1    def max_consecutive_with_k_boosts(projected_sales, k):
2      l, r = 0, 0
3      used_boosts = 0
4      cur_max = 0
5      while r < len(projected_sales):
6        can_grow = used_boosts + max(10 - projected_sales[r], 0) <= k
7        if can_grow:
8          used_boosts += max(10 - projected_sales[r], 0)
9          r += 1
10         cur_max = max(cur_max, r - 1)
11       elif l == r:
12         r += 1
13         l += 1
14       else:
15         used_boosts -= max(10 - projected_sales[l], 0)
16         l += 1
17     return cur_max
```

SOLUTION 38.12   LONGEST PERIOD AT-MOST K DISTINCT

We need to keep track of the number of distinct books in the window. Again, we can use a *frequency map* from book titles in the window to their number of occurrences. When we shrink the window, if a count goes down to 0, we remove the corresponding key from the map. This way, the size of the map reflects the number of distinct elements in the window, and the window is valid if the map's size is at most k.

```
1    def max_at_most_k_distinct(best_seller, k):
2      l, r = 0, 0
3      window_counts = {}
4      cur_max = 0
5      while r < len(best_seller):
6        can_grow = best_seller[r] in window_counts or len(window_counts) + 1 <= k
7        if can_grow:
8          if not best_seller[r] in window_counts:
9            window_counts[best_seller[r]] = 0
10         window_counts[best_seller[r]] += 1
11         r += 1
12         cur_max = max(cur_max, r - 1)
13       else:
14         window_counts[best_seller[l]] -= 1
15         if window_counts[best_seller[l]] == 0:
16           del window_counts[best_seller[l]]
17         l += 1
18     return cur_max
```

LIMITATIONS OF MAXIMUM WINDOWS

All the problems we solved with a maximum window (as well as a resetting window) have this property: *Growing an invalid window never makes it valid.*

We call this the *maximum window property*, and it is critical—without it, the maximum window recipe may not work. The intuition is that, without it, we may have to grow through invalid solutions in order to get to the optimal one, making it hard to know when to grow or shrink.

For example, consider a simplified version of Problem 43.7: Longest Subarray With Sum K (pg 620): Given an array of integers, which may be negative, return if any subarray adds up to 0.

This problem looks like a maximum window problem because it asks for the longest subarray satisfying a constraint, but we can't follow the typical maximum window policy of "grow when you can, shrink when you must."

For instance, if the input starts with [1, 4, -2, -2, 5, ...] and we (somehow) grow the window up to [1, 4, -2, -2], should we shrink it in order to find a valid window of length 3, or keep growing because there may be a longer solution with the initial 1, like [1, 4, -2, -2, 5, -6]? It is impossible to say.

For problems without the maximum window property, it is better to ditch the sliding window approach entirely and think of different approaches. A linear-time algorithm may also be less realistic (although it is possible for this particular problem using prefix sums, pg 620).

Sliding windows often don't work with negative values.[9]

Finally, there are also problems that have the maximum window property, meaning that the maximum window recipe gives the optimal answer, but it is just really hard to implement efficiently. Here is an example of a classic problem:

✦✦   **PROBLEM 38.13**   **LONGEST REPEATED SUBSTRING**

Given a string, s, return the longest substring that appears more than once in s (overlapping is allowed) or the empty string if there is none.

▸ **Example:** s = "murmur"
  Output: "mur"
▸ **Example:** s = "murmurmur"
  Output: "murmur"
▸ **Example:** s = "aaaa"
  Output: "aaa"

SOLUTION 38.13   LONGEST REPEATED SUBSTRING

This can be seen as a maximum window problem because we are looking for the longest window with some property. Further, it has the maximum window property: if a substring is not repeated, it won't suddenly become repeated if we make it longer.

The challenge for this problem is assessing whether a substring is valid or not is not easy because it depends on what is *outside* the window instead of what is inside of it.

For problems like this, where the maximum window recipe works but is hard to implement efficiently, we recommend trying something other than sliding windows.

---

9 Kadane's algorithm (Solution 38.6: Max Subarray Sum (pg 520) for the maximum subarray sum problem is an exception.

For this particular problem, we can try the **guess-and-check technique** we learned in the Binary Search chapter (pg 338). That is, we can try to *binary search over the length of the optimal window*. This approach starts by asking: "If I somehow knew the length of the optimal window, would that make the problem easier?" The answer is often yes because then we can use the fixed-length window recipe, which is the most straightforward one. In this case, the fixed-length window version of the problem is "For a given k, is there a substring of length k that appears more than once?" If we can solve this efficiently, we can then binary search for the transition point in the range of values of k where the answer goes from "yes" to "no". The fixed-length window version can be solved in $O(n)$ time using a rolling hash (bctci.co/set-and-map-implementations, Rolling Hash Algorithm section), leading to $O(n \log n)$ total time.

\#   When a problem has the maximum window property, but you cannot find an efficient way to check if the window is valid or evaluate the window, consider using the guess-and-check technique. For an 'extra' factor of $O(\log n)$ in the runtime, it turns the problem into a potentially easier fixed-length window problem.

MINIMUM WINDOWS

Minimum window problems are the opposite of maximum window problems. We try to find a window as short as possible, but the constraint restricts how small valid windows can be. We'll use 'minimum windows', which *grow when they must and shrink when they can*.

Recall the fourth opening bookstore problem:

✦   **PROBLEM 38.14**   **SHORTEST PERIOD WITH OVER 20 SALES**

Given an array, sales, return the length of the shortest period of time with over 20 sales, or -1 if there isn't any.

▶ **Example:** sales = [5, 10, 15, 5, 10]
  Output: 2. The subarray [10, 15] has over 20 sales.
▶ **Example:** sales = [5, 10, 4, 5, 10]
  Output: 4. [5, 10, 4, 5] and [10, 4, 5, 10] have over 20 sales.
▶ **Example:** sales = [5, 5, 5, 5]
  Output: -1. There is no subarray with more than 20 sales.

SOLUTION 38.14   SHORTEST PERIOD WITH OVER 20 SALES

This is a minimum window problem because we are trying to find a window as short as possible.

For minimum window problems, the empty window is invalid (in this problem, because it has fewer than 20 sales). We need to grow it until it becomes valid, similar to how we did for fixed-length window problems. We can follow this strategy for when to grow and shrink the window:

1. If the window has 20 sales or fewer: grow it.
2. Otherwise, shrink it to look for a shorter one with over 20 sales.

```
 1  def shortest_over_20_sales(sales):
 2    l, r = 0, 0
 3    window_sum = 0
 4    cur_min = math.inf
 5    while True:
 6      must_grow = window_sum <= 20
 7      if must_grow:
 8        if r == len(sales):
 9          break
10        window_sum += sales[r]
11        r += 1
12      else:
13        cur_min = min(cur_min, r - 1)
14        window_sum -= sales[l]
15        l += 1
16    if cur_min == math.inf:
17      return -1
18    return cur_min
```

sales: | 5 | 10 | 15 | 5 | 10 |

window_sum

| 5 10 15 5 10 | 0 ✗
  lr

| 5 10 15 5 10 | 5 ✗
  l r

| 5 10 15 5 10 | 15 ✗
  l r

| 5 10 15 5 10 | 30 ✓
  l   r

| 5 10 15 5 10 | 25 ✓
    l   r

| 5 10 15 5 10 | 15 ✗
      l r

| 5 10 15 5 10 | 20 ✗
      l   r

| 5 10 15 5 10 | 30 ✓
      l   r

| 5 10 15 5 10 | 15 ✗
        l   r

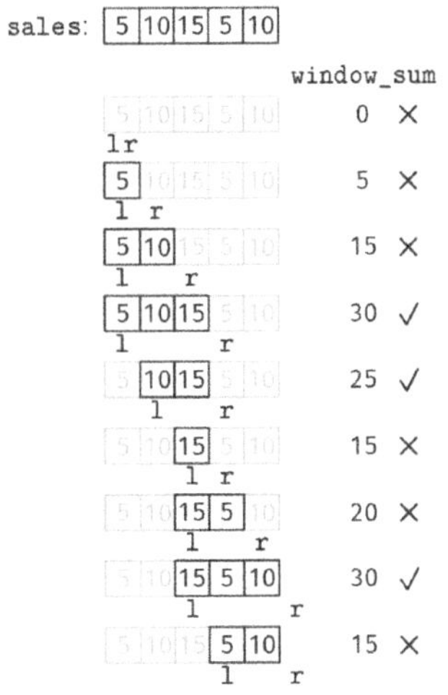

Figure 5. Illustration of the sliding window of short-est_over_20_sales().

Unlike the other recipes, we initialize the result (cur_min) to infinity because we update it by taking the minimum. At the end, we need to check if it is still infinity, which means that we didn't find any valid windows. It is a common mistake to forget this final check!

In the main loop, we start each iteration by declaring a variable must_grow (instead of can_grow for maximum windows) which indicates if the *current* window is invalid. If we must grow, there is one edge case to consider: if r == len(sales), we ran out of elements to grow, so we break out of the loop. We have this edge case for minimum windows but not maximum windows because the while-loop condition is different: we don't stop as soon as r gets to the end because it might still be possible to make the window smaller and get a better answer.

If must_grow is false, then we have a valid window, so we update the current minimum *first* and then shrink the window to see if we can make it even smaller.

We can put these ideas together in a general recipe for minimum window problems.

🗐 RECIPE 4. MINIMUM WINDOW RECIPE.

```
minimum_window(arr):
  initialize:
  - l and r to 0 (empty window)
  - data structures to track window info
  - cur_best to infinity
  while true
    if the window must grow to become valid
      if the window cannot grow (r == len(arr))
        break
      grow the window (update data structures and increase r)
    else
      update cur_best if needed
      shrink the window (update data structures and increase l)
  return cur_best
```

Recall that maximum windows only work for problems that have what we call the maximum window property? For the minimum window recipe to work, we need the opposite property: **Shrinking an invalid window never makes it valid**. We call this the **minimum window property**. It means that if the current window is invalid, we definitely need to grow it.

SUCCESSFULLY SOLVES MINIMUM SLIDING WINDOW PROBLEM		INTERVIEW REPLAY
View Online:	bctci.co/sliding-windows-replay-2 @ 4:15 - 43:23	
The Question:	Find the smallest substring in s containing all characters of t (including duplicates).	
What You'll See:	The candidate successfully applied a minimum sliding window solution.	
Who:	*Interviewer*: Staff Software Engineer at Meta *Candidate*: 1 year exp.	
Outcome:	The candidate got the job at Amazon!	

MINIMUM WINDOWS PROBLEM SET

✦ *Try these problems with AI Interviewer: bctci.co/sliding-windows-problem-set-4*

PROBLEM 38.15   SHORTEST WITH ALL LETTERS

Given a string, s1, and a shorter but non-empty string, s2, return the length of the shortest substring of s1 that has every letter in s2 (as many times as they appear in s2). If there is no such substring, return -1.

▸ **Example:** s1 = "helloworld", s2 = "well"
  Output: 5. The substring "ellow" in s1 has all the letters in s2.
▸ **Example:** s1 = "helloworld", s2 = "weelll"
  Output: -1. s1 does not have 2 e's.

PROBLEM 38.16   SMALLEST RANGE WITH K ELEMENTS

Given an array of integers, arr, and an integer k with 1 ≤ k ≤ len(arr), return a pair of values, [low, high], with low ≤ high, representing the smallest range such that there are at least k elements in arr with values at least low and at most high. If there are multiple valid answers, return any of them.

▸ **Example:** arr = [1, 2, 5, 7, 8], k = 3
  Output: [5, 8]. The range has 3 elements in arr (5, 7, and 8) and it is
             smaller than other ranges with 3 elements, such as [1, 5].
▸ **Example:** arr = [5, 5, 2, 2, 8, 8], k = 3
  Output: [2, 5]. The range has 4 elements in arr (5, 5, 2, and 2) and there
             is no smaller range with at least 3 elements. [5, 8] is also a valid
             answer.
▸ **Example:** arr = [0], k = 1
  Output: [0, 0].

| PROBLEM 38.17 | STRONG START AND ENDING |

We have an array, projected_sales, with the number of book sales we expect each day of the fall season. We would like to start and close the season strong. We want to have as many consecutive good days as possible starting from day 0 and as many consecutive good days as possible ending on the last day (a *good day* is a day with at least 10 sales). We can pick k days to boost with advertising, which we expect to boost the sales on those specific days by at least 20. What's the maximum number of combined initial good days and final good days we can have?

▸ **Example:** projected_sales = [10, 0, 0, 0, 10, 0, 0, 10], k = 2
  Output: 5. We should boost days 5 and 6 so that the projected sales after
             boosting are [10, 0, 0, 0, 10, 20, 20, 10]. This way, we have 1
             initial and 4 final good days.
▸ **Example:** arr = [0, 10, 0, 10], k = 1
  Output: 3. We can boost either day 0 or day 2.

✦ PROBLEM SET SOLUTIONS

SOLUTION 38.15   SHORTEST WITH ALL LETTERS

This is a minimum window problem since we have to minimize the window length. A window is valid if the count for each letter is at least as big as the count in s2.

The key information we need to maintain about the window is a *frequency map* counting how many times each letter from s2 is missing. We can also keep a separate count of the number of distinct letters that are missing. When this counter is at 0, the window is valid.

```
 1  def shortest_with_all_letters(s1, s2):
 2      l, r = 0, 0
 3      missing = {}
 4      for c in s2:
 5          if not c in missing:
 6              missing[c] = 0
 7          missing[c] += 1
 8      distinct_missing = len(missing)
 9      cur_min = math.inf
10      while True:
11          must_grow = distinct_missing > 0
12          if must_grow:
13              if r == len(s1):
14                  break
15              if s1[r] in missing:
16                  missing[s1[r]] -= 1
```

```
17            if missing[s1[r]] == 0:
18                distinct_missing -= 1
19          r += 1
20        else:
21          cur_min = min(cur_min, r - 1)
22          if s1[l] in missing:
23            missing[s1[l]] += 1
24            if missing[s1[l]] == 1:
25              distinct_missing += 1
26          l += 1
27    return cur_min if cur_min != math.inf else -1
```

SOLUTION 38.16   SMALLEST RANGE WITH K ELEMENTS

This is an interesting problem because we are not looking for a subarray of the input but rather a window on the *values* in the array. Nonetheless, we can still use a minimum window to find this range.

First, we sort the input since we do not care about the original order, and it will help us find values in arr that are close together. After sorting, the problem can be *REFRAMED* as follows:

Find the window containing at least k elements, minimizing the difference between its maximum and minimum. Now that we have a constraint and an objective for the window, this is a standard minimum window problem.

Thanks to sorting, the minimum and maximum in the window are easy to calculate as they are the first and last elements. Sorting is the runtime bottleneck in this solution, so it takes $O(n \log n)$ time instead of $O(n)$ as usual.

```
1   def smallest_range_with_k_elements(arr, k):
2     arr.sort()
3     l, r = 0, 0
4     best_low, best_high = 0, math.inf
5     while True:
6       must_grow = (r - l) < k
7       if must_grow:
8         if r == len(arr):
9           break
10        r += 1
11      else:
12        if arr[r - 1] - arr[l] < best_high - best_low:
13          best_low, best_high = arr[l], arr[r - 1]
14        l += 1
15    return [best_low, best_high]
```

SOLUTION 38.17   STRONG START AND ENDING

It is not obvious at all how a problem about maximizing prefix and suffix lengths is related to minimum windows, but we will show a clever trick to *REFRAME THE PROBLEM* into a minimum window problem.

What is between a prefix and a suffix? A window! Finding a prefix and a suffix is the twin problem of finding the subarray between them. The next question is: "If we look for a subarray instead of for a prefix and a suffix, what property should the subarray have?"

Let's say projected_sales has B bad days in total. We know we can flip k of them into good days, so we will end up with B - k bad days (if B - k is 0 or negative, we can convert all bad days into good days, so the answer is the length of the input array). If we can find the *smallest* window with B - k bad days, then we can flip every bad day *outside* the window and maximize the prefix and suffix without bad days.

With this reframing, the problem becomes a standard minimum window problem.

EXTRA CREDIT: COUNTING PROBLEMS

By this point, we have seen many sliding window problems in which the constraint that the window must satisfy is of the form "at most/at least/exactly k of something." In this section, we talk about how to count the number of subarrays under a constraint like that, including the final three opening bookstore problems.

AT-MOST-K COUNTING

PROBLEM 38.18 **COUNT SUBARRAYS WITH AT MOST K BAD DAYS**

Given an array, `sales`, count the number of subarrays with at most k bad days (days with fewer than 10 sales).

▸ **Example:** `sales = [0, 20, 5]`, `k = 1`
  Output: 5. `[20]` has 0 bad days, and `[0]`, `[0, 20]`, `[20, 5]`, and `[5]` have 1 bad day each.

SOLUTION 38.18 **COUNT SUBARRAYS WITH AT MOST K BAD DAYS**

We can leverage an interesting property about the maximum window recipe: if a problem has the maximum window property (pg 525), whenever we grow the window by adding an element `arr[r - 1]`, the new window is the longest valid window that ends at `arr[r - 1]`. This means that the valid subarrays ending at `arr[r - 1]` are those starting at `arr[l]`, `arr[l + 1]`, and so on, up to `arr[r - 1]` itself. Thus, there are `r - l` valid subarrays ending `arr[r - 1]`.

As we saw in the Problem-Solving Boosters chapter, we can often leverage properties into algorithmic ideas. In this case, we can follow the maximum window recipe—as if we were trying to find the longest window with at most k bad days—and whenever we grow the window by adding an element `arr[r - 1]`, we add `r - l` to a running count of valid subarrays.

Here is a full solution based on this idea:

```
1  def count_at_most_k_bad_days(sales, k):
2    l, r = 0, 0
3    window_bad_days = 0
4    count = 0
5    while r < len(sales):
1      can_grow = sales[r] >= 10 or
2                 window_bad_days < k
3      if can_grow:
4        if sales[r] < 10:
5          window_bad_days += 1
6        r += 1
7        count += r - l
8      else:
9        if sales[l] < 10:
10         window_bad_days -= 1
11       l += 1
12   return count
```

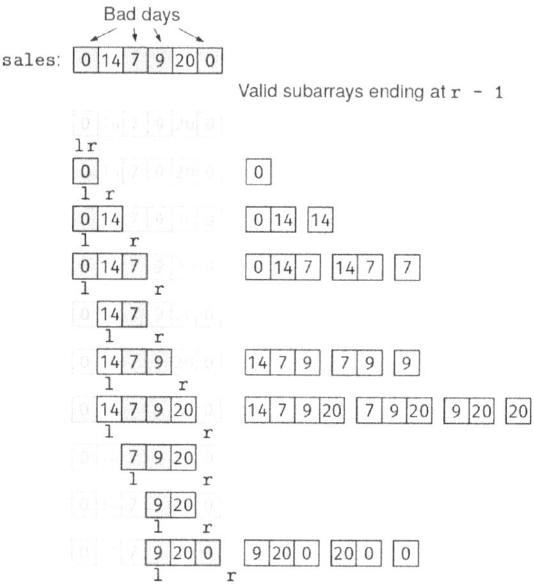

Figure 6. Sliding window for count_at_most_k_bad_days(sales, 2). Every time we grow the window, we show all the valid subarrays that we add to the running count (16 in total).

Note that the code is exactly the same as max_at_most_3_bad_days() from the previous section except for computing count instead of cur_max (and k instead of 3).

If a problem has the maximum window property, the maximum window recipe also works for At-Most-K counting problems. Whenever we add an element to the window, we add to the running count all the valid subarrays ending at that element.

Fortunately, At-Most-K counting problems are a bit of a 'freebie' because we can reuse the maximum window recipe. In the next section, we'll see a trick that makes Exactly-K counting problems equally easy!

As mentioned, this only works if the problem has the maximum window property. For instance, if we allow negative numbers in the array in this problem, we cannot use the algorithm anymore.

EXACTLY-K COUNTING

✦✦ | PROBLEM 38.19 | **COUNT SUBARRAYS WITH EXACTLY K BAD DAYS**

Given an array, sales, count the number of subarrays with *exactly* k bad days (days with fewer than 10 sales).

▸ **Example:** sales = [0, 20, 5], k = 1
  Output: 4. The subarrays [0], [0, 20], [20, 5], and [5] have 1 bad day each.

SOLUTION 38.19   **COUNT SUBARRAYS WITH EXACTLY K BAD DAYS**

This time, we will start with the solution and then break it down:

```
1  def count_exactly_k_bad_days(sales, k):
2    if k == 0:
3      return count_at_most_k_bad_days(sales, 0)
4    return count_at_most_k_bad_days(sales, k) -
5           count_at_most_k_bad_days(sales, k-1)
```

We re-used the At-Most-K counting function count_at_most_k_bad_days() from the previous section.

For k == 0, 'at most 0' and 'exactly 0' are the same. For k == 1, the code works because the number of subarrays with exactly 1 bad day is equal to the number of subarrays with at most 1 bad day (meaning 0 or 1 bad days) minus the number of subarrays with at most 0 bad days. This applies to any higher k as well!

For example, Figure 7 shows an example sales array and all 16 subarrays with at most 2 bad days. Of those, 10 have at most 1 bad day, meaning there are 16 - 10 = 6 subarrays with **exactly** 2 bad days. By the same logic, there are 10 - 2 = 8 subarrays with exactly 1 bad day.

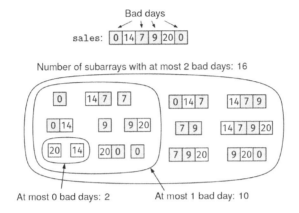

Figure 7. The set of all subarrays with at most 2 bad days, which contains the set of subarrays with at most 1 bad day, which contains the set of subarrays with no bad days.

Since we need to make two calls to the At-Most-K solution, the runtime is twice as long, which is still O(n).

Exactly-K counting problems can also be solved in linear time with prefix sums: see Problem 38.6: Max Subarray Sum (pg 519). The prefix-sums approach works *even if the array has negative numbers.*

AT-LEAST-K COUNTING

✦ **PROBLEM 38.20** **COUNT SUBARRAYS WITH AT LEAST K BAD DAYS**

Given an array, sales, count the number of subarrays with *at least* k bad days (days with fewer than 10 sales).

▶ **Example:** sales = [0, 20, 5], k = 1
  Output: 5. The subarrays [0], [0, 20], [20, 5], and [5] have 1 bad day each, and the subarray [0, 20, 5] has 2.

SOLUTION 38.20 COUNT SUBARRAYS WITH AT LEAST K BAD DAYS

We will see how to reuse the At-Most-K counting solution once again. First, we need to know the total number of subarrays.

What's the total number of subarrays?

An array of length n has (n+1)*n/2 non-empty subarrays.

Each subarray is defined by a pair of indices, [start, end]. There are n^2 [i, j] pairs where i and j are valid indices (0 ≤ i, j < n). Of those, there are n pairs where i == j, which define single-element subarrays. Of the remaining n^2 - n pairs, half have i < j and half have i > j.

The latter half does not identify valid subarrays, so we don't count them. In total, we have $n + (n^2 - n)/2 = (n+1)*n/2$ subarrays.

The subarrays with at least k bad days are those with k bad days, those with k+1 bad days, those with k+2 bad days, and so on. Therefore, to count the subarrays with at least k bad days, we can start with the count of *all* subarrays (of which there are $n*(n+1)/2$) and subtract the number of subarrays with at most k-1 bad days. Something we already saw how to compute!

```
1   def count_at_least_k_bad_days(sales, k):
2       n = len(sales)
3       total_subarrays = n*(n+1)//2
4       if k == 0:
5           return total_subarrays
6       return total_subarrays - count_at_most_k_bad_days(sales, k-1)
```

\# If the At-Most-K version of a counting problem has the maximum window property, it can be reused to solve the At-Least-K version.

♻ REUSABLE IDEA: TRANSFORM EXACTLY-K/AT-LEAST-K COUNTING TO AT-MOST-K COUNTING

> If the At-Most-K version of a counting problem has the maximum window property, it can be reused to solve the Exactly-K and At-Least-K versions.
>
> 1. 'Exactly k' is equivalent to 'at most k' minus 'at most k - 1'.
>
> 2. 'At Least k' is equivalent to 'total count' $(n*(n+1)/2)$ minus 'at most k - 1'.
>
> The At-Most-K version can be solved by tweaking the maximum window template, as in Solution 18.

There are counting problems that do not fit into any of the At-Most-K / Exactly-K / At-Least-K categories. We should tackle such problems on a case-by-case basis. Here is an example:

✦ PROBLEM 38.21   COUNT SUBARRAYS WITH GOOD START AND ENDING

Given an array, sales, return the number of subarrays that start and end on a good day (a day with at least 10 sales).

SOLUTION 38.21   COUNT SUBARRAYS WITH GOOD START AND ENDING

For this particular problem, the key property to leverage is that each distinct pair of good days in sales contributes 1 to the final count. Thus, the answer is $g*(g + 1)/2$, where g is the number of good days in sales.

COUNTING PROBLEM SET

✦ *Try these problems with AI Interviewer: bctci.co/sliding-windows-problem-set-5*

PROBLEM 38.22   COUNT SUBARRAYS WITH DROPS

Given an array of integers, arr, and an integer k, count how many subarrays have (1) at most k drops, (2) exactly k drops, and (3) at least k drops. A *drop* is a sequence of two consecutive numbers where the first is larger than the second.

▸ **Example:** arr = [1, 2, 3], k = 1
  Output: (1) 6. The array has no drops, so every subarray has 0 drops.

```
(2) 0. The array has no drops.
(3) 0. The array has no drops.
```

▶ **Example:** arr = [3, 2, 1], k = 1
  Output: (1) 5. [3, 2] and [2, 1] have 1 drop and [3], [2], and [1] have 0
             drops.
             (2) 2. [3, 2] and [2, 1] have exactly 1 drop.
             (3) 3. [3, 2] and [2, 1] have 1 drop and [3, 2, 1] has 2 drops.

PROBLEM 38.23 **COUNT SUBARRAYS WITH BAD DAYS IN RANGE**

Given the array sales and two numbers k1 and k2 with 0 ≤ k1 ≤ k2, count the number of subarrays with *at least* k1 bad days and *at most* k2 bad days (days with fewer than 10 sales).

▶ **Example:** sales = [0, 20, 5], k1 = 2, k2 = 2
  Output: 1. [0, 20, 5] has 2 bad days.
▶ **Example:** sales = [0, 20, 5], k1 = 1, k2 = 2
  Output: 5. [0, 20, 5] has 2 bad days, and [0], [0, 20], [20, 5], and [5]
             have 1 bad day.

PROBLEM 38.24 **COUNT SUBARRAYS WITH ALL REMAINDERS**

Given an array of positive integers, arr, return the number of subarrays that have at least one of each of the following:

- a multiple of 3,
- a number with remainder 1 when divided by 3, and
- a number with remainder 2 when divided by 3.

▶ **Example:** arr = [9, 8, 7]
  Output: 1. [9, 8, 7] counts because 9 % 3 is 0, 7 % 3 is 1, and 8 % 3 is 2.
▶ **Example:** arr = [1, 2, 3, 4, 5]
  Output: 6. The subarrays are [1, 2, 3], [2, 3, 4], [3, 4, 5], [1, 2, 3, 4],
             [2, 3, 4, 5], and [1, 2, 3, 4, 5].
▶ **Example:** arr = [1, 3, 4, 6, 7, 9]
  Output: 0. There are no numbers with remainder 2 when divided by 3.

PROBLEM 38.25 **COUNT GOOD SUBARRAYS WITH AT LEAST K SALES**

Given an array, sales, and a positive integer k, return the number of subarrays with no bad days and at least k total sales (bad days are days with fewer than 10 sales).

▶ **Example:** arr = [15, 20, 5, 30, 25], k = 50
  Output: 1. The subarrays with no bad days are [15], [15, 20], [20], [30],
             [30, 25], and [25]. Of those, only [30, 25] has at least 50 sales.

✦ PROBLEM SET SOLUTIONS

SOLUTION 38.22 COUNT SUBARRAYS WITH DROPS

This is a direct application of the techniques we discussed.

```
1  def count_at_most_k_drops(arr, k):
2    l, r = 0, 0
```

```
3      window_drops = 0
4      count = 0
5      while r < len(arr):
6        can_grow = r == 0 or arr[r] >= arr[r-1] or window_drops < k
7        if can_grow:
8          if r > 0 and arr[r] < arr[r-1]:
9            window_drops += 1
10         r += 1
11         count += r - 1
12       else:
13         if arr[l] > arr[l+1]:
14           window_drops -= 1
15         l += 1
16     return count
17
18   def count_exactly_k_drops(arr, k):
19     if k == 0:
20       return count_at_most_k_drops(arr, 0)
21     return count_at_most_k_drops(arr, k) - count_at_most_k_drops(arr, k-1)
22
23   def count_at_least_k_drops(arr, k):
24     n = len(arr)
25     total_count = n*(n+1)//2
26     if k == 0:
27       return total_count
28     return total_count - count_at_most_k_drops(arr, k-1)
```

SOLUTION 38.23   COUNT SUBARRAYS WITH BAD DAYS IN RANGE

The same idea for Exactly-K counting problems also applies to a range:[10]

```
1   def count_bad_days_range(sales, k1, k2):
2     if k1 == 0:
3       return count_at_most_k_bad_days(sales, k2)
4     return count_at_most_k_bad_days(sales, k2) -
5             count_at_most_k_bad_days(sales, k1-1)
```

SOLUTION 38.24   COUNT SUBARRAYS WITH ALL REMAINDERS

Every number has a remainder of 0, 1, or 2 when divided by 3. The count of subarrays that have a number from each group is equal to the total number of subarrays $(n*(n+1)/2)$ minus the subarrays that have numbers from at most 2 of those groups. For the latter, we use the at-most-k counting technique.

```
1   def count_all_3_groups(arr):
2     n = len(arr)
3     total_count = n * (n + 1) // 2
4     return total_count - count_at_most_2_groups(arr)
5
6   def count_at_most_2_groups(arr):
7     l, r = 0, 0
8     window_counts = {}
9     count = 0
10    while r < len(arr):
11      can_grow = arr[r] % 3 in window_counts or len(window_counts) < 2
```

---

10   This is the same logic behind how we use prefix sums to answer range sum queries (pg 614).

```
12      if can_grow:
13        if not arr[r] % 3 in window_counts:
14          window_counts[arr[r] % 3] = 0
15        window_counts[arr[r] % 3] += 1
16        r += 1
17        count += r - l
18      else:
19        window_counts[arr[l] % 3] -= 1
20        if window_counts[arr[l] % 3] == 0:
21          del window_counts[arr[l] % 3]
22        l += 1
23    return count
```

We could have made the code a bit more efficient by replacing the dictionary with an array of length 3, since the set of keys that we are using is {0, 1, 2}.

SOLUTION 38.25   COUNT GOOD SUBARRAYS WITH AT LEAST K SALES

We can use the 'break down the problem' booster:

1. First, we can use a resetting window to find all maximal subarrays without any bad days. Then, we can focus on each subarray we found without worrying about bad days.

2. For each subarray, sub, from Step 1, we need to count the number of subarrays of sub with at least k total sales. To do this, we can use the trick for At-Least-K counting: counting the total number of subarrays in sub and subtracting the number of subarrays in sub with at most k-1 total sales.

KEY TAKEAWAYS

If you want to try using a sliding window, your first goal should be identifying the *constraint* and the *objective*. Based on those, you can choose the most appropriate window type: see the fixed-length window recipe (pg 515), the resetting window recipe (pg 518), the maximum window recipe (pg 522), and the minimum window recipe (pg 528).

Once you choose a recipe, the next question is:

▸   What information do I need about the window to check its *validity* and *evaluation* efficiently?

Based on the answer, we will pick which window data structures to *maintain* as we slide the window (and remember, if you can't find appropriate window data structures, you can always try the binary search **guess-and-check technique** (pg 338).

Finally, we implement the sliding window. We recommend following some conventions such as those described on page 513. Here are some edge cases to keep an eye for:

•   Make sure to consider the case where no valid window is found, especially for minimization problems.

•   Make sure not to shrink an empty window or grow a window past the end of the array.

Even better, update your own personal Bug List (pg 172) with the edge cases that *you* tend to forget about.

Counting problems are less common, but we can use the trick to adapt the maximum window recipe to At-Most-K counting problems (pg 532). For Exactly-K/At-Least-K counting problems, see the reusable idea for transforming them to At-Most-K problems (pg 534).

For maximization problems without the maximum window property (pg 525) or minimization problems without the minimum window property (pg 528), sliding windows may be the wrong technique! Consider other techniques commonly used on subarray problems, like two pointers, prefix sums, and dynamic programming.

Sliding window triggers: The input type is just an array of numbers or a string, and maybe a number. The lower bound is linear.

Keywords: subarray, substring, length, contiguous, consecutive, range, longest, or shortest.

At this point, you should be ready to start adding sliding window problems to your practice rotation. You can find the problems in this chapter and additional problems in the companion AI interviewer.

 **ONLINE RESOURCES**

Online resources for this chapter include:

- A chance to try each problem in this chapter in AI Interviewer
- Interview replays that show specific mistakes people make with sliding windows problems
- Full code solutions for every problem in the chapter in multiple programming languages

Try online at bctci.co/sliding-windows.

## CHAPTER 39

BACKTRACKING

▶ *Prerequisites: Trees*

Our next three topics are tightly interrelated: backtracking, dynamic programming, and greedy algorithms. We want to introduce all three together because you'll often find yourself having to choose among them in an interview. This is best explored with an example:

✦ PROBLEM 39.1   MAX-SUM PATH

Given a non-empty grid of positive integers, grid, find the path from the top-left corner to the bottom-right corner with the largest sum. You can only go down or to the right (not diagonal).

▶ **Example:** grid = [[1, 4, 3],
                       [2, 7, 6],
                       [5, 8, 9]]
    Output: 29. The maximum path is 1 -> 4 -> 7 -> 8 -> 9.

▶ **Example:** grid = [[5]]
    Output: 5

We'll slowly build toward a solution to this problem, considering each approach.

Greedy Algorithm

If you tried to solve Example 1 for this problem by hand, your first thought might be to start at the top-left corner and look at the available choices: go down to the 2 or right to the 4. Since the goal is to maximize the sum, should we pick the direction of the larger one (4)? In this case, yes, the maximum path goes through the 4. But, can this be generalized? Should we *always* continue the path by going to the larger cell? This would be a *greedy algorithm*.

The idea of the greedy approach is to build the output step-by-step, **always picking the choice with the most instant gratification without taking into account the longer-term consequences.**

It is a promising idea, but it doesn't always lead to the max-sum path. Can you see why? Consider this input:
[[1, 5, 1],
 [2, 3, 1],
 [20, 1, 1]]

Greedy would see 2 and 5 as the options for the first choice and pick 5. However, that forces us to miss the 20 in the bottom-left corner later. This *counterexample* shows that Greedy is *suboptimal* for this problem—it returns a path, but it is not the max-sum path for every input. Check out Greedy Algorithms for more on greedy algorithms.

Usually, we use 'optimal' and 'suboptimal' to refer to the runtime and space analysis of an algorithm. In the context of optimization problems, we use 'optimal solution' to describe the output for a specific input which maximizes the objective of the problem, and we also say an algorithm is 'optimal' if it always finds the optimal solution/output (independently of how long it takes). Conversely, a 'suboptimal' algorithm is one that doesn't always find the optimal solution/output.

Backtracking

The path constructed by the greedy algorithm can be seen as following a path through a *decision tree*, where the root is the empty path, the internal nodes are partial paths, and the leaves are full paths:

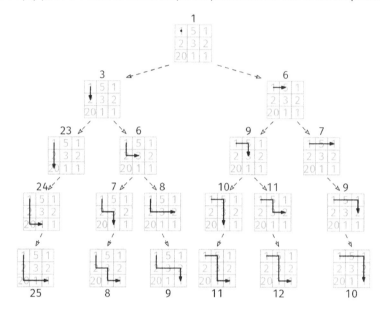

Figure 1. Decision tree for Problem 1. The number next to each partial path is the current sum for that partial path.

For the grid in Figure 1, Greedy doesn't follow the decisions that lead to the optimal solution (25). It would go `1 -> 5 -> 3 -> 2 -> 1`.

To guarantee we find the optimal path, instead of trying to be smart like Greedy, we can be exhaustive and *consider all possible paths in the decision tree.* That is the core idea of backtracking. Like in Greedy, backtracking starts with an *empty solution* and builds up an answer by making decisions until we have a *complete solution*. The 'backtracking' part is not stopping at the first one. Instead, we undo our last decision and try the next option we haven't explored yet. Even if it takes a long time, backtracking eventually finds the best solution.

The downside of being exhaustive is that it blows up the time complexity. For instance, in a `10x10` grid, the number of paths is already `48,620`.[1] As we'll see, **backtracking algorithms typically take exponential time or worse.**

To find all the possible paths, we'll revisit a familiar algorithm later in this chapter: depth-first search (DFS).

> The core idea of backtracking is doing a DFS through a decision tree rather than a given binary tree (like in the Tree chapters, pg 435) or a graph (pg 464).

---

1   The exact number of such paths on a nxn grid is (`2n-2 choose n-1`) because the paths have `2n-2` steps, of which `n-1` of them are 'down' and we can choose any of the `2n-2` steps to be the 'down' ones. In big O terms, this is $O(4^n/\sqrt{n})$.

Dynamic Programming

We've seen that greedy algorithms are fast but may miss the optimal solution (depending on the problem), whereas backtracking always finds the optimal solution but is slow. The third related technique, dynamic programming (DP), sometimes allows us to get the best of both worlds (again, it depends on the problem).

The key idea of DP is that the exhaustive nature of backtracking sometimes leads to repeated work that can be eliminated. In Figure 1, we can see that backtracking reaches cell (1, 1) in two different ways. No matter how we get there, the optimal path from there to the bottom-right corner won't change. It is wasteful and repetitive to fully explore the decision tree from the same cell (r, c) more than once. Instead, the idea of DP is that we can do it only once and store the optimal path for the next time we get to (r, c). Conceptually, we can think of each subgrid as a *subproblem*[2] with its own solution that we can *store (or 'memoize', in DP parlance) and reuse:*

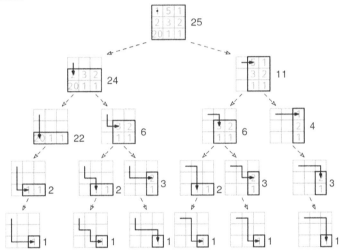

Figure 2. In the decision tree, the remaining subgrid from each cell in the path can be seen as a subproblem with its own optimal solution. The subproblem at each node is highlighted with a box with its optimal solution next to it. We can see that even in a small 3x3 grid, there are many *overlapping subproblems.*

Avoiding recalculating answers pays big! We will see an O(R*C) solution for this problem in the Dynamic Programming chapter (pg 571).

GREEDY VS DP VS BACKTRACKING

It's hard to know whether you should use greedy, DP, or backtracking. Even though backtracking is slow, it can still be the right answer in a technical interview under the right circumstances.

Should I use Greedy, DP, or backtracking?

- **Greedy is the right choice when...** you can show that it always finds the optimal solution (there are no counterexamples). Due to its simplicity, when it works, it will often be the best choice in terms of time and space complexity. Whether a greedy algorithm exists or not depends on the problem, and it can be hard to tell (more on that on page 587).

- **DP is the right choice when...** you can find overlapping subproblems.[3]

---

2 Another piece of confusing notation: by "subproblem" we mean "a smaller input for the same problem," like a subgrid of a grid.

3 Even if you think Greedy works, sometimes it can be easier to implement DP than to prove that greedy works. For instance, see Problem 24.6: Hiring And Training (pg 258).

- **Backtracking is the right choice when...** there are no overlapping subproblems that can be stored and reused (i.e., DP cannot be applied) and an exponential runtime is acceptable according to our boundary thinking. Backtracking always finds the optimal solution, so we don't have to worry about that.

One reason why it is hard to choose between the three is that slight variations on the problem statement can change the best choice. For instance:

- DP is the best choice for Problem 1 (max-sum path).
- On page 589, we show a variant where Greedy *does* work and is faster than DP.
- Question 4: 4-Directional Max-Sum Path (pg 547) is a variant where DP *doesn't* work and backtracking is optimal.

This means we can't have a simple trigger like, "Use <X> for grid path problems." It depends on the details.

Boundary thinking can be incredibly helpful in deciding when to use backtracking. There are three main conditions:

1. A small maximum input size (in the low 2 digits) means exponential runtimes are acceptable, and backtracking is likely the sought solution.
2. The problem is an *enumeration problem*, meaning that it asks to return all possible solutions (e.g., all top-left to bottom-right paths in a grid). Enumeration problems often have exponential-size outputs, making an exponential runtime not only acceptable but required. This makes backtracking optimal, so we don't need to consider other options.
3. If you identify that the problem is a well-known *NP-complete problem* (pg 226), in which case exponential time is the best we can do.

Without these conditions, we often must decide between DP and a greedy approach. Statistically, DP is more common in interviews than Greedy.

> Backtracking itself is a *trigger* to try Greedy and DP approaches, so if you're considering a backtracking solution, be sure to consider if these better options can work before coding anything.
>
> That said, candidates often spend a whole interview searching for a better solution to a problem when it does not exist. Use cues from the interviewer, express your concern about large input sizes, and leverage boundary thinking. Don't fear coding a "bad backtracking answer" in a Big Tech interview. Sometimes backtracking is the best you can do.

We recommend reading the DP and Greedy chapters directly after this one.

TYPES OF BACKTRACKING PROBLEMS

Backtracking can help us solve four main problem types: *feasibility*, *enumeration*, *counting*, and *optimization*. To illustrate them all, consider the classic subset sum problem:

Given an array of integers, arr, return whether there is a non-empty subset that adds up to 0.

▶ **Example:** arr = [5, 1, -2, 7, -14, -4]
  Output: True. 5 + 1 + (-2) + (-4) = 0.
▶ **Example:** arr = [5, 1, -2, 7, -14, -2]
  Output: False.
▶ **Example:** arr = [2, -3, 0]
  Output: True. 0 = 0.
▶ **Example:** arr = [2, 2, -4]
  Output: True. 2 + 2 + (-4) = 0.

Subset sum is a 'feasibility' problem because it asks whether it is feasible to find a *valid solution* (a non-empty subset with sum 0). We could also formulate enumeration, counting, and optimization variants of this problem:

Type	Objective	Subset Sum Variant	Output
Feasibility	Is there *any* valid solution?	Is there any non-empty subset that adds up to 0?	True/False (or the valid solution found)
Enumeration	Find *all* valid solutions.	Find all subsets that add up to 0.	A list of solutions.
Counting	*How many* valid solutions are there?	How many subsets add up to 0?	A number.
Optimization	Among all valid solutions, return the one *optimizing* some objective.	Find the smallest non-empty subset that adds up to 0 (if any).	The value of the optimal solution (or the solution itself).

Table 1. Types of backtracking problems.

All four variations of this problem have the same decision tree, and they can all be solved by doing a DFS on that same decision tree.[4] *In all cases, the solutions are subsets, which we can build by starting with an empty subset and making a decision for each element: pick it for the subset or not.*

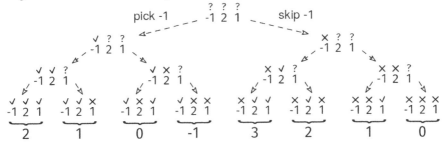

Figure 3. Decision tree for subset sum. At each step, we decide to pick (left child) or skip (right child) one element. At the leaves, we have decided on each element. The sum of the subset at each leaf is shown under it.

The only difference is what we do with the tree:

- **Feasibility version:** return whether there is *any* leaf with sum 0 (other than the empty subset, which doesn't count in any of the versions).
- **Enumeration version:** return *all* leaves with a sum of 0.
- **Counting:** count the number of leaves with a sum of 0.
- **Optimization:** among all the leaves with sum 0, return the one with the *smallest* subset.

In a feasibility problem, we can stop the decision tree DFS as soon as we find one valid solution, but in the worst case, we'll still traverse the whole tree. For the other types, we are usually stuck exploring the whole tree.

DECISION TREE MODELING

Backtracking can be broken down into two steps:

3. Model the problem as a decision tree.

---

4 Subset sum is one of those NP-complete problems, meaning that no polynomial-time algorithm is known. Greedy and DP cannot help us beat the exponential runtime.

4. Implement a DFS through the decision tree.

In this section, we'll go over the first step. It has little to do with coding—it's only about modeling how to get to the solution (or all solutions) as a sequence of decisions. We haven't shown any code yet because if we can first get a clear picture of the decision tree, the implementation part will feel a lot more intuitive.

If you can clearly visualize the decision tree, implementing backtracking will become a lot easier. We recommend drawing it out when possible, on paper if necessary.

We've already seen decision trees for a couple of problems. Here are a few more:

Jumping Numbers: A *jumping number* is a positive integer where every two consecutive digits differ by one, such as 2343. We can design a decision tree to find all jumping numbers smaller than some value n (Problem 39.6: Jumping Numbers, pg 557). We start with 0 digits and, at each step, we add one more digit. For the first digit, we have 9 choices. After that, we have two choices, the next larger digit or the next smaller digit (except for 0 and 9, which only have one choice).

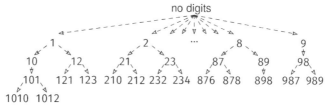

Figure 4. Decision tree for finding all jumping numbers smaller than 1200. Some of the children of the root are omitted for brevity.

In this decision tree, jumping numbers are not only in the leaves—all the numbers in internal nodes are also jumping numbers.

Balanced Parentheses: On page 385, we talked about strings of balanced parentheses, such as "(())()". We can design a decision tree to find all balanced parentheses strings of some (even) length, n. We can model this as a decision tree where we start with an empty string and, at each step, we decide whether to add '(' or ')'.

Further, we don't always need to go all the way down to length n. We can avoid partial strings that are already unbalanced. For instance, any string starting with ()) cannot be 'fixed' later, so we don't need to visit it nor extend it into longer strings like ())(and ())). This is called *pruning*. The more we prune, the smaller the decision tree, making the backtracking DFS faster (at least in the constant factors).

When generating balanced parentheses, we can prune:

- Any partial string with more closing parentheses than opening ones.

- Any partial string with more than n/2 opening parentheses.

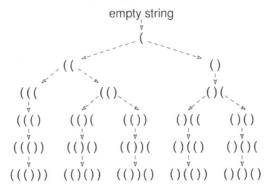

Figure 5. Decision tree for finding all balanced parentheses strings of length 6.

In backtracking, **pruning** is an optimization where we "prune" (i.e., don't visit) branches of the decision tree when we know for sure that it won't lead to a valid solution.

Pruning is problem-specific, so look for opportunities to do it. It usually does not change the asymptotic size of the decision tree, but it is one of the ways in which we can showcase problem-solving skills when using backtracking.

Traveling Salesperson Problem (TSP): This is a classic graph optimization problem. One of the versions goes as follows: given a set of cities represented by points in the plane, what is the shortest path that goes through all of them and ends at the starting city?

We can model this as a decision problem: we pick an arbitrary city as a starting point (it doesn't matter which one since they all need to be in the cycle). Then, we build a path step by step by choosing where to go next among the remaining unvisited cities. Once we've visited every city, the only thing that remains is going back to the initial city.

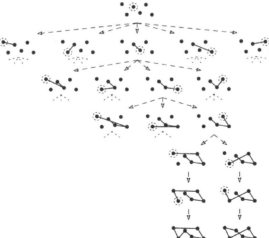

Figure 6. Decision tree for TSP with six cities. We omitted most of it for brevity, showing only the children of one node at each level. The circled city at each node is the one from which we are extending the path.

In Figure 6, we omitted most of the decision tree because it grows really fast: with 6 cities, after picking one of them as a starting point, we have 5 choices for where to go next, and then 4, and then 3, and so on. In total, there are over (n-1)! nodes.

Drawing Advice

Even candidates who know how backtracking works still get stuck figuring out the implementation. We advise taking the time to draw the decision tree before implementing anything.

Our advice for drawing decision trees is similar to the drawing advice in the Trees chapter (pg 435). However, in backtracking questions, the tree may be huge. We recommend using either a tiny input or drawing just enough to give you a sense of the tree structure.

Finally, it may be a good idea to keep pen and paper close in case it's hard to draw the tree in an editor.

DECISION TREE MODELING PROBLEM SET

Model each of the following problems as finding a leaf or set of leaves in a decision tree. Think about the sequence of decisions that you need to make and whether you can prune any of them. We recommend drawing the decision tree for each problem. Do not code anything yet.

QUESTION 1   N-QUEENS PUZZLE

In Problem 28.1: Chess Moves (pg 314), we described the movement of a queen in chess.[5] Find all the ways to place n queens on an nxn board without any two of them being in the same row, column, or diagonal.

Figure 7. One of the possible solutions to the 8-queens puzzle.

QUESTION 2   K-COMBINATION SUM

Given an array of unique integers, arr, and a positive number k, find whether there is any subset of arr of size k that adds up to 0.

QUESTION 3   GRAPH COLORING

Given an undirected, connected graph, and a positive number k, find whether it is possible to assign a color to each node, using only k different colors, in such a way that adjacent nodes always have different colors (there is no limit for how many nodes can have the same color, as long as they are not adjacent).

---

5   The queen can move any number of cells in any direction, including diagonals.

Figure 8. A valid coloring of a graph with 2 colors.

| QUESTION 4 | 4-DIRECTIONAL MAX-SUM PATH |

Given an RxC grid with positive and negative integers, find the path from the top-left cell to the bottom-right cell that maximizes the sum. You can go in all four directions (diagonals not allowed), but you **can't visit a cell more than once**.

PROBLEM SET SOLUTIONS

ANSWER 1   N-QUEENS PUZZLE

There are a few ways we could model this puzzle as a decision tree. One *PROPERTY* we can use is that, to have n queens on an nxn board, each row must have exactly one queen. We can start with an empty grid. Then, we decide where to put a queen in the first row. At each step, we decide where to put a queen in the next empty row. We can **prune** columns and diagonals that already have a queen.

ANSWER 2   K-COMBINATION SUM

This would be like the decision tree for Subset Sum (Figure 3), except we stop at nodes that already picked k elements.

ANSWER 3   GRAPH COLORING

At the beginning, every node is uncolored. Then, we need to make a decision for each node: which of the k colors to assign to it. When choosing colors for a node, we can **prune** the colors of any neighbor that has already been colored.

ANSWER 4   4-DIRECTIONAL MAX-SUM PATH

This would be like the decision tree for the Max-Sum Path problem (Figure 1) except that we would have extra children to also go up and left when the cells in those directions are not visited yet. We would also have to avoid revisiting cells already in the path, which means we could end at a dead end surrounded by already-visited cells (Figure 9). We should **prune** such branches. We'll later see a full solution (pg 563).

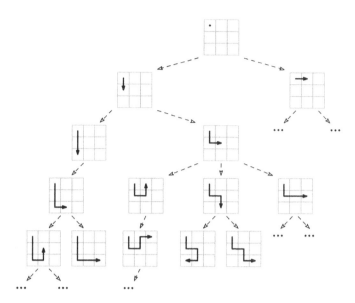

Figure 9. Part of the decision tree, including two full solutions (paths that reach the bottom-right corner) and a dead end.

Can there be more than one valid decision tree for a problem?

For most problems, yes! In the N-Queens problem, we could model a decision tree by placing queens by:

- By row,
- By column,
- With a binary choice per cell to place a queen or not.

Some decision trees may be larger than others. The best decision trees are those with the fewest nodes—we should keep that in mind when modeling a problem as a decision tree.

IMPLEMENTATION

When you think 'backtracking', think 'recursion'. We explore the decision tree through recursion.

At each point, we have a decision to make, such as: Do we go down or to the right? We'll try both. Go down (recursively). Then, after that's done, go right (recursively).

Another way to think about this is that we're doing DFS on the decision tree, just like we might on a binary tree. But, in this case, the tree doesn't actually fully exist in memory. Instead, we'll use the DFS to carry the required information about the partial solution at each node as we visit them.

SOLUTION 39.1   MAX-SUM PATH

As we mentioned, the optimal solution to this problem uses DP, and we'll see it in the next chapter (pg 573). But just to make this 'DFS on a decision tree' idea concrete, this is how we implement a DFS through the decision tree in Figure 1 to solve Problem 1.

```
1   def max_sum_path(grid):  # Inefficient backtracking solution. DP is better!
```

```
2      max_sum = -math.inf
3      R, C = len(grid), len(grid[0])
4      def visit(r, c, cur_sum):
5        nonlocal max_sum
6        if r == R - 1 and c == C - 1:
7          max_sum = max(max_sum, cur_sum)
8          return
9        if r+1 < R:
10         visit(r + 1, c, cur_sum + grid[r + 1][c]) #  Go down.
11       if c+1 < C:
12         visit(r, c + 1, cur_sum + grid[r][c + 1]) #  Go right.
13       visit(0, 0, grid[0][0])
14       return max_sum
```

If we run the code with the same input as in Figure 1, there will be one `visit()` call for each node in Figure 1. Each `visit()` call receives the current endpoint of the partial path (r and c) and the sum of the cells in the partial path so far (the numbers on top of each node in Figure 1).

Note that:

- The *root* of the decision tree corresponds to `(r, c)` = `(0, 0)` and `cur_sum` = `grid[0][0]`.
- At each node, we obtain the *children* by considering our choices: either increasing r or c (as long as it doesn't push us out of bounds). As in normal DFS, we recursively explore the children one by one.
- We know we are at a *leaf* (i.e., a full solution) when `(r, c)` is `(R - 1, C - 1)`.

A common theme is that backtracking solutions can often be optimized with DP. We should only use backtracking for the *enumeration* version of this problem, where we want to list all different paths through the grid.

> Using backtracking on a grid-based problem like this problem is not like doing a traditional grid-based DFS (pg 482), where we keep track of a `visited` set to avoid exploring a cell more than once. With backtracking, the "head" of the partial path may reach the same cell in multiple ways after retracing previous steps (see Figure 1).

We can capture a generic decision tree DFS in a recipe:

📋 **RECIPE 1. BACKTRACKING.**

```
def visit(partial_solution):
  if full_solution(partial_solution):
    # Process leaf/full solution.
  else:
    for choice in choices(partial_solution):
      # Prune children where possible.
      child = apply_choice(partial_solution)
      visit(child)
visit(empty_solution)
```

How is this different from a traditional tree DFS?

Binary Tree DFS

- The binary tree is given to us as an *explicit* input.

- The size of the input corresponds to the number of nodes in the tree.

- The time and space analysis is typically measured in terms of the number of nodes in the input, which we call n.

Backtracking DFS

- We need to model the problem as a decision tree ourselves.

- The input format could be almost anything.

- The size of the tree is typically exponential on the size of the input.

- The time can be analyzed with the **BAD method** (pg 402).

DESIGN CHOICES

For each problem, we'll need to fill in concrete details in Recipe 1 make some implementation choices:

1. **Solution state:** What data structures do we need to represent partial solutions?

2. **Child creation:** When we create a child, should we make new data structures for its state or modify the parent's state in place? As a rule of thumb, we'll modify data structures with non-constant-size like arrays or grids, as modifying is cheaper than creating new ones.

3. **Pruning:** Should we prune eagerly (when generating the children) or lazily (as a base case in visit())? In particular, do we check boundary conditions before recursing or after?

4. **Leaf processing:** What should we do with full solutions?

5. **Additional work optimization:** Can we improve the runtime per node (or per leaf) by passing any extra information down the call tree?

'Leaf processing' is the part that depends on the problem type. First, it involves checking if the full solution is valid. If it is, what we do with it differs:

- **Feasibility:** save it so we can return it at the end.

- **Enumeration:** appending the full solution to a 'global' array.[6]

- **Counting:** incrementing a 'global' counter.

- **Optimization:** updating a 'global' variable tracking the best solution so far, if it's better.

We don't need a different recipe for each problem type!

Let's see the decisions we made for the Max-Sum Path problem:

1. **Solution state:** for each partial solution, we only need the end of the partial path and the accumulated sum. Since we are just looking for the value of the solution and not the solution itself, we didn't need the entire partial path, so we don't bother passing it down the tree.

2. **Child creation:** since the data structures consist of just three integers, it is straightforward to create new integers. Modifying the data structures in place makes sense only when they are more complicated.

3. **Pruning:** we eagerly check if the children are out of bounds.

4. **Leaf processing:** all full solutions end at the bottom-right corner, so we don't need a validity check. Since this is an optimization problem, we update a 'global' variable with the best value seen so far.

5. **Additional work optimization:** we already spend O(1) time at each node, so there is no possible optimization here.

We'll see different design choices throughout the chapter.

---

6   As we discussed in the Trees chapter (pg 437), when we say 'global' we mean "shared by the entire recursive search, rather than a single call." It could also be a variable passed around by reference. The idiomatic way to do this depends on the language. In Python, we'll usually declare such variables in a function containing visit() as a nested function. In other languages, it could be a class-scoped variable.

SUBSETS & PERMUTATIONS

The two most important problems in backtracking are generating *subsets*[7] and *permutations* of a group of elements. Many backtracking problems are just extensions of these two ideas. For instance, the valid parentheses and subset sum problem decision trees we modeled earlier were subset-based problems, while the TSP and N-queens problems are examples of permutation-based problems.

✦ PROBLEM 39.2   SUBSET ENUMERATION

Given a set of elements, S, a subset of S is another set obtained by removing any number of elements from S (including none or all of them). As usual with sets, order does not matter. Given an array of unique characters, return all possible subsets in any order.

▸ **Example:** S = ['x', 'y', 'z']
  Output: [[], ['x'], ['y'], ['z'], ['x', 'y'], ['x', 'z'], ['y', 'z'],
             ['x', 'y', 'z']]

SOLUTION 39.2   SUBSET ENUMERATION

Each subset is created by making a *decision* for each input element: pick it or skip it. For instance, the empty set excludes each element, and the full set includes every element. The decision tree is like the one in Figure 3 (pg 431).

We'll first look at the code and then explain the implementation choices we made:

```
1   def all_subsets(S):
2     res = []    # Global list of subsets.
3     subset = [] # State of the current partial solution.
4     def visit(i):
5       if i == len(S):
6         res.append(subset.copy())
7         return
8       # Choice 1: pick S[i].
9       subset.append(S[i])
10      visit(i + 1)
11      subset.pop()  # Cleanup work: undo choice 1.
12      # Choice 2: skip S[i].
13      visit(i + 1)
14    visit(0)
15    return res
```

Unlike in the recipe, we don't need a for loop for the choices because, for this problem, there are only 2.

- **Solution state:** subset is the current subset at each node in the decision tree, while i is the next element for which we need to make a decision.
- **Child creation:** we share the same subset array between parents and children by modifying it in place in O(1) time. The complication that comes with that is that, after we add S[i] and recursively visit the child, we need to do the **cleanup work** of popping S[i] out again (see Figure 10). We recommend experimenting with this code, printing out subset at each step with and without this cleanup step.
- **Pruning:** there's no pruning—to generate all subsets, we must always visit both children.

---

7 Also sometimes called **combinations** in the coding interview setting.

- **Leaf processing:** we append a copy of subset to a global solution array. It must be a copy, or we would mess it up after the fact as we start popping from subset further up the recursion tree.[8]
- **Additional work optimization:** we spend O(1) time at internal nodes and O(n) time at the leaves, which is needed to make a copy of subset, so there's no room to optimize anything for this problem.

The line that people find most confusing is:

```
11    subset.pop()  # Cleanup work: undo choice 1.
```

Figure 10 illustrates how subset changes throughout the lifetime of the program:

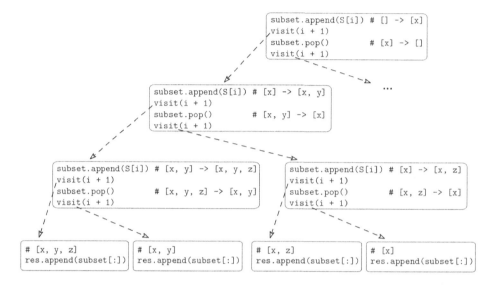

Figure 10. First half of the call tree in Solution 2. The comments show the evolution of the subset state.

 REUSABLE IDEA: MODIFY -> RECURSE -> UNDO

> When you make a mess, clean it up. In backtracking, if you modify a global variable before calling visit() recursively, you must do the opposite change immediately upon returning from visit(). Code how you make the mess and how you clean it up symmetrically. For example, if you append to an array right before your recursive call, pop from it right after (not in the recursive function).[9]

There isn't a single option when it comes to design choices. There are often trade-offs. Here are some common alternatives for generating subsets:

- **Solution state**: a perfectly fine alternative would be to use a boolean array with a boolean for each element, indicating whether we picked it or not. At the leaves, we would then use this array to construct the subset.

  An example of a non-ideal choice would be storing the remaining elements for which we still have to make a decision in a separate variable. Using the index i is cleaner.

---

8 One of the most common—and most vexing—backtracking mistakes is forgetting to store a copy in the result variable. If you forget to do this, and your language defaults to storing references rather than copies, you'll end up with 2^n references in your result array all with the same final global state! If your output is a list of empty lists, this could be the reason.

9 You can avoid having to worry about cleanups by making copies of the parent's state for each child. This can simplify the code but it increases the time and space we use at each node.

View online materials for Beyond Cracking the Coding Interview at bctci.co

- **Child creation:** we could make a copy of subset for each child. Avoiding shared state between parents and children makes the implementation easier because we wouldn't need to do the cleanup step undoing the modification. However, it increases the time per internal node to O(len(S)).

Poor design choices can lead to verbose and clunky solutions.

PROBLEM 39.3   PERMUTATION ENUMERATION

A *permutation* of a list is a list with the same elements but in any order. Finding all permutations means finding all possible orderings of the input elements. Given a non-empty array of unique characters, arr, return all possible permutations, in any order.

▶ **Example:** arr = ['x', 'y', 'z']
  Output: [['x', 'y', 'z'], ['x', 'z', 'y'], ['y', 'x', 'z'], ['y', 'z', 'x'],
            ['z', 'x', 'y'], ['z', 'y', 'x']]

SOLUTION 39.3   PERMUTATION ENUMERATION

First, we should model the decision tree. We start with an empty list, but we no longer make a binary choice to include or exclude each element. Instead, each decision is a choice about which of the remaining elements to put next:

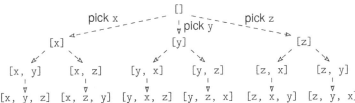

Figure 11.

We can use an array, perm, to store the elements we picked so far. This raises two questions:

1. How do we pick the next element of our current permutation?

2. How do we know which elements we have already used and which are still remaining?

At each node, we could (1) iterate through the input array to find elements to add next, and (2) for each one, iterate through the current partial permutation to check if it is already picked or not.

This would work, but there is a trick we can use to simplify the logic: we keep all the elements in perm, but use an index i to separate those already picked and the remaining ones. Before i is the list we picked so far, and the remaining ones are after that. The index i starts at 0. At each step, we can pick any elements between index i and n-1. When we pick an element at some index j, with j > i, we move it to index i, and swap the element that was at index i to j (it doesn't matter where the element that was at index i ends up—it only matters that it is in the "not picked yet" region).

Figure 12. The partial solution at each node when using the trick of keeping the remaining elements in the same array. The underlined elements are the picked ones. All the remaining elements can be picked next.

```
1   def generate_permutations(arr):
2     res = []
3     perm = arr.copy()
4     def visit(i):
5       if i == len(perm) - 1:
6         res.append(perm.copy())
7         return
8       for j in range(i, len(perm)):
9         perm[i], perm[j] = perm[j], perm[i]  # Pick perm[j].
10        visit(i + 1)
11        perm[i], perm[j] = perm[j], perm[i]  # Cleanup work: undo change.
12      visit(0)
13      return res
```

A couple of details:

- The base case is len(arr) - 1 because, when there is only one element left, there are no choices left (the nodes at level 2 in Figure 11 only have one child). Using len(arr) would work as well.

- For the first choice, when i == j, the swap has no effect, but that is working as intended. We could handle that case separately and start the loop at i + 1, but that takes one extra line of code.

As usual, there isn't a single way to represent solutions. If we didn't know the "swapping" trick, we could, e.g., use a set to track remaining elements.

▶ **AN IMMEDIATELY RECOGNIZABLE BACKTRACKING QUESTION**   INTERVIEW REPLAY

View Online:	bctci.co/backtracking-replay-1 @ 3:07 - 56:33
The Question:	Generate all valid strings up to a given length with a set of `allowed` characters.
What You'll See:	The candidate quickly identified that the question is a backtracking algorithm. The interviewer guided them towards increasing their algorithm's efficiency as much as possible.
Who:	*Interviewer*: Senior Software Engineer at Google *Candidate*: College student

ANALYSIS

DECISION TREE SIZE

The biggest factor in the runtime of a backtracking algorithm is the size of the decision tree.

In the Trees chapter (pg 450), we saw that a tree with depth d and maximum branching factor $b \geq 2$ has $O(b^d)$ nodes.

If you look at the decision trees we have seen so far, you'll notice that the depth is usually *linear* on the input size, and the branching factor is usually at least 2. This means that the number of nodes in a decision tree is usually exponential or worse. Backtracking often needs to traverse all of them, and that's why it is slow.

The number of leaves specifically is also $O(b^d)$ because, in a perfect binary tree, leaves alone account for more than half of the nodes (pg 450). For branching factors larger than 2, the portion of leaves is even larger.

APPLYING THE BAD METHOD

For the total runtime of backtracking, we can use the **BAD method** (pg 402):

BAD Method: If we have to traverse a decision tree with maximum branching factor $b \geq 2$, maximum depth d, and we do $O(A)$ *additional* work (not counting recursion) at every node/leaf, we can bound the runtime of backtracking by $O(b^d * A)$.

Let's apply it to the subset generation and permutation generation problems.

Subset generation analysis:

- Branching factor: 2 because we pick or skip each element.
- Depth: n+1 (see Figure 3).
- Additional work: $O(n)$ because we copy the array into our result variable at each leaf.
- Total runtime: $O(2^n * n)$.

Permutation generation analysis:

For permutation-based problems, the BAD method overshoots the analysis:

- Maximum branching factor: n, at the root.
- Depth: n (see Figure 12).
- Additional work: $O(n)$ because we copy the array into our result variable at each leaf.
- BAD method upper bound: $O(n^n * n)$

This is correct in the upper bound sense, but it is not tight. In order to give an upper bound, the BAD method assumes the worst-case scenario where the branching factor is as large as possible at every node.

For permutation-based problems, the root has n children, which have n-1 children, which have n-2 children, and so on. The total number of nodes is

$$n * (n-1) * (n-2) * \ldots * 1 = n!$$

Correcting for that in the BAD formula, the actual runtime is $O(n! * n)$ (we can also say that this is $O((n+1)!)$, but this is *not* equivalent to $O(n!)$).

> As a rule of thumb, subset-based problems have decision trees with size $O(2^n)$, while permutation-based problems have decision trees with size $O(n!)$.
>
> If you try to go beyond the BAD method, the analysis of the size of decision trees can get quite mathy. Luckily, the most important part is realizing that the complexity is not polynomial. Most interviewers won't be too concerned if we correctly call out that the complexity is exponential or factorial, but our analysis is not quite tight.

SPACE ANALYSIS

Enumeration problems, such as generating all subsets or permutations (Problems 2 and 3), are special in that their output size is exponential ($O(2n * n)$ and $O(n! * n)$, respectively), which is the bottleneck in the space complexity.

For other types of backtracking problems (feasibility, counting, and optimization), the space bottleneck is likely to be the global state or the recursion call stack (pg 392). The call stack is largest when we are at a leaf, at which point it takes $O(d * S)$ space, where d is the decision tree depth, and S is the space used at each node along the way.[10]

The child creation design choice often affects S: if we reuse the same data structures, S is usually constant. If we make a copy of the data structures, S is usually linear.

OPTIMIZING BACKTRACKING

The runtime of backtracking algorithms largely depends on how big the decision tree is. While we usually can't do better than exponential size, we can reduce its size in two ways:

Approach 1. Picking the best decision tree when modeling the problem. There can be many ways to model a problem as a decision tree. Some will be smaller than others.

For instance, in the 8-queens puzzle, we can (from worst to best):

1. Make a decision for each square whether to put a queen or not. This results in $O(2^{n*n}) \approx 2^{64}$ leaves.
2. Make a decision for each square whether to put a queen or not, but stop at n queens. The number of leaves becomes $O(n^2 \text{ choose } n) \approx 2^{48}$.
3. Choose a square for each row. This results in $O(n^n) \approx 8^8 = 2^{24}$ leaves.
4. Find all permutations of $[1, 2, \ldots, n]$, and, for each permutation perm, assign a queen to $(i, perm[i])$. This avoids placing two queens in the same column, resulting in $O(n!) \approx 8! < 2^{16}$ leaves.

While still not polynomial, we went from super-exponential size to factorial size.

Approach 2. Pruning. Once we have a decision tree, we can proactively look for nodes that won't lead to valid solutions and remove them from the tree.

For instance, in the 8-queens puzzle, we can rule out any squares already attacked by a queen. If we do so proactively, we'll only reach 92 leaves, which is the actual number of solutions.

> It depends on the problem, but pruning usually doesn't affect the runtime complexity class since it typically doesn't change the depth or the maximum branching factor of the decision tree. In contrast, choosing a better decision tree in the first place can easily improve the runtime.

If pruning is like chopping branches off a tree, picking the best decision tree is like having a Bonsai tree instead of a sprawling oak tree in the first place.

Finally, we can optimize the additional work at each node by making careful design choices (pg 550). However, the sub-exponential factor of the runtime should not be the main focus.

PROBLEM SET

✦✦ *Try these problems with AI Interviewer: bctci.co/backtracking-problem-set-1*

Backtracking requires practice, so try out the following problems. Don't be afraid to start by drawing out the decision tree. Consider which design choices will make your life easiest before coding, and don't forget to analyze the runtime.

---

10 The space usage is also why it is almost never a good idea to use BFS rather than DFS to traverse a decision tree. It works, but the space complexity is usually a lot worse. In BFS, we need to store all the nodes for a given level at the same time, which would take exponential space. With recursion, we only need to store a path a nodes from the root, which is linear.

TO BE OR NOT TO BE

Inspired by Shakespeare's iconic line, you decide to write a function, `shakespearify()`, which takes in a string, `sentence`, consisting of lowercase letters and spaces. For each word in the string, the function chooses if it should "be" or "not be" included in the sentence, returning all possible outcomes. The order of the output strings does not matter.

▸ **Example:** `sentence = "I love dogs"`
    `Output:  ["", "I", "love", "dogs", "I love", "I dogs", "love dogs",`
             `"I love dogs"]`

THESAURUSLY

Given a non-empty string, `sentence`, and a non-empty map, `synonyms`, where each key is a single word in the sentence, and its value is a list of synonyms, return all possible sentences that can be created by replacing the words in the sentence with their synonyms. Words without synonyms should remain unchanged. The input `sentence` only contains lowercase letters and spaces, while the words in `synonyms` only contain lowercase letters. The order of the generated sentences in the output does not matter.

▸ **Example:** `sentence = "one does not simply walk into mordor"`
            `synonyms = {`
               `"walk": ["stroll", "hike", "wander"],`
               `"simply": ["just", "merely"]`
            `}`
    `Output: ["one does not just stroll into mordor",  "one does not just hike`
            `into mordor",  "one does not just wander into mordor",  "one does`
            `not merely stroll into mordor",  "one does not merely hike into`
            `mordor",  "one does not merely wander into mordor"]`

JUMPING NUMBERS

A *jumping number* is a positive integer where every two consecutive digits differ by one, such as 2343. Given a positive integer, n, return all jumping numbers smaller than n, ordered from smallest to largest.

▸ **Example:** n = 34.
    `Output: [1, 2, 3, 4, 5, 6, 7, 8, 9, 10, 12, 21, 23, 32]`

IKEA SHOPPING

A magazine has rated every IKEA item from 1 to 10 in terms of style. We have gone to IKEA with a limited budget and the goal of maximizing the sum of style ratings of the items we buy. We also don't want to pick more than one of each item. We are given 3 things:

- `budget`, a positive integer,
- `prices`, an array of n positive integers,
- `ratings`, an array of n positive floating-point numbers between 0 and 10 (inclusive).

There are n items. Item i has price `prices[i]` and style rating `ratings[i]`. Return an array with the indices of the items that we should buy.

▸ **Example:** `budget = 20`
            `prices =  [10,  5,   15,  8,   3]`
            `ratings = [7.0, 3.5, 9.0, 6.0, 2.0]`
    `Output:  [0, 3]. With items 0 and 3, we get a rating sum of 13 without`
            `exceeding the budget.`
▸ **Example:** `budget = 10`

```
            prices = [2,   3,   4,   5]
            ratings = [1.0, 2.0, 3.5, 4.0]
    Output: [2, 3]
    Constraints: n ≤ 15
                 budget ≤ 10⁶
                 prices[i] ≤ 10⁴ for all i
```

PROBLEM 39.8   **WHITE HAT HACKER**

You are trying to hack into an account (for good reasons, I'm sure). You know that the password:

- has at least 1 and at most 10 letters,
- uses only lowercase English letters,
- does not repeat any letter.

You have a script that tries to log in with a given password and returns a boolean indicating if it was successful. Write a function to find the password. You can call check_password(s) to check if s is the password.

▸ **Example:** check_password("a")   # returns False
            check_password("abc") # returns False
            check_password("ac") # returns False
            check_password("ab") # returns False
            check_password("bc") # returns True
  Output: "bc"

PROBLEM 39.9   **COUNT UNIQUE SUBMULTISETS WITH SUM ZERO**

A *multiset* is a set that allows repeated elements. A *submultiset* of a multiset S is another multiset obtained by removing any number of elements from S. We are given an array with n integers representing a multiset (it can have *duplicates*). Return the number of *unique submultisets* of S with sum 0, ignoring which position in S the values came from.

▸ **Example:** S = [1, 1, -1, -1]
  Output: 3. The unique submultisets with sum 0 are [], [1, 1, -1, -1] and
            [1, -1]. The last one can be obtained in more than one way.
▸ **Example:** S = []
  Output: 1. [] is a submultiset of [] with sum 0.
▸ **Example:** S = [-1, 2, 1, 0, 3]
  Output: 4. The unique submultiset with sum 0 are [-1, 1], [-1, 1, 0],
            [0], and [].

PROBLEM 39.10   **4-DIRECTIONAL MAX-SUM PATH**

Given an RxC grid of integers (which can be negative), grid, return the path from the top-left corner to the bottom-right corner with the largest sum. You can go in all four directions (diagonals not allowed), but you *can't visit a cell more than once*.

▸ **Example:** grid = [[1, -4, 3],
                  [-2, 7, -6],
                  [5, -4, 9]]
  Output: [[0, 0], [0, 1], [1, 1], [1, 0], [2, 0], [2, 1], [2, 2]]
            The maximum path is 1 -> -4 -> 7 -> -2 -> 5 -> -4 -> 9, which has
            sum 12.

| PROBLEM 39.11 | ESCAPE WITH ALL CLUES |

We are building an escape room puzzle where a player has to collect all the clues in a room to unlock the way out. The room is represented by a non-empty grid, room, consisting of walkable spaces (0), obstacles (1), and clues (2). The player starts on the top-left cell of the grid, which is guaranteed to be an open space, and can move to adjacent cells (diagonals not allowed). If it is possible to collect all the clues *without repeating any cell,* return an array with the list of cells in the shortest path to collect them, starting with [0, 0]. Otherwise, return an empty array. If there are multiple shortest paths, return any of them. It is guaranteed that there is at least one clue.

▶ **Example:** room = [[0, 1, 0],
                      [0, 2, 0],
                      [0, 0, 2]]
   Output: [[0,0], [1,0], [1,1], [1,2], [2,2]]. The other valid output is
             [[0,0], [1,0], [1,1], [2,1], [2,2]].

▶ **Example:** room = [[0, 0, 0],
                      [2, 1, 2]]
   Output: []. It is not possible to get both clues without revisiting a cell.

▶ **Example:** room = [[0, 0, 1, 2],
                      [0, 1, 0, 0]]
   Output: []. It is not possible to reach the clue.

✣ PROBLEM SET SOLUTIONS

SOLUTION 39.4   TO BE OR NOT TO BE

This problem is a variant of the Subset Enumeration problem. Instead of focusing on individual characters, we must pick or skip entire words. The simplest way is to split the string into words in a **preprocessing step** before doing the recursive DFS. The picked words can be joined again into a string at the leaves.

SOLUTION 39.5   THEASAURUSLY

We can build the output sentences one word at a time. For words without synonyms, keeping the word the same is the only choice. For words with synonyms, we have a choice per synonym.

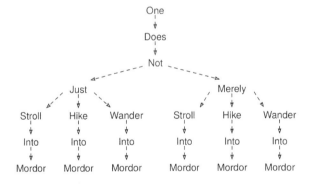

Figure 13.

```
1   def generate_sentences(sentence, synonyms):
2       words = sentence.split()
3       res = []
```

```
4      cur_sentence = []
5      def visit(i):
6        if i == len(words):
7          res.append(" ".join(cur_sentence))
8          return
9        if words[i] not in synonyms:
10         choices = [words[i]]
11       else:
12         choices = synonyms.get(words[i])
13       for choice in choices:
14         cur_sentence.append(choice)
15         visit(i + 1)
16         cur_sentence.pop()  # Undo change.
17     visit(0)
18     return res
```

The depth of the decision tree is n, the number of words in sentence. The maximum branching factor is the maximum number of synonyms of any word. Since this is a decision tree where many nodes could have a single child, instead of using the BAD method, we can try to be a bit more precise.

When a word in sentence has k synonyms, the nodes in the decision tree split into k children. Thus, the total number of leaves is the product of the number of synonyms of each word in sentence. Let's call this L. In the example in Figure 13, L = 2 * 3 = 6. Since each level has at most L nodes, the size of the decision tree is O(n * L). The total runtime is O(n * L * w), where w is the maximum length of an output sentence.

SOLUTION 39.6   JUMPING NUMBERS

We already saw the decision tree for this problem (Figure 4, pg 544): we start with no digits, and we add digits one by one, respecting the 'jumping number' constraint. There are two things to keep in mind:

1. The numbers at non-leaf nodes are valid jumping numbers too, so we need to add to the global output array at every node, not only the leaves.

2. The backtracking visit order is not the sorted order. In the sorted order, 2 goes after 1, but in the recursive DFS order, we would find all numbers starting with 1, like 12, before getting to 2. We can add a sorting **postprocessing step** at the end.[11]

```
1    def jumping_numbers(n):
2      res = []
3      def visit(num):
4        if num >= n:
5          return
6        res.append(num)
7        last_digit = num % 10
8        if last_digit > 0:
9          visit(num * 10 + (last_digit - 1))
10       if last_digit < 9:
11         visit(num * 10 + (last_digit + 1))
12     for num in range(1, 10):
13       visit(num)
14     return sorted(res)
```

---

11 To avoid having to sort, we could use BFS instead of DFS. Since this is an enumeration problem and we need to store all jumping numbers in the output array, the BFS queue would not be the space bottleneck. While BFS is faster by a logarithmic factor for this problem, it's probably not worth the effort learning to BFS over decision trees when DFS covers the majority of cases.

The logic for extracting and adding the least significant digit works as follows:

- If x is a positive integer, x % 10 is the least significant digit.
- If x is a positive integer and we want to add a new least significant digit, d, we can do x = x * 10 + d.

We prune numbers that are too large. For convenience, we do it lazily.

For the analysis, we can apply the BAD method:

- Besides the root, the maximum branching factor is 2. The root has a branching factor of 9 but, since it is only one node, we can ignore it. Having 9 children at the root blows up the runtime by a factor of 9, which is a constant factor.
- The depth of the tree is the number of digits of n, i.e., $\log_{10}(n)$.
- The additional work at each node is $O(1)$.

Per the BAD method, the total runtime is $O(2^{\log\_10(n)})$. If we remember the property of logarithms that $O(a^{\log\_b(c)}) = O(c^{\log\_b(a)})$, we can further simplify it to $O(n^{\log\_10(2)}) = O(n^{0.302})$.[12]

Upon seeing this problem, some people think, "Since backtracking is so slow, I might as well simply iterate through all the numbers from 1 to n and check which ones are jumping numbers." However, $O(n^{0.302})$ is much smaller than $O(n)$. For instance, $1000^{0.302} \approx 16$.

 REUSABLE IDEA: EXTRACTING AND ADDING DIGITS

In some problems, we need to handle integers digit by digit. The following loop extracts all the digits of x and returns them as an array, from least to most significant:

```
1   arr = []
2   while x > 0:
3       arr.append(x % 10)   # Extract the last digit.
4       x = x // 10   # Remove the last digit.
```

If x = 123, we'll get arr = [3, 2, 1]. We can reassemble x like this (note that we reverse arr):

```
1   x = 0
2   for digit in reversed(arr):
3       x = x * 10 + digit
```

The same idea applies if we need to handle integers bit by bit instead.

SOLUTION 39.7   IKEA SHOPPING

This is a variation of the classic Knapsack problem, a subset-based optimization problem.

We can start with an empty shopping cart, and make a decision for each item: pick it or not. We can prune subsets that exceed our budget. At the leaves, we check if the current subset has the best sum of ratings so far, in which case we save it in a global variable.

```
1   def maximize_style(budget, prices, ratings):
2       best_rating_sum = 0
3       best_items = []
4       n = len(prices)
5       items = []
6       def visit(i, cur_cost, cur_rating_sum):
7           nonlocal best_items, best_rating_sum
8           if i == n:
9               if cur_rating_sum > best_rating_sum:
```

---

12 Remember, the base of the logarithm *cannot* be simplified away when the logarithm is in the exponent!

```
10            best_rating_sum = cur_rating_sum
11            best_items = items.copy()
12          return
13        # Choice 1: skip item i.
14        visit(i + 1, cur_cost, cur_rating_sum)
15        # Choice 2: pick item i (if within budget).
16        if cur_cost + prices[i] <= budget:
17          items.append(i)
18          visit(i + 1, cur_cost + prices[i], cur_rating_sum + ratings[i])
19          items.pop()
20      visit(0, 0, 0)
21      return best_items
```

As usual with subset-based problems, the runtime is $O(2^n * n)$.[13]

SOLUTION 39.8   WHITE HAT HACKER

The fact that the "password size" constraint is 10 is a *trigger* to use backtracking.

We can generate all permutations of the alphabet, stopping at length 10. Non-leaf nodes are also potential passwords, so we can call check_password() for those partial permutations too.

In the worst case, the number of check_password() calls will be $26*25*24*...*17 \approx 2 * 10^{13} = O(1)$.[14]

SOLUTION 39.9   COUNT UNIQUE SUBMULTISETS WITH SUM 0

First of all, this is a counting problem, which is a *trigger* for trying to optimize with DP. However, just finding one subset with sum 0—i.e., the subset-sum problem—is already an NP-complete problem, so we definitely cannot expect to do better than exponential time. Backtracking is the best we can do.

Since this is a subset-based problem, we could follow the typical backtracking where we make a decision for each element: pick it or skip it. This would work perfectly if the elements were all unique. The issue is that different sequences of choices can lead up to the same submultiset. For instance, if the input is [1, 1, -1, -1], we can get the submultiset [1, -1] with (pick, skip, pick, skip) and also with (skip, pick, pick, skip).

One workaround is to store all submultisets with sum 0 in a global set, which will take care of removing duplicates. At the end, we can return the size of the set. The issue with this approach is that our space complexity becomes exponential.[15]

Recall that the main way of optimizing backtracking is picking a better decision tree (pg 556). Is there a better way to model the problem as a decision tree? Yes! Instead of deciding individually for each element whether to pick it or not, our choice can be: "how many copies of this element should I pick?"

For instance, if the input is [1, 1, 2, 2, 2, 3, 3, 4], the first choice is "should I include zero, one, or two 1's? The second choice is "should I include zero, one, two, or three 2's? And so on. See Figure 14.

---

13 There is also a DP algorithm for the knapsack problem that we could use here. It takes $O(n*budget)$ time. This is a bit of an outlier because DP is not strictly better than backtracking. It depends on how big budget is relative to 2^n. In the constraints for this problem, we said that $n \leq 15$ and budget $\leq 10^6$, so backtracking could be faster in the worst case ($2^{15} < 15 * 10^6$).

14 Fun fact: assuming that we can call the script one million times per second, it would take approximately 223 days to try them all, but we can check all passwords of length up to 8 in less than one day. That's why short passwords are a bad idea!

15 The worst-case input might be something like [1, -1, 2, -2, 3, -3, ..., n/2, -n/2], which has more than $O(2^{n/2})$ subsets with sum 0 (there are n/2 pairs of indices [0, 1], [2, 3], [4, 5], ... which we can independently add or remove from any subset while keeping the sum at 0).

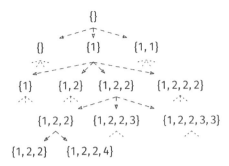

Figure 14. Part of the decision tree for input [1, 1, 2, 2, 2, 3, 3, 4], including two leaves.
The first decision is the number of 1's to include.

This decision tree guarantees that we never generate repeated submultisets, allowing us to skip the global set and reduce the space complexity to $O(n)$. In the best case (e.g., if all the input elements are the same), the decision tree will also be much smaller. However, in the worst case (e.g., if all elements in the input are unique), the decision tree will have $O(2^n)$ leaves, as usual.

In the implementation, we can start by building a **frequency map** (pg 347) mapping elements to how many times they appear in S. Each *key* in the frequency map becomes one of the decisions, and the *value* becomes the number of choices for that decision (plus one more choice for skipping the element altogether).

SOLUTION 39.10   4-DIRECTIONAL MAX-SUM PATH

As we mentioned in the introduction, this variation of the Max-Sum Path cannot be optimized with DP—it is NP-complete (it's a variant of the longest-path problem). Backtracking is the best we can do.

We already saw the decision tree for this problem (Figure 9, pg 548), so now we just need to implement it. The biggest challenge is not revisiting cells (which could get us stuck in an infinite loop). We could iterate through the path we built so far to make sure we don't. Or, we can do an **additional work optimization** (pg 550) and maintain a set of cells in the current path. This way, the additional work at each node will be $O(1)$.

Using the BAD method, the runtime will be $O(3^{R*C})$.

SOLUTION 39.11   ESCAPE WITH ALL CLUES

If you found this problem challenging, you're in good company—it's NP-complete! In fact, it is a mashup of two well-known problems: the Traveling Salesperson Problem (pg 543) and the Hamiltonian Path Problem (pg 226). It's a prime example of a difficult FAANG-style question: deceptively simple to describe but loaded with nuances that can lead to dead ends or overlooked edge cases.

To succeed (escape), you must first address the invalidating scenarios and tricky edge cases:

- Is the player completely blocked by obstacles?
- Are one or more clues inaccessible?

Then, we must pick the right algorithm and code it. In a chapter about backtracking, it was hopefully clear that we'd need backtracking, but in an interview, it's easy to get lost in the false triggers for this problem:

- The problem asks for the shortest path, which is a *trigger* for a shortest path algorithm such as BFS or Dijkstra's algorithm. But wait—a shortest-path algorithm heads straight to its destination, which might block its own path in the future. Counterintuitively, sometimes we must move away from the immediate goal to maintain a viable route.
- After shortest path algorithms fail, greedy and DP are the logical next choices to try. Neither work.

Let's follow a backtracking approach. We generate every path from the starting point that does not revisit any cells (like in Problem 39.10: 4-Directional Max-Sum Path, pg 558, but also avoiding obstacles). Our leaves are paths that contain every clue. While we generate all paths, we keep track of the shortest path so far in a 'global' variable. We can prune paths that hit dead ends.

▶ NERVOUS CANDIDATE CRUSHES THEIR GRAPH-BASED CODING ROUND   INTERVIEW REPLAY

View Online: bctci.co/backtracking-replay-2 @ 50:30 - end

The Question: Given a grid representing an "escape room," perform an increasingly difficult set of tasks with it (three separate graph-based questions in the interview are discussed).

What You'll See: The candidate was nervous, but they did an excellent job providing solutions to a problem that got harder as the interview progressed. The interviewer gave feedback to help the candidate get faster and optimize their interview flow.

Who: *Interviewer*: Software Engineer at Google
                     Candidate: 17 years exp.

Outcome: The candidate got the job at a FAANG+ company!

KEY TAKEAWAYS

Perhaps the biggest challenge in backtracking is knowing when to use it. Besides the triggers at the end, we discussed when to use it vs Greedy vs DP in the introduction (pg 541). Reading the Greedy and DP chapters next will give you a more complete picture of where each piece fits.

Conceptually, we tried to demystify backtracking by presenting it as a variation of an algorithm we already know: tree-based DFS. Our main advice is to *always draw the decision tree* in advance, which should make traversing it more intuitive.

When it comes to the implementation, perhaps the most confusing part is recursively making changes to a global state and then undoing it (see the reusable idea: 'Modify -> Recurse -> Undo' (pg 552)). Hopefully, the step-by-step illustration on page 552 helps you understand it, but if that's still confusing, you can always copy the state at each node. This is one of the design choices we discussed on page 550.

We didn't discuss a couple of more niche backtracking algorithms, such as 'iterative deepening' and 'minimax'. These could be considered extra credit, but we didn't include them in the book for space constraints.

> **Backtracking Triggers.** Problems with maximum input sizes in the lower 2-digits; enumeration problems or problems with exponential-sized outputs in general; NP-complete problems, especially optimization ones; games and puzzles (like N-queens, sudoku, knight's tour problem); subset-based or permutation-based problems; problems where you'd think of using DP but there are no overlapping subproblems.

ONLINE RESOURCES

Online resources for this chapter include:

- A chance to try each problem in this chapter in AI Interviewer
- Interview replays that show specific mistakes people make with backtracking problems
- Full code solutions for every problem in the chapter in multiple programming languages

Try online at bctci.co/backtracking.

## CHAPTER 40

DYNAMIC PROGRAMMING

AI interviewer, replays, and more materials for this chapter at bctci.co/dynamic-programming

> I thought dynamic programming was a good name. It was something not even a Congressman could object to.
>
> Richard Bellman, inventor of dynamic programming.

▶ *Prerequisites: Backtracking*

Although dynamic programming has a reputation for being intimidating, applying it to solve a problem is actually a very formulaic process. We've seen candidates flip from considering DP their worst topic to one of their best once they understand the steps they are supposed to follow.

At a high level, we apply DP in two steps:

Problem-Solving: Come up with a recurrence relation that computes the solution (output) to your problem.

Implementation: Turn the recurrence relation into efficient code with memoization or tabulation.

Let's unpack these steps.

Problem-solving step

We introduced the concept of *recurrence relations* in the Recursion chapter. A *recurrence relation* is a function or formula defined in terms of itself with smaller inputs. A classic example are Fibonacci numbers, F_n, which are defined as follows for any $n \geq 0$:

```
F₀ = 1
F₁ = 1
For n > 1, Fₙ = Fₙ₋₁ + Fₙ₋₂
```

Unlike in the case of Fibonacci, where the recurrence relation is established from the start (because it is part of the definition), we will mostly tackle problems where we are *not* given a recurrence relation and need to find one. In fact, this will often be the most challenging step.

This may seem vague at first, but it will probably click once we look at concrete examples.

Implementation step

Once we have a recurrence relation, we need to convert it into code. The two main approaches are *memoization* and *tabulation*.

Memoization   This starts by implementing the recurrence relation with a recursive function. We'll talk about how *overlapping subproblems*[1] are the main source of inefficiency and how we can fix it with *caching*. In fact, we already saw the gist of memoization in the Recursion chapter (pg 407), and we used it to solve Problem 33.4: Lego Castle (pg 409)

Tabulation   This is a way to implement recurrence relations iteratively. See the extra-credit Tabulation section (pg 583).

Memoization is also called *top-down* DP, and tabulation is also called *bottom-up* DP. For the large majority of interview problems, your interviewer will be fine with both approaches and let you choose. In this chapter, we'll focus on memoization because recursion is a natural fit for recurrence relations, so it tends to be a bit more intuitive.

\#   Focus on mastering one of memoization and tabulation. This will provide the most value.

RECURRENCE RELATIONS

In this section, we'll explain how to find recurrence relations—the key to DP.

Recall the concept of a *decision tree* from the backtracking chapter. The idea is to construct all possible solutions one choice at a time.

- The root is the empty solution.
- At each node, we have a child for each choice.
- Internal nodes represent partial solutions.
- The leaves represent complete solutions.

The idea of backtracking is to perform a DFS through the decision tree to find all the complete solutions. The downside is that decision trees often have exponential size, so the DFS is very slow.

If any of this is fuzzy for you, revisit the Decision Tree Modeling section (pg 543).

The decision tree for a problem is closely related to the recurrence relation. We just shift the focus of what we care about at each node. Instead of worrying about how we arrived at a partial solution, we focus on the **subproblem** that remains to be solved to reach a complete solution. The subproblem is usually a smaller part of the original input.

\#   In Backtracking, we care about partial solutions. In dynamic programming, we care about remaining subproblems.

We can find a recurrence relation with these steps:

1. Start by modeling the problem as a **decision tree**, just like we did in backtracking.
2. Define the **subproblems** that remain at each node.
3. Define a **recurrence relation** that, for each node, aggregates the outputs to the subproblems at the children into an output to the subproblem at the node.

If we can do that, the solution (output) to the entire problem will be the value of the recurrence relation at the root of the decision tree.

Let's make this concrete with an interview question:

---

1   A notation quirk: in this context, it is customary to use 'problem' to refer to an individual input for a problem (rather than the problem definition itself) and 'solution' to refer to the corresponding output (instead of using 'solution' to refer to our algorithm). So, when we say 'subproblem', we really mean "a smaller input for the same problem."

✦✦ **PROBLEM 40.1**   **ROAD TRIP**

We are driving down a road with n rest stops between us and our destination. For each rest stop, our mapping software tells us how long of a detour it would be to stop there. We start before the first rest stop and our destination is past the last one.

We are given an array of n positive integers, `times`, indicating the delay incurred to stop at each rest stop. If we don't want to go more than 2 rest stops without taking a break, what's the least amount of time we have to spend on detours?

▶ **Example:** times = [8, 1, 2, 3, 9, 6, 2, 4]
  Output: 6. The optimal rest stops are underlined: [8, 1, 2, 3, 9, 6, 2, 4]
▶ **Example:** times = [8, 1, 2, 3, 9, 3, 2, 4]
  Output: 5. The optimal rest stops are: [8, 1, 2, 3, 9, 3, 2, 4]
▶ **Example:** times = [10, 10]
  Output: 0. We don't need to make any stops.

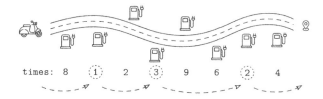

Figure 1. Example 1 for Problem 1.

SOLUTION 40.1   ROAD TRIP

You might be tempted to always just pick the smallest delay between the next three indices, but, as shown in Example 1, this is suboptimal. For the second stop, we must pick 3 and not 2.

We can find the optimal stops with DP. We start by finding the recurrence relation with the steps above:

1. **Decision tree:** The root is where we start the road trip. The decisions are where to take the next break. We have three choices: we can go to the next rest stop, skip one rest stop, or skip two. Each partial solution is a list of breaks we have taken so far. A leaf is when we don't need more breaks.

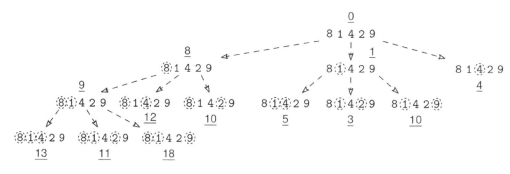

Figure 2. Decision tree for this problem for input [8, 1, 4, 2, 9]. The circles indicate the stops chosen at each partial solution. The total detour time so far for each partial solution is underlined. Leaves are partial solutions where we can reach the end without any more breaks.

2. **Subproblems:** For each partial solution, the remaining subproblem is the *suffix* of rest stops after our location. It's like starting the road trip from a rest stop in the middle of the road.

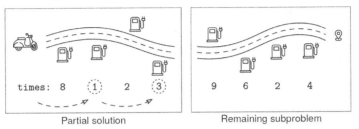

Partial solution   Remaining subproblem

Figure 3.

3. **Recurrence relation:** This is where it all comes together. Let's say we stop at the rest area at index i. We want to find a formula, `delay(i)`, that returns the minimum delay needed to get from rest stop i to the final one. Our choices are to go to rest areas `i + 1`, `i + 2`, or `i + 3`. Of the three options, we want to pick the shortest one overall, so we can **aggregate** them by taking the min.

```
delay(i) = times[i] + min(delay(i+1), delay(i+2), delay(i+3))
```

We need to be careful around edge cases: this only works if there are at least three rest stops. If there are fewer than three, we can jump directly to the goal. Those are our base cases:

```
delay(n-1) = times[n-1]
delay(n-2) = times[n-2]
delay(n-3) = times[n-3]
```

	General case					Base cases		
times:	8	1	2	3	9	6	2	4
i:	0	1	2	3	4	5	6	7
delay(i):	14	6	7	5	11	6	2	4

delay(2) = 2 + min(5, 11, 6)

Figure 4. All the values of `delay(i)` for Example 1.

Our initial three choices are rest areas 0, 1, and 2. This means that the solution to the *original problem* is `min(delay(0), delay(1), delay(2))`.

In the next section, we'll turn this recurrence relation into efficient code. First, let's recap everything we need to specify a recurrence:

Elements of a Recurrence Relation

- **Signature:** The name and arguments of the recurrence relation. The arguments are how we identify a subproblem, so they depend on the 'shape' of the subproblems. For instance, if each subproblem is a suffix of the input array, we can identify them with the index where the suffix starts.

- **Description:** What the recurrence relation computes, in words. It should reference the arguments.[2]

- **Base cases:** Subproblems where we can compute the solution directly.

- **General case:** this is where we:

  » Identify the **choices** at each step,

  » Map the choices to smaller subproblems,

  » Get their solutions recursively, and

  » **Aggregate** them to compute the solution to the current subproblem. The typical aggregation methods are:[3]

    · Max for maximization problems.

    · Min for minimization problems.

    · Sum for counting problems.

    · Logical 'or' for feasibility problems.

- **Original problem:** How to use the recurrence relation to solve the original problem.

We recommend writing down the recurrence relation in a comment in the shared editor before starting to code. We'd write something like this:

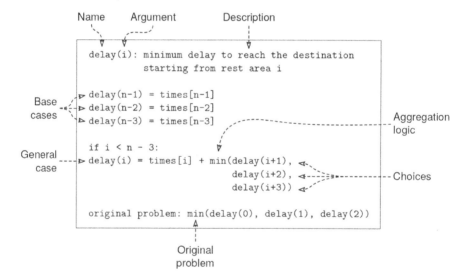

Figure 5. Recurrence relation for Problem 40.1, as we would type it in an editor, with annotations identifying each part.

\#   For the recurrence relation to be correct, make sure every valid index is covered by either a base case or the general case. Correctly identifying the thresholds will simplify our implementation later.

---

2   We recommend writing this down in an interview. It's not strictly necessary, but if you can't express in words what you are trying to compute, it's much more likely you'll get confused. It will also be harder for the interviewer to understand your formula.

3   See a discussion on problem types on page 542. One problem type mentioned there which we are not listing here is *enumeration* problems. Those are usually better tackled with backtracking than DP.

MEMOIZATION IMPLEMENTATION

If we have fully specified a recurrence relation, turning it into recursive code is straightforward. Here is the code for the recurrence relation of Problem 40.1:

```
1   def delay(times): # Inefficient -- do not use in interviews.
2     n = len(times)
3     if n < 3:
4       return 0
5     def delay_rec(i):
6       if i >= n - 3:
7         return times[i]
8       return times[i] + min(delay_rec(i+1), delay_rec(i+2), delay_rec(i+3))
9     return min(delay_rec(0), delay_rec(1), delay_rec(2))
```

This code correctly solves Problem 40.1, but it is *very inefficient*. This code makes one call to delay() for each node in the decision tree (Figure 2), and, like most decision trees, it grows exponentially on the input size. The point of DP is that this is not necessary. In Figure 2, we can see that we can get to the rest area at index 2 (4) in three different ways. That means we compute the recurrence relation for subproblem [2, 9] three times. This is what we call overlapping subproblems. *Overlapping subproblems are repeated work.* As you can imagine, the amount of repeated work grows exponentially as n grows.

Thankfully, the fix is straightforward: we just need to *cache* or 'memoize'[4] the solutions to subproblems the first time we compute them. Then, if we reach that subproblem again, we just return the cached value. We *never* recurse again for the same subproblem.

In practice, this memoization looks like a hash map with subproblems as keys and subproblem solutions as values (we call it memo). Let's do that for Problem 40.1:

```
1   def delay(times):
2     n = len(times)
3     if n < 3:
4       return 0
5     memo = {}
6
7     def delay_rec(i):
8       if i >= n - 3:
9         return times[i]
10      if i in memo:
11        return memo[i]
12      memo[i] = times[i] + min(delay_rec(i+1), delay_rec(i+2), delay_rec(i+3))
13      return memo[i]
14
15    return min(delay_rec(0), delay_rec(1), delay_rec(2))
```

And just like that, the runtime went from exponential to linear (more on that later).

Why are the base cases at the end and not the beginning?

In Problem 40.1, our base cases are n-1, n-2, and n-3, rather than 0, 1, and 2. This may seem unusual. Where the base cases end up is a consequence of how we define our recurrence relation.

For Problem 40.1, we defined:

---

4   Just because an algorithm caches 'something' doesn't mean it is a DP algorithm. For instance, you could say that we cache node distances during a graph BFS, but that doesn't mean BFS is DP. DP is about the special case of caching *overlapping subproblems*.

- delay(i): minimum delay to reach the destination starting from rest area i

We could have also said:

- delay(i): minimum delay to reach rest area i from the start

Then, the direction of everything would be reversed: the base cases would be at the beginning, the choices would be to the left, and the original problem would be at the end.

We can think of the first one as a 'forward' recurrence relation and the other as a 'backward' recurrence relation. Both are equally correct and extensively used,[5] so you can pick your favorite. In this chapter, we'll stick to 'forward' recurrences because they more closely match decision trees in backtracking.

Let's capture this logic as a recipe. We can use this recipe to solve virtually any DP problem.

▢ RECIPE 1. MEMOIZATION

```
memo = empty map

f(subproblem_id):
  if subproblem is base case:
    return result directly
  if subproblem in memo map:
    return cached result
  memo[subproblem_id] = recurrence relation formula
  return memo[subproblem_id]

return f(initial subproblem)
```

MEMOIZATION ANALYSIS

DP analysis is straightforward. We care about two things:

- The number of subproblems.
- The non-recursive work for each subproblem (when it is not cached).

We multiply the two to get the overall amount of work. This works because, thanks to memoization, we only compute each subproblem once.

The space is typically the number of subproblems, since we usually only store an integer value for each one in the memo map.

For Problem 40.1 (Road Trip), we have:

- Subproblems: n.
- Non-recursive work: $O(1)$.
- Total time: $O(n)$.
- Extra space: $O(n)$.

We haven't discussed tabulation yet, but the time and space analysis comes out to be the same. That's the main reason we can freely choose between the two. The fine print is that while they have the same space complexity by default, tabulation often enables a space optimization known as a *rolling array*, which we can't

---

5 The fact that both 'forward' and 'backward' recurrences are extensively used is one reason why we recommend writing down the description of the recurrence relation in words. It will help the interviewer understand which one you are trying to do, as they may default to the opposite one than you.

do with memoization (pg 584). For instance, for Problem 40.1, it allows us to improve the extra space to O(1). As established, we care much less about space than time, so focus on whatever method clicks better.

DP VARIATIONS

2D Input

The same recipe applies to any kind of input. For instance, recall Problem 39.1: Max-Sum Path (pg 539), where the input is a grid:

Given a non-empty RxC grid of positive integers, grid, find the path from the top-left corner to the bottom-right corner with the largest sum. You can only go down or to the right (not diagonal).

▸ **Example:** grid = [[1, 5, 1],
                       [2, 3, 2],
                       [20, 1, 1]]
  Output: 25. The maximum path is 1 -> 2 -> 20 -> 1 -> 1.

▸ **Example:** grid = [[5]]
  Output: 5

A partial solution is a partial path through the grid, and a remaining subproblem is a subgrid starting from the current position.

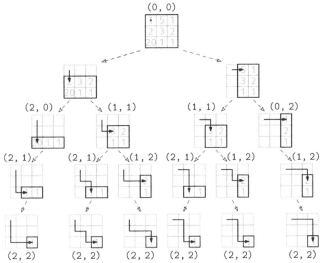

Figure 6. Partial solution and remaining subproblem at each node of the decision tree. The partial solution is the path ending with an arrow. The subproblem is the highlighted subgrid. Each subproblem is identified by the top-left coordinates (r, c). We can see that the decision tree has *overlapping subproblems*.

The main thing with 2D inputs is that we have more out-of-bounds checks:

- If we are in the last row, we can only go right.
- If we are in the last column, we can only go down.

When writing down the recurrence relation, we need to be systematic about all the edge cases:

```
max_path(r, c): the maximum path sum starting from grid[r][c]
bottom-right corner (r == R-1, c == C-1):
  max_path(r, c) = grid[r][c]
last row (r == R-1, c < C-1):
```

```
      max_path(r, c) = grid[r][c] + max_path(r, c+1)   # we can only go right
   last column (r < R-1, c == C-1):
      max_path(r, c) = grid[r][c] + max_path(r+1, c)   # we can only go down
   general case (r < R-1, c < C-1):
      max_path(r, c) = grid[r][c] + max(max_path(r+1, c),   # go down
                                        max_path(r, c+1))   # go right
   original problem: max_path(0, 0)
```

Now, we can translate it into code and add caching, as in Recipe 1:

```
1    def max_path(grid):
2      R, C = len(grid), len(grid[0])
3      memo = {}
4
5      def max_path_rec(r, c):
6        if r == R - 1 and c == C - 1:
7          return grid[r][c]
8        if (r, c) in memo:
9          return memo[(r, c)]
10        elif r == R - 1:
11          memo[(r, c)] = grid[r][c] + max_path_rec(r, c + 1)
12        elif c == C - 1:
13          memo[(r, c)] = grid[r][c] + max_path_rec(r + 1, c)
14        else:
15          memo[(r, c)] = grid[r][c] + max(max_path_rec(r + 1, c), max_path_rec(r, c + 1))
16        return memo[(r, c)]
17
18      return max_path_rec(0, 0)
```

Analysis:

- Subproblems: $R * C$.
- Non-recursive work: $O(1)$.
- Total time: $O(R * C)$.
- Extra space: $O(R * C)$.

Should you cache the base cases or only the general case?

Add to the memo map any subproblem solutions that require recursive calls or take more than constant time to compute. For instance, in Problem 40.2: Minivan Road Trip (pg 576), we should cache the subproblems for the final row and column.

It doesn't matter if you cache constant-time base cases or not.

Non-constant number of choices

Next, let's see an example where the number of choices is not constant. Recall Problem 29.9: Min-Subarray-Sum Split (pg 338):[6]

Given a non-empty array with n positive integers, arr, and a number k with $1 \leq k \leq n$, the goal is to split arr into k non-empty subarrays so that the largest sum across all subarrays is minimized. Return the largest sum across all k subarrays after making it as small as possible. Each subarray must contain at least one value.

---

6 We saw a $O(n \log S)$-time binary search solution in Problem 29.9: Min-Subarray-Sum Split (pg 338), where S is the sum of arr. Here, we will show a DP solution that takes $O(n*k)$ time.

▶ **Example:** `arr = [10, 5, 8, 9, 11], k = 3`
  Output: 17. There are six ways of splitting the array into three subarrays.
         The optimal split is: `[10, 5]`, `[8, 9]`, and `[11]`. The largest sum
         among the three subarrays is 17.

▶ **Example:** `arr = [10, 10, 10, 10, 10], k = 2`
  Output: 30.

If we modeled this as a decision tree, we could start with an empty list of subarrays. Then, we decide which subarray should be the first in the split. For instance, if `arr` is `[1, 2, 3, 4]`, we could start with `[1]`, `[1, 2]`, `[1, 2, 3]`, or `[1, 2, 3, 4]`. Then, at each step, we decide which subarray to add next. For instance, if we picked `[1, 2]` as the first one, the next one can be `[3]`, or `[3, 4]`. Once we have added `k - 1` subarrays, we don't have any more choice. All remaining elements must go in the final subarray.

Now, let's turn this into a recurrence relation. Let's identify all the parts systematically:

1. **Signature:** we can identify each subproblem, `min_split(i, x)`, with two things:

   » an index `i` of the beginning of the suffix of elements that still need to be added to a subarray. $0 \le i < n$.

   » a value `x` of how many subarrays we can put them in. $1 \le x \le k$.

2. **Description:** `min_split(i, x)` the minimum possible largest subarray-sum after splitting `arr[i:n]` into x subarrays.

3. **Base cases:**

   » If there are x elements left (`len(arr[i:n]) == x`), we must put each one in its own subarray: `min_split(i, x) = max(arr[i:n])`

   » If `x == 1`, we must put all remaining elements in a single subarray: `min_split(i, 1) = sum(arr[i:n])`.

4. **General case:**

   » **Choices:** we have one choice for each subarray starting at index `i`. We just need to make sure that we leave at least a suffix with `x - 1` elements for the remaining `x - 1` subarrays.

   » We can compute what would be the value of `min_split(i, x)` if we pick a specific subarray, say, `arr[i:p]`. It would be the maximum between two things:

     · the sum of that array, `sum(arr[i:p])`, and
     · the solution to the remaining subproblem: `min_split(p, x-1)`.

   » **Aggregation logic:** Of all the options, we pick the one that minimizes this value.

5. **Original problem:** `min_split(0, k)`.

We can write this as a recurrence relation and then code it with Recipe 1. Since we have a non-constant number of choices, we use a loop to explore all of them.

```
1  def min_split(arr, k):
2      n = len(arr)
3      memo = {}
4      def min_split_rec(i, x):
5          if (i, x) in memo:
6              return memo[(i, x)]
7          # Base cases
8          if n - i == x:  # Put each element in its own subarray.
```

```
 9        memo[(i, x)] = max(arr[i:])
10     elif x == 1:    # Put all elements in one subarray.
11       memo[(i, x)] = sum(arr[i:])
12     else:  # General case
13       current_sum = 0
14       res = math.inf
15       for p in range(i, n - x + 1):
16         current_sum += arr[p]
17         res = min(res, max(current_sum, min_split_rec(p + 1, x - 1)))
18       memo[(i, x)] = res
19     return memo[(i, x)]
20   return min_split_rec(0, k)
```

Analysis:

- Subproblems: n * k.
- Non-recursive work: O(n) for the inner loop.
- Total time: O(n² * k).
- Extra space: O(n * k).

▶ **IN DP PROBLEMS, EVEN THE BRUTE FORCE RECURSION IS DIFFICULT**   INTERVIEW REPLAY

View Online: bctci.co/dynamic-programming-replay-1 @ 50:29 - 1:02:05

The Question: Given a matrix where each cell represents the height of a location in a ski area, return the longest path the skier can travel if they start in the optimal location going downhill.

What You'll See: Identifying a brute force solution for a dynamic programming problem can be tricky. The candidate was able to go from brute force to the optimized solution.

Who: *Interviewer*: Software Engineer at Google
                     Candidate: 6 years exp.

PROBLEM SET

✦ *Try these problems with AI Interviewer: bctci.co/dynamic-programming-problem-set-1*

PROBLEM 40.2   **MINIVAN ROAD TRIP**

Consider the setting from Problem 40.1: Road Trip (pg 568). We're doing the same road trip, except this time in a comfortable minivan. In addition to the times array, we are also given a positive integer k, indicating the number of consecutive rest areas we can skip.

What's the least amount of time we have to spend on detours?

▸ **Example:** times = [8, 1, 2, 3, 9, 6, 2, 4], k = 2.
   Output: 6. The optimal rest stops are underlined: [8, 1, 2, 3, 9, 6, 2, 4].
               The k = 2 case is equivalent to Problem 1.

▸ **Example:** times = [8, 1, 2, 3, 9, 6, 2, 4], k = 3.
   Output: 4. The optimal rest stops are underlined: [8, 1, 2, 3, 9, 6, 2, 4].

PROBLEM 40.3   **RESTAURANT RATINGS**

We are doing a road trip and trying to plan where to stop to eat. There are n restaurants along the route. We are given an array, `ratings`, with the ratings of all the restaurants in the order we will find them. Ratings are floating-point numbers. Our goal is to choose restaurants maximizing the sum of ratings of the places where we stop. The only constraint is that we don't want to stop at 2 consecutive restaurants, as we would be too full. Return the optimal sum of ratings.

▶ **Example:** `ratings = [8, 1, 3, 9, 5, 2, 1]`
  `Output:` 19. The optimal restaurants are underlined: [8̲, 1, 3, 9̲, 5, 2̲, 1]
▶ **Example:** `ratings = [8, 1, 3, 7, 5, 2, 4]`
  `Output:` 20. The optimal restaurants are underlined: [8̲, 1, 3̲, 7, 5̲, 2, 4̲].

PROBLEM 40.4   **COUNT 0-SUM PATHS**

Given a non-empty RxC binary grid, `grid`, return the number of paths from the top-left corner to the bottom-right corner with a sum of 0. You can only go down, to the right, or diagonally down and to the right.

▶ **Example:** `grid = [[0, 1, 1],`
                `[0, 0, 0],`
                `[1, 0, 0]]`
  `Output:` 7. See Figure 7.
▶ **Example:** `grid = [[1]]`
  `Output:` 0.

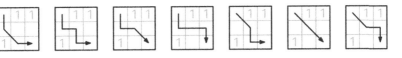

Figure 7. Possible paths for Example 1. Empty cells are 0's.

PROBLEM 40.5   **MAGIC BLACKJACK**

You're given a magic deck of cards. When one card is removed, an identical card spawns as a replacement. Each card is a number between 1 and 10 (suits do not matter). When a card is drawn, each value from 1 to 10 has a 10% chance of appearing. A dealer repeatedly draws cards until one of two things happen:

· The sum of the cards is between 16 and 21.
· The sum of the cards exceeds 21. When this happens, we say the dealer *busts*.

Return the number of different ways the dealer can bust.

For instance, if the dealer draws 10, 2, 10, they bust. If they draw 2, 10, 10, that counts as a different way to bust. If the dealer draws 10, 1, 10, they don't bust.

PROBLEM 40.6   **MINIMUM STEPS TO ONE**

Write a function that accepts a positive integer, n, and returns the minimum number of operations to get to 1, assuming we can choose between the following operations:

· Subtract 1.
· Divide by 2. We can only do this if the number is divisible by 2.
· Divide by 3. We can only do this if the number is divisible by 3.

✦ PROBLEM SET SOLUTIONS

SOLUTION 40.2   MINIVAN ROAD TRIP

We need to generalize Solution 40.1: Road Trip (pg 568) from 3 choices to k+1 choices. We do this with an inner loop. Here is the modified recurrence:

```
delay(i): minimum delay to reach the destination
          starting from rest area i
Base case: k or fewer remaining stops (i ≥ n - k - 1)
  delay(i) = 0
General case: i < n - k - 1
  delay(i) = times[i] + min(delay(i+p) for p from 1 to k+1)


original problem:
  min(delay(p) for p from 0 to k)
```

We can implement the recurrence relation with Recipe 1.

Analysis:

- Subproblems: n.
- Non-recursive work: $O(k)$ for the inner loop.
- Total time: $O(n * k)$.
- Extra space: $O(n)$.

SOLUTION 40.3   RESTAURANT RATINGS

We can think about our initial choices in two ways:

1. We can ask, "At which restaurant should I stop first?",
2. or we can ask, "Should I stop at the first restaurant or not?"

Each way of thinking about it leads to slightly different decision trees and recurrence relations. We'll try the second way.

1. **Signature:** we'll have one subproblem, rating_sum(i), per suffix of the input array.
2. **Description:** rating_sum(i) is the maximum sum of ratings we can get if the route consisted only of restaurants i to n-1.
3. **Base case:**

   » rating_sum(n) = 0 (there are no restaurants left).

4. **General case:**

   » **Choices:** eat at restaurant i or not.
   » If we stop at restaurant i, we add ratings[i] to our total, but we have to skip restaurant i+1.
   » **Aggregation logic:** We pick the maximum between the two options:

   rating_sum(i) = max(ratings[i] + rating_sum(i+2), rating_sum(i+1))

5. **Original problem:** rating_sum(0).

We can implement the recurrence relation with Recipe 1.

Analysis:

- Subproblems: n.
- Non-recursive work: $O(1)$.
- Total time: $O(n)$.
- Extra space: $O(n)$.

SOLUTION 40.4   COUNT 0-SUM PATHS

This is a grid-based problem with 3 choices (down, right, and diagonal), but not all the choices are valid at every cell—it depends on where the 1's are located. Also, since it's a *counting* problem, we aggregate the three options with 'sum.'

```
num_paths(r, c): the number of paths without any 1's starting from grid[r]
[c]
any cell (r, c) with a 1:
  num_paths(r, c) = 0
for cells with a 0:
bottom-right corner (r == R-1, c == C-1):
  num_paths(r, c) = 1
last row (r == R-1, c < C-1):
  num_paths(r, c) = num_paths(r, c+1)   # we can only go right
last column (r < R-1, c == C-1):
  num_paths(r, c) = num_paths(r+1, c)   # we can only go down
general case (r < R-1, c < C-1):
  num_paths(r, c) = num_paths(r+1, c) +   # go down
                    num_paths(r, c+1) +   # go right
                    num_paths(r+1, c+1)   # go diagonal
original problem:
  num_paths(0, 0)
```

We can implement the recurrence relation with Recipe 1.

SOLUTION 40.5   MAGIC BLACKJACK

The '10% chance' part is a bit of a red herring that causes many candidates to think they need to use probabilities or start generating random numbers.[7] This is really just a counting problem.

There is no input for this problem, which technically means that any algorithm for it takes constant time. However, that doesn't mean we should just use backtracking—the decision tree has a branching factor 10 and a maximum depth 16 (if we repeatedly draw 1's), so it is still unpractically large.

We'll have one subproblem, num_ways(i), for each possible sum. Each subproblem denotes the number of ways to bust starting from that sum. Our base cases are $i > 21$ (1 way) and $16 \le i \le 21$ (0 ways). The original problem is num_ways(0). Here is the code with memoization:

```
1  def num_ways():
2    memo = {}
3    def num_ways_rec(i):
4      if i > 21:
5        return 1
6      if 16 <= i <= 21:
7        return 0
8      if i in memo:
```

---

7 Randomness is almost never needed for DS&A interviews, with the notable exception of selecting a pivot in quicksort and quickselect (pg 372).

```
 9        return memo[i]
10      memo[i] = 0
11      for card in range(1, 11):
12        memo[i] += num_ways_rec(i + card)
13      return memo[i]
14    return num_ways_rec(0)
```

SOLUTION 40.6   MINIMUM STEPS TO ONE

First of all, we may ask—do we really need DP? It seems intuitive that we should always pick whichever operation gets us closer to 1. So, if n is 9, we would divide by 3, not subtract 1.

This is what is known as a *greedy* algorithm, which we'll talk about in the next chapter. However, it does **not** work for every input. Can you find one where it doesn't work?

For instance, if n = 10, it is a *mistake* to divide by 2. This results in 4 steps: 10 -> 5 -> 4 -> 2 -> 1. A better solution is 10 -> 9 -> 3 -> 1. We say that 10 is a *counterexample* for this greedy algorithm. Since Greedy doesn't work, let's tackle it with DP.

We'll have one subproblem, num_steps(i), for each number from n to 1. Each subproblem denotes the minimum number of steps to get to 1 starting from i. At each step, we have up to 3 choices, which we aggregate with min() because it's a minimization problem. Our base case is i == 1, and our original case is num_steps(n).

▶	**A DIFFICULT STRING-BASED DP PROBLEM**	INTERVIEW REPLAY

View Online:	bctci.co/dynamic-programming-replay-2 @ 3:47 - end
The Question:	Given two strings, a and b, determine the minimum number of operations required to convert the first string into the second string if each 'operation' is either to (1) add a character, (2) remove a character, or (3) substitute one character for another.
What You'll See:	The candidate made no progress on this challenging question throughout the interview but still managed to learn a lot as the interviewer walked them through it to the optimal answer.
Who:	*Interviewer*: Software Engineer at FAANG+
	Candidate: 5 years exp.

SOLUTION RECONSTRUCTION

So far, for optimization problems, we have looked at problems where we were asked the *value* of the solution. What if we want to find the actual solution that achieves this value? We'll illustrate this with a classic problem, the longest common subsequence (LCS). We'll start with the version that asks for the value.

✦ **PROBLEM 40.7**   **LONGEST COMMON SUBSEQUENCE**

Given two strings, s1 and s2, find the length of the longest subsequence that is common to both s1 and s2. A *subsequence* of a string s is a sequence that appears in s in the same relative order but not necessarily consecutively. The two strings consist of uppercase English letters only.

▸ **Example:** s1 = "HAHAH", s2 = "AAAAHH"
   Output: 3. There are two common subsequences of length 3: "AAH" and "AHH".
▸ **Example:** s1 = "", s2 = "AA"
   Output: 0.

SOLUTION 40.7   LONGEST COMMON SUBSEQUENCE

It is often helpful to start by examining the initial choices. If the first letter in s1 and the first letter in s2 are the same, we can add it to the LCS. If they don't, they can't both be in the LCS—we'll need to 'discard' at least one of them. The challenge is that just by looking at the first letter of each string, it is not obvious which one to discard.

Consider the case where s1 = "ABC" and s2 = "BCA", it is important that we discard the 'A' in s1, **not** the 'B' in s2.

Let's specify a recurrence relation:

1. **Signature:** we'll have one subproblem, lcs(i1, i2), where i1 identifies a suffix of s1, and i2 identifies a suffix of s2.

2. **Description:** lcs(i1, i2) is the longest common subsequence of the two suffixes.

3. **Base cases:**

   » lcs(n1, i2) = 0 (the first suffix is empty).
   » lcs(i1, n2) = 0 (the second suffix is empty).

4. **General case:**

   » If s1[i1] == s2[i2], lcs(i1, i2) = 1 + lcs(i1 + 1, i2 + 1).
   » If not, our options are to discard s1[i1] or discard s2[i2].
   » **Aggregation logic:** We pick the maximum:

   lcs(i1, i2) = max(lcs(i1 + 1, i2), lcs(i1, i2 + 1))

5. **Original problem:** lcs(0, 0).

We implement it with Recipe 1 as follows:

```
1   def lcs(s1, s2):
2     memo = {}
3     def lcs_rec(i1, i2):
4       if i1 == len(s1) or i2 == len(s2):
5         return 0
6       if (i1, i2) in memo:
7         return memo[(i1, i2)]
8       if s1[i1] == s2[i2]:
9         memo[(i1, i2)] = 1 + lcs_rec(i1+1, i2+1)
10      else:
11        memo[(i1, i2)] = max(lcs_rec(i1+1, i2), lcs_rec(i1, i2+1))
12      return memo[(i1, i2)]
13    return lcs_rec(0, 0)
```

Analysis:

- Subproblems: n1 * n2, where n1 is the length of s1 and n2 is the length of s2.
- Non-recursive work: O(1).
- Total time: O(n1 * n2).
- Extra space: O(n1 * n2).

Next, let's look at the version where we need to return the actual LCS:

✦✦ **PROBLEM 40.8**   **RECONSTRUCT LONGEST COMMON SUBSEQUENCE**

Given two strings, s1 and s2, return the longest subsequence that is common to both s1 and s2. A *subsequence* of a string s is a sequence that appears in s in the same relative order but not necessarily consecutively. In case of a tie, return any of common subsequence of maximum length. The two strings consist of uppercase English letters only.

▸ **Example:** s1 = "HAHAH", s2 = "AAAAHH"
  Output: "AAH". The other valid output is "AHH".

▸ **Example:** s1 = "", s2 = "AA"
  Output: "".

SOLUTION 40.8   RECONSTRUCT LONGEST COMMON SUBSEQUENCE

We can adapt our solution that only returns the length of the LCS, into a solution that returns the LCS itself. The straightforward approach is to store the strings themselves in the memo table instead of their length. So, for Example 1, instead of memo[(2, 0)] = 2, we store memo[(2, 0)] = "HH".

```
 1   def lcs_reconstruction(s1, s2):
 2     memo = {}
 3     def lcs_rec(i1, i2):
 4       if i1 == len(s1) or i2 == len(s2):
 5         return ""
 6       if (i1, i2) in memo:
 7         return memo[(i1, i2)]
 8       if s1[i1] == s2[i2]:
 9         memo[(i1, i2)] = s1[i1] + lcs_rec(i1+1, i2+1)
10       else:
11         opt1, opt2 = lcs_rec(i1+1, i2), lcs_rec(i1, i2+1)
12         if len(opt1) >= len(opt2):
13           memo[(i1, i2)] = opt1
14         else:
15           memo[(i1, i2)] = opt2
16       return memo[(i1, i2)]
17     return lcs_rec(0, 0)
```

The downside to this approach is that it increases the time and space per subproblem:

- Subproblems: n1 * n2.
- Non-recursive work: O(n1 + n2).
- Total time: O(n1 * n2 * (n1 + n2)).
- Extra space: O(n1 * n2 * (n1 + n2)).

There is a technique we can use to avoid the extra time and space. We call it *solution reconstruction*. We start by implementing the normal recurrence relation with memoization (as in Solution 40.7). The difference is that, instead of returning the original problem at the end (with return lcs_rec(0, 0)), that's where we start reconstructing the solution.

We build it one character at a time with parallel pointers (pg 294). We use two pointers, i1 and i2, initialized to 0. If s1[i1] and s2[i2] match, we can add that character to the solution and advance both pointers. Otherwise, we know that we need to advance one of the two pointers without adding anything to the solution. Which one? We use lcs_rec() to answer that. If lcs_rec(i1 + 1, i2) is higher than lcs_rec(i1, i2 + 1), it is better to advance i1. Otherwise, it's better to advance i2. We keep going until either pointer reaches the end of the string, which means we are done.

```
1   def lcs_reconstruction_optimal(s1, s2):
2     memo = {}
3     def lcs_rec(s1, s2):
4       ...  # Same as Solution 7.
5     i1, i2 = 0, 0
6     res = []
7     while i1 < len(s1) and i2 < len(s2):
8       if s1[i1] == s2[i2]:
9         res.append(s1[i1])
10        i1 += 1
11        i2 += 1
12      elif lcs_rec(i1+1, i2) > lcs_rec(i1, i2+1):
13        i1 += 1
14      else:
15        i2 += 1
16    return ''.join(res)
```

Analysis:

- Subproblems: n1 * n2, where n1 is the length of s1 and n2 is the length of s2.
- Non-recursive work: O(1).
- Total time: O(n1 * n2). The two-pointer step takes linear time.
- Extra space: O(n1 * n2).

This solution reconstruction idea isn't specific to LCS. It is reusable for any DP problem.

REUSABLE IDEA: SOLUTION RECONSTRUCTION

DP problems asking for the *value* of the solution are easier than problems that ask for the solution itself.

A practical way to return full solutions to DP problems instead of just their values is to store them in the memo table. It can piggyback along with the value, if the value is also needed (see 'Reusable Idea: Piggy-backing Extra Info', pg 382). However, this increases the time and space complexity.

The more efficient approach is to start by implementing the recurrence relation for values only. Then, we reconstruct the solution step by step, essentially following a path down the decision tree. The key is to use the function for the value-based recurrence relation to determine the best choice at each step. This is analogous to how we build our partial solution in backtracking, except we only go down one path, so we don't need to do it recursively.

EXTRA-CREDIT: TABULATION

Tabulation starts by finding a recurrence relation, just like memoization. Ask yourself: if you wanted to implement a recurrence relation without using recursion, how would you do it?

The main idea is to use a loop to fill in every subproblem in the memo map. Following convention, we'll use an array (the 'table') instead of a map, and we'll call it dp.

We start by filling in the base cases directly in the table. Then loop over all the indices of the general case. *The iteration order is very important.* We must iterate in an order that respects the *dependencies* between subproblems.

For instance, for Chapter 40: Road Trip (pg 568), the general case of the recurrence relation was:

▶   `delay(i) = times[i] + min(delay(i+1), delay(i+2), delay(i+3))`

In tabulation, this becomes:

▸ `dp[i] = times[i] + min(dp[i+1], dp[i+2], dp[i+3])`

Notice how `dp[i]` depends on subproblems with *greater* indices? That means that we must iterate from right to left. Here is Solution 40.1: Road Trip (pg 568) using tabulation:

```
1   def delay(times):
2       n = len(times)
3       if n < 3:
4           return 0
5       dp = [0]*n
6       dp[n-1], dp[n-2], dp[n-3] = times[n-1], times[n-2], times[n-3]
7       for i in range(n-4, -1, -1):
8           dp[i] = times[i] + min(dp[i+1], dp[i+2], dp[i+3])
9       return min(dp[0], dp[1], dp[2])
```

Analysis:

- Subproblems: n.
- Work per iteration: $O(1)$.
- Total time: $O(n)$.
- Extra space: $O(n)$.

The main advantage of memoization over tabulation is that we don't need to worry about the order in which we fill the table. This can start to get tricky for recurrence relations with multiple arguments, which involve 2D tables (or more). There's a lot more to say about how to know the correct iteration order to fill 2D tables, but it is an advanced topic niche enough to belong in Tier 3. Also, there are diminishing returns to learning both memoization and tabulation.

ROLLING ARRAY OPTIMIZATION

As we mentioned, there is a space optimization that only works for tabulation. If we want to signal the most problem-solving skills, this is one reason why we might choose it over memoization.[8]

The idea is that we often don't need to store the solution to every subproblem. For instance, in the loop in `delay()` in the previous section, we only ever read the next three indices of the table. Everything after that is 'wasted' space. Instead of an array of length n, we can use three standalone variables to store the values we need. After each iteration, we shift them over by one.

```
1   def delay(times):
2       n = len(times)
3       if n < 3:
4           return 0
5       dp1, dp2, dp3 = times[n-3], times[n-2], times[n-1]
6       for i in range(n-4, -1, -1):
7           cur = times[i] + min(dp1, dp2, dp3)
8           dp1, dp2, dp3 = cur, dp1, dp2
9       return min(dp1, dp2, dp3)
```

This improves the space complexity to $O(1)$ without increasing the time complexity.[9]

---

8 Though practically speaking, in an interview, we've never seen someone fail to pass just because they chose memoization rather than tabulation, so don't stress over this.

9 Without getting into the details, for some 2D problem like Problem 40.4: Count 0-Sum Paths (pg 577), we can reduce the space complexity from $O(RxC)$ to $O(C)$ (or $O(R)$). That is because we can fill the DP table row by row (or column by column), and, for each row, we only need the subproblems from the previous row (or column).

KEY TAKEAWAYS

We recommend always starting DP by writing down a recurrence relation. This feels mathy and abstract at first, but, in our experience, it starts to click if you stick to it for a few practice problems. After you have a recurrence, applying memoization (Recipe 1) is straightforward.

DP does not work for every problem. Sometimes, the choices we've made so far to get to a specific partial solution influence the remaining subproblem, which means that we can't reuse subproblems as easily. See the discussion in the Backtracking chapter (pg 541) about when to use Backtracking vs DP vs Greedy.

> **Dynamic programming triggers:** it's an optimization or counting problem, and the naive solution is backtracking. You have to make a sequence of choices. Path-finding problems where you can't go back.

ONLINE RESOURCES

Online resources for this chapter include:

- A chance to try each problem in this chapter in AI Interviewer
- Interview replays that show specific mistakes people make with dynamic programming problems
- Full code solutions for every problem in the chapter in multiple programming languages

Try online at bctci.co/dynamic-programming.

## CHAPTER 41

GREEDY ALGORITHMS

AI interviewer, replays, and more materials for this chapter at bctci.co/greedy-algorithms

▶ *Prerequisites: Backtracking*

A greedy algorithm is like a kid eating a meal and starting with their favorite foods. At each bite, they maximize instant gratification. Like the kid, the defining characteristic of a greedy algorithm is that it **always picks the choice with the most instant gratification without taking into account the longer-term consequences**.

Greedy algorithms are mostly for *optimization problems*, which go something like "of all the <things> that satisfy <given constraints>, find the one that optimizes <a given objective>." The 'things' could be strings, paths, subsets, subarrays, assignments, etc. In this context, we call the 'things' *solutions* and the one that we must find the *optimal solution*. We also say an algorithm is 'optimal' if it always finds the optimal solution (independently of how long the runtime is).[1]

In Backtracking, we discussed the idea of constructing solutions by making a sequence of choices, and we visualized this as navigating a *decision tree* (pg 543): we start with an *empty solution* (the root of the *decision tree*) and grow it step by step into larger and larger *partial solutions* by considering our options for how to expand it (children in the decision tree). Eventually, we reach a *full solution* (a leaf). In those terms, a greedy algorithm is one that always grows the partial solution in the way that contributes the most to the objective. That is, when picking a child in the decision tree, the greedy algorithm picks based only on those children and not on what may be further down the tree.

For some problems, making locally best choices always leads to the optimal solution. When that happens, a greedy algorithm is awesome! Easy to implement and often with optimal runtimes. The catch is that, depending on the problem, a greedy algorithm can seem very convincing and intuitive and even find the optimal solution for many inputs, but not all. The inputs where it finds a suboptimal solution are called *counterexamples*.

> The most common interview mistake related to greedy algorithms is using one without realizing that it doesn't always reach the optimal solution. Each individual choice by itself looks right, so sometimes, it is hard to notice the long-term consequences.

---

1 This notation is overloaded because we usually use "solution" to refer to a program that solves the problem and "optimal solution" to a program that solves the problem with the optimal asymptotic runtime. We already discussed how this notation is potentially confusing on page 540.

The most important skill when it comes to greedy algorithms is the ability to find counterexamples to the greedy algorithms you come up with.[2]

We've already seen examples of Greedy thinking in previous chapters, even if we didn't call it that. For instance, in Solution 37.7: Make Playlist (pg 507), we greedily chose to put a song from the artist with the most songs.

FINDING COUNTEREXAMPLES

When considering a greedy algorithm, we should think about possible counterexamples before we even think about the implementation.

Recall Problem 39.7: IKEA Shopping (pg 557): A magazine has rated every IKEA item from 1 to 10 in terms of style. We go to IKEA with a limited budget and the goal of maximizing the sum of style ratings of the items we buy. We also don't want to pick more than one of each item. The input is the price and the rating of each item and our overall budget. The output is the list of items we should pick.

A greedy algorithm for this problem would start with an empty shopping cart and would add items to it one by one according to some greedy choice until we run out of budget (the *greedy choice* is the rule we use to pick an option at each step).

Spoiler alert: there is no greedy algorithm for this problem—which is a variant of the classic Knapsack problem—that always finds the optimal set of items. But we can propose greedy algorithms and use them to practice finding counterexamples.

Counterexamples Problem Set.

For each of the following greedy choices for the IKEA Shopping problem, find a counterexample—that is, an input where a greedy algorithm following that criterion for making choices will end up with a suboptimal collection of items.

QUESTION 1

At each step, pick the cheapest item.

QUESTION 2

At each step, pick the highest-rated item.

QUESTION 3

At each step, pick the item with the highest rating/price ratio.

PROBLEM SET SOLUTIONS

ANSWER 1

Counterexample: Budget: $10. Items: [($5, 5.0), ($5, 5.0), ($4, 4.0)]

The optimal answer is [0, 1] with a rating sum of 10.0, but Greedy would start by picking 2 because it's the cheapest item.

---

2 Finding counterexamples is not limited to greedy algorithms—it's a fundamental problem-solving skill, and you should always look for cases where your algorithm won't work. Finding counterexamples is similar to finding problematic edge cases. We focus on counterexamples here because this is a common mistake when choosing a greedy approach.

ANSWER 2

Counterexample: Budget: $10. Items: `[($5, 5.0), ($5, 5.0), ($6, 6.0)]`

The optimal answer is `[0, 1]` with a rating sum of `10.0`, but Greedy would start by picking 2 because it's the highest-rated item.

ANSWER 3

Counterexample: Budget: $10. Items: `[($5, 5.0), ($5, 5.0), ($4, 4.5)]`

The optimal answer is `[0, 1]` with a rating sum of `10.0`, but Greedy would start by picking 2 because the first two items have a rating/price ratio of 1 and item 2 has a rating/price ratio >1.

\# We don't need to think about the implementation when we look for counterexamples. Just think about what Greedy would choose. Try to "set a trap" for greedy when constructing the input: make it so greedy starts with two options for the first choice, where choice A is slightly preferred by Greedy, but picking A restricts later options more.

One more example: recall the Traveling Salesperson Problem (TSP) (pg 545). A greedy algorithm may start at a random city and repeatedly go to the nearest yet-to-visit city. Can you draw an input where that leads to a longer-than-necessary cycle?

▶ DISPROVING A GREEDY APPROACH WITH A COUNTEREXAMPLE   INTERVIEW REPLAY

View Online:	bctci.co/greedy-replay-1 @ 4:55 - 14:12
The Question:	Given a positive integer, n, return the minimum number of steps to get to 1, assuming we can repeatedly either (a) subtract 1, (b) divide by two if evenly divisible, or (c) divide by three if evenly divisible.
What You'll See:	The candidate suggested an intuitive, greedy approach to the problem. Then they found a counterexample that made them change their approach
Who:	*Interviewer*: Senior Software Engineer at Microsoft *Candidate*: 3 years exp.
Outcome:	The candidate got the job at a FAANG+ company!

JUSTIFYING GREEDY IN AN INTERVIEW

It's hard to tell if a greedy algorithm is optimal for two reasons:

1. You can't check every possible input, so it is hard to rule out that there really aren't any counterexamples.
2. Often, a subtle change in the problem formulation can be the difference between there being a greedy algorithm being optimal or not.

To illustrate this, recall Chapter 39: Max-Sum Path (pg 539): Given a grid of positive integers, find the path from the top-left corner to the bottom-right corner with the largest sum. You can only go down or to the right (not diagonal).

A greedy algorithm would start on the top-left corner and always choose to move to the next cell with the largest value. In the Backtracking chapter (pg 539), we saw that this greedy algorithm does not work. The best solution for this problem uses dynamic programming (DP), as we saw on page 573. For instance, here's a counterexample:

```
[[0, 0, 2],
 [1, 0, 0]]
```

Greedy would get a path with sum 1, while the optimal is 2.

Now, consider a variation of the Max-Sum Path problem, where we add this extra condition: each row is sorted, and the last element of each row is smaller than the first element of the next row.

▸ **Example:** `grid = [[ 1,  2,  3,  4],`
                   `[20, 21, 30, 32],`
                   `[53, 57, 59, 60]]`
   Output: `250`. `The maximum path sum is 1 + 20 + 53 + 57 + 59 + 60.`

In this variation, we don't need DP anymore; Greedy always maximizes the sum. In fact, Greedy always does the same thing: it goes down until the last row, and then it goes right.

But how can we be sure that's always optimal? And how can we justify our choice to use Greedy to an interviewer?

We usually stay away from formal proofs of optimality in coding interviews, as it is notoriously difficult to prove that greedy algorithms are always optimal. However, we should still try to explain the intuition behind why they work to the interviewer (with examples and diagrams if it helps).

For comparison, we'll take this variant of the Max-Sum Path problem and give:

1. The intuitive explanation that's probably enough to satisfy an interviewer, and
2. A formal proof that would be overkill in an interview.

Intuitive explanation. Going down is better than going right, so the greedy path goes straight down and then right. If we deviate from that by going right at an earlier point, we eventually end up at the same place, but each intermediate step in the 'detour' is worse than if we stuck to the greedy path. We can illustrate this with Figure 1: it shows a 'detour' from the Greedy path that takes 5 steps (marked with an x) to 'merge back' into the greedy path. For each cell marked with an x, there is a cell in the Greedy path with a larger value because it is further down in the grid.

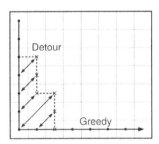

Figure 1.

This is not quite a proof, but it should be enough to signal strong problem-solving skills to the interviewer. In contrast, if you just state you'll use a greedy algorithm without any justification, even if it works, that would send a negative signal to the interviewer (they may think you've memorized the answer or made a lucky guess). Justifying all your technical choices is important—see the 'Name-and-Justify' technique on page 199. At the very least, show that Greedy works for specific inputs and explain *why* it works for those inputs. It's better than nothing, but it may not be enough for a strong problem-solving score.

\# A word of caution: Many candidates run into trouble because they *think* the Greedy approach works when it doesn't. If you can't explain why it works for the selected inputs, consider that maybe it doesn't work for other inputs.

FORMAL PROOF

Any path from the top-left cell to the bottom-right cell visits the same number of cells, $k = nr + nc - 2$. Let $G = g_1, g_2, g_3, \ldots, g_k$ be the greedy path and $P = p_1, p_2, p_3, \ldots, p_k$ be a different path. We want to show that

$$g_1 + g_2 + g_3 + \ldots + g_k \geq p_1 + p_2 + p_3 + \ldots + p_k$$

G and P both start at the same place and end at the same place ($g_1 = p_1$ and $g_k = p_k$), so they share a common prefix and suffix. Let's say they differ from step a to step b, with $1 < a \leq b < k$. So, at step a, G goes down and P goes right.

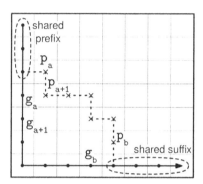

The two paths don't meet again until the last row, so we can say that $row(g_a) < row(p_a), row(g_{a+1}) < row(p_{a+1}), \ldots, row(g_b) < row(p_b)$. Since the grid is sorted, that means that $g_a > p_a, g_{a+1} > p_{a+1}, \ldots, g_b > p_b$. So:

- If $1 \leq i < a, g_i = p_i$.
- If $a \leq i \leq b, g_i > p_i$.
- If $b < i \leq k, g_i = p_i$.

Adding over i from 1 to k, we see that the sum of the g_i is more than the sum of the p_i. This completes the proof.

As you can see, formally proving that greedy finds the optimal solution is quite an exercise, even for a problem where it is intuitive.

Most interviewers won't expect a formal proof that a greedy algorithm finds the optimal solution. Instead:

1. Show that you checked a broad set of inputs for counterexamples, and
2. Explain the intuition why greedy always finds the best solution, with examples and diagrams if it helps.

FINDING THE CORRECT GREEDY CHOICE

We have seen problems where no greedy strategy is optimal (e.g., any NP-complete problem) and problems with an obvious greedy algorithm. In between these camps, there are problems where greedy algorithms work, but **only if we use the correct greedy choice**. Those are some of the most interesting (and challenging) problems when it comes to greedy algorithms.

✦✦ **PROBLEM 41.1**   **MOST NON-OVERLAPPING INTERVALS**

We are given a list, `intervals`, where each element is a pair of integers $[1, r]$, with $1 \leq r$, representing an interval (with both endpoints included). Return the largest number of non-overlapping intervals.

▶ **Example:** intervals = [[2, 3], [1, 4], [2, 3], [3, 6], [8, 9]]
   Output: 2. For instance, [2, 3] and [8, 9] don't overlap. We can't add [3, 6]
              because it overlaps with [2, 3] at value 3.
▶ **Example:** intervals = [[1, 2], [2, 3], [3, 4]]
   Output: 2

SOLUTION 41.1   MOST NON-OVERLAPPING INTERVALS

We have to find a subset of non-overlapping intervals as large as possible. For each interval, we need to make a *decision* whether to pick it for the subset or not. All intervals contribute 1 to the solution size, so we can't pick them based on how much they add to the objective. Instead, we should pick intervals that conflict the least with other intervals. Intuitively, shorter intervals are 'better'.

Based on this logic, we can propose a greedy algorithm:

1. Start with an empty subset.
2. Always pick the shortest remaining interval 'available', meaning that it doesn't overlap with intervals we already picked.

Figure 2. Greedy algorithm for Problem 41.1 that always picks the shortest interval available.
Unavailable intervals are marked with x.

Can you find a counterexample? Here is one:

Figure 3. Counterexample for a greedy algorithm that always picks the shortest interval available.

In this counterexample, we should have picked the leftmost interval, which would have allowed us to also pick the rightmost one. So, perhaps the key is to always pick the available interval that starts the earliest. Can you find a counterexample for this new rule? Here is one:

Figure 4. Counterexample for a greedy algorithm that always picks the available interval that starts the earliest.

This counterexample shows that how early an interval starts is not a good choice criterion because it could be super long. What if we always pick the available interval that *ends* the earliest instead? Try to find a counterexample.

This greedy choice actually works—there are no counterexamples. If we can't find counterexamples, the next step should be to explain the intuition for why it works to the interviewer (with examples and diagrams, if it helps). Something like this:

Imagine [2, 7] is the interval that ends the earliest. All intervals that overlap with it reach further to the right than 7. So, if we don't pick [2, 7] to pick another interval that overlaps with it, we'd just be restricting our options more than if we picked [2, 7]. So, picking [2, 7] is a safe bet (it might not be better, but it's definitely not worse). We can repeat the same logic for the remaining intervals.[3]

\#   Aim for the simplest and smallest counterexample you can think of (like we have done for every problem in this chapter). This often helps you diagnose the faulty logic in your algorithm and see whether it can be fixed or if you need a different approach altogether (e.g., DP).

Finally, let's talk about the implementation. A very common pattern is using a *custom-comparator sort* (pg 365) to sort the input elements in the order that greedy would consider them. For this problem, that means:

1. Sorting the input intervals based on the right endpoint.
2. Iterating through them, keeping track of which ones we can add.

```
1   def most_non_overlapping_intervals(intervals):
2       intervals.sort(key=lambda x: x[1])
3       count = 0
4       prev_end = -math.inf
5       for l, r in intervals:
6           if l > prev_end:
7               count += 1
8               prev_end = r
9       return count
```

The sorting step dominates the runtime, $O(n \log n)$, and extra space, $O(n)$ (even though we sorted the intervals in-place, most in-place sorting algorithms still use $O(n)$ extra space. See page 369.

> To be able to implement greedy algorithms, make sure you know how to implement custom sorts (pg 365). Sorting is often the bottleneck in greedy algorithms.

Now consider a version of Problem 41.1, where each interval also has a *weight*, and we need to maximize the sum of the weights of the non-overlapping intervals.

For the greedy choice, we can think of at least two options that make intuitive sense:

1. Always pick the available interval with the highest weight.
2. Always pick the available interval with the earliest end time (same choice as Solution 1).

Can you find counterexamples for each greedy choice?

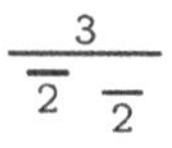

$$\frac{3}{2 \quad \frac{}{2}}$$

Figure 5. A counterexample for Greedy choice (1).

$$\frac{1}{2}$$

Figure 6. A counterexample for Greedy choice (2).

---

3   Another greedy choice that works for this problem is to always pick the available interval that starts the latest. It is symmetric to the greedy choice that picks the available interval that ends the earliest.

With practice, we can develop a "feel" for when problems don't have a greedy solution, and we should be willing to pivot into a different strategy. For this problem, greedy doesn't work and we should pivot to dynamic programming instead.

GREEDY END-TO-END

Let's formalize the steps to use a greedy algorithm:

1. Brainstorm for different options for the greedy choice.

2. Hunt for counterexamples. If you find one, go back to Step 1 or consider non-greedy solutions.

3. Explain to the interviewer the intuition for why it is correct.

4. As usual, before implementing, check with the interviewer. If there is some flaw in your logic, they may help you discover it.

Yes, steps 2 and 3 are tricky. But if you get through them, you should be in a good place. The implementation and analysis are usually the easy part of greedy algorithms.

Follow these steps to tackle the problems in the following problem set (the only step we can't do is check with the interviewer).

PROBLEM SET

✦ *Try these problems with AI Interviewer: bctci.co/greedy-problem-set-1*

> **PROBLEM 41.2**   **TIME TRAVELER**

You are a time traveler who is stuck in the past and trying to reach a future point. Fortunately, in addition to just letting time pass naturally, you can use an emergency system to jump forward in time—but there are constraints:

- Jumping Points: The emergency system can only jump to the next year specified in a sorted list called `jumping_points`, which contains n ≥ 2 unique years.

- Jumps: You have a limited number of jumps k, which lets you instantly move forward to the next jumping point of your choice. Once you're out of jumps, you must live through the years naturally to reach your target year. $0 \leq k \leq n-1$.

- Maximum Aging: You want to avoid aging more than a certain limit, `max_aging`, which is the total number of years you live naturally during your journey. `max_aging > 0`.

Your starting point is the first year in `jumping_points` and your goal is to reach the last year in the list. To achieve this, you can use any mix of:

- Jumping to the next jumping point instantaneously (up to a limit of k jumps).

- Let time pass naturally.

Return whether you can reach the final jumping point without exceeding the `max_aging` limit.

▸ **Example:** jumping_points = [2020, 2024], k = 0, max_aging = 3
    Output: false. We don't have jumps, and aging naturally from 2020 to 2024
            would take 4 years.

▸ **Example:** jumping_points = [2020, 2024], k = 1, max_aging = 1
    Output: true. We can use the jump to go from 2020 to 2024, so we get to 2024
            in 0 years.

▸ **Example:** jumping_points = [1803, 1861, 1863, 1865, 1920, 1929, 1941, 1964,

```
            2001, 2021], k = 4, max_aging = 45
```
Output: true. We start at 1803. We use our first jump to get to 1861. We let
             time flow naturally for four years, carrying us to 1865. We use our
             second jump to fast forward to 1920. We bide our time until 1941.
             The third jump takes us to 1964, and we jump again immediately to
             2001. Out of jumps, we endure the final stretch of 20 long years. In
             total, we have aged 4 + 9 + 12 + 20 = 45 years, the maximum we could
             afford.

PROBLEM 41.3   CENTER ASSIGNMENT

You are given:

1. A list of points on a 2D plane, points, where each point is represented as [x, y] (floating-point
    coordinates). The list always contains an even number of points.

2. Two additional points, center1 and center2, each also represented as [x, y].

Your task is to divide the points in points into two groups of equal size:

- Assign half of the points to center1.

- Assign the other half to center2.

The goal is to minimize the sum of the (Euclidean) distance from each point to its assigned center. Return
the sum of distances for an optimal assignment.

▸ **Example:** points = [[0, 1], [1, 0],
                        [-1, 0], [0, -1]]
            center1 = [0, 0]
            center2 = [1, 1]
   Output: 4. We can assign [-1, 0]
            and [0, -1] to center1
            and [0, 1] and [1, 0] to
            center2.

▸ **Example:** points = [[0, 0], [0, 0]]
            center1 = [0, 0]
            center2 = [1, 1]
   Output: 1.414. One of the points
            has to be assigned to
            center2, which is at
            distance √2 from [0, 0].

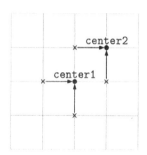

Figure 7. Example 1 for Problem 3. The points are shown
with x.

PROBLEM 41.4   MINIMUM TRIPLET MEDIANS

You are given a non-empty list of distinct integers, arr, where the length of arr is guaranteed to be a
multiple of three. Your task is to group the numbers into triplets such that the sum of the medians of each
triplet (the middle value in sorted order) is minimized.

▸ **Example:** arr = [6, 5, 8, 2, 1, 9]
   Output: 8. One optimal grouping is [1, 2, 8], [5, 6, 9].

▸ **Example:** arr = [6, 5, 8, 2, 1, 9, 12, 15, 14]
   Output: 17. One optimal grouping is [5, 6, 14], [1, 2, 12], [8, 9, 15].

| PROBLEM 41.5 | FEWEST SCRIPT RUNS |

There are n meetings scheduled, each with a start time and an end time. We have a script that, when run, captures some information about all ongoing meetings. Given an array, meetings, where each element is a tuple [l, r] with l < r, what's the minimum number of times we need to run the script to capture information from all meetings? If the script runs at the same time that a meeting starts or ends, it captures the information for that meeting.

▸ **Example:** meetings = [[2, 3], [1, 4], [2, 3], [3, 6], [8, 10]]
  Output: 2. We can run the script at t = 3 and t = 9.

| PROBLEM 41.6 | TIME TRAVELER MAX YEAR |

Consider the same setting as Problem 41.2: Time Traveler (pg 593). Instead of returning whether you can get to the final jumping point, return the latest year you can reach.

▸ **Example:** jumping_points = [2020, 2024], k = 0, max_aging = 2
  Output: 2022
▸ **Example:** jumping_points = [2020, 2024], k = 1, max_aging = 1
  Output: 2025
▸ **Example:** jumping_points = [1803, 1861, 1863, 1865, 1920, 1929, 1941, 1964, 2001, 2021], k = 4, max_aging = 45
  Output: 2021

✦ PROBLEM SET SOLUTIONS

SOLUTION 41.2   TIME TRAVELER

At each jumping point, we have a choice: use one of the remaining jumps to get to the next one and not age, or age naturally until the next one. We could use backtracking to try all possible jump choices, but we might already be too old by the time it finishes running. Intuitively, we should use our jumps on the biggest gaps between consecutive jumping points.

Greedy choice: find the k biggest gaps in jumping_points and use our jumps on those.

Intuitive explanation: Greedy is optimal because if we use a jump to cross a gap that is not one of the k largest ones, we will have to age through it, which will age us more.

```
1   def can_reach_goal(jumping_points, k, max_aging):
2     n = len(jumping_points)
3     gaps = []
4     for i in range(1, n):
5       gaps.append(jumping_points[i] - jumping_points[i - 1])
6     gaps.sort()
7     total_aging = sum(gaps[:n - 1 - k])
8     return total_aging <= max_aging
```

As usual in Greedy algorithms, the runtime bottleneck is sorting (the input was already sorted chronologically, but we had to sort the gaps instead).

SOLUTION 41.3   CENTER ASSIGNMENT

Intuitively, points closer to center1 should be assigned to center1.

Greedy choice: take the closest n/2 points to center1 and assign them to center1, and the rest to center2.

However, this is a **counterexample**:

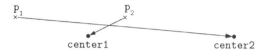

Figure 8.

Let's try something different: start with every point assigned to its closest center. A center may have more than $n/2$ points, so we need to pick some of them to assign to the other center. The cost for switching a point p from center1 to center2 is dist(p, center2) - dist(p, center1). We can greedily switch the points with the smallest switching cost until the balance is restored. For instance, in Figure 8, we would switch p_2 because it has a smaller switching cost than p_1.

Greedy choice 2: switch the point assigned to the overloaded center with the smallest switching cost.

Intuitive explanation: assigning each point to its nearest center produces a baseline assignment that is locally minimal for each individual point. Then, when rebalancing the assignments to ensure each center has exactly half the points, choosing the points that incur the smallest additional cost to switch guarantees that no alternative reassignment could produce a lower total distance.

```
1   def minimize_distance(points, center1, center2):
2     n = len(points)
3     assignment = [0] * n
4     baseline = 0
5     c1_count = 0
6     for i, p in enumerate(points):
7       if dist(p, center1) <= dist(p, center2):
8         assignment[i] = 1
9         baseline += dist(p, center1)
10        c1_count += 1
11      else:
12        assignment[i] = 2
13        baseline += dist(p, center2)
14    if c1_count == n // 2:
15      return baseline
16    switch_costs = []
17    for i, p in enumerate(points):
18      if assignment[i] == 1 and c1_count > n // 2:
19        switch_costs.append(dist(p, center2) - dist(p, center1))
20      if assignment[i] == 2 and c1_count < n // 2:
21        switch_costs.append(dist(p, center1) - dist(p, center2))
22    res = baseline
23    switch_costs.sort()
24    for cost in switch_costs[:abs(c1_count - n // 2)]:
25      res += cost
26    return res
```

SOLUTION 41.4   MINIMUM TRIPLET MEDIANS

We don't need to consider all the ways to partition arr into triplets. We can greedily form triplets with the smallest possible middle value:

- Consider the smallest number. It cannot be the middle element of a triplet, but it has to go in some triplet.

- We should put the second-smallest value in the same triplet as the smallest value. If we didn't, it would end up as the smallest element of a different triplet, which would be suboptimal.
- The third element doesn't affect the contribution of this group to the overall sum, so we may as well pick the largest number. It's a "safe bet."
- We can repeat this logic for the remaining elements.

```
1   def minimize_middle_sum(arr):
2     arr.sort()
3     middle_sum = 0
4     for i in range(len(arr) // 3):
5       middle_sum += arr[i * 2 + 1]
6     return middle_sum
```

SOLUTION 41.5 FEWEST SCRIPT RUNS

We want to maximize the number of meetings we take care of with each run. Intuitively, we want to "check off" as many meetings as possible in a single run.

Greedy choice: run the script at the time with the most meetings, discard those meetings, and repeat.

However, here is a **counterexample**:

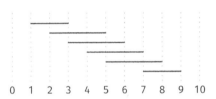

Figure 9. Greedy would pick 5 first because it overlaps with the most intervals (4), and end up with a solution of size 3 like [5, 2, 8]. However, the optimal solution is [3, 7].

Instead, let's focus on the meeting, [1, r], with the earliest end time. We need to run the script at some point between l and r. Of all the options, r will overlap the most with other meetings, so r is a "safe bet."

Greedy choice: run the script at the end time of the meeting that ends the earliest. Repeat for meetings not covered yet.

Here is the implementation:[4]

```
1   def minimum_script_runs(meetings):
2     meetings.sort(key=lambda x: x[1])
3     count = 0
4     prev_end = -math.inf
5     for l, r in meetings:
6       if l > prev_end:
7         count += 1
8         prev_end = r
9     return count
```

\# Interval problems are a common application of greedy algorithms. It often helps to focus on processing them based on the earliest end time.

---

4 A perceptive reader may have noticed that this is exactly the same code as Solution 41.1. This shows that, for any set of intervals, the maximum number of non-overlapping intervals equals the minimum number of numbers intersecting all the intervals.

SOLUTION 41.6   TIME TRAVELER MAX YEAR

Recall the solution to Problem 41.2: Time Traveler (pg 593). This problem is trickier because we don't know ahead of time how far we can get. There may be a big gap far in the future, but if it is unreachable with at least 1 jump left, we should use our jumps on smaller gaps. The greedy choice of using the jumps on the largest gaps no longer works! Here's a concrete **counterexample**:

▶ **Example:** `jumping_points = [1, 10, 30], k = 1, max_aging = 5`
   Output: 15

In this counterexample, we *must* use the jump on the small gap. We are at a tough crossroads where we must decide whether to try a different greedy choice or switch to a different approach altogether.

While we often pivot from Greedy to DP, the binary search guess-and-check technique (pg 338) works well for this problem: we can binary search for the latest reachable jumping point. Each check inside the binary search asks whether we can reach a specific year, which is equivalent to Problem 41.2 which we already solved. By sorting the gaps in a preliminary step, we could do each binary search check in $O(n)$ time, leading to total $O(n \log n)$ time.

We can *also* stick with Greedy for this problem. The idea is to iterate through the jumping points one by one. When we get to jumping point i, we ask: *can I get here with the available jumps?* The Greedy part is that, to answer this question, we should **use our jumps for the biggest gaps up to jumping point** i. The set of gaps to jump over will evolve as i advances and we reach longer gaps. For instance:

```
jumping_points = [1, 3, 6, 7, 11, 16, 17, 19], k = 2, max_aging = 4
- Getting to 1, 3, and 6 is trivial because we have 2 jumps.
- Can we get to 7? The two biggest jumps are 1->3 and 3->6, so we need to
age 1 year (6 to 7). The answer is yes.
- Can we get to 11? The two biggest jumps are 3->6 and 7->11, so we need to
age 3 years (1 to 3 and 6 to 7). The answer is yes.
- Can we get to 16? The two biggest jumps are 7->11 and 11->16, so we need
to age 6 years (1 to 7). The answer is no.
```

We can stop here—the answer is 12. We use our 2 jumps to get to 11, and we have 1 year left.

The tricky part about this problem is the implementation: a naive approach would take $O(n)$ time per jumping point, for a total time of $O(n^2)$. We can use a min-heap to keep track of the k largest gaps so far (see the reusable idea 'Heap Size Restriction', pg 501). The sum of the elements in the min-heap is the total number of years we can jump over. Now, for each iteration, we just need to do some min-heap operations, which take $O(\log k)$ time each. The total time is $O(n * \log k)$.

```
1   def latest_reachable_year(jumping_points, k, max_aging):
2     gaps = []
3     for i in range(1, len(jumping_points)):
4       gaps.append(jumping_points[i] - jumping_points[i-1])
5
6     min_heap = Heap()
7     total_gap_sum = 0
8     sum_heap = 0
9     for i, gap in enumerate(gaps):
10      aged = total_gap_sum - sum_heap
11      min_heap.push(gap)
12      sum_heap += gap
13      total_gap_sum += gap
14      if min_heap.size() > k:
15        smallest_jump = min_heap.pop()
16        sum_heap -= smallest_jump
```

```
17    new_aged = total_gap_sum - sum_heap
18    if new_aged > max_aging:
19      # We can't reach the end of gap i.
20      # We get to jumping_points[i] and age naturally from there.
21      remaining_aging = max_aging - aged
22      return jumping_points[i] + remaining_aging
23
24  # Reached the last jumping point
25  aged = total_gap_sum - sum_heap
26  remaining_aging = max_aging - aged
27  return jumping_points[len(jumping_points)-1] + remaining_aging
```

KEY TAKEAWAYS

There are pros and cons of greedy algorithms, especially in contrast to backtracking and DP, which are often used for similar problems:

Pros:

- Easy to code. No need for recursion like in backtracking, and no need for a recurrence equation like in DP. You'll need to know how to use a custom sort, or perhaps even a heap.
- Easy to analyze the runtime. Sorting is often the bottleneck.
- When it works, its runtime is often optimal.

Cons:

- Greedy algorithms can be optimal for some (even most) inputs, but not all. Your intuition may give you a false sense of optimality. You need to get good at finding counterexamples.
- It's hard to prove a greedy algorithm finds the optimal solution. We usually avoid formal proofs in coding interviews, but you should still be able to give an intuitive explanation of why the output is *always* optimal.
- Greedy algorithms are less common in interviews than backtracking and DP. So, when picking between them, statistically, Greedy is less likely to be right. Most problems that can be solved efficiently with Greedy can also be solved efficiently with DP, but not the other way around.

We recommend following the steps on page 593. Specifically, finding counterexamples is key to avoiding the most common mistake with greedy algorithms: thinking they are always optimal when they are not.

> **Greedy Algorithm triggers:** optimization problems; interval problems; problems where you'd use backtracking but you need better-than-exponential runtime.

ONLINE RESOURCES

Online resources for this chapter include:

- A chance to try each problem in this chapter in AI Interviewer
- Interview replays that show specific mistakes people make with greedy algorithms problems
- Full code solutions for every problem in the chapter in multiple programming languages

Try online at bctci.co/greedy-algorithms.

## CHAPTER 42

TOPOLOGICAL SORT

AI interviewer, replays, and more materials for this chapter at bctci.co/topological-sort

▶ *Prerequisites: Graphs*

Imagine you're managing a complex project with dozens of interdependent tasks. Some tasks must be completed before others can even begin—like designing a blueprint before starting construction or securing permits before ordering materials. How would you determine the order to tackle these tasks?

This is exactly the kind of problem that topological sorting solves. It's a way to organize the nodes in a directed acyclic graph (DAG) so that for every directed edge u -> w, u appears before w in the topological ordering. In other words, it finds a valid sequence that respects all the dependencies.

Topological sort is more than just a theoretical concept—it's a practical tool used in areas like course scheduling, build systems in software development, and even supply chain management. By the end of this chapter, you'll not only understand how to implement a topological sort but also know how to apply it to solve dependency problems efficiently in coding interviews and beyond.

DAGS: DIRECTED ACYCLIC GRAPHS

A *directed acyclic graph*, commonly abbreviated to DAG, has directed edges and no cycles (that is, it is *acyclic*):

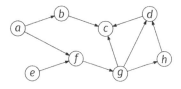

Figure 1. A DAG.

DAGs can be used to model things like dependencies and prerequisites, where cycles do not make sense. Settings like:

- Chapter prerequisites in a book, like the DAG on page 171.
- Course prerequisites in college.
- Parts that get combined into bigger parts in a car assembly line.
- Project management, where tasks depend on other tasks.
- Parallel execution threads that depend on other threads.

Every DAG has at least one *topological ordering*—an ordering of nodes where each directed edge goes from a node appearing earlier in the ordering to one appearing later:

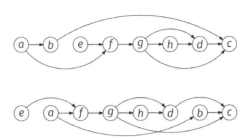

Figure 2. Two topological orderings for the graph from Figure 1. There can be many topological orderings for the same DAG.

Can a non-DAG graph have a valid topological sort? No.

- If a graph has a cycle, you have a circular dependency. You can't have an ordering of nodes that respects a circular dependency. At least one edge in the cycle would have to go to a predecessor (i.e., from right to left).
- If a graph is not directed, we have no concept of dependencies.

In that sense, DAGs and topological sorts are tightly linked. A topological sort exists if and only if the graph is a DAG.

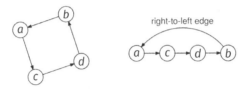

Figure 3. Topological orderings do not exist for graphs with cycles.

The fundamental DAG questions are:

- Find if a directed graph is a DAG.
- Find a topological ordering in a DAG.
- Find the shortest or longest path in a DAG.
- Count the number of topological orderings.

There is a class of coding problems—DAG problems, if you will—based on the type of settings described above which ultimately can be reduced to one of the questions above. DAG problems are often handled in two steps:

1. Compute a topological ordering.
2. Process the nodes in that order.

The good news is that Step (1) is the same for every problem, so we just need to learn an algorithm for computing a topological ordering and be able to reproduce it in an interview.

Next, we will learn an algorithm for computing a topological ordering. After that, we will use it to solve DAG problems.

COMPUTING A TOPOLOGICAL ORDERING

An algorithm for computing a topological ordering is known as a topological sort. Two widely used approaches for this are Kahn's algorithm (also called the "peel-off algorithm") and a DFS-based method.

Both have equivalent runtimes, allowing you to choose the one you prefer. In this chapter, we'll focus on Kahn's algorithm due to its simplicity and intuitive design.

If you were to create a topological ordering, which node would you put first? Any node with incoming edges won't work since there's another node that needs to come before it. This brings us to this: **Topological orderings must start with a node that has an in-degree of 0.**

The peel-off algorithm takes advantage of this by selecting such a node, adding it to the ordering, and then "peeling it off" the graph. This involves removing the node and all its outgoing edges, which reduces the in-degree of its neighbors, potentially making them eligible to be picked next.

🗎 RECIPE 1. PEEL-OFF ALGORITHM

```
topo_order = empty list
while not every node is in topo_order:
  pick a node with in-degree 0
  add it to topo_order
  decrease the in-degree of its neighbors by 1
if not all nodes were peeled off, there is a cycle
```

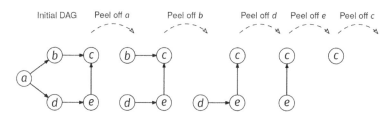

Figure 4. Peel-off algorithm steps.

To implement this algorithm, we need to track (1) the in-degree of each node, and (2) nodes ready to be picked. The order in which we pick nodes with in-degree 0 does not matter; we'll just get different but valid topological orderings as a result.

```
1   def topological_sort(graph):
2     # Initialization
3     V = len(graph)
4     in_degrees = [0 for _ in range(V)]
5     for node in range(V):
6       for nbr in graph[node]:  # For weighted graphs, unpack edges: nbr, _
7         in_degrees[nbr] += 1
8     degree_zero = []
9     for node in range(V):
10      if in_degrees[node] == 0:
11        degree_zero.append(node)
12    # Main 'peel-off' loop
13    topo_order = []
14    while degree_zero:
15      node = degree_zero.pop()
16      topo_order.append(node)
17      for nbr in graph[node]:  # For weighted graphs, unpack edges: nbr, _
18        in_degrees[nbr] -= 1
19        if in_degrees[nbr] == 0:
20          degree_zero.append(nbr)
21    if len(topo_order) < V:
22      return []  # There is a cycle; some nodes couldn't be peeled off
```

```
23    return topo_order
```

The algorithm offers a way to detect if a directed graph is a DAG. If there is a cycle, the process of peeling off nodes will eventually stall because no nodes with an in-degree of 0 will remain.

The peel-off algorithm processes each edge once, so it takes $O(V+E)$ time and $O(V)$ space (the space becomes $O(V+E)$ if we are only given the edge list and we have to build the adjacency list ourselves, which is common in interviews).

CORE DAG PROBLEMS

We already tackled the cycle detection problem, which is one of the most common. The other core DAG problems can be solved with the DAG problem recipe:

RECIPE 2. DAG PROBLEM RECIPE

```
compute a topological ordering (Khan's peel-off algorithm)
for node in topological ordering
  for each edge node -> nbr
    update some information about nbr
```

SHORTEST PATHS

You may already know that BFS can be used to find shortest paths in unweighted graphs in $O(V + E)$ time (pg 474), while Dijkstra's algorithm can do the same in graphs with positive edge weights in $O(V + E \log E)$ time. In DAGs, we'll see a topological-ordering-based solution can match the runtime of BFS **even if the DAG is weighted and has negative weights**.

✦ PROBLEM 42.1   DAG DISTANCES

Given the adjacency list of a DAG with edge weights, graph, and a node, start, return the distances from start to every other node in an array of length V (the number of nodes). Element i should be the distance from start to node i. If i cannot be reached from start, that element should be +∞. The edge weights can be negative.

▸ Example:
```
  graph = [
    [[1, 10]],
    [],
    [[1, 10]],
    [[4, 12]],
    [[1, 11], [2, 21], [5, 14]],
    [[2, -30]]
  ]
  start = 4
  Output: [+∞, -6, -16, +∞, 0, 14]
  Nodes 0 and 3 are unreachable from node
  4. Node 4 is at distance 0 from itself.
  The shortest path from node 4 to node 1
  is 4 -> 5 -> 2 -> 1.
```

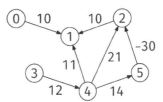

Figure 5. Example DAG for Problem 1.

SOLUTION 42.1   DAG DISTANCES

We follow Recipe 2. We start computing a topological ordering, as usual:

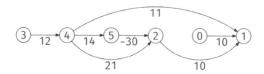

Figure 6. A topological ordering for the graph in Figure 5.

Similar to BFS and Dijkstra's algorithm, we maintain a distances map, where distances[u] is the short-est distance we have found *so far* from start to u.[1] Initially, all we know is that distances[start] is 0.

We iterate through the topological ordering from left to right. Nodes before start are unreachable, so we can ignore them. Starting from start, when we process a node u, we check if any of the outgoing edges u -> w produces a shorter path to w. For instance, imagine that start is node 4 in Figure 6. When processing node 4, since distances[4] is 0 and there is an edge with length 11 from node 4 to node 1, we can set distances[1] to 11. This indicates that, at worst, there is a path from 4 to 1 of length 11. However, this distance is not definitive. There is, in fact, a shorter path, which is 4 -> 5 -> 2 -> 1. The point of the algorithm is that, since we are following a topological ordering, we will visit nodes 4, 5, 2, and 1 in that order, and we'll find the correct distance by doing a sequence of updates:

- Initialization: distances[4] = 0
- Processing edge 4 -> 5: distances[5] = distances[4] + 14 = 14.
- Processing edge 5 -> 2: distances[2] = distances[5] - 30 = -16.
- Processing edge 2 -> 1: distances[1] = distances[2] + 10 = -6.

Here is how we implement this idea:

```
1   def distance(graph, start):
2     topo_order = topological_sort(graph)  # Recipe 1.
3     distances = {start: 0}
4     for node in topo_order:
5       if node not in distances: continue
6       for nbr, weight in graph[node]:
7         if nbr not in distances or distances[node] + weight < distances[nbr]:
8           distances[nbr] = distances[node] + weight
9     res = []
10    for i in range(len(graph)):
11      if i in distances:
12        res.append(distances[i])
13      else:
14        res.append(math.inf)
15    return res
```

The distances map contains all the reachable nodes and their distances. What we do with it depends on the problem. For Problem 42.1, we transformed it into an array.

✦✦ **PROBLEM 42.2**   **DAG PATH RECONSTRUCTION**

Given the adjacency list of a DAG with edge weights, graph, and a pair of nodes, start and goal, return the shortest path from start to goal, or an empty array if goal cannot be reached from start. The edge weights can be negative.

---

1   Instead of a map, we could also use an array of length V where each element is initialized to +∞ except the start index, which is initialized to 0.

SOLUTION 42.2 DAG PATH RECONSTRUCTION

We need to compute the distances, as in Problem 42.1, while also tracking the best way to reach each node. We'll follow the **path reconstruction** reusable idea from the Graphs chapter. It involves tracking predecessors in a predecessors map.

```
1   def shortest_path(graph, start, goal):
2     topo_order = topological_sort(graph)   # Recipe 1.
3     distances = {start: 0}
4     predecessors = {}
5     for node in topo_order:
6       if node not in distances: continue
7       for nbr, weight in graph[node]:
8         if nbr not in distances or distances[node] + weight < distances[nbr]:
9           distances[nbr] = distances[node] + weight
10          predecessors[nbr] = node
11    if goal not in distances:
12      return []
13    path = [goal]
14    while path[-1] != start:
15      path.append(predecessors[path[-1]])
16    path.reverse()
17    return path
```

This shortest-path algorithm for DAGs has some advantages over other shortest-path algorithms.

- It **works with negative edge weights**, whereas Dijkstra's algorithm does not.
- It can be adapted to finding longest paths, which is an NP-complete problem for graphs with cycles (even unweighted ones).

   » Topological sort should be our go-to algorithm for finding distances and shortest/longest paths in weighted DAGs.

✦ **PROBLEM 42.3** **DAG LONGEST PATH**

Given the adjacency list of a DAG with edge weights, graph, and a node, start, return an array of length V (the number of nodes) with the length of the longest path from start to every other node (or -∞ if the node is unreachable). The edge weights can be negative.

▶ Example:
```
graph = [
  [[1, 10]],
  [],
  [[1, 10]],
  [[4, 12]],
  [[1, 11], [2, 21], [5, 14]],
  [[2, -30]]
]
start = 4
```
Output: [-∞, 31, 21, -∞, 0, 14]
Nodes 0 and 3 are unreachable from node 4.
The longest path from node 4 to node 1 is
4 -> 2 -> 1.

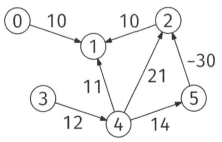

Figure 7. Example DAG for Problem 42.3 (same as **Figure 5**).

SOLUTION 42.3   DAG LONGEST PATH

We can do the same as for shortest paths, with one difference: when we process a node, we check if each outgoing edge produces a *longer* path to the neighbor node. This condition:

▸   `if nbr not in distances or distances[node] + weight < distances[nbr]:`

becomes:

▸   `if nbr not in lengths or lengths[node] + weight > lengths[nbr]:`

✦   **PROBLEM 42.4**   **COUNTING PATHS**

Given the adjacency list of an *unweighted* DAG, graph, and a node, start, return an array of length V (the number of nodes) with the number of different paths from start to every node.

▸ **Example:**
```
graph = [
  [1],
  [],
  [1],
  [4],
  [1, 2, 5],
  [2]
]
start = 4
Output: [0, 3, 2, 0, 1, 1]
Nodes 0 and 3 are unreachable from node 4. There
is a single path from 4 to itself, the empty
path. There are 3 paths from node 4 to node 1:
  4 -> 1
  4 -> 2 -> 1
  4 -> 5 -> 2 -> 1
```

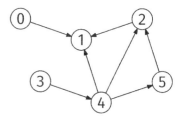

Figure 8. Example DAG for Problem 4.

SOLUTION 42.4   COUNTING PATHS

We follow a very similar approach to the one for shortest and longest paths. This time, instead of a `distances` map, we have a `counts` map, which starts at 1 for start. When we process a node, u, if `counts[u]` is k, we increase the count of all its neighbors by k.

For instance, if the starting node is 4 in Figure 8, the counts evolve as follows:

- Initialization: {4: 1}
- After processing 4: {4: 1, 5: 1, 2: 1, 1: 1}
- After processing 5: {4: 1, 5: 1, 2: 2, 1: 1}
- After processing 2: {4: 1, 5: 1, 2: 2, 1: 3}

Since there are 2 ways of getting from 4 to 2 (4 -> 2 and 4 -> 5 -> 2), when we process edge 2 -> 1, we increase `counts[1]` by 2 to account the two paths from 4 to 1 that go through 2 (4 -> 2 -> 1 and 4 -> 5 -> 2 -> 1).

```
1  def path_count(graph, start, goal):
2    topo_order = topological_sort(graph)  # Recipe 1.
3    counts = {start: 1}
4    for node in topo_order:
5      if node not in counts:
```

```
6          continue
7        for nbr in graph[node]:
8          if nbr not in counts:
9            counts[nbr] = 0
10         counts[nbr] += counts[node]
11     if goal in counts:
12       return counts[goal]
13     return 0
```

In most actual problems, the setting will be about task dependencies, course prerequisites, or something like that. They may look something like this:

PROBLEM 42.5 **PARALLEL COMPILATION**

A compiler needs to compile a program consisting of n packages, numbered from 0 to n - 1. We are given an array of n positive integers, seconds, where seconds[i] indicates the time it takes to compile package i, in seconds. An additional array, imports, of length n, specifies the package dependencies, where imports[i] is the list of packages that package i depends on.

Constraints:

1. There are no circular dependencies (no cycles in the dependency graph).
2. We cannot start compiling a package until all the packages it depends on have finished compiling.
3. There is no limit to how many packages can be compiled *in parallel*, provided they don't depend on each other.
4. The program is considered fully compiled when all packages are compiled.

Determine the minimum time required to compile the entire program.

▸ **Example:** seconds = [10, 20, 30],
　　　　　　　imports = [
　　　　　　　　　[],
　　　　　　　　　[],
　　　　　　　　　[0, 1]
　　　　　　　]
　　Output: 50. Packages 0 and 1 can be compiled in parallel. Package 2 takes
　　　　　　　30s and cannot start until packages 0 and 1 finish, which takes 20s.

▸ **Example:** seconds = [10, 20, 30], imports = [[], [], []]
　　Output: 30. We can compile all packages in parallel.

SOLUTION 42.5   PARALLEL COMPILATION

It's easy to see that the program forms a DAG in which the packages are nodes and the imports are edges. But can you tell which core DAG question is being asked?

We can start compiling all the packages without any imports in parallel, and then, as they finish, start compiling packages that depend only on packages that are already compiled. Any path in the DAG must be compiled sequentially, so this is really a variant of the *longest path problem*[2] (Problem 42.4) with some tweaks:

- The imports array is like an adjacency list, but for *incoming* edges, not outgoing ones. We need to construct the normal adjacency list in order to compute the topological order.

2　In the context of task dependencies, it is also called the *critical path* because it denotes the bottleneck for parallelizing the tasks. No matter how much parallelization you throw at the problem, you can never finish faster than the critical path.

- We don't have a start node. Instead, we can treat all the packages without imports (i.e., nodes without incoming edges) as starting nodes.
- We have weights in the nodes, not the edges. We need to tweak how we update the longest-path lengths to add node weights instead of edge weights.
- Since we need to wait for all the packages to finish, we return the maximum among all durations.

Here is the final algorithm:

```
def compile_time(seconds, imports):
  V = len(seconds)
  graph = [[] for _ in range(V)]
  for package in range(V):
    for imported_package in imports[package]:
      graph[imported_package].append(package)
  topo_order = topological_sort(graph)  # Recipe 1.
  durations = {}
  for node in topo_order:
    if node not in durations:
      durations[node] = seconds[node]
    for nbr in graph[node]:
      if nbr not in durations:
        durations[nbr] = 0
      durations[nbr] = max(durations[nbr], seconds[nbr] + durations[node])
  return max(durations.values())
```

GRAPH MODELING

In the Graph Modeling section (pg 485), we saw there are problems where the input is not a graph, but we can find a way to reframe it as a graph problem and solve it with a graph algorithm. This idea does not only apply to DFS and BFS, but also to topological sort (and other graph algorithms). Try to convert the following problems into DAG questions and then solve them with a DAG algorithm.

The full solutions are online—here we focus on how to formulate the problem as a DAG question.

✦ **PROBLEM 42.6**   **LONGEST PATH OF INCREASING DEGREES**

Given the number of nodes and the edge list of an unweighted, *undirected* graph, V and edges, find the longest path where every node has a higher degree than the previous one and return its length.

Figure 9. Graph from the example for Problem 6.

▸ **Example:** V = 8, edges = [[0, 1], [1, 2], [2, 3], [0, 2], [0, 4], [2, 6], [3, 7], [2, 7], [4, 5], [5, 6], [6, 7]]
Output: 3. One of the longest paths with increasing degrees is 5 -> 6 -> 2 (degrees 2, 3, and 5). Other longest paths include 1 -> 0 -> 2.

SOLUTION 42.6   LONGEST PATH OF INCREASING DEGREES

At first, it may seem that topological order cannot be used because the graph is undirected and may have cycles. However, we can only follow edges in one direction, from smaller to larger degrees. And, more importantly, we cannot have a cycle of increasing degrees. Thus, when we restrict the edges to the directions we can use, the graph becomes a DAG (Figure 10), and we can **REFRAME THE PROBLEM** as finding the longest path in a DAG (Problem 42.3).

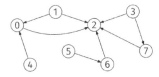

Figure 10.

In the implementation, we can do the same as Problem 42.3, with the only exception that, whenever we need to iterate through the neighbors of a node, we skip those with lower or equal degree. We can encapsulate this in a helper function, e.g.:

```
1  def dag_neighbors(graph, node):
2    return [nbr for nbr in graph[node] if len(graph[nbr]) > len(graph[node])]
```

And then replace

▶   `for nbr in graph[node]:`

for

▶   `for nbr in dag_neighbors(node):`

✦ **PROBLEM 42.7**   **SUPERSEQUENCE**

A *supersequence* of a string s is another string that contains all the same letters of s in the same relative order. For instance, `"aabbcc"` is a supersequence of `"abc"`, but not of `"bca"`. Given a non-empty array of strings, `arr`, where each string consists only of lowercase English letters, determine if it is possible to construct a *single* supersequence of all the strings in `arr` such that no letter appears more than once. Return `true` if such a supersequence exists and `false` otherwise.

▶ **Example:** arr = ["abc", "bde", "df", "cfe"]
   `Output:` True. "abcdfe" is a supersequence.
▶ **Example:** arr = ["ab", "ba"]
   `Output:` False. Any supersequence would have to include 'a' twice (like "aba")
             or 'b' twice (like "bab").
▶ **Example:** arr = ["aa"]
   `Output:` False.

SOLUTION 42.7   SUPERSEQUENCE

Even though the input consists of strings, the clue that this might be a graph-related problem is that we have **pairwise relationships** between letters. The fact that those relationships indicate dependencies of the kind "letter x must go before letter y" further narrows it down to a DAG. Interestingly, the DAG's nodes are not the input strings, but rather individual letters.

We can model this problem as a graph where there is one node per English letter and edges represent that a letter must appear before another. If we have a string in `arr` like `"xyz"`, we add edges x -> y and y -> z (we could also add x -> z, but that is redundant). See Figure 11 for an example. After building this graph, the problem becomes the cycle detection problem, which we saw how to tackle with the peel-off algorithm (Recipe 1).

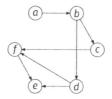

Figure 11. DAG for strings "abc", "bde", "df", and "cfe" (Example 1).

✦‡ PROBLEM 42.8   NUMBER OF PALINDROMIC SPLITS

A *palindromic split* of a string is a way of dividing a string into substrings where every substring is a palindrome (a palindrome is a string that reads the same forward and backward). For instance, abbaab has six palindromic splits: a|b|b|a|a|b, a|bb|a|a|b, a|b|b|aa|b, a|bb|aa|b, abba|a|b, and a|b|baab. Given a string, s, return the number of palindromic splits.

▶ **Example:** s = "abbaab"
  Output: 6.

▶ **Example:** s = "aabaa"
  Output: 6. The palindromic splits are a|a|b|a|a, aa|b|a|a, a|a|b|aa,
       aa|b|aa, a|aba|a, and aabaa.

▶ **Example:** s = "aaaaa"
  Output: 31.

SOLUTION 42.8   NUMBER OF PALINDROMIC SPLITS

This is a *counting* problem, which is a trigger for backtracking and dynamic programming (pg 543), and it can indeed be solved efficiently with DP. The topological sort solution is probably less intuitive, but it shows just how many problems can be modeled as graphs.

The nodes of our DAG are all the palindromic substring of s. The **pairwise relationship** between two palindromic substrings is "substring x ends where substring y starts." For instance, if the string is "abacdc", one of the edges would be "aba" -> "cdc". This relationship forms directed edges that cannot have cycles.

Now we can *REFRAME THE PROBLEM* as counting the number of paths that cover the whole string. To make it a bit simpler, we can also add a special start node to the DAG with an edge to every node corresponding to a substring starting at the first character, and a special goal node with an incoming edge from every substring ending at the last character (see Figure 12). Then, the problem can be reframed as counting the number of paths in a DAG from start to goal (Problem 42.4).

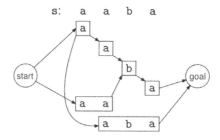

Figure 12. DAG for "aaba". It has 3 palindromic splits: a|a|b|a, a|aba, and aa|b|a.

The tedious part of this problem is first creating the DAG. First, we need to find the nodes. For this, we start at each character in s, which is a palindrome by itself, and then try to grow outward for as long as possible while remaining a palindrome. E.g., if s is "aabaa" and we start at b, we will find three nodes: "b", "aba", and "aabaa". This will find all palindromes of odd length. For the ones with even length, we need to grow outward from every pair of consecutive characters.

We actually don't care about the letters in the substring, only where it starts and where it ends, so we can encode each node as an interval; for s = "aabaa", "b" becomes [2, 2], "aba" becomes [1, 3], and "aabaa" becomes [0, 4]. Next, we need to find the edges. For this, we can build two maps: one from indices in s to palindromic substrings starting at that index, and the other from indices in s to palindromic substrings that end there. The two maps allow us to find all edges.

A CLASSIC TOPOLOGICAL SORT PROBLEM		INTERVIEW REPLAY
View Online:	bctci.co/topological-sort-replay-1 @ 6:20 - 47:55	
The Question:	Given a directed acyclic graph of tasks, determine task dependencies.	
What You'll See:	The candidate was given a classic topological sort problem but didn't recognize it.	
Who:	*Interviewer*: Principal Software Engineer at Amazon *Candidate*: Junior engineer	

KEY TAKEAWAYS

The best advice to nail DAG questions is to learn a topological sort algorithm (like the peel-off algorithm from Recipe 1) and get comfortable implementing it on the spot. Of course, you should also be comfortable building the adjacency list data structure and working with it (pg 460).

Once you have a topological order, most DAG problems can be solved with the approach illustrated in Recipe 2. It often comes down to some variation of a few core DAG questions: detecting cycles, finding shortest/longest paths, or counting paths.

> **Topological sort triggers.** The input is a DAG, or at least a directed graph; there is some notion of dependencies or prerequisites (even if the input is not a graph); the question is about distances or paths; the runtime upperbound is linear.

ONLINE RESOURCES

Online resources for this chapter include:

- A chance to try each problem in this chapter in AI Interviewer
- Interview replays that show specific mistakes people make with topological sort problems
- Full code solutions for every problem in the chapter in multiple programming languages

Try online at bctci.co/topological-sort.

## CHAPTER 43

PREFIX SUMS

AI interviewer, replays, and more materials for this chapter at bctci.co/prefix-sums

▶ *Prerequisites: None*

In this chapter, we will tackle problems about *range queries* and the technique commonly used to solve them, *prefix sums*. What's a range query? We're glad you asked.

In this context, *range* is a synonym for subarray (like 'window'), and a 'range query' is a question requiring us to aggregate some information about a subarray. Here's an example of a problem about *range sums*:

✦ **PROBLEM 43.1** **CHANNEL VIEWS**

A YouTuber wants to analyze their channel's performance to see if viewer engagement varies during certain times of the year. We are given:

- An array, views, of length n > 0, where views[i] represents the number of views on day i.
- An array, periods, of length p > 0, where each element is a pair [l, r] with 0 ≤ l ≤ r < n. Each pair represents a time period from day l to day r *inclusive*.

Return an array, results, of integers with length p, where result[i] is the number of views during period i.

▶ **Example:** views = [3, 5, 4, 8, 7, 2, 5, 3, 2, 3]
          periods = [[0, 1], [0, 5], [5, 8], [3, 3]]
  Output: [8, 29, 12, 8]. For instance, element 0 is 8 because 3 + 5 = 8.

SOLUTION 43.1   CHANNEL VIEWS

In this problem, each period is a range, and we have queries asking for the sum of each range.

A naive solution would iterate from l to r for each period [l, r]. In the worst case, when l is 0 and r is n-1, this would take O(n) time, resulting in O(p*n) total time.

Can you think of a way to use the *PREPROCESSING PATTERN* (pg 250) to optimize the naive solution? If not, try using the **tackle an easier problem** booster first: what if the left boundary was always fixed at 0?

When l is 0, the range becomes a prefix of the array, and the sum becomes a *prefix sum*. We can build an **array of prefix sums** to handle such sums in O(1) time:[1]
    views =   [3, 5, 4, 8, 7, 2, 5, 3, 2, 3]
    prefix_sum = [3, 8, 12, 20, 27, 29, 34, 37, 39, 42]

---

1 If you work in a language with fixed-size bit representations for integers, like C++ or Java, be aware that repeatedly adding prefixes could lead to integer overflow for large enough inputs. A common trick is to use a wider type for the prefix sum array. E.g., if the input are 32-bit integers, you can use 64-bit integers for the prefix sum array.

The sum of views from index 0 to index r is prefix_sum[r]. What about general queries, where l may not be 0?

The neat thing about prefix sums is that they also help us in that case:

    views[l] + ... + views[r] = prefix_sum[r] - prefix_sum[l-1]

To build some intuition for this formula, consider this interaction:

> Bartender: Your running tab is up to $300. When are you planning to pay?
>
> Albert: $300?! Earlier it was $200. You mean the wine was $100?!
>
> Bartender: Oh, why don't you go whine about it.
>
> Albert: Hey! That's not very punny.

Albert[2] computes the cost of the wine by taking the total after the wine and subtracting the total before the wine. Similarly, to get the sum from arr[l] to arr[r], we take the running total up to index r and subtract the running total before index l. Let's take the example of period [3, 7]:

```
index            0   1    2    3    4    5    6    7    8    9
views        = 3,   5,   4,   8,   7,   2,   5,   3,   2,   3
prefix_sum   = 3,   8,  12,  20,  27,  29,  34,  37,  39,  42
sum([0, 7]) = 3 + 5 + 4 + 8 + 7 + 2 + 5 + 3               = 37
sum([0, 2]) = 3 + 5 + 4                                   = 12
sum([3, 7]) =                 8 + 7 + 2 + 5 + 3           = 37 - 12 = 25
```

Edge case! If our query's left index is 0, there is nothing to subtract—if we tried to subtract prefix_sum[l - 1], we would go out of bounds. Instead, we shouldn't subtract anything.

With this change, each query can be answered in constant time, so the total is O(n + p).

```
 1   def channel_views(views, periods):
 2     prefix_sum = [0] * len(views)
 3     prefix_sum[0] = views[0]
 4     for i in range(1, len(views)):
 5       prefix_sum[i] = prefix_sum[i-1] + views[i]
 6     res = []
 7     for l, r in periods:
 8       if l == 0:
 9         res.append(prefix_sum[r])
10       else:
11         res.append(prefix_sum[r] - prefix_sum[l-1])
12     return res
```

This idea of subtracting a prefix from a larger prefix is the key to many problems about range queries. We can capture the logic in a recipe:

---

2 Most people call him AI, but his friends usually just call him by his last name, Gorithm.

RECIPE 1. RANGE SUM QUERIES.[3]

```
# Initialization
Initialize prefix_sum with the same length as the input array
prefix_sum[0] = arr[0]  # There must be at least one element.
for i from 1 to len(arr) - 1:
  prefix_sum[i] = prefix_sum[i-1] + arr[i]

# Query: sum of subarray [l, r]
if l == 0:
  return prefix_sum[r]
return prefix_sum[r] - prefix_sum[l-1]
```

GENERALIZED PREFIX SUMS

Now that we've learned the basic technique, we'll see other applications. The name of the technique is a bit misleading because **it is not limited to either prefixes or sums**:

1. We could compute other information about the prefixes instead of their sum.

2. Sometimes, we need to precompute information about suffixes instead of prefixes. This is sometimes called a *postfix sum array*.

We can say that any algorithm that precomputes information about the prefixes or suffixes of the input array uses the "prefix-sum technique."

The prefix-sum technique can be useful even beyond range queries. For instance, it can be useful if you have to compute 'something' for each element in an array which depends on (1) every previous element, (2) every subsequent element, or (3) every other element.

PREFIX SUMS PROBLEM SET

✦ *Try these problems with AI Interviewer: bctci.co/prefix-sums-problem-set-1*

PROBLEM 43.2   YOUTUBE VIDEO RECEPTION

A YouTuber has fetched the number of likes and dislikes of a video each day since its publication. We say a day is *positive* if it has more likes than dislikes.

We are given:

- Two arrays, likes and dislikes, of length n, representing the likes and dislikes on each day (likes and dislikes are positive integers).

- An array periods of length p, where each element is a pair [l, r] with $0 \le l \le r < n$. Each pair represents a time period from day l to day r *inclusive*.

Return an array, results, of length p, where results[i] is the number of positive days during period[i].

▸ **Example:** likes   = [6, 3, 4, 8, 7, 2, 6, 5, 0, 1]
            dislikes = [6, 0, 8, 0, 0, 0, 1, 8, 0, 2]
            periods = [[0, 1], [0, 5], [5, 8], [3, 3]]
    Output: [1, 4, 2, 1]. For instance, element 0 (for the period [0, 1]) is 1
            because day 0 doesn't have more likes than dislikes, but day 1 does.

---

3   Some people consider prefix sums a type of dynamic programming because each prefix sum is computed from the previous one, but, in DP, each subproblem usually depends on multiple other subproblems.

EXCLUSIVE PRODUCT

Given an array of non-negative integers, arr, return an array with the same length where index i contains the product of all the elements in arr except arr[i]. Since the values could be very large, return them modulo $10^9 + 7$.

▶ **Example:** arr = [1, 3, 2, 1]
   Output: [6, 2, 3, 6]. For instance, index 0 is 3*2*1 = 6.

▶ **Example:** arr = [0, 1, 0]
   Output: [0, 0, 0]
   Constraints: For any i, 0 ≤ arr[i] ≤ 10000.
                  $2 ≤ n ≤ 10^6$, where n is the length of arr.

Note: the "obvious" solution is to compute the total product and then divide it by each element. However, the total product could be up to $10000^n = 10^{4000000}$. Even if your language supports arbitrary integers, we don't want to work with numbers that large (at that point, arithmetic operations are not 'constant time' anymore). Instead, we should use the reusable idea 'Apply Modulo At Each Step' (pg 406) to keep any products we compute below $10^9 + 7$. However, applying the modulo at each step only works for addition, subtraction, and multiplication, not division. Dividing first and then applying modulo yields different results than applying modulo and then dividing: (12 / 3) % 5 != (12 % 5) / 3. This means that we need to find a way to solve this problem without using division at the end.

BALANCE POINT

Given an array of integers, arr, return the first *balanced index*, if there is any, or -1 otherwise. An index is balanced if the sum of the elements to its left is the same as the sum of the elements to its right.

▶ **Example:** arr = [3, 5, -2, 7, 2, 2, 2]
   Output: 3. Index 3 is balanced because 3 + 5 + (-2) equals 2 + 2 + 2.

YOUTUBE VIDEO UNUSUAL DAYS

A YouTuber has fetched the number of likes and dislikes of a video each day since its publication, with the goal of finding days with unusually high or low like-to-dislike ratios.

We are given two arrays, likes and dislikes, of length n, representing the likes and dislikes on each day (likes and dislikes are positive integers).

The *reception score* of a day is the number of likes minus the number of dislikes. The *deviation* between two days is the absolute value of the difference in their reception scores. The *total deviation* of a given day is the sum of the deviations between it and every other day.

Find the highest *total deviation* of any day and return it.

▶ **Example:** likes   = [3, 6, 1]
          dislikes = [0, 1, 9]
  Output: 24. The reception scores are [3, 5, -8]. The total deviation of each
          day is:
          day 0: |3 - 5| + |3 - (-8)| = 2 + 11 = 13
          day 1: |5 - 3| + |5 - (-8)| = 2 + 13 = 15
          day 2: |-8 - 3| + |-8 - 5| = 11 + 13 = 24

✦ PROBLEM SET SOLUTIONS

SOLUTION 43.2   YOUTUBE VIDEO RECEPTION

The queries in this problem are similar to *range sum* queries, but instead of directly computing prefix sums for the likes or dislikes, we first transform the input arrays into a more usable format: a binary array where 1s represent positive days. The problem then becomes a standard problem about range sum queries on this array, and we can use Recipe 1.

```
1   def good_reception_scores(likes, dislikes, periods):
2       positive_days = [0] * len(likes)
3       for i in range(likes):
4         if likes[i] > dislikes[i]:
5           positive_days[i] = 1
6       # Use the 'Range sum queries' recipe to build the prefix sums for
7       # the positive_days array and query it with each period
```

We could have computed the prefix sum array directly without first creating the positive_days array. However, we transformed the input to make our lives simpler.

SOLUTION 43.3   EXCLUSIVE PRODUCT

Whenever a problem requires us to compute something at each index based on all other indices, it is an excellent candidate for the prefix-sum technique. In this case, we need to customize it as follows:

- We need to compute prefix products instead of prefix sums.
- We need to compute products for all prefixes *and* suffixes. To compute the postfix products, we can iterate backward through the array.
- We apply the modulo at each step to prevent the intermediate prefix or suffix products from getting too large.

Then, we can compute the result at each index i as:

```
res[i] = prefix[i-1] * postfix[i+1]
```

If i-1 or i+1 is out of bounds, we just omit that term. For example:

```
index                   0  1  2  3
arr               = [1, 3, 2, 1]
prefix_product    = [1, 3, 6, 6]
postfix_product   = [6, 6, 2, 1]
res               = [6, 2, 3, 6]
```

Here is the implementation:

```
1   def exclusive_product_array(arr):
2       m = 10**9 + 7
3       n = len(arr)
4       prefix_product = [1] * n
5       prefix_product[0] = arr[0]
6       for i in range(1, n):
7         prefix_product[i] = (prefix_product[i - 1] * arr[i]) % m
8       postfix_product = [1] * n
9       postfix_product[n - 1] = arr[n - 1]
10      for i in range(n - 2, -1, -1):
11        postfix_product[i] = (postfix_product[i + 1] * arr[i]) % m
12      res = [1] * n
13      res[0] = postfix_product[1]
```

```
14    res[n - 1] = prefix_product[n - 2]
15    for i in range(1, n - 1):
16      res[i] = (prefix_product[i - 1] * postfix_product[i + 1]) % m
17    return res
```

SOLUTION 43.4   BALANCE POINT

After solving the 'Exclusive Product' problem, you might reasonably consider building two separate arrays to store prefix and postfix sums for this question. However, we don't need to. We just need to check if the sum to the left of each index is the same as the sum to the right, and we can update both of these while iterating through the original array—no extra array needed!

```
1   def balanced_index(arr):
2     prefix_sum = 0
3     postfix_sum = sum(arr) - arr[0]
4     for i in range(len(arr)):
5       if prefix_sum == postfix_sum:
6         return i
7       prefix_sum += arr[i]
8       if i + 1 < len(arr):
9         postfix_sum -= arr[i+1]
10    return -1
```

SOLUTION 43.5   YOUTUBE VIDEO UNUSUAL DAYS

First, it is clear that 'likes' and 'dislikes' are not what really matters. We can start by computing a scores array with the reception score (likes minus dislikes) for each day.

The naive solution would take $O(n^2)$ time to compute the 'total deviation' of each day one by one. Improving the naive algorithm is hard because we can't simply compute "prefix absolute differences"—they depend on each element. To tackle this problem, we can **break it down** into two parts. For each day, we can:

1. Compute the contribution of days with larger scores to the total deviation.
2. Compute the contribution of days with smaller scores to the total deviation.

If we can do that, then we can add up the two parts.

Sorting the reception scores as a preprocessing step is helpful here because:

1. It puts all the smaller elements on one side and all the larger elements on the other.
2. We do not care about the original order of the videos.

So, let's focus on the first part, assuming the input is sorted. For a value at index i, each larger index j contributes scores[j] - scores[i] (since the input is sorted, we don't need to worry about computing absolute values anymore). **Drawing a sketch** can help us come up with a formula to compute all those contributions at once:

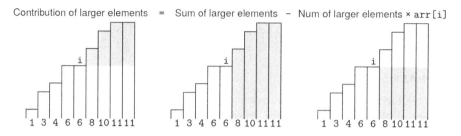

Figure 1. The contribution of larger scores to the 'total deviation' of day i is the sum of the larger scores minus the area of a rectangle. The base of the rectangle is the number of larger scores and the height is `scores[i]`.

Similar to how we use prefix sums to answer 'range sum' queries, Figure 1 shows the same idea of "calculating a sum that's too large and then subtracting the unwanted portion."

Working out the index math, the contribution of all larger elements is:

$$\text{range\_sum(i + 1, n - 1) - (n - i - 1) * scores[i]}$$

We already know how to compute range sums, so we can calculate this expression.

Next, let's tackle smaller elements, again assuming the input is sorted. For a value at index i, each smaller index j contributes `scores[i] - scores[j]`. We can draw a similar sketch to figure out the formula to compute all those contributions at once:

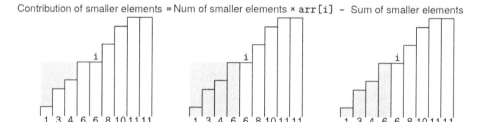

Figure 2.

In other words, the contribution of all larger elements is:

```
i * scores[i] - range_sum(0, i-1)
```

The following code implements this approach.

```
1   def max_total_deviation(likes, dislikes):
2     scores = [likes[i] - dislikes[i] for i in range(len(likes))]
3     scores.sort()
4     n = len(scores)
5     prefix_sum = [0] * n
6     prefix_sum[0] = scores[0]
7     for i in range(1, n):
8       prefix_sum[i] = prefix_sum[i - 1] + scores[i]
9     max_deviation = 0
10    for i in range(n):
11      left, right = 0, 0
12      if i > 0:
13        left = i * scores[i] - prefix_sum[i - 1]
```

```
14      if i < n - 1:
15          right = prefix_sum[n - 1] - prefix_sum[i] - (n - i - 1) * scores[i]
16      max_deviation = max(max_deviation, left + right)
17  return max_deviation
```

So far, we have only worked with arrays of numbers, but the prefix-sum technique is not limited to numbers. For instance, recall Problem 30.11: Largest Set Intersection (pg 355):

You are given a non-empty array, sets, where each element is an array of unique integers representing a set. Return the index of the set that should be excluded to maximize the size of the *intersection* of the remaining sets. The intersection of a list of sets is the set of elements that appears in every set.

▶ **Example:** sets = [[1, 2, 3], [3, 2, 1], [1, 4, 5], [1, 2]]
    Output: 2. Excluding the third set (index 2) yields a set intersection of
               size 2: {1, 2}. This is the largest set intersection size after
               removing a set, so we return index 2.

This is similar to the 'Exclusive Product' problem in that we need to compute something for each input element that is a function of every other element. The only difference is changing the operation from "product of numbers" to "intersection of sets."

Imagine we compute the intersection of every prefix of sets and every suffix of sets. Then, the intersection of all sets *excluding* the one at index i, is

```
intersection(prefix_intersection[i-1], postfix_intersection[i+1])
```

We have to mind our edge cases, but a prefix-sum-based solution will probably be easier to implement and reason about than the solution we saw on page 355.

\# The prefix-sum technique is not restricted to *prefixes*, *sums*, *arrays*, or even *numbers*.

2D PREFIX SUMS STRUGGLES   INTERVIEW REPLAY

View Online:	bctci.co/prefix-sums-replay-1 @ 1:01:02 - 1:10:32
The Question:	Given a matrix and a function, query(1, r), which is repeatedly called with different square coordinates, you must determine the sum within the square.
What You'll See:	The candidate was able to get a brute force solution but couldn't optimize it.
Who:	*Interviewer:* Principal Engineer at Roblox
Candidate: 8 years exp.

SUBARRAYS WITH SUM K

We'll show one final advanced application of the prefix-sum technique. It can be useful in problems about finding subarrays with a specific sum:

PROBLEM 43.6   COUNT SUBARRAYS WITH SUM K

Given an array of integers, arr, and an integer k, return the number of subarrays in arr with sum k.

▶ **Example:** arr = [1, 2, 3, 2, 1], k = 3
    Output: 3. The subarrays with sum 3 are [1, 2], [3], and [2, 1].
▶ **Example:** arr = [-1, -2, -3, 2, 1], k = -3
    Output: 4. The subarrays with sum -3 are [-1, -2], [-3], [-2, 3, 2], and [-1,
             -2, -3, 2, 1].

SOLUTION 43.6   COUNT SUBARRAYS WITH SUM K

This problem seems hard until you *REFRAME* it in terms of the input array's prefix sums: instead of counting subarrays with sum k, we can count pairs of indices in prefix_sum with a difference of k.

We can compute prefix_sum in a preprocessing step. Then, the problem becomes:

Given an array of n integers, prefix_sum, and an integer k, return the number of pairs of indices, [1, r], with 0 ≤ 1 ≤ r < n, such that prefix_sum[r] - prefix_sum[1-1] == k (or just prefix_sum[r] if 1 == 0).

We can iterate through the prefix_sum array with a pointer, r, and for each element prefix_sum[r], add 1 to the running counter for each previous index with value prefix_sum[r] - k. To know the number of such elements, we can use a map mapping prefix sums to the number of times they appear. This is the **frequency map** reusable idea (pg 348).

```
 1    def count_subarrays(arr, k):
 2      prefix_sum = ... # Recipe 1.
 3      prefix_sum_to_count = {0: 1}  # For the empty prefix.
 4      count = 0
 5      for val in prefix_sum:
 6        if val - k in prefix_sum_to_count:
 7          count += prefix_sum_to_count[val - k]
 8        if val not in prefix_sum_to_count:
 9          prefix_sum_to_count[val] = 0
10        prefix_sum_to_count[val] += 1
11      return count
```

The runtime and space complexities are both linear.[4]

Problems about subarrays with a specific sum often become easier when reframed in terms of the prefix sum array.

See if you can apply a similar reframe to the following problem:

✦   **PROBLEM 43.7**   **LONGEST SUBARRAY WITH SUM K**

Given an array of integers, arr, and an integer k, return the length of the longest subarray in arr with sum k, or -1 if there is no such subarray.

▸ **Example:** arr = [1, 2, 3, 2, 1], k = 3
   Output: 2. The longest subarrays with sum 3 are [1, 2] and [2, 1].
▸ **Example:** arr = [-1, -2, -3, 2, 1], k = -3
   Output: 5. The longest subarray with sum -3 is [-1, -2, -3, 2, 1].

SOLUTION 43.7   LONGEST SUBARRAY WITH SUM K

The approach is the same as Problem 43.6: Assuming we precompute the prefix_sum array, we can reframe it as:

Given an array of numbers, prefix_sum, and an integer k, return the longest range [1, r], with 0 ≤ 1 ≤ r < n, such that prefix_sum[r] - prefix_sum[1 - 1] == k (or just prefix_sum[r] if 1 == 0).

The implementation also uses a *map with prefix sums as keys;* the only difference is that the values are not counts, but the earliest index of that prefix sum:

---

4 Problems about counting subarrays can often be tackled with sliding windows (see Problem 38.19: Count Subarrays With Exactly K Bad Days (pg 532). However, this problem is not a good fit for sliding windows because of the negative numbers, which break the *maximum window property* (pg 525).

```
1   def longest_subarray_with_sum_k(arr, k):
2     prefix_sum = ... # Recipe 1.
3     prefix_sum_to_index = {0: -1}  # For the empty prefix.
4     res = -1
5     for r, val in enumerate(prefix_sum):
6       if val - k in prefix_sum_to_index:
7         l = prefix_sum_to_index[val - k]
8         res = max(res, r - l)
9       if val not in prefix_sum_to_index:
10        prefix_sum_to_index[val] = r
11    return res
```

| ▶ | **HOW TO MAKE A DIFFICULT PREFIX SUM PROBLEM LOOK EASY** | INTERVIEW REPLAY |

| **View Online:** | bctci.co/prefix-sums-replay-2 @ 23:12 - 47:14 |

| **The Question:** | Given an unsorted array of integers, find the number of continuous subarrays having a sum exactly equal to a given number k. |

| **What You'll See:** | The candidate expertly navigated this tricky prefix sum problem after first crushing a tree problem. |

| **Who:** | *Interviewer*: Principal Engineering Manager at Microsoft
Candidate: 1 year exp. |

EXTRA CREDIT: RANGE UPDATES

We've seen range queries; in this section, we'll talk about its cousin, range updates. A *range update* is when we *modify* an entire subarray of an array in one operation. Here is an example:

✦✦ **PROBLEM 43.8**   **SEGMENTED VIDEO VOTES**

YouTube is testing an experimental API that allows users to like or dislike specific segments of a video instead of the entire video. You are provided with:

- n: the length of the video in minutes.
- votes: an array where each element represents a user's vote and is structured as an array with 3 integers:

  » l: the starting minute of the vote (inclusive).
  » r: the ending minute of the vote (inclusive).
  » v: the type of vote, where 1 indicates a like and -1 indicates a dislike.

Each vote satisfies $0 \leq l \leq r < n$. The votes can be in any order and may overlap. Your task is to return an array of length n, where each index i contains the *net vote count* at minute i (calculated as the total likes minus total dislikes).

▶ **Example:** n = 6, votes = [[3, 4, 1], [0, 0, 1], [1, 3, 1], [0, 5, -1]]
  Output: [0, 0, 0, 1, 0, -1]. The net vote counts after applying each vote
          are:
              [0, 0, 0, 1, 1, 0]
              [1, 0, 0, 1, 1, 0]
              [1, 1, 1, 2, 1, 0]
              [0, 0, 0, 1, 0, -1]

SOLUTION 43.8   SEGMENTED VIDEO VOTES

Let's start with the 'indented English' version of the naive solution:

```
initialize an array of 0s of length n
for each update [l, r, v]
  for each index from l to r
    increment or decrement it accordingly
```

This is inefficient because each update could span the entire array and take $O(n)$ time, for a total time of $O(n*k)$, where k is the number of votes.

A more efficient solution is to process the updates in *chronological order*. For each vote [l, r, v], we can create two individual "instructions" that can be applied as we process the video from left to right:

- When we reach time l, change the current vote by v.
- When we reach time r, change the current vote by -v.

If we sort all these individual instructions from left to right and iterate through them, we can track how the vote count evolves over time.

We *could* use a two-pointer solution, one to process the sorted instructions and the other to apply them to the output array. However, a simplification allows us to avoid sorting and having to use two pointers.

The idea is to write the instructions directly at the index where they should happen. That is, for an update like [l, r, v], we do:

- diff[l] += v
- diff[r+1] -= v (if r+1 is in bounds)

The array with the "instructions" written directly into it is known as a *difference array*. The key property is that *the prefix sum of the difference array is the solution after applying all the range updates.* This is because if we add an update value, v, at index l, we will "carry" that value through the rest of the array as we calculate our prefix sum. Then, when we get to r+1, we will "undo" the change by applying the opposite operation.

```
 1  def range_updates(n, votes):
 2    diff = [0] * n
 3    for l, r, v in votes:
 4      diff[l] += v
 5      if r + 1 < n:
 6        diff[r + 1] -= v
 7    # Recipe 1.
 8    prefix_sum = [0] * n
 9    prefix_sum[0] = diff[0]
10    for i in range(1, n):
11      prefix_sum[i] = prefix_sum[i - 1] + diff[i]
12    return prefix_sum
```

Difference arrays are often useful for problems where we need to apply a series of range updates.

RANGE UPDATES PROBLEM SET

✦ *Try these problems with AI Interviewer: bctci.co/prefix-sums-problem-set-2*

PROBLEM 43.9   **MOST BOOKED SLOT**

In a mock interview booking system, there is a list of n time slots available to book interviews. We are given:

- An array, slots, of length n > 0, where slots[i] is the number of bookings already made for slot i.
- An array, bookings, of length k > 0, where each element represents a bulk booking for a given range. Each element is an array of 3 integers, [l, r, c], where [l, r] is the range of requested slots (both inclusive), and c is the number of clients booked for the entire range. We can assume that $0 \le l \le r < n$ and $0 < c$.

Determine the most booked slot and return its index. If there is more than one, return the earliest one.

▶ **Example:** slots = [0, 0, 0, 0, 0, 0]
              bookings = [[0, 3, 4], [2, 5, 1], [4, 4, 3]]
   Output: 2. The final number of bookings at each slot is [4, 4, 5, 5, 4, 1].
              Slots at indices 2 and 3 are the most popular, and 2 is earlier.

▶ **Example:** slots = [1, 1, 0, 0, 2, 3]
              bookings = [[0, 3, 4], [2, 5, 1], [4, 4, 3]]
   Output: 4. Counting the initial bookings, the final number of bookings at
              each slot is [5, 5, 5, 5, 6, 4].

PROBLEM 43.10   **ALL OVERBOOKED SLOTS**

Consider the same setting as Problem 43.9, but we are also given a positive integer, cap, representing the maximum number of interviews that can be accommodated at any given slot. Return the number of slots that are *overbooked*.

▶ **Example:** slots = [0, 0, 0, 0, 0, 0]
              bookings = [[0, 3, 4], [2, 5, 1], [4, 4, 3]]
              cap = 5
   Output: 0. The number of bookings at each slot is [4, 4, 5, 5, 4, 1]. None
              of them is over the cap.

▶ **Example:** slots = [1, 1, 0, 0, 2, 3]
              bookings = [[0, 3, 4], [2, 5, 1], [4, 4, 3]]
              cap = 4
   Output: 5. The number of bookings at each slot is [5, 5, 5, 5, 6, 4].

✲ PROBLEM SET SOLUTIONS

SOLUTION 43.9   MOST BOOKED SLOT

This is a straightforward application of difference arrays. After computing the prefix sums for the difference array, we can add the initial bookings to get the total for each slot.

```
1   def most_booked_slot(slots, bookings):
2       n = len(slots)
3       diff = [0] * n
4       for l, r, c in bookings:
5           diff[l] += c
6           if r + 1 < n:
7               diff[r + 1] -= c
8
9       # Recipe 1.
10      prefix_sum = [0] * n
11      prefix_sum[0] = diff[0]
```

```
12    for i in range(1, n):
13      prefix_sum[i] = prefix_sum[i - 1] + diff[i]
14
15    max_bookings, max_index = 0, -1
16    for i in range(n):
17      total_bookings = prefix_sum[i] + slots[i]
18      if total_bookings > max_bookings:
19        max_bookings, max_index = total_bookings, i
20    return max_index
```

SOLUTION 43.10   ALL OVERBOOKED SLOTS

We start by computing the final bookings at each slot, like in Solution 9. Once we have this, it is straightfor-ward to count overbooked ones by comparing them to cap.

RANGE QUERIES AND UPDATES TOGETHER

We've seen that prefix sums allow us to do range queries efficiently, while difference arrays allow us to do range updates efficiently. What if we need both? That is, how can we answer range queries efficiently if they are intermixed with range updates touching that same array?

Fenwick Trees (also known as *Binary Indexed Trees*) and *Segment Trees* are tree-based data structures that can handle this scenario. The former is typically easier to implement, while the latter supports complex operations (like 'range min' and 'range max'). Both are *usually* outside the expectation of interviews, so we don't recommend spending time learning them for coding interviews. The following table breaks down the trade-offs between their runtimes.

Data Structure	Initialization Time	Range queries	Range updates
Prefix sums	$O(n)$	$O(1)$	$O(n)$
Difference arrays	$O(n)$	$O(n)$[5]	$O(1)$
Fenwick Tree (a.k.a. BIT)	$O(n \log n)$[6]	$O(\log n)$	$O(\log n)$
Segment Tree	$O(n)$	$O(\log n)$	$O(\log n)$

Table 1. Range query/update techniques, ordered from most common and easy to implement (prefix sums) to most niche and hard to implement (segment trees). The initialization time assumes that we are given an initial array of size n upon which we want to do subsequent range queries and updates.

KEY TAKEAWAYS

The most valuable thing you can take away from this chapter is learning how to implement range sum queries on the fly (Recipe 1, pg 614), while also being aware that the **prefix-sum technique** is neither restricted to prefixes nor sums. The section 'Generalized Prefix Sums' (pg 614) gives an overview of the type of problems where it can be useful.

Prefix sums are closely related to sliding windows. When one technique doesn't work, the other can be a good option to try next. In particular, sliding windows often don't work if negative values are allowed because it

---

5 We need $O(n)$ time to build the prefix sums of the difference array, after which we can answer range queries in $O(1)$ time, but any further range updates will require us to rebuild the prefix array.

6 Can be improved to $O(n)$, but, for interviews, we'd recommend sticking to the naive initialization of doing n single-element range updates, which takes $O(n \log n)$ time.

is not clear when to grow or shrink the window (see the maximum window property on page 525), while prefix sums usually work with negative numbers, as seen in most examples in this chapter.

Prefix Sum triggers: The input consists of an array/strings. We need to use $O(1)$ extra memory or modify the input in place. Problems with multiple subarrays, especially when sliding windows don't seem to work. The input is sorted. The naive solution is $O(n^2)$, and we want to get to $O(n)$. Problems with ranges or intervals.

Keywords: prefix, suffix, partition.

EXIT()

PART VIII

Watch for these speech-bubble icons, which mean there is online content.

✦ **AI Interviewer:** Each problem can be tried online with the AI Interviewer.

▶ **Interview Replay:** Recordings of actual mock interviews.

📄 **Snippet:** Material to copy/paste online, including email templates and code recipes.

↗ **Resource:** Bonus chapters, worksheets, and other material.

EXIT()

ACKNOWLEDGMENTS

Books like this aren't so much written as built. And like complex software, they require iteration, debugging, and plenty of cross-functional help. Along the way, we've been lucky to have friends, colleagues, and sometimes total strangers who stress-tested our ideas, refactored our rough drafts, and kept us from shipping something not quite production-ready. We're especially grateful to those who shared their own interview experiences—their wins, their struggles, and everything in between. Their stories added real-world depth to these pages, making this book more than just a set of problems, but a reflection of the journey engineers take to land their dream roles.

With that, a huge thank you to…

The whole core interviewing.io team, and especially Dwight Gunning, for going above and beyond, for months on end, to make this project possible.

The core interviewing.io team:

Liz Graves	Richard Graves	Dwight Gunning	Drew Lazzeri
Eamonn MacConville			

The engineers, designers, and data scientists who contributed to this project:

David Anthony Archuleta Jr.	Adam Bhula	Jaroslav Getman	Dwight Gunning
Stanislav Kryshtal	Drew Lazzeri	Brandon Lyons	Maxim Massenkoff
Jonathon Mroczka	Muhammad Daniyal Saqib	Rupal Totale	Brian Githire Wahome
Joe Yu			

Everyone who read chapters and/or helped test the physical book and online materials:

Nishant S Agarwal	Estevan Aguayo	Alex Allain	Gabriel Bitis
Rafael Dolores	Daniel Farlow	Alex Feerst	Scott Gerenser
Bruno Guardia	Mahmudul Hasan, PhD	Marcell Himawan	Justin Hoyt
Ambareesh Jayakumari	Tikhon Jelvis	Sonia Jindal	Ben Katin
Euvin Keel	Jacob Kerr	Nick Knowles	Harikrishnan Lakshmanan
Chris G Lee	Kevin Ma	Tahiya Mahin	Sanyasi Naidu Malla
Sreekar Mankala	Andrew Marsh	Austen McDonald	Rishi Mehta
Marc Merino	Chara Lilith Moradian	Francis J Nickels III	Brendin Nye
Shannon Ogborn, MIOP	Christopher Onyiuke	Osman (Ozzie) Osman	Blaine Rister
Arjan Singh	Glenn Stroz	William Sun	Jay Huynh Thinh
Chloe G. Tran	Jos Visser	Thomas Vollmer	Yu Zhou

All the interviewing.io users and interviewers who were brave enough to let us use their interview replays in the book, as well as everyone in the interviewing.io community who lent their beautiful brains to this project:

Aaron Crow	Aaron Hammer	Abhishek Srinivasa Raju Padmavathi	Adam Zhang
Adil Aliyev	Aditya Nath	Alex Barganier	Alex Bowe
Alex C.	Alex Lee	Alexis Olmos-Cortes	Aliya Rysbek
Alonso Gutierrez	Arash Nikoo	Ash Sundar	Asim Ihsan
Ayden Mason	Bailey Berro	Ben Lamm	Benjamin Erichsen
Brian Githire Wahome	Bruno Albuquerque	Caleb Albers	Camilo Quintas Meneses
Charley Cunningham	Chris Li	Christopher Boudreau	Clinton Kelly
Connor Viani Maas	Conor Sweeney	Constance Jiang	Continuous Warrior
Cyrus Hadavi	Daniel Tatarkin	David Fann	Dennis Wu
Yu Zhou	Devang Arvind Shah	Devin Gamble	Devon Anderson
Diamond Buffalo	Dima Korolev	Durlabh Malik	Ekagra Gupta
Elliot Bonneville	Elrich Groenewald	Ernesto G. Grabowski	Ethan Nicholas
FAANG-manager	Farley Knight	Federico	Fizuli V.
Gabriel Dos Santos Davila	Gaziza Yestemirova	Graham P Heath	Hambear
Haris Hussain	Harry Wang	Hemant Sethi	Henryk Sarat
Ho Jung Kim	Howard Tucker	Hozefa Jodiawalla	Hunter Heston
Igor Garin	Itamar Belson	Jacques Bernier	Jacques Chester
Jada Forrester	Jake Mathias	James Valentine	jefQuery
Jonathan Ho	Joshua Goller	Justin Maltese	Kavya Kushnoor
Kevin Melkowski	Leonardo Jimenez	Lev Glick	Lucia Tseng
Madhuri Devidi	Mahesh Coimbatore	Marcell Himawan	Maria Castro
Mike Laurence	Ming Wong	Muhammad Daniyal Saqib	Murugan Ayyappan
Namita Singh Manhas	Nataliia Bondarevska	Nick McMahon	Nikolai Anikevich
Nina Schiff	Nino Obanor	Noah Ruderman	Noah Shpak
Omsai Jadhav	Paulina Ramos	Pavel Sherman	Philip B
Princess Sopeju	Pulkit Kapoor	Puneet Jain	Rahul Sunil Purohit
Rashmi Kishore	Ravi Nanavati	Razvan Darju	Robert Skonieczny
Rodrigo Quezada	Rohan Bansal	Rohit Mukerji	Rose Wang
Russ Schick	Ruzaik Rafeek	Ryan Clements	Ryan Loughlin
Saadi N.	Sahand Saba	Sam Gamer	Sanjeev Qazi
Sarp Centel	Satyanarayana Reddy Janga	Sauhard Sharma	Scott Urman
Sehoon Shon	Sergey Zaika aka @fewald	Shadab Ahmed	Shahraiz Niazi
Shehbaj Dhillon	Sherzod Kariev	Shuo Qian	Simon Ayzman
Skanda Narendra Bhargav	Smitha Venkatesh	Spencer Corwin	Sreekar Mankala
Steven Joseph Priest	Suprita Pramanik	Takumi McAllister	Teddy Lo
Timur Sadykov	Toli Zaslavskiy	Tony Brix	Trevor Miranda
Trupti Bavalatti	Van	Vishnu Malikireddy	Vivek Ramamoorthy
Wenxiang Guan	Wolfgang E. Sanyer	Yi Zhang	Zichun

WITH GRATITUDE...

To my husband, John, and my sons, Davis and Tobin, thank you for your love and support during this journey. John, your encouragement kept me grounded and focused, making this project possible.

To my children, Davis and Tobin—Davis, your creative input (especially making—and repeatedly remaking—our custom fonts) added an invaluable touch to this work. Tobin, your humor, boundless energy, and knack for making me laugh provided the perfect escape when I needed it most.

To my friends, thank you for cheering me on and understanding my absences during this long slog. I will consider answering your phone calls now.

Gayle

Rachel Mroczka, thank you for getting me through this book—your sacrifices helped make my dream possible. Jonathon Mroczka & Daniyal Saqib, way to come in clutch at the end there, you two! To my parents, Eric & Michele Mroczka, thanks for letting me take over your house in the final stages of this book. To Kevin Landucci for believing in this project before it began. To Percy, who is the only reason I left the house at all this past year.

Thanks to Gayle for letting us carry on her brand and not strangling me over my poor grammar. Thanks, Aline, for dreaming big with me—you're an unshakeable badass and one hell of a partner. And to the smartest person I know, Nil, this book is all it could have been because you agreed to help. Thank you all for working so hard on this.

Lastly, thank you for showing me what it means to be a great mentor, engineer, and person: Marissa Levy, Sean Corgan, & Geeta Chaudhry.

Mike

To E.K., the love of my life.

To my brilliant daughter for being such a good sport while your silly mom hid in a cave to write this book.

Finally, to the two grand heroes in my life, my parents, Rachel and Arcady. Thank you for your love, your bravery that brought us to this country, and for modeling everything that good parenting should be (which I appreciate all the more now that I'm a parent myself). Thank you to Arcady specifically for teaching me math, getting me into computers, and letting me copy his assembly programming homework that summer when we ended up in two computer science classes together... even if it only got me a B.

Aline

Many thanks to Michele and Eric Mroczka for letting me take over their kitchen while writing the book; to Timothy Johnson, who contributed many solutions in the book—especially the clever ones; to Ngoc Vo for her support.

Nil

POST-MORTEM EXAMPLE LOG

After each practice question, we recommend completing a post-mortem to pinpoint what went well and what could use improvement. Common mistakes will surface over time, which can be added to a bug list for heightened awareness. Access an editable / printable version at bctci.co/post-mortem.

POST-MORTEM EXAMPLE

PROBLEM: COUNT ISLANDS	DATE: JAN 22, 2025
Time to design the algorithm:	7 minutes
Time to code:	19 minutes
What solutions did I consider/miss?	I identified DFS and BFS, but missed the union-find solution.
Analysis: Was your solution optimal?	T: O(R*C) S: O(R*C) It was optimal :)
What triggers did I find/miss?	Grid cells connected four-directionally is a trigger for grid graphs (similar to the 'rotting oranges' problem). Missed: "merging" adjacent 1's together (into the same island) is a trigger for union-find.
Any mistakes I keep making? Any bugs to add to the Bug List?	Yes! I forgot to check if a cell had been visited before recursing in the DFS, resulting in an infinite loop
What could I have done differently?	I could have used BFS to avoid the possibility of stack overflow.
Takeaways:	I need to review the DFS recipe, so I don't waste time one this part of the interview next time. Missing the union-find solution was silly since this problem is clearly about connected components. Union-find is slightly slower than DFS for this problem, but I will focus on exploring union-find when I see that trigger in the future.
Anything to add to my cheat sheet?	The 'connected component loop' recipe.

Rubric self-rating:		
	Problem solving:	4/5. Missed a possible solution
	Coding:	4/5
	Verification:	5/5. Found the DFS bug before running the code.
	Communication:	0/5. Totally forgot to talk out loud

REFERENCE MATERIALS

TRIGGERS

TWO POINTERS	
Trigger	**Keywords**
The input consists of one or two arrays/strings/linked lists. We need to use O(1) extra memory or modify the input in place. The input is sorted. The naive solution is O(n²), and we want to get to O(n).	palindrome, reverse, swap, merge, partition

BINARY SEARCH	
Trigger	**Keywords**
The input is a sorted array/string. The brute force involves repeated linear scans. We are given an optimization problem that's hard to optimize directly.	sorted, threshold, range, boundary, find, search, minimum/ maximum, first/last, smallest/largest

SETS & MAPS	
Trigger	**Keywords**
There is some "key-like" concept in the problem. We are doing multiple linear scans in arrays. The input and/or output order is irrelevant in our algorithm. Linear-time target complexity. The problem is a sliding window problem.	frequency, unique, duplicate, grouping, union, intersection, anagram, caching

STACKS & QUEUES	
Trigger	**Keywords**
Right-to-left combinations/transformations; undo/redo actions; balanced parenthesis. Brackets like [ ], ( ), { }, and <>, quotation marks, code comment markers like /* */, and *even* the double asterisks (**) used to bold text in Markdown. Next Greatest Element.	nested, bracket, parentheses

RECURSION	
Trigger	**Keywords**
The input data is a recursive data structure or has a recursive or "nesting" nature (e.g., a binary tree or an array where each element can itself be an array). The problem statement includes a self-referential definition (e.g., Fibonacci). You find yourself wanting to write a number of nested loops that depend on the input. The problem is related to merge sort or quicksort.	nested, quicksort, merge sort

LINKED LISTS	
Trigger	**Keywords**
The input is a linked list. We need O(1) access to both the beginning and the end of a data structure while maintaining insertion order. Data structure design questions.	

GRAPHS	
Trigger	**Keywords**
The input is an edge list or a grid. The topic is related to connectivity, reachability, or distance. Problems involving pairwise relationships between input elements. Geometric problems.	path, source, destination, goal, steps, travel, maze, points

HEAPS	
Trigger	**Keywords**
The data is dynamic, like in 'data structure design' questions where the answer changes over time; top-k type problems; the naive solution uses sorting; the goal is to optimize the extra space.	top/bottom, minimum/maximum, largest/smallest, median

SLIDING WINDOWS	
Trigger	**Keywords**
The input type is just an array of numbers or a string, and maybe a number. The lower bound is linear.	subarray, substring, length, contiguous, consecutive, range, longest, or shortest

BACKTRACKING	
Trigger	**Keywords**
Problems with maximum input sizes in the lower 2-digits; enumeration problems or problems with exponential-sized outputs in general; NP-complete problems, especially optimization ones; games and puzzles (like N-queens, sudoku, knight's tour problem); subset-based or permutation-based problems; problems where you'd think of using DP but there are no overlapping subproblems.	

DYNAMIC PROGRAMMING	
Trigger	**Keywords**
It's an optimization or counting problem, and the naive solution is backtracking. You have to make a sequence of choices. Path-finding problems where you can't go back.	

GREEDY	
Trigger	**Keywords**
optimization problems; interval problems; problems where you'd use backtracking but you need better-than-exponential runtime.	

TOPOLOGICAL SORT	
Trigger	**Keywords**
The input is a DAG, or at least a directed graph; there is some notion of dependencies or prerequisites (even if the input is not a graph); the question is about distances or paths; the runtime upperbound is linear.	

PREFIX SUMS	
Trigger	**Keywords**
The input consists of an array/strings. We need to use O(1) extra memory or modify the input in place. Problems with multiple subarrays, especially when sliding windows don't seem to work. The input is sorted. The naive solution is O(n²), and we want to get to O(n). Problems with ranges or intervals.	prefix, suffix, partition, subarray

BIG O

UPPER & LOWER BOUNDS

TIME COMPLEXITY	MAX N (LOW END)	MAX N (HIGH END)
$O(n!)$	11	9
$O(2^n)$	27	20
$O(n^3)$	584	125
$O(n^2)$	14,142	1,414
$O(n \log n)$	8,677,239	118,649
$O(n)$	200,000,000	2,000,000
$O(\log n)$	Super high	Super high
$O(1)$	Infinite	Infinite

COMMON COMPLEXITY CLASSES

COMPLEX-ITY CLASS	NOTATION	DESCRIPTION	EXAMPLES OF FUNCTIONS IN THE CLASS
Constant	$O(1)$	The growth rate does not depend on the input.[1]	$18, 3 * 3 * 3, 10!$ $\min(n, 10)$
Logarithmic	$O(\log n)$	Very slow growth rate. When the input doubles, the value only increases by a constant.	$\log_2(n), \log_3(n)$ $6*\log_2(2n+1)$
Linear	$O(n)$	When the input doubles, the value at most doubles.	$n, n/10, 3n + 5$ $n + \log_2(n)$
Linearithmic	$O(n \log n)$	Slightly faster growth than linear. When the input doubles, the value grows by a bit more than double.	$7n * 3\log_2(n)$ $n * \log_2(n) + n$
Quadratic	$O(n^2)$	When the input doubles, the value at most quadruples.	$n(n-1)/2$ $1 + 2 + 3 + \ldots + n$
Cubic	$O(n^3)$	When the input doubles, the value grows at most eight-fold.	$n^3 + n^2*\log_2(n)$
Exponential (with base 2)	$O(2^n)$	Extremely fast growth rate. When the input grows by one, the value can double.	$2^n, 2^{(n+1)}, 2^n + n^2$
Exponential (with base 3)	$O(3^n)$	Extremely fast growth rate. When the input grows by one, the value can triple.	$3^n, 3^{(n+4)}, 3^n + 2^n$
Factorial	$O(n!)$	Even faster growth rate. When the input grows by one, the value gets multiplied by a factor that increases each time.	$n! + n!$ $1 * 2 * 3 * \ldots * n$

---

1   Even though we learned in Rule 1 to get rid of constants, the constant complexity class is the exception as it is denoted by $O(1)$. It contains all functions where the value does not depend on the input, like $f(n) = 5$. It also contains functions where the value is below some constant for any input, like $f(n) = \min(n, 10)$. This function is never bigger than 10, so $\min(n, 10) = O(1)$.

REUSABLE IDEAS

PROBLEM-SOLVING BOOSTERS

Transform the Input
Often, transforming the input in a preprocessing step is not strictly necessary, but it can simplify the logic of the final solution. If it retains the same time and space complexities, it can be worth doing to simplify your life and reduce the risk of bugs.

Length-26 Array
When the input is a string of lowercase letters, we often can use an array of length 26 where index 0 corresponds to 'a', index 1 corresponds to 'b', and so on. This is more efficient than using a map data structure.

For instance, if we want to count how many times each letter appears in a string:

```
1    # We are told that s only contains lowercase letters.
2    def letter_counts(s):
3      counts = [0] * 26
4      for c in s:
5        index = ord(c) - ord('a')
6        counts[index] += 1
7      return counts
```

If we want to support all ASCII characters, then we can use an array of length 128 instead (and not subtract ord('a')).

STRING MANIPULATION

Building Strings With Dynamic Arrays
Check if strings are mutable in your language of choice. If you need to build a string character by character, and the strings in your language are immutable, put the characters in a dynamic array instead. When you are done, convert the array to a string with the built-in join method.

TWO POINTERS

Searching With Inward Pointers
In problems where we have to find an index or pair of indices in a sorted array, we can often 'discard' the largest value based on the smallest one or vice versa. Such problems are a natural fit for inward pointers.

GRIDS & MATRICES

Directions Array To Visit Grid Neighbors
Navigating through a grid by checking neighbor cells is common in graphs, backtracking, and other topics. We can do this compactly with a directions array that contains all the possible offsets to add to the current position to generate its neighbors.

We can easily extend the directions array with additional directions (e.g., diagonals) depending on the problem.

Factor Out Validation To A Helper Function
When checking if a cell is valid, embedding the logic directly in your main algorithm can clutter the code. Instead, consider encapsulating the validation logic in a dedicated is_valid() function.

Beyond grid cells, this applies anywhere you must validate 'something' before using it.

Handle Wraparounds With Mod

For problems involving 'circular arrays,' where the last element wraps around to the first one, modular arithmetic can simplify indexing logic: the next element after index i is always (i + 1)%n, where n is the length of the array.

BINARY SEARCH

Grid Flattening

If we want to iterate or search through a grid with dimensions RxC as if it was a 'normal' array of length R*C, we can use the following mapping from grid coordinates to "flattened-grid array" coordinates:

   [r, c] → r * C + c

and the reverse mapping to go from "flattened-grid array" coordinates to grid coordinates:

   i → [i // C, i % C]

For instance, cell [1, 2] in Figure 5 (the 9) becomes index 1 * 4 + 2 = 6, and, conversely, index 6 becomes cell [6 // 4, 6 % 4] = [1, 2].

Exponential Search

Whenever we need to search for a value in a range, but the upper bound (or even lower bound) of the range is unknown, we can find it efficiently with repeated doubling.

This is often useful in the guess-and-check technique (e.g., Problem 29.10: Water Refilling (pg 340)).

SETS & MAPS

Frequency Maps

A *frequency map* is a map from elements to counts. It can be initialized in O(n) time and is useful in questions about duplicate detection, counting, and most frequent elements.

Leverage the Input Range

When the input range is small, leveraging it can lead to significantly more efficient solutions. For instance, when it comes to sorting, we may be able to use specialized algorithms like counting sort (pg 363). Similarly, the difference array technique in Prefix Sums (pg 624) works well for interval problems when the maximum value in the range is constrained—like 24 to represent the hours in a day.

Impose A Canonical Order

If a problem deals with arrays and we want to treat two arrays as the same when they have the same elements regardless of the order (like [1, 2] and [2, 1]), we can sort them and compare (or hash) their sorted versions rather than comparing them directly.

SORTING

Sort To Track The Smallest/Largest Elements

If we need to repeatedly find the smallest/largest elements of an array without modifying the array itself, we can sort the indices instead, and iterate through the indices.

If we do not have all the elements upfront, it tends to be more efficient to use a heap (Problem 37.3: Top Songs Class (pg 501)).

STACKS & QUEUES

Piggybacking Extra Info

When storing elements in a data structure, it may help to store extra fields with information to help you process the element once you fetch it from the data structure. In Python, we can use tuples.

In Problem 32.2: Compress Array By K (pg 382), the count piggybacks along with the number. For additional examples, see the 'node–height queue' recipe for trees, where the height piggybacks along with the node, or Chapter 37: K Most Played (pg 501), where the title of the song piggybacks in the heap along with the number of plays.

If you think about it, a *map* is just a *set* with extra info piggybacking along with each key.

Reframe Balanced Parentheses As Plot Heights

We can visualize a string of parentheses as a plot that starts at 0 and goes up for each opening parenthesis and down for each closing parenthesis:

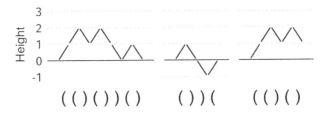

Figure 4. An example of a balanced string (left) and two unbalanced ones (center and right).

The plot for a balanced string creates a valid 'mountain range outline:'

- it never goes below height 0, and
- it ends at height 0.

Balanced parentheses questions are often easier to solve when reframed in terms of this plot.

RECURSION

Pass Indices, Not Copies

By referencing positions within an original array or string using indices, we can eliminate the overhead of slicing and copying, improving time and space efficiency.

Avoiding copies does not only apply to recursion, but it can stack up quickly in recursive algorithms. It is very language dependent, so do some research on your language of choice about how to avoid them (we touched on this in section 'The space complexity of copies' (pg 223).

Applying Modulo At Each Step

Some problems involve math operations that could result in really large integers that overflow in some languages. As a workaround, many questions ask to return the solution modulo some large prime (we'll use 10^9+7 in this book).

When we see that, we should apply the modulo at each step rather than at the very end, to avoid overflow/working with really large numbers. The neat property of modulo is that, if an operation only involves sums, subtractions, and multiplications (but not divisions), applying it at each step does not change the final output.

E.g., `(10 + 3 + 10 + 6) % 5` is 4, and so is `(10 % 5) + (3 % 5) + (10 % 5) + (6 % 5)`.

Division is the exception: dividing first and then applying modulo yields different results than applying modulo first and then dividing: (12 / 3) % 5 != (12 % 5) / 3.

LINKED LISTS

Dummy Node
Adding a dummy node at the head simplifies edge cases by reducing null checks—just don't forget that the real head is dummy.next!

Linked List Reversal Break Down
If a problem asks to reverse only a part of a linked list, we can use the break down the problem booster and do it in steps:

1. Find the bounds of the section that need to be reversed.
2. Break that section out of the linked list without losing the before/after parts of the list.
3. Reverse the section (as in Solution 6).
4. Reattach the section.

Each of these steps should be easier to tackle. Using a dummy head will simplify the cases where the real head is part of the section being reversed.

TREES

Finding The Node In The Path With Minimum Depth
A useful property in problems about finding paths in binary trees is that a path has a single node with minimum depth.

Finding this node is often easier than finding the endpoints because there are only n candidates as opposed to $O(n^2)$ possible pairs of endpoints. If you can find this node, it's then usually easy to find the rest of the path.

For instance, this property would have helped us solve Problem 24.12: Tree diameter (pg 268).

GRAPHS

Edge List To Adjacency List
```
1    def build_adjacency_list(V, edge_list):
2        graph = [[] for _ in range(V)]
3        for node1, node2 in edge_list:
4            graph[node1].append(node2)
5            graph[node2].append(node1)
```

For directed graphs, each edge [node1, node2] in edge_list represents an edge from node1 to node2. Thus, we would add node2 to the adjacency list of node1, but not the other way around.

Path Reconstruction
In DFS when we mark a node as visited, we can also track their *predecessor* in the DFS. The mapping from each node to its predecessor defines a 'DFS visit tree' rooted at the starting node. The predecessor of each node is the parent in this DFS tree (the starting node has no predecessor). Given any node, node, reachable from the starting node, start, we can follow a chain of predecessors to find a path from node to start.

Every chain of predecessors leads to the starting node, so we can keep going until we reach start:
```
1    path = [node]
2    while path[-1] != start:
```

```
3       path.append(predecessors[path[-1]])
```

Path reconstruction also works the BFS, in which case it doesn't just find any path, it finds the shortest path.

Computing averages
When computing averages, it is often easiest to focus on computing the numerator and denominator separately and dividing at the very end.

Multisource BFS
In O(V+E) time, we can find the distance from every node to its closest node in a designated subset with multisource BFS. It's like a normal BFS except for the initialization: we start by putting all the designated nodes in the queue and setting their distances to 0.

HEAPS

Heap Size Restriction
Depending on the problem, restricting the size of the heap to the size of the output can save space and even time.

For a 'largest k' problem, you can use either a max-heap or a restricted-size min-heap.

- Max-heap: dump all elements in the max-heap with heapify and pop the largest k. This takes O(n + (k log n)) time and O(n) space.
- Min-heap: add the elements one by one to a min-heap of the k largest elements so far. This takes O(n log k) time and O(k) space.

There is an interesting trade-off between the time and space of the two solutions.

Two-Heap Median Tracking
Tracking the median in a dynamic dataset is possible by keeping the lower half in a max-heap and the upper half in a min-heap.

Each addition takes O(log n) time, and returning the median takes O(1) time.

M-way Merge
We can efficiently merge m sorted lists into a single sorted list by tracking m pointers in a heap pointing to the first non-added element from each list.

SLIDING WINDOWS

Transform Exactly-K/At-Least-K Counting to At-Most-K Counting
If the At-Most-K version of a counting problem has the maximum window property, it can be reused to solve the Exactly-K and At-Least-K versions.

- 'Exactly k' is equivalent to 'at most k' minus 'at most k - 1'.
- 'At Least k' is equivalent to 'total count' (n*(n+1)/2) minus 'at most k - 1'.

The At-Most-K version can be solved by tweaking the maximum window template, as in Solution 18.

BACKTRACKING

Modify -> Recurse -> Undo
When you make a mess, clean it up. In backtracking, if you modify a global variable before calling visit() recursively, you must do the opposite change immediately upon returning from visit(). Code how you

make the mess and how you clean it up symmetrically. For example, if you append to an array right before your recursive call, pop from it right after (not in the recursive function).[2]

Extracting And Adding Digits

In some problems, we need to handle integers digit by digit. The following loop extracts all the digits of x and returns them as an array, from least to most significant:

```
1    arr = []
2    while x > 0:
3        arr.append(x % 10)  # Extract the last digit.
4        x = x // 10  # Remove the last digit.
```

If x = 123, we'll get arr = [3, 2, 1]. We can reassemble x like this (note that we reverse arr):

```
1    x = 0
2    for digit in reversed(arr):
3        x = x * 10 + digit
```

The same idea applies if we need to handle integers bit by bit instead.

DYNAMIC PROGRAMMING

Solution Reconstruction

DP problems asking for the *value* of the solution are easier than problems that ask for the solution itself.

A practical way to return full solutions to DP problems instead of just their values is to store them in the memo table. It can piggyback along with the value, if the value is also needed (see 'Reusable Idea: Piggybacking Extra Info', pg 382). However, this increases the time and space complexity.

The more efficient approach is to start by implementing the recurrence relation for values only. Then, we reconstruct the solution step by step, essentially following a path down the decision tree. The key is to use the function for the value-based recurrence relation to determine the best choice at each step. This is analogous to how we build our partial solution in backtracking, except we only go down one path, so we don't need to do it recursively.

---

2 You can avoid having to worry about cleanups by making copies of the parent's state for each child. This can simplify the code but it increases the time and space we use at each node.

MY NOTES & REMINDERS

Made in the USA
Las Vegas, NV
02 February 2025

17438452R00354